THE PAPERS OF
BENJAMIN FRANKLIN

SPONSORED BY

The American Philosophical Society
and Yale University

THE PAPERS OF

Benjamin Franklin

VOLUME 2 *January 1, 1735, through December 31, 1744*

LEONARD W. LABAREE, *Editor*

WHITFIELD J. BELL, JR., *Associate Editor*

Helen C. Boatfield and Helene H. Fineman, Assistant Editors

New Haven YALE UNIVERSITY PRESS

The reprinting of this volume was made possible by a grant from the
Charles E. Culpeper Foundation to the Friends of Franklin, and by a grant
from the National Historical Publications and Records Commission.

Library of Congress catalogue number: 59-12697.
International standard book number: 0-300-00651-9.

∞ The paper in this book meets the guidelines for permanence and durability of
the Committee on Production Guidelines for Book Longevity of the Council on
Library Resources.

Printed in the United States of America.

10 9 8 7 6 5 4 3

Contents

List of Illustrations

Franklin met him in 1739. This painting is so unlike Wollaston's other work that it is thought he may have had the assistance of another hand. John Faber made an engraving, which was printed by John Bowles, Cornhill, London. George C. Groce, "John Wollaston (Fl. 1736–1767): A Cosmopolitan Painter in the British Colonies," *Art Quarterly*, XV (1952), 133–48. Reproduced by permission of the National Portrait Gallery, London.

In a race with Andrew Bradford for the distinction of publishing the first magazine in America, Franklin lost by three days; the first, or "January," issue of Bradford's *American Maga*ine* appeared on February 13, 1741, that of Franklin's *General Maga*ine*, similarly dated, on February 16. Neither publication was a success; Bradford's lasted only three months, Franklin's six. The title pages of all issues of the *General Maga*ine* are alike. For a central decoration Franklin adopted the plumed badge of the Prince of Wales. Reproduced by permission of the Yale University Library.

Often regarded as the finest example of printing done at Franklin's press, James Logan's translation of Cicero's *Cato Major*, or *De senectute* as it is perhaps better known, was certainly a publication on which he took especial pains. The title page, which measures 8½ by 6 inches, appears in two colors, the lines "Cato Major," "Old-Age:" and "Philadelphia:" being in red. Reproduced by permission of the Yale University Library.

Drawn by Lewis Evans of Philadelphia and probably engraved by James Turner of Boston, this diagram appears on page 17 of Franklin's pamphlet, *An Account Of the New Invented Pennsylvanian Fire-Places*. It explains the installation of the device and illustrates its operation. Arrows, smoke lines, and some lettering were added by hand after printing. Reproduced by permission of the Library Company of Philadelphia.

The several parts of the fireplace and a perspective view of the assembled whole appear on this plate, which measures 6½ inches square in the original. It was inserted as a folded sheet at the end of Franklin's pamphlet. Drawn by Lewis Evans and probably engraved by James Turner. Reproduced by permission of the Yale University Library.

This map shows places and buildings in Philadelphia associated with Benjamin Franklin between 1723, when he came to the city, and 1776, when he went to France to represent the United States. Based on the Clarkson and Biddle map of 1762, with additional information from Grant M. Simon's map of old Philadelphia (published in American Philosophical Society *Transactions*, n.s., XLIII, pt. 1, 1953), from Hannah Benner Roach, "Benjamin Franklin Slept Here," *Pennsylvania Magazine of History and Biography*, LXXXIV (April, 1960), 127–74, and from manuscripts in The Papers of Benjamin Franklin. Drawn by Crimilda Pontes.

Contributors to Volume 2

The ownership of each manuscript, or the location of the particular copy used by the editors of each contemporary pamphlet or similar printed work, is indicated where the document appears in the text. The sponsors and editors are deeply grateful to the following institutions for permission to print in the present volume manuscripts or other materials which they own:

American Philosophical Society
Boston Public Library
Chicago Historical Society
Columbia University Library
Department of Records,
    City of Philadelphia
Harvard College Library
Haverford College Library
Historical Society of Haddonfield
Historical Society of
    Pennsylvania

Land Office, Department of Internal
    Affairs, Commonwealth of Pennsylvania
Library Company of Philadelphia
Library of Congress
Massachusetts Historical Society
New-York Historical Society
The Royal Society
Royal Society of Arts
University of Pennsylvania Library
Yale University Library

Method of Textual Reproduction

An extended statement of the principles of selection, arrangement, form of presentation, and method of textual reproduction observed in this edition appears in the Introduction to the first volume, pp. xxxiv-xlvii. A condensation and revision of the portion relating to the method of reproducing the texts follows here.

Printed Material:

In general Franklin's writings printed under his direction should be regarded as his ultimate intention and should therefore be reproduced without change, except as modern typography requires. In fact, however, newspapers and pamphlets were often set by two or more journeymen with different notions of spelling, capitalization, and punctuation. Although the resulting inconsistencies and errors did not represent Franklin's intentions, they are not eliminated by the editors. Again, in cases where Franklin's writings were printed by another, they were sometimes carelessly or willfully revised without his consent. He once complained, for example, that an English printer had so corrected and excised one of his papers "that it can neither scratch nor bite. It seems only to paw and mumble."[1] What was thus printed was obviously not what Franklin wrote, but, in the absence of his manuscript, the editors have no alternative but to reprint it as it stands. Still other Franklin letters are known only in nineteenth-century printings, vigorously edited by William Temple Franklin, Duane, or Sparks. Here, too, the editors follow the texts as printed, only noting obvious misreadings.

In reproducing printed materials, the following general rules are observed:

1. The place and date of composition of letters are set at the top, regardless of their location in the original printing.

2. Proper nouns, including personal names, which were often printed in italics, are set in roman, except when the original was italicized for emphasis.

1. BF to William Franklin, Jan. 9, 1768.

3. Prefaces and other long passages, though italicized in the original, are set in roman. Long italicized quotations are set in roman within quotation marks.

4. Words in full capitals are set in small capitals, with initial letters in full capitals if required by Franklin's normal usage.

5. All signatures are set in capitals and small capitals.

6. Obvious typographical errors are silently corrected. An omitted parenthesis or quotation mark, for example, is inserted when the other of the pair was printed.

7. Every sentence is closed with a period or other appropriate mark of punctuation (usually a question mark).

8. Longhand insertions in the blanks of printed forms are set in italics, with space before and after.

Manuscript Material:

a. *Letters* are presented in the following form:

1. The place and date of composition are set at the top, regardless of their location in the original.

2. The complimentary close is set continuously with the text.

3. Addresses, endorsements, and docketing are so labeled and printed at the end of the letter.

b. *Spelling* of the original is retained. When, however, it is so abnormal as to obscure meaning, the correct form is supplied in brackets or footnote, as: "yf [wife]."

c. *Capitalization* has been retained as written, except that every sentence is made to begin with a capital. When there is doubt whether a letter is a capital, it is printed as like letters are in the same manuscript, or, that guide failing, as modern usage directs.

d. Words underlined once in the manuscript are printed in *italics;* words underlined twice or written in large letters or full capitals are printed in SMALL CAPITALS.

e. *Punctuation* has been retained as in the original, except:

1. Every sentence ends with a period or other appropriate mark (usually a question mark), unless it is not clear where the sentence ends, when the original punctuation (or lack of it) is preserved.

xviii

2. Dashes used in place of commas, semicolons, colons, or periods are replaced by the appropriate marks; and when a sentence ends with both a dash and a period, the dash is omitted.

3. Commas scattered meaninglessly through a manuscript are eliminated.

4. When a mark of punctuation is not clear or can be read as one of two marks, modern usage is followed.[2]

5. Some documents, especially those of a legal character, lack all punctuation. This is supplied with restraint, and the fact indicated in a footnote. In some other, inadequately punctuated documents, it is silently added when needed for clarity, as in a long series of names.

f. *Contractions and abbreviations* in general are expanded except in proper names. The ampersand is rendered as "and," except in the names of business firms, in the form "&c.," and in a few other cases. Letters represented by the thorn or tilde are printed. The tailed "p" is spelled out as per, pre, or pro. Symbols of weights, measures, and monetary values follow modern usage, as: £34. Superscript letters are lowered. Abbreviations in current use are retained, as: Col., Dr., N.Y., i.e.

g. *Omitted or illegible words or letters* are treated as follows:

1. If not more than four letters are missing, they are silently supplied when there is no doubt what they should be.

2. The omission of more than four letters or one or more words is supplied conjecturally within brackets. The addition of a question mark within the brackets indicates uncertainty as to the conjecture.

3. Other omissions are shown as follows: [*illegible*], [*torn*], [*remainder missing*], or the like.

4. Missing or illegible digits are indicated by suspension points in brackets, the number of points corresponding to the estimated number of missing figures.

5. Blank spaces are left as blanks.

2. The typescripts from which these papers are printed have been made from photocopies of the manuscripts, and marks of punctuation are sometimes blurred or lost in photography. It has often been impossible to consult the originals in these cases.

h. *Author's additions and corrections.*

1. Interlineations and brief marginal notes are brought into the text without comment. Longer notes are brought into the text with the notation: [*in the margin*].

2. Author's footnotes are printed at the bottom of the appropriate pages between the text and any editorial footnotes.

3. Canceled words and phrases are in general omitted without notice; if significant, they are printed in footnotes. The canceled passages of important documents, such as drafts of treaties, are brought into the text enclosed in angle brackets *before* the words substituted.

4. When alternative words and phrases have been inserted in a manuscript but the original remains uncanceled, the alternatives are given in brackets, preceded by explanatory words in italics, as: "it is [*written above:* may be] true."

5. Variant readings of several versions are noted if important.

Abbreviations and Short Titles

ADS	Autograph document signed.[1]
ALS	Autograph letter signed.
APS	American Philosophical Society.
BF	Benjamin Franklin.
Bigelow, *Works*	John Bigelow, ed., *The Complete Works of Benjamin Franklin* . . . (10 vols., N.Y., 1887–88).
Colden Paps.	*The Letters and Papers of Cadwallader Colden.* New-York Historical Society *Collections* for 1917–23, 1934, 1935.
DAB	*Dictionary of American Biography.*
DNB	*Dictionary of National Biography.*
DS	Document signed.
Darlington, *Memorials*	William Darlington, *Memorials of John Bartram and Humphry Marshall* (Phila., 1849).
Dexter, *Biog. Sketches*	Franklin B. Dexter, *Biographical Sketches of the Graduates of Yale College* . . . (6 vols., N.Y. and New Haven, 1885–1912).
Duane, *Works*	William Duane, ed., *The Works of Dr. Benjamin Franklin* . . . (6 vols., Phila., 1808–18). Title varies in the several volumes.
Evans	Charles Evans, *American Bibliography* (13 vols., Chicago and Worcester, Mass., 1903–55). Surviving imprints are reproduced in full in microprint in Clifford K. Shipton, ed., *Early American Imprints, 1639–1800* (microprint, Worcester, Mass.).
P. L. Ford, *Franklin Bibliog.*	Paul L. Ford, *Franklin Bibliography. A List of Books written by, or relating to Benjamin Franklin* (Brooklyn, 1889).
Laws of Pa.	*A Collection of all the Laws of the Province of Pennsylvania: Now in Force* (Phila., 1742).

1. For definitions of this and other kinds of manuscripts, see above, I, xliv–xlvii.

Lib. Co. Phila.	Library Company of Philadelphia.
LS	Letter signed.
MS, MSS	Manuscript, manuscripts.
Montgomery, *Hist. Univ. Pa.*	Thomas H. Montgomery, *A History of the University of Pennsylvania from its Foundation to A.D. 1770* (Phila., 1900).
OED	*Oxford English Dictionary.*
PMHB	*Pennsylvania Magazine of History and Biography.*
Pa. Arch.	Samuel Hazard and others, eds., *Pennsylvania Archives* (9 series, Phila. and Harrisburg, 1852–1935).
Pa. Col. Recs.	*Minutes of the Provincial Council of Pennsylvania* . . . (16 vols., Phila., 1838–53). Title changes with volume 11 to Supreme Executive Council.
Pa. Gaz.	*The Pennsylvania Gazette.*
Par. Text edit.	Max Farrand, ed., *Benjamin Franklin's Memoirs. Parallel Text Edition* . . . (Berkeley and Los Angeles, 1949).
Parton, *Franklin*	James Parton, *Life and Times of Benjamin Franklin* (2 vols., N.Y., 1864).
Phil. Trans.	The Royal Society, *Philosophical Transactions.*
Sibley's Harvard Graduates	John L. Sibley, *Biographical Sketches of Graduates of Harvard University* (Cambridge, Mass., 1873–). Continued from volume 4 by Clifford K. Shipton.
Smyth, *Writings*	Albert H. Smyth, ed., *The Writings of Benjamin Franklin* . . . (10 vols., N.Y., 1905–07).
Sparks, *Works*	Jared Sparks, ed., *The Works of Benjamin Franklin* . . . (10 vols., Boston, 1836–40).
Thomas, *Printing*	Isaiah Thomas, *The History of Printing in America, with a Biography of Printers* . . . (2 vols., American Antiquarian Society *Transactions and Collections*, V–VI, 1874).

Tyerman, *Whitefield*   Luke Tyerman, *The Life of the Rev. George Whitefield* . . . (2 vols., London, 1876–77).

Van Doren, *Franklin*   Carl Van Doren, *Benjamin Franklin* (N.Y., 1938).

Van Doren,   Carl Van Doren, ed., *The Letters of Ben-*
Franklin-Mecom   *jamin Franklin & Jane Mecom* (*Memoirs* of the American Philosophical Society, XXVII, Princeton, 1950).

WTF, *Memoirs*   William Temple Franklin, ed., *Memoirs of the Life and Writings of Benjamin Franklin, LL.D., F.R.S. &c.* . . . (3 vols., 4to, London, 1817–18).

Watson, *Annals*   John F. Watson, *Annals of Philadelphia, and Pennsylvania, in the Olden Time* . . . (3 vols., Phila., 1891).

Genealogical references. An editorial reference to one of Franklin's relatives may be accompanied by a citation of the symbol assigned to that person in the genealogical tables and charts in volume 1 of this work, pp. xlix-lxxvii, as, for example: Thomas Franklin (A.5.2.1), Benjamin Mecom (C.17.3), or Benjamin Franklin Bache (D.3.1).

Chronology

January 1, 1735, through December 31, 1744

1735

April–September: BF engages in controversy over Samuel Hemphill.

1736

October 15: BF appointed clerk of the Assembly.
November 21: Francis Folger Franklin dies.
December 7: Union Fire Company formed.

1737

October 5: BF opens his account as postmaster of Philadelphia.

1739

October 19: Great Britain declares war on Spain.
November 2: George Whitefield arrives at Philadelphia on first visit.

1740

November 9: The "New Building" in Philadelphia used for the first time.

1741

February 16: BF publishes the first issue of *The General Magazine, and Historical Chronicle.*

1742

February 20: BF forms a partnership with James Parker to run a printing office in New York City.

1743

May 14: BF publishes *A Proposal for Promoting Useful Knowledge.*

May–June: BF visits Boston and meets Dr. Adam Spencer there; meets
 Cadwallader Colden on the journey.
August 31: Sarah Franklin born; October 5: baptized.

1744

March 15: France declares war on Great Britain.
November 15: BF announces *An Account of the New Invented Pennsylvanian Fire-Places* as "just published."

THE PAPERS OF
BENJAMIN FRANKLIN

VOLUME 2

January 1, 1735, through December 31, 1744

Poor Richard, 1735

Poor Richard, 1735. An Almanack For the Year of Christ 1735 . . . By Richard Saunders, Philom. Philadelphia: Printed and sold by B. Franklin, at the New Printing-Office near the Market. (Yale University Library)

Courteous Reader,   Octob. 30. 1734.

This is the third Time of my appearing in print, hitherto very much to my own Satisfaction, and, I have reason to hope, to the Satisfaction of the Publick also; for the Publick is generous, and has been very charitable and good to me. I should be ungrateful then, if I did not take every Opportunity of expressing my Gratitude; for *ingratum si dixeris, omnia dixeris:* I therefore return the Publick my most humble and hearty Thanks.

Whatever may be the Musick of the Spheres, how great soever the Harmony of the Stars, 'tis certain there is no Harmony among the Stargazers; but they are perpetually growling and snarling at one another like strange Curs, or like some Men at their Wives: I had resolved to keep the Peace on my own part, and affront none of them; and I shall persist in that Resolution: But having receiv'd much Abuse from Titan Leeds deceas'd, (Titan Leeds when living would not have us'd me so!) I say, having receiv'd much Abuse from the Ghost of Titan Leeds, who pretends to be still living, and to write Almanacks in spight of me and my Predictions, I cannot help saying, that tho' I take it patiently, I take it very unkindly. And whatever he may pretend, 'tis undoubtedly true that he is really defunct and dead. First because the Stars are seldom disappointed, never but in the Case of wise Men, *Sapiens dominabitur astris,* and they fore-show'd his Death at the Time I predicted it. Secondly, 'Twas requisite and necessary he should die punctually at that Time, for the Honour of Astrology, the Art professed both by him and his Father before him. Thirdly, 'Tis plain to every one that reads his two last Almanacks (for 1734 and 35) that they are not written with that *Life* his Performances use to be written with; the Wit is low and flat, the little Hints dull and spiritless, nothing smart in them but Hudibras's Verses against Astrology at the Heads of the Months in the last, which no Astrologer but a *dead one* would have inserted, and no Man *living* would or could write such Stuff as the rest. But lastly, I shall convince him from his own Words, that he is dead, (*ex ore suo condemnatus est*) for in his Preface to his

3

Almanack for 1734, he says, "Saunders adds another GROSS FALS-HOOD in his Almanack, viz. that by my own Calculation I shall *survive* until the 26th of the said Month October 1733, which is as *untrue* as the former." Now if it be, as Leeds says, *untrue* and a *gross Falshood* that he surviv'd till the 26th of October 1733, then it is certainly *true* that he died *before* that Time: And if he died before that Time, he is dead now, to all Intents and Purposes, any thing he may say to the contrary notwithstanding. And at what Time before the 26th is it so likely he should die, as at the Time by me predicted, viz. the 17th of October aforesaid? But if some People will walk and be troublesome after Death, it may perhaps be born with a little, because it cannot well be avoided unless one would be at the Pains and Expence of laying them in the Red Sea; however, they should not presume too much upon the Liberty allow'd them; I know Confinement must needs be mighty irksome to the free Spirit of an Astronomer, and I am too compassionate to proceed suddenly to Extremities with it; nevertheless, tho' I resolve with Reluctance, I shall not long defer, if it does not speedily learn to treat its living Friends with better Manners. I am, Courteous Reader, Your obliged Friend and Servant,   R. SAUNDERS

> Says ♄ to ♂, Brother, when shall I see
> Penn's People a scraping Acquaintance with thee?
> Says ♂, only ♃ knows; but this I can tell,
> They neglect me for Hermes, they love him too well.
> O, if that be Case, says ♄ , ne'er fear,
> If they're tender of Hermes, and hold him so dear,
> They'll solicit thy Help e'er I've finish'd my Round,
> Using ♂ Hermes' Foes to deter or confound.

XI Mon. January hath xxxi days.

The two or three Necessaries.

Two or three Frolicks abroad in sweet May,
Two or three civil Things said by the way,
Two or three Languishes, two or three Sighs,
Two or three *Bless me's!* and *Let me die's!*
Two or three Squeezes, and two or three Towzes,

4

With 2 or 3 hundred Pound spent at their Houses,
Can never fail cuckolding two or three Spouses.

Look before, or you'll find yourself behind.

Bad Commentators spoil the best of books,
So God sends meat (they say) the devil Cooks.

Approve not of him who commends all you say.

By diligence and patience, the mouse bit in two the cable.

Full of courtesie, full of craft.

XII Mon. February hath xxviii days.

Among the vain Pretenders of the Town,
Hibham of late is wondrous noted grown;
Hibham scarce reads, and is not worth a groat,
Yet with some high-flown Words and a fine Coat,
He struts and talks of Books, and of Estate,
And learned J---s he calls his Intimate.
The Mob admire! Thus mighty Impudence
Supplies the want of Learning, Wealth and Sense.

A little House well fill'd, a little Field well till'd, and a little Wife
well will'd, are great Riches.

Old Maids lead Apes there, where the old Batchelors are turn'd
to Apes.

Some are weatherwise, some are otherwise.

I Mon. March hath xxxi days.

There's many Men forget their proper Station,
And still are meddling with th' Administration
Of Government; that's wrong, and this is right,
And such a Law is out of Reason quite;
Thus spending too much Thought on State Affairs
The Business is neglected which is theirs.
So some fond Traveller gazing at the Stars
Slips in next Ditch and gets a dirty Arse.

Dyrro lynn y ddoeth e fydd ddoethach.[1]

The poor man must walk to get meat for his stomach, the rich man to get a stomach to his meat.

He that goes far to marry, will either deceive or be deceived.

Eyes and Priests
Bear no Jests.

II Mon. April hath xxx days.

William, because his Wife was something ill,
Uncertain in her Health, indifferent still,
He turn'd her out of Doors without reply:
I ask'd if he that Act could justifie.
In Sickness and in Health, says he, *I'm bound*
To keep her; when she's worse or better found
I'll take her in again: And now you'll see,
She'll quickly either mend or end, says he.

The Family of Fools is ancient.

Necessity never made a good bargain.

If Pride leads the Van, Beggary brings up the Rear.

There's many witty men whose brains can't fill their bellies.

Weighty Questions ask for deliberate Answers.

III Mon. May hath xxxi days.

There's nought so silly, sure, as Vanity,
It self its chiefest End does still destroy.
To be commended still its Brains are racking,
But who will give it what it's always taking?
Thou'rt fair 'tis true; and witty too, I know it;
And well-bred, Sally, for thy Manners show it:
But whilst thou mak'st Self-Praise thy only Care,
Thou'rt neither witty, nor well-bred, nor fair.

1. "Give drink to a wise man [and] he will be wiser."

6

When ♂ and ♀ in ♂ lie,
Then, Maids, whate'er is ask'd of you, deny.

Be slow in chusing a Friend, slower in changing.

Old Hob was lately married in the Night,
What needed Day, his fair young Wife is light.

Pain wastes the Body, Pleasures the Understanding.

The cunning man steals a horse, the wise man lets him alone.

IV Mon. June hath xxx days.

When will the Miser's Chest be full enough?
When will he cease his Bags to cram and stuff?
All Day he labours and all Night contrives,
Providing as if he'd an hundred Lives.
While endless Care cuts short the common Span:
So have I seen with Dropsy swoln, a Man,
Drink and drink more, and still unsatisfi'd,
Drink till Drink drown'd him, yet he thirsty dy'd.

Nothing but Money,
Is sweeter than Honey.

Humility makes great men twice honourable.

A Ship under sail and a big-bellied Woman,
Are the handsomest two things that can be seen common.

Keep thy shop, and thy shop will keep thee.

The King's cheese is half wasted in parings: But no matter, 'tis
made of the peoples milk.

V Mon. July hath xxxi days.

On *LOUIS the XIV. of France.*

Louis ('tis true, I own to you)
Paid Learned Men for Writing,
And valiant Men for Fighting:
Himself could neither write nor fight,

7

Nor make his People happy;
Yet Fools will prate, and call him *Great;*
Shame on their Noddles sappy.

What's given shines,
What's receiv'd is rusty.

Sloth and Silence are a Fool's Virtues.

Of learned Fools I have seen ten times ten,
Of unlearned wise men I have seen a hundred.

Three may keep a Secret, if two of them are dead.

Poverty wants some things, Luxury many things, Avarice all things.

A Lie stands on 1 leg, Truth on 2.

VI Mon. August hath xxxi days.

Sam had the worst Wife that a Man could have,
Proud, Lazy, Sot, could neither get nor save,
Eternal Scold she was, and what is worse,
The D---l burn thee, was her common Curse.
Forbear, quoth Sam, that fruitless Curse so common,
He'll not hurt me who've married his Kinswoman.

There's small Revenge in Words, but Words may be greatly revenged.

Great wits jump (says the Poet) and hit his Head against the Post.

A man is never so ridiculous by those Qualities that are his own as by those that he affects to have.

Deny Self for Self's sake.

VII Mon. September hath xxx days.

Blind are the Sons of Men, few of the Kind
Know their *chief* Interest, or knowing, mind:
Most, far from following *what* they know is best,

Trifle in earnest, but mind *that* in jest.
  So Hal the Fiddle tunes harmoniously,
While all is Discord in's Oeconomy.
Tim moderate fare and abstinence much prizes,
In publick, but in private gormandizes.

Ever since Follies have pleas'd, Fools have been able to divert.

It is better to take many Injuries than to give one.

Opportunity is the great Bawd.

VIII Mon. October hath xxxi days.

  Little Half-wits are wondrous pert, we find,
Scoffing and jeering on whole Womankind,
ALL false, ALL Whores, ALL this and that and t'other,
Not one Exception left, ev'n for their Mother.
But Men of Wisdom and Experience know,
That there's no greater Happiness below
Than a good Wife affords; and such there's many,
For every Man has one, the best of any.

Early to bed and early to rise, makes a man healthy wealthy and
  wise.

To be humble to Superiors is Duty, to Equals Courtesy, to In-
  feriors Nobleness.

Here comes the Orator! with his Flood of Words, and his Drop of
  Reason.

IX Mon. November hath xxx days.

  The Lying Habit is in some so strong,
To Truth they know not how to bend their Tongue;
And tho' sometimes their Ends Truth best would answer
Yet Lies come uppermost, do what they can, Sir,
Mendacio delights in telling News,
And that it may be such, himself doth use
To make it; but he now no longer need;
Let him tell Truth, it will be News indeed.

9

An old young man, will be a young old man.

Sal laughs at every thing you say. Why? Because she has fine Teeth.

> If what most men admire, they would despise,
> 'Twould look as if mankind were growing wise.

The Sun never repents of the good he does, nor does he ever demand a recompence.

X Mon. December hath xxxi days.

> 'Tis not the Face with a delightful Air,
> A rosy Cheek and lovely flowing Hair;
> Nor sparkling Eyes to best Advantage set,
> Nor all the Members rang'd in Alphabet,
> Sweet in Proportion as the lovely Dies,
> Which bring th' etherial Bow before our Eyes,
> That can with Wisdom Approbation find,
> Like pious Morals and an honest Mind;
> By Virtue's living Laws from every Vice refin'd.

Are you angry that others disappoint you? remember you cannot depend upon yourself.

One Mend-fault is worth two Findfaults, but one Findfault is better than two Makefaults.

> Reader, I wish thee Health, Wealth, Happiness,
> And may kind Heaven thy Year's Industry bless.

Of the ECLIPSES, 1735.

There will be four Eclipses this Year, two of the Sun and two of the Moon.

The first will be of the Moon the 27th of March, in the Morning; the Moon, being near setting, will be below our Horizon before the greatest Obscuration; so that we shall not see above 5 Digits eclipsed; but those who live far enough westward may see the whole, which will be near seven Digits.

The second is of the Sun, April 11. invisible in these Parts.

The third is of the Moon, September 20. beginning at 15 minutes after 7 Afternoon; the middle at 20 min. after 8, the End at 11 minutes after 10; total Duration 2 ho. 56 min. Digits eclipsed 6 and a quarter.

The fourth and last is an Eclipse of the Sun, October 4. at 9 afternoon, invisible.

I shall not say much of the Signification of the Eclipses this Year, for in truth they do not signifie much; only I may observe by the way, that the first Eclipse of the Moon being celebrated in ♎ Libra or the Ballance, foreshews a Failure of Justice, where People judge in their own Cases. But in the following Year 1736, there will be six Eclipses, four of the Sun, and two of the Moon, which two Eclipses of the Moon will be both total, and portend great Revolutions in Europe, particularly in Germany; and some great and surprizing Events relating to these northern Colonies, of which I purpose to speak at large in my next.

The COURTS.

When Popery in Britain sway'd, I've read,
The *Lawyers* fear'd they should be damn'd when dead,
Because they had no Saint to hand their Pray'rs,
And in Heav'n's Court take Care of their Affairs.
Therefore consulting, Evanus they sent
To Rome with a huge Purse, on this Intent
That to the Holy Father making known
Their woful Case, he might appoint them One.
Being arriv'd, he offers his Complaint
In Language smooth, and humbly begs a Saint:
For why, says he, when others on Heav'n wou'd call,
Physicians, Seamen, Scholars, Tradesmen, all
Have their own Saints, we *Lawyers* none at all.
  The Pope was puzzel'd, never puzzel'd worse,
For with pleas'd Eyes he saw the proffer'd Purse,
But ne'er, in all his Knowledge or his Reading,
He'd met with one good Man that practis'd Pleading;
Who then should be the Saint? he could not tell.
At length the Thing was thus concluded well.
Within our City, says his Holiness,
There is one Church fill'd with the Images

Of all the Saints, with whom the Wall's surrounded,
Blindfold Evanus, lead him three times round it,
Then let him feel (*but give me first the Purse*)
And take the first he finds, for better or worse.
Round went Evanus till he came where stood
St. Michael with the Devil under's Foot;
And groping round, he seiz'd old Satan's Head,
This be our Saint, he cries; *Amen,* the Father said.
   But when they open'd poor Evanus' Eyes,
   Alack! he sunk with Shame and with Surprize!

On Protection of Towns from Fire[1]

Printed in *The Pennsylvania Gazette*, February 4, 1734/5.

Mr. Franklin,

Being old and lame of my Hands, and thereby uncapable of assisting my Fellow Citizens, when their Houses are on Fire; I must beg them to take in good Part the following Hints on the Subject of Fires.

In the first Place, as *an Ounce of Prevention is worth a Pound of Cure,* I would advise 'em to take Care how they suffer living Brands-ends, or Coals in a full Shovel, to be carried out of one Room into another, or up or down Stairs, unless in a Warmingpan shut; for Scraps of Fire may fall into Chinks, and make no Appearance till Midnight; when your Stairs being in Flames, you may be forced, (as I once was) to leap out of your Windows, and hazard your Necks to avoid being over-roasted.

And now we talk of Prevention, where would be the Damage, if, to the Act for preventing Fires, by regulating Bakehouses and Coopers Shops, a Clause were added to regulate all other Houses in the particulars of too shallow Hearths, and the detestable Practice of putting wooden Mouldings on each side the Fire Place,

---

1. Franklin remembered in his autobiography that he had prepared a paper "(first to be read in Junto, but it was afterwards publish'd) on the different Accidents and Carelessnesses by which Houses were set on fire, with Cautions against them, and Means proposed of avoiding them. This paper was much spoken of as a useful Piece," a consequence of which was the formation of Philadelphia's first fire company. See below, p. 150.

which being commonly of Heart-of-Pine and full of Turpentine, stand ready to flame as soon as a Coal or a small Brand shall roul [roll] against them.

Once more; if Chimneys were more frequently and more carefully clean'd, some Fires might thereby be prevented. I have known foul Chimneys burn most furiously a few Days after they were swept: People in Confidence that they are clean, making large Fires. Every Body among us is allow'd to sweep Chimneys, that please to undertake that Business; and if a Chimney fires thro' fault of the Sweeper, the Owner pays the Fine, and the Sweeper goes free. This Thing is not right. Those who undertake Sweeping of Chimneys, and employ Servants for that Purpose, ought to be licensed by the Mayor; and if any Chimney fires and flames out 15 Days after Sweeping, the Fine should be paid by the Sweeper; for it is his Fault.

We have at present got Engines enough in the Town, but I question, whether in many Parts of the Town, Water enough can be had to keep them going for half an Hour together. It seems to me some Publick Pumps are wanting; but that I submit to better Judgments.

As to our Conduct in the Affair of Extinguishing Fires, tho' we do not want Hands or Good-will, yet we seem to want Order and Method, and therefore I believe I cannot do better than to offer for our Imitation, the Example of a City in a Neighbouring Province.[2] There is, as I am well inform'd, a Club or Society of active Men belonging to each Fire Engine; whose Business is to attend all Fires with it whenever they happen; and to work it once a Quarter, and see it kept in order: Some of these are to handle the Firehooks, and others the Axes, which are always kept with the

2. The Boston Fire Society, established 1717, was, according to Carl Bridenbaugh, the model for Franklin's Union Fire Company, 1736. No copy of the Boston Articles of Agreement, 1734, has been found. In February 1712, the General Court authorized the selectmen and justices of Boston to appoint ten firewards to care for the public apparatus and to "give such necessary orders as may best serve the said Town in Suppressing and Extinguishing Fires." Ladders, pails, axes, engines, and other equipment were purchased; by 1720 these firewards were directing a fire department of six engines and twenty men. Bridenbaugh, *Cities in the Wilderness* (N.Y., 1938), pp. 210–2, 369; Samuel G. Drake, *The History and Antiquities of Boston* (Boston, 1856), pp. 542, 557.

Engine; and for this Service they are consider'd in an Abatement or Exemption in the Taxes. In Time of Fire, they are commanded by Officers appointed by Law, called *Firewards,* who are distinguish'd by a Red Staff of five Feet long, headed with a Brass Flame of 6 Inches; And being Men of Prudence and Authority, they direct the opening and stripping of Roofs by the Ax-Men, the pulling down burning Timbers by the Hookmen, and the playing of the Engines, and command the making of Lanes, &c. and they are impowered to require Assistance for the Removing of Goods out of Houses on fire or in Danger of Fire, and to appoint Guards for securing such Goods; and Disobedience, to these Officers in any, at such Times, is punished by a Fine of 40s. or Ten Days Imprisonment. These Officers, with the Men belonging to the Engine, at their Quarterly Meetings, discourse of Fires, of the Faults committed at some, the good Management in some Cases at others, and thus communicating their Thoughts and Experience they grow wise in the Thing, and know how to command and to execute in the best manner upon every Emergency. Since the Establishment of this Regulation, it seems there has been no extraordinary Fire in that Place; and I wish there never may be any here. But they suffer'd before they made such a Regulation, and so must we; for Englishmen feel but cannot see; as the Italian says of us. And it has pleased God, that in the Fires we have hitherto had, all the bad Circumstances have never happened together, such as dry Season, high Wind, narrow Street, and little or low Water: which perhaps tends to makes us secure in our own Minds; but if a Fire with those Circumstances, which God forbid, should happen, we should afterwards be careful enough.

Let me say one thing more, and I will be silent. I could wish, that either Tiles would come in use for a Covering to Buildings; or else that those who build, would make their Roofs more safe to walk upon, by carrying the Wall above the Eves, in the Manner of the new Buildings in London, and as Mr. Turner's House in Front-Street, or Mr. Nichols's in Chesnut-Street,[3] are built; which I conceive would tend considerably to their Preservation.

Let others communicate their Thoughts as freely as I have done

3. Possibly Joseph Turner and Anthony Nicholas, both later members of the Union Fire Company. Harrold E. Gillingham, "Philadelphia's First Fire Defences," *PMHB,* LVI (1932), 355–77.

mine, and perhaps something useful may be drawn from the Whole.
I am yours, &c.   A. A.

A Man of Sense

Printed in *The Pennsylvania Gazette*, February 11, 1734/5.

Franklin wanted his newspaper to instruct as well as inform, and sometimes published in it, he wrote in the autobiography, "little Pieces of
my own which had been first compos'd for Reading in our Junto. Of
these are a Socratic Dialogue, tending to prove, that, whatever might
be his Parts and Abilities, a vicious Man could not properly be called
a Man of Sense. And a Discourse on Self denial, showing that Virtue
was not secure, till its Practice became a Habitude, and was free from
the Opposition of contrary Inclinations. These may be found in the
Papers about the beginning of 1735."[4] He originally indicated that the
first of these had been "printed in Feb." but crossed out the words out.
These two pieces follow.

Mr. Franklin,
   Being the other Day near the Meeting-House Corner with some
Gentlemen, in the open Street, I heard the following Piece of Conversation; and penn'd it down as soon as I came home. I am confident it varies scarce any thing from what really passed; and as it
pleased the By-standers, it may possibly please the Publick, if you
give it a Place in your Paper.
   It not being proper to name the Persons discoursing, I shall call
one of them Socrates, his manner of Arguing being in my Opinion,
somewhat like that of Socrates: And, if you please, the other may
be Crito. I am Yours, &c.   A. A.

   Socrates. Who is that well-dress'd Man that passed by just
now?
   Crito. He is a Gentleman of this City, esteem'd a *Man of Sense,*
but not very honest.
   S. The Appellation of *a Man of Sense* is of late frequently given,
and seems to come naturally into the Character of every Man we

   4. See Alfred Owen Aldridge, "Franklin's 'Shaftesburian' Dialogues Not
Franklin's: A Revision of the Franklin Canon," *Amer. Lit.,* XXI (1949–50),
151–9.

are about to praise: But I am at some Loss to know whether a Man who *is not honest* can deserve it.

C. Yes, doubtless; There are many vicious Men who are nevertheless Men of very good Sense.

S. You are of Opinion, perhaps, that a Man of Knowledge is *a Man of Sense.*

C. I am really of that Opinion.

S. Is the Knowledge of Push-pin, or of the Game at Ninepins, or of Cards and Dice, or even of Musick and Dancing, sufficient to constitute the Character of a Man of Sense?

C. No certainly; there are many silly People that understand these Things tolerably well.

S. Will the Knowledge of Languages, or of Logic and Rhetoric serve to make a Man of Sense?

C. I think not; for I have known very senseless Fellows to be Masters of two or three Languages; and mighty full of their Logic, or their Rhetoric.

S. Perhaps some Men may understand all the Forms and Terms of Logic, or all the Figures of Rhetoric, and yet be no more able to convince or to perswade, than others who have not learnt those Things?

C. Indeed I believe they may.

S. Will not the Knowledge of the Mathematicks, Astronomy, and Natural Philosophy, those sublime Sciences, give a Right to the Character of *a Man of Sense?*

C. At first Sight I should have thought they might: But upon Recollection I must own I have known some Men, Masters of those Sciences, who, in the Management of their Affairs, and *Conduct of their Lives,* have acted very weakly, I do not mean viciously but foolishly; and therefore I cannot find in my Heart to allow 'em the Character of *Men of Sense.*

S. It seems then, that no Knowledge will serve to give this Character, but the Knowledge of our *true Interest;* that is, of what is best to be done in all the Circumstances of Humane Life, in order to arrive at our main End in View, HAPPINESS.

C. I am of the same Opinion. And now, as to the Point in Hand, I suppose you will no longer doubt whether a vicious Man may deserve the Character of a Man of Sense, since 'tis certain that there are many Men who *know* their true Interest, &c. and are

16

therefore *Men of Sense*, but are nevertheless vicious and dishonest Men, as appears from the whole Tenour of their Conduct in Life.

S. Can Vice consist with any Man's true Interest, or contribute to his Happiness?

C. No certainly; for in Proportion as a Man is vicious he loses the Favour of God and Man, and brings upon himself many Inconveniences, the least of which is capable of marring and demolishing his Happiness.

S. How then does it appear that those vicious Men have the Knowledge we have been speaking of, which constitutes *a Man of Sense*, since they act directly contrary?

C. It appears by their Discoursing perfectly well upon the Subjects of Vice and Virtue, when they occur in Conversation, and by the just Manner in which they express their Thoughts of the pernicious Consequences of the one, and the happy Effects of the other.

S. Is it the Knowledge of all the Terms and Expressions proper to be used in Discoursing well upon the Subject of making a good Shoe, that constitutes a Shoemaker; or is it the Knowing how to go about it and do it?

C. I own it is the latter, and not the former.

S. And if one who could only *talk finely* about Shoemaking, were to be set to work, would he not presently discover his Ignorance in that Art?

C. He would, I confess.

S. Can the Man who is only able to talk justly of Virtue and Vice, and to say that "Drunkenness, Gluttony and Lewdness destroy a Man's Constitution; waste his Time and Substance, and bring him under many Misfortunes, (to the Destruction of his Happiness) which the contrary Virtues would enable him to avoid;" but notwithstanding his talking thus, continues in those Vices; can such a Man deserve the Character of a Temperate and Chaste Man? Or does not that Man rather deserve it, who having *a thorough Sense* that what the other has said is true, *knows* also *how* to resist the Temptation to those Vices, and embrace Virtue with a hearty and steady Affection?

C. The latter, I acknowledge. And since Virtue is really the true Interest of all Men; and some of those who talk well of it, do not put it in Practice, I am now inclined to believe they speak only by rote, retailing to us what they have pick'd out of the Books or Con-

17

versation of wise and virtuous Men; but what having never enter'd or made any Impression on their Hearts, has therefore no Influence on the Conduct of their Lives.

S. Vicious Men, then, do not appear to have that Knowledge
which constitutes *the Man of Sense.*

C. No, I am convinced they do not deserve the Name. However, I am afraid, that instead of *defining* a Man of Sense we have
now entirely *annihilated* him: For if the Knowledge of his true Interest in all Parts of the Conduct of Life, and a constant Course of
Practice agreeable to it, are essential to his Character, I do not
know where we shall find him.

S. There seems no necessity that to be a Man of Sense, he should
never make a Slip in the Path of Virtue, or in Point of Morality;
provided he is sensible of his Failing and diligently applys himself
to rectify what is done amiss, and to prevent the like for the future.
The best Arithmetician may err in casting up a long Account; but
having found that Error, he *knows how* to mend it, and immediately
does so; and is notwithstanding that Error, an Arithmetician; But
he who *always* blunders, and cannot correct his Faults in Accounting, is no Arithmetician; nor is the habitually-vicious Man *a Man
of Sense.*

C. But methinks 'twill look hard, that all other Arts and Sciences
put together, and possess'd by one Man in the greatest Perfection,
are not able to dignify him with the Title of *a Man of Sense,* unless
he be also a Man of Virtue.

S. We shall agree, perhaps, that one who is *a Man of Sense,* will
not spend his Time in learning such Sciences as, if not useless in
themselves, will probably be useless to him?

C. I grant it.

S. And of those which may be useful to him, that is, may contribute to his Happiness, he ought, if he is a Man of Sense to know
how to make them so.

C. To be sure.

S. And of those which may be useful, he will not (if he is a Man
of Sense) acquire all, except that One only which is the most useful
of all, to wit, the Science of Virtue.

C. It would, I own, be inconsistent with his Character to do so.

S. It seems to follow then, that the vicious Man, tho' Master of
many Sciences, must needs be an ignorant and foolish Man; for

being, as he is vicious, of consequence unhappy, either he has acquired only the useless Sciences, or having acquired such as might be useful, he knows not how to make them contribute to his Happiness; and tho' he may have every other Science, he is ignorant that the SCIENCE OF VIRTUE is of more worth, and of more consequence to his Happiness than all the rest put together. And since he is ignorant of what *principally* concerns him, tho' it has been told him a thousand Times from Parents, Press, and Pulpit, the Vicious Man however learned, cannot be *a Man of Sense,* but is a Fool, a Dunce, and a Blockhead.

Self-Denial Not the Essence of Virtue[5]

Printed in *The Pennsylvania Gazette,* February 18, 1734/5.

New-Castle, Feb. 5. 1734/5.

To the Printer of the *Gazette.*

That SELF-DENIAL *is not the* ESSENCE OF VIRTUE.

It is commonly asserted, that without *Self-Denial* there is no Virtue, and that the greater the *Self-Denial* the greater the Virtue.

If it were said, that he who cannot deny himself in any Thing he inclines to, tho' he knows it will be to his Hurt, has not the Virtue of *Resolution* or *Fortitude,* it would be intelligible enough; but as it stands it seems obscure or erroneous.

Let us consider some of the Virtues singly.

If a Man has no inclination to *wrong* People in his Dealings, if he feels no Temptation to it, and therefore never does it; can it be said that he is not a just Man? If he is a just Man, has he not the Virtue of Justice?

If to a certain Man, idle Diversions have nothing in them that is tempting, and therefore he never relaxes his Application to Business for their Sake; is he not an Industrious Man? Or has he not the Virtue of Industry?

I might in like manner instance in all the rest of the Virtues: But to make the Thing short, As it is certain, that the more we strive against the Temptation to any Vice, and practise the contrary Virtue, the weaker will that Temptation be, and the stronger will be

5. See the headnote on p. 15 above for evidence of BF's authorship of this essay.

that Habit; 'till at length the Temptation has no Force, or entirely vanishes: Does it follow from thence, that in our Endeavours to overcome Vice, we grow continually less and less Virtuous; till at length we have no Virtue at all?

If Self-Denial be the Essence of Virtue, then it follows, that the Man who is naturally temperate, just, &c. is not virtuous; but that in order to be virtuous, he must, in spight of his natural Inclinations, wrong his Neighbours, and eat and drink, &c. to excess.

But perhaps it may be said, that by the Word *Virtue* in the above Assertion, is meant, *Merit;* and so it should stand thus; Without Self-Denial there is no Merit; and the greater the Self-Denial the greater the Merit.

The Self-denial here meant, must be when our Inclinations are towards Vice, or else it would still be Nonsense.

By Merit is understood, Desert; and when we say a Man merits, we mean that he deserves Praise or Reward.

We do not pretend to merit any thing of God, for he is above our Services; and the Benefits he confers on us, are the Effects of his Goodness and Bounty.

All our Merit then is with regard to one another, and from one to another.

Taking then the Assertion as it last stands,

If a Man does me a Service from a natural benevolent Inclination, does he deserve less of me than another who does me the like Kindness against his Inclination?

If I have two Journeymen, one naturally industrious, the other idle, but both perform a Days Work equally good, ought I to give the latter the most Wages?

Indeed, lazy Workmen are commonly observ'd to be more extravagant in their Demands than the Industrious; for if they have not more for their Work, they cannot live so well: But tho' it be true to a Proverb, *That Lazy Folks take the most Pains,* does it follow that they deserve the most Money?

If you were to employ Servants in Affairs of Trust, would you not bid more for one you knew was naturally honest, than for one naturally roguish, but who had lately acted honestly? For Currents whose natural Channel is damm'd up, (till the new Course is by Time worn sufficiently deep and become natural,) are apt to break their Banks. If one Servant is more valuable than another, has he not more Merit than the other? And yet this is not on Account of Superior Self-denial.

Is a Patriot not praise-worthy, if Publick Spirit is natural to him?

Is a Pacing-Horse less valuable for being a natural Pacer?

Nor in my Opinion has any Man less Merit for having in general natural virtuous Inclinations.

The Truth is, that Temperance, Justice, Charity, &c. are Virtues, whether practis'd with or against our Inclinations; and the Man who practises them, merits our Love and Esteem: And Self-denial is neither good nor bad, but as 'tis apply'd: He that denies a Vicious Inclination is Virtuous in proportion to his Resolution, but the most perfect Virtue is above all Temptation, such as the Virtue of the Saints in Heaven: And he who does a foolish, in-decent or wicked Thing, meerly because 'tis contrary to his Inclination, (like some mad Enthusiasts I have read of, who ran about naked, under the Notion of taking up the Cross) is not practising the reasonable Science of Virtue, but is lunatick.[6]

Reply to a Piece of Advice[7]

Printed in *The Pennsylvania Gazette*, March 4, 1734/5.

Mr. Franklin,

In your Paper of the 18th past, some Verses were inserted, said to be design'd as a PIECE OF ADVICE to a good Friend.[8] As this

6. Franklin's views were rejected by a contributor to *American Weekly Mercury*, March 4, 1735.

7. Here attributed to BF for stylistic reasons and because the signature "A.A." is the one he used to sign the essays on fire-protection and on "A Man of Sense" during the preceding month. See above, pp. 12–19.

8. The verses by "M. B." to which this essay replies were printed in the *Gazette*, Feb. 18.

> How mighty silly your Resolves,
> And Designs to change our [your?] State,
> Your Wishes crown'd, your Bliss dissolves
> To Cares in Bondage; Curse Compleat.
> Thy wonted Gaiety regain,
> Let Fools in Life content to wed,
> Submit to MISS's Tyrant Reign,
> I hope it's your's to be obey'd. [*Continued on next page*]

Piece of Advice, if it had been intended for a particular Friend alone, might have been as well convey'd to him privately; I suppose the Author by getting it publish'd, thinks it may be of Use to great Numbers of others, in his Friend's Circumstances. The import of it is, "That 'tis mighty silly for a single Man to change his State; for assoon as his Wishes are crown'd, his expected Bliss dissolves into Cares in Bondage, which is a compleat Curse; That only Fools in Life wed, for every Woman is a Tyrant: That he who marries, acts contrary to his Interest, loses his Liberty and his Friends, and will soon perceive himself undone; and that the best of the Sex are no better than a Plague." So ill-natur'd a Thing must have been written, either by some forlorn old Batchelor, or some cast-away Widower, that has got the Knack of drowning all his softer Inclinations in his Bowl or his Bottle. I am grown old and have made abundance of Observations, and I have had three Wives my self; so that from both Experience and Observation I can say, that this Advice is wrong and untrue in every Particular. It is wrong to assert *that tis silly in a single Man to change his State:* For what old Batchelor can die without Regret and Remorse, when he reflects upon his Deathbed, that the inestimable Blessing of Life and Being has been communicated by Father to Son through all Generations from Adam down to him, but in him it stops and is extinguished; and that *the Humane Race divine* would be no more, for any Thing he has done to continue it; he having, like the wicked Servant, *wrapt up and hid his Talent in a Napkin,* (i. e. his Shirt Tail,) while his Neighbours the Good and Faithful Servants, had some of them produced *Five* and some *Ten.* I say such an one shall not only die with Regret, but he may justly fear a severe Punishment. Nor is it true that *assoon as a Man weds, his expected Bliss dissolves into slavish Cares ana Bondage.* Every Man that is really a Man is Master of his own

---

> To Interest, Friendship, Freedom, lost,
> Dear Purchase for this mighty Boon,
> Of Hours of Bliss you'll not long boast,
> But pining, owning yourself undone.
>   Accept as Cordial what has past,
> Your Debonnair, with me approve,
> Confess the Sex a Plague at best,
> Nor one, nor other ever love.

Family; and it cannot be *Bondage* to have another submit to one's Government. If there be any Bondage in the Case, 'tis the Woman enters into it, and not the Man. And as to the *Cares,* they are chiefly what attend the bringing up of Children; and I would ask any Man who has experienced it, if they are not the most delightful Cares in the World; and if from that Particular alone, he does not find the *Bliss* of a double State much greater, instead of being less than he expected. In short this *Bondage* and these *Cares* are like the Bondage of having a beautiful and fertile Garden, which a Man takes great Delight in; and the Cares are the Pleasure he finds in cultivating it, and raising as many beautiful and useful Plants from it as he can. And if common Planting and Gardening be an Honourable Employment, (as 'tis generally allow'd, since the greatest Heroes have practic'd it without any Diminution to their Glory) I think *Human Planting* must be more Honourable, as the Plants to be raised are more excellent in their Nature, and to bring them to Perfection requires the greater Skill and Wisdom.

As to the Adviser's next Insinuation, that *only Fools wed, and every Woman is a Tyrant;* 'tis a very severe and undutiful Reflection upon his own Father and Mother; and since he is most likely to know best the Affairs of his own Family, I shall not contradict him in that particular, so far as relates to his own Relations: for perhaps his Aversion to a Wife arises from observing how his Mamma treated his Daddy; for she might be a Xantippe tho' he was no Socrates; it being probable that a wise Man would have instill'd sounder Principles into his Son. But in general I utterly dissent from him, and declare, that I scarce ever knew a Man who knew how to command in a proper Manner, but his Wife knew as well how to show a becoming Obedience. And there are in the World infinitely more He-Tyrants than She-Ones.

In the next Place he insinuates, that *a Man by marrying, acts contrary to his Interest, loses his Liberty and his Friends, and soon finds himself undone.* In which he is as much mistaken as in any of the rest. A Man does not act contrary to his Interest by Marrying; for I and Thousands more know very well that we could never thrive till we were married; and have done well ever since; What we get, the Women save; a Man being fixt in Life minds his Business better and more steadily; and he that cannot thrive married, could never have throve better single; for the Idleness and Negligence

23

of Men is more frequently fatal to Families, than the Extravagance of Women. Nor does a Man *lose his Liberty* but encrease it; for when he has no Wife to take Care of his Affairs at Home, if he carries on any Business there, he cannot go Abroad without a Detriment to that; but having a Wife, that he can confide in, he may with much more Freedom be abroad, and for a longer Time; thus the Business goes on comfortably, and the good Couple relieve one another by turns, like a faithful Pair of Doves. Nor does he *lose Friends* but gain them, by prudently marrying; for there are all the Woman's Relations added to his own, ready to assist and encourage the new-married Couple; and a Man that has a Wife and Children, is sooner trusted in Business, and can have Credit longer and for larger Sums than if he was single, inasmuch as he is look'd upon to be more firmly settled, and under greater Obligations to behave honestly, for his Family's Sake.

I have almost done with our Adviser, for he says but one thing more; to wit, *that the best of the Sex are no better than Plagues.* Very hard again upon his poor Mother, who tho' she might be the best Woman in the World, was, it seems, in her graceless Son's Opinion, no better than a Pestilence. Certainly this Versifyer never knew what a Woman is! He must be, as I conjectur'd at first, some forlorn old Batchelor. And if I could conjure, I believe I should discover, that his Case is like that of many other old He-Maids I have heard of. Such senseless Advice as this can have no Effect upon them; 'tis nothing like this, that deters them from marrying. But having in some of their first Attempts upon the kinder Sort of the Fair Sex, come off with Shame and Disgrace, they persuade themselves that they are, (and perhaps they are) really Impotent: And so durst not marry, for fear of those dishonourable Decorations of the Head, which they think it the inevitable Fate of a Fumbler to wear. Then, like the Fox who could not use his Tail, (but the Fox had really lost it) they set up for *Advisers,* as the Gentleman I have been dealing with; and would fain persuade others, that the Use of their own Tails is more mischievous than beneficial. But I shall leave him to Repentance; and endeavour to make the Reader some Amends for my Scribble, by adding the following Verses from the two best English Poets that ever were; only hinting, that by the first two Lines 'tis plain from whence our Poetical Adviser had his Inspiration.

Our Maker bids increase; who bids abstain,
But our *Destroyer*, foe to GOD and Man?
Hail wedded Love! mysterious Law, true source
Of human Offspring, sole propriety
In Paradise! of all Things common else.
By thee adult'rous Lust was driv'n from Men,
Among the bestial Herds to range; by thee,
(Founded in Reason, loyal, just, and pure)
Relations dear, and all the Charities
Of Father, Son, and Brother, first were known.
Perpetual Fountain of domestic Sweets!
Whose Bed is undefil'd, and chaste, pronounc'd.
Here, Love his golden shafts employs; here lights
His constant Lamp; and waves his purple Wings;
Reigns here, and revels: not in the bought smile
Of harlots; loveless, joyless, un-endear'd;
Casual fruition!   Milton[9]

But happy they! the happiest of their Kind!
Whom gentler Stars unite, and in one Fate
Their Hearts, their Fortunes, and their Beings blend.
'Tis not the coarser Tie of human Laws,
Unnatural oft, and foreign to the Mind,
Which binds their Peace, but Harmony itself,
Attuning all their Passions into Love;
Where Friendship full-exerts his softest Power,
Perfect Esteem enliven'd by Desire
Ineffable, and Sympathy of Soul,
Thought meeting Thought, and Will preventing Will,
With boundless Confidence; for nought but Love
Can answer Love, and render Bliss secure.
——— those whom Love cements, in holy Faith,
And equal Transport, free as Nature, live,
Disdaining Fear; for what's the World to them,
It's Pomp, it's Pleasure, and it's Nonsense all!
Who in each other clasp whatever fair
High Fancy forms, and lavish Heart can wish,

9. *Paradise Lost*, IV, 748–67, except 758–9 and 762.

Something than Beauty dearer, should they look
Or on the Mind, or mind-illumin'd Face;
Truth, Goodness, Honour, Harmony and Love,
The richest Bounty of indulgent *Heaven.*
Mean-time a smiling Offspring rises round,
And mingles both their Graces. By degrees,
The human Blossom blows; and every Day,
Soft as it rolls along, shows some new Charm,
The Father's Lustre, and the Mother's Bloom.
Then infant Reason grows apace, and calls
For the kind Hand of an assiduous Care;
Delightful Task! to rear the tender Thought,
To teach the young Idea how to shoot,
To pour the fresh Instruction o'er the Mind,
To breathe th' inspiring Spirit, and to plant
The generous Purpose in the glowing Breast.
Oh speak the Joy! You, whom the sudden Tear
Surprizes often, while you look around,
And nothing strikes your Eye but Sights of Bliss,
All various Nature pressing on the Heart,
Obedient Fortune, and approving *Heaven.*
These are the Blessings of diviner Love;
And thus their Moments fly; the *Seasons* thus,
As ceaseless round a jarring World they roll,
Still find them happy; and consenting SPRING
Sheds her own rosy Garland on their Head:
Till Evening comes at last, cool, gentle, calm;
When after the long vernal Day of Life,
Enamour'd more, as Soul approaches Soul,
Together, down they sink in social Sleep.   Thomson.[1]

I am, Sir, Your most humble Servant, A. A.

1. *The Seasons*, "Spring" (London, 1731), 1030–87, except 1043–51. BF's apostrophes in the three possessives in the line: "Its Pomp, its Pleasure, and its Nonsense all" have (unwittingly?) changed its meaning.

Dialogue between Two Presbyterians

Printed in *The Pennsylvania Gazette*, April 10, 1735.

Franklin was deeply involved in 1735 in the controversy about the Reverend Mr. Samuel Hemphill.[2] Ordained in Ireland, coming with recommendations from the Presbytery of Strabane, Hemphill was received by the Synod of Philadelphia, September 21, 1734. In Ireland a charge of unorthodoxy had been made against him, but was found to be unsupported. A report of this affair, Hemphill charged, was sent to Pennsylvania expressly to harm him; it brought about an inquiry by the Presbytery of New Castle into two sermons he had preached at New London in Chester County. Acquitted by the Presbytery, Hemphill was then invited by the aging Reverend Jedediah Andrews,[3] minister of the congregation in Philadelphia since 1698, to assist him by taking a service there each Sabbath.

Andrews' sermons, as Franklin remembered, "were chiefly either polemic Arguments, or Explications of the peculiar Doctrines of our Sect, and were all to me very dry, uninteresting and unedifying, since not a single moral Principle was inculcated or enforc'd, their Aim seeming to be rather to make us Presbyterians than good Citizens." Andrews succeeded as Franklin's spiritual adviser only to the extent of bringing him to church five Sundays in succession. Then Franklin stopped going and worshiped instead according to his private ritual. Hemphill's sermons, very different from those of Andrews both in content and style, brought Franklin into church again. Hemphill was young, vigorous, an effective speaker; his sermons contained "little of the dogmatical kind, but inculcated strongly the Practice of Virtue, or what in the religious Stile are called Good Works." To explain and urge the eternal laws of morality, Hemphill declared, was "not only a truly Christian, but beyond Comparison the most useful Method of Preaching."[4] Such sermons attracted and pleased not only Franklin, but many others as well, and Hemphill soon had large congregations, including many from other churches. Andrews described the attendants afterwards as "Freethinkers, Deists, and Nothings."[5]

2. For a general account of the affair, see Merton A. Christensen, "Franklin on the Hemphill Trial: Deism Versus Presbyterian Orthodoxy," *Wm. and Mary Quar.*, 3d ser., X (1953), 422–40.

3. *Sibley's Harvard Graduates*, IV (1933), 219–24.

4. *An Extract of the Minutes Of the Commission of the Synod, Relating to the Affair of The Reverend Mr. Samuel Hemphil* [sic] (Phila., 1735).

5. *Sibley's Harvard Graduates*, IV, 222; William B. Sprague, *Annals of the American Pulpit* (N.Y., 1859), III, 11; William M. Engles, ed., *Records of*

Inevitably, orthodox Presbyterians disapproved Hemphill's eloquently expounded views. Andrews attended his services all winter but, perhaps a little jealous of the younger man's popularity, thought his opinions dangerous. On April 7, 1735, he brought charges in the Synod. A commission was appointed to examine them.

To Franklin the issue was not merely whether Hemphill's "subverting opinions" were acceptable doctrine, but whether elder churchmen might silence and dismiss a man for preaching what they disapproved. He tried to organize supporters, and since Hemphill was a poor writer Franklin "lent him my Pen." His first defense was published only one week before the Commission was to meet.

MR. FRANKLIN,

You are desired by several of your Readers to print the following DIALOGUE. *It is between Two of the Presbyterian Meeting in this City. We cannot tell whether it may not be contrary to your Sentiments, but hope, if it should, you will not refuse publishing it on that Account: nor shall we be offended if you print any thing in Answer to it. We are yours, &c.* A.B.C.D.

S. Good Morrow! I am glad to find you well and abroad; for not having seen you at Meeting lately, I concluded you were indispos'd.

T. *Tis true I have not been much at Meeting lately, but that was not occasion'd by any Indisposition. In short, I stay at home, or else go to Church, because I do not like Mr. H. your new-fangled Preacher.*

S. I am sorry we should differ in Opinion upon any Account; but let us reason the Point calmly; what Offence does Mr. H. give you?

T. *Tis his Preaching disturbs me: He talks of nothing but the Duties of Morality: I do not love to hear so much of Morality: I am sure it will carry no Man to Heaven, and I do not think it fit to be preached in a Christian Congregation.*

S. I suppose you think no Doctrine fit to be preached in a Christian Congregation, but such as Christ and his Apostles used to preach.

T. *To be sure I think so.*

the Presbyterian Church in the United States of America (Phila., 1841), p. 107; Richard Webster, A History of the Presbyterian Church in America (Phila., 1857), pp. 416–20.

S. I do not conceive then how you can dislike the Preaching of Morality, when you consider, that Morality made the principal Part of their Preaching as well as of Mr. H's. What is Christ's Sermon on the Mount but an excellent moral Discourse, towards the End of which, (as foreseeing that People might in time come to depend more upon their *Faith* in him, than upon *Good Works,* for their Salvation) he tells the Hearers plainly, that their saying to him, *Lord, Lord,* (that is, professing themselves his Disciples or *Christians*) should give them no Title to Salvation, but their *Doing* the Will of his Father; and that tho' they have prophesied in his Name, yet he will declare to them, as Neglecters of Morality, that he never knew them.

T. But what do you understand by that Expression of Christ's, Doing the Will of my Father?

S. I understand it to be the Will of God, that we should live virtuous, upright, and good-doing Lives; as the Prophet understood it, when he said, *What doth the Lord require of thee, O Man, but to do justly, love Mercy, and walk humbly with the Lord thy God.*[6]

T. But is not Faith recommended in the New Testament as well as Morality?

S. Tis true, it is. Faith is recommended as a Means of producing Morality: Our Saviour was a Teacher of Morality or Virtue, and they that were deficient and desired to be taught, ought first to *believe* in him as an able and faithful Teacher. Thus Faith would be a Means of producing Morality, and Morality of Salvation. But that from such Faith alone Salvation may be expected, appears to me to be neither a Christian Doctrine nor a reasonable one. And I should as soon expect, that my bare Believing Mr. Grew to be an excellent Teacher of the Mathematicks,[7] would make me a Mathematician, as that Believing in Christ would of it self make a Man a Christian.

6. Micah 6:8.

7. Theophilus Grew (d. 1759), a successful private teacher of mathematics, compiler of almanacs; appointed professor of mathematics in the Academy and College of Philadelphia, 1751; author of *Description and Use of the Globes,* 1753; A.M., College of Philadelphia, 1757. BF sent his son William to Grew's school, 1738. Thomas H. Montgomery, *A History of the University of Pennsylvania* (Phila., 1900), pp. 146–7, 286. See above, I, 379.

T. *Perhaps you may think, that tho' Faith alone cannot save a Man, Morality or Virtue alone, may.*

S. Morality or Virtue is the End, Faith only a Means to obtain that End: And if the End be obtained, it is no matter by what Means. What think you of these Sayings of Christ, when he was reproached for conversing chiefly with gross Sinners, *The whole,* says he, *need not a Physician, but they that are sick;* and, *I come not to call the Righteous, but Sinners, to Repentance:* Does not this imply, that there were good Men, who, without Faith in him, were in a State of Salvation? And moreover, did he not say of Nathanael, while he was yet an Unbeliever in him, and thought no Good could possibly come out of Nazareth, *Behold an Israelite indeed, in whom there is no Guile!* that is, *behold a virtuous upright Man.* Faith in Christ, however, may be and is of great Use to produce a good Life, but that it can conduce nothing towards Salvation where it does not conduce to Virtue, is, I suppose, plain from the Instance of the Devils, who are far from being Infidels, *they believe,* says the Scripture, *and tremble.* There were some indeed, even in the Apostles' Days, that set a great Value upon Faith, distinct from Good Works, they meerly idolized it, and thought that a Man ever so righteous could not be saved without it: But one of the Apostles, to show his Dislike of such Notions, tells them, that not only those heinous Sins of Theft, Murder, and Blasphemy, but even *Idleness,* or the Neglect of a Man's Business, was more pernicious than meer harmless Infidelity, *He that neglects to provide for them of his own House,* says he, *is* WORSE *than an Infidel.* St. James, in his second Chapter, is very zealous against these Cryers-up of Faith, and maintains that Faith without Virtue is useless, *Wilt thou know, O vain Man,* says he, *that Faith without Works is dead;* and, *shew me your Faith without your Works, and I will shew you mine by my Works.* Our Saviour, when describing the last Judgment, and declaring what shall give Admission into Bliss, or exclude from it, says nothing of *Faith* but what he says against it, that is, that those who cry *Lord, Lord,* and profess to have *believed* in his Name, have no Favour to expect on that Account; but declares that 'tis the Practice, or the omitting the Practice of the Duties of Morality, *Feeding the Hungry, cloathing the Naked, visiting the Sick,* &c. in short, 'tis the Doing or not Doing all the Good that lies in our Power, that will render us the Heirs of Happiness or Misery.

T. But if Faith is of great Use to produce a good Life, why does not Mr. H. preach up Faith as well as Morality?

S. Perhaps it may [be] this, that as the good Physician suits his Physick to the Disease he finds in the Patient, so Mr. H. may possibly think, that though Faith in Christ be properly first preach'd to Heathens and such as are ignorant of the Gospel, yet since he knows that we have been baptized in the Name of Christ, and educated in his Religion, and call'd after his Name, it may not be so immediately necessary to preach *Faith* to us who abound in it, as *Morality* in which we are evidently deficient: For our late Want of Charity to each other, our Heart-burnings and Bickerings are notorious. St. James says, *Where Envying and Strife is, there is Confusion and every evil Work:* and where Confusion and every evil Work is, *Morality* and Good-will to Men, can, I think, be no unsuitable Doctrine. But surely *Morality* can do us no harm. Upon a Supposition that we all have Faith in Christ already, as I think we have, where can be the Damage of being exhorted to Good Works? Is Virtue Heresy; and Universal Benevolence False Doctrine, that any of us should keep away from Meeting because it is preached there?

T. Well, I do not like it, and I hope we shall not long be troubled with it. A Commission of the Synod will sit in a short Time, and try this Sort of Preaching.

S. I am glad to hear that the Synod are to take it into Consideration. There are Men of unquestionable Good Sense as well as Piety among them, and I doubt not but they will, by their Decision, deliver our Profession from the satyrical Reflection, which a few uneasy People of our Congregation have of late given Occasion for, to wit, That the Presbyterians are going to persecute, silence and condemn a good Preacher, for exhorting them to be honest and charitable to one another and the rest of Mankind.

T. If Mr. H. is a Presbyterian Teacher, he ought to preach as Presbyterians use to preach; or else he may justly be condemn'd and silenc'd by our Church Authority. We ought to abide by the Westminster Confession of Faith; and he that does not, ought not to preach in our Meetings.

S. The Apostacy of the Church from the primitive Simplicity of the Gospel, came on by Degrees; and do you think that the Reformation was of a sudden perfect, and that the first Reformers knew at once all that was right or wrong in Religion? Did not Luther at first preach only against selling of Pardons, allowing all

31

the other Practices of the Romish Church for good? He afterwards went further, and Calvin, some think, yet further. The Church of England made a Stop, and fix'd her Faith and Doctrine by 39 Articles; with which the Presbyterians not satisfied, went yet farther; but being too self-confident to think, that as their Fathers were mistaken in some Things, they also might be in some others; and fancying themselves infallible in *their* Interpretations, they also ty'd themselves down by the Westminster Confession. But has not a Synod that meets in King George the Second's Reign, as much Right to interpret Scripture, as one that met in Oliver's Time? And if any Doctrine then maintain'd is, or shall hereafter be found not altogether orthodox, why must we be for ever confin'd to that, or to any, Confession?

T. *But if the Majority of the Synod be against any Innovation, they may justly hinder the Innovator from Preaching.*

S. That is as much as to say, if the Majority of the Preachers be in the wrong, they may justly hinder any Man from setting the People right; for a *Majority* may be in the wrong as well as the *Minority*, and frequently are. In the beginning of the Reformation, the *Majority* was vastly against the Reformers, and continues so to this Day; and, if, according to your Opinion, they had a Right to silence the *Minority*, I am sure the *Minority* ought to have been silent. But tell me, if the Presbyterians in this Country, being charitably enclin'd, should send a Missionary into Turky, to propagate the Gospel, would it not be unreasonable in the Turks to prohibit his Preaching?

T. *It would, to be sure, because he comes to them for their good.*

S. And if the Turks, believing us in the wrong, as we think them, should out of the same charitable Disposition, send a Missionary to preach Mahometanism to us, ought we not in the same manner to give him free Liberty of preaching his Doctrine?

T. *It may be so; but what would you infer from that?*

S. I would only infer, that if it would be thought reasonable to suffer a Turk to preach among us a Doctrine diametrically opposite to Christianity, it cannot be reasonable to silence one of our own Preachers, for preaching a Doctrine exactly agreeable to Christianity, only because he does not perhaps zealously propagate all the Doctrines of an old Confession. And upon the whole, though the *Majority* of the Synod should not in all respects approve of Mr.

H.'s Doctrine, I do not however think they will find it proper to condemn him. We have justly deny'd the Infallibility of the Pope and his Councils and Synods in their Interpretations of Scripture, and can we modestly claim *Infallibility* for our selves or our Synods in our way of Interpreting? Peace, Unity and Virtue in any Church are more to be regarded than Orthodoxy. In the present weak State of humane Nature, surrounded as we are on all sides with Ignorance and Error, it little becomes poor fallible Man to be positive and dogmatical in his Opinions. No Point of Faith is so plain, as that *Morality* is our Duty, for all Sides agree in that. A virtuous Heretick shall be saved before a wicked Christian: for there is no such Thing as voluntary Error. Therefore, since 'tis an Uncertainty till we get to Heaven what true Orthodoxy in all points is, and since our Congregation is rather too small to be divided, I hope this Misunderstanding will soon be got over, and that we shall as heretofore unite again in mutual *Christian Charity.*

T. *I wish we may. I'll consider of what you've said, and wish you well.*

S. Farewell.[8]

Library Company to John Penn[9] and Reply

Printed in *The Pennsylvania Gazette*, June 5, 1735; also MS Minute Book, Library Company of Philadelphia.

The Directors of the Library Company on October 14, 1734, named Franklin and William Coleman to draft an address to John Penn, recently arrived from England. Coleman prepared it, and submitted it to the Directors on October 21, but consideration was postponed until the spring of 1735, when it was apparently rejected. On April 14 Franklin, Coleman, Thomas Hopkinson, and Joseph Breintnall were appointed

8. For the next stage in the controversy, see p. 37.
9. John Penn (1700–1746), called "the American" because he was born in Philadelphia during his father's second visit to Pennsylvania; an amiable and sensitive young man, he inherited a half-interest in William Penn's proprietorship. He visited Pennsylvania in September 1734 (see above, I, 381), but returned to England a year later. He bequeathed his share of the proprietorship to his brother Thomas. Howard M. Jenkins, "The Family of William Penn," *PMHB*, XX (1896), 439–43.

to write another, which was read on May 5, "and after a few small alterations 'twas generally approved of." It was delivered to the Proprietor on May 31.[1]

[May 31, 1735]

To the Honourable JOHN PENN, Esq; one of the Proprietors of Pennsylvania.

The humble ADDRESS of the LIBRARY COMPANY of Philadelphia.

May it please your Honour,

The Library Company of Philadelphia, as they are Pennsylvanians, finding themselves under the strongest Ties of Gratitude and Affection to your honourable Family, from which so many valuable Privileges are derived to the People of this Province; take this first Opportunity of expressing the Satisfaction they feel, in thus having two of their honourable Proprietors among them.

As nothing can be more glorious than the true Patriot, whose sole View is the Publick Good, so no one ever merited that Title more justly than the great and honourable Founder of this Province; That excellent Constitution it enjoys, so perfectly adapted to the true Ends of Government, Security and Freedom, clearly demonstrates the Wisdom and Humanity of that great and good Man your Father, who first modelled and established it; And with Pleasure we observe, that the same Wisdom, and the same benevolent Disposition is the distinguishing Character of his Successors.

As so excellent a Form of Government hath been answerable to the beneficent Views of the Author of it, in making this a flourishing Colony, it is not to be wondered at that some Men, (proceeding upon different Schemes, and of Course falling vastly short in the great Work of Peopling a new Country) should burn with Envy and Ill-will against your honourable House; and labour, tho' we hope impotently, to injure those whom they have not Minds generous enough to imitate.

Addresses are sometimes look'd upon as Matter of meer Form and Compliment, and perhaps to such who make Use of Power only to serve themselves and promote their own particular Interests, they can consist of little else; but he must be a Stranger to

1. Lib. Co. Phila., MS Minutes, May 31, June 5, 1735. For the Library Company's address to Thomas Penn, May 16, 1733, see above, I, 320.

our Charter, and the singular Privileges we enjoy, who suspects of Insincerity the highest Expressions of Gratitude, from the People of Pennsylvania to their Proprietors.

What now seems most necessary to increase the Happiness of a Country, possessed of so many Advantages, is the promoting of Knowledge and Virtue, that the Inhabitants may know how to esteem those Advantages as they ought, and appear not unworthy of them. To which End, the Erecting a *Publick Library* in this City, we hope may in some Measure contribute.

That Virtue, Learning and true Religion, may increase and flourish, under the Encouragement and Protection of your honourable House, is our earnest Wish and hearty Endeavour.

Signed by Order of the Library Company,

JOSEPH BREINTNALL, Secr.

The Proprietor's ANSWER

Gentlemen,

I am obliged to You for the Regard You express for my Self and Family in this Address. I agree with You that the encouraging of Virtue and useful Knowledge will be of very great Service to this Province; and I shall always be ready with Pleasure to promote so good and necessary an Undertaking, as the erecting a Publick Library in this City.

From Joseph Morgan[2]   ALS: American Philosophical Society

Mr. Franklin   Maidenhead   7. July 1735.

Sir, I have long expected to See the new Edition of The Temp. Inter.[3] If it Sell like that which you last printed of mine, you may

2. Joseph Morgan (1671–c.1745), Presbyterian minister at Maidenhead and Hopewell, N.J., since 1729; formerly Congregational minister in Greenwich, Conn., Bedford and East Chester, N.Y., 1697–1709, and minister of the Presbyterian church at Freehold, N.J., 1709–29; honorary M.A., Yale College, 1719. Undisciplined, cantankerous, drinking excessively, and experimenting with judicial astrology, he neglected his parochial duties, and was suspended by the Synod during 1736–39. He wrote several theological tracts, a novel, and many letters to scholars and learned societies about science and invention, especially as related to navigation. BF printed in the

print many; for they are all gone and people enquire for more, and none to be had. I Sent, as you desired, the places marked in the Margin, where the Additions Should be Set. Have you the Manuscript of Additions, It refers to the Same places: and you have nothing to puzzel you, except to that against Usury, add yet

[The Second Councel at Lateran under Lotharius the Emperour increased to near a thousand Bishops, in the year 1131 deprived *Userers* of Christian Burial, and cursed them to Hell. See Prideux's Synopsis of Councels, Pag. 23.

Of this I writ to you Several Times.

And to the End of all you may add

[If an Act were made that no Debt Should be recovered by Law in the Space of three years (except from Persons moving out of the Province) I think in that Time most Debts would be paid, and people in a way to Live: but as it now goes it will be worse and worse; people more and more in Debt, and never better till the country is quite undone.

This I think highly necessary. If you will print it I will Serve you much in Selling and put the Books into better hands. Yet I have first and last paid you Six pounds for Books of the 2 former Sold:[4] and more I expect from men afar off. I remain Your Friend and Servant   JOSEPH MORGAN

The £7 is long paid to Mr. Peace as you ordered.

Addressed: To   Mr Benjamin Franklin   at the New Printing Office   near the Market   in Philadelphia   These

---

Gazette, 1732, two letters of his: on locks to improve navigation and on fish-ladders (see above, I, 192). Dr. Alexander Hamilton described this village philosopher, whom he met at Kingston, N.J., 1744, in *Gentleman's Progress*, ed. Carl Bridenbaugh (Chapel Hill, 1948), p. 36. Whitfield J. Bell, Jr., "The Reverend Mr. Joseph Morgan, An American Correspondent of the Royal Society, 1732–1739," APS *Proc.*, xcv (1951), 254–61; Richard Schlatter, ed., *The History of the Kingdom of Basaruah* (Cambridge, Mass., 1946), pp. 11–19. The brackets in the text of this letter are in the original.

3. *The Temporal Interest of North America*, published by BF, 1733; no second edition was printed.

4. Probably *The Nature of Riches*, published by BF, 1732, and *The Temporal Interest of North America*.

Observations on the Proceedings against Mr. Hemphill

Some Observations on the Proceedings against The Rev. Mr. Hemphill; with a Vindication of his Sermons. The Second Edition. Philadelphia: Printed and Sold by B. Franklin. 1735. (Yale University Library)

The Commission of the Synod of Philadelphia appointed to hear Jedediah Andrews' charges against Samuel Hemphill[5] met April 17. The evidence consisted of the testimony of witnesses and Hemphill's own notes of seven of his sermons, which, after first "positively and peremptorily" refusing to produce, he finally agreed to read. Ten days later he was unanimously censured and suspended from his ministerial office for doctrines "Unsound and Dangerous, contrary to the sacred Scriptures and our excellent Confession and Catechisms." This action against a popular preacher provoked "much Discourse" throughout the city and forced the Commission to print, the first week in May, an extract of their minutes explaining and defending their action.[6]

This pamphlet listed six points on which Hemphill's opinions, as expressed in supporting evidence, were judged to be in error. Although it showed that Hemphill "had free Liberty to offer any thing in his own Defence," and that he and others spoke in his behalf, it gave no hint of what he or his supporters said. Accordingly, it brought Franklin once more to Hemphill's side. In his *Observations* on this *Extract,* Franklin reviewed Hemphill's career, reprinted Andrews' charges, and examined each of the six indictments in the light of the entire evidence offered or available. These *Observations* were announced on June 12 as in the press, and were advertised as "just published" in the *Gazette* of July 17. The first edition sold out in two weeks; a second was run off in August.[7] No copy of the first edition has been found.

ADVERTISEMENT.

The Commission of the Synod having published what they thought proper of their Proceedings in Hemphill's Tryal, it is therefore thought expedient to give a true Narrative of the whole Affair, in order to clear his Character from the false Aspersions which

5. See above, pp. 27–8.

6. *An Extract of the Minutes Of the Commission of the Synod, Relating to the Affair of The Reverend Mr. Samuel Hemphil* [sic] was printed by Andrew Bradford at Philadelphia.

7. Beginning June 19 the *American Weekly Mercury* announced for several weeks that there was "now in the Press at New-York" *Some Observations on the Sentence passed against the Reverend Mr. Hemphill;* but this pamphlet seems not to have been published.

have been cast upon it, and to convince the World how unjustly some Men will act, when they have their own private Ends in View.

The Commission promis'd Hemphill a Copy of the Minutes as soon as they could be transcrib'd; which Promise if they had comply'd with, this *Answer* might have been published before the Printer was taken sick, whose Illness unexpectedly continuing six or seven Weeks has thus long retarded its Publication.

Some Observations, &c.

It will be necessary by way of Introduction, to give a brief Account of the first Cause which gave Rise to the unchristian Treatment which Mr. Hemphill has met with since he came to America.

This was a Letter which Mr. Vance, a Presbyterian Minister in the North of Ireland, sent to his Brother-in-law J. Kilpatrick in Pennsylvania, to the prejudice of Hemphill's Character, of which Letter more hereafter. The Difference between Vance and Hemphill arose thus; Vance having preach'd at a neighbouring Congregation call'd Burt near London-derry, Hemphill soon after preach'd in the same Place and upon the same Subject. Some of those who heard Hemphill's Sermon, told Vance that his Sermon was oppos'd by Hemphill; and altho' neither Vance nor Hemphill were acquainted with each other, nor had they ever heard one another preach, yet this inflam'd Vance's Zeal to that degree, that he took all the care in his Power to defame Hemphill, calling him a vile Heretick, and said that no christian Minister should allow him to preach in his Pulpit, and that he would have him suspended next Synod. The Synod meeting soon after, Vance thought proper to invite Hemphill to a private Conference in order to accomodate the Affair in a christian manner; and accordingly both met, with four other Ministers, viz. Messrs. Ross, Ferguson, Donaldson and Harvey. It was there propos'd by one of the Ministers, that both Sermons should be preach'd before the Synod, which Hemphill agreed to, but Vance would not, altho' he had traduced him in so vile a manner. At length Vance freely own'd he had reported Things of Hemphill which he himself did not believe, that he believ'd Hemphill was wronged, that he was sorry for it, and would use all the means in his Power to inform his Neighbours that Hemphill was very ill used.

Notwithstanding this solemn Promise, Vance acted with more Malice and Envy than ever; and being accused in a second Conference by Hemphill, when two of the aforesaid Ministers were present, that he not only reported Lies of him, but also violated the solemn Promise he had made at the Synod; he absolutely deny'd that he had said any thing to Hemphill's Disadvantage since their last Meeting at the Synod; this he did upon the Word of a christian Minister, and with uplifted Hands, altho' it could have been sufficiently prov'd against him. And Vance having further an Opportunity of stopping Hemphill's Ordination, being present when his Name was publish'd in the Synod in the usual manner, "desiring if any Member knew any Cause why Hemphill should not be ordain'd, they would tell it to the Synod"; this one would think was the most proper time and place for Vance to have told what he knew of Hemphill, and which without doubt he would have been very fond of, had there been any Truth in what he reported of him before, or afterwards wrote to America. And here I'm amaz'd that Vance could find so many Men in these Parts of his own Principles, who will not only venture to violate the peculiar Duties of Christianity, but even every thing that is human. One would think, that neither Vance, nor those who are the Executioners of his religious Vengeance in America, can be ignorant of that noble moral Precept of *doing as they would be done by*.

In the Letter which Vance sent to J. Kilpatrick, he tells him, that there is a Preacher, Hemphill by name, gone over to Pennsylvania, who is a vile Heretick, a Preacher of Morality, and giving him all the invidious Names that Malice could invent, he desires him to prevent his Settlement in America if possible; at the same time desiring that his Name may not be made use of; from whence it may justly be concluded, that it was not a Regard for Christianity, but Malice, that was his Motive in writing so scandalous a Letter, and none but those of his own Stamp would have given any Credit to it.

When Kilpatrick received said Letter, he took a particular care to publish it; he went to the neighbouring Congregations, reading it as often as he could find Hearers, and showing it to the Ministers, who copied after Vance's Example; for soon after, Hemphill was represented by several Ministers to be a *New-Light Man*, a *Deist*, one who preach'd nothing but *Morality*, a Missionary sent from Ireland to corrupt the Faith once delivered to the Saints; in short, he was every thing a persecuting Spirit could invent; altho' neither they nor Vance had ever heard him preach, nor did they know at that Time but he was as full of Enthusiasm and a persecuting Zeal as themselves.

But this was not all, for they made use of all the means they were capable of, to excite the People of New-London in Chester County, where Hemphill had preach'd two Sermons, to prosecute and give Evidence against him for some Heresy or other, and prevail'd upon two Men for that purpose; upon which Hemphill being summoned by the Presbytery of New-Castle, he appear'd and was acquitted, to the great Grief of several of the Members, who since endeavoured to have another Presbytery call'd, in order to suspend him; nay some of them consulted the Records of the Church of Scotland, in order to find a Precedent for deposing him before the Sentence of Suspension.

I should inform my Reader, when Mr. Hemphill came to Philadelphia, immediately after his Arrival in Pennsylvania, Mr. Andrews invited him to preach in his Pulpit once a day, and even told him, that if the Congregation of Philadelphia should chance to be pleased with his Preaching, Mr. Andrews would leave the Place to himself: But some time after this, Mr. Andrews, moved it seems by Envy at hearing Hemphill's Preaching universally applauded, and observing the large Audiences when he preached, thought fit to go from House to House among his Congregation, declaring Hemphill to be a Preacher of erroneous Doctrine, calling him *Deist, Socinian,* and the like, and was pleased to be very angry with those who could not agree with him in his Notions of Hemphill and his Sermons.

Mr. Andrews is an old Man, and therefore in Compassion to his Weakness, one would chuse to pass over in Silence any part of his Conduct upon this Occasion, which seemed not to be very consistent with the Character of a christian Minister. Notwithstanding all the hard Treatment Hemphill met with from Mr. Andrews, he kept so far within the Bounds of christian Charity, as not to make him any Returns of the like Usage, thinking if he knew better he would act otherwise: This Behaviour of Hemphill's had this Effect on Mr. Andrews, that he could not help saying to many People, that Hemphill was a Man of an excellent Temper. However, at last, perceiving that much the largest part of the Congregation approv'd of Hemphill's Conduct and Sermons, he was pleas'd to represent the Affair in such a Light to the Moderator and other Ministers, that the Commission of the Synod met the 17th of April, 1735, in order to the Trial of Hemphill; at which time the Articles of Accusation exhibited by Mr. Andrews were read, and follow in these Words, viz.

ARTICLES *to be presented to the Consideration of the Reverend Commission of the Synod and Correspondents, exhibiting an Account of sundry Doctrines advanced by the Reverend Mr. Samuel Hemphill, that have been and are dissatisfactory to the Subscriber.*

"1. That Christianity is nothing else but a Revival or new Edition of the Laws and Precepts of Nature, except two positive Precepts and worshipping of God by a Mediator. Text, Rom. 8:18.[8]

"2. Whether the Sentiments some had of his Opinion about the new Creature from his Sermon on Gal. 6:15,[9] were well grounded, I shall not determine: But his saying in that Sermon that the Sacrament of the Lord's Supper is only a Means to promote a good and pious Life, and afterwards denying any Communion in it, is what I don't agree to. I was also not satisfied at his speaking against the need of spiritual Pangs in order to Conversion.

"3. In his Sermon on Acts 24:25,[1] there were many Things that I was displeased with. He appeared to me and others as declaiming with great Earnestness against the Doctrine of Christ's Merits and Satisfaction, as a Doctrine that represented God as stern and inexorable, and fit only for Tyrants to impose and Slaves to obey. There were also some complained of, as if they made a Charm of the Word *Christ* in their preaching, thereby working up their Hearers to Enthusiasm.

"4. Preaching upon Mark 16:16,[2] he described Saving Faith to be nothing else but an Assent to or Persuasion of the Truth of the

8. "For I reckon, that the sufferings of this present time are not worthy to be compared with the glory which shall be revealed in us."

9. "For in Christ Jesus neither circumcision availeth any thing, nor uncircumcision, but a new creature."

1. "And as he reasoned of righteousness, temperance, and judgment to come, Felix trembled and answered, Go thy way for this time, when I have a convenient season, I will call for thee."

2. "He that believeth and is baptized, shall be saved, but he that believeth not, shall be damned."

Doctrines of the Gospel on rational Grounds. He also said, that the Mysteries mentioned in the Epistles concerned only those Times in which they were wrote, and not us. And that Faith and Obedience are the same Thing.

"5. In his Sermon on Acts 10:34, 35,[3] he appeared to me and others as designing to open the Door of the Church wide enough to admit all honest Heathens, as such, into it, upon a supposition that Cornelius was a Heathen when Peter was sent to him.

"6. In his Sermon on Psalm 41:4, *Lord heal my Soul,* &c.[4] when an Account was given how our Souls came to be distempered, no Distemper by original Sin, as I heard, was mentioned, but only such Distempers and Diseases as are contracted by evil Practices, and the want of a due Government of our Passions and Affections by Reason; which Passions and Affections were declared right and sound or good in themselves, and made or put into us so by God. And when he came to speak of the Cure of those Distempers and Maladies, there was no mention made (as I remember) of Prayer or the Blood or Spirit of Christ, or any thing said of him; but the whole Cure seemed to me by what he said, to be performed by ourselves. He had also a peculiar Notion, as I took it, about Hell, in the Application, which the perusal of the Sermon will discover.

"7. Preaching upon Eph. 3:8,[5] after having brought again his Account wherein the Nature of Christianity consists, namely in a Revival or new Edition of the Law of Nature, he went on to run down (as I understood him) the Protestant Doctrine of Justification by Faith, saying, among other Things, to this Effect, that what the Apostle says of that Doctrine, concerned new converted Heathens and not us. And to make this good, he set up St. James against St. Paul, saying, is not the Authority of St. James as good as the Authority of St. Paul?

"*Lastly,* In his Prayer he constantly omits to pray for any Church either Catholick or particular, or any Ministers of it, but only for

3. "Then Peter opened his mouth, and said, Of a truth I perceive that God is no respecter of persons: But in every nation, he that feareth him, and worketh righteousness, is accepted with him."

4. "I said, Lord, be merciful unto me: heal my soul; for I have sinned against thee."

5. "Unto me, who am less than the least of all Saints, is this grace given, that I should preach among the Gentiles the unsearchable riches of Christ."

Mankind in general. It is also common with him in his Prayers, and sometimes in his Sermons, to say that Reason is our Rule, and was given us for a Rule.

"Some other things might be mentioned, that were displeasing to many when spoken, which, whether there will be any Notice taken of them in the Process I know not, and so say nothing of 'em here.

"If I am mistaken in any of the above-mentioned particulars, I shall be abundantly more ready to retract than I was to accuse.

"April 7. 1735.   J. ANDREWS."

How trifling some of these Accusations are, may be left to the Observation of every Reader; and how groundless the rest are will appear when we come to the particular Consideration of them; which before we enter upon, I shall endeavour to give a true and faithful Account of the Proceedings of this reverend Commission, and if in any thing I deviate from the Truth, I may be contradicted by those who were present during the whole Tryal.

After the Articles were read, Mr. Hemphill objected to Messrs. Thompson and Gillespie,[6] as not being proper Persons to be of the Number of his Judges, by reason that they had condemn'd him already; having declar'd their Sentiments that he was guilty of preaching great Errors; and that they had done this without any personal Acquaintance with him, nor had they ever heard him preach. This was clearly made to appear with relation to Thompson, by several Gentlemen who had seen his Letters. What concern'd Gillespie had been so notorious, that Hemphill referr'd it to himself, whether he had not upon a particular Occasion, before many People, asserted that Mr. Hemphill was a New-Light Man, and other Words importing that he was guilty of preaching Errors? Mr. Gillespie made answer, that he did not remember that he ever said any such thing. In Charity we are to suppose that he had forgot it; but the Allegation was nevertheless true, as can be incontestably prov'd. However, neither of these Objections were allow'd to have any Weight with the Commission.

6. John Thomson (d. 1753?) was minister of the Presbyterian church at Chestnut Level. George Gillespie (1683–1760), minister of the congregation on White Clay Creek, Del., was the author of *A Treatise against the Deists of* [sic] *Freethinkers, proving the Necessity of Revealed Religion* (Phila., 1735).

Then Mr. Hemphill being requested to deliver up his Sermons for their Perusal, denied to do it for these Reasons, viz. 1st, It was contrary to the common Rights of Mankind, no Man being obliged to furnish Matter of Accusation against himself. 2dly, It was contrary to the Usage of the Church of Scotland, from whence they pretend to take a Pattern of their Church Government. 3dly, He was inform'd from all Hands that his Cause was prejudg'd, that there was a strange Spirit of Bitterness rais'd up against him among the People by the Ministers, and that there was little Probability of obtaining a fair and impartial Decision in his Case. And how just these Reasons were, the Sequel of this will plainly show. Upon his Refusal to deliver up ʌis Notes, tho' they acknowledged they had no Right to insist upon it, yet they were charitable enough to make Suggestions, that Hemphill's Guilt was the Occasion of his not delivering up his Sermons. How becoming such a Conduct as this was, in Judges who had not as yet heard any thing more of the Cause than barely the reading of the Charges, let the Reader judge. Sure in a civil Case such Judges would not deserve the Character of very impartial ones; however, it is very necessary to make Allowances for some Clergymen.

In answer to what they alledge of his Promise; Hemphill declar'd he had let Mr. Andrews know in private Conversation, being inform'd by him that he intended to draw up a Charge against him, that if he would call at his House, he would act so friendly as to show him his Notes, in order to set him right in any Part, if he should be wrong; which Andrews never thought proper to do: And two Gentlemen that were present, declared, That some little time after this Conversation had with Andrews, Hemphill had told 'em separately the Story in the same manner. And as to the Evidences produc'd to prove the Promise, he alledges that they mistook him when he told this Story, it being well known to many Gentlemen that are his Friends, that he had ever since the Information he had receiv'd of the unfair Usage he was like to meet with, resolv'd not to show his Notes; in which Resolution he was strengthen'd by their Advice. Further, if Mr. Andrews had depended upon such a Promise of Hemphill's, as he declar'd he did, (giving it as a Reason for the Weakness and Imperfection of his Charges) he must have depended upon that Promise long before he himself said it was made, for the Charges antecedent to that Promise are much more imperfectly drawn up, than those consequent upon it; which in my humble Opinion, plainly proves that Andrews had no Dependance on any such Promise, neither did he expect that the Notes would be given to the Commission, but only made use of it as an Excuse for the Nonsense and Inconsistencies with which these Charges are stuffed.

After this, the Commission proceeded to hear such Evidence as was brought before 'em, the Credibility and Faithfulness of which they say *they had no Reason to object against,* which can't but be very surprizing to all Persons present at the Tryal. The main Evidence, or rather, to make use of the Moderator's own Words, the *plumb* Evidence, deposed that he heard Mr. Hemphill in his Sermon say, *That to preach up Christ's Merits and Satisfaction, his Death and Sufferings, was to preach up a Charm,* with many other Things equally absurd as false. This Man's Evidence exceedingly surprized all the Members of the Congregation then present, who then positively declared that no such Words had been utter'd; and forty People could have been adduced to contradict his Testimony; but this they were told by the Commission was admitting of negative Evidence; nor could they by any means prevail so far as to have Leave to set the Matter in its true Light, by declaring the Truth; tho' sundry Persons remember'd the very Words of the Sentence in which the Word *Charm* was contain'd; and the Commission was told, that Mr. Andrews's Charge corroborated what they had to say. And when nothing would prevail with them, a Gentleman of the Congregation appealed to the Accuser, who had brought this Evidence, Whether he did not believe that what that Evidence said was untrue? To which, to the great Surprize of many, he was forced to make this disingenuous Reply, *That he was not obliged to answer the Question.* This Answer, together with his adducing a Person to depose a thing that he knew was false, has stagger'd many People who formerly had received a good Opinion of his Integrity. And to give you a Sample of the Spirit that was then predominant, one of the Ministers, and who was one of Hemphill's Judges too, justified this vile Action of Andrews in Conversation afterwards; he call'd it, *an innocent Wile,* and said, *there was no harm in admitting a false Evidence in order to force the Accused to confess the Truth.* This needs no Remark; for I can't help thinking the bare reading of it is sufficient to fill the Mind of every candid Reader with Horror!

There were several other Evidences produced, particularly one who declared, that the Accused said in his Sermon, *there were no Mysteries in Christianity*. This, together with several other things, was offer'd to be invalidated by the Testimony of a great many ingenious Persons then present; but it was at that time absolutely refused, as admitting negative Evidence: Notwithstanding it was urged to 'em, that their Duty was to find out Truth, and that good End ought not to be impeded by any Quirks or Evasions; and surely that Affair of negative Evidence deserved no better Name. It was urged likewise, that it might be any of their own Cases, that one or two of the most ignorant Members of their Congregations, might accuse 'em in the like manner, and if the Testimony of the rest could not be allow'd to invalidate it, they might be brought to the Circumstances of Hemphill, and condemned upon very false Evidence; and that such a Method of Proceedure would destroy all Safety both in Church and State. All this and much more was said, but to no purpose. True indeed it is, after they had adjourn'd, being somewhat abated from the Heat they were in the Evening before, and reflecting how this Conduct of theirs would be censured by the World, they agreed to let Hemphill adduce Evidences, to invalidate the Depositions given in against him: But in order to render their Indulgence ineffectual, they peremptorily refus'd to let him have a Copy of them. Which Action of theirs was a strange Piece of Mockery; for how can any Man invalidate the Testimony of another without knowing what it is; especially where there were so many Evidences, and where it is in Relation to Words spoken, which was then the Case.

And here I shall conclude this Head, by observing, if they gave any Credit to the Sermons upon which they afterwards condemned him; and which they were pleas'd to declare they believ'd to be genuine, and read to 'em as they were preached, they had then the highest Reason to object to the Credibility and Faithfulness of the Evidence; seeing the Sermons plainly prov'd most of the Evidences to be false: Nor can these reverend Gentlemen make it appear, that either Andrews's Charges or Evidences were justly founded on these Sermons they heard read. But this will more fully appear in the Sequel of these Papers.

Having spent the remaining Part of the Week in examining the Evidences, they then adjourn'd to Monday, the Moderator and

Mr. Cross being appointed to preach on Sunday;[7] tho' at that time the Affair of Mr. Hemphill was still under consideration, and he being the next Day to offer what he thought proper in his Defence, yet, I say, these two charitable Men, these impartial Judges, were pleased to deliver such Sermons as plainly convinc'd all indifferent Persons, that they had condemned Hemphill before they left their own Homes: Their Discourses were calculated to exasperate the People against him, to represent him as a Preacher of erroneous Doctrine, a Seducer, &c. And lest they should not be understood against whom their Discourses were levelled, they cautioned the Hearers against Preachers who *deny'd the Merits and Satisfaction of Christ*, which was one of the Crimes upon which Hemphill was falsly accus'd, and afterwards unjustly condemn'd. How proper such Sermons as these were in the Time of this Tryal, how consistent with Christian Moderation or with their own Reputations as Men, or what Justice was to be expected from such Judges, let the Reader imagine. They have indeed upon this Occasion given such Impressions of themselves as will not be very soon forgotten in Philadelphia.

Mr. Hemphill by this time perceiving that he was not to expect any fair Usage, from Men who upon all Occasions gave such evident Proofs of their Bitterness against him, had Thoughts of taking his Leave of them, without saying any thing further in his own Defence: But at length, out of a Regard to his own Reputation, and to clear himself from the Aspersions thrown upon him by the Evidences, and the uncharitable Invectives deliver'd in the Sermons abovementioned; he determin'd to make the Commission of the Synod an Offer of publickly Reading of his Sermons to 'em; which Offer of his, after some short Time, they accepted of: And this publick Method he chose to take, that the World might be convinced how far he had been injured in his Reputation, and what little Reason he had given for the unchristian Usage he afterwards met with. His Sermons were then read, which for the Strain of Christian Charity that run thro' the whole of them, and their con-

7. The sermons were by Ebenezer Pemberton (1705–1777), minister at New York, and moderator of the Synod of 1735, *A Sermon Preach'd before the Commission of the Synod at Philadelphia, April 20, 1735* (N.Y., 1735), and by Robert Cross (1689–1766), minister at Jamaica, Long Island, *The Danger of Perverting the Gospel of Christ* (N.Y., 1735).

stantly urging the Necessity of a holy Life and Conversation in order to our final Acceptance with God, were approved of by People of all Persuasions; and I believe I may venture to affirm, that few People present discover'd the Heresies that seemed so plain and obvious afterwards to the Commission of the Synod and Correspondents.

After the Sermons were read over, and such Extracts taken out of them as any Member of the Commission thought proper, they then proceeded to desire Hemphill to appear before 'em the next Day, to offer what he had to say in his own Defence. But what Meaning they had in this, no one but they can devise. Hemphill at first imagined, they intended to have examined him the next Day, upon the Extracts they had taken from his Notes, and to have shown him in what Sense they thought them worthy of Censure, and have heard him to the several Points; but herein he was greatly mistaken.

And here I can't help being fill'd with Amazement, to see what Lengths the crafty Malice of some, and the hot distemper'd Zeal of others will carry them! The Day following Hemphill appear'd before the Commission of the Synod, and was then prepared to answer any Objections made to the Doctrines he had preach'd, or to have explained his Words where they might have been misunderstood; but to his very great Surprize, they refused to let him know what in particular they objected to, nor would they by any means point out to him, in what part of the Extracts they had taken, they had deemed him to be erroneous; altho' they had told him when he read the first Sermon, that he should have an Opportunity to vindicate every part they would object against; but this was promis'd with a View to end a Dispute between the Moderator and Hemphill. Indeed some of them contended that he had no Right to explain his own Words; tho' that was offered to them only for their own Satisfaction, and it was not expected that the Explications should have any further Weight with them than what the natural Construction of the Words would bear, and this was declared to them at the same time. This Point was afterwards given up by 'em, but in Words only; for when he was told he might explain his own Words, they at the same time refused to let him know what part of the Extracts wanted explaining, or in their Opinion contained Errors. No, a more just Method of Proceeding would not have been conducive to the End they had in View; the malicious, or to give it the most charitable Name it can bear, their mistaken Manner of taking down Parts of his Sermons, and the false Glosses they were pleased to put upon 'em, would then have been manifest to the World. The Truth of which Assertion will plainly appear to the Reader in the Sequel of this; where he may perceive, that in some Places they have falsly recited his Words, in others taken only Parts of Sentences, and left out the remaining Parts which would have cleared up their Objections, and render'd ridiculous the pretended Heresies for which they condemned him. If they had at that time in the face of the World, declared in what they judged him to be erroneous, and produced Authority from Scripture to support their Opinions, and *then* given him an Opportunity to offer what he thought proper in his own Defence; they then surely would have acted a more Christian and justifiable Part, and would not have brought such a Reproach on themselves and their Profession as they have done.

And here I am sorry, that I am obliged to say, that they have no Pattern for their Proceedings, but that hellish Tribunal the *Inquisition,* who rake up all the vile Evidences, and extort all the Confessions they can from the wretched Object of their Rage, and without allowing him any Means of invalidating the Evidence, or convincing 'em of their own Mistakes, they assemble together in secret, and proceed to Judgment. No Precedent from the Church of Scotland will warrant these their Proceedings; for when any Affair of this kind is laid before their Judicatures, they debate amongst themselves publickly, and the Members of which it is compos'd do separately give Reasons for their Opinions, and point out what they take to be subversive of the Gospel of Christ, and their well known Confession of Faith; and give an Opportunity to the Person accused to answer their several Objections, and to take all just Methods of clearing himself: And this is done in order to demonstrate to the World, the Sincerity and Candour of their Actions, and upon what Motives they have proceeded. These Gentlemen on the contrary, only took Extracts out of Hemphill's Sermons, and without acquainting him or any other Person of their Sentiments in relation to 'em, or publickly declaring in what manner they understood 'em, they assembled together in secret, refusing to admit any Persons to be present at any of their Debates (if they had any) and proceeded to devise Reasons for their condemning of him. This indeed took them several Days; for as they could not give good Reasons for their so doing, it was necessary to invent some plausible ones: which I shall here transcribe from the *Extract of their Minutes*, in order to answer them one after another.

EXTRACT page 6.

"The Commission proceeded to consider the Affair of Mr. Hemphill, in order to form a Judgment, and accordingly determined to take each Article of the Charge distinctly, and to compare them with the Extracts of his Sermons; and upon mature Consideration of the first Article, we find that agreeable to the first Charge brought in against him, viz. That Christianity, which he calls the second Revelation of God's Will agreeable to the first, is by him asserted to be only an Illustration and Improvement of the Law of Nature, with the Addition of some few positive Things, such as the two Sacraments, and our going to God and making our approaches to him in the Name and Mediation of his Son Jesus Christ. And what, in our Apprehension, further supports this Charge, is what he asserts when he is professedly treating of such Things as are more purely and properly Christian; after an Enumeration of several Particulars, he has these Expressions, viz. *This is no more than to live and act according to our Nature, and to have the Government of our selves in our own Hands*. And this is further confirmed by an Extract of his Sermon on Mark 16: 16, wherein he asserts, That *the Gospel is, as to its ultimate End and most essential Parts, implanted in our very Nature and Reason;* which Description of Christianity we judge to be inconsistent with our well-known Confession of Faith, and subversive of the Gospel of Christ."

Allowing freely that Hemphill deliver'd such a Description of Christianity as this, he nevertheless denies the Assertion of these Gentlemen, that it is inconsistent with their Confession of Faith, and more especially he denies that it is subversive of the Gospel of Christ. What he means in his Account of Christianity, is, that our Saviour's Design in coming into the World, was to restore Mankind to the State of Perfection in which Adam was at first created, and that all those Laws which he has given us are agreeable to that original Law, as having such a natural Tendency to our present

Ease and Quiet, that they carry their own Reward, tho' there were nothing to reward our Obedience or punish our Disobedience in another Life; and that to this very End he has given us some few positive Precepts, such as the two Sacraments, and going to God and making our Approaches to him in the Name and thro' the Mediation of his Son Jesus Christ; and that all those Duties are inforced by new and stronger Motives than either the Light of Nature or the Jewish Religion could furnish us with.

This, I say, is so far from being subversive of the Gospel, that the opposite Opinion is destructive both of the Gospel, and all the Notions we have of the moral Perfections of God, and the disinterested Love and Benevolence which appears throughout his whole Conduct towards Mankind. I would desire these Gentlemen to point out to the World those Duties which are not included in his Description of Christianity. 'Tis surprizing to me, that Men who call themselves Christians, and more especially those who pretend to preach Christianity to others, should say that a God of infinite Perfections would make any thing our Duty, that has not a natural Tendency to our Happiness; and if to our Happiness, then it is agreeable to our Nature, since a Desire of Happiness is a natural Principle which all Mankind are endued with.

And in order to make the World believe the Justice of their Censure, they have perverted and altered the very Words of Hemphill's Sermon. They declare in their Minutes that he says, *the Gospel is, as to its ultimate End and most essential Parts,* &c. These two Words they have falsly added, viz: *Gospel* and *End,* which changes the Meaning of the Whole. What Hemphill has in his Sermon is this, "That the Doctrines absolutely necessary to be believed, are so very plain and nigh unto us, that they are, as to their ultimate and most essential Parts implanted in our very Nature and Reason, and more distinctly and authoritatively delivered in the Discourses of our Saviour, and in the Writings of the Apostles." That is, Those Doctrines delivered by our Saviour and the Apostles, which are absolutely necessary to be believed, are so very plain, that the meanest Capacities, may easily understand 'em, they being so reconcilable to our Reason, and so agreeable to our Nature, as having such a Tendency even to our present Happiness; and this he illustrated from our Saviour's Sermons upon the Mount, which are so very plain, that every impartial Man who reads 'em, may easily

51

reconcile to his Reason, as being wisely calculated to serve that noble End of Man's Happiness. Now let any impartial Reader consider what a poor State these Men have brought themselves to, that they are forced, in order to answer their own base Views, to change the very Meaning of the Paragraph, by adding some Words, and leaving out others. If what they have inserted in the Minutes were true, with what immediately follows in the same Paragraph, the whole would amount to this, *that the Gospel was contained in the Gospel,* which would not have been Sense, neither did he ever preach any such thing; but the Words in Truth were as they are inserted above.

And if these Reverend Gentlemen were as well acquainted with what they call their *well-known* Confession of Faith as they pretend to be, they would not have found Hemphill's Sermons inconsistent with it; he will undertake to prove that all his Discourses are agreeable to the *fundamental* Articles of it, which was all he declared to at his Admittance into the Synod: And surely they would not offer to condemn him for differing with them about extra-essentials.

EXTRACT page 7.

"*2dly.* As to the second Article which concerns the new Creature or Conversion, upon mature Consideration, we find by the Extract of Mr. Hemphill's Sermon on Gal. 6: 15, that he denies the necessity of Conversion to those that are born in the Church, and are not degenerated into vitious Practice; particularly in these Words, viz. *Such as are born of Christian Parents, and brought up in a Christian Country, cannot be so properly called new Creatures, when compared with themselves, because they were always what they are, except the progress and improvement which they daily make in Virtue;* which Doctrine we judge to be contrary to the sacred Scriptures and to our Confession of Faith."

With a Design to amuse the World, they assert, that they have acted upon mature Consideration; whereas nothing but Envy and Malice could move 'em to act so unjustly as they have done. In the Extract taken out of Hemphill's Sermon, they have omitted to insert those Parts of it in their Minutes, that would have explained the rest, and only inserted the middle of a Paragraph; the whole runs thus, "Altho' that Change was most visible in the first Conversion of Heathens to Christianity, or of wicked Professors of Christianity to a Conversion becoming the Gospel of Christ, yet the Effects of Christianity truly believed and duly practiced, is the same in those who were neither Heathens nor wicked Christians, but are born of Christian Parents, brought up in a christian Country, and had the Benefit of a virtuous Education, and were never engaged in vicious Practices; such as these, I say, tho' they can't so properly be call'd new Creatures, when compared with themselves, because they were always what they are, except the Progress and Improvement which they daily make in Virtue; yet when compar'd with others they may be so call'd; they are new Creatures, different Men and of another Sort, from those who either never heard of the Gospel of Christ, or never firmly believed and practiced it; so that still the Design of Christianity is the same, to make us new Creatures, quite other Men from what we should have been without the Gospel, to cure the Corruption and Depravity of Human Nature, and restore it to the Image of the Divine Nature in which Man was at first created, and from which by Transgression he fell."

And even suppose nothing had followed to clear what they have inserted in the Minutes, 'tis surprizing to me that those Gentlemen should look upon Mankind, to be so very weak and ignorant, as to be persuaded to believe, that it contradicted the sacred Scriptures. I would advise these Reverend Gentlemen impartially to read the Scriptures, and they will find that it is said, *the Day begins in an insensible Dawn, and the Path of the Just shines more and more unto a perfect Day,*[8] that is, Men don't become very good or very bad in an Instant, both vicious and virtuous Habits being acquired by Length of Time and repeated Acts. And the Kingdom of Heaven, that is Christianity, is compar'd to *Leaven hid in so many Measures of Meal,* to a *Grain of Mustard Seed,* to a *Field sown with Corn,*[9] &c. all which Things do not obtain their several Effects in an Instant, or any particular Time we can fix on: We can't say, that the Leaven wrought just that Moment, or that the Mustard Seed shot up into a Tree that very Minute, or that the Corn appear'd above-

8. "But the path of the just is as the shining light, that shineth more and more unto the perfect day." Prov. 4:18.

9. The figures are found in Jesus' sermon reported in Matt. 13: esp. 24, 31, and 33.

ground at that very Instant. And then we are told, that there are some *converted from the very Womb*,[1] and that *little Children are quali- fied for Heaven*,[2] which is the same thing. Now if all these Texts of Scripture are true, how is it possible their Conversion should be so sensible either to themselves or others, as that of Heathens or wicked Christians? I have said, it cannot; which is all that can be justly founded upon the Extract of the Sermon they have con- demn'd. I may add, that whoever preaches up the absolute neces- sity of spiritual *Pangs* and Convulsions in those whose Education has been in the Ways of Piety and Vertue, and who therefore are not to pass from a State of Sin to a State of Holiness, but to go on and improve in the State wherein they already are, represent Christianity to be unworthy of its divine Author.

EXTRACT, page 8.

"The Commission reassuming the third Article of Accusation against Mr. Hemphill, and considering it with all seriousness and impartiality that we are capable of, we cannot but judge that the most plain and obvious scope of the Extract of the Sermon now be- fore us appears subversive of the true and proper Satisfaction of Christ (notwithstanding of any Sound or Orthodox Expressions made use of by him, particularly in that summary of Principles de- livered to the Commission, taken from his Sermon on Mark 16: 16) inasmuch as the said Paragraph, wherein he professedly takes upon him to shew what is not and what is to preach Christ aright, while he amply insists upon Christ, as a King and Law-giver, giving the best System of Laws, he takes no Notice of his making Satisfaction to the Justice of God, but once barely mentions him as a Saviour, which any Socinian in the World might do. And this will be more clearly evident if it be considered what he says in the same Para- graph, wherein he speaks of those who maintain that God doth demand a full Satisfaction for the Offences of Sinners, as exalting the Glory of Christ as a kind condescending Saviour, to the dis- honour of the supreme unlimited Goodness of the Creator and

1. No precisely appropriate text has been found in either Testament for this statement. Perhaps BF had in mind the last half of Luke 1:15, foretelling the birth of John the Baptist: "... and he shall be filled with the Holy Ghost, even from his mother's womb."
2. Matt. 18:3; 19:14.

Father of the Universe, representing him as stern and inexorable, expressing no indulgence to his guilty Creatures; which will be further evident from what is expressed towards the close of the same Sermon, inference the Second, viz. *To explain and press the eternal Laws of Morality is not only a truly Christian, but beyond Comparison the most useful Method of Preaching.* And also by what he speaks in his Sermon on Acts 10: 34, 35, viz. *That God hath no Regard to any thing but Mans inward merits and deserts.* And also in the same Sermon it is said, *it cannot be deny'd but that they* (viz. good Works performed by the Light of Nature) *put Men in God's Way, reconcile him to them, and whatever else is wanting, dispose him to reveal even that unto them;* and tho' some Gentlemen, to whose Evidence we give an intire Credit, declared that it was his Manner in his publick Prayer, to give Thanks to God for sending his own Son Jesus Christ into the World to redeem poor lost Mankind; the Attonement he has made for the Sins of Mankind; and that he ends his Prayers by saying, *all petitioned for is upon the Account, and for the Sake of Jesus Christ;* yet we cannot think these or any such Expressions can justify his declaiming against this Doctrine in many Places of his Sermons."

The former Part of this Minute relates to the Merits and Satisfaction of Christ, as they word it; if they mean by that the Doctrine of Christ's Satisfaction, as held by Protestants, if Hemphill endeavoured to subvert That, he will not only be condemned by them, but by all good Christians. This is a very heavy Charge, and surely ought to be well made out, before any Minister should be deemed guilty of it. In this Case I can't help believing that every impartial Reader will be convinced, that this was done purely to blacken the Man; and here introduced in order to deceive the World, well knowing there are a sort of People who think no Usage can be too bad for such as they deem Hereticks, by whom the Commission imagined they should be applauded, let other Parts of their Conduct in this Affair be never so unjust, could they but once persuade 'em that he was guilty of opposing this important Doctrine of Christianity, which by all Christians is esteem'd a fundamental Article of Belief: Except this one Article, every thing for which they have been pleased to censure him, truly considered, will, I make no doubt, redound more to his Praise and Reputation, than to his Discredit; and that the Generality of the World, instead of censuring him, will rather condemn them for holding Doctrines full of Uncharitableness, and giving People unworthy and dishonourable Notions of the supreme Being. They therefore thought it absolutely necessary to condemn him upon this Point, which they could not have been guilty of doing, if Reason, Justice or Charity had had any Weight with them. In order to support what I have said, I shall now give the Reader the Paragraph upon which the Censure is grounded.

"To preach Christ is universally allowed to be the Duty of every christian Minister, but what does that mean? 'Tis not to use his Name as a *Charm,* to work up the Hearers to a warm Pitch of Enthusiasm, without any Foundation in Reason to support it: 'Tis not to make his Person or his Offices incomprehensible: 'Tis not to exalt his Glory as a kind condescending Saviour, to the Dishonour of the unlimited Goodness of the Creator and Father of the Universe, who is represented as stern and inexorable, expressing no Indulgence to his guilty Creatures, but demanding full and rigorous Satisfaction for their Offences: 'Tis not to encourage undue and presumptuous Reliances on his Merits and Satisfaction to the Contempt of Virtue and Good Works. No, but to represent him as a Law-giver as well as a Saviour, as a Preacher of Righteousness, as one who hath given us the most noble and compleat System of Morals inforced by the most substantial and worthy Motives; and shows that the whole Scheme of our Redemption is *a Doctrine according to Godliness.*"

Mr. Hemphill is here preaching against the Antinomians, who hold, that Christ's Merits and Satisfaction will save us, without our performing Good Works, which they say are unnecessary, and some of them even hold to be sinful; because, say they, to believe that Good Works or a holy Life is necessary in order to our Acceptance with God, is depreciating the Sufferings of Christ, who is sufficient without our Compliance; and therefore they never look upon him as a Lawgiver, but only in their mistaken Notion of a Saviour. This is the most impious Doctrine that ever was broached, and it is the Duty of every christian Minister to explode such Errors, which have a natural Tendency to make Men act as if Christ came into the World to patronize Vice, and allow Men to live as they please. Surely they who preach up Christ in this manner, do

Dishonour both to the Father and the Son. If the Reader will consider the Paragraph, he will find the whole Meaning of it to be this, We are not to preach up Christ so as to dishonour God the Father, nor are we to make such undue Reliances upon his Merits, as to neglect Good Works; but we are to look upon him in both Characters of Saviour and Lawgiver; that if we expect he has attoned for our Sins, we must sincerely endeavour to obey his Laws. I am afraid, that it is the Antinomian Doctrine of Christ's Merits and Satisfaction, which they call the true and proper One, with whose Principles these Gentlemen seem to be too much tinctured. However that be, I shall leave the World to judge how fond these Men were to condemn Hemphill, when they ground their Censure upon his taking *no Notice* of Satisfaction made to the Justice of God; and if this be a just Method of judging Men's Sermons, there is no Preacher safe; even the soundest that ever preach'd, may be proved guilty of all the Heresies that have ever been in the World; seeing a Man's *omitting* any particular Doctrine proves his *denying* of it. In order to show that his Words were wrested, and that there is no Probability he should mean any such Thing as they have falsly fathered upon him, I shall here subjoin an Extract taken from his Sermon on Mark 16: 16, which he calls *a Summary of the Principles necessary for a Christian to believe,* and which they promised to insert in their Minutes, viz. "That there is one God the Father and Lord of all Things: That he sent his eternal Son, who was the Brightness of his Glory, and the express Image of his Person, both to condemn Sin in the Flesh, and also to obtain Pardon for it, by the shedding of his own Blood; and that to this end, the Son of God freely and willingly left the Bosom of the Father, was incarnate and made in the Likeness of Man, became subject to all the Infirmities and Frailties of Human Nature, Sin only excepted; preached and declared the Will of his Father to Mankind, died for our Sins upon the Cross, rose the third Day from the Dead, ascended up into Heaven and sate down on the right Hand of God, where he is continually making Intercession for us." And another Extract which they likewise promised to insert, viz. "This is the Design of the Death of Christ, and the Redemption purchased for us by his Blood; for he gave himself for us, that he might redeem us from all Iniquity, and purify unto himself a People zealous of Good Works." In both these, this Doctrine is

57

owned in express Words; and what will put it beyond Dispute with all unprejudiced Men, is, that Mr. Hemphill constantly in his Prayers gave Thanks to God for sending his Son into the World, to redeem poor lost Mankind, and for the Atonement made for their Sins. Now how is it probable he should preach, or what End could he have in preaching against a Doctrine which he so solemnly own'd in his Addresses to God every Day? Would it not be giving himself the Lie in the Face of the World? Would it not be prevaricating both with God and Man?

Now let the Reader judge, after so much positive Evidence of his acknowledging the Doctrines of Christ's Merits and Satisfaction, all which was laid before the Commission, how charitable, how just and reasonable these Men were when they condemned him. And what makes the Judgment in this Case more surprizing, especially when they say they had not one dissenting Vote in their whole Transactions, is, that one of the Ministers, the supposed Compiler of the Minutes, and one of the chief Managers in the whole Tryal, being shewn the very Paragraph upon which they pretend to ground their Censure concerning the Satisfaction of Christ, by a Gentleman in Philadelphia, he after Perusal declared his Sentiments in this Manner, *For my part, I do not know what other People may think of it, I can't see any Heresy in it, it is all very right.* This Man surely wanted either Courage or Honesty afterwards, when he did not dissent from the rest. Where they say that Hemphill declaims against that Doctrine in many places of his Sermon, few People will believe them, for they have given so many Samples of their Disposition (especially where they put down Words which they had not from his Extracts, and leave out Parts of Sentences necessary to have been inserted in order to explain the rest) that if there were these *many Places,* they would have pointed out at least some of them, and not have set down those that are nothing to the purpose: For Example, *To explain and press the eternal Laws of Morality, is not only a truly christian, but beyond comparison the most useful Method of Preaching.* And because the whole would not have answered their Ends, they have omitted the explaining part which immediately followed, viz. *in this I include the enforceing the Rules of Virtue by all the peculiar Motives which the christian Religion suggests, making all its Doctrines subservient to Holiness.* Which I say is the End and Design of the christian Scheme, for Christ gave himself for us that he might redeem us from all Iniquity, and purify to himself a peculiar People zealous of Good-Works. And there is scarcely a Chapter in the whole Gospels or Epistles from which this Doctrine can't be prov'd. And the next Extract they produce, viz: *God hath no Regard to any thing but Mens inward Merit and Desert,* is in my humble Opinion as little to the purpose as the other. I would ask these reverend Gentlemen, Does God regard Man at all? The Answer I suppose will be, That he does, but that it is upon the Account of Christ's Merits; which I shall grant them, and allow it to be the Merits and Satisfaction of Christ that purchased such easy and plain Conditions of Happiness; but still it is our Compliance with these Conditions that I call inward Merit and Desert which God regards in us. For to say that God regards Men for any thing else besides Goodness and Virtue, is such a Notion as makes all Men both virtuous and vicious capable of being equally regarded by him, and consequently there is no Difference between Virtue and Vice. And the Apostle Peter is, with Hemphill, condemn'd by these Men for a Heretick, in saying, that *God is no Respecter of Persons, but in every Nation he that feareth him and worketh Righteousness is accepted of him.* I shall make no more Remarks upon this Minute, but conclude with saying, If these Gentlemen had regarded their own Honour, (not to talk of the Honour of Christianity, which breathes such a Spirit of Benevolence, Justice and Charity through the whole of it) they would not have condemned Hemphill upon a single Expression, supposing there had been any such; but would have compared the whole Extracts of his Sermons in order to understand his Meaning, which is common in every such Case, where Men are impartial and desirous to find out the Truth; but this is inconsistent with a Spirit of Persecution, with which these Gentlemen were possessed.

EXTRACT, page 9.

"*4thly.* As to the fourth Article, viz. The Description of saving Faith in his Sermon on Mark 16: 16. We acknowledge that saving Faith doth include (as Mr. Hemphill asserts) a firm Perswasion of Mind of the Truths of the Gospel upon good and rational Grounds, and producing proper and suitable Effects; yet we cannot but apprehend that this is too general a Description of saving Faith, as not explicitly mentioning our receiving of Christ upon the Terms of the Gospel, which is so essential an act or ingredient of the Faith which is unto Salvation, that without it our Faith will be vain and ineffectual; and so the Description may be apt dangerously to mislead Persons in this important Article, and incourage them to trust to a naked assent to the Gospel Revelation, especially if this their assent be accompanied with an externally regular Conversation."

I am at a Loss what could move these Gentlemen (unless it was to shew their Learning) to censure Hemphill's Description of Saving Faith as being too general, when at the same time they have given a more general one; but in their Illustration they seem not to have understood either of them; where they say, that it has a Tendency to make Men rely upon a bare Assent to the Truths of the Gospel; which is impossible; for how can such a Faith, in the Description of which Good Works are expressly mentioned, be a Means to lead Men from Good Works.

EXTRACT page 10.

"5thly. As to the fifth Article of the Charge, respecting the Salvation of Heathens while they continue such, we judge it abundantly supported by the Extracts of his Sermon on Acts 10: 34, 35. Wherein he evidently contradicts the Necessity of Divine Revelation, and asserts the sufficiency of the Light of Nature to bring us to Salvation; particularly in these Expressions, viz. *They who have no other Knowledge of God and their Duty, but what the Light of Nature teacheth them, no Law for the Government of their Actions but the Law of Reason and Conscience, will be accepted if they live up to the Light they have, and govern their Actions accordingly:* And further he asserts, *That Cornelius, who,* as he affirms, *had neither imbraced the Jewish nor Christian Religion, was for this accepted of God and highly Favoured.*"

In this 5th Article, Mr. Hemphill is censured as denying the necessity of a divine Revelation, from these Words: "They who have no other Knowledge of God and their Duty, but what the Light of Nature teaches, no Law for the Government of their

Actions but the Law of Reason and Conscience, will be accepted of God if they live up to the Light which they have, and govern their Actions accordingly." But they have omitted the latter part of the Paragraph which explains the former, viz. "This was the Case of Cornelius, who worshipped God and did Good to Men, he pray'd to God always and gave much Alms to the People, and this he did from the meer Light of Nature, not having embraced either the Jewish or Christian Religion; for this he was accepted of God, and had a farther Revelation of his Will. So that tho' it may be disputed how far such Righteousness as this, such Good Works as these, are of themselves available for Salvation, yet it can't be denied but that they put Men in God's Way, reconcile him to 'em, and whatever else is wanting dispose him to reveal even that unto them."

Now from the whole of the Extract, (part of which they left out, for what End I shall leave the World to judge) I believe no unprejudiced Person can see a just Foundation of this Censure: For all that they can found it upon, is this, that Hemphill maintains it was the Good Works of Cornelius, (a Heathen) which disposed God to give him a miraculous Revelation of the Gospel. But to corroborate their Censure, they assert a downright Falshood, viz. That Hemphill says it was upon the Account of Cornelius's not having embraced either the Jewish or Christian Religion that he was accepted of God; Whereas in the Extract taken from his Sermon, it is said, it was his praying to God always, and giving much Alms to the People that rendered him acceptable to God. And this is sufficient to show the base Conduct of these Men, who to accomplish their wicked Ends, will not only venture to change the Meaning but the very Words themselves.

EXTRACT page 11.

"*6thly.* As to that Article of the Charge wherein he is alledged to pervert the Doctrine of Justification by Faith, we find it sufficiently supported by the Extracts from his Sermon on Eph. 3: 8, Wherein he has these Words, viz. *It will not be amiss to consider what the Apostle means when he says that Christians are saved by Faith; it may be well said of them, because it is their Faith that saves them from the Guilt of their Sins committed before their Faith, a Privilege which peculiarly belonged to the first Christians, converted at*

Years of Discretion from a Life of Sin and impurity; and therefore this first Justification is often inculcated by St. Paul in his Epistles, and attributed to Faith; but this doth not concern those who have been educated and instructed in the Knowledge of the Christian Religion. And by asserting, towards the close of the said Sermon, *That all Hopes of Happiness, but what are built on purity of Heart and a virtuous Life, are, according to the Christian Scheme, vain and delusory, and will certainly end in Disappointment and Confusion;* which Expressions we cannot but look upon as subversive of the Scripture Doctrine of Justification by Faith, tho' we zealously maintain the indispensible Necessity of universal Holiness in order to Salvation."

In this 6th Article they assert, that they find Mr. Andrews's Charge against Hemphill sufficiently supported. What is it that they would not find supported from his Sermons, if Andrews had charged him with it? In this Discourse Hemphill was endeavouring to show the Folly of those who make that first Justification by Faith, which the Apostle mentions, an Encouragement to us, that if we believe even at our Death, tho' we have wilfully persisted in Disobedience to Christ's Commands, we shall be equally entitled to Salvation with those who, assoon as they heard Christianity preached, embraced it, and who therefore had their Faith imputed to them for Righteousness. And I suppose all Christians, Antinomians excepted, will allow this, that Faith will not be imputed for Righteousness to those Men who have been educated in the Christian Religion, and yet have never endeavoured to practice its Precepts; I say that such Men have no Reason to expect that they shall be justified by a bare Faith, as the primitive Christians were, who embraced Christianity assoon as they heard it preached. And then he went on to show, that we may be said to be justified by Faith, because it is impossible we should embrace those Terms offered by Christ for our Salvation and Happiness until we once believe them to be true, or as it is the Means of our Obedience. This, say they, is plainly denying Justification by Faith, and this they confirm from another Part of the Sermon, viz. "that all Hopes of Happiness but what are built on Purity of Heart and a virtuous Life, are, according to the christian Scheme vain and delusory, and will certainly end in Disappointment and Confusion." This they absolutely condemn in Hemphill, altho' they at the same time confess, that they zealously maintain the very same thing; or, in their own orthodox Words, the indispensible necessity of universal Holiness in order to Salvation.

EXTRACT page 12.

"*Ordered*, That our whole Minutes since Monday last be read.

"Upon reading of which we find that we have gone through the several Articles of Charge exhibited against Mr. Hemphill, and tho' we have past over many Particulars, as either not being clearly supported by the Extracts taken out of his Sermons, or not of sufficient Weight to deserve a Censure, yet to our great Grief we cannot but judge, that many of the Articles of most considerable Weight and Importance, are fully supported by said Extracts, as will more clearly appear by our preceeding Minutes, reference thereunto being had: Many of these Doctrines therefore which he hath delivered in these Sermons, we are obliged to declare unsound and dangerous, contrary to the sacred Scriptures and our excellent Confession and Catechisms, having an unhappy tendency to corrupt the Faith once delivered to the Saints, and that such Doctrines should be delivered by Mr. Hemphill is the more surprizing to us, when we consider that the said Mr. Hemphill solemnly declared, last September, before the Synod, his Assent to the Westminster Confession, and adopted it as the Confession of his Faith."

Having gone thro' the several Charges exhibited by Andrews, they declare with great Solemnity, that it was their great Grief to find so many of these Charges justly grounded upon the Extracts of the Sermons. I must confess they are the best Judges of their own Grief; yet it appears to me and many others, that their great Grief was because Andrews's Charges were not more justly founded upon the Sermons; which plainly appears from the whole Trial. And then they are not ashamed to say, *We are obliged to declare many of these Doctrines unsound and dangerous, contrary to the sacred Scriptures and our most excellent Confession.* If there be any Meaning in this, it must be, that they were obliged to it, as they designed to defend Andrews's Character, tho' never so unjustly. I shall give these Gentlemen my Word, that 'tis as surprizing to me, as it was to them, that they should affirm that Hemphill solemnly declared last September before the Synod, his Assent to the Westminster Confession of Faith; whereas it was only to the

63

fundamental Articles of it that he declared, and not the Whole of it; and it seems very hard that they should make this Book the Standard and Test, when at the same time they own'd to him, that *they knew not how many fundamental Articles were in it.* He himself is sufficiently satisfied, that he has not preached any thing contrary to his Declaration at the Synod, and he offered to the Commission, that he would reconcile all his Doctrines to the Confession as he had adopted it, provided they would but point out to him the Parts they thought he had contradicted. But this would not have answered the Ends they had in View, and therefore they refus'd it. I shall only add, that many of these reverend Gentlemen, who are now so zealous for the Confession, that they seem to give it the Preference to the Holy Scriptures, were of late Years more indifferent than Hemphill has yet appear'd to be; and altho' they then agreed, that there were some Articles in it of no great Moment whether Men believed 'em or not, nay some publickly declared they did not understand many of 'em, (which I sincerely believe was very true) yet they would now make 'em all Fundamentals, in order to serve a Turn.

EXTRACT page 13.

"And now we are come to the Conclusion of this weighty Affair, we cannot but observe, with the utmost Gratitude to Divine Providence, that all our Consultations have been carried on with an undisturbed Unanimity, such a remarkable Harmony and good Agreement has subsisted among us, that in the whole Transaction we have not had one dissenting Vote."

And here they conclude this weighty Affair, with acknowledging their utmost Gratitude to divine Providence for their Unanimity. This I suppose they mention as an Argument of the Justice of their Censure: But this will likewise prove that the Spanish Inquisition is in the right, which is as unanimous in all its Transactions as the Commission. The Reverend Inquisitors go to Prayer, they call upon God to direct them in every [one] of their Censures (altho' they have unanimously determined to condemn all who are so unfortunate as to be call'd before them) and, I am sorry to say it, all this is too applicable to the present Case: For these Reverend Gentlemen came to Philadelphia with the same

Spirit, proceeded in the same manner, and have gone as far in proportion to their Power as ever the Inquisition went.

I shall conclude with an Extract out of the *Layman's Sermon*,[3] and therewith take my Leave of the Reverend Commission. It is as follows,

"What adds to this Evil and Insolence, this Cruelty on the Score of Opinion, and makes it still more provoking and intolerable, is, that it is all perpetrated in the Name of Christ, of the meek Jesus, and said to be for his Church and Cause: A Declaration so impudent and incredible, that it could only be made by Men who wanted Shame, to Men who had no Eyes. It is as false as the Gospel is true, nor could a Revelation which inspired or warranted any Degree of Bitterness or Cruelty, ever have come from God, or from any but the Antagonist of God and Enemy of Man, from Hypocrites reigning, that is, tyrannizing in the Name of the Lord.

"And all Persecution is Popery, and every Degree of it, even the smallest Degree, is an Advance towards the Inquisition: As negative Penalties are the first Degree, so Death and Burning is the last and highest: All the other Steps are but natural Gradations following the first Degree, and introducing the last: For the smallest implies the necessity of a greater where the former fails, and consequently of the greatest of all, which is the Inquisition."

A Letter to a Friend in the Country

A Letter to a Friend in the Country, Containing the Substance of a Sermon Preach'd at Philadelphia, in the Congregation of The Rev. Mr. Hemphill, Concerning the Terms of Christian and Ministerial Communion. Philadelphia: Printed and Sold by B. Franklin at the New Printing-Office near the Market. 1735.[4] (Yale University Library)

The *Pennsylvania Gazette* advertised September 18 that this sermon in the form of a letter would be published on the following Monday. The next week it was reported as being "just published." The Preface is probably Franklin's, though it is by no means certain that he wrote the body of the pamphlet. He may, however, have revised it.

3. [Thomas Gordon], *A Sermon Preached before the Learned Society of Lincoln's Inn, On January 30, 1732* (London, 1733), pp. 6–7, 20.
4. The title page quotes as texts II Cor. 3:17 and Gal. 5:1.

THE PUBLISHER TO HIS LAY-READERS.

It is sufficiently known to all the thinking Part of Mankind, how difficult it is to alter Opinions long and universally receiv'd. The Prejudices of Education, Custom and Example, are generally very strong; it may therefore seem, in a manner, needless to publish any Thing contrary to such long imbib'd and generally receiv'd Opinions. It were, however, much to be wish'd, that Men would consider how glorious a Conquest they make, when they shake off all manner of Prejudice, and bring themselves to think *freely, fairly,* and *honestly.*

This is to think and act like Men; 'tis a Privilege common to Mankind; 'tis the only way to promote the Interests of Truth and Liberty in the World; and surely, none but Slaves and Lovers of Dominion and Darkness can be out of humour at it; nor would any Man, or any Set of Men, pretend to hinder others from a free impartial Enquiry into Matters of Religion especially, if they had not some sinister Designs in so doing.

My Brethren of the Laity, as it is to you that this Letter is address'd, and chiefly for your Sakes that I take the Liberty of Publishing it, it is hop'd you'll seriously consider the Contents of it. The Generality of the Clergy were always too fond of Power to quit their Pretensions to it, by any thing that was ever yet said by particular Persons; but my Brethren, how soon should WE humble their Pride, did we all heartily and unanimously join in asserting our own natural Rights and Liberties in Opposition to their unrighteous Claims. Besides, WE could make use of more prevailing Arguments than any that have been yet advanc'd, I mean such as oppose their temporal Interests. It is impossible they could long stand against the united Force of so powerful Antagonists. Truth manag'd by the Laity in Opposition to them and their temporal Interests, would do much. Their pretending to be the Directors of Men's Consciences, and Embassadors of the meek and lowly Jesus, ('twere greatly to be wish'd they study'd more to imitate so perfect a Model of Meekness and Humility, and pretended less to a Power that belongs not to 'em) and their assuming such like fine Titles, ought not to frighten us out of a good Cause, *The glorious Cause of Christian Liberty.* It is very probable, indeed, that according to their laudable Custom, they will make very free with

66

the Characters of those that oppose their Schemes, and like sound, orthodox Divines, call them Hereticks, unsound in the Faith, and so on; but there is no Argument in such kind of Language, nor will it ever persuade. And we ought to value such ridiculous Epithets just as little as St. Paul did, Acts 24:14,[5] since instead of a Reproach, they may be our greatest Glory and Honour. Such kind of Treatment was always look'd upon to be a strong Argument either of a bad Cause or a weak side. That it is our Duty to make a vigorous Opposition to them, is plain from these two Considerations: *First,* that when and wherever Men blindly submitted themselves to the Impositions of Priests, whether Popish, Presbyterian or Episcopal, &c. Ignorance and Error, Bigotry, Enthusiasm and Superstition, more or less, and in Proportion to such Submission, most certainly ensu'd, And *Secondly,* That all the Persecutions, Cruelties, Mischiefs and Disturbances, that ever yet happen'd in the Church, took their rise from the usurp'd Power and Authority of her lawless Sons. Let us then to the utmost of our Power endeavour to preserve and maintain Truth, Common Sense, universal Charity, and brotherly Love, Peace and Tranquility, as recommended in the Gospel of Jesus, in this our infant and growing Nation, by steadily opposing those, whose Measures tend to nothing less than utterly to subvert and destroy all. Nothing, in all Probability, can prevent our being a very flourishing and happy People, but our suffering the Clergy to get upon our Backs, and ride us, as they do their Horses, where they please.

I shall make no other Apology to the Author, or any one else, who may think it unfair to publish what was only a private Letter to my self, than this, viz. that I believ'd it might be useful.

Your affectionate Brother, and hearty Well-wisher,

A LAYMAN

A LETTER, &c.

SIR,

It is somewhat surprizing, that a Sermon, which you tell me in yours is said to be preach'd here by a Stranger, (whom you believe to be your humble Servant) should make so great a Noise

5. "But this I confess unto thee, that after the way which they call heresy, so worship I the God of my fathers, believing all things which are written in the Law and in the Prophets."

already, as you speak of, especially at the Distance you live from Philadelphia. As I have no Reason to induce me to conceal it, I own I did give a Discourse, in the sermonizing way, upon the Subject you mention.

You say, the Representation made of it in your Part of the Country, has given Occasion to much Speculation, not only among some of the Clergy of the Presbyterian Denomination, but many of the Priest-ridden Laity, who, it seems are put into a Pannick, and much alarm'd at the suppos'd Tendency of it. I would not willingly offend any; but some People's being offended at important Truths, ought not to hinder their being urg'd and inculcated. All I have to say about the Load of hard Names which you tell me they begin already to heap upon me, is, that their Reproaches, however inveterate, cannot at all hurt me; nor can they affect me any farther than to excite Pity and Compassion towards the Authors of them. I am not much surpriz'd at the Conduct of a certain Set of Clergy, especially since Calumny and Reproach, where they could not command the civil Sword, were (for want of Argument) always the Weapons with which they fought, whenever their exorbitant Claims to Power and Authority were oppos'd. I most heartily wish them a better temper. Christianity teaches us *to bless them that curse us, to pray for them that despitefully use and persecute us.* And I think indeed, the Names of the aforesaid Persons ought to be given in, to all well-dispos'd Christian Congregations in the Province, to be publickly pray'd for every Sabbath.

As I was always a Lover of Truth and Christian Liberty, my only Design in the Discourse was to promote the Interests of both.

I had almost forgot to tell you, that (if we may believe Report) a Gentleman of this City, in a Sermon which he preached here not long ago, out of his great and abundant Zeal for Orthodoxy and the Safety of the Church, suggested to his Audience, that there were some Preachers lately come into this Country, who might be Jesuits, (a most surprizing Discovery!) and whose Credentials, for that Reason, ought to be enquir'd into. Some of those that heard him, say it was very easy, by the Tenor and Strain of his Discourse, to apprehend who were pointed at in the Insinuation; and think the Probability of their Conjecture greatly strengthen'd, by the vast Care, godly Pains, and pious Industry made use of by this wonderfully charitable Son of the Church, to hinder Mr. H--p--ll, whose Story you know, from getting a Place to preach in.

How well founded the Charge of *Jesuitism* is, where this Reverend and worthy Gentleman (if Report be true) would fix it, is not difficult to apprehend: Some are ill-natur'd enough to suggest, the Charge may much more justly, be laid elsewhere, and that the Occasion of his Clamours is his Fear of losing some of his Parishioners. How strangely censorious the World is grown!

Your Advice to print the Sermon in my own Defence, as you call it, is what I do not at all relish, nor can I comply with for very obvious Reasons. Yet upon the Supposition which you make of my refusing this; since you insist upon it as the only Evidence I can give of that Esteem and Regard which I always profess'd for you, I so far comply with your Desire, as to send you some loose Hints of what was advanc'd in that Sermon. And as I only write this Letter for the Perusal of a Friend, so I hope you will excuse Want of Method and Exactness in it, which I really resolve to be no way sollicitous about, nor shall I strictly confine myself to the Method, or Manner of Expression made use of in the Sermon, lest we turn too grave upon it. Without any farther Preamble, then, let us come to the Point. After the Formalities of an Introduction and Textual Explication, which I shan't trouble you with, the Question propos'd to be consider'd was,

Whether it be lawful to impose any other Term of Communion, Christian or Ministerial, than the Belief of the Holy Scriptures? Or, Whether a Man that professes to believe the Holy Scriptures, and the Christian Scheme of Religion as contain'd in them, ought not to be admitted to Christian and Ministerial Communion, if no Reason can be alledg'd against him in other respects, why he should not?

The general Method in which it was propos'd to manage this Point, was to consider the principal Arguments offer'd by those who contend for other Terms of Communion than the Belief of the holy Scriptures, &c. and to endeavour to shew their Weakness.

The first ARGUMENT examin'd was this:

A Thing agreed on by almost all Christian Churches, of all Denominations: A Thing universally practic'd in the early Times of

69

Christianity, &c. ought not to be abolish'd without the strongest Reasons. For tho' it be acknowledg'd that even the greatest Unanimity of the Christian Church in general, does not amount to a full Proof of the Truth of any Position, or the Reasonableness of any Custom or Practice, yet it must be confess'd, that the said Unanimity forms at least a very strong Presumption in Behalf of the Position asserted, or the Practice establish'd. Now for the Point in question, we have Antiquity, Unanimity, and the Practice of the Church Time out of mind.

ANSWER.

As there is no great Stress laid upon this Argument, since it is confess'd that Antiquity, Unanimity, &c. cannot amount to a full Proof, and do at best but form a strong Presumption, so I might without much Prejudice to that Cause that I here contend for, *The Cause of* LIBERTY, leave said Argument wholly unanswer'd; but to evince that the Cause of Liberty in this Case, seems to have the Advantage on all sides, let it be observ'd that the Custom contended for is not Apostolical. We see nothing of it in the Holy Scriptures; nay the very contrary may most probably be deduc'd from several Passages. When the Eunuch, when Cornelius, when Three Thousand Souls at once, were converted,[6] there is not the least Hint, that any of the Articles of Faith now stiffly maintain'd by some Sects of Christians as essential ones, and esteem'd by others not necessary, and altogether rejected by others as erroneous, were impos'd as Terms of Communion, or even mention'd at all. It rather appears, that nothing more was required of these new Converts, but that they should acknowledge Jesus Christ to be the Messiah promised by the Prophets, the Son of God; and that they should to the best of their Power, act agreeable to his Precepts, and obey his Laws. And really there was hardly a Possibility, that one Discourse should inform them of all the metaphysical Notions, nice Distinctions, which are now brought into our Confessions of Faith as necessary Articles. Had infinite Wisdom thought it any way necessary, or useful, to frame long Confessions of Faith, or to establish numerous Tests of Orthodoxy, as is now done in most Christian Churches, is it to be suppos'd, that

6. The conversion of the Eunuch is related in Acts 8:27–39; of Cornelius in Acts 10:1–48; and of the 3000 souls in Acts 2:6–41.

70

neither our Saviour nor his Apostles would have left any such thing in their Writings; especially if it be consider'd that many Things are wrote, which in point of Importance are not to be compar'd to the Necessity or Usefulness of Creeds contended for by the Imposers of them?

In the two or three first Centuries of Christianity, those acquainted with the History of those Times, tell us, they can find no Signs, no Footsteps of such Confessions of Faith, or Tests of Orthodoxy. The Creed commonly called the Apostles' Creed, is on all hands allow'd to be an ancient Piece; it is suppos'd by some, to be compos'd in the Beginning of the third Century; and this is the utmost Antiquity that the Learn'd will allow it. This Creed, however, is rather for than against the Principle here contended for: And indeed it is very observable, that it is couch'd in so loose a Manner, with respect to the Points chiefly controverted among Christians, that it is highly probable it was fram'd on purpose with that remarkable Latitude, in order to let into the Church all such as in general sincerely believe the Holy Scriptures, tho' with respect to many metaphysical Speculations, they should widely differ from other Christians, or, if you will, from the far greatest Number of the Members of the Catholick Church. This having in all Probability been the prudent Practice of the two first Centuries, the Framers of this Creed thought it proper not to recede much from that discreet Proceeding, whatever it was that induc'd them to make the said Creed, and engag'd afterwards the Church to receive and impose it. Upon the whole, The Practice of the Apostles, and of the purest Ages of Christianity, with respect to the Matter in Debate, seeming to be on the Side of *Liberty* in this Case, a good deal of Advantage might be taken from it; but having Arguments to offer which I think of much greater Weight, I will infer nothing from the aforesaid Observations, but that they are more than sufficient to remove the first Difficulty alledg'd. What has been done since those primitive Times, may be look'd upon as a general Corruption, and the Authority of the Church in this Case is of no greater Force, than it was in respect to the many Abuses which our Reformers have successfully oppos'd: Nor indeed can our happy Reformation from Popery and religious Slavery be defended upon any other Principle than what is here asserted.

71

Another ARGUMENT consider'd was this;

Every Society, say Creed-Imposers, *has a Right to make such Laws as seem necessary for its Support and Welfare: The very Nature of a Society requires, nay supposes this; else it would lie open to all kinds of Enemies; there would be no Provision, no Remedy against the Intrusion of Adversaries, that might destroy its very Vitals; in a Word, no Means to keep them off, or turn them out. And why of all imaginable Societies, a Christian one alone should be depriv'd of such a Right, is not to be accounted for. It is acknowledg'd,* say they, *that in a christian Civil Society, penal Laws may be justly made, to punish even to Death notorious Transgressors of the Rules of Morality; now, either you must suppose that all speculative Matters of Religion are indifferent, or, in other Words, that there are no Articles of Faith necessary to Salvation; or else you must own, that such Persons as obstinately refuse to believe such necessary Articles, may lawfully, nay ought to be excluded that christian Society, wherein the said Articles are receiv'd as essential to Christianity.*

ANSWER.

The Parallel that is so frequently drawn between a Society consider'd meerly as civil, or as concern'd only in Temporals, is very lame, or rather, it is no Parallel at all. A civil Society may lawfully indeed make what Laws it pleases for its Defence, Preservation and Welfare; It is not accountable for such Laws to any superior earthly Power; it has no other Master here besides the Consent of the Plurality, or the Will of one or more whom the Plurality has appointed to act for the Good of the whole Body. But a christian Society has no manner of Right to make any Laws that may any how infringe upon the Laws already made by our common King Jesus; or that may in any Measure encroach upon the Rights and Privileges of his Subjects. Our King is absent, he has left us a System of Laws which is on all Hands own'd to be perfect and compleat (and for that Reason, no Occasion for new Laws) and they that acknowledge him for their King and Head, and believe that System to contain his Will in full, and seem resolv'd to act accordingly, are upon that very Account to be admitted Members of the Christian Society or Church. For this our spiritual King has not deputed any one to be here on Earth his

Vicegerent, or to interpret that Will as he pleases, and impose that Interpretation on any. Every Subject is equal to any other Subject; their Concerns have nothing to do with this World; every one is accountable for his Belief to Christ alone. Let no Man then presume to judge of another Master's Servant. One Man's Salvation does not interfere with the Salvation of another Man, and therefore every Man is to be left at Liberty to work it out by what Method he thinks best.

Speculative Points are not indifferent, but then their Necessity or Importance varies; it increases or diminishes according to the various Circumstances and Capacities of those to whom they are proposed. Those Articles of Faith which the Society is pleas'd to declare to be essential, or necessary to Salvation, may not appear so to this or t'other Man, altho' he acknowledge Jesus Christ to be his Redeemer or spiritual Monarch: Now the Society's insisting upon the Essentiality or Necessity of such Articles, does not add to them one Grain of Importance with respect to this or t'other Man's spiritual Welfare.

If Jesus Christ has not most distinctly and positively pronounc'd that such and such a speculative Point, understood so and so and not otherwise, is necessary to Salvation; then the Society's peremptorily pronouncing and imposing the Belief of it, according to its own Interpretation, as a Term of Christian or Ministerial Communion, seems plainly to be an unjustifiable assuming of a Power that belongs to Christ alone, a Tyrannical Treating as a Rebel, a Man whom perhaps Jesus Christ himself loves as one of his most faithful Subjects, and a manifest Infringement upon the most sacred Laws of christian Charity.

The Words *obstinate, obstinately,* and the like, are of no Force here; God alone knows whether a Man that refuses to believe such or such a speculative Point, be guilty of *Obstinacy* or no. What seems to Men to be the Effect of Obstinacy, may in reality be the noble Result of a steady Sincerity, and a real Love of Truth.

Here perhaps it will be said, that by this Scheme all manner of Power and Authority is taken away from the Church, even with respect to Matters of Indifferency, as suppose Settling the outward Modes and Circumstances of Worship. And it is very true, indeed; I know no proper Legislative Authority she is invested

73

with, no Power to make Laws which Christ has not already made, and impose those Laws as Terms of Communion.

The Church, according to the very Notion of our Antagonists, must be resolv'd into the Majority. By the by it may happen, that a Blockhead, or a wicked Man may have the Casting Vote, for establishing this or that Rite or Ceremony, or this or that Doctrine. A very comfortable Thing indeed, that Terms of Communion should be impos'd by the Decision of such a Man! A mistaken, I had almost said a ridiculous Notion of Unity, is the Spring of all those tyrannical Pretences which occasion the Dispute before us. Some of our Adversaries seem to think it essential, or at least highly useful to the Interests of Christianity; that there should be not only an Unity of Opinion, but an outward Uniformity in Worship, (and indeed, as to Worship, as well as Opinion, an outward Uniformity is all that the most absolute Church Authority can effect; for as to the secret Thoughts and Sentiments it cannot reach them) whereas in reality such an Uniformity is neither the One nor the Other. And if it be of some Advantage, I cannot help thinking, that allowing Christians as much Liberty as is here contended for, is the likeliest Means to produce that very Unity, or Uniformity, so much recommended. The Reason is plain; many a Man who justly and with Indignation rejects an erroneous Opinion, or an insignificant Rite, which the Church or Religious Society would impose upon him as a Term of Christian Communion, that is, as a Thing essential to the Being or at least to the Purity of Christianity, would let People quietly go on in such an Opinion if it were not of an evil Tendency, and join with them in the insignificant Rite if it were left to his Choice.

In abundance of Things in Life, but most peculiarly in Religion, a rational Creature may easily be led, but will not be driven. And tho' a Thing be in itself of little Consequence, yet the Making or Declaring it essential, renders it highly prejudicial to Religion; and therefore out of a discreet Zeal, not any Obstinacy, a good Man may reject and oppose it, because enforc'd as material: Whereas if look'd upon and left as what it really is, he would scarcely mind it, much less would he scruple to comply.

But suppose that an outward Uniformity could be introduc'd into the Catholick Church, yet at least an inward Unity, a Unity of Affection, which is infinitely preferable, would in all Probability soon spring from Liberty. Truth having then full Room to play, would soon diffuse it self, and settle in almost every Man's Breast, at least with respect to Matters of Importance in Religion.

On the other Hand, that same Liberty would probably soon lead People to lay aside all impertinent Practices, and cause them perfectly to forget, or at least hardly to think it worth while Disputing about a Number of metaphysical useless Points, which the Spirit of Pride and a Love of Power and Authority on one side, and Impatience of spiritual Servitude on the other, turn into so many Engines of Contention and War.

Here it may be farther ask'd; Must there not be some Form of Worship? Must not that be agreed on? Must it not be carried by the Majority either of the whole Church, or of those who are appointed to preside in it, and settle such Matters? Yes. Well what then? Why if there be in the Church some refractory Person, who not liking the Form of Worship, or, if you will, the Confession of Faith agreed on, What must be done with him? Why truly, just nothing.

If a Man thinks your Worship inconsistent with the Purity of Christianity, or your Confession of Faith subversive of some fundamental Tenets, and that you (i.e. the Church in general, or the acknowledg'd Rulers of it) on the other Hand, be convinc'd that all your Tenets or Rites, or some of them, which are rejected by that Man, are either necessary, or so highly useful, that the Salvation of others would be endanger'd, or that their Instruction and Edification cannot so well be carried on without them; then indeed (and not perhaps in any other Case; for it were better to erase out of your Creed twenty uncertain Tenets, which, if true, have little or no Influence on the Conduct of Men; and abolish twenty trivial Formalities in publick Worship, than to offend one single weak Brother, and move him to separate from you) then indeed, I say, you may retain such Tenets, and keep up the Practice of such external Acts of Devotion: For surely you, i.e. a Number of Men, have the same Liberty to think and act in Religion as that one Man has.

But then, what will authorize you, or the Church to impose these your Tenets and Forms upon him as Terms of Communion? You cannot say he is not a Christian, for he solemnly professes to believe the holy Scriptures. Let him alone as to his Belief. Nay,

75

hear him patiently if he be willing to preach to you; for he *may* be in the right; and as to publick Worship, why should you hinder him from joining with you if he pleases? He certainly is or may be (and that *May be* is equivalent to a Certainty with respect to our Duty to him) I say, he is, or *may be,* a true Christian, and as such I think one may defie all the World to show from Scripture or Reason, that Jesus Christ, the sole King and Governor of the Christian Church, allows any Man, or any Set of Men, or any Nation, to refuse him Admittance to all the Advantages and Comforts of Christian, and consequently Ministerial Communion.

To make Judging of a Man's Soundness in the Faith, who professes himself a Christian, to make that, I say, a Matter of Prudence, and to invest any Set of Men with a Power of thus Judging, and Censuring and Excommunicating according to their Determinations, is prodigiously odd among Protestants. It seems the Assertors of such Maxims do not consider that they make such Judges just so many *Popes.*

As to those Texts of Scripture which are sometimes adduc'd to prove such an Authority in the Church, they are, in my humble Opinion, just nothing to the purpose. That we ought to pay a certain Respect and Civility to such Persons as are appointed to teach others, to preside in the Church, and to take Care that Things be done decently and in order, is not, I believe, deny'd by any body; and that is all that can be fairly infer'd from some of those Passages of Scripture. And it appears too, that the rest of the said Passages are applicable only to the Apostles, or to those Pastors who in the Apostolical Times were endued with the Gifts of the Holy Ghost. And really, common Observation shews us, that your stiff Maintainers of Church-Authority, are as far, if not farther, than any other Men, from being bless'd with those heavenly Qualifications.

Another ARGUMENT consider'd was this;

Private Judgment in Matters of Religion, will surely be allow'd of by Creed-Opposers; *Now, if every Man may judge for himself, then he may join with such other Men as think as he does. They may form a Society, and separate themselves from all others, who in their Way of Thinking maintain pernicious Errors. They may reject any Teacher that entertains erroneous Notions in Points which they look upon as essential. It were very hard truly,* say Creed-Imposers, *that Men should not have the Liberty of chusing their Teachers. If a Man that offers to be a Minister or Teacher, refuse to subscribe the* Confesson of Faith *receiv'd in that Society into which he would be introduc'd as a Teacher, that Society has reason to think that that Man entertains and might broach Heretical Doctrines; and if they have a Right to reject him, 'twould be very imprudent to admit him. And those Proceedings,* say they, *can by no Means be stiled Persecution, or any thing like it. The Man thus excluded Christian or Ministerial Communion, does not thereby suffer in his Person, Interest or Reputation; far be it from us,* say they, *to make use of Gibbets, Tortures, &c. nay to do a Man any Harm for Heretical Principles, that have no Tendency to subvert the civil Society. Nor do we imagine, that a Man's being excluded Communion with this or that Christian Society, can affect his spiritual Concerns. We do not judge of the State of his Conscience, much less do we pronounce Damnation, &c. Therefore there is here no placing our selves in the Judgment-Seat of Christ, there is no usurping an Authority that belongs to him alone, &c.*

ANSWER.

How from the Right of private Judgment (and as to that Right, we had as good give up at once, our Reason, our Religion and all, as part with it) how from that Right, I say, it is infer'd, that you may refuse a Man Christian or Ministerial Communion, upon Account of his differing from you in Matters disputable, I confess I am utterly at a Loss to see. Before I proceed, I must observe, that by Matters disputable amongst Christians, I mean all such as are or may be controverted. Perhaps it will be said, that a Man may dispute even the Truth of Christianity itself, reject Christ, look upon him as an Impostor, &c. Well, what then? Why, say they, must even that Man be admitted into Christian Communion with us? The Answer is obvious: That Man does not at all pretend to Communion, for he declares himself no Christian; he denies the Truth of Christianity in general. We don't exclude him, he excludes himself. But this is altogether out of the Question: For the Person here suppos'd, is one that professes to believe the Holy Scriptures, or who declares himself a Christian. But to return.

The Right of private Judgment seems to me most fairly and evidently to lead us to a Consequence directly opposite to the one

77

that was deduc'd. If I allow my self the Privilege of private Judgment, surely I cannot without Injustice deny it to another. I happen to differ widely from this or that Man, concerning this or that Speculative Point; I should certainly think it very rash in him to declare I am no Christian; since I am conscious I believe in Christ, and exert my best Endeavours to understand his Will aright, and strictly to follow it. By that grand Law of Christianity, *whatsoever ye would that Men should do unto you, do ye likewise unto them,* I ought not to pass on him that Judgment, which I should think very presumptuous as well as uncharitable in him. Now, the Case between a whole Society and one Man, is exactly the same as between Man and Man; the Number of Persons on one side, and their Fewness on the other, does not make any Alteration in it.

Shall WE refuse that Man Communion with us Christians, who perhaps is deem'd by the Almighty himself a good Christian? What Authority have we for doing so? Infinite Wisdom has not thought it proper to appoint any infallible Interpreters of his Reveal'd Will, and to impose this Interpretation of theirs as a Term of Communion. And if he has not, how come any Set of Men to pretend to a Power of determining the Sense of the Holy Scriptures for others? Why should I pretend to impose my Sense of the Scriptures, or of any part of them, upon you, any more than you yours upon me? and since a Pretence to Infallibility is absurd, these Interpretations may in many Instances be wrong, and when this is the Case (as it is much to be fear'd, it but too often happens) Error and Falshood is impos'd instead of Truth.

But suppose nothing but Truths be impos'd, it can never answer the End intended. The Man on whom they are impos'd is either convinc'd of, and consequently believes them, or he is not, and consequently does not believe them. If he be convinc'd, there is no Occasion for such Imposition at all, it is altogether unnecessary and foolish. If he be not, this Method will never clear up his Understanding; will never set the Evidences, by which those suppos'd Truths are supported, in a Light which shall convince him. He may play the Hypocrite indeed, '*dissemble and speak a Language foreign to his Heart*' (I wish there was less Ground for suspecting it to be too often the Case) nor, can I conceive any other End that can be answer'd by the Imposition of Creeds and Confessions. At best, if a Man pretends to believe the Truth of such and such Propositions

78

or Articles, the Evidences of which he does not see, but meerly upon the Authority of other Men like himself, or because they tell him they are true, his Faith can be no other than human, not divine, or rather indeed it is altogether a blind implicit Faith. The only Way to convince a Man of his Errors, is to address his Understanding. One solid Argument will do more than all the human Creeds and Confessions in the Universe; and if a Man once clearly sees the Truth of any Proposition or Article, his assent necessarily follows, and in all Cases of this Nature his Assent will be in Proportion to Evidence perceiv'd.

And as to Ministerial Communion, does it not at first View appear extreamly odd, not to say whimsical, to deny it to a Man of Piety and Virtue, Learning and good Sense. These are the only Qualifications, that I know of, necessary to entitle him to it.

Suppose he differs much from the Sentiments of the Church, or Society to whom he offers his Ministry, if these Differences in Opinion do not affect his Christianity, what Reason can be assign'd for rejecting him? Why, he may, say you, preach dangerous Doctrines; that is, Doctrines which you now think dangerous; but those very Doctrines, for what you know at present, may prove vastly conducive to the Interests of Religion in general, and Christianity in particular. Take Care that you do not obstruct the Propagation of Truth, by rejecting a Man, who is perhaps a very wise and good Man. What are you afraid of? Let him be heard; and if he cannot convince you that you are in the Wrong, retain your present Notions. If you have the Truth on your Side, his unsuccessful Attacks upon it, will rather root it deeper in your Mind, than shake it. Trust your self to Reason and to God's kind Providence; but never do any Thing that may hinder the Discovery of any useful and important Truth. You say, you may be led into Error, but if you be sincerely persuaded an erroneous Opinion is a true one, do you imagine our good and just God will punish you for it? No, surely; or else what would become of all Mankind. Sincerity is the Touchstone. 'Tis that will decide our future Condition. The Justness of our Reasonings, in all Instances, we cannot absolutely answer for; but we can know whether we be sincere in our Enquiries and Searches after, or Love for any Truth, whereby we suppose God's Glory, and the Good of our Fellow-Creatures may be promoted. Nor can I think it too bold to say, that it were better for

79

a Man to fall into many Errors, by earnestly and sincerely endeavouring to find out Truth, than accidentally to stumble upon it.

It were hard, say they, *that we should not have the Liberty of chusing our Teachers; and what if we will not receive any but such as do in the Main believe as we do, what Injury or Wrong is done to them? Are we in Duty bound to receive any one that desires it?*

In answer to this, let it be observ'd, that I do assert our own spiritual Liberty, and that of our Fellow-Creatures, by allowing every Man qualified according to the Scripture Rules, to teach, and we our selves to mind and consider what he takes to be Truth. No Man ought to resign his Liberty: Let him make Choice of his Minister as his Judgment and Conscience direct him. The Circumstances of the World require that some Men be establish'd among us constantly to do the Functions of a Minister, and they are maintain'd for that purpose. Now as a Maintenance can be afforded only to a certain Number of such constant Ministers, so People are necessitated to single out some Persons among those that pretend to that Office. It is very proper to prefer a Man of Learning and good Sense, to one that is known to be an ignorant Person. Discretion, Good Nature, and an exemplary Life, are chiefly to be minded: But to reject a Man in other Respects preferable, to reject him, I say, because he does not in the Whole believe as we do, is to declare we will not upon any Account, or for any Reason, alter our Opinions whatever they be. It is to declare that we are infallibly in the right: It is to profess we will not be taught any material Truth but what we know and are persuaded of already. How absurd would it not be to say to a Man, *Sir, we acknowledge you to be a very learned and diligent Person, we believe you know a vast deal more than the Generality of Christians; upon these Accounts we pitch upon you to be our Teacher or Minister, with this one little Proviso, that you will teach us nothing but such and such Truths which we perfectly know and are fully convinc'd of.* As ridiculous as this appears to be, 'tis exactly the Case before us.

But, say they, *that learn'd Person whom we make choice of, and who submits himself to the Laws of our Society, may adorn, illustrate, and set those Truths in a clearer Light,* &c. But yet the Absurdity still remains as to the most material Points; and in a Word, I cannot see how a fix'd Resolution to remain invariably in the Belief of such and such Articles, can be freed from the heavy Imputation of either a Pretence to Infallibility, or a wilful Blindness. Neither can I see what great Occasion there is for a Teacher at all, except it be to save Parents and Masters the Trouble of Instructing their Children and Servants. It looks prodigiously odd that any should think That an Act of Christian Liberty which in reality appears the very contrary. To confine our selves to listen only to such Teachers as are sworn to tell us nothing but what we do sufficiently know and believe, is actually to forsake our Liberty, to fetter our Understandings, and limit ourselves to a poor, slavish, narrow Circle of Thought.

Allow me here to observe by the by, that it were greatly to be wish'd that we had Teachers among us, who could live independently of the Gratuities and Voluntary Contributions of the People, who upon Occasion would give us the Fruits of their studious Piety. Any Man in easy Circumstances, that had a competent Share of Learning, and a fair Character in the World, should at first Request be with Gratitude admitted into the Number of our Teachers. It is easy to see what Advantages might probably flow from his Instructions. But to proceed.

As to the Wrong done to a Man who is deny'd Communion with a Society of Christians, tho' he declares his Belief of the Holy Scriptures, it is obvious that the Thing is not so harmless as our Creed-Imposers alledge. How afflicting must it not be to a Man who is conscious of his sincere Affection to Christianity, and consequently for all those that profess it, to be look'd upon by his Brethren as a Heretick and Infidel, &c. Thus in the first Place he suffers in his Reputation. 'Tis well known how the Generality of Men, shun, dread, and even hate a Person branded with Heresy by the Rulers of a Church or spiritual Society. No Advantages, no Places of publick Trust and Honour or Profit, no temporal Favours to be expected for him wherever they can prevent it. Thus he suffers in his Worldly Circumstances. Poverty, Contempt, Aspersion often pursue him, and destroy his Health and Constitution: Thus our suppos'd Heretic suffers in his very Person. Now you may call this what you will; but if it be not Persecution, it is something so very like it, that for my own Part I confess, it shocks all my Notions, Sentiments and Affections of Humanity and Christian Char-

81

LETTER TO A FRIEND, 1735

ity to a very high Degree. So also as to a Teacher; a Man may have spent his Substance and Youth to fit himself for the Ministry, if he be rejected when there is nothing against him but his refusing to subscribe Creeds which perhaps he does not well understand, or in the Belief whereof he cannot rest entirely satisfied, or if he refuses it for some other Reason, it is or may be a very great Disappointment. Then follows the general Odium that constantly pursues a poor Soul once call'd a Heretick. The Case is yet worse with a Man that has been a Minister for some Time, and who in his Search after Truth having dropt into an Opinion deem'd erroneous, is so ingenuous and fond of doing what he thinks advantageous to Mankind, as to confess or declare the Alteration of his Sentiments. The Case is worse indeed, for he is immediately depriv'd of Office and Benefice, and may, for ought I know, he and his Family, go and starve on a Dunghill with his fine Discoveries. And is this then their Separating themselves from such a Man, (as they mildly express it) is their Refusing him Christian or Ministerial Communion, so inconsiderable, so easy, so harmless a Thing? Who is it that does not see how inconsistent it is with Christian Charity? And tho' these Men tell us, they would not be for making use of Racks, Tortures, Gibbets, Death, &c. yet it is plain that if they have a Right to make Use of the lowest Degrees of Persecution, or to lay a Man under any Restraints for religious Speculations; they have a Right to proceed to higher degrees, if the lowest don't answer the End, and so to go on to the highest that even a Spanish Inquisition cou'd invent, if nothing less will do. O rare Protestants! It is well observ'd by an ingenious Gentleman,[7] that *whoever would convince by Stripes and Terror, proclaims open War against Christianity and Common Sense, against the Peace of Society and the Happiness of Mankind. Persecution,* says he, *for any Opinion whatsoever, justifies Persecution for any Opinion in the World; and every Persecutor is liable to be persecuted, upon his own Principles, by every Man upon Earth of a different Opinion and more Strength. What dismal Butcheries would such a cruel Spirit raise!* But to proceed.

To alledge that a Person truly heretical can by no means deserve the Name of a true Christian, would not be to the Purpose; for the very Point in question is, Whether a Person that believes the Holy Scriptures, and that differs from the Generality of Christians only

7. Not identified.

in Points determined and interpreted by Creed-makers and not by Christ, be undoubtedly a Heretick or no. Or even, Whether real Errors in Matters not most distinctly and evidently declar'd essential by Christ and his Apostles, but afterwards denominated such by Creed-Makers, do constitute a Man a Heretick, or blot out of him the noble Character of a sincere and real Christian. Now in this Case to declare against that Man what Christ or his Apostles have not declar'd, is demonstrably, as was observ'd before, to usurp his Authority, and venture to act in direct Opposition to his Design and Will. Who can deny, that to say as the Romanists do, *We are certainly in the Right, and Heretics cannot plead the same*, is grossly to beg the Question? And in a Word, to deny Christian or Ministerial Communion with a Man only because he does not think as we do, is evidently to make a moral Impossibility a Term of such Communion. How injurious this to the Spirit and Design of the Christian Scheme of Religion, which breathes forth nothing but Concord and Harmony: How injurious to the great and benevolent Author of it, who is all Love, Truth, Meekness and Charity! It is, I say, to make a moral Impossibility a Term of Christian or Ministerial Communion. For as long as Men are made by God himself, of different Constitutions, Capacities, Genius's, &c. and since in his all-wise Providence he affords them very different, very various Opportunities of Education, Instruction and Example, a Difference in Opinion is inevitable. Besides a Man's Sentiments are not in his own Power; Conviction is the necessary Result or Effect of Proof and Evidence; and where the Proof does not appear sufficient, a Man cannot believe or assent to the suppos'd Truth of any Proposition if he would. But to proceed to the Consideration of another ARGUMENT offer'd by our Creed-Imposers.

The strange Mixture of various and jarring Opinions, the Confusion which it is imagined would inevitably, upon the Principles here asserted, rush into the Church of Christ, is the grand Difficulty often objected and insisted upon.

ANSWER.

Indeed if Creeds were a sure Means to form and preserve the Unity of the Church; if they could prevent that Confusion, that Anarchy which it is suppos'd would be introduc'd upon the Scheme of *Liberty* in this Case, then truly our Creed-Imposers would have an Advantage much to be regarded: But it seems, indeed, that Creeds and Confessions are so far from bringing into or keeping up in the Catholick Church, that Unity, that Concord and Harmony which we ought all most earnestly to wish and pray for, that they have been one of the chief Causes of the cruel Divisions whereby the Church has been as it were rent and torn into so many Parties or Sects, and do still as much or more than any Thing else, contribute to perpetuate and heighten Feuds, Animosities and Dissensions; so that as long as such a Use of them as is here oppos'd, remains in Force, there will be little or no Hopes of a Coalition or Re-Union of the Christian Sects into one Body.

In fact, the Catholick Church of Christ (and this must be granted, except you confine the Catholicism of the Church to this or that particular Sect, and will not allow any other Sect to belong to the Church Universal, which I believe no thinking Person will do) the Catholick Church of Christ, I say, actually groans under all those mighty Inconveniences aforesaid; and in fact, all the Creeds and Confessions now extant do not in the least mend the Matter. Things, with respect to a strange Mixture of Opinions, Confusion, Anarchy, &c. cannot be worse than they are. Even in this City we have half a Dozen, for aught I know half a Score, different Sects; and were the Hearts of Men to be at once opened to our View, we should perhaps see a thousand Diversities more. Many a Man who in Appearance is of this or that Profession, entertains many Notions quite opposite to it, or to the Notions of others of the same Denomination. Creeds or Confessions may perhaps bring upon some small Christian Societies, an external Show, an outside Appearance of Unanimity in religious Sentiments. And this is the very best Effect they can produce. A poor, an inconsiderable, a bad one indeed! so that the Scheme here contended for can do no Harm but what by the opposite one is sufficiently done already, and remains utterly unremedy'd. Fact is against the Advocates for Creeds and Confessions, but they have nothing against the other Party in the present Argument but Conjecture. Besides do we not plainly see that the greatest Absurdities and Falshoods are supported by this goodly Method of imposing Creeds and Confessions: Such as Cringings, Bowings, Mortifications, Penances, Transubstantiations, praying to Saints and Angels, Indulgences, Persecution or playing the Devil

84

for God's Sake, &c. and if the Church has a Power of imposing at all, she has a Power of imposing every thing she looks upon to be Truth, and consequently the aforesaid Impertinences, if she in her great Wisdom thinks proper to do so. And can any Man in his Senses imagine that to be a proper Method of promoting the Interests of Truth in the World, which will as certainly propagate Falshood, Superstition, Absurdity, Cruelty, &c?

It is readily granted, that according to the common Proverb, *As many Men as many Minds,* so in all probability, very great would still be the Diversity of Opinion, should Creeds and Confessions be abolish'd. But then first, there would be among Christians a full Liberty of declaring their Minds or Opinions to one another both in publick and private. And secondly Heresy, that huge Bugbear would no more frighten People, would no more kindle among us the hellish Fires of furious Zeal and Party Bigotry. We might peaceably, and without the least Breach upon Brotherly Love, differ in our religious Speculations as we do in Astronomy or any other Part of natural Philosophy. Those two invaluable Blessings, full Liberty and universal Peace would in all likelyhood make the Ways of Truth so easy, that the greater Number of Christians would even come to think alike in many Cases in which they now widely differ. And, in a Word, that mighty Diversity of Opinions look'd upon as such a horrid and monstrous Thing, (and such indeed it is, when it carries along with it the Venom and Claws of religious Animosity, Tyranny and Persecution) that mighty Diversity of Opinions, I say, would be look'd upon as a harmless, innocent Thing, if Men would bring it under the amiable Power of mutual Love and Forbearance. Let the Church but enjoy Unity in Point of reciprocal Benevolence, make all the various Members of it one Body by the Bonds of Charity and mutual Forbearance, and then let them differ as much as you will in their Speculations, it will not occasion any thing like Confusion or Anarchy. Whereas imposing this or that System of Articles, this or that Rite or Ceremony, enslaving People's Minds, excluding them from Christian or Ministerial Communion, in short, unjustly vexing them will hardly ever change their Sentiments; but it will surely tend to turn their Hearts against such Imposers, Enslavers, &c. and Animosities will soon greatly encrease the speculative Differences.

Thus, Sir, you have a random Account of the principal Things advanc'd in that frightful and monstrous Sermon; and a longer one than I at first intended. There are several Things in it, which would require farther Illustration: But I thought it needless, since I write to you, *Verbum Sapienti satis;* besides, I was afraid of tiring you overmuch; and indeed if the Reading of this Scroll tires you as much as the Writing of it has me, you'll be provok'd to commit it to the Flames. I am, Sir, Your most Humble Servant.

Philadel. Aug. 30. 1735.

POSTSCRIPT.

Allow me here, however, to subjoin, by way of Postscript, some Observations of a very worthy and ingenious Gentleman, concerning the Argument drawn by Creed-Imposers from the Rights of *Private Judgment*.[8] This I add, because in our last Conversation you seem'd not to be altogether satisfied with any Thing I could offer upon this particular Argument. What follows, will, I hope, thoroughly convince you; wherein the Author shews that the Principle of the opposite Party, pursu'd thro' its just and natural Consequences, gives all manner of Encouragement to the Popish Usurpation.

The Principle (of Creed-Imposers) says he, is this, That even where the religious Rights of others are affected by our private Judgments, we must judge for our selves, and are in so doing only maintaining our own just Rights, that are concern'd in these Judgments. The opposite Principle is, That where the religious Rights of others are affected, we ought to rest in the express Decisions of Scripture. I believe this, says the candid Author, is a very fair State of the Controversy. If it be not so, 'tis owing to Mistake and not Design.

Now if we are to pursue our private Judgments, even in those Cases in which the religious Rights of others are affected, *where shall we stop?* Are we not to go as far as our private Judgments direct us, and are not all Men right in doing so? To this Argument, it is no matter, whether the particular Judgments Men form, are just and according to Truth, or not; for Truth consider'd as abstracted from the Discerning of the Mind, is no Rule of Action to any Man, nor can any Thing be Truth to us but as we apprehend it to be so,

8. Not identified.

86

and *see* the Agreement *between the Ideas* compar'd in our Minds. So that in *receiving* the Truth ourselves, or *imposing* it upon others it must be the *Apprehension* or *Perception* of our Minds that must be our Rule. And this Rule must equally direct Men, whether they are really in the Right, or only *think* themselves so, seeing Truth not known or perceiv'd by the Mind, can be no Rule at all. And so even supposing Men are wrong in their Particular Decisions, yet they are right in following their Judgment, while they continue of it; which is only saying that they are right in not contradicting the Light of their own Minds; and this, I suppose, no body will dispute. Now if all Men are right in following their private Judgments, even where the religious Rights of others are affected, will not this justifie any Encroachments upon our religious Rights, that any Man or body of Men shall judge necessary and just? To apply this to the Popish Usurpations, (which I do to shew the Tendency of the Principle, without intending a Reflection upon any Protestant, as if he approv'd what I know in his Heart he abhors) Pray what has the Popish Church been doing all this while, but pursuing *this very Principle?* Has she not judg'd for herself in all the Creeds she has ever published? Has not she judg'd for herself that she is *infallible?* Has she not as the natural Consequence of this, judg'd *that all Men ought to submit to her?* has she not judg'd for herself *that she ought to use Force?* and *that Hereticks ought not to live at all?* Has she not judg'd for her self *that the Magistrate ought to execute her Sentences?* and *that the Civil Power should wait upon the Ecclesiastick?* These are very wrong Judgments, I own; but yet they are the *Judgments* of *that Church.* They own no Conviction that they are in the Wrong, and no doubt Thousands thro' strong Prejudice believe they are in the right. Well then, they must not contradict the Light of their own Minds, but are right in going on according to it. And here is no Stop. Let a Man or Body of Men be never so far wrong, let him never so much injure the civil or religious Rights of his Fellow-Creatures in following his private Judgment; yet according to this Scheme, while he is of that Judgment he is in the right to follow it. So that no Protestant whatsoever can condemn a Papist, for doing what he does, while he judges he ought to do so. This is so obvious, that I cannot make it more so. Now it is not possible that a Principle should be a good and just one, in Pursuance of which such odious Things can be and have been done. —— And this may be applied to all Imposition that ever was in the World, and to all that ever shall be in it. Let Men be never so far in the Wrong, let their Impositions be never so *unscriptural,* while *they have that way of Thinking,* they *do right* in imposing their Errors; there never can be any Security for Truth from such Impositions, and every Church that ever was or shall be, is right in fixing such Terms of Communion, and such Doctrines and Usages, as shall be agreeable *to the Sentiments of such Men as have the greatest Numbers or Interest on their Side, when the Constitution is fram'd, and the publick Confessions compos'd.* So that here we can never have any fix'd Rule or Standard, either for Faith or the Terms of Christian Communion; and a Man that's accepted as a good Christian in one Place, may stand excommunicated in another; while 'tis certain, he is equally the Object of Divine Favour in every Place. In a Word, Private Judgment in this Scheme, is just another Name for *Arbitrary Power,* and no Man can set a Limit to it.

The other Way of Thinking furnishes a very clear Answer to Papists, and all others that are guilty of Imposition, if it be but *a just one,* viz. that their whole Scheme is wrong, for they are wrong in forming Judgments so as to affect the religious Rights of others, other than the express Decisions of Scripture: This cuts the very *Nerves* of all Anti-Christian Authority, and leaves us a fix'd Point to rest at.[9]

9. This pamphlet was answered by *Remarks Upon a Pamphlet, Entitled, A Letter to a Friend in the Country,* possibly by Jonathan Dickinson, minister of the Presbyterian church at Elizabeth, N.J., and later president of the College of New Jersey before it moved to Princeton. It admitted the strength of the arguments in the *Letter,* but asserted that each church should have liberty to accept and reject whom it would. "Men may pretend that it affects their *religious Rights,* to be denied Communion in any Society, to which they are pleased to offer themselves. But don't it affect the *religious Rights* of the Society much more, to be forced to admit them, when convinced that they are altogether unqualified Subjects, either for the Kingdom of Grace or Glory?" And the author concluded with a quotation from Locke's first *Letter concerning Toleration,* that a "spontaneous Society" has "Power to remove any of its Members who transgress the Rules of its Institution."

A
DEFENCE
Of the Rev. Mr. *Hemphill's*

OBSERVATIONS:

OR, AN

A N S W E R

TO THE

VINDICATION of the Reverend *COMMISSION.*

---

1 TIM. i. 4. and iv. 7. *Neither give heed to Fables, and endless Genealogies, which minister Questions, rather than godly Edifying, which is in Faith.* ----- *But refuse profane and old Wives Fables, and exercise thy self unto Godliness.*

Equidem, ut vere quod res est scribam, prorsus decrevi fugere omnem Conventum Episcoporum : nullius enim Concilii bonum exitum unquam vidi : Concilia enim non minuunt mala, sed augent potius. *Augustine.*

I never knew any Good to come from the Meetings of Priests.
Tillotson.

TIT. i. 13. *This Witness is true : Wherefore rebuke them sharply, that they may be found in the Faith.*

PHILADELPHIA:
Printed and Sold by B. FRANKLIN at the *New Printing-Office* near the Market. 1735.

A Defense of Mr. Hemphill's Observations[1]

A Defence Of the Rev. Mr. Hemphill's Observations: or, an Answer to the Vindication of the Reverend Commission. Philadelphia: Printed and Sold by B. Franklin at the New Printing-Office near the Market. 1735.[2] (Boston Public Library)

Franklin's *Observations on the Proceedings against the Rev. Mr. Hemphill* (see above, pp. 37–65) was answered by *A Vindication of the Reverend Commission of the Synod: In Answer to Some Observations on their Proceedings Against the Reverend Mr. Hemphill,* advertised as "This Day is Published," in the *American Weekly Mercury,* September 4. Ascribed to Jonathan Dickinson, the *Vindication* defended the Synod against Hemphill's charges that it had violated the standard of fair conduct and infringed his rights; and it examined again, this time with a fuller display of the evidence, the articles against Hemphill. That person, asserted the author, had the right to "declare non-communion with us, if he sees Reason for it," just as the Synod has the right to judge the qualifications of its own members.

Franklin's rejoinder to the *Vindication* was this *Defence of Mr. Hemphill's Observations.* Before it appeared, however, not only was Hemphill's case losing in interest, but his cause was irretrievably lost. During the summer, one of the clerical party discovered that Hemphill's sermons were not his own, but those of notorious Arians. Putting on the best face he could, Franklin stoutly affirmed he would rather hear Hemphill deliver "good sermons composed by others than bad ones of his own Manufacture"; but the "detection gave many of our party disgust" and cost Hemphill many supporters. Refusing to defend himself before the Synod, declaring that the pamphlet then in the press contained his defense, he defiantly challenged them to excommunicate him. The Synod

1. *Pa. Gaz.*, Oct. 30, announced this pamphlet as "just published."
2. The title-page contains five quotations: I Tim. 1:4; I Tim. 4:7; Titus 1:13; a sentence from Archbishop Tillotson: "I never knew any Good to come from the Meetings of Priests," which has not been located in his writings; and a longer Latin quotation ascribed to Augustine, though quite out of character, expressing the same sentiment. It is, in fact, a literal translation from the Greek of an epistle of Gregory Nazianzen to Procopius. J.-P. Migne, *Patrologia Graeca* (Paris, 1857), XXXVII, 225. In 382 Gregory, Patriarch of Constantinople, was summoned to a synod; he wrote to Procopius, the prefect of the city, declining, "on the ground of his great dislike to Episcopal Synods, from which, he said, he had never known any good to result." *A Select Library of Nicene and post-Nicene Fathers of the Christian Church,* 2d ser. (Oxford, 1894), VII, 478.

ignored the challenge, but, September 22, unanimously made his suspension permanent and his destruction complete.[3]

Hemphill left Philadelphia, and no more is known of him. As for Franklin, he "quitted the congregation, never joining it after," though he continued to give its ministers financial support for many years.[4]

A DEFENCE, &c.

When I first read the Rev. Commission's Vindication, I was in doubt with my self, whether I should take any publick Notice of it. I had reason to believe this Part of the World was troubled with Impertinence enough already, and that a Reply would be only affording our Authors a new Occasion for more of it by another Publication. Besides, I had little Reason to hope, that the most obvious Refutation of what our Reverend Authors have said to flatter and deceive their unthinking Readers into an Opinion of their honest Zeal and inflexible Justice, should ever gain one Proselyte from the Dominion of Bigotry and Prejudice.

As for the discerning Part of Men in this Place, especially those who were immediate Witnesses of the Proceedings which gave Rise to this Controversy, they must be own'd to be the most impartial Judges of this Affair; And those who were not present at the Tryal, if they are at all concern'd about the Merits of the Cause, will depend rather upon the Relation of those who attended it, as they are respectively influenc'd by an Opinion of the Veracity and Judgment of the Relater, than upon any Vindication of the Parties themselves.

For these Reasons then, tho' Occasion be taken to address this Part of the World once more about this Affair, yet I shan't undertake a formal Answer to every trifling Impertinence in the Vindication. It were but an ill Complement paid to the intelligent Reader,

3. William M. Engles, ed., *Records of the Presbyterian Church in the United States of America* (Phila., 1841), p. 115.

4. This pamphlet was answered by Obadiah Jenkins, *Remarks upon the Defence of the Reverend Mr. Hemphill's Observations: In a Letter to a Friend.* The principal teachings of orthodox Protestant churches were compared in parallel columns with Hemphill's views. "Obadiah Jenkins" was probably a pseudonym; a contemporary note on the copy in Hist. Soc. Pa. indicates that Jonathan Dickinson was the author. It was dated at New York Nov. 24, 1735, and its publication was announced in the *American Weekly Mercury*, Jan. 6, 1736.

to pretend helping him to see Absurdities in such *Meridian Lustre,* as our Authors elegantly phrase it. There is good Reason to believe the Opinion of thinking Men, who know the Affair, is not much chang'd by it, and that they entertain much the same Sentiments of the Rev. Commission which they did before. Perhaps the more Pains they have taken, by invented Surmises, wrested Constructions of Hemphill's Words and Actions, and sinister and palpable Prostitutions of Scripture-Phrase, to hang him up, as a Scare-crow to the People, and represent him as a dangerous Innovator; the more Occasion they have given to many to call in question their slavish and arbitrary Principles; and the more they have convinc'd them, even in these remote Parts of the Earth, (where they thought themselves secure) of their Inconsistency to every Thing that is real Virtue, Religion and Christian Liberty. Actions, and the Principles from whence they flow, do mutually illustrate each other; at least we can have no other Way in judging of either, but by comparing them respectively: However it must be own'd, that here the most curious Observers of Men, their various Affections and Desires, in many Instances make erroneous Conclusions; but 'tis evident, that nothing can render such Error or Mistake excusable, but a fair and candid Enquiry, free from all Humour and Interest, and a Consciousness of Honesty in Searching after Truth. Now whether the Authors of the Vindication had this latter more in view, than an Impatience to justify themselves by any Methods they could contrive, not to be too obviously reprehended by the Bulk of their Readers; and to raise a religious Pannick among the People, by pointing out one as professedly disclaiming the most important Doctrines in the Christian Scheme, I would even leave to their own Consciences upon a serious Self-Examination.

But this is not the first Time, that such pretended Defenders of *the Faith once delivered to the Saints,* have us'd the same Artifice, and let loose the popular Rage upon their Adversaries.

A Defender of the Faith, must be own'd a truly great and venerable Character; But I can't forbear quoting the Advice of a great Author, and applying it to the Gentlemen, Members of the Commission, "That since they have of late been so elated by some seeming Advantages which they are ill-suited to bear; they would at least beware of accumulating too hastily, those high Characters, Appellations, and Titles, which may be Tokens perhaps of what they expect hereafter, but which as yet don't answer the real Power and Authority bestowed on them."

If Truth stands in no need of false and deceitful Arts to support it, as our Rev. Authors themselves own; I wonder that they should in the very next Paragraph, use so much Flourish, either to palliate what they were asham'd to own, or to publish a palpable False-hood. Certainly had they been more honest to have told the Truth, or more ingenious in the Texture of their Inventions, they would not have expos'd themselves so much; I speak with Reference to the Sermons preach'd by Messrs. Cross and Pemberton during the Tryal; which were mention'd by Hemphill, as an Evidence of their having prejudg'd his Cause; Here they say, "they thought they could recommend the great Doctrines of the Gospel to their Hearers, and warn them against destructive Errors, and the pre-vailing Errors of the Day, without being charg'd with reflecting upon Mr. Hemphill, or accusing him as a guilty Person, and that Mr. Hemphill was neither accus'd nor condemn'd in them." But if these Discourses were not calculated against Hemphill, against whom then? who besides himself had at that time stirr'd up their watchful Zeal? None surely. For they say themselves in the second Page of their Performance, "that they had no Suspicion of being call'd into the Field of Battle, and oblig'd to defend the great Doc-trines of the Christian Religion, 'till Complaints were deliver'd in against Mr. Samuel Hemphill, a Minister who arriv'd at Phila-delphia the last September." Now if they had been enclin'd to have spoke Truth, they would have said, That Mr. Andrews's long establish'd Character for Virtue and Integrity, was sufficient Evi-dence of the Truth of any Charge they might have received against Hemphill from him, and that it was high Time to bestir themselves, and exorcise the Demon out of Philadelphia.

What occasion'd, say our Authors, *Hemphill's Removal from his native Country, we know not,* &c. What it was that occasion'd his Removal is not material to enquire. He may return to his native Country, when he will, which is more than a certain Person (and a principal one too) among them dare do. But I forbear ——

Page the 5th our Authors say, "Now let the World judge, whether our declaring our selves of an Opinion different from Mr. Hemphill, and refusing to own him as one of our Members, while his Principles were so contrary to ours, gave him any Ground to

93

load us with so many hard Reflections, and represent us as Men fir'd with a persecuting Spirit, and fill'd with Malice and Prejudice against him. Have not we an undoubted Right to judge for our selves, and to declare what our Opinions are?"

Tho' I believe no body will deny their undoubted Right to declare *their* Opinions, yet 'tis certain that to go farther, and deprive him as far as they can of Liberty to declare *his;* to deprive him of the Exercise of his Ministerial Function, and of a Livelihood as far as it depends on it, because his Principles were thought contrary to theirs, gave him a just Occasion to *represent them as Men fir'd with a persecuting Spirit,* since this was Persecution, as far as they could carry it. They farther add "Has not the Commission that Liberty which is common to all Societies, of Judging of the Qualifications of their own Members? Mr. Hemphill is possess'd with the same Right, and may declare Non-Communion with us, if he sees Reason for it." If, by judging of their Members Qualifications, they mean, that they have a Right to censure them, as they have done him, and expel 'em their Society; I think it is clear they have no such Right; for, according to this way of Reasoning, the Spanish Inquisitors may say to a Person they imagine heretical, You, 'tis true, have a Right to judge for your self, to quit our Communion, and declare yourself Protestant; but we have likewise the common and natural Right of Societies, to expel you our civil and ecclesiastical Society, destroy your Reputation, deprive you of your Estate, nay your Life, or in other Words do you all the Mischief we please, notwithstanding your Right of declaring Non-Communion with us. How so? Because we have the Power, and Inclination to do it. Are not these Reasons by which they vindicate themselves every whit as good to justify the Practice of the Inquisition? Neither do, nor can the Synod or Commission give any better, for expelling a Man their Society, branding him with the Name of Heretick, and depriving him of a Livelyhood, as much as lies in their Power, for a meer Difference in Opinion: And after all, out of their great Goodness, declare, they neither gagg his Mouth nor cut off his Hands; or in other Words, allow him Liberty to declare Non-communion with them. A great Favour this! A most extraordinary Act of Grace indeed! But how long he would enjoy it, if 'twas in their Power to dispossess him of it, is not difficult to guess, if we may judge of what Men would do by what they have already done. How then

94

were they injur'd by a Comparison with the Inquisition, when thus they justify themselves by the same Reasons, and copy them as far as they can, or dare do?

How then must we act, say they; have we no Power to suppress Error and advance Truth? Yes, all the Power that any Set of calm, reasonable, just Men can wish for. They may consider his Assertions and Doctrines expose their evil Tendency, if such they have, and combat the Falshood they find in them with Truth, which will ever be the most effectual Way to suppress them and to attempt any other Method of doing it, is much more likely to propagate such suppos'd Errors or false Doctrines, than suppress them: In this free Country where the Understandings of Men are under no civil Restraint, and their Liberties sound and untouch'd, there is nothing more easy than to shew that a Doctrine is false, and of ill Consequence, if it really be so; but if not, no Man, or Set of Men can make it so, by peremptorily declaring it unsound or dangerous, without vouchsafing to shew how or where, as the Commission did at the Beginning of this Affair, and indeed have yet done no better.

Upon the whole, if the controverted Points be false and of ill Consequence, let them be expos'd to the World, if not, the Sentence which the Commission hath pronounc'd against them, will prove their own Condemnation; for, to alledge they may treat any Doctrines they please to call false, and the Believers of them, as they have done Hemphill and his Doctrines, is to give them an unbounded Latitude, an unlimited Power of discouraging and oppressing Truth it self, when it happens to clash with their private Judgment and mercenary selfish Views, as I dare say it will often do. See this Argument farther discuss'd in a late Pamphlet entitled, *A Letter to a Friend in the Country, containing the Substance of a Sermon, &c.*

Page 6. Our Rev. Authors observe, that "in the greatness of his (Hemphill's) Modesty, he takes Care to inform us, *how universally his Sermons were applauded, to what large Audiences he preach'd, and how much (upon their being read in the Synod) they were approv'd by People of all Perswasions, for the Strain of Christian Charity that runs thro' them, &c.*"

This aukward, ill-tim'd, and unjust Raillery is level'd against Hemphill for his being, as they elegantly phrase it, *the Trumpeter of his own Praises;* 'Tis true, he says, his Sermons were applauded, &c. but this they shou'd have omitted [for] their own sakes, for if it be Matter of Fact that they were so approv'd (on being read in the Synod) as they neither do nor can deny, 'tis a very fair and weighty Argument against them, and plainly shews they proceeded against and censur'd what was the avowed Common Sense of all unbias'd and disinterested Judges at the time; and surely we may suppose, he inserted it from some other Motive than meer Vanity, when it was so much to his purpose in helping to strengthen his Argument, and set their candid Proceedings in a fair Light.

Here they also endeavour to lessen Hemphill, by representing him as a Plagiary, and say, *They are apt to think, that if he had honestly given Credit to the several Authors from whom he borrowed much of what he deliver'd, it wou'd have made a considerable Abatement of the Reputation he supposes he gain'd, &c.*

But which of these Gentlemen, or their Brethren, is it, that does give due Credit for what he borrows? Are they beholden to no Author, ancient or modern, for what they know, or what they preach; Why then must we be told, that Ministers ought to have a good Salary, because they are at great Expence in Learning, and in purchasing Books? If they preach from their own natural Fund or by immediate Inspiration, what need have they either of Learning or Books? Yet Books they have, and must have, and by the help of them are their Sermons compos'd: But why then, you will ask, are we entertain'd with such dull, such horrid Stuff, for the most part? 'Tis the want of the *Bongoût* [good Taste][5] that spoils all. Their Taste is corrupted, and like a bad Stomach will corrupt the best Food in digesting it. They chuse the dullest Authors to read and study, and retail the dullest Parts of those Authors to the Publick. It seems as if they search'd only for Stupidity and Nonsense. If there be in a Book a weak Piece of Reasoning on any Point of Religion, That they remark, and keep it safely to be adopted upon Occasion. If an Author otherwise good has chanc'd to write one Impertinency, 'tis all they retain of him. But when Hemphill had Occasion to borrow, he gave us the best Parts of the best Writers of the Age. Thus the Difference between him and most of his Brethren, in this part of the World, is the same with that between

5. Here and hereafter throughout the pamphlet the brackets are in the original.

the Bee and the Fly in a Garden. The one wanders from Flower to Flower, and for the use of others collects from the whole the most delightful Honey; while the other (of a quite different Taste) places her Happiness entirely in Filth, Corruption, and Ordure.

Page 6 and 7. We have a lively Instance of their boasted Candor, Truth and Probity, both in their Proceedings at the Trial, and in their Writing of the Vindication. They acknowledge the Charge against 'em for admitting Thompson and Gillespie as Hemphill's Judges, (who, it was alledg'd *had condemn'd him already, having declar'd their Sentiments that he was guilty of preaching great Errors)* wou'd have some Weight in it, were it true; But these Men have the Confidence to say, No EVIDENCE *appear'd to the Commission, that these Gentlemen had prejudg'd his Cause, or declar'd him guilty.* 'Tis true, the Letters written by Thompson cou'd not be produc'd; They were burnt; by whose Instance I know not; But was there therefore (as these Authors are hardy enough to say) No EVIDENCE? Were there not three Gentlemen of undoubted Credit, that declar'd they had seen those Letters? Men of unquestionable Understanding, and therefore capable of giving an Account of what they had read? Did they not evidence, that the whole Tenor of these Letters discover'd a manifest Prejudice in Thompson towards Hemphill? and did they not repeat one Sentence that made it evident to the whole Congregation? If this was not EVIDENCE, I wou'd fain know what EVIDENCE is. But it cou'd not be admitted by our wise Commission as EVIDENCE; and the Case must have been the same with regard to the Words spoken against Hemphill by Gillespie. That Thompson had written in Prejudice of Hemphill, was prov'd; But That Proof, it seems, must pass for nothing, unless the Writing appear'd to the Commission; By the same Rule, if Evidence had been brought of Gillespie's Speaking against Hemphill, it wou'd have signify'd nothing with these righteous Judges, unless Gillespie had been pleas'd to repeat the Words before them. Senseless therefore is the Introduction of their Latin Scrap, *De non entibus et non apparentibus, idem est Judicium.* A Maxim, which if it prov'd what they wou'd have it, wou'd prove that no Fact, how atrocious soever, and witness'd by ever so many credible Persons, shou'd be punish'd unless done in open Court, that the Judges themselves might see it. Extraordinary Doctrine truly! and worthy none but it's reverend Authors; who have giv'n us this Sample that they are able to outdo the Jesuits themselves, in *Subterfuge, Distinction and Evasion.*

> *And therefore topical Evasions*
> *Of subtil Turns and Shifts of Sense*
> *Serve best with th' Wicked for Pretence,*
> *Such as the learned Jesuits use,*
> *And Presbyterians, for Excuse.*   Hud.[6]

But when Hemphill had with so much Justice excepted against these Gentlemen, how mean, how ungentlemanlike, how scandalous, was their earnest Insisting to be continued his Judges! A strong Evidence of that Partiality and Enmity which they deny'd and labour'd to conceal!

I dare venture to say, that, except themselves, there was not a Man so mean in that Congregation, who being call'd upon a Jury, in a common Court, if he had been excepted against by the Prisoner, tho' without cause, but wou'd have thrown up the ungrateful Office with Pleasure, and scorn'd to open his Mouth, or say the least Syllable tending to continue himself in the Place. But the Zeal of having a hand in the Condemnation of a Heretick carried them beyond all other Considerations. The Synod upon the whole unanimously voted them proper Judges; which Unanimity, in the Extract of their Minutes, they ascribe to God as the Work of divine Providence. To make God the Author of a palpable Piece of Injustice, is little better than Blasphemy, and I charge it on 'em as such. And their saying, in the case of Thompson, that there was no Evidence; I charge upon 'em, as a downright Falsehood. Of these two Burthens, I leave them to disengage their Shoulders as well as they can. But

> *Tis the Temptation of the Devil,*
> *That makes all human Actions evil,*
> *For Saints may do the same thing by*
> *The Spirit in Sincerity*
> *Which other Men are tempted to,*
> *And at the Devil's Instance do.*   Hud.[7]

6. Samuel Butler, *Hudibras*, II, ii, 262–6.
7. *Ibid.*, 233–8.

Page 8. of the Vindication, it is said, *Nor was it any Breach of Charity in the Commission, to suppose, that his Persisting in the Refusal,* (of his giving up his Notes) *look'd too much like a Consciousness of his own Guilt, when the first Reason he gave for this his Refusal, was,* that no man was oblig'd to furnish Matter of Accusation against himself. *What was this but a tacit Acknowledgment of his Guilt, otherwise his producing his Notes wou'd have been his best and noblest Defence, and no Accusation against him.*

But however they censure Hemphill for refusing to give up his Notes, it appears from all their Proceedings, that he was in the right to do so, since the worthy, candid and impartial Commission was determin'd to find Heresy enough in them, to condemn him; nor cou'd any thing annex'd to the Paragraphs objected against, (which explain'd or obviated their suppos'd heretical meaning) have any weight at all with them; for elsewhere in their Performance, when they allow that Hemphill in his Sermons and Prayers gave several Proofs of his Orthodoxy; yet, to invalidate this, they charitably insinuate at the same time, that he cloaks his real Sentiments, in order to have the more ample Occasion of doing secret Mischief to the Cause he publickly professes to espouse. A Suspicion truly replete with christian Charity, and in every Respect worthy it's Authors.

But say they, they cou'd not allow some Gentlemen to contradict the Evidence against Hemphill, *by affirming that they heard no such Words in his Sermon,* as *their* Evidences said they had heard, because they were a negative Evidence, or cou'd only swear they did not hear such Words; But that was not the case; and here as in other places, their pious Fraud, their sanctify'd Prevarication stands them in great Stead; for at the same time, that those illiterate Evidences were sworn against Hemphill, there were Gentlemen of undoubted Probity and good Sense ready to affirm to the particular Expressions, as they really were deliver'd by Hemphill, the meaning of which widely differ'd from that of those sworn to, by his Accuser's Witness which when Mr. Moderator saw, he stifled the Motion by crying out, He wou'd have no clashing of Evidences so that tho' the Evidence in Hemphill's Favour was beyond Comparison, the least likely to mistake the Expression, (and as much a positive Evidence as the other or any Evidence cou'd be in such a case) yet their appearing for him was Cause sufficient to make the

99

impartial Commission disregard or suppress their Testimony. What was this, but chusing to credit the Evidence against Hemphill at all hazards; to encourage his Accusers, and stifle every Truth that seem'd to make in his Favour?

These Reverend Gentlemen have always made a mighty Noise about a pretended Promise of Hemphill's to produce his Sermons to the Commission; and now they tell us, that *three Gentlemen of undoubted Veracity solemnly declar'd that they heard Hemphill say, he wou'd give up his Notes to the Commission of the Synod, if requir'd.* Two of these Gentlemen of undoubted Veracity, were the Rev. Mr. Tenant, and one of his Sons, of whose Evidence having taken particular Notice, I shall beg leave to set it in its true Light.

Mr. Tenant the Father[8] was ask'd What he knew of the Affair? (the Clerk being ready to write down what he shou'd say) and he answer'd thus, *Being with Mr. Hemphill, I ask'd him, if he thought he shou'd be willing, when the Commission met, to shew them his Notes, if requir'd; and he answer'd,* Yes. The Clerk minuted it thus, *I ask'd him, if when the Commission met, he wou'd shew them his Notes, if requir'd; and he answer'd,* he wou'd.

Thus by a *Hocus Pocus* slight of hand in the management of this Evidence, they converted an Opinion of Hemphill's of what he might be willing to do some Months afterwards, into an absolute Promise of what he really wou'd do. And thus alter'd and wrapt up, the Rev. Witnesses took their solemn Affirmation to the Truth of what the Clerk had written.

> *For if the Devil to serve his turn*
> *Can tell truth, why the Saints shou'd scorn,*
> *When it serves theirs to swear or lye,*
> *I think there's little reason why.*   Hud.[9]

But, as they pretend, It was the glorious Cause of Christ and his Church, and in behalf of *the Faith once delivered to the Saints,* and who can doubt, after what one of the Commission has said concerning *innocent Wiles,* but that in such a Cause, 'tis lawful to say or swear any thing.

8. William Tennent (1673–1745), minister at Neshaminy; in 1736 he erected the "Log College" to train his sons and other young men for the ministry. *DAB.*

9. *Hudibras,* II, ii, 123–6.

However, since the Vindicators declare their Abhorrence of the Principles of that unknown Member of theirs, who thinks any Method of promoting a good Cause, innocent and lawful; I imagine it not improper to inform them who he is, if it were only to see how far their Abhorrence will carry them in their Dealings with him, and whether their Zeal against Impiety be equal to their Zeal for Orthodoxy. The Rev. Gentleman's Name therefore is Nath. Hubbel.

I pass by, and leave to the Observation of every Reader, what sad Work the Vindicators, *Page* 10, make on't, when they wou'd justify Andrews upon the Charge of adducing a false Evidence. Vain is their Endeavour to wipe out the indelible Stain he has fix'd upon his Character by his Conduct in that Affair. They flounder and wallow in his Quagmire, and cover themselves with that Dirt, which before belong'd to him alone; bringing as a Proof of his Innocence, That, which in the strongest Manner confirms his Guilt; Since it shews that he knew the Truth at the same time, that he procur'd a Witness to swear the direct contrary. But to proceed,

In this Page, They put the Trial on the Credit of Hemphill's Notes, and yet out of their usual Good-nature and Charity, suppose that Evidence true, which is utterly falsify'd by his Notes, and rather believe he had delivered some Heresy from the Pulpit omitted in his Notes, than mistrust the Memory or Integrity of a crazy, weak, furious and partial Evidence. Behold the Men and their Impartiality! Lo the Desire they profess to have of seeing him vindicated from every Article of Accusation!

They farther insinuate that Hemphill had no right to expect their particular Objections to the Extracts, and for this reason, because they were there, not as his Accusers, but Judges; and tell us, that their *sincere Design was to give him full Opportunity of explaining his Sense, defending his Doctrines, &c.*

I shall not now dispute what was their sincere Design, which, I believe, is by this time very evident to every impartial and discerning Man, nor whether they came there with an Intent to judge or condemn him, tho' the latter plainly appear'd to all By-standers. But they ask, *how* they *cou'd point out his Errors to him, before they found him guilty of any; how* they *cou'd acquaint him with the Censures they thought him worthy of, before they had concluded him censurable, &c.*

101

I wou'd gladly have seen these Gentlemen, when they were writing this; they must certainly have been in great pain to keep Countenance, with all their saint-like Assurance, when they assert a thing so ridiculous, false and absurd; for, Who mark'd out the several Passages objected against in Hemphill's Sermons? I suppose the Commission. What did they mark 'em out for? They thought them not Orthodox; or did they mark 'em at random without understanding their Meaning, or without meaning any thing themselves. I believe they'll hardly allow this to be the Case, tho' one wou'd almost think it was, from reading their Minutes and the Extracts. I take it then for granted that the Extracts were made by the Commission, because they were thought Heterodox: Now with what Face can they say that they cou'd not shew him his Error because they had not discover'd it, when they themselves had cull'd out those Passages from his Sermons, as containing the most flagrant Heterodoxy and Error. Is not this then a vile, canting, false, prevaricating Excuse? For who were they that ought to have shewn the Errors and Falsehoods of the Doctrines contain'd in the Extracts? Certainly those Men who had made the Extracts, and thought 'em unsound and erroneous. And did not they, by making them, shew themselves the Supporters of Andrews's Charge, and the Abettors of the Accusation? For to prove the Charge on Hemphill was properly the Business of his Accuser, (Andrews) but lest the Accuser shou'd not be able sufficiently to support and make out the Impeachment, the *merciful* and *impartial* Judges took it upon themselves. *Behold that Spirit that wou'd have rejoic'd to see Hemphill vindicate himself; and brought them there, as merciful Judges, not Supporters of the Accuser!*

Nor can they by any Means extricate themselves out of this Difficulty, by alledging they gave him an Opportunity of vindicating himself from the Charge, and explaining what he meant in the Extracts; For, was it to be suppos'd that Hemphill, who did not think them faulty, shou'd happen to pitch upon every particular Article in the Extracts, which they consider'd as objectionable? And to put him upon a general Explanation was to impose a tedious, and indeed a useless Task; for he who had an Opinion of the Extracts, and their Tendency, quite different from the Commission, was very likely in such a Number of them to expatiate sometimes, where *They* wou'd think it needless, or entirely omit what they thought most heterodox. For, as he neither meant to preach, nor thought he had preach'd any dangerous Error, he cou'd not of himself find out where it lay, to explain it, or defend himself upon it, till they who were convinc'd he had done it, wou'd shew him where and how he had done so, and in what Sense they understood him; and this was absolutely the Business of the Commission.

Their Endeavours to justify Cross, p. 39, for changing his Sentiments, and condemning for Heresy, what but a day or two before he acquitted, need not be much insisted on. I shall only say, 'tis strange a Gentleman of his acute Penetration cou'd not 'till after much Consideration discover Heresy in a Paragraph, that shock'd an illiterate Evidence at the first Hearing, and oblig'd him to run out of the Church in the midst of it. But they have, methinks, giv'n up the Point entirely, in blaming the Philadelphia Gentleman for publishing what was spoken in private Conversation, since this is a tacit Acknowledgment that Cross then spoke his true Sentiments in *Confidence,* however he intended to act in Publick. But who, 'till now, cou'd have imagin'd, that the Sentiments of a Minister of the Gospel, deliver'd to one of the Laity upon a Matter of Religion, ought by all Means to have been kept a Secret?

Let us now consider a little their Remarks on Hemphill's Observations upon the Articles of Accusation exhibited against him in their Minutes.

It is a very melancholy and affecting Consideration to find any, who pretend they *are set for the Defence of the Gospel,* taking so much Pains (tho' perhaps ignorantly) to propagate Doctrines tending to promote Enthusiasm, Demonism, and Immorality in the World. This may be look'd upon to be a very heavy Charge upon the Authors of the Pamphlet now before me; yet the Charge is so easily made good, that it looks like an Affront to the Reason and a distrusting the Common Sense of Men to be at any trouble in doing it. But before I come to a particular Examination of the Accusations, &c. it is necessary to consider briefly the main End and Design of the christian Scheme of Religion, which our Authors seem, by their Performance, not at all to understand.

It is well observ'd by an ingenious Writer,[1] "That the common Mistake to which the Folly and Superstition of Men, in all Ages, has led them, is to over-value things of lesser Importance in Re-

1. Not identified.

ligion in comparison with greater; to substitute the Means in Place of the End; or rest on these as in themselves sufficient. Now if in any case the Worth and Excellency of Means lies in their Subserviency to the End, whence they derive their Value, there can hardly be a grosser Blunder in Practice, than to substitute the Means in place of the End; or to use them otherwise than with Regard, and in Subserviency to it. But if we once justly fix the main End of the christian Institution; a due Regard to that will lead us to a right understanding of the comparative Worth and Excellency of the several things contain'd in it; will direct us what we ought chiefly to be concern'd about, and shou'd have in view, in our use of all the Means Christianity points out to us."

Now the surest way to find out the End and Design of the Christian Revelation, or what View the Author of it had in coming into the World, is, to consult the Revelation itself. And he himself (the great and glorious Author) tells us, *he came to call Sinners to Repentance*;[2] that is, not only to a hearty Concern for Sin, but to an actual Amendment and Reformation of what was amiss in their Conduct. And Jesus Christ, the Redeemer of Mankind, elsewhere gives us a full and comprehensive View of the Whole of our Religion, and of the main End and Design of the christian Scheme, when he says, *thou shalt love the Lord thy God with all thy heart, and with all thy Soul, and with all thy Mind, and thy Neighbour, as thyself,* and he plainly tells us, that these are the most necessary and essential parts of God's Law, when he adds, *on these two Commandments hang all the Law and the Prophets.*[3] "These are what Nature and eternal Reason teach us; and these are the two great moral Precepts, which the Revelations the Almighty has made to Mankind, are design'd to explain and enforce." Moreover St. Paul in his First Epistle to Timothy expressly tells us, that *the End of the Commandment,* (i.e. of the christian Institution) *is Charity,* or Love, (as the original word might as well, or better, be translated here, and in several other Places) i.e. Love to God, and Love to Mankind.[4]

It wou'd be needless to quote any more Texts of Scripture to this Purpose; they are to be found in almost every Page of the New Testament. So that upon the whole, it may justly be concluded, that the main Design and ultimate End of the christian Revelation,

2. Matt. 9:13.   3. Matt. 22:37–40.   4. I Tim. 1:5.

or of Christ's coming into the World, was to promote the Practice of Piety, Goodness, Virtue, and Universal Righteousness among Mankind, or the Practice of the moral Duties both with Respect to God and Man, and by these Means to make us happy here and hereafter. All the Precepts, Promises, Threatnings, positive Institutions, Faith in Jesus Christ, and all the Peculiarities and Discoveries in this Revelation tend to this End; and if God gives a Revelation to Mankind at all, it is this, and this only that can make it worthy of him.

Now that natural Religion, or that the Laws of our Nature oblige us to the highest Degrees of Love to God, and in consequence of this Love to our almighty Maker, to pay him all the Homage, Worship and Adoration we are capable of, and to do every thing we know he requires; and that the same Laws oblige us to the Love of Mankind, and in consequence of this Love, as well as of our Love to God, (because he requires these things of us) to do good Offices to, and promote the general Welfare and Happiness of our Fellow-creatures: That the Laws of our Nature, I say, oblige us to these things, even the Rev. Vindicators themselves, will hardly be altogether so absurd as to deny, since they acknowledge, p. 20, of their learn'd Performance, the christian Revelation *to be agreeable to our Nature.* By what Accident such an Acknowledgment slipt from their Pen is not easy to guess; I imagine it to be a Mistake of the Printer; if not, how consistent it is with other parts of their wise Scheme is obvious to the lowest Capacity.

What Hemphill means *by the first Revelation which God made to us by the Light of Nature,* is the Knowledge, and our Obligations to the Practice of the Laws of Morality, which are discoverable by the Light of Nature; or by reflecting upon the human Frame, and considering it's natural Propensities, Instincts, and Principles of Action, and the genuine Tendencies of them.

Now, that to promote the Practice of the great Laws of Morality and Virtue both with Respect to God and Man, is the main End and Design of the christian Revelation has been already prov'd from the Revelation itself. And indeed as just now hinted at, it is obvious to the Reason of every thinking Person, that, if God almighty gives a Revelation at all, it must be for this End; nor is the Truth of the christian Revelation, or of any other that ever was made, to be defended upon any other Footing. But quitting these things; if the above Observations be true, then where lies the Absurdity of Hemphill's asserting,

ARTICLE I.

That *Christianity,* [as to it's most essential and necessary Parts,] *is plainly Nothing else, but a second Revelation of God's Will founded upon the first Revelation, which God made to us by the Light of Nature.* Let it not be pretended, that these Words, [*as to it's most essential and necessary parts,*] are here added to get over a Difficulty; for, it is plain even from the Extracts themselves, mangl'd as they are, that this is his Meaning; Nor can any Mortals upon Earth be suppos'd stupid enough, (our Authors, and the Rev. Commission excepted) to understand what he says otherwise. Where lies the Absurdity of his saying, that *this second Revelation of God's Will is agreeable to the first, and is an Illustration and Improvement of the Law of Nature, with the Addition of some positive Things, such as two Sacraments, and going to God and making our Approaches to him, in the Name and Mediation of his Son Jesus Christ;* and so of the rest of the Propositions under this Article. These Gentlemen surely, wou'dn't take upon them to say that the contrary Propositions are true and orthodox; for Instance, That this second Revelation of God's Will, is *not* agreeable to the first, nor is it an Illustration and Improvement of the Law of Nature, &c. If what Hemphill has asserted be false, this must be true. But, whether they look upon what he has advanc'd, to be true or false, they do not directly say, only in general find Fault with it.

What they say, is this, p. 16, *What farther serves to illustrate the meaning of all this,* [of what Hemphill has said] (I wish *they* had plainly told us how they understand him) *is his consideration of these things, which are properly christian, wherein Christianity, as being an Improvement of natural Religion, carries our Duty higher than Men generally thought themselves oblig'd to by the Light of Nature.* Among *all which Peculiars of Christianity,* say they, *wherein (if in any thing) it is distinguish'd from the Law of Nature, we hear not one word of Faith in Jesus Christ, of the Necessity of our Interest in the Benefits of his Redemption, of Justification by his Righteousness, or of Sanctification by his holy Spirit; nor one Word of any thing but what we find urg'd by the Heathen Moralists from the same Sort of Arguments.*

Surely these Gentlemen must have a strong Itch for wrangling, and be greatly inclin'd to Suspicion and *evil Surmises*. Does it follow from Hemphill's not mentioning *Faith in Jesus Christ* among the Instances which he gave of the Peculiarities of Christianity, that therefore he does not look upon *Faith in Jesus Christ* to be a *Peculiar* of it? Besides does he not expressly mention (as in the Extracts themselves) our *going to God, and making our Approaches to him in the Name and Mediation of his Son Jesus Christ*, as an Addition [i. e. a Peculiar] *of this Second Revelation of God's Will* [i.e. of Christianity?] Now can any one imagine that Hemphill, or any one else, that is a Christian, wou'd thus make his Approaches to God without believing in Jesus Christ? But to proceed,

Has Hemphill any where deny'd the Benefits of our Redemption by Christ, or the Assistances of the holy Spirit to all good Men in the Work of their Sanctification? 'Tis possible indeed he may not understand these things, as these Gentlemen do; and since they have not explain'd what they mean by them, nothing more need be here said about 'em, but that it is certain, they were intended, as Means, to promote the great End and Design of the christian Revelation, viz. The Practice of Piety and Virtue; and if this End be not answer'd by the Peculiarities of the christian Revelation, they can be of no Advantage to us with Respect to our Acceptance with God. But again,

What do these mysterious Authors mean here, by these Words, *Justification by his (Christ's) Righteousness*, or as they elsewhere call it *his imputed Righteousness to justify us in the Sight of God?* Do they mean, that the Almighty transfers the personal and perfect Righteousness of Christ to Men, or that he infuses it into them, and looks upon it, as the same thing with their own actual Obedience to his Law, and that in him they fulfil the Law?

Such a Notion is abominably ridiculous and absurd in itself; and is so far from being a Peculiar of Christianity, that the holy Scripture is absolutely a Stranger to it; Nor does the Notion tend to any thing less than the utter Subversion of Religion in general, and Christianity in particular. To prove this, I shall here transcribe the Reasonings of a Pious and learn'd Divine, the late Rev. Mr. Boyse of Dublin in Ireland.[5]

5. Joseph Boyse (1660–1728), *Works . . . Being a Complete Collection of all the Discourses, Sermons, and other Tracts, Which have been already Published* (London, 1728), I, 455–6.

"First," says he, "This Scheme [of imputed Righteousness] renders Christ's Satisfaction to the Justice of God, by offering up himself as our expiatory Sacrifice, needless and superfluous.

"The divine Law never subjects any to Punishment, who are regarded and accepted by God any Way as perfect Fulfillers of it. They may have transgress'd it in their *natural Persons;* but if another by God's own Appointment, is constituted their legal Proxy, and his sinless Obedience to the Law be in God's Account, and by an Act of strict Imputation made their personal Obedience, then after such an Act of Imputation, no Sins commited by them in their *natural Persons,* can be any longer charg'd upon them as *theirs;* and as a noted Writer (tho' no profess'd Antinomian) speaks, as to the Elect, *there was never any Guilt upon them in the Judgment of God.* And this shews the Confusion that those run into, who supposing Christ to be in the strictest sense our *Surety,* assert him to have both discharg'd our Debt of *perfect Obedience,* and our Debt of *Punishment* too. Whereas he that has fully discharg'd the Debt of Obedience by another, as a legal Surety, can never be liable to the Debt of Punishment. For the Penalty of a Law never extends to any that are justify'd as perfect Fulfillers of it by one that God himself has constituted their legal Proxy, made his sinless Obedience to become theirs by his own Act of Imputation. We need indeed both the Merit of Christ's sinless Obedience and Satisfaction too to obtain for us that Act of Grace, by which we are pardon'd and entitl'd to Life upon our Compliance with the gracious, and indeed necessary Terms of it. But if his sinless Obedience be made by a strict Imputation, our Personal Obedience, we need no Satisfaction to attone for the past Disobedience of our natural Persons.

"2*dly.* This Scheme of theirs is subversive of the Gospel Doctrine of Forgiveness.

"For, he that is accounted and accepted as a sinless Observer of the Law, by one that by God's Allowance and Estimation was the same Person with himself, stands in no need of Forgiveness for what he may have done in his natural Person, and is only dealt with according to the sinless Obedience of his legal Proxy, whose Obedience was perfect and sinless from his Birth to his Death, and whose Performance of it is suppos'd by God's Act of Imputation, to be made theirs, whose strict Representative he was. And therefore as far as I can see the Antinomian Writers very justly infer from this rigid Notion of Imputation, that *God sees no Sin in Believers, that there never was any Guilt upon them in God's Judgment, that they have no Occasion or Need to pray for the Pardon of it.* And how this can be reconcil'd with that perfect Pattern of Prayer which our Lord has taught, that directs us as much to pray for the daily *Forgiveness of our Trespasses,* as, for *our daily Bread,* the Favourers of this unscriptural Scheme, wou'd do well to consider. And how this can be consistent with the constant Practice of all christian Churches, as well as private Christians, who are wont in their publick Assemblies, their Families, and their secret Devotions to implore divine Forgiveness, needs to be resolv'd by the Patrons of this Scheme. For sure the Meaning of those Prayers, is not barely that God wou'd manifest our Pardon to our own Consciences. For Desert of Punishment inseparably attends all Sin. For Sins of Ignorance, meer inadvertency, &c. God's Act of Grace provides for their Pardon, upon a general Repentance. For Sins that are wilful, a particular Pardon, upon a particular Repentance; and as to both we need to sue for Pardon, and this is God's appointed Means of our obtaining it.

"3*dly.* This Scheme weakens the Force of those powerful Motives which the Gospel sets before us to persuade us to Holiness of Heart and Life.

"The Gospel manifestly supposes us to be reasonable and free Agents plac'd in a State of Trial, and Probation for the Rewards and Punishments of a future State. And accordingly makes Use of a great Variety of Arguments to disswade us from *all ungodliness and worldly lusts,* and to perswade us to *live righteously, and soberly, and godly in this present world.* And those Arguments are suited to those various Passions of human Nature, that are the usual Springs of our moral Actions. Sometimes it uses Arguments to work upon our Fears; and such are all Threatnings of eternal Punishment it denounces against all unbelieving, impenitent and finally disobedient Sinners, against all that refuse to believe this Gospel, or to obey it when publish'd to them. Sometimes it makes Use of Arguments proper to work upon our Hopes; and such all those *exceeding great, and precious Promises* furnish us with, which assure us of God's gracious Acceptance, and liberal Reward of our sincere and persevering Obedience. Sometimes it makes use of Arguments proper to work upon our Ingenuity and Gratitude; and such are those that are drawn from the manifold Blessings of common Providence, but especially from the Consideration of the unexampled and astonishing Love of our heavenly Father, and of our Redemption and Salvation.

"Now whatever persuasive Force the Defenders of this Scheme may suppose to be in the Arguments proper to work upon our Ingenuity and Gratitude, yet their Scheme enervates the Force of all those that are proper to work upon our *Fears* and *Hopes,* those two powerful Springs of our moral Actions. For he that has already satisfy'd divine Justice, by One consider'd and allow'd to be his legal Surety, is fully secure from all Danger of Punishment for Sins committed in his *natural Person,* and he that has perform'd Sinless Obedience by the same *Legal Surety,* whose Performance of it is by Imputation made and accepted as his, has an immediate Right to the Reward, and has nothing to do as any appointed Means to obtain the actual Possession of it. And therefore not only do the Antinomian Writers make these their favourite Maxims, *that Sin can do a Believer no Hurt, and that God is not displeas'd with him on Account of it. He must work from Life, and not for Life,* (i.e. must not yield sincere Obedience as an appointed Means to obtain it) *that the Holiness of his Life, is not one Jot of the Way to his Salvation:* But even other Writers that disclaim the Title of Antinomians, yet thro' this mistaken Sense of the *Imputation of Christ's Righteousness,* adopt the same false Maxims." Thus far our judicious Author. Now let any unprejudic'd Person judge of the Tendency of this Enthusiastick Doctrine; Whether it does not tend to destroy all Religion, and to introduce all Immorality and Wickedness into the World. Is it not then the Duty of every body to disapprove and discourage the Propagation of such a Notion, that not only tends to subvert the Doctrines of the Gospel, but the Happiness and Welfare of human Society? Even heathen Moralists themselves, how inferiour soever these Theological Wits may suppose 'em to be to them, wou'd blush to teach such a palpable Absurdity. It is easy then to apprehend who they are that endeavour to render *the Cross of Christ of none Effect, to frustrate the Grace of God, and render Christ's Death in vain,* how strongly soever, they may boast themselves to be *set for the Defence of the Gospel.* Noble and Worthy Defenders undoubtedly! and if this be the Way to defend it, *Know all men by these Presents,* That, according to our Rev. Authors, the

Way to defend the Gospel, is to promote Immorality and Wicked-ness among Mankind.

But they next proceed to observe, that *He* (*Hemphill*) tells us, that *allowing freely, that he deliver'd such a Description of Christianity as this, he nevertheless denies the Assertion of these Gentlemen, that it is inconsistent with their Confession of Faith, and more especially he denies, that it is subversive of the Gospel of Christ.*

Whether Hemphill's Notions of Christianity be or be not incon-sistent with the darling Confession of Faith, he is not at all con-cern'd to enquire; whatever Notions he might have formerly enter-tain'd of this Idol Confession, he now declares it to be no more *his* Confession, &c. That his Description of Christianity is not incon-sistent with, or subversive of the Gospel of Christ, is already prov'd. But our Authors attempt to prove the contrary; and indeed in such a manner as every Man of Common Sense laughs at. Hemphill has said in his *Observations,* "That what he means in his Account of Christianity, is, that our Saviour's Design in coming into the World, was to restore Mankind to that State of Perfection, in which Adam was at first created; and that all those Laws that he has given us, are agreeable to that original Law, as having such a natural Tend-ency to our own Ease and Quiet, that they carry their own Reward, &c." That is, that our Saviour's Design in Coming into the World, was to publish such a System of Laws, as have a natural Tendency to restore Mankind to that State of Perfection, in which Adam was at first created, &c. Hemphill's Meaning being thus in a few Words explain'd, it is altogether needless to say any thing about the Ob-servations of these incomprehensible Writers upon this part of Hemphill's Doctrine. The Scriptures they have adduc'd to prove it false, and every thing they say about it are altogether impertinent and foreign to the Purpose, as every common Reader (our Authors excepted) will easily apprehend. And indeed if they (our Authors) had purposely endeavour'd to give the World an Idea of their impenetrable Stupidity they cou'd hardly have fallen upon more effectual Methods to do it, than they have (I'll not say in this Part of their Performance only, but) thro' the whole of it.

But before we proceed to the Consideration of the next Article, let us observe *(en passant)* how grosly these orthodox Writers, page 20, mistake the Question between them and Hemphill. The true State of the Question is, *Whether Christianity* [*as to its most essential and necessary Parts*] *be not a second Revelation of God's Will founded upon the first Revelation (the Law of Nature)?* Or, *Whether Christianity,* [*as to its most essential and necessary Parts*] *be not a Reinforcement of the Religion of Nature?* And, *Whether our Redemption by the Blood of Christ, and all the Peculiarities of the Christian Revelation, were not ultimately intended to promote the Practice of Piety, Virtue and universal Righteousness among Mankind?* Nothing need be further said upon the Question thus fairly stated, than what has been already said, 'till these Men please to put Pen to Paper again, and let us know their Sentiments about it; and the World may undoubtedly expect a wise Scheme from this quadruple Alliance. Let us then proceed to the Consideration of their Remarks upon

ARTICLE II.

Which is, That Mr. Hemphill denies the Necessity of Conversion to those born in the Church, and not degenerated into wicked Practices. This our Reverend Authors think is sufficiently justified by the Extracts mentioned in their Performance. Let us then see how sufficiently they have made their Charge good. Hemphill in his Discourse upon these Words, *For in Christ Jesus, neither Circumcision availeth any thing, nor Uncircumcision, but a new Creature,* attempted among other Things to explain this Phrase, *a new Creature;* and he observ'd that this metaphorical Expression is sometimes made use of in Scripture, to denote that Change or Alteration made by the Grace of God in a Man, when he passes from the State or Character of a Heathen or a Jew to the happy State or Condition of a true and sincere Christian; and that it is sometimes made use of to denote in general the Change and Alteration made by the same Grace of God in wicked and immoral Persons, tho' profess'd Christians, when they sincerely endeavour to practise the Laws of the Gospel: And Hemphill in his Enlargement took Notice, that *this Change is most visible in the Conversion of Heathens to Christianity; and of wicked Professors of Christianity to a Conversation becoming the Gospel of Christ, and that it may be truly affirm'd of such, that they are new Creatures, different from what they were, and scarce to be known for the same Persons;* and that, tho' this be so, yet (as in the Extract) *the Effect of Christianity truly believ'd and duly practis'd, is the same upon those who were neither Heathens, nor wicked Christians, but were born of christian Parents, and brought up in a christian Country,*

*and had the happiness of a virtuous Education, and were never engag'd
in vicious Courses. Such as these,* he says, *tho' they can't properly be
call'd new Creatures,* (that is, in the same Sense and so properly as
Heathens or Jews converted to Christianity, or wicked, immoral
Persons, tho' profess'd Christians, brought to a Sense of their
Crimes, and a virtuous Course of Action, may be said to be New
Creatures) *when compar'd with themselves, because they were always
what they are,* (i.e. Christians) *except the Progress which they daily
make in Virtue.*

How the Charge of Hemphill's denying the Necessity of Conversion, i.e. in one Sense of every Man's believing the Truth of
Christianity, that has a fair Opportunity of being convinced of it,
and of practising every Thing that Christianity recommends, or the
Necessity of Conversion with Respect to wicked, immoral Christians, i.e. the Necessity of forsaking their evil Courses, and sincerely endeavouring to practise all Holiness, and Virtue; how, I
say, this Charge is founded upon this Extract, and the others mention'd in the Vindication, I confess, I am utterly at a Loss to see;
and I believe, every Man of common Sense will be as much at a
Loss.

Hemphill indeed supposes that Persons, who have all along had
the Happiness of a christian and virtuous Education, and who have
sincerely endeavour'd to practise the Laws of the Gospel, cannot
so properly in the Scripture Sense be stil'd *new Creatures;* therefore
say his wise Adversaries, he denies the Necessity of a Sinner's Conversion to God: Admirable Reasoning! —— To which I answer,
that

> *Asses are grave and dull Animals,*
> *Our Authors are grave and dull Animals; therefore*
> *Our Authors are grave, dull,* or if you will, *Rev. Asses.*

This Reasoning is every Whit as conclusive, and as infallibly just
as theirs.

It wou'd be a needless spending of Time to make any farther
Remarks upon what they say under this Article, or to take Notice
of what little Use the Texts of Scripture, they mention, are to prove
the Necessity of inward Pangs and Convulsions to all truly sincere
Christians; they are only different Expressions signifying the same
Thing; viz. pointing to us the Necessity of Holiness and Virtue, in

order to be entitl'd to the glorious Denomination of Christ's real Disciples, or true Christians.

But lest they shou'd imagine that one of their strongest Objections hinted at here, and elsewhere, is designedly overlook'd, as being unanswerable, viz. *our lost and undone State by Nature,* as it is commonly call'd, proceeding undoubtedly from the Imputation of old Father Adam's first Guilt. To this I answer once for all, that I look upon this Opinion every whit as ridiculous as that of Imputed Righteousness. 'Tis a Notion invented, a Bugbear set up by Priests (whether *Popish* or *Presbyterian* I know not) to fright and scare an unthinking Populace out of their Senses, and inspire them with Terror, to answer the little selfish Ends of the Inventors and Propagators. 'Tis absurd in it self, and therefore cannot be father'd upon the Christian Religion as deliver'd in the Gospel. Moral Guilt is so personal a Thing, that it cannot possibly in the Nature of Things be transferr'd from one Man to Myriads of others, that were no way accessary to it. And to suppose a Man liable to Punishment upon account of the Guilt of another, is unreasonable; and actually to punish him for it, is unjust and cruel.

Our Adversaries will perhaps alledge some Passages of the sacred Scriptures to prove this their Opinion; What! will they pretend to prove from Scripture a Notion that is absurd in itself, and has no Foundation in Nature? And if there was such a Text of Scripture, for my own Part, I should not in the least hesitate to say, that it could not be genuine, being so evidently contrary to Reason and the Nature of Things. But is it alledg'd, that there are some Passages in Scripture, which do, at least, insinuate the Notion here contradicted? In answer to this, I observe, that these Passages are intricate and obscure. And granting that I could not explain them after a manner more agreeable to the Nature of God and Reason, than the Maintainers of this monstrous System do, yet I could not help thinking that they must be understood in a Sense consistent with them, tho' I could not find it out; and I would ingeniously confess I did not understand them, sooner than admit of a Sense contrary to Reason and to the Nature and Perfections of the Almighty God, and which Sense has no other Tendency than to represent the great Father of Mercy, the beneficent Creator and Preserver of universal Nature, as arbitrary, unjust and cruel; which is contrary to a thousand other Declarations of the same holy

Scriptures. If the teaching of this Notion, pursued in its natural Consequences, be not teaching of Demonism, I know not what is.

All that Hemphill has to say about the Mistake of citing Words for Scripture Expressions, which he owns are not, is, that such a Mistake is not so bad, nor of so dangerous Consequence, as perverting the holy Scriptures, which these Authors are most miserably guilty of; and he thinks his Opinions still just, and agreeable to the sacred Scriptures, for any thing they have said to the contrary. Now for

ARTICLE III.

Which is, that Hemphill has declaim'd against the Doctrine of Christ's Merit and Satisfaction. A heavy Charge indeed; and to support it they produce several Extracts from his Sermons. Now, if what is advanc'd in these Extracts be false and heterodox, the contrary Propositions must be true and orthodox. Let us then compare Hemphill's Sentiments and the opposite together in the subsequent Manner. After Hemphill had observ'd that to preach Christ is universally allow'd to be the Duty of every Gospel Minister; he asks, What does this mean? and observes that "It is not to use his Name as a Charm, to work up the Hearers to a warm Pitch of Enthusiasm, without any Foundation of Reason to support it. 'Tis not to make his Person and Offices incomprehensible. 'Tis not to exalt his Glory, as a kind condescending Saviour, to the dishonouring of the supreme and unlimited Goodness of the Creator and Father of the Universe, who is represented as stern and inexorable, as expressing no Indulgence to his guilty Creatures, but demanding full and rigorous Satisfaction for their Offences."

The opposite and orthodox Principles of the Presbyterian Ministers of Pensylvania are, that *to preach Christ is to use his Name as a Charm, to work up the Hearers to a warm Pitch of Enthusiasm, without any Foundation of Reason to support it. 'Tis to make his Person and Offices incomprehensible. 'Tis to exalt his Glory as a kind, condescending Saviour, to the dishonouring of the supreme and unlimited Goodness of the Creator and Father of the Universe, who is really a stern and inexorable Being, expressing no Indulgence to his guilty Creatures but demanding full and rigorous Satisfaction for their Offences.* Well, these are glorious Principles, and a most excellent Method of preaching Christ.

These gloomy Writers after a Story of a Cock and a Bull, observe that Hemphill can't pretend to instance in any Preachers of Christ, that ever directly or in Terms applied these Epithets, *stern, rigorous,* &c. to the glorious God. Suppose this granted; yet it is easy to mention some who pretend to preach Christ, that maintain Doctrines, which, if pursued thro' their just and natural Consequences, would lead any unprejudic'd Mind to entertain such unworthy Conceptions of our glorious, good and beneficent God.

But Hemphill is charg'd with denying the Merits and Satisfaction of Christ, and that too for preaching the Laws of Christ. Let us then consider what the Scripture Doctrine of this Affair is, and in a Word it is this: Christ by his Death and Sufferings has purchas'd for us those easy Terms and Conditions of our Acceptance with God, propos'd in the Gospel, to wit, Faith and Repentance: By his Death and Sufferings, he has assur'd us of God's being ready and willing to accept of our sincere, tho' imperfect Obedience to his reveal'd Will; By his Death and Sufferings he has atton'd for all Sins forsaken and amended, but surely not for such as are wilfully and obstinately persisted in. This is Hemphill's Notion of this Affair, and this he has always preach'd; and he believes, 'tis what no wise Man will contradict.

That the ultimate End and Design of Christ's Death, of our Redemption by his Blood, &c. was to lead us to the Practice of all Holiness, Piety and Virtue, and by these Means to deliver us from future Pain and Punishment, and lead us to the Happiness of Heaven, may, (besides what has been already suggested) be prov'd from innumerable Passages of the holy Scriptures. If St. Paul's Authority be of any Weight with these Rev. and Ghostly Fathers, he distinctly tells us that the Design of Christ's giving himself for us, was, *that he might redeem us from all Iniquity, and purify unto himself a peculiar People, zealous of good Works.*[6] And he elsewhere tells us, that *Christ dyed for all, that they which live, should not henceforth live unto themselves, but unto him,* (i.e. in Obedience to his Laws) *which died for them, and rose again.*[7] And St. Peter expresly tells us the same thing, when he says, that *Jesus Christ bore our Sins in his own Body on the Tree, that we being dead unto Sin should live unto Righteousness.*[8] Our Saviour himself, as was before

6. Titus 2:14.   7. II Cor. 5:15.   8. I Pet. 2:24.

116

observ'd, tells us, that he *came to call Sinners to Repentance*. But what need I trouble the Reader with quoting any more Passages to this Purpose? To proceed then,

It is most astonishing to find those who pretend to be christian Ministers finding Fault with Hemphill, p. 40, for teaching, that *to preach Christ is not to encourage undue and presumptuous Reliances on his Merits and Satisfaction, to the Contempt of Virtue and good Works?* This, say they, *is a most dangerous Doctrine.*

And wou'd they really have Hemphill preach the contrary Doctrine? Wou'd they have him encourage impenitent Sinners with the Hopes of Salvation, by teaching them an undue and presumptuous Reliance on Christ's Merits and Satisfaction? And was it for this that God sent his Son into the World? If then Christ has shed his Blood to save such as wilfully continue in their Sins, and obstinately persist in a vicious Course of Action, then in Order to evidence our Trust and Reliance upon the Merits and Satisfaction of our Lord Jesus Christ, we must continue quietly in a State of Impenitence and Wickedness, and promise ourselves Favour and Acceptance with God, notwithstanding all our Sins.

If this be not Antinomianism, if it be not to preach the Doctrine of Devils, instead of the Gospel of Jesus, I know not what is. How great and valuable soever the Merits and Satisfaction of Christ may be (as undoubtedly they are great and valuable beyond Conception) yet, they are no more with Respect to us, than what God in his Word has declar'd them to be. They will be of no Use to us, without sincerely endeavouring to conform to his Will. And when Christians sincerely endeavour to obey God's Commands, and perform their Duty really and affectionately, tho' very imperfectly; to rely then and depend upon the Merits and Satisfaction of Christ for our final Acceptance with God, is undoubtedly not only the Duty, but the Comfort of all Christians. This is a Trust and Reliance founded upon the Gospel. But when Men continue in a vicious Course of Action, and imagine that God, notwithstanding their Impenitence, will save them at last, and that because of the Merits and Satisfaction of our Lord and Redeemer Jesus Christ, provided they at particular Times, when they happen to fall into a Paroxysm of Devotion, confidently declare their Trust and Dependence thereupon, and apply them to themselves, as our unmeaning Authors sometimes talk; when Sinners, I say, trust and rely upon this; it is a foolish, presumptuous and extravagantly unreasonable Reliance, and it is obvious to the meanest Capacity (our Authors still excepted) that such a Dependance is no way founded upon the Gospel. Besides, such a Trust and Reliance as this, is to injure and affront the great Redeemer of Mankind in the most extravagant manner imaginable; as if he came from Heaven, as if he suffer'd so much, not *to lead Sinners to Repentance,* but to encourage them in their Impenitence. But enough of this; every unbias'd Reader will easily see how ill-grounded the Charge of Hemphill's denying the Merits and Satisfaction of Christ is, and also the ridiculous Impertinence of the Whole of what our Reverend Authors have said upon the Affair; and they will easily apprehend too, the Truth of this Position of Hemphill's, found so much Fault with by our Authors, viz. *That God hath no Regard to any thing but Men's inward Merits and Deserts;* that is, no Regard to any thing *in Men* but their inward Merits; What else can the Almighty regard in them?

'Twould be a needless Trouble (and the Reader would hardly forgive the doing it) to follow these dark Authors Step by Step, thro' all their incoherent Starts and Hints. I shall therefore only take Notice of one Thing more under this Article. Hemphill is condemn'd for advancing this Piece of Heresy, viz. *They who have no other Knowledge of God and their Duty, but what the Light of Nature teaches them; no Law for the Government of their Actions, but the Law of Reason and Conscience; will be accepted, if they live up to the Light which they have, and govern their Actions accordingly.* To this our stern Authors answer, *Will the Heathen be accepted of God, by living up to the Light which they have, and governing their Actions accordingly?* then, say they, *there is no need of Christ's Merits and Satisfaction, in order to our Acceptance with God.* Well concluded! Pray, how came these Rev. Gentlemen to know that the Heathen, living up to the Light of Nature, may not have an Interest in the Merits and Satisfaction of Christ, or that they may not be accepted of God upon account thereof. The Merits of Christ's Death and Sufferings may be so great as to extend to the Heathen World, they may reap the Advantages of it, tho' they never had an Opportunity of hearing of him, provided they make a good Use of their Reason, and other Principles of Action within them. And to say otherwise is actually to lessen and diminish the Merits

118

of the Redeemer of Mankind: The Holy Scriptures represent his Mission as a general Benefit, a Benefit which Regards all Men, and in Fact, tell us that *Christ dyed for all*. And can any imagine that our good God, as is here suppos'd, will eternally damn the Heathen World for not obeying a Law they never heard of; that is, damn them for not doing an Impossibility. Surely none can imagine such a thing; except such as form their Ideas of the great Governor of the Universe, by reflecting upon their own cruel, unjust and barbarous Tempers, as our Authors seem to do. If God requir'd Obedience to an unknown Law, Obedience to the Gospel from those that never heard of it, or who never were in a Capacity or Circumstances of being reasonably convinc'd of it, it would be in the first Place manifest Injustice; for surely, Promulgation or Publishing of a Law must be allow'd necessary, before Disobedience to it can be accounted criminal. It is utterly impossible to reconcile the contrary Notion with the Idea of a good and just God; and is a most dreadful and shocking Reflection upon the Almighty. In the next Place, we should find the Mission of our Saviour so far from being a general Benefit, as the Scripture teaches, that on the contrary it would be but a particular one, distributed only to the smallest Part of Mankind: But, which is more, this Mission of our Saviour wou'd be a very great Misfortune and Unhappiness to the greatest Part (three Fourths) of Mankind. For it is probable, that without this Necessity of Obedience to an unknown Law, many would be able to save themselves by a good Use of their Reason and the Light of Nature; whereas by the Mission of our Redeemer, and the Imposition of an unknown Law, a Law which they could not observe (I mean what is peculiar to Christianity) they are reduc'd to an utter Impossibility of being sav'd. I do not think that these Observations can be contradicted without saying Things very injurious to the Deity, and therefore erroneous. Agreable to the general Notion here advanc'd are the Sentiments of St. Paul in Rom. 4:15 where he says, *For where no Law is there is no Transgression*. And Rom. 5:13 *Sin is not imputed when there is no Law*. See also Rom. 2:14, 15.

I know that some Passages of Scripture are adduc'd by the Maintainers of this Notion to prove the Truth of it. But some of the Observations made in page 32 [above, p. 114], are applicable here, which I need not repeat. And give me leave to remark here by the by, that if after all requisite Care and Pains, Reason clearly teaches the Truth of such or such a Proposition, and that we find in the holy Scriptures some Passage that seems to contradict the clear Decisions of Reason, we ought not, for we really cannot, admit that Sense of the Passage that does so, altho' it shou'd be receiv'd by all the Divines, that call themselves *orthodox,* upon Earth; So that any Man must be altogether in the right to look out for another Sense of the Passage in Question, which will not contradict the clear Decisions of Reason.

This Principle is to be extended only to Propositions, which evidently contradict the clear and manifestly well-founded Decisions of Reason in general (as in the Case before us;) and I say that such Propositions, such Doctrines cannot be contain'd in divine Revelation; so that we must look for another Sense of the Passages, by which they wou'd pretend to establish these Propositions or Doctrines; we must, I say, look for a Sense agreeable to Reason and the known Perfections of God; and it is absolutely impossible to reconcile the Opinion here contradicted to either; and if this Notion be not to represent the Almighty, as stern, arbitrary, inexorable, &c. pray what is?

As for those Passages of Scripture, which are often adduc'd to prove the absolute Necessity of all Men's believing in Jesus Christ without Distinction, in order to Salvation; Reason, common Sense, Equity and Goodness oblige us to understand and apply them only to those to whom infinite Wisdom has thought proper to send the Gospel.

These Gentlemen can hardly take it amiss to be advis'd to take the utmost Care of saying any thing, or interpreting Scripture after a Manner injurious to the infinite Justice, Goodness and Mercy of God, and contradictory to Reason. If the christian Scheme of Religion be not a reasonable one, they wou'd make but a dull Piece of Work on't in attempting to vindicate the Truth of it.

But they ask, What are the Benefits and Advantages of the christian Revelation, if the Heathen World living up to the Light of Nature and Reason may be sav'd? For Answer to this, I refer them to that excellent Defence of Christianity by Mr. Foster, Chap. 1.[9] But not to insist any more upon this Point, their remain-

9. James Foster (1697–1753), *The Usefulness, Truth, and Excellency of the Christian Revelation Defended* (London, 1731).

ing Objections against Hemphill, under this Article are easily obviated from what has been already said.

ARTICLE IV.

The next Article of Accusation exhibited against Hemphill, is that *he describ'd saving Faith, but an Assent to, or Perswasion of the Gospel upon rational Grounds;* as they word it. Which Article, say they, is supported by this Extract; viz. *That by saving Faith is always intended such a firm Perswasion of Mind of the Truths of the Gospel, as is founded on reasonable and good Grounds, and produces suitable Effects.* "The Commission," say the Vindicators, "complain that this Description is too general, as not explicitly mentioning our receiving of Christ upon the Terms of the Gospel."

Pray, what do the Commission or their learn'd Advocates mean by this Enthusiastick Cant, more than what is included in Hemphill's Definition? What is it to receive Christ upon the Terms of the Gospel? I should be apt to suspect some Charm in this, and the Authors of Sorcery and Witchcraft, had they not given so many Instances of a contemptible Stupidity; and among the rest is the following, viz. their concluding that Hemphill's Description of Saving Faith *may be apt dangerously to mislead Persons, and encourage them to trust to a naked Assent to the Gospel Revelation,* when the very contrary is included in the Definition itself. Saving Faith, in Hemphill's Sense, is always attended with suitable Effects; that is, with Piety and Virtue, or Love to God and Mankind; this in the Opinion of our worthy Authors and Rev. Commission, is apt dangerously to mislead People, &c. This is New-Light indeed! But *How,* as Hemphill has already said in his Observations, *can such a Faith, in the Description of which Good Works are mention'd, be a Means to lead Men from Good Works,* or mislead them?

One would imagine these Men were jesting about this Affair, or that they really wrote with a Design to burlesque Christianity, did not a dull, phlegmatic Air of Seriousness run thro' their whole Performance; when they in the very next Page condemn him for saying, *the only End of Faith is Obedience.* Pray what is the End of it, if Obedience be not? Is Disobedience the End of it? He, surely, must deserve to be as heartily laught at, as our Authors themselves, that would undertake a formal Refutation of what so

121

sufficiently refutes it self. Let's try if we can find any better Sense in the Accusation contain'd in

ARTICLE V.

And here we are told, that Hemphill has *open'd the Door of the Church wide enough to admit all honest Heathens as such into it.* Well, these Men have the rarest Knack of Writing unintelligibly of any I ever met with! What do these Words of theirs mean? Would they be for shutting the Doors of their Churches against honest Heathens that had a mind to come in, and so deprive them of any Opportunity of being convinc'd of the Truth of the Christian Religion? Wonderful Charity indeed! of a Piece with their damning them to all Eternity for an Impossibility. What Connexion there is between the Accusation, and the Extracts upon which they say it is founded, I own I am not able to see. And till they please to explain themselves, if they know what they would be at, I have nothing further to say, but *Darapti Felapton Disamis Datisi Ferison Bocardo Bamarip Cameres Dimatis Festapo Fresison.*[1]

ARTICLE VI.

The next and last Article of Accusation is, *that Hemphill has subverted the Doctrine of Justification by Faith.* The Observations of these unlucky Writers, and their pretended Proofs of this, are every whit as impertinent and senseless as the rest.

In the Discourse from whence the Extracts are taken, upon which this ridiculous Censure is foolishly suppos'd to be grounded, Hemphill, among other Things considered how, or in what Senses, Christians might be said to be sav'd by Faith. One Sense in which he alledg'd they might be said to be sav'd by their Faith in Jesus Christ was, that this their *Faith saves them from the Guilt of their Sins committed before their Faith;* that is, when, for Instance, a Jew or a Gentile commenc'd Christian, or profess'd his Faith in Jesus Christ, all Sins committed while a Jew or a Gentile, were forgiven him upon Account of this his first sincerely professing to believe, &c. and this Notion seems still to be agreeable to the christian Scheme of Religion: And he farther observ'd this to be a *Priviledge*

1. "Darapti . . . Fresison:" some of the mnemonic names given by Petrus Hispanus in the thirteenth century to various moods in the second, third, and fourth figures of syllogism. BF rendered some of these words incorrectly.

peculiarly belonging to the first Christians, converted at Years of Discretion from a Life of Sin and Impurity; and therefore, this first Justification, or Forgiveness of past Sins, *is often inculcated by St. Paul in his Epistles, and attributed to Faith; but this doth not concern those who have been educated and instructed in the Knowledge of the Christian Religion.* And it is very true indeed, that Justification, or Forgiveness of past Sins, in the Sense here mention'd, is not, nor can it be applicable to such as were always Christians, or *were educated and instructed in the Knowledge of the Christian Religion;* except you'll suppose, that those that were always Christians, were notwithstanding Jews or Gentiles, before they were Christians, tho' they were always Christians. An Absurdity which our Rev. Authors alone are capable of.

Tho' Hemphill, upon farther Reflection, will own that Justification, in the Sense above, is not a Privilege so peculiarly belonging to the first Christians, but that it may be applicable now-a-days; yet this will not at all answer their foolish Design, because the Case is exactly the same with that of the first Christians, or those converted from Judaism or Gentilism to Christianity, at the first Propagation of it. What Hemphill means, is this; Suppose an Indian, for Instance, now converted to Christianity, Justification in the Sense above might as well be apply'd to him, as to the first Christians: If the Reason of Things continue the same, God Almighty, according to the Christian Scheme of Religion, would forgive our suppos'd Indian, upon his Conversion, all his past Sins, as he did the Sins of the first Christians upon their Conversion, or upon Account of their believing in Jesus Christ. Now the Question with respect to our new Convert, or new Christian, is, What are the Terms or Conditions of *his* final Acceptance with God? In Hemphill's Opinion, and according to his Notions of Christianity, a sincere Endeavour to conform to all the Laws of true Goodness, Piety, Virtue, and universal Righteousness, or the Laws of Morality both with respect to God and Man, are the Terms of his final Acceptance with God; and when he fails in any Instances, a sincere Repentance and a renew'd Endeavour, begging divine Assistance, to practise the contrary Virtues; and when our Convert, and all other Christians, have thus endeavour'd sincerely to conform to the Laws of Piety and Virtue, tho' their Obedience be attended with many Imperfections, they will, as Christians, or as

123

Believers in Christ Jesus, be accepted of by God, according to the christian Scheme of Religion, the Imperfections of their Virtue will be forgiven upon account of the Merits and Satisfaction of Christ, as was before observ'd. So that what Hemphill farther says (as in the Extract) is still true, if rightly understood, viz. *that all Hopes of Happiness but what are built upon Purity of Heart and a virtuous Life, are, according to the Christian Scheme, vain and delusory.* That is, *all Hopes of Happiness* to Christians, as such, consider'd separately and distinctly from the Practice of the Moral Virtues, *are vain and delusory.* If these Gentlemen assert the contrary, they must infallibly run into Antinomianism, how angry soever, they may appear to be at the Charge. Now, how justly the Accusation of Hemphill's denying our Justification by Faith is founded upon the Extracts before us, is obvious to every body. The first Extract has nothing to do with us at all, who were all along educated and instructed in the Christian Religion; the second has been shewn to contain in it the Terms or Conditions of our Acceptance with God, as Christians, for Christ's Sake, or upon Account of his Merits and Satisfaction. How ridiculously silly and impertinent then are all their Observations upon these Extracts!

These Authors in very angry Terms condemn a Remark of Hemphill's in his Observations, which yet appears to be a very just one. *He* (Hemphill) *supposes, that all Christians (Antinomians excepted) will allow, that Faith will not be imputed for Righteousness to those Men who have been educated in the Christian Religion, and yet have never endeavour'd to practise its Precepts; that such Men,* says he, *have no reason to expect that they shall be justify'd by a bare Faith, as the primitive Christians were, who embrac'd Christianity assoon as they heard it preached;* that is, have no reason to expect the Forgiveness of their Sins upon account of a bare Faith, as the primitive Christians were forgiven their past Sins upon their first Conversion, or their Believing in Jesus Christ.

To this our very reverend Authors, with a pious and orthodox Sneer, answer, *It is scarce possible for a Man to bind together a greater Bundle of Error, Ignorance and Impertinence in so few Words, than this Gentleman has done.* Hah! a home Thrust! a bold Stroke! next Turn's mine. Here they suppose this Position of Hemphill's to be erroneous, &c. And yet in the next Paragraph tell us, with a sanctify'd Leer, that *the whole Protestant World, the Antinomians only excepted, have constantly taught, that those Men who have been edu-*

cated in the Christian Religion, are justifyed by a Faith, that from the very Nature of it is necessarily accompanied with Good Works, by a Faith that can no more exist without good Works, than the Body can live without the Spirit, &c. So then we are now justify'd by a Faith, the very Life and Soul of which consists in good Works, as certainly as the Life of the Body consists in the Spirit. Such Inconsistency! Such Self-contradiction! Surely these Men's Spirits must be strangely muffled up with Phlegm, and their Brains, if they have any, *encompass'd with a Fence of a most impenetrable Thickness.*

Thus, I think, I have examin'd the principal Things in this Vindication of the Rev. Commission; and upon the whole, it appears even from a plain Narration of Matter of Fact, that they (the leading Men among them at least) came to Philadelphia with Malice, Rancour and Prejudice in their Hearts, resolv'd at all Hazards to condemn the Man and his Doctrines; and their Aversion to both carry'd them those shameful Lengths which we have here shewn in their true Light. For if to justify a known Perjury, to lye openly and frequently in the Face of the World; if to condemn Doctrines agreeable to the main End and Design of the Gospel, and calculated for the common Welfare of Men; if to stamp an Appearance of Sanctity upon Animosity, false Zeal, Injustice, Fraud, Oppression, by their own open Example as well as Precept; and to behave as bitter Adversaries instead of impartial Judges; if to do all this be truly *christian Candour, Charity and Truth,* then will I venture to say, these Rev. Gentlemen have given the most lively Instances of theirs. For all these Things have been so strongly charg'd and fairly prov'd upon 'em, that they must of Necessity confess their Guilt in Silence, or by endeavouring a Refutation of the plain Truth, plunge themselves deeper into the Dirt and Filth of Hypocrisy, Falsehood and Impiety, 'till at length they carry their quibbling Absurdities far enough to open the Eyes of the weakest and most unthinking Part of the Laity, from whom alone they can expect Support and Proselytes.

I have one Thing to desire of the Vindicators, before I come to a Conclusion, viz. that they wou'd, for Shame, take in the Motto they have hung out in the Title Page of their Performance, from II Tim. 3,* since 'tis plainly applicable to none but themselves, and

---

*II Tim. 3:5, 6, 7. *Having a Form of Godliness, but denying the Power thereof, from such turn away. For this Sort are they which creep into Houses, and lead captive silly Women, laden with Sins, led away with divers lusts.*

can by no means touch Hemphill; for, he contended for the *Power of Godliness*, denying the *Form*; and 'tis well known, that none but the Men of Sense were on his Side, and that all the *silly Women* of the Congregation were inveterately bent against him, being zealous Abettors of Mr. Andrews, who *crept into their Houses, and led them away captive* to the Commission to say and swear whatever he had prepar'd for them. This Motto therefore was the most improper one they cou'd possibly have pick'd out of the whole Bible.

The Rev. Mr. David Evans, one of the Commission, in his Sermon at the Ordination of Mr. Treat, says, Page 49,[2] *That it is a* WONDER *to see* ANY *truly gracious, considerate wise Man in the Gospel Ministry*. And confirms it at the End of the Paragraph, by saying, *It is no* Wonder *to see thousands of Ignorant, inconsiderate, carnal Ministers, but a* WONDER *to see* ANY *truly understanding, considerate, gracious ones*. I am really inclin'd to be of his Opinion; especially, if he confines his Observations to the Presbyterian Ministers of this Part of the World. I am sure, however, that their Proceedings against Hemphill has convinc'd Multitudes, that this WONDER was not to be seen in the late Commission.

I might therefore divide the Gentlemen that were concern'd in this Affair (and I trust, I should do them no Injustice), into these three Classes; first, the Men of Honesty who wanted Sense; secondly the Men of Sense, who wanted Honesty; and lastly, those who had neither Sense, nor Honesty. And I believe this Division may comprehend the whole Commission.

[Of the Usefulness of Mathematics]

Printed in *The Pennsylvania Gazette*, October 30, 1735.

First reprinted by Duane (*Works*, IV, 377) and later by William Temple Franklin, Sparks, and Bigelow, but not by Smyth, this essay is omitted here for lack of evidence of Franklin's authorship. See above, I, 170. Julius F. Sachse asserted, without indicating authority or evidence, that it was originally delivered by Franklin before the brethren of St. John's

---

2. *The Minister of Christ, and the Duties of his Flock; as it was Delivered in a Sermon at Abington in Pensilvania, December 30, 1731* (Phila., 1732), pp. 49, 51. David Evans (c.1690–1751) was minister at Tredyffryn. Amer. Antiq. Soc. *Proc.*, LXVI (Oct., 1956), 215.

Masonic Lodge in response to their by-laws of 1732 (see above, I, 231), which Franklin helped draft.[3] There is, however, no connection between the essay and the Lodge's by-laws except that both declare the importance of geometry and architecture.

Shop Book, 1735–39

MS Account Book: American Philosophical Society

The Shop Book is a manuscript volume and business record like the Journal (see above, I, 172). It covers the period from November 14, 1735, to August 3, 1739, with the number of entries falling off sharply after 1736. The cover bears, in addition to doodlings, the words "Shop Book 1738" and the name of Deborah Franklin; Benjamin Franklin's name is written on the first leaf. From November 14, 1735, when the Shop Book was opened, until December 7, 1737, when the Journal was closed, the Franklins seem to have recorded sales on credit in one volume or the other without distinction, Deborah mainly using the Shop Book, her husband mainly the Journal. Franklin posted accounts from both records alphabetically in his Ledger (see above, I, 173).

In the pages of this narrow folio Mrs. Franklin recorded much of the daily, over-the-counter business: the sale of all kinds of printed forms and printing and writing materials—bonds, bills of lading, servants' indentures, powers of attorney, bills of sale, paper by the ream or quire, blank books, ink, pencils, quills, slates, lampblack, sealing-wax, parchment, wafers, pasteboard. There was a steady sale for primers, Bibles, psalters, dictionaries, and grammars, as well as for the books Franklin printed, notably *Cato's Moral Distichs* (see below, p. 130) and Logan's *Charge* to the Grand Jury, 1736. He sold dozens of copies of John Peter Zenger's *Narrative* of his trial in New York, published in 1736. At year's end the New Printing-Office was selling and shipping almanacs —Jerman's, Taylor's, and "Poor Dicks," as Mrs. Franklin called her husband's best-seller. The Shop Book shows, for example, the sale of more than 3000 copies of the 1738 *Poor Richard*. "Sister Franklin"— Ann Franklin of Newport, James's widow—took a thousand; John Peter Zenger ordered 18 dozen and then 200 more; two gross and a dozen went to Lewis Timothy in Charleston, and the same number to Thomas Fleet in Boston. The Franklins sold much chocolate, especially in 1737, some cloth, clothing, and even spectacles, while the Proprietor Thomas Penn bought and charged a cake of the family's famous crown soap.

3. *Benjamin Franklin as a Free Mason* (Phila., 1906), p. 23.

The customers of the New Printing-Office were as varied as the goods they bought. All Franklin's Junto friends came, as did many of the local political and merchant grandees: Governor Thomas, James Logan, Isaac Norris, ("for a set of Votes"), William Allen, Charles Willing, Anthony Morris, Andrew Hamilton, Lawrence Growden. Customers from out of town visited the shop: Isaac DeCow, whom Franklin had met at Burlington, Charles Read of Trenton, and others from Bristol, Salem, New Castle, and Lewes. Daniel Dulany of Maryland bought two Greek grammars and some other books; and Benjamin Lay, Conrad Weiser, Dr. John DeNormandie, Anthony Benezet, and Hesselius the limner also appear in the pages of the Shop Book. Many entries record payments or sales to "My Mother Read" and to Deborah Franklin's brother-in-law John Croker. An almanac, some paper, an ounce of ink went to people whom Deborah identified only as "Cristefer the Fishman," "Mary the Papist that is at Cozen Willkisons," and "the seck stone of the Church." It seems that nothing was unaccounted for: Franklin has debited a sixpence, "Lent the Stranger from Boston."

[Of True Happiness]

Printed in *The Pennsylvania Gazette*, November 20, 1735

Reprinted by Duane twice with minor variations (*Works*, IV, 350-2, 372-4), and later by William Temple Franklin, Sparks, and Bigelow but not by Smyth, this essay is omitted here for the reasons explained above, I, 170.

Advice to a Pretty Creature and Replies

Printed in *The Pennsylvania Gazette*, November 20 and 27, 1735.[4]

Mr. Franklin,

Pray let the prettiest Creature in this Place know, (by publishing this) That if it was not for her Affectation, she would be absolutely irresistible.

The little Epistle in our last, has produced no less than six, which follow in the order we receiv'd 'em.

4. The advice was published November 20, the six replies the following week.

Mr. Franklin,

I cannot conceive who your Correspondent means by *the prettiest Creature* in this Place; but I can assure either him or her, that she who is truly so, has no Affectation at all.

Sir,

Since your last Week's Paper I have look'd in my Glass a thousand Times, I believe, in one Day; and if it was not for the Charge of Affectation I might, without Partiality, believe myself the Person meant.

Mr. Franklin,

I must own that several have told me, I am the prettiest Creature in this Place; but I believe I should not have been tax'd with Affectation if I could have thought as well of them as they do of themselves.

Sir,

Your Sex calls me pretty; my own affected. Is it from Judgment in the one, or Envy in the other?

Mr. Franklin,

They that call me affected are greatly mistaken; for I don't know that I ever refus'd a Kiss to any Body but a Fool.

Friend Benjamin,

I am not at all displeased at being charged with Affectation. Thou know'st the vain People call Decency of Behaviour by that Name.

[On Human Vanity]

Printed in *The Pennsylvania Gazette*, December 11, 1735.

Duane printed this essay (*Works*, IV, 346–50), but later editors have not followed his lead. Except for a completely rewritten first paragraph and minor verbal changes this piece first appeared in *The Free-Thinker: or, Essays of Wit and Humour*, April 24, 1719, as Alfred Owen Aldridge has shown in "The Sources of Franklin's 'The Ephemera,'" *New Eng.*

Quar., XXVII (1954), 388–91. Franklin used the central idea of this essay—that of the short-lived insect—in the bagatelle "The Ephemera," which he addressed to Mme. Brillon, September 20, 1778.

Preface to Cato's Moral Distichs

Cato's Moral Distichs Englished in Couplets. Philadelphia: Printed and Sold by B. Franklin, 1735. Pp. iii–iv. (Yale University Library)

[December 18, 1735][5]

The PRINTER to the READER.

The Manuscript Copy of this Translation of *Cato's Moral Distichs,* happened into my Hands some Time since, and being my self extreamly pleased with it, I thought it might be no less acceptable to the Publick; and therefore determined to print it as soon as I should have convenient Leisure and Opportunity. It was done by a Gentleman amongst us (whose Name or Character I am strictly forbid to mention, tho' it might give some Advantage to my Edition) for the Use of his own Children;[6] But in my Opinion, it is no unfit or unprofitable Entertainment for those of riper Years. For certainly, such excellent Precepts of Morality, contain'd in such short and easily-remember'd Sentences, may to Youth particularly be very serviceable in the Conduct of Life, since there can scarce happen any Affair of Importance to us, in which we may need Advice, but one or more of these Distichs suited to the Occasion, will seasonably occur to the Memory, if the Book has been read and studied with a proper Care and Attention.

When I obtained Leave to make this Publication, I procured also the following Account of the Author and his Work: for I thought something of the kind necessary to be prefix'd to it.[7]

In most Places that I am acquainted with, so great is the present Corruption of Manners, that a Printer shall find much more Profit in such Things as flatter and encourage Vice, than in such as tend to promote its contrary. It would be thought a Piece of Hypocrisy

---

5. The work was advertised in the *Gazette,* Dec. 18, 1735, as "just publish'd."

6. James Logan. See above, I, 191 n.

7. By Logan; printed on pp. v–vi, following BF's preface.

and pharisaical Ostentation in me, if I should say, that I print these *Distichs* more with a View to the Good of others than my own private Advantage: And indeed I cannot say it; for I confess, I have so great Confidence in the common Virtue and Good Sense of the People of this and the neighbouring Provinces, that I expect to sell a very good Impression.

Extracts from the Gazette, 1735

Printed in *The Pennsylvania Gazette*, January 2 to December 30, 1735.

[ADVERTISEMENT] Any Township or Neighbourhood in the Country, wanting a School-Master, to teach Reading, Writing, or Arithmetick, may hear of one well qualified by enquiring of the Printer hereof. [January 9]

[ADVERTISEMENT] By the Indulgence of the Honourable Col. Spotswood, Post-Master General, the Printer hereof is allow'd to send the *Gazettes* by the Post, Postage free, to all Parts of the Post-Road from Virginia to New England: So that all Gentlemen and others, living on the Post Roads, may have this Paper sent them by every Post, as usual before the late Obstruction.[8] [January 23]

[ADVERTISEMENT] A QUANTITY of Spanish PISTOLES to be disposed of, enquire of the Printer hereof. [March 4]

Saturday Night last a House in Strawberry-Alley was broke open, and about 10 Pounds in Money, and some other odd Things taken out of a little Trunk that was lock'd up in a Chest: Three Servants belonging to different Masters being missing next day, were suspected of the Theft, and being taken at Byberry and brought to Town, they confess'd the Fact, and are now confin'd in

8. Andrew Bradford, postmaster of Philadelphia and publisher of the *American Weekly Mercury*, forbade the post-riders to carry the *Gazette;* BF bribed them to distribute his papers secretly. This announcement followed an order of Colonel Alexander Spotswood, deputy postmaster general for North America, that Bradford must allow rival papers to be carried like his own. Ruth L. Butler, *Doctor Franklin, Postmaster General* (Garden City, N.Y., 1928), p. 33; see also below, p. 275 n.

Goal in order to a Tryal. One of them is a Lad about 18 Years of Age. The Money belong'd to some poor People, who had been some Years getting it together, in order to put themselves into some better Way of Business. [March 27]

Wednesday Night last a Fire broke out near the Prison, in a Smith's Shop, which was presently consumed; together with another Smith's Shop, and two Wheelwrights Shops, they being all of Wood. The Prison was in great Danger, as also a Row of Houses to the Westward of the Fire, one of which was considerably Damag'd; but by the extraordinary Diligence and Activity of the People, the Fire was at length suppress'd, with only the entire Loss of those four Shops. [April 10]

Thursday next a Commission of the Presbyterian Synod meet, to try the Reverend Mr. Hemphill, upon a Charge of Heterodoxy.[9] [April 10]

We hear from Chester County, that last Week at a Vendue held there, a Man being unreasonably abusive to his Wife upon some trifling Occasion, the Women form'd themselves into a Court, and order'd him to be apprehended by their Officers and brought to Tryal: being found guilty he was condemn'd to be duck'd 3 times in a neighbouring Pond, and to have one half cut off, of his Hair and Beard (which it seems he wore at full length) and the Sentence was accordingly executed, to the great Diversion of the Spectators. [April 17]

[ADVERTISEMENT] The Subscribers to the Library in Philadelphia are advertised, that Monday the 5th of May ensuing, at Two in the Afternoon, is the Time appointed for the Choice of Directors and a Treasurer for the succeeding Year, and for making the third annual Payment, at the House of John Roberts in High-Street.
JOSEPH BREINTNAL, Secr.
[April 24]

[ADVERTISEMENT] Lately lost out of a Boat, between Bristol and Philadelphia, a large Portmantua covered with blue Cloth; and having within it sundry Holland Shirts, a Plad Night-Gown

9. See above, pp. 27–8, 37.

lin'd with blue Sattin, and other valuable Things. Whoever may have taken up the same, and shall forthwith deliver the Whole to the Printer hereof, shall receive a Reward of *Five Pounds*.

[May 1]

Sunday last in the violent Thunder Storm about 7 in the Evening, a Boat with five Servant-Men overset about a Mile this side Gloucester, four of them held by the Boat and Masts for two Hours, till they drove against the Upper Part of this City, when their crying for Help was accidentally heard; the other a Servant belonging to Mr. Simon Edgel, was shook off by the Boat's shifting, and drowned.

[May 22]

[ADVERTISEMENT] All Persons who are indebted to Henry Flower, late Postmaster of Pennsylvania, for Postage or otherwise, are desired to pay the same to him at the old Coffee-House in Philadelphia.

[May 29]

To BE SOLD, By the Printer hereof, very good Chocolate at 4*s*. per Pound by the Dozen, and 4*s*. 6*d*. by the single Pound.

[May 29]

Wednesday Morning died suddenly at Germantown Meeting, of an Apoplectic fit, Isaac Norris, of Fairhill, Esq; He had been many Years one of the Council, was often chosen a Representative in Assembly, had born several other Offices of Honour and Trust, and was esteemed one of the most considerable Men in the Province.[1]

[June 5]

Sunday last one Rachel Twells of this City died suddenly and the Coroner's Inquest having sat on the Body brought in their Verdict, that by drinking too plentifully of Rum and other strong Liquors she came by her Death. 'Tis said she had drank sixteen Drams of Rum and two Mugs of strong Beer that Day.

[June 19]

---

1. Isaac Norris (1671–1735), Philadelphia merchant, member and speaker of the Assembly, mayor, member of the Provincial Council, chief representative (after James Logan) of the proprietary interests in Pennsylvania from 1708 until his death. *DAB*.

The Person that borrow'd B. Franklin's Law-Book of this Province, is hereby desired to return it, he having forgot to whom he lent it.   [July 24]

Sunday last the Rev. Mr. Hemphill, (who was lately suspended by the Commission of the Synod) preached twice to a very numerous Congregation, at the House where the Assembly used to meet. The first Edition of the Observations on the Proceedings against him being all sold, a Second Edition is in the Press and will speedily be published.[2]   [July 31]

[ADVERTISEMENT] Very Good COFFEE sold by the Printer hereof.   [July 31]

Wednesday last arrived here two Frenchmen Deserters from Missisipi. They reckon they have travell'd 1500 Miles thro' the Woods, subsisting only upon what they could kill by the Way. They were five in all, Soldiers, that deserted, but they parted at Albany, and some went towards Boston. They brought with them from Missisipi a Man that was half French half Indian: He had kill'd a Frenchman in a Quarrel, and was condemn'd to die; but they help'd him to break Prison, on condition of his guiding them to these Parts. They say they deserted because they were neither paid, fed, nor cloath'd; that there are but few People settled on that River, only here and there a Fort for Security of Trade; and that there are more Soldiers than other Inhabitants. [August 28]

Saturday last in the Morning, the Honourable JOHN PENN, Esq; the eldest of our Proprietors, being attended by the principal Magistrates and Gentlemen of this City, &c. set out on his Journey for New-Castle, in order to embark on board Capt. Budden's Ship, which lay there ready to receive him. And the next Day he set sail from thence for London.   [September 25]

†‡†This Paper Numb. 355, ends the sixth Year since we undertook printing the Gazette. Those who are indebted for more than a Year, are desired to make Payment.   [September 25]

2. See above, pp. 37–65.

Thursday last being the Anniversary of His Majesty's Birth Day, the same was solemnly observed here. An elegant Entertainment was made by our Honourable Proprietor, for the Principal Gentlemen, Merchants, &c. of this City, at which all the Loyal Healths were drank under the Discharge of Cannon, and the Day concluded with the usual Demonstrations of Joy.   [November 6]

[ADVERTISEMENT] On Wednesday Night the 19th Instant, Thieves broke into a House in this City, and stole some Paper Money, with a parcel of double worsted-flower'd Caps: Several Drops of Blood were found about the Drawer from whence the Money was taken, whence 'tis probable that the Money also may be bloodied. If such Money is offered to be passed, or such Caps to be sold, by any such suspicious Person, 'tis desired that Information may [be] given to the Printer hereof.   [November 27]

JUST PUBLISHED. John Jerman's[3] and Poor Richard's ALMANACKS, for the Year 1736.
Jacob Taylor's,[4] is now in the Press, and will speedily be published and sold by the Printer hereof.   [December 4]

JUST PUBLISH'D. CATO's Moral Distichs newly translated into English Verse. Very proper to be put into the Hands of young Persons, Sold by the Printer hereof. Price 1s. cover'd.[5]
[December 18]

PHILADELPHIA: printed by B. FRANKLIN, at the New-Printing-Office near the Market. *Price* 10s. a Year. Where Advertisements are taken in, and BOOK-BINDING is done reasonably, in the best Manner.

3. For Jerman's *Almanack* see above, I, 280–1.
4. Jacob Taylor, surveyor-general of Pennsylvania, 1706–33, prepared almanacs for each year from 1702 through 1746. The great majority were published by the Bradfords; the issue for 1736, here advertised, is the only one of his brought out by BF, although Evans 3963 erroneously attributes this one also to Bradford.
5. See above, p. 130.

Poor Richard, 1736

Poor Richard, 1736. An Almanack For the Year of Christ 1736, ... By Richard Saunders, Philom. Philadelphia: Printed and sold by B. Franklin, at the New Printing-Office near the Market. (Yale University Library)

Loving Readers,

Your kind Acceptance of my former Labours, has encouraged me to continue writing, tho' the general Approbation you have been so good as to favour me with, has excited the Envy of some, and drawn upon me the Malice of others. These Ill-willers of mine, despited at the great Reputation I gain'd by exactly predicting another Man's Death, have endeavour'd to deprive me of it all at once in the most effectual Manner, by reporting that I my self was never alive. They say in short, *That there is no such a Man as I am;* and have spread this Notion so thoroughly in the Country, that I have been frequently told it to my Face by those that don't know me. This is not civil Treatment, to endeavour to deprive me of my very Being, and reduce me to a Non-entity in the Opinion of the publick. But so long as I know my self to walk about, eat, drink and sleep, I am satisfied that *there is really such a Man as I am,* whatever they may say to the contrary: And the World may be satisfied likewise; for if there were no such Man as I am, how is it possible I should appear publickly to hundreds of People, as I have done for several Years past, in print? I need not, indeed, have taken any Notice of so idle a Report, if it had not been for the sake of my Printer, to whom my Enemies are pleased to ascribe my Productions; and who it seems is as unwilling to father my Offspring, as I am to lose the Credit of it. Therefore to clear him entirely, as well as to vindicate my own Honour, I make this publick and serious Declaration, which I desire may be believed, to wit, *That what I have written heretofore, and do now write, neither was nor is written by any other Man or Men, Person or Persons whatsoever.* Those who are not satisfied with this, must needs be very unreasonable.

My Performance for this Year follows; it submits itself, kind Reader, to thy Censure, but hopes for thy Candor, to forgive its Faults. It devotes itself entirely to thy Service, and will serve thee faithfully: And if it has the good Fortune to please its Master, 'tis Gratification enough for the Labour of Poor   R. SAUNDERS

136

Presumptuous Man! the Reason wouldst thou find
Why form'd so weak, so little, and so blind?
First, if thou canst, the harder reason guess
Why form'd no weaker, blinder, and no less?
Ask of thy Mother Earth, why Oaks are made,
Taller or stronger than the Weeds they shade?
Or ask of yonder argent Fields above,
Why JOVE's Satellites are less than JOVE?

XI Mon. January hath xxxi days.

Some have learnt many Tricks of sly Evasion,
Instead of Truth they use Equivocation,
And eke it out with mental Reservation,
Which to good Men is an Abomination.
Our Smith of late most wonderfully swore,
That whilst he breathed he would drink no more;
But since, I know his Meaning, for I think
He meant he would not breath whilst he did drink.

He is no clown that drives the plow, but he that doth clownish things.

If you know how to spend less than you get, you have the Philosophers-Stone.

The good Paymaster is Lord of another man's Purse.

Fish and Visitors stink in 3 days.

XII Mon. February hath xxix days.

Sam's Wife provok'd him once; he broke her Crown,
The Surgeon's Bill amounted to Five Pound;
This Blow (she brags) *has cost my Husband dear,*
He'll ne'er strike more. Sam chanc'd to over-hear.
Therefore before his Wife the Bill he pays,
And to the Surgeon in her Hearing says:
Doctor, you charge Five Pound, here e'en take Ten;
My Wife may chance to want your Help again.

137

He that has neither fools, whores nor beggars among his kindred, is the son of a thunder gust.

Diligence is the Mother of Good-Luck.

He that lives upon Hope, dies farting.

Do not do that which you would not have known.

I Mon. March hath xxxi days.

>   Whate'er's desired, Knowledge, Fame, or Pelf,
> Not one will change his Neighbour with himself.
> The learn'd are happy Nature to explore,
> The Fool is happy that he knows no more.
> The Rich are happy in the Plenty given;
> The Poor contents him with the Care of Heav'n.
> Thus does some Comfort ev'ry State attend,
> And Pride's bestow'd on all, a common Friend.

Never praise your Cyder, Horse, or Bedfellow.

Wealth is not his that has it, but his that enjoys it.

Tis easy to see, hard to foresee.

In a discreet man's mouth, a publick thing is private.

II Mon. April hath xxx days.

>   By nought is Man from Beast distinguished
> More than by Knowledge in his learned Head.
> Then Youth improve thy Time, but cautious see
> That what thou learnest some how useful be.
> Each Day improving, Solon waxed old;
> For Time he knew was better far than Gold:
> Fortune might give him Gold which would decay,
> But Fortune cannot give him Yesterday.

Let thy maidservant be faithful, strong, and homely.

Keep flax from fire, youth from gaming.

138

Bargaining has neither friends nor relations.

Admiration is the Daughter of Ignorance.

There's more old Drunkards than old Doctors.

III Mon. May hath xxxi days.

> Lalus who loves to hear himself discourse
>   Keeps talking still as if he frantick were,
> And tho' himself might no where hear a worse,
>   Yet he no other but himself will hear.
> Stop not his Mouth, if he be troublesome,
> But stop his Ears, and then the Man is dumb.

She that paints her Face, thinks of her Tail.

Here comes Courage! that seiz'd the lion absent, and run away from the present mouse.

He that takes a wife, takes care.

Nor Eye in a letter, nor Hand in a purse, nor Ear in the secret of another.

He that buys by the penny, maintains not only himself, but other people.

IV Mon. June hath xxx days.[6]

> Things that are bitter, bitterer than Gall
> Physicians say are always physical:
> Now Women's Tongues if into Powder beaten,
> May in a Potion or a Pill be eaten,
> And as there's nought more bitter, I do muse,
> That Women's Tongues in Physick they ne'er use.
> My self and others who lead restless Lives,
> Would spare that bitter Member of our Wives.

6. A forecast for June 21 reads:
> If we have rain about the Change [solstice],
>   Let not my reader think it strange.

139

He that can have Patience, can have what he will.

Now I've a sheep and a cow, every body bids me good morrow.

God helps them that help themselves.

Why does the blind man's wife paint herself?

V Mon. July hath xxxi days.

> Who can charge Ebrio with Thirst of Wealth?
> See he consumes his Money, Time and Health,
> In drunken Frolicks which will all confound,
> Neglects his Farm, forgets to till his Ground,
> His Stock grows less that might be kept with ease;
> In nought but Guts and Debts he finds Encrease.
> In Town reels as if he'd shove down each Wall,
> Yet Walls must stand, poor Soul, or he must fall.

None preaches better than the ant, and she says nothing.

The absent are never without fault, nor the present without excuse.

Gifts burst rocks.

> If wind blows on you thro' a hole,
> Make your will and take care of your soul.

The rotten Apple spoils his Companion.

VI Mon. August hath xxxi days.

> The Tongue was once a Servant to the Heart,
> And what it gave she freely did impart;
> But now Hypocrisy is grown so strong
> The Heart's become a Servant to the Tongue.
> Virtue we praise, but practise not her good,
> (Athenian-like), we act not what we know,
> As many Men do talk of Robin Hood
> Who never did shoot Arrow in his Bow.

He that sells upon trust, loses many friends, and always wants money.

Don't throw stones at your neighbours, if your own windows are glass.

The excellency of hogs is fatness, of men virtue.

Good wives and good plantations are made by good husbands.

Pox take you, is no curse to some people.

VII Mon. September hath xxx days.

> Briskcap, thou'st little Judgment in thy Head,
> More than to dress thee, drink and go to Bed:
> Yet thou shalt have the Wall, and the Way lead,
> Since Logick wills that simple Things precede.

> Walking and meeting one not long ago,
> I ask'd who 'twas, he said, he did not know.
> I said, I know thee; so said he, I you;
> But he that knows himself I never knew.

Force shites upon Reason's Back.

Lovers, Travellers, and Poets, will give money to be heard.

He that speaks much, is much mistaken.

Creditors have better memories than debtors.

Forwarn'd, forearm'd, unless in the case of Cuckolds, who are often forearm'd before warn'd.

VIII Mon. October hath xxxi days.

> Whimsical Will once fancy'd he was ill,
> The Doctor's call'd, who thus examin'd Will;
> *How is your Appetite?* O, as to that
> I eat right heartily, you see I'm fat.
> *How is your Sleep anights?* 'Tis sound and good;
> I eat, drink, sleep as well as e'er I cou'd.
> *Well,* says the Doctor, clapping on his Hat;
> *I'll give you something shall remove all that.*

141

Three things are men most liable to be cheated in, a Horse, a Wig, and a Wife.

He that lives well, is learned enough.

Poverty, Poetry, and new Titles of Honour, make Men ridiculous.

He that scatters Thorns, let him not go barefoot.

There's none deceived but he that trusts.

IX Mon. November hath xxx days.

When you are sick, what you like best is to be chosen for a Medicine in the first Place; what Experience tells you is best, is to be chosen in the second Place; what Reason (i.e. Theory) says is best, is to be chosen in the last Place. But if you can get Dr. Inclination, Dr. Experience and Dr. Reason to hold a Consultation together, they will give you the best Advice that can be given.

God heals, and the Doctor takes the Fees.

If you desire many things, many things will seem but a few.

Mary's mouth costs her nothing, for she never opens it but at others expence.

Receive before you write, but write before you pay.

I saw few die of Hunger, of Eating 100000.

X Mon. December hath xxxi days.

☉ nearer the Earth in Winter than in Summer 15046 miles, *(his Lowness and short Appearance making Winter cold.)* ☽ nearer in her *Perigeon* than *Apogeon* 69512 miles: ♄ nearer 49868 miles; ♃ nearer 38613 miles: ♂ nearer 80608 miles: ♀ nearer 6209 miles: ☿ 181427 miles. And yet ☿ is never distant from the ☉ a whole Sign, nor ♀ above two: You'll never find a ✳ ☉ ☿, nor a ☐ ☉ ♀.[7]

Maids of America, who gave you bad teeth?
Answ. Hot Soupings: and frozen Apples.

7. For the meaning of these signs, see the almanac for 1733, above, I, 289.

Marry your Daughter and eat fresh Fish betimes.

If God blesses a Man, his Bitch brings forth Pigs.

> He that would live in peace and at ease,
> Must not speak all he knows, nor judge all he sees.

Adieu.

Of the ECLIPSES, 1736.

There will be this Year six Eclipses, four of the Sun, and two of the Moon; those of the Moon both visible and total.

The first is a small Eclipse of the Sun, March the first, 35 minutes past 9 in the Morn. Scarcely visible in these Parts.

The second is an Eclipse of the Moon, March 15, beginning 30 minutes after 4 a Clock, P. M. the Moon being then beneath our Horizon, and rises totally dark, and continues so till 25 minutes after 7, and the Eclipse is not entirely ended till 20 minutes after 8. This Eclipse falls in Libra, or the Balance. Poor Germania! *Mene, mene, tekel upharsin!*

The Third is of the Sun, March 31. 30 minutes past 2 in the Morning. Invisible here.

The Fourth is of the Sun likewise, Aug. 25. 35 minutes after three in the Morning; no more to be seen than the former; the Sun at the Conjunction being under the Horizon.

The Fifth is of the Moon, Sept. 8. 18 minutes after 8 at Night; Beginning of total Darkness 18 min. after 9. Time of Emergence 57 min. after 10. End of the Eclipse at midnight.

The 6th and last, is of the Sun, September 23 at Noon: Invisible here tho' the Sun itself be visible. For there is this Difference between Eclipses of the Moon and of the Sun, viz. All Lunar Eclipses are universal, i.e. visible in all Parts of the Globe which have the Moon above their Horizon, and are every where of the same Magnitude: But Eclipses of the Sun do not appear the same in all Parts of the Earth where they are seen; being when total in some Places, only partial in others; and in other Places not seen at all, tho' neither Clouds nor Horizon prevent the Sight of the Sun it self.

As to the Effects of these two great Eclipses, suffer me to observe, that whoever studies the Eclipses of former Ages, and compares them with the great Events in the History of the Times and Years in which they happened (as every true Astrologer ought to do) shall find, that the Fall of the Assyrian, Persian, Grecian and Roman

143

Monarchies, each of them, was remarkably preceded by great and total Eclipses of the Heavenly Bodies. Observations of this kind, join'd with the ancient and long-try'd Rules of our Art, (too tedious to repeat here) make me tremble for an Empire now in being. O Christendom! why art thou so fatally divided against thy self? O Poland! formerly the Bulwark of the Christian Faith, wilt thou become the Flood-gate to let in an Inundation of Infidelity? O mischievous Crescent! when shall we see thee at the Full, and rejoice at thy future Waning? May Heaven avert these presag'd Misfortunes, and confound the Designs of all wicked and impious Men![8]

COURTS.[9]

For Gratitude there's none exceed 'em,
(Their Clients know this when they bleed 'em).
Since they who give most for their Laws,
Have most return'd, and carry th' Cause.
All know, except an arrant Tony,
That Right and Wrong's meer Ceremony.
It is enough that the Law Jargon,
Gives the best Bidder the best Bargain.

In my last Year's Almanack I mention'd, that the visible Eclipses of this Year, 1736, portended some great and surprizing Events relating to these Northern Colonies, of which I purposed this Year to speak at large. But as those Events are not to happen immediately this Year, I chuse rather, upon second Thought, to defer farther Mention of them, till the Publication of my Almanack for that Year in which they are to happen. However, that the Reader may not be entirely disappointed, here follow for his present Amusement a few

ENIGMATICAL PROPHECIES

Which they that do not understand, cannot well explain.

8. In the War of the Polish Succession, 1733–34, Russia and the Austrian Empire had successfully supported Augustus of Saxony for the Polish crown against Stanislaus Leszczynski, who was supported by France. Before the peace treaty was signed Russia opened an attack on Turkey, 1736, claiming Austrian support, while France incited Turkey to attack Austria. Thus Poland was used to divide Christendom and open the gates of Europe to the infidel Turks.

9. These verses immediately precede the calendars of court meetings.

144

1. Before the middle of this Year, a Wind at N. East will arise, during which the *Water of the* Sea and Rivers will be in such a manner raised, that great part of the Towns of Boston, Newport, New-York, Philadelphia, the low Lands of Maryland and Virginia, and the Town of Charlstown in South Carolina, will be *under Water*. Happy will it be for the Sugar and Salt, standing in the Cellars of those Places, if there be tight Roofs and Cielings overhead; otherwise, without being a Conjurer, a Man may easily foretel that such Commodities will receive Damage.

2. About the middle of the Year, great Numbers of Vessels fully laden will be taken out of the Ports aforesaid, by a *Power* with which we are not now at War, and whose Forces shall not be *descried or seen* either coming or going. But in the End this may not be disadvantageous to those Places.

3. However, not long after, a visible Army of 20000 *Musketers* will land, some in Virginia and Maryland, and some in the lower Counties on both sides of Delaware, who will over-run the Country, and sorely annoy the Inhabitants: But the Air in this Climate will agree with them so ill towards Winter, that they will die in the beginning of cold Weather like rotten Sheep, and by Christmas the Inhabitants will get the better of them.

Note, In my next Almanack these Enigmatical Prophecies will be explained.[1]   R. S.

[On Government]

Printed in *The Pennsylvania Gazette*, April 1 and 8, 1736.

The first two essays of an untitled series on government which ran in the *Gazette* from April 1 to June 10, 1736, were reprinted by Duane (*Works*, IV, 340–6) in the apparent belief that Franklin wrote them. Sparks also included the two essays (*Works*, II, 278–84), but pointed out that he had no reason for assuming that Franklin was the author except that they had appeared in the *Gazette*. He added: "The internal evidence does not appear very strong." Bigelow likewise reprinted them, without comment (*Works*, I, 425–31), but Smyth correctly omitted them. The author, who wrote under the pseudonym "Z," declared in the *Gazette*, July 15, 1736, that all the essays so signed, i.e., all those on govern-

1. See below, p. 172.

ment, "were written by the same Hand, without the Participation or Knowledge of a second Person." John Webbe acknowledged authorship in the *Gazette*, July 28, 1737.

On Amplification[2] Printed in *The Pennsylvania Gazette*, June 17, 1736.

Amplification, or the Art of saying *Little in Much,* seems to be principally studied by the Gentlemen Retainers to the Law. 'Tis highly useful when they are to speak at the Bar; for by its Help, they talk a great while, and appear to say a great deal, when they have really very little to say. But 'tis principally us'd in Deeds and every thing they write. You must abridge their Performances to understand them; and when you find how little there is in a Writing of vast Bulk, you will be as much surpriz'd as a Stranger at the Opening of a *Pumpkin.*

It is said, that in the Reign of William the Conqueror, the Conveyance of a large Estate, might be made in about half a dozen short Lines; which was nevertheless in every Respect sufficiently authentick. For several Hundred Years past, Conveyances and Writings in the Law have been continually encreasing in Bulk, and when they will come to their full Growth, no Man knows: For the Rule, *That every thing past and present ought to be express'd, and every thing future provided for,* (tho' one would think a large Writing might be made by it) does not serve to confine us at present; since all those things are not only to be express'd, but may (by the Modern Licence) be express'd by all the *different Words* we can think of. Probably the Invention of Printing, which took from the Scribes great Part of their former Employment, put them on the Contrivance of making up by a Multitude of Words, what they wanted in real Business; hence the plain and strong Expression, *shall be his own,* is now swoln into, *shall and may at all Times hereafter forever, and so from time to time, freely, quietly and peaceably, have, hold and enjoy, &c.* The Lawyer, in one of Steele's Comedies, instructs his Pupil, that *Tautology* is the first, second, and third Parts of his Profession, that is to say, *the whole of it:* And adds, *That he hopes to see*

2. Attributed to BF for reasons of both style and content. Compare this definition of Amplification with that in his essay on Literary Style. See above, I, 328. The essay was reprinted in *Boston Evening-Post*, Oct. 11, 1736.

the Time, when it will require as much Parchment to convey a Piece of Land as will cover it. That time perhaps is not far off: For I am told, that the Deeds belonging to the Title of some small Lotts, (which have gone thro' several Hands) are nearly sufficient for the Purpose.

But of all the Writings I have ever seen, for the Multiplicity, Variety, Particularity, and prodigious Flow of Expression, none come up to the Petition of Dermond O'Folivey, an Attorney of the Kingdom of Ireland: As the Petition is curious in itself, and may serve as a Precedent for young Clerks, when they would acquire a proper Stile in their Performances, I shall give it to the Publick entire, as follows.

"To the Right Honourable Sir William Aston,[3] Knight, and Lord Judge of Assize of the Munster Circuit.
    "The humble Petition of Dermond O Folivey[4] a well and most accomplished Gentleman.

"Most humbly, and most submissively, and most obediently, and most dutifully, by shewing, and expressing, and declaring to your Lordship, that whereby, and whereas, and wherein, the most major, and most greater, and most bigger, and the most stronger Part of the most best, and the most ablest, and the most mightiest Sort of the People of the Barony of Torrough and County of Kerry, finding, and knowing, and certifying themselves, both hereafter, and the Time past, and now, and then, and at the present time, to be very much oppressed, and distressed, and overcharged in all Taxes, and Quit-rents, and other Levies, and accidental Applotments, and Collections, and Gatherings-together in the Barony of Torrough and County of Kerry aforesaid, And for the future Prevention of all, and every such, henceforth, hereafter, heretofore, and for the time to come, and now, and then, and at this time, and forever, the aforesaid most major, and most bigger, and most better, and most

3. William Aston (d. 1671) was senior puisne judge of the Chief Place (the equivalent in Ireland of the King's Bench). He was knighted at the Restoration for his loyalty to the Crown and appointed, Nov. 3, 1660, a justice of the King's Bench. Francis E. Ball, "Some Notes on the Irish Judiciary in the Reign of Charles II," Cork Hist. and Arch. Soc., *Jour.*, 2d ser., VII (1901), 215–16.

4. Dermond (Desmond or Dermot?) O'Folivey has not been identified, but the name O'Falvey is that of an old Kerry family. Jeremiah King, *King's History of Kerry* (Liverpool, 1908), *passim*, esp. p. 103.

stronger Part of the most best, and most ablest, and most mightiest
Sort of the People of Torrough and County of Kerry aforesaid,
HATH appointed, nominated, constituted, ordained, declared,
elected, and made me Mr. Dermond O Folivey to solicite, and
make mention to your Lordship, looking upon me now, and then,
and there, and here, the said Mr. Dermond O Folivey, to be the
fittest, and the most mightiest, and the most ablest, and the most
best, and the most accomplished, and the most eloquentest Spokesman within the said Barony and County, their granded, and well
beloved, and well bestowed, and better merited Agent and Sollicitor, to represent Oppression, and Suppression, and Extortion, for
all such, and for all much, and whereof, and whereby, and whereupon, your Petitioner fairly, and finely, and honestly, and ingeniously, and deservedly appointed, nominated, constituted, and ordained, and elected, and approved, and made choice of me the said
Mr. Dermond O Folivey as an Agent and Sollicitor, to undergo,
and overgo, and under-run, and over-run, and manage this much,
big, and mighty Service.

"These are therefore to will, and to shall be, now, and then, and
there, and at this time, and at the time past, and heretofore, and
formerly, and at the present, and forever, the humble, and special,
and important, and mighty, and irrefatigable Request of me, your
Petitioner and Sollicitor-General aforesaid; THAT your Lordship
will be pleased, and satisfied, and resolved, to grant, and give, and
deliver, and bestow, upon me Mr. Dermond O Folivey, your
before recited, and nominated Petitioner and Sollicitor-General
aforesaid, an Order and Judgment, and Warrant, and Authority of
Preference to my Lord Kerry, and Mr. Henry Punceby, Esq; and
Justice of the Peace and Quorum, or to any four or five or more or
less, or either or neither of them, now, and then, and there, and
here, and any where, and every where, and somewhere, and no-
where, to call and bring, and fetch, and carry, before him, or them,
or either of them, or neither, or both, such Party or Parties as they
shall imagine, and conceive, and consider, and suppose, and assent,
and esteem, and think fit, and meet, and necessary, and decent,
and convenient, all, and every, and either, or neither of them, to
call, to examine, and call to a strict Account; and that Part, and
most Part, Extortion; and then, and there, when, and where, and
whether, to establish, and elect, and direct, and impower, and

authorize all such, and all much, Bailiffs, and under Receivers, and Collectors and Gatherers-together of Money, as your Petitioner did, or do, or have, or had, or shall, or will, or may, or might, or should, or could, or ought to chuse, or pitch upon with, and punctually to desire my self Mr. Dermond O Folivey that they, them, and these, and every, and either, and neither of them, that shall, and did, and have, and do, and will him in Peace, and Unity, and Amity, and Concord, and Tranquility, henceforth, and for the time to come, and hereafter, and for the time past, and not past, and the time present, and now, and for everlasting; and especially not to molest, or trouble, or hinder, or disturb, or hurt, or meddle with the Petitioner, my self, Mr. Dermond O Folivey, in his Possession of 72 Acres of Land in Gertogolinmore in the Barony of Torrough and County of Kerry.

"*Given, and granted, and dated, and signed, and sealed by my own Hand and with my own Hand, and so my own Hand, and under my own Hand and Seal this   Day of Anno Dom.*"   } MR. DERMOND O FOLIVEY."

[On Discoveries]

Printed in *The Pennsylvania Gazette*, October 14, 1736.

Reprinted by Duane (*Works*, IV, 374–7) and later by William Temple Franklin, Sparks, and Bigelow, but not by Smyth (see above, I, 170), this essay, as Alfred Owen Aldridge has shown,[5] originally appeared in *The Prompter*, a London literary periodical, June 11, 1736. It was reprinted, without the opening paragraph and with other excisions and changes, in the *London Magazine*, V (June 1736), 297–8, and the *Gentleman's Magazine*, VI (June 1736), 313–14. The *New England Weekly Journal* reprinted it from the *London Magazine*, Sept. 21, 1736. Typographical similarities indicate that Franklin probably reprinted it from the *Weekly Journal*.

5. "Benjamin Franklin and Jonathan Edwards on Lightning and Earthquakes," *Isis*, XLI (1950), 162–4.

[The Waste of Life]

Printed in *The Pennsylvania Gazette*, November 18, 1736.

First printed by Duane (*Works*, IV, 367–70) and later by William Temple Franklin, Sparks, and Bigelow, but not by Smyth, this essay is omitted here for the reasons given above, I, 170.

Articles of the Union Fire Company[6]

MS Minute Book, Union Fire Company: Library Company of Philadelphia

THE seventh Day of *December,* in the Year of our Lord One thousand seven hundred and thirty six, WE whose Names are hereunto subscribed, reposing special Confidence in each others Friendship, Do, for the better preserving our Goods and Effects from Fire, mutually agree in Manner following, *That is to say.*

1. THAT we will each of us at his own proper Charge provide Two Leathern Buckets, and Four Baggs of good Oznabrigs or wider Linnen, Whereof each Bagg shall contain four Yards at least, and shall have a running Cord near the Mouth; Which said Buckets and Baggs shall be marked with the Initial Letters of our respective Names and Company Thus [*A.B. & Company*][7] and shall be apply'd to no other Use than for preserving our Goods and Effects in Case of Fire as aforesaid.[8]

2. THAT if any one of us shall fail to provide and keep his Buckets and Baggs as aforesaid he shall forfeit and pay unto the Clerk for the Time being, for the Use of the Company, the Sum of *Five Shillings* for every Bucket and Bagg wanting.

6. Established to supplement the city's inadequate provisions, the Union Fire Company was the first of several volunteer organizations which provided most of Philadelphia's fire protection after mid-century (Harrold E. Gillingham, "Philadelphia's First Fire Defences," *PMHB*, LVI, 1932, 355–77). The Company may have been patterned on Boston's Fire Society of 1717, whose Articles of Association were adopted March 7, 1734. See above, p. 12 n., and below, p. 375.

7. Brackets in the MS.

8. The Union got a fire engine from England, 1743; in cooperation with the Hand-in-Hand Company it erected a fire-bell on the Academy building, 1752. *Ibid.*, 366, 367. For the bell's odyssey until 1945, when it finally returned home to the University of Pennsylvania, see Joseph S. Hepburn, "The Academy Bell . . .," *Jour. Franklin Inst.*, CCLXII (1956), 45–52.

150

3. THAT if any of the Buckets or Baggs aforesaid shall be lost or damaged at any Fire aforesaid The same shall be supplyed and repaired at the Charge of the whole Company.

4. THAT we will all of us, upon hearing of Fire breaking out at or near any of our Dwelling Houses, immediately repair to the same with all our Buckets and Baggs, and there employ our best Endeavours to preserve the Goods and Effects of such of us as shall be in Danger by Packing the same into our Baggs: And if more than one of us shall be in Danger at the same time, we will divide our selves as near as may be to be equally helpful. And to prevent suspicious Persons from coming into, or carrying any Goods out of, any such House, Two of our Number shall constantly attend at the Doors until all the Goods and Effects that can be saved shall be secured in our Baggs, and carryed to some safe Place, to be appointed by such of our Company as shall be present, Where one or more of us shall attend them 'till they can be conveniently delivered to, or secured for, the Owner.

5. THAT we will meet together in the Ev'ning of the last Second Day of the Week commonly called Monday, in every Month, at some convenient Place and Time to be appointed at each Meeting, to consider of what may be further useful in the Premises; And whatsoever shall be expended at every Meeting aforesaid shall be paid by the Members met. And if any Member shall neglect to meet as aforesaid, he shall forfeit and pay the Sum of *One Shilling*.

6. THAT we will each of us in our Turns, according to the Order of our Subscriptions, serve the Company as Clerk for the Space of one Month, Viz. That Member whose Name is hereunto first subscribed shall serve first, and so on to the last, Whose Business shall be to inspect the Condition of each of our Buckets and Baggs, and to make Report thereof at every Monthly Meeting aforesaid, To collect all the Fines and Forfeitures accruing by Virtue hereof; To warn every Member of the Time and Place of Meeting, at least Six Hours before Hand. And if any new Member be proposed to be admitted, or any Alteration to be made in any of the present Articles, he shall inform every Member thereof at the Time of Warning a[foresaid.] And shall also read over a Copy of these Presents, and a List of all the Subscribers Names, at every Monthly Meeting, before the Company proceeds to any other Bu[siness,] Which said Clerk shall be accountable to the Rest of the Company

for, and pay [to] the next succeeding Clerk, all the Monies accruing or belonging unto the Company by virtue of these presents. And if any Member shall refuse to serve as Clerk in his Turn aforesaid, he shall forfeit the Sum of *Five Shillings*.

7. THAT our Company shall not exceed the Number of twenty-five Persons a[t a] time, no new Member be admitted, nor any Alteration made in these present Ar[ticles] until the Monthly Meeting after the same is first proposed, and the whole Company acquainted therewith by the Clerk as aforesaid; Nor without the Consent of Three Fourths of our whole Number, the whole Three Fourths being met. But the other Affairs relating to the Company shall be determined by Three Fourths of Members met. And that the Time of entring upon Business shall be one Hour after the Time appointed for Meeting as aforesaid.

8. THAT each Member shall keep two Lists of all the Subscribers Names, [one] to be fixed in open View near the Buckets and Baggs, and the Other to be pr[oduced] at every Monthly Meeting if required under pain of forfeiting the Sum of [six?] Pence.

9. THAT all Fines and Forfeitures arising by Virtue hereof, shall be paid unto the Clerk for the Time being, for the Use of the Company, and shall be erected into a common Stock. And if any Member shall refuse to pay any Fine or Forfeiture aforesaid when due, his Name shall be razed out, And he shall from thenceforth be excluded the Company.

10. LASTLY THAT upon the Death of any of our Company, the Survivors shall in time of Danger as aforesaid, be aiding to the Widow of such Decedent during her Widowhood, in the same Manner as if her Husband had been living; she only keeping the Buckets and Baggs as aforesaid. IN WITNESS whereof we have hereunto set our Hands; Dated the Day and Year abovesaid.[9]

9. The Company's minute book, immediately following the Articles, records in BF's hand the meeting of Third Month [May] 30, 1737:

"The Union Fire Company have met once a month for some Months past, but as the foregoing Articles were not till now fully compleated and agreed on, no regular Minutes have hitherto been kept.

"This Evening the Company (which at present consists of Twenty Persons) met at the House of John Roberts. Absent only Wm Rawle, Wm Parsons and Edward Shippen.

JOSEPH PASCHALL[1]	1	GEORGE HOUSE	15
SAML: COATES	2	WM PLUMSTED	16
JOHN ARMITT	3	JOHN DILLWYN	17
WM. RAWLE	4	WM. COOPER	18
BENJA. SHOEMAKER	5	EDWD. SHIPPEN	19
HUGH ROBERTS	6	LLOYD ZACHARY	20
B. FRANKLIN	7	P[ost] S[cripti]	
PHILIP SYNG JUNR.	8	SAML. POWEL JUNR.	
WM. PARSONS	9	THOMAS LLOYD	
RICHD: SEWELL	10	GEORGE EMLEN	
JAMES MORRIS	11	CHS. WILLING	
STEPN. ARMITT	12	THO. LAWRENCE	
THO HATTON	13	WILLM. BELL	
EDWARD ROBERTS	14	JO TURNER	

"Several Persons being nominated as desirous of joining with the Company, the four following were by Ballot unanimously chosen, to wit, Samuel Powel, junr. Thos Lloyd, George Emlen, and Charles Willing.

"Hugh Roberts officiated as Clerk, and at the Conclusion of the Meeting deliver'd to his Successor B. Franklin the Company's Book, and 17/6 in Cash, which is the Company's present Stock. I receiv'd it,   B. FRANKLIN."

1. The signers of the Articles of 1737 were: Joseph Paschall (1699–1741), common councilor; Samuel Coates (1711–1748), merchant; John Armitt (1702–1762), Philadelphia agent of Cadwallader Colden; William Rawle (d. 1741), director of Library Company, operated a ferry between Philadelphia and West Jersey; Benjamin Shoemaker (1704–1767), distiller, city official, provincial councilor; Hugh Roberts (1706–1786), merchant, member of the Junto and APS, hospital director, close friend of BF; Philip Syng (1703–1789), see above, I, 209n; William Parsons (1701–1757), see above, I, 359 n; Richard Sewell, later sheriff of Philadelphia; James Morris (1707–1751), assemblyman, trustee of Loan Office; Stephen Armitt (1705–1751), joiner, brother of John; Thomas Hatton (c. 1718–1772), probably a shipowner; Edward Roberts (1680–1741), mayor of Philadelphia, 1739–41; George House, overseer of the poor, common councilor (name struck through on the list of signers); William Plumsted (1708–1765), merchant, city official, assemblyman from Northampton County, register general, vestryman of Christ Church, trustee of College and Academy, grand master of Pennsylvania; John Dillwyn (1693–1748), common councilor; William Cooper, not identified; Edward Shippen (1703–1781) "of Lancaster," merchant, partner of James Logan and later of Thomas Lawrence, city official, judge of Common Pleas in Philadelphia and of Lancaster County, prothonotary, trustee of College of New Jersey; Lloyd Zachary (1701–1756), physician,

On the Death of His Son[2]

Printed in *The Pennsylvania Gazette*, December 30, 1736.

Understanding 'tis a current Report, that my Son Francis, who died lately of the Small Pox, had it by Inoculation; and being desired to satisfy the Publick in that Particular; inasmuch as some People are, by that Report (join'd with others of the like kind, and perhaps equally groundless) deter'd from having that Operation perform'd on their Children, I do hereby sincerely declare, that he was not inoculated, but receiv'd the Distemper in the common Way of Infection: And I suppose the Report could only arise from its being my known Opinion, that Inoculation was a safe and beneficial Practice; and from my having said among my Acquaintance, that I intended to have my Child inoculated, as soon as he should have recovered sufficient Strength from a Flux with which he had been long afflicted.   B. FRANKLIN

---

health officer of port of Philadelphia, physician to Pennsylvania Hospital; Samuel Powel, Jr. (1705–1759), merchant, common councilor; Thomas Lloyd (d. 1754), merchant; George Emlen (1694–1754), brewer, common councilor, benefactor of Hospital; Charles Willing (1710–1754), merchant, city official, trustee of College and Academy (name struck through on the list of signers); Thomas Lawrence (1689–1754), merchant, city official, lieutenant colonel of City Regiment, provincial councilor, partner of James Logan and later of Edward Shippen; William Bell, not identified; Joseph Turner (1701–1783), sea captain and merchant, iron manufacturer, trustee of College of Philadelphia, city official.

2. Francis Folger Franklin, born Oct. 20, 1732, died of smallpox Nov. 21, 1736. BF regretted to the end of his life, he wrote in his autobiography, that he had not had the boy inoculated. To Jane Mecom he wrote, Jan. 13, 1772, that accounts of his grandson Benjamin Franklin Bache brought "often fresh to my Mind the Idea of my Son Franky, ... whom I have seldom since seen equal'd in every thing, and whom to this Day I cannot think of without a Sigh." His parents placed on his gravestone the words: "The DELIGHT of all that knew him."

Afterword to Every Man his own Doctor

Printed in [John Tennent], *Every Man his own Doctor: or, The Poor Planter's Physician.* . . . The Fourth Edition. Philadelphia: printed and Sold by B. Franklin, near the Market, M,DCC,XXXVI. (Historical Society of Pennsylvania)

In 1734 Franklin reprinted John Tennent's *Every Man his own Doctor*, which had been published earlier that year in a "second edition" in Williamsburg, Va.[3] Franklin may have concluded this "third edition" with the address to his readers, which is reprinted below; but no complete copy is known.[4] In 1736 he reprinted Tennent's pamphlet in a "fourth edition" with the address to his readers and a postscript based on Tennent's *Essay on Pleurisy*, published at Williamsburg in 1736.[5]

The PRINTER to the READER wisheth HEALTH.

This Book entituled, *Every Man his own Doctor,* was first printed in Virginia, for the Use of which Colony it was written by a Gentleman residing there. Great Numbers have been distributed among the People both in Virginia and Maryland, and 'tis generally allow'd that abundance of Good has been thereby done: And as some Parts of Pennsylvania, the Jerseys, and the Lower Counties on Delaware, are by the lowness and moistness of their Situation, subject to the same kind of Diseases, I have been ad-

3. John Tennent (*c.* 1700–1748), English physician, came to Virginia about 1725. His *Essay on the Pleurisy* (Williamsburg, Va., 1736), advocating seneca rattlesnake root, excited lively controversy in America and abroad. See below, pp. 239, 254. Returning to London in 1737, he began to prepare a book on the diseases of Virginia; his proposals for printing it, issued when he returned to America, 1738, appeared in *Pa. Gaz.*, Aug. 3, 1738, and later; but subscriptions fell short of the required 1,000, and it did not appear. BF also reprinted *Every Man his own Doctor* in *The American Instructor* (Phila., 1748), and a German translation was published by BF and Johann Boehm in 1749. For Tennent's later publications, most of which continued his crusade for snakeroot, and for his troubled career in London, see *DAB* and Wyndham B. Blanton, *Medicine in Virginia in the Eighteenth Century* (Richmond, Va., 1931), pp. 119–29. Tennent went to Jamaica in 1740 but soon returned to England, where he died Oct. 27, 1748. *Gent. Mag.*, XVIII (1748), 524.

4. Evans 3844.

5. No advertisement for *Every Man his own Doctor* has been found in *Pa. Gaz.* for 1736. The pamphlet was advertised, however, in *Pa. Gaz.*, Oct. 27, 1737 (see below, p. 188); but no copy of a 1737 imprint (Evans 4202) has been located. It is possible that BF's "fourth edition," with the 1736 imprint date, did not actually appear until the next year.

vised to reprint this Book here, for the Use and Benefit of such People in these Countries, as live at too great a Distance from good Physicians. It is necessary, however, to give the Reader this one Caution, that the *Ipecacuania* or *Indian Physick* so frequently prescribed by the Author, is much weaker in Virginia, than that which grows in Pennsylvania; so that whereas he prescribes 80 Grains for a Vomiting Potion, and 70 for a Purge; 12 Grains of our *Indian Physick*, or *Ipecacuania*, will be sufficient for a Vomit, and 10 for a Purge: There is another Sort which comes to us from Europe, and is to be found in the Apothecaries Shops, of which 30 or 32 Grains is commonly given for a Vomit, and 27 Grains for a Purge, which will work most Constitutions sufficiently.

Postscript.

A Physician in Virginia has lately published an Essay on the *Pleurisy,* in which he discovers a Method of treating that fatal Distemper, that he says he always found to succeed. The principal Part of the Cure depends on the Use of a Simple that begins to be known in this Country by the Name of *Rattle-Snake Root,* being the same that the Indians use in curing the Bite of that venemous Reptile. The Method which the Author practices and recommends, is as follows.[6]

"Let the Patient first have 10 Ounces of Blood taken from the Arm of the well Side, or Foot if both Sides are affected; and every 6 Hours 3 Spoonfuls of the following Tincture is to be given, the first Dose immediately after, and continued 'till the Symptoms abate.

"Take of the *Rattle-Snake Root,* 3 Ounces, *wild Valerian Root,* an Ounce and a Half, let them be well bruised in a Mortar, then mix them with a Quart of old *Canary,* and digest in a proper Vessel in a Sand-Heat for Six Hours, afterwards decant for Use.

"Let fifteen Drops of *Balsam Capivi,* and as many of *Sal volatile Oleosum,* be given in a little ordinary Drink, twice between each Dose of the Tincture, beginning with the first Dose two Hours after the Tincture; and give the second Dose two Hours after.

"Let the ordinary Drink be a Tea made of *Marsh-mallow Roots,* always given warm.

6. The quoted material is from Tennent's *Essay on the Pleurisy*, pp. 32–4.

"If the Patient has been ill some Days before any thing administred, the *Balsom* is to be continued for some Days after a considerable Amendment.

"Bloodletting is to be repeated the second Day, and in the same Quantity as the first, if the Patient is not much better, or the same Day unless something better in 4 Hours: But such is the Efficacy of this Medicine, that there is seldom Occasion. The Symptoms generally abate considerably in 24 Hours, and the Recovery CERTAIN."

But because every one may not have Conveniency for preparing this Tincture, nor have the other Medicines mentioned at hand, and do not live within reach of a Physician, it is necessary to acquaint the Reader with what the Author adds further, viz.

"A Decoction of the *Rattle-Snake Root* alone in Spring Water, 3 Ounces to about one Quart; together with Pectoral Teas sweetned with Honey *will prove effectual,* without *any thing else;* if the Patient has been let Blood as soon as taken, and this Decoction immediately given afterwards."

This is to be understood of the genuine *Pleurisy* or *Peripneumony* attended with a Fever.

As for the other Disease, which often personates a *Pleurisy* in these Parts, the Symptoms of which are, that the Patient is cold in a *somniferous* State, and sometimes convulsed.

In this Case the Author omits Bloodletting as pernicious; but says the Tincture aforesaid is as effectual here as in the genuine *Pleurisy,* only advises that the *Rattle-Snake Root* and Valerian be in equal Quantities.

We have not room to add more out of the abovementioned Essay; and indeed the greatest Part of it being taken up in abstracted Reasonings on the Texture of the Blood, and the Operations of different Medicines, &c. to make a larger Extract would be of little Use to the unlearned Reader, for whom this Book was originally intended; and 'tis supposed that in Cases of Danger, the Patient will always consult a skilful Physician where it can possibly be done.

But while we are solicitous about the Health of the Body, let us not forget, that there are also *Diseases of the Mind,* which concern us no less to be thoroughly cured of. The divine Assistance and Blessing on our Endeavours is absolutely necessary in both

Cases; which we ought therefore piously and devoutly to request. And being healed, let us gratefully bless and praise that GREAT PHYSICIAN, from whose Goodness flows every Virtue, and the Discovery of every useful Medicine.

Extracts from the Gazette, 1736

Printed in *The Pennsylvania Gazette*, January 6 to December 30, 1736.

[ADVERTISEMENT] This is to certify, that I Robert Jesson, late Merchant of Philadelphia, having been afflicted with a DROPSEY, insomuch that my Life was despaired of, am now effectualy cured by an Elixir which Mr. Edward Jones of this City, Gent. has the Secret of making.

In Gratitude for the Favour, and for the Benefit of Mankind, I make this Publick; by which, all under the same Misfortune may know where to apply. ROBERT JESSON
[February 11]

The Subscribers to the Library in Philadelphia are advertised, that Monday the 3d of May ensuing, at Two in the Afternoon, is the Time appointed for the Choice of Directors and a Treasurer for the succeeding Year, and for making the fourth annual Payment, at the House of John Roberts in High-Street.
JOSEPH BREINTNALL, Secr.
[April 22]

Friday night last died here Mr. Henry Flower, in a very advanc'd Age. He was one of the first Settlers,[7] and had been Post-Master of this Place for many Years. A vast number of People of all Ranks testified the Respect they bore him, by attending his Funeral, which was performed on Sunday Evening. [May 20]

Tuesday last, during the Fair, a Fire broke out at one end of the long Row of Buildings near the Draw-bridge, and had like to have carried the whole Row; but by the Diligence, Courage and Resolution of some active Men, it was suppress'd beyond Expectation, having only consum'd the Roofs of two Houses, and damaged several others. The Engines did great Service. [May 20]

7. Henry Flower came to Philadelphia before 1693. Watson, *Annals*, 1, 54.

[ADVERTISEMENT] Glaz'd Fulling-Papers and Bonnet-Papers, Sold by the Printer hereof. [June 17]

[ADVERTISEMENT] To be Sold by the Printer hereof; The following Books, viz.

Michaelis Etmulleri Philos. & Med. D. Opera omnia: In 3 Vols. Folio.

Testamentum novum, in folio, having the Greek, the vulgate Translation, and Beza's, in opposite Columns; with Beza's large Annotations.

Concordantiae Bibliorum, id est, Dictiones omnes quae in vulgata Editione Latina Librorum veteris novi Testamenti leguntur, ordine digesta, & ita distinctae ut maximae and [sic] absolutissimae (quas offert haec Editio) Concordantiae dici possint.

Gulielmi Pisonis Medici Amstelaedamensis De Indiae Utriusque Re Naturali & Medica, Libri quatuordecim.

Scapula's Lexicon, Greek and Latin, Folio, printed at Basil. 1600. [July 15]

The Printer hopes the irregular Publication of this Paper will be excused a few times by his Town Readers, on consideration of his being at Burlington with the Press, labouring for the publick Good, to make Money more plentiful. [August 2]

Early on Thursday Morning last the Honourable PATRICK GORDON, Esq; our Lieutenant Governor; after a long and tedious Indisposition, departed this Life in the 73d Year of his Age.[8] His Honour arrived here in June 1726, vested with the Government of this Province, and Counties of New-Castle, Kent and Sussex on Delaware.

It may be justly said of him, that, during the whole course of his Administration, the true Interest and Happiness, Prosperity and

8. Major Patrick Gordon (1663–1736), lieutenant governor of Pennsylvania from 1726 to his death, had a comparatively tranquil administration, during which the State House was completed and a law enacted confirming trusts for religious purposes. The appointment of Ferdinand John Paris as the colony's agent in London was at his suggestion. Charles P. Keith, *Chronicles of Pennsylvania* (Phila., 1917), II, 685–97, 703–29. For the announcement of his wife's death, see above, I, 380.

Welfare of his Majesty's Subjects in these Parts seemed to be his chief Concern and peculiar Care. [August 7]

We hear from Virginia, that not long since a Flash of Lightning fell on a House there, and struck dead a Man who was standing at the Door. Upon examining the Body they found no Mark of Violence, but on his Breast an exact and perfect (tho' small) Representation of a Pine Tree which grew before the Door, imprest or printed as it were in Miniature. This surprizing Fact is attested by a Gentleman lately come from thence, who was himself an Eye-witness of it; and 'tis added that great Numbers of People came out of Curiosity, to view the Body before it was interr'd. [August 12]

[ADVERTISEMENT] Lost last Week in removing the Printing Press, and either left on the Wharff at Burlington, or dropt off the Dray between the Waterside and the Market in Philadelphia, A Pine water-tite Trough, containing sundry odd Things and Utensils belonging to the Press. Whoever brings it to B. Franklin shall have *Five Shillings* Reward. [September 16]

Thursday last WILLIAM ALLEN, Esq; Mayor of this City for the Year past, made a FEAST for his Citizens at the Statehouse, to which all the Strangers in Town of Note were also invited. Those who are Judges of such Things, say, That considering the Delicacy of the Viands, the Variety and Excellency of the Wines, the great Number of Guests, and yet the Easiness and Order with which the whole was conducted, it was the most grand and the most elegant Entertainment that has been made in these Parts of America. [September 30]

Our late Honourable Proprietor, having from the first Settlement of this Province, made it his principal Care, to cultivate and maintain a good Understanding with all the Indians, to the Preservation of which, nothing hath contributed more than the Practice which he set on Foot, and hath since been continued, of purchasing their Claims to Lands, before he would suffer them to be taken up by his Authority: and Col. Dongan one of the Governors of New-York having about Fifty Years since, purchased for our late Proprietor, from the Indians of the Six (then the Five) Nations, all the Lands lying upon Susquehannah; We are told that the Chiefs of these Nations, now here, who are about Twenty in Number, have confirmed that Purchase made by Col. Dongan, and have absolutely released to Our present Honourable Proprietors all the Lands from about the Mouth of Susquehannah as high up that River as those called by the Indians the Twhagasachata or Endless Mountains, with all the Lands on both Sides the said River, and its Streams as far Westward as the Setting of the Sun.[9]

[October 14]

JUST PUBLISHED, POOR RICHARD'S ALMANACKS for the Year 1737, containing besides what is usual, a particular Description of the Herb which the Indians use to cure the Bite of that venemous Reptile a RATTLE-SNAKE, an exact Print of the Leaf of the Plant, an Account of the Places it grows in, and the Manner of using it, &c. made publick for the general Good. With Variety of other Matters serious and Comical. Printed and Sold by B. Franklin.

Where may be had Cole's Dictionaries Latin and English, and Variety of other School-Books just imported.   [November 11]

[ADVERTISEMENT] Just imported and sold by B. Franklin, the following Books, viz.

Bibles, Testaments, Psalters and Primmers of several Sorts.

The *British School-Master,* teaching to read, spell and write true English, exactly, without learning of Latin, and in less than a quarter of the Time usually spent therein. In a new Method, for the Use of English Schools. *price* 1*s.*

English Liberties, or the Free-born Subjects' Inheritance.

Religious Courtship, being historical Discourses on the Necessity of marrying religious Husbands and Wives only: As also

9. A conference or treaty with the Six Nations took place Sept. 28–Oct. 14, 1736, with sessions at James Logan's house Stenton and in the Great Meeting House in Philadelphia. BF printed the proceedings in 1737, the first of the series of Indian treaties to be issued from his press. It is reproduced in facsimile in Carl Van Doren, ed., *Indian Treaties Printed by Benjamin Franklin, 1736–1762* (Phila., 1938), pp. 1–14. Thomas Dongan (1634–1715) was governor of New York, 1682–88. The Indian deed here referred to is in 1 *Pa. Arch.,* I, 494–8.

of Husbands and Wives being of the same Opinions in Religion with one another.

Henry, on Prayer.

Cole's Latin and English Dictionary.

Clark's ⎰ Introduction to making Latin. ⎱ For the Use of young
        ⎱ Cordery.   ⎰ Beginners in Latin.
        ⎰ Erasmus.

Ruddiman's Rudiments of Grammar, Latin and English. Lilly's Grammar. Virgil. Caesar's Commentaries. Juvenal and Persius. Eutropius. Ovid's Metamorphosis and Ovid de Tristibus. Cornelius Nepos. Hoole's Accidence, and sundry other School-Books. Also Writing Paper of several Sorts, Dutch Quills, Inkhorns, Pen-knives, Seals, Gilt Pocket-Books, Memorandum Books and other Stationary-ware.   [November 25]

[ADVERTISEMENT] Lent, or left somewhere abroad, about three or four Months ago, a very large Kersey GREAT-COAT, burnt almost through in one or two Places, with the Edge of the Taylor's Goose, in making it. Whoever brings it to the Printer hereof, shall be thankfully rewarded.   [December 9]

PHILADELPHIA: Printed by B. FRANKLIN, at the New Printing-Office near the Market. *Price* 10s. a Year. Where Advertisements are taken in, and BOOK-BINDING is done reasonably, in the best Manner.

Poor Richard, 1737

Poor Richard, 1737. An Almanack For the Year of Christ 1737, ... By Richard Saunders, Philom. Philadelphia: Printed and sold by B. Franklin, at the New Printing-Office near the Market. (Yale University Library)

Courteous and kind Reader,

This is the fifth Time I have appear'd in Publick, chalking out the future Year for my honest Countrymen, and foretelling what shall, and what may, and what may not come to pass; in which I have the Pleasure to find that I have given general Satisfaction. Indeed, among the Multitude of our astrological Predictions, 'tis no wonder if some few fail; for, without any Defect in the Art itself, 'tis well known that a small Error, a single wrong Figure overseen in a Calculation, may occasion great Mistakes: But however we Almanack-makers may *miss it* in other Things, I believe it will be generally allow'd *That we always hit the Day of the Month,* and that I suppose is esteem'd one of the most useful Things in an Almanack.

As to the Weather, if I were to fall into the Method my Brother J----n[1] sometimes uses, and tell you, *Snow here or in New England, —Rain here or in South-Carolina, —Cold to the Northward, —Warm to the Southward,* and the like, whatever Errors I might commit, I should be something more secure of not being detected in them: But I consider, it will be of no Service to any body to know what Weather it is 1000 miles off, and therefore I always set down positively what Weather my Reader will have, be he where he will at the time. We modestly desire only the favourable Allowance of *a day or two before* and *a day or two after* the precise Day against which the Weather is set; and if it does not come to pass accordingly, let the Fault be laid upon the Printer, who, 'tis very like, may have transpos'd or misplac'd it, perhaps for the Conveniency of putting in his Holidays: And since, in spight of all I can say, People will give him great part of the Credit of making my Almanacks, 'tis but reasonable he should take some share of the Blame.

I must not omit here to thank the Publick for the gracious and kind Encouragement they have hitherto given me: But if the generous Purchaser of my Labours could see how often his *Fi'-pence* helps to light up the comfortable Fire, line the Pot, fill the Cup and make glad the Heart of a poor Man and an honest good old Woman, he would not think his Money ill laid out, tho' the Almanack of his Friend and Servant   R. SAUNDERS were one half blank Paper.

1. John Jerman, whose almanac computations for 1734–36 BF had printed, sold his copy for 1737 to Andrew Bradford. With his almanac for 1740 he returned to BF, but three years later was back with Bradford.

RATTLE-SNAKE HERB.[2]

The Indians long made a Secret of the Herb they used in curing the Bite of that venemous Reptile a RATTLE-SNAKE: but since some curious Persons among the English have fully discover'd and are now well acquainted with it, I hope it will be an acceptable Service to these Parts of the World, if I make it more publick by the following Description, with the Figure of a Leaf of it.

The Top and Branches of the Plant are thick set with small yellow flowers in August and September. It is a Species of Golden-Rod, known from the other Sorts by the smoothness of the Leaf, and its pungent Taste, and occasioning when chewed and swallow'd, a small Stoppage of the Breath, and Contraction in the Throat; and the Stalk, which is in some Places less than a yard in height when at full Growth, in others more, is of a dull purple colour, and smooth, and cover'd with a fine blue Dust, like that on many of the English Plums. It grows in most Wood-Lands, but under the Shade of Trees is seldom rank or large, or with more than one, two or three Stalks. It is also found on the Banks of dry Ditches, and sometimes in them, and in Hedge-Rows: But it is most luxuriant near to Run Sides, if the Soil be rich, and not too moist, nor too much shaded. The Root continues over the Winter, and if set in a good Garden, will send forth (in the 2d or 3d Year) at least 50 Stalks. The Plant shoots early in the Spring and withers late in the Fall.

The Indians use it variously; sometimes they bruise it between Stones, sometimes chew it and spit in the Patient's Mouth, some lay it to the Wound, others about the Wound, sometimes they boil it and give the Water to drink, washing the Wound with it likewise:

2. A MS draft of these paragraphs, dated Sept. 6, 1736, in Joseph Breintnall's hand, is in Lib. Co. Phila. Breintnall was much interested in the properties of herbs: Peter Collinson in a letter to Bartram, Jan. 20, 1735, refers to "Joseph Breintnall's Snake-root." This may have been the *Polygala senega*, about which John Tennent wrote (see above, p. 155 n.); but Breintnall described it as a goldenrod and Collinson seems to have thought it *Sanicula canadensis*. Darlington, *Memorials*, pp. 61, 78. The designation snakeroot includes several species. In the almanac, alongside these paragraphs, is the impression of the goldenrod leaf, 3½ inches long. Breintnall acquired skill and reputation for making such impressions. See above, I, 344 n. His widow gave the Library Company some of her husband's MSS, 1746, "together with a large Collection of Prints of Leaves of Plants growing near Philadelphia. . . ." Lib. Co. Phila., Minutes, May 5, 1746.

but always some of it is to be swallowed, either with the Spittle or with Water.

The Leaf figur'd in the Margin is one of the largest; for the most part they are not near so big though the Shape be the same.

HINTS for those that would be Rich.

The Use of Money is all the Advantage there is in having Money.

For £6 a Year, you may have the Use of £100 if you are a Man of known Prudence and Honesty.

He that spends a Groat a day idly, spends idly above £6 a year, which is the Price of using £100.

He that wastes idly a Groat's worth of his Time per Day, one Day with another, wastes the Privilege of using £100 each Day.

He that idly loses 5s. worth of time, loses 5s. and might as prudently throw 5s. in the River.

He that loses 5s. not only loses that Sum, but all the Advantage that might be made by turning it in Dealing, which by the time that a young Man becomes old, amounts to a comfortable Bag of Money.

Again, He that sells upon Credit, asks a Price for what he sells, equivalent to the Principal and Interest of his Money for the Time he is like to be kept out of it: therefore

He that buys upon Credit, pays Interest for what he buys.

And he that pays ready Money, might let that Money out to Use: so that

He that possesses any Thing he has bought, pays Interest for the Use of it.

Consider then, when you are tempted to buy any unnecessary Housholdstuff, or any superfluous thing, whether you will be willing to pay *Interest,* and *Interest upon Interest* for it as long as you live; and more if it grows worse by using.

Yet, in buying Goods, 'tis best to pay ready Money, because,

He that sells upon Credit, expects to lose 5 *per Cent.* by bad Debts; therefore he charges, on all he sells upon Credit, an Advance that shall make up that Deficiency.

Those who pay for what they buy upon Credit, pay their Share of this Advance.

He that pays ready Money, escapes or may escape that Charge.

A Penny sav'd is Twopence clear, A Pin a day is a Groat a Year. Save and have. Every little makes a mickle.

XI Mon. January hath xxxi days.

> God offer'd to the Jews Salvation
> And 'twas refus'd by half the Nation:
> Thus, (tho' 'tis Life's great Preservation)
> Many oppose *Inoculation.*
>   We're told by one of the black Robe
> The Devil inoculated Job:
> Suppose 'tis true, what he does tell;
> Pray, Neighbours, *Did not Job do well?*

The greatest monarch on the proudest throne, is oblig'd to sit upon his own arse.

The Master piece of Man, is to live to the purpose.

He that steals the old man's supper, do's him no wrong.

XII Mon. February hath xxviii days.

> The Thracian Infant, entring into Life,
> Both Parents mourn for, both receive with Grief:
> The Thracian Infant snatch'd by Death away,
> Both Parents to the Grave with Joy convey.
> This, Greece and Rome, you with Derision view;
> This is meer Thracian Ignorance to you:
> But if you weigh the Custom you despise,
> This Thracian Ignorance may teach the wise.

A countryman between 2 Lawyers, is like a fish between two cats.

He that can take rest is greater than he that can take cities.

The misers cheese is wholesomest.

Felix quem, &c.

I Mon. March hath xxxi days.

> Doris, a Widow, past her Prime,
>   Her Spouse long dead, her Wailing doubles;
> Her real Griefs increase by Time;
>   What might abate, improves her Troubles.

166

Those Pangs her prudent Hopes supprest,
    Impatient now, she cannot smother,
How should the helpless Woman rest?
    One's gone; — nor can she get another.

Love and lordship hate companions.

The nearest way to come at glory, is to do that for conscience
which we do for glory.

There is much money given to be laught at, though the purchasers
don't know it; witness A's fine horse, and B's fine house.

II Mon. April hath xxx days.

    A Nymph and a Swain to Apollo once pray'd;
The Swain had been jilted, the Nymph been betray'd.
They came for to try if his Oracle knew
E'er a Nymph that was chast or a Swain that was true.
Apollo stood mute, and had like t'have been pos'd;
At length he thus sagely the question disclos'd:
He alone may be true in whom none will confide,
And the nymph may be chast that has never been tryd.

He that can compose himself, is wiser than he that composes books.

Poor Dick, eats like a well man, and drinks like a sick.

After crosses and losses men grow humbler and wiser.

Love, Cough, and a Smoke, can't well be hid.

III Mon. May hath xxxi days.

    Rich Gripe does all his Thoughts and Cunning bend
T'encrease that Wealth he wants the Soul [to] spend:
Poor Shifter does his whole Contrivance set,
To spend that Wealth he wants the Sense to get.
How happy would appear to each his Fate,
Had Gripe his Humour, or he Gripe's Estate?

167

Kind Fate and Fortune, blend 'em if you can,
And of two Wretches make one happy Man.

Well done is better than well said.

Fine linnen, girls and gold so bright,
Chuse not to take by candle-light.

He that can travel well afoot, keeps a good horse.

There are no ugly Loves, nor handsome Prisons.

No better relation than a prudent and faithful Friend.

IV Mon. June hath xxx days.

Boy, bring a Bowl of China here,
Fill it with Water cool and clear:
Decanter with Jamaica right,
And Spoon of Silver clean and bright,
Sugar twice-fin'd, in pieces cut,
Knife, Sieve and Glass, in order put,
Bring forth the fragrant Fruit, and then
We're happy till the Clock strikes Ten.

A Traveller should have a hog's nose, deer's legs, and an ass's back.

At the working man's house hunger looks in but dares not enter.

A good Lawyer a bad Neighbour.

V Mon. July hath xxxi days.

Impudent Jack, who now lives by his Shifts,
Borrowing of Driblets, boldly begging Gifts;
For Twenty Shillings lent him t'other Day
(By one who ne'er expected he would pay)
On his Friend's Paper fain a Note wou'd write;
His Friend, as needless, did refuse it quite;
Paper was scarce, and 'twas too hard, it's true,
To part with Cash, and lose his Paper too.

Certainlie these things agree,
The Priest, the Lawyer, and Death all three:
Death takes both the weak and the strong.
The lawyer takes from both right and wrong,
And the priest from living and dead has his Fee.

The worst wheel of the cart makes the most noise.

VI Mon. August hath xxxi days. .

On his Death-bed poor Lubin lies;
    His Spouse is in Despair;
With frequent Sobs, and mutual Cries,
    They both express their Care.
A diff'rent Cause, says Parson Sly,
    The same Effect may give;
Poor Lubin fears that he shall die;
    His Wife, that he may live.

Don't misinform your Doctor nor your Lawyer.

I never saw an oft-transplanted tree,
Nor yet an oft-removed family,
That throve so well as those that settled be.

VII Mon. September hath xxx days.

To-morrow you'll reform, you always cry;
In what far Country does this Morrow lie,
That 'tis so mighty long e'er it arrive?
Beyond the Indies does this Morrow live?
'Tis so far-fetch'd, this Morrow, that I fear,
'Twill be both very old, and very dear.
To-morrow I'll reform, the Fool does say:
To day it self's too late; the Wise did yesterday.

Let the Letter stay for the Post, and not the Post for the Letter.

Three good meals a day is bad living.

169

Tis better leave for an enemy at one's death, than beg of a friend in one's life.

> To whom thy secret thou dost tell,
> To him thy freedom thou dost sell.

VIII Mon. October hath xxxi days.

> *On T.T. who destroy'd his Landlord's fine Wood.*
> Indulgent Nature to each kind bestows,
> A secret Instinct to discern its Foes:
> The Goose, a silly Bird, avoids the Fox;
> Lambs fly from Wolves; and Sailors steer from rocks;
> A Rogue the Gallows, as his Fate, foresees,
> And bears the like Antipathy to Trees.

If you'd have a Servant that you like, serve your self.

He that pursues two Hares at once, does not catch one and lets t'other go.

If you want a neat wife, chuse her on a Saturday.

If you have time dont wait for time.

IX Mon. November hath xxx days.

> You say you'll spend Five hundred Pound
>   The World and Men to know,
> And take a Tour all Europe round,
>   Improving as you go.
> Dear Sam, in search of others Sense,
>   Discover not your own;
> But wisely double the Expence
>   That you may pass unknown.

Tell a miser he's rich, and a woman she's old, you'll get no money of one, nor kindness of t'other.

Don't go to the doctor with every distemper, nor to the lawyer with every quarrel, nor to the pot for every thirst.

X Mon. December hath xxxi days.

> Women are Books, and Men the Readers be,
> Who sometimes in those Books Erratas see;
> Yet oft the Reader's raptur'd with each Line,
> Fair Print and Paper fraught with Sense divine;
> Tho' some neglectful seldom care to read,
> And faithful Wives no more than Bibles heed.
>   Are Women Books? says Hodge, then would mine were
>   An *Almanack,* to change her every Year.

The Creditors are a superstitious sect, great observers of set days and times.

The noblest question in the world is *What Good may I do in it?*

Nec sibi, sed toto, genitum se credere mundo.[3]

Nothing so popular as GOODNESS.

Of the ECLIPSES, 1737.

There will be four Eclipses this Year, two of the Sun and two of the Moon.

The first is a great and visible Eclipse of the Sun, Feb. 18. beginning at 8 h. 1 m. A.M. middle at 9 h. 11 m. end at 10 h. 20 m. Digits eclipsed near nine, on the upper side of the Sun.

The second is of the Moon, March 5. at 10 h. 34 m. in the morning, therefore invisible here.

The third is of the Sun, Aug. 14. at 7 h. 30 m. P.M. invisible also.

The fourth is a visible Defect of the Moon, Aug. 28. beginning 9 h. 40 m. P.M. the middle at 10 h. 51 m. End near midnight. Digits eclipsed five and a quarter.

In my last, on the second Eclipse which was of the Moon, March 1736, celebrated in ♎ or *the Balance,* I hinted, *That Germany would be weighed and found wanting.* The Course of the Year (I speak without Boasting) has verified that Prediction; for that Empire now weighed in the *Balance of Europe,* is found to want two Kingdoms, to wit Naples and Sicily.[4] May the Doubts I expressed concerning

3. [This was Cato's rule of life,] To believe that one is born not for himself, but for the whole world. Lucan, *Civil War,* II, 383.

4. Naples and Sicily were under Austrian domination, 1707-33, but became the independent Kingdom of the Two Sicilies, 1735.

the Empire itself, prove groundless as to Germany, and be verified in the Turkish Dominion. *Tekel, Peres.*

In my last I published some *Enigmatical Prophecies,*[5] which I did not expect any one would take for serious Predictions. The Explanation I promised, follows, viz.

1. The Water of the Sea and Rivers is raised in Vapours by the Sun, is form'd into Clouds in the Air, and thence descends in Rain. Now when there is Rain overhead, (which frequently happens when the Wind is at N.E.) the Cities and Places on the Earth below, are certainly *under Wat*. .

2. The Power with which *we were not then at War,* but which, it was said, would take many full laden Vessels out of our Ports before the End of the Year, is The WIND, whose Forces also *are not descried either coming or going.*

3. The Army which it was said would *land* in Virginia, Maryland, and the Lower Counties on Delaware, were not *Musketeers* with Guns on their Shoulders as some expected; but their Namesakes, in Pronunciation, tho' truly spelt *Moschitos,* arm'd only with a sharp Sting. Every one knows they are Fish before they fly, being bred in the Water; and therefore may properly be said *to land* before they become generally troublesome.

A WONDERFUL PROPHECY
For January 1737, which consists entirely of odd Figures.

E'er of this odd odd Year one Month has roll'd,
What Wonders, Reader, shall the World behold!
Four Kings with mighty Force shall Albion's Isle
Infest with Wars and Tumults for a while;
Then some shall unexpected Treasures gain,
While some mourn o'er an empty Purse in vain:
And many a christian's Heart shall ake for Fear,
When they the dreadful Sound of Trump shall hear.
Dead Bones shall then be tumbled up and down,
In every City and in every Town.

5. See above, pp. 144–5.

The Drinker's Dictionary

Printed in *The Pennsylvania Gazette*, January 13, 1736/7.

In his Silence Dogood Letter, No. 12 (see above, I, 39) Franklin listed nineteen terms signifying drunkenness. Fifteen of them, some with slight changes, appear in The Drinker's Dictionary. This congruity is the principal reason for attributing the piece to Franklin.

Nothing more like a Fool than a drunken Man.   Poor Richard.[6]

'Tis an old Remark, that Vice always endeavours to assume the Appearance of Virtue: Thus Covetousness calls itself *Prudence;* *Prodigality* would be thought *Generosity;* and so of others. This perhaps arises hence, that, Mankind naturally and universally approve Virtue in their Hearts, and detest Vice; and therefore, whenever thro' Temptation they fall into a Practice of the latter, they would if possible conceal it from themselves as well as others, under some other Name than that which properly belongs to it.

But DRUNKENNESS is a very unfortunate Vice in this respect. It bears no kind of Similitude with any sort of Virtue, from which it might possibly borrow a Name; and is therefore reduc'd to the wretched Necessity of being express'd by distant round-about Phrases, and of perpetually varying those Phrases, as often as they come to be well understood to signify plainly that A MAN IS DRUNK.

Tho' every one may possibly recollect a Dozen at least of the Expressions us'd on this Occasion, yet I think no one who has not much frequented Taverns would imagine the number of them so great as it really is. It may therefore surprize as well as divert the sober Reader, to have the Sight of a new Piece, lately communicated to me, entitled

The DRINKERS DICTIONARY.[7]

A

He is Addled,	He's Afflicted,
He's casting up his Accounts,	He's in his Airs.

6. *Poor Richard's Almanack*, 1733 (above, I, 317).

7. The list of synonyms may have been suggested by similar lists in Rabelais' works. Of the 225 words and phrases BF gives for drunkenness, most are English, but 90 have been shown to be "possibly not of English usage," and therefore possibly American. Edward D. Seeber, "Franklin's 'Drinker's

B

He's Biggy,
  Bewitch'd,
  Block and Block,
  Boozy,
  Bowz'd,
  Been at Barbadoes,
  Piss'd in the Brook,
  Drunk as a Wheel-
    Barrow,
  Burdock'd,
  Buskey,
  Buzzey,
Has Stole a Manchet out of
  the Brewer's Basket,
His Head is full of Bees,
Has been in the Bibbing Plot,
Has drank more than he has
  bled,
He's Bungey,
  As Drunk as a Beggar,
He sees the Bears,
He's kiss'd black Betty,
He's had a Thump over the
  Head with Sampson's
  Jawbone,
He's Bridgey.

C

He's Cat,
  Cagrin'd,
  Capable,
  Cramp'd,
  Cherubimical,
  Cherry Merry,

Wamble Crop'd,
  Crack'd,
  Concern'd,
  Half Way to Concord,
Has taken a Chirriping-
  Glass,
  Got Corns in his Head,
  A Cup too much,
  Coguy,
  Copey,
He's heat his Copper,
He's Crocus,
  Catch'd,
He cuts his Capers,
He's been in the Cellar,
He's in his Cups,
  Non Compos,
  Cock'd,
  Curv'd,
  Cut,
  Chipper,
  Chickery,
  Loaded his Cart,
He's been too free with the
  Creature,
Sir Richard has taken off his
  Considering Cap,
He's Chap-fallen.

D

He's Disguiz'd,
He's got a Dish,
  Kill'd his Dog,
  Took his Drops,
It is a Dark Day with him,
He's a Dead Man,

Dictionary' Again," *Amer. Speech*, xv (1940), 103–5. The list was reprinted in *N.-Y. Weekly Jour.*, Feb. 7, and *South-Carolina Gaz.*, April 30, 1737.

174

Has Dipp'd his Bill,
He's Dagg'd,
He's seen the Devil.

E

He's Prince Eugene,
  Enter'd,
    Wet both Eyes,
    Cock Ey'd,
    Got the Pole Evil,
    Got a brass Eye,
    Made an Example,
He's Eat a Toad and half for
    Breakfast,
In his Element.

F

He's Fishey,
  Fox'd,
  Fuddled,
  Sore Footed,
  Frozen,
  Well in for 't,
  Owes no Man a Farthing,
  Fears no Man,
  Crump Footed,
  Been to France,
  Flush'd,
  Froze his Mouth,
  Fetter'd,
  Been to a Funeral,
  His Flag is out,
  Fuzl'd,
  Spoke with his Friend,
  Been at an Indian Feast.

G

He's Glad,
  Groatable,

Gold-headed,
  Glaiz'd,
  Generous,
  Booz'd the Gage,
  As Dizzy as a Goose,
  Been before George,
  Got the Gout,
  Had a Kick in the Guts,
  Been with Sir John Goa,
  Been at Geneva,
  Globular,
  Got the Glanders.

H

Half and Half,
  Hardy,
  Top Heavy,
  Got by the Head,
  Hiddey,
  Got on his little Hat,
  Hammerish,
  Loose in the Hilts,
  Knows not the way
    Home,
  Got the Hornson,
  Haunted with Evil
    Spirits,
  Has Taken Hippocrates
    grand Elixir.

I

He's Intoxicated,
  Jolly,
  Jagg'd,
  Jambled,
  Going to Jerusalem,
  Jocular,
  Been to Jerico,
  Juicy.

K

He's a King,
   Clips the King's
      English,
   Seen the French King,
   The King is his Cousin,
   Got Kib'd Heels,
   Knapt,
   Het his Kettle.

L

He's in Liquor,
   Lordly,
   He makes Indentures
      with his Leggs,
   Well to Live,
   Light,
   Lappy,
   Limber.

M

He sees two Moons,
   Merry,
   Middling,
   Moon-Ey'd,
   Muddled,
   Seen a Flock of
      Moons,
   Maudlin,
   Mountous,
   Muddy,
   Rais'd his Monuments,
   Mellow.

N

He's eat the Cocoa Nut,
   Nimptopsical,
   Got the Night Mare.

O

He's Oil'd,
   Eat Opium,
   Smelt of an Onion,
   Oxycrocium,
   Overset.

P

He drank till he gave up his
      Half-Penny,
   Pidgeon Ey'd,
   Pungey,
   Priddy,
   As good conditioned as a
      Puppy,
   Has Scalt his Head Pan,
   Been among the
      Philistines,
   In his Prosperity,
He's been among the
      Philippians,
He's contending with
      Pharaoh,
   Wasted his Paunch,
He's Polite,
   Eat a Pudding Bagg.

Q

He's Quarrelsome.

R

He's Rocky,
   Raddled,
   Rich,
   Religious,
   Lost his Rudder,
   Ragged,
   Rais'd,

Been too free with Sir
  Richard,
Like a Rat in Trouble.

S

He's Stitch'd,
  Seafaring,
  In the Sudds,
  Strong,
  Been in the Sun,
  As Drunk as David's Sow,
  Swampt,
His Skin is full,
He's Steady,
He's Stiff,
He's burnt his Shoulder,
He's got his Top Gallant
  Sails out,
  Seen the yellow Star,
  As Stiff as a Ring-bolt,
  Half Seas over,
  His Shoe pinches him,
  Staggerish,
  It is Star-light with him,
He carries too much
  Sail,
  Stew'd,
  Stubb'd,
  Soak'd,
  Soft,
Been too free with
  Sir John Strawberry,

He's right before the Wind
  with all his Studding
  Sails out,
Has Sold his Senses.

T

He's Top'd,
  Tongue-ty'd,
  Tann'd,
  Tipium Grove,
  Double Tongu'd,
  Topsy Turvey,
  Tipsey,
Has Swallow'd a Tavern
  Token,
He's Thaw'd,
He's in a Trance,
He's Trammel'd.

V

He makes Virginia Fence,
  Valiant,
  Got the Indian Vapours.

W

The Malt is above the Water,
He's Wise,
He's Wet,
He's been to the Salt Water,
He's Water-soaken,
He's very Weary,
  Out of the Way.

The Phrases in this Dictionary are not (like most of our Terms of Art) borrow'd from Foreign Languages, neither are they collected from the Writings of the Learned in our own, but gather'd wholly from the modern Tavern-Conversation of Tiplers. I do not doubt but that there are many more in use; and I was even tempted to add a new one my self under the Letter B, to wit, *Brutify'd:* But upon Consideration, I fear'd being guilty of Injustice to the Brute Creation, if I represented Drunkenness as a beastly Vice, since, 'tis well-known, that the Brutes are in general a very sober sort of People.

Philadelphia Post Office Record Books, 1737–53

Seven MS record books: American Philosophical Society

"In 1737," Franklin wrote in his autobiography, "Col. Spotswood, late Governor of Virginia, and then Post-master, General,[8] being dissatisfied with the Conduct of his Deputy at Philadelphia, respecting some Negligence in rendering, and Inexactitude of his Accounts, took from him the Commission and offered it to me. I accepted it readily, and found it of great Advantage." Franklin's commission has not been found and the exact date of his appointment has not been determined. The earliest entries in his surviving record books are dated October 5, 1737, and the *Gazette* of October 6 advertises goods "to be sold by B. Franklin at the Post-Office in Market Street", so it may be assumed that he began his new duties early in October 1737. He held the office until he was commissioned (with William Hunter) joint deputy postmaster general for North America in 1753. The last date entered in his surviving Philadelphia post office records is June 19, 1753.

Among the Franklin Papers in the American Philosophical Society are seven record books which Franklin kept for the business of the local Philadelphia post office. None of them shows his accountings with Spotswood or later deputy postmasters general; all concern his local operations. Since postage was rarely prepaid in the eighteenth century, the addressee was almost always liable for the charge. Small change was scarce and the postmaster had to extend credit to the many individuals and business firms in his area for whom letters arrived in his office. Most of Franklin's books are therefore the records of the letters received and the charges entered against their addressees. The thousands of entries are individually of no historical importance and are not reproduced here; rather, each book is described in sufficient detail to make clear its nature and to suggest the light it may shed on Franklin's operations as postmaster at Philadelphia.

1. *Post Office Ledger, No. 1, October 5, 1737–September 29, 1742.* A thin volume of 92 unnumbered pages with thumb index, inscribed on the

8. On Spotswood, see below, p. 235 n.

marbled cover "Post-Office Leidger No. 1." More than 350 names are listed by their initial letters with dated entries after each name showing charges for letters received and notations of payment. While many individuals received only one letter each during these five years, others ran up substantial debts; the largest accumulated charge stands against the name of the merchant Peter Baynton for a total of £36 15s. 11d. which, like some others, was "Carry'd to New Ledger."

2. *Post Office Ledger, No. 2, September 29, 1742–June 19, 1753.* A stout volume of 324 unnumbered pages with board covers and index tabs, inscribed on the first page "Philadelphia Sepr 29.1742 Sept B. Franklin," above which is the notation "There is a Post Office Leidger preceding this, being a thin 8vo Book in Marble Cover." This book carries on the record begun in No. 1 above. In a few instances, charges dated before September 29, 1742, are transferred individually; more often the accumulated debit total is brought over from the first ledger. The last charges entered are dated June 19, 1753. In most of the accounts which stretch over a considerable period subtotals of charges are entered from time to time, especially in 1743 and 1748 (see Nos. 3 and 4 below). Some accounts are marked "Paid," others are struck through, presumably to indicate the same thing; but the great majority are noted at the bottom as "Carried to Leger E. fo.—," or more briefly "L.E.," followed by a folio number. These entries are explained by a memorandum at the back of the book, probably in William Temple Franklin's hand: "Every Account is transfer'd to Leger E. Philadelphia: May 11th 1786."[9]

The extent to which postal business in eighteenth-century America operated on credit is indicated by the totals of these transfers. After sixteen years as postmaster of Philadelphia Franklin had nearly 700 outstanding and unpaid accounts for letters received entered in this

9. Between 1757, when BF went to England, and 1786, after his return from France, he made little effort to collect his unpaid business accounts because of his involvement in public affairs. In the latter year he went over his Ledger D, which recorded those business accounts (see below, p. 232) and this Post Office Ledger and transferred all outstanding debts to a new Ledger E. These debts, he wrote in his will, had "become in a manner obsolete, yet are nevertheless justly due." Accordingly he bequeathed them all, as recorded in "my great Folio Leger E," to the Pennsylvania Hospital, "hoping that those Debtors and the Descendants of such as are deceased, who now as I find make some Difficulty of satisfying such antiquated Demands, as just Debts, may however be induced to pay or give them as Charity to that excellent Institution." Last Will and Testament, July 17, 1788. The Hospital Managers found it so difficult to collect these debts that they finally returned Ledger E to BF's heirs, and it has since disappeared.

ledger, totaling more than £800. Most of these debts were for small sums: thirteen men owed less than a shilling apiece, and two-thirds of all the accounts were for under 10 shillings. On the other hand, some individuals and firms allowed their postal debts to accumulate for very long periods and to reach surprisingly large totals. The longest and largest account was that of the merchant Israel Pemberton, which ran with no credit entries from November 8, 1739, to June 14, 1753, when it amounted to £80 15s. 6d. The columns of dates and figures are struck through, so one can assume that Pemberton eventually paid what he owed. The largest uncollected account transferred to Ledger E was that of William Vanderspiegle, another merchant, who ran up a debt of £56 16s. 1d. between 1741 and 1753; it was still unpaid in 1786. Altogether, 119 men owed more than £1 apiece, 19 of them more than £10.

Franklin, of course, was under obligation to transmit to the general postal authorities the money due for mail received in the Philadelphia office. In the absence of his accounts with the deputy postmaster general or the comptroller, we can merely assume that in his periodic accounting he entered the total due as a debit against himself, paid in whatever balance was owing, and hoped to reimburse himself from future collections. That he regarded the outstanding debts for letters received and delivered as money owing to himself personally is indicated by the fact that he transferred these accounts in 1786 to Ledger E, in which he also entered all other small debts accumulated during his personal business career and still unpaid. As an efficient businessman Franklin certainly tried to collect these postal debts, sometimes individually and as opportunity offered, again systematically and in organized fashion, as the next two record books show.

3. *Post Office Accounts, November 1743.* A small volume of 56 unnumbered pages with marbled paper covers inscribed on the first page "Post Office Accounts drawn out Nov. 1743." There follows a list of 372 names, arranged by initial letters, opposite each of which is placed the sum due for letters received as shown at this time in the ledger described as No. 2 above. A slip of paper is attached to the inside back cover, on which Franklin wrote: "This Bundle contains two Books [i.e., this No. 3, and No. 4 described below], One with the Foot of the Post-Office Accounts as they stood when L. Evans posted them: The other as they stood when Jos. Kent posted them;[1] Also a Number of Accounts drawn out, but not yet deliver'd." Against nearly

1. "L. Evans" is almost certainly Lewis Evans (*c.* 1700–1756), engraver and mapmaker (see below, p. 419). While no other evidence has been found that he served BF as a postal clerk, the personal connection between the two men

half of the names on this list are penciled notations of "dd Acct" (i.e., "delivered Account"), "Paid," or both, or occasionally something else such as "dd Acct to his Boy," "mischarged," or "denyes the Acct." The totals due, entered at the bottom of each page, amount to £417 2s. 8d. for the entire record, of which Franklin succeeded in collecting £42 9s. 3d. at this time.

4. *Post Office Accounts, May 18, 1748.* A volume of 68 unnumbered pages similar to No. 3, and clearly the second book referred to in the memorandum attached to No. 3. The first page is inscribed simply "Post Office Accounts," but the date is shown by the first entry: "Mr. Wm. Allens Account to May 18 48 £65. 11. 10." This book contains 656 names, with the amounts owed by each corresponding to the sub-totals entered in May 1748 in the ledger described above as No. 2. The total of outstanding charges was £964 14s. 9d. As there are no penciled notations next to the names as in No. 3 above, it is impossible to determine how much Franklin collected at this time, although a few items are noted in ink as paid—one dated as late as April 16, 1764. A spot check of some of the entries with the corresponding ones in Ledger No. 2 suggests that very few of Franklin's postal debtors paid up what they owed him in this effort of 1748.

5. *List of Letters in the Post Office (c. 1741).* A narrow volume of 52 unnumbered pages with thumb index, inscribed on the last page "A List of Letters in the Post-Office," but without date. There are 680 names. No weights of letters or amounts of money due are entered with these names, but many of them are followed by "Philadel.," "City," "P.," or "B.C.," "C.C.," "L.C.," or "P.C.," which stand for Bucks, Chester, Lancaster, or Philadelphia County respectively. A few note individual towns in Pennsylvania or nearby provinces, and others more distant places, such as "N. England," "N. Jersey," "Virginia," or "S. Carolina," and one is even marked "Ireland." The names correspond in part, but only in part, with a list of some 775 individuals printed in the *Pennsylvania Gazette,* January 15, 1741, as the addressees of letters "which have been brought into the Post Office at Philadelphia, and remain unredeem'd." Franklin warned that if they were not redeemed before March 25 following they would be "sent away as dead Letters to the General Post-Office."

6. *List of Letters, April 18, 1744.* A small narrow booklet of 32 unnumbered pages dated at the top of the first page "1744. 18 April," with 275 alphabetically arranged names, with corresponding figures indicating the weights in pennyweight and grains of one or more letters.

---

was close and lasting. Joseph Kent was a clerk of the Philadelphia Lotteries in 1748.

Some entries also carry check marks. This list is presumably one of persons for whom letters had been received; it may have been prepared for a purpose similar to that of No. 5 above, but no comparable list of names was published in the *Gazette*. Some amounts, but not all, match entries in Ledger No. 2.

7. *Post Office Book, May 25, 1748*. A tall narrow volume of 372 pages, of which only the first 15 were originally numbered, inscribed on the first page "Post-Office Book, 1748, May 25." Except for the last few pages, it constitutes a record of the mails received in, or dispatched from, Philadelphia between May 25, 1748, and July 23, 1752. The kind of information this book contains can be shown by summarizing the entries for the week commencing June 21, 1749. On that day the post rider arrived in Philadelphia from the north bringing twenty-five letters from Boston, four from Rhode Island, thirty from New York, and one "Way Letter" picked up along the route. The names of the addressees are listed, with the weight of each letter in pennyweight and grains given in one column, and this weight translated into the postal charge in shillings and pence in another column. Four of the letters were recorded as "free," and two as prepaid; the total charges for the others add up to £6 5s. 6d. (Postage rates in the colonies were high.) On June 22 the post rider from the south arrived with ten letters from Williamsburg, twelve from Annapolis, and one from Boyd's Hole on the Potomac. With one letter from Annapolis prepaid, the total charge to be collected from the addressees was £2 6s. 5d. On the same day Franklin sent the northern rider off on his return trip, with letters for Boston, New York, Rhode Island, Perth Amboy, and Trenton in his saddlebags. Franklin's record of mail dispatched is shorter than that of mail received because he did not list individual addressees or the charges to be collected. Instead he entered for each destination the number of single-sheet, double-sheet, and triple-sheet letters, and the number of packets to be charged at the ounce rate. Then he added the total weight of mail for that town. Thus the mail for Boston on this day consisted of thirty single-sheet letters, nine double, and one triple, but no packets, for a total of 360 dwt. 16 grs. The mail for New York was made up of twenty-four single-sheet letters, nine double, no triple, and one packet, totaling 151 dwt. 8 grs., of which 6 dwt. had been paid for in advance.[2] On June 27 the southern rider set off with nine letters for Annapolis and five for Williamsburg, recorded in the same way.

2. Three examples of the printed form called a "Post-Master's Bill" that BF used in dispatching mail from Philadelphia have been found. All three were used for mail sent to Boston and are dated respectively June 13 and July 11, 1745, and May 22, 1746. The form provides spaces for listing the numbers of

The northern post arrived and departed on a weekly schedule from April through November and on a biweekly schedule during the season of bad weather. The rider was commendably regular; except during the change-over periods between seasons he was a day late in reaching Philadelphia only eight times in more than four years. The southern post, which carried much less mail, operated at longer intervals and was much more irregular. At first the plan seems to have been that mail would reach Philadelphia once in about two weeks during the warmer months, but the rider by no means succeeded in meeting such a schedule. In 1750 he slowed down to an erratic monthly arrival in the summer, but managed to get back to a biweekly schedule with considerable success in 1751. In winter he put in an appearance in Philadelphia at intervals which varied from four weeks to as much as seven, and he sometimes brought very little mail when he did arrive. Philadelphia's most important postal business during these years was clearly with the northern colonies.

Following the last regular entry in this volume and preceding some miscellaneous jottings and notes on the last few pages, appears a table listing by dates all mails received in Philadelphia from January 3, 1750, through June 19, 1753 (the last entry being about eleven months after the final entry in the main part of the book, and corresponding to the date of the latest entries in No. 2 above). In ruled columns there is recorded for each date the weight of mail received in Philadelphia that day, under the several headings of "Unpaid Letters," "Paid Letters," and "Forwarded Letters." There are no daily totals, but there are totals for each category of mail for two entire years and again for the whole period. The last series shows that for the approximately three and a half years covered by the table the unpaid letters constituted 97.4 per cent by weight of all those received in Philadelphia, paid letters 1.8 per cent, and forwarded letters 0.8 per cent.

These seven bound volumes, which vary greatly in size and in detail, together with a few loose papers and fragmentary lists of little or no value, constitute the surviving records of Franklin's service as postmaster of Philadelphia from 1737 to 1753. Inadequate as they are for a complete reconstruction of his operations, they do shed some light on the conduct of an important colonial post office in the middle of the eighteenth century, and indicate some of the problems Franklin faced during his tenure of the Philadelphia postmastership.

---

single, double, triple, and packet letters of different weights under each of the three main headings of unpaid, paid, and free. BF signed and dated each bill and in two instances used the margins to write short notes to the Boston postmaster. MS printed forms: APS, Bostonian Soc., and Mass. Hist. Soc.

[On Freedom of Speech and the Press]

Printed in *The Pennsylvania Gazette*, November 17, 1737, and following issues.

Duane (*Works*, IV, 319–40) and, on his authority, though less certain, Sparks (*Writings*, II, 285–311), printed this long historical essay with its examples drawn mainly from Roman and English history. It is signed "X." No evidence, internal or external, persuades the present editors that Franklin wrote it.

[Causes of Earthquakes]

Printed in *The Pennsylvania Gazette*, December 15 and 22, 1737.

An earthquake felt in the Middle Colonies on December 7, 1737, was the occasion for publishing these essays. Duane printed them (*Works*, IV, 380–91), as did Sparks and Bigelow, but Alfred Owen Aldridge has shown them to be almost verbatim reprints from Chambers' *Cyclopaedia; or, an Universal Dictionary of Arts and Sciences*. . . . (London, 1728), I, 266–8.[3] See above, I, 170.

To James Logan   Transcript: Harvard College Library (Sparks)[4]

[1737?]

Having read the Chapter on Moral Good or Virtue,[5] with all the Attention I am Capable of, amidst the many little Cares that Con-

3. "Benjamin Franklin and Jonathan Edwards on Lightning and Earthquakes," *Isis*, XLI (1950), 162–4.

4. This transcript was made for Sparks, according to the copyist, "from a Paper found at Stenton," Logan's home; and the copyist has added the information, "Indorsed by Jas. Logan. B. Franklin on my 5th Chapt. Of Moral Good. 1727." Another hand has written after "1727," the words "this date may be wrong," and has inserted "(3?)" above the "2."

5. The chapter is from Logan's treatise on ethics, entitled "The Duties of Man Deduced from Nature," begun in 1735, but never finished and now lost. Logan's practice was to submit a chapter for criticism to a learned friend, sometimes, as in this case, as though from a third person. Some of the ideas of the treatise are found in Logan's *Charge delivered from the Bench to the Grand Inquest . . . April 13, 1736*, which BF printed, and in Logan's letters to Thomas Story, 12th 5 mo. 1736, and Nov. 15, 1737, in Norman Penney, ed., *The Correspondence of James Logan and Thomas Story, 1724–1741* (Phila., 1927), pp. 56–66. Frederick B. Tolles, *James Logan and the Culture of Provincial America* (Boston, 1957), pp. 208–11.

tinually infest me, I shall, as the Author Condescends to desire, give my Opinion of it, and that with all Sincerity and Freedom, neither apprehending the Imputation of Flattery on the one hand, nor that of Ill Manners on the other.

I think the Design excellent—and the Management of it in the Main, good; a short Summary of the Chapter plac'd at the Beginning, and little Summaries of each Paragraph in the Margin being only necessary, and what will in my Opinion sufficiently remove any Disgust that the Authors dilate Manner of Writing may give to some Readers; And the whole is so curious and entertaining, that I know not where any thing can be spared.

It seems to me that the Author is a little too severe upon Hobbes, whose Notion, I imagine, is somewhat nearer the Truth than that which makes the State of Nature a State of Love: But the Truth perhaps lies between both Extreams.

I think what is said upon Musick, might be enlarg'd to Advantage by showing that what principally makes a Tune agreeable, is the Conformity between its Air or Genius, and some Motion, Passion or Affection of the Mind, which the Tune imitates.

I should have been glad to have seen the Virtues enumerated, distinguish'd, and the proper Ideas affix'd to each Name; which I have not yet seen, scarce two Authors agreeing therein, some annexing more, others fewer and different Ideas to the Same Name. But I think there is some Incorrectness of Sentiment in what the Author has said of Temperance concerning which I have not time to explain myself in writing. [*caetera desunt*].[6]

Extracts from the Gazette, 1737

Printed in *The Pennsylvania Gazette*, January 6 to December 29, 1737.

Thursday Evening last [*should be* Wednesday, Dec. 29], the Weather being very cold and clear, we had a fair and surprizing Appearance of the *Aurora Borealis,* or *Northern Twilight*. It was more red and luminous than that which we saw here about Six Years ago: Insomuch that People in the Southern Parts of the Town, imagin'd there was some House on Fire near the North

6. The words in brackets and the corrected date mentioned in note 4 are in the same hand.

End; and some ran to assist in extinguishing it. The following Account of this kind of Meteor taken from the *Philosophical Transactions,* perhaps may not be disagreeable to our Readers.[7]

[January 6]

On Thursday last Died here, after a lingring Illness, in the 51st Year of his Age, and on Saturday last was decently Interr'd, the Honourable Charles Read, Esq; of this Place.[8] He was heretofore several Times elected Mayor, and Sheriff of this City, and one of the Representatives for the County; and 'till his Decease he held the Office of Judge of the Vice-Admiralty, one of the Council, one of the Commissioners of the Loan-Office, and several other Posts of Honour and Profit, in this Province, and Collector of the Port of Burlington in New-Jersey; always Discharging his respective Trusts with Applause, and has left behind him an excellent Character.

[January 13]

JUST PUBLISHED, THE ARTICLES OF AGREEMENT made and concluded upon May 10. 1732, between the Right Honourable the Lord Proprietary of Maryland, and the Honourable the Proprietaries of Pennsylvania. . . . To which is prefixed a MAP. . . . Printed and sold by B. Franklin, price 6d.[9]   [February 3]

There are several private Letters in Town from London, that mention the Appointment of Col. THOMAS (a Gentleman of Antigua) to the Government of this Province.[1]   [May 19]

We hear from Burlington County, that on the 11th Inst. died there of a Stoppage in his Urine, Dr. John Browne, a Gentleman

7. The extract that followed is from Edmund Halley, "An Account of the late surprising Appearance of the Lights seen in the Air, on the 6th of March last [1716]," *Phil. Trans.,* XXIX, 406.

8. Charles Read was related to John Read, father of BF's wife Deborah. Carl R. Woodward, *Ploughs and Politicks: Charles Read of New Jersey* (New Brunswick, N.J., 1941), p. 28.

9. For BF's bill to the proprietors for printing this agreement and map, see above, I, 324.

1. George Thomas (*c.* 1695–1774), speaker of the Antigua Assembly, 1727–28, member of the Council of the Leeward Islands, 1728–38. He was appointed deputy governor of Pennsylvania, 1737, and confirmed by the King, February 1738. He reached Philadelphia June 1, 1738. He resigned in 1747. *DAB.*

of singular Skill in the Profession of Surgery, which he practiced in those Parts many Years with great Success, and was well esteemed by all that knew him.[2]   [May 19]

The same Day [Monday last] arrived Capt. Farra, who has long been given over for lost. In his Voyage from Jamaica hither, he was cast away in Palachee Bay within Cape Florida, among the Cannibal Indians, who were extreamly kind and assisted in saving the Cargo, Rigging, &c. And News of the Wreck coming to Augustine, the Spaniards sent Periagua's and other small Vessels round to take in what was sav'd, and bring it to that Port; where Capt. Farra hir'd a Rhode-Island Sloop to bring it hither. Had this English Vessel been forc'd ashore on the civil, polite, hospitable, christian, protestant Coast of Great-Britain, Query, *Might they have expected kinder Treatment from their own Countrymen?*   [June 2]

We hear that on Monday Night last, some People pretending to be Free-Masons, got together in a Cellar with a young Man who was desirous of being made one, and in the Ceremony, 'tis said, they threw some burning Spirits upon him either accidentally or to terrify him, which burnt him so that he was oblig'd to take his Bed, and died this Morning. The Coroners inquest are now sitting on the Body.[3]   [June 16]

The Coroners Inquest on the Body of the young Man, mentioned in our last, found that his Death was occasioned by the burning Spirits thrown on him, but that, as far as it appeared to them by the Evidence they had, the Throwing those Spirits on him was accidental. 'Tis said however that since the Inquest, farther Evidence has been given to the Magistrates, that it was a voluntary Action.   [June 23]

2. Dr. John Browne (*c.* 1667–1737), physician, innkeeper, iconoclast, had befriended BF on the way to Philadelphia in 1723. "Our Acquaintance continu'd as long as he liv'd," BF wrote in the autobiography. The sale of his 230-acre plantation some nine miles from Burlington, N.J., was advertised in *Pa. Gaz.*, Feb. 23, 1731. Fred B. Rogers, "Dr. John Browne: Friend of Franklin," *Bull. Hist. Med.*, xxx (1956), 1–6.

3. For the aftermath of this tragic accident, see BF's defense of his conduct in the affair, below, p. 198.

[ADVERTISEMENT] Taken out of a Pew in the Church some Months since, a Common Prayer Book, bound in Red, gilt, and letter'd DF on each Corner.[4] The Person who took it, is desir'd to open it and read the *Eighth* Commandment, and afterwards return it into the same Pew again; upon which no further Notice will be taken.   [June 30]

Monday last, Sampson the Negro Man mentioned in our last, had his Tryal for burning the House near the President's Country Seat. He made a long, artful and pathetick Defence, which wanted nothing to make it effectual but good English and Truth. The Evidence was too clear against him. He was found guilty and received Sentence of Death.   [September 1]

[ADVERTISEMENT] CYPHERING SLATES and Pencils, ALEPPO INK and Holman's Ink-Powder, LINSEED OIL, and LAMPBLACK, sold by the Printer hereof.   [September 8]

JUST PUBLISHED, *A Treaty of Friendship held with the Chiefs of the Six Nations, at Philadelphia, in September and October, 1736.* Printed and Sold by B. Franklin, price 8*d*.   [September 22]

JUST PUBLISHED, Every Man his own Doctor, or, the Poor Planter's Physician. Prescribing Plain and Easy Means for Persons to cure themselves of all, or most of the Distempers, incident to this Climate, and with very little Charge, the Medicines being chiefly of the Growth and Production of this Country. With a Postscript containing a new discover'd Method of curing the Pleurisy. Printed and Sold by the Printer hereof. Price One Shilling.[5]   [October 27]

Last Week Schich Sidi, the Eastern Prince arrived here, with his Attendants, and is treated with great Respect. 'Tis said he is recommended by His Majesty to the Charity of all good Christians.[6]   [November 3]

4. Deborah Read attended Christ Church before her marriage; BF became a pewholder and made financial contributions to it; their children were baptized there, and their son was interred in Christ Church burying ground, 1736.
5. See above, p. 155, and below, pp. 239–40.
6. Sheik Sidi (or Shedid Allhazar) of Beirut, reached Boston from Bristol,

Notice is hereby given, that the POST-OFFICE of Philadelphia, is now kept at B. Franklin's in Market-Street. And that Henry Pratt is appointed RIDING POST-MASTER for all the Stages between Philadelphia and Newpost in Virginia, who sets out about the Beginning of each Month, and returns in 24 Days, by whom Gentlemen, Merchants and others, may have their Letters, &c. carefully convey'd, and Business faithfully transacted, he having given good Security for the same to the Hon. Col. SPOTSWOOD, Post-Master General of all his Majesty's Dominions in America.
[November 3]

JUST PUBLISHED, POOR RICHARD's ALMANACKS, For the Year 1738. Printed and Sold by the Printer hereof.   [November 3]

Yesterday during the Fair, the House in which the eastern Prince lodges, took Fire, and alarm'd the Neighbourhood, but was soon extinguished. It was occasioned by a Fire left in the Chamber above that of the Prince, part of which Fire falling on the Floor had spread over a great Part of the Room, and occasion'd a great Heat in the Room below, by which Means it was discover'd.   [November 17]

[ADVERTISEMENT] A HONORARY Reward is proposed to any *Cabalist,* who shall demonstrate that the Letter Z contains more occult virtues than the Letter X.

A PECUNIARY Gratification is offered to any of the learned or unlearned, who shall *Mathematically* prove, that a Man's having a Property in a Tract of Land, more or less, is thereby entitled to any Advantage, *in point of understanding,* over another Fellow, who has no other Estate, than "THE AIR——*to breath in,* THE EARTH——*to walk upon,* and ALL THE RIVERS OF THE WORLD ——*to drink of.*"[7]   [December 8]

[ADVERTISEMENT] To be Sold by the Printer hereof, A Brief Narrative of the CASE and TRYAL of John Peter Zenger, Printer of the *New-York Weekly-Journal.* Price 2s. 6d.   [December 8]

England, in the summer of 1735, visited Newport and New York before coming to Philadelphia with an introduction to James Logan. He returned to London via Jamaica. Watson, *Annals,* I, 552, *New-York Weekly Jour.,* Aug. 29, 1737.
7. This was reprinted in *Boston Evening Post,* Dec. 26, 1737.

The Earthquake which surpriz'd us here on Wednesday Night the 7th Inst. was not felt at Annapolis in Maryland, but the Accounts we have from New-Castle on Delaware, represent the Shake to be nearly as violent there as here. We have not as yet heard of it from any Place farther to the Southward than New-Castle. But it was felt at Conestogoe near 100 Miles Westward of this City, where some Clouds at the same time were seen to waver, dance, disappear and appear again in an uncommon and surprizing manner. And all the Accounts we have hitherto received from the Northward, make us suspect that the most violent Shock was in that Quarter. Three or four Evenings successively after the Earthquake an unusual Redness appeared in the Western Sky and southwards, continuing about an hour after Sunset, gradually declining. It reach'd near 45 Degrees above the Horizon.   [December 15]

Thursday last the Eastern Prince left this City, on board Capt. Loftus, bound for Barbadoes.   [December 15]

We hear from Derby, that on Saturday Night last, a Woman there, was delivered of three Daughters, and all likely to live.
                    [December 15]

[ADVERTISEMENT] The Person who borrow'd B. Franklin's Book of Laws of this Province, is desired to return it he having forgot to whom he lent it.   [December 15]

PHILADELPHIA: Printed by B. FRANKLIN, POST-MASTER, at the New Printing-Office near the Market. *Price* 10s. a Year. Where ADVERTISEMENTS are taken in, and BOOK-BINDING is done reasonably, in the best Manner.

Poor Richard, 1738

Poor Richard, 1738. An Almanack For the Year of Christ 1738, . . . By Richard Saunders, Philom. Philadelphia: Printed and sold by B. Franklin, at the New Printing-Office near the Market. (Yale University Library)

PREFACE by Mistress SAUNDERS

Dear Readers,

My good Man set out last Week for Potowmack, to visit an

old Stargazer of his Acquaintance, and see about a little Place for us to settle and end our Days on. He left the Copy of his Almanack seal'd up, and bid me send it to the Press. I suspected something, and therefore as soon as he was gone, I open'd it, to see if he had not been flinging some of his old Skitts at me. Just as I thought, so it was. And truly, (for want of somewhat else to say, I suppose) he had put into his Preface, that his Wife Bridget —was this, and that, and t'other.—What a peasecods! cannot I have a little Fault or two, but all the Country must see it in print! They have already been told, at one time that I am proud, another time that I am loud, and that I have got a new Petticoat, and abundance of such kind of stuff; and now, forsooth! all the World must know, that Poor Dick's Wife has lately taken a fancy to drink a little Tea now and then. A mighty matter, truly, to make a Song of! 'Tis true, I had a little Tea of a Present from the Printer last Year; and what, must a body throw it away? In short, I thought the Preface was not worth a printing, and so I fairly scratch'd it all out, and I believe you'll like our Almanack never the worse for it.

Upon looking over the Months, I see he has put in abundance of foul Weather this Year; and therefore I have scatter'd here and there, where I could find room, some *fair, pleasant, sunshiny,* &c. for the Good-Women to dry their Clothes in. If it does not come to pass according to my Desire, I have shown my Good-will, however; and I hope they'll take it in good part.

I had a Design to make some other Corrections; and particularly to change some of the Verses that I don't very well like; but I have just now unluckily broke my Spectacles; which obliges me to give it you as it is, and conclude Your loving Friend,

BRIDGET SAUNDERS

Lo as a Giant strong, the lusty Sun
Multiply'd Rounds in one great Round doth run.
Twofold his Course, yet constant his Career
Changing the Day and finishing the Year.
Again when his descending Orb retires
And Earth perceives the Absence of his Fires
The Moon affords us her alternate Ray,
And with kind Beams distributes fainter Day.

XI Mon. January hath xxxi days.

> Dick's Wife was sick, and pos'd the Doctor's Skill,
> Who differ'd how to cure th'inveterate Ill.
> Purging the one prescrib'd. No, quoth another,
> That will do neither Good nor Harm, my Brother.
> *Bleeding's the only Way;* 'twas quick reply'd,
> That's certain Death;—But e'en let Dick decide.
> *Ise no great Skill,* quo' Richard, *by the Rood;*
> *But I think Bleeding's like to do most good.*

There are three faithful friends, an old wife, an old dog, and ready money.

Great talkers should be cropt, for they've no need of ears.

If you'd have your shoes last, put no nails in 'em.

Who has deceiv'd thee so oft as thy self?

XII Mon. February hath xxviii days.

> In Christendom we all are *Christians* now,
> And thus I answer, if you ask me how;
> Where with *Christ's Rule* our Lives will not comply,
> We bend it like a Rule of Lead, say I;
> Making it thus comply with what we be,
> And only thus our Lives with th' Rule agree.
> But from our Fathers we've the Name (perchance)
> Ay, so our King is call'd *the King of France.*

Is there any thing Men take more pains about than to render themselves unhappy?

Nothing brings more pain than too much pleasure; nothing more bondage than too much liberty, (or libertinism.)

Read much, but not many Books.

I Mon. March hath xxxi days.

Jack's Wife was born in Wiltshire, brought up in Cumberland, led much of her Life in Bedfordshire, sent her Husband into Huntingdonshire in order to bring him into Buckinghamshire: But he took Courage in Hartfordshire, and carry'd her into Staffordshire, or else he might have liv'd and dy'd in Shrewsbury.

He that would have a short Lent, let him borrow Money to be repaid at Easter.

Write with the learned, pronounce with the vulgar.

Fly Pleasures, and they'll follow you.

Squirrel-like she covers her back with her tail.

II Mon. April hath xxx days.

The old Gentry.
That all from Adam first begun,
   Sure none but Whiston[8] doubts,
And that his Son, and his Son's Son
   Were Plowmen, Clowns and Louts;
Here lies the only Difference now,
   Some shot off late, some soon;
Your Sires i' th' Morning left the Plow,
   And ours i' th' Afternoon.

Caesar did not merit the triumphal Car, more than he that conquers himself.

Hast thou virtue? acquire also the graces and beauties of virtue.

Buy what thou has no need of; and e'er long thou shalt sell thy necessaries.

If thou has wit and learning, add to it Wisdom and Modesty.

III Mon. May hath xxxi days.

A frugal Thought.

In an Acre of Land are 43560 square feet, In 100 Acres are

8. William Whiston (1667–1752). Perhaps a reference to his *New Theory of the Earth* (London, 1696).

4356000 square feet; Twenty Pounds will buy 100 Acres of the Proprietor. In £20 are 4800 pence; by which divide the Number of Feet in 100 Acres; and you will find that one penny will buy 907 square Feet; or a Lot of 30 Feet square.—*Save your Pence.*

You may be more happy than Princes, if you will be more virtuous.

> If you wou'd not be forgotten
> As soon as you are dead and rotten,
> Either write things worth reading,
> Or do things worth the writing.

Sell not virtue to purchase wealth, nor Liberty to purchase power.

IV Mon. June hath xxx days.

> Epitaph on a talkative old Maid.
> Beneath this silent Stone is laid,
> A noisy antiquated Maid,
> Who from her Cradle talk'd 'till Death,
> And ne'er before was out of Breath.
> Whither she's gone we cannot tell;
> For, if she talks not, she's in Hell:
> If she's in Heaven, she's there unblest,
> Because she hates a Place of Rest.

God bless the King, and grant him long to Reign.

Let thy vices die before thee.

Keep your eyes wide open before marriage, half shut afterwards.

The ancients tell us what is best; but we must learn of the moderns what is fittest.

V Mon. July hath xxxi days.

> One Month a Lawyer, thou the next wilt be
> A grave Physician, and the third a Priest:
> Chuse quickly one Profession of the three,

Marry'd to her thou yet may'st court the rest.
Resolve at once; deliberate no more;
Leap in, and stand not shiv'ring on the Shore.
On any one amiss thou can'st not fall:
Thou'lt end in nothing, if thou grasps at all.

Since I cannot govern my own tongue, tho' within my own teeth,
how can I hope to govern the tongues of others?

'Tis less discredit to abridge petty charges, than to stoop to petty
Gettings.

Since thou art not sure of a minute, throw not away an hour.

VI Mon. August hath xxxi days.

While faster than his costive Brain indites
Philo's quick Hand in flowing Nonsence writes,
His Case appears to me like honest Teague's,
When he was run away with by his Legs.
Phaebus, give Philo o'er himself Command;
Quicken his Senses, or restrain his Hand;
Let him be kept from Paper, Pen and Ink;
So may he cease to write, and learn to think.

If you do what you should not, you must hear what you would
not.

Defer not thy well doing; be not like St. George, who is always
a horseback, and never rides on.[9]

Wish not so much to live long as to live well.

VII Mon. September hath xxx days.

These Lines may be read backward or forward.
Joy, Mirth, Triumph, I do defie;
Destroy me Death, fain would I die:

9. Some years later, describing Lord Loudon's dilatoriness, BF recalled that one of his lordship's messengers used this simile to characterize the man. Par. Text edit., p. 398.

Forlorn am I, Love is exil'd,
Scorn smiles thereat; Hope is beguil'd;
   Men banish'd bliss, in Woe must dwell,
   Then Joy, Mirth, Triumph all farewell.

As we must account for every idle word, so we must for every idle silence.

I have never seen the Philosopher's Stone that turns lead into Gold; but I have known the pursuit of it turn a Man's Gold into Lead.

Never intreat a servant to dwell with thee.

VIII Mon. October hath xxxi days.

A Doubtful Meaning:
The Female kind is counted ill:
And is indeed; The contrary;
No Man can find: That hurt they will:
But every where: Shew Charity;
To no Body: Malicious still;
In word or Deed: Believe you me.

Time is an herb that cures all Diseases.

Reading makes a full Man, Meditation a profound Man, discourse a clear Man.

If any man flatters me, I'll flatter him again; tho' he were my best Friend.

IX Mon. November hath xxx days.

A Monster in a Course of Vice grown old,
Leaves to his gaping Heir his ill-gain'd Gold;
The Preacher fee'd, strait are his Virtues shown;
And render'd lasting by the sculptur'd Stone.
If on the Stone or Sermon we rely,
Pity a Worth, like his, should ever die!
If Credit to his real Life we give,
Pity a Wretch like him, should ever live.

Wish a miser long life, and you wish him no good.

None but the well bred man knows how to confess a fault, or acknowledge himself in an error.

Drive thy business; let not that drive thee.

There is much difference between imitating a good man, and counterfeiting him.

X Mon. December hath xxxi days.

> The Wiseman says, *It is a Wiseman's Part*
> *To keep his Tongue close Prisoner in his Heart.*
> If he then be a Fool whose Thought denies
> *There is a God,* how desp'rately unwise,
> How much more Fool is he whose Language shall
> Proclaim in publick, *There's no God at all:*
> What then are they, nay Fools in what degree
> Whose Actions shall maintain 't? *Such Fools are we.*

Wink at small faults; remember thou hast great ones.

Eat to please thyself, but dress to please others.

Search others for their virtues, thy self for thy vices.

Never spare the Parson's wine, nor Baker's Pudding.

> Each year one vicious habit rooted out,
> In time might make the worst Man good throughout.

Of the ECLIPSES 1738.

There will be two, and both of the SUN. The First on Feb. 7 at 1 afternoon, hardly visible here, but a great Eclipse in Brasil, Peru, Paragua and other southern Countries in America. And to the Astrologers of those Parts we leave it, to harangue on its terrible Effects.

The other on August 4. A.M. beginning at 4 h 20 m. Middle at 5 h 29 m. End at 6 h. 38 m. Digits Eclipsed 5 and three quarters on the north or upper Side. They that would see Phaebus with his Night-cap on this Morning, should be out of Bed before him to watch his Rising; and perhaps after all may be disappointed, by his intercepting Window-Curtains.

You will excuse me, dear Readers, that I afford you no Eclipses of the Moon this Year. The Truth is, I do not find they do you any Good. When there is one you are apt in observing it to expose yourselves too much and too long to the Night Air, whereby great Numbers of you catch Cold. Which was the Case last Year, to my very great Concern. However, if you will promise to take more Care of your selves, you shall have a fine one to stare at, the Year after next.

A Defense of Conduct

Printed in *The Pennsylvania Gazette*, February 15, 1737/8.

Dr. Evan Jones, "chymist" at the Golden Paracelsus' Head in Philadelphia, had a simple-minded apprentice Daniel Rees, who thought he wanted to be a Mason. With several cronies, one a renegade Mason, Jones, thinking to have some agreeable sport, set up a burlesque initiation ceremony, complete with scandalous oath of allegiance to Satan. One John Tackerbury was responsible for the ceremony; John Remington, a lawyer, wrote the oath. In the garden of Jones's house young Rees was "initiated" with meaningless, ludicrous, and obscene signs and ceremonies, pledging his loyalty to the Prince of Darkness, and drinking from a "sacramental" cup, which contained a strong purgative; "after which one of the Company indecently discovered his Posteriors, to which the Lad . . . was led to kiss, as a Book to swear upon." Jones and Remington enjoyed repeating their account of the affair. Franklin heard it, laughed heartily, and asked for a copy of the oath, which he showed and read to various friends in the ensuing days.

The "initiation" had been such fun that Jones invited a number of people to watch Rees receive another "degree" in Freemasonry on the evening of June 13, in the cellar of his (Jones's) house. One Sullivan, dressed in a cow's hide with horns, impersonated the devil. Through the bluish flames of a bowl of brandy, which the doctor lighted, the faces of those officiating appeared ghastly and hideous. Young Rees seems to have regarded the performance too stolidly for the amusement of his audience. Jones, to make things livelier and more frightening, raised the flaming bowl and, grimacing through the haze, approached the boy. Suddenly he threw, or accidentally spilled, the burning spirits, and Daniel Rees died of his burns two days later (see above, p. 187).

198

The news spread rapidly. The Masons immediately disavowed any connection with it or the participants. Franklin reported what he knew to the authorities. A coroner's inquest found it only an unfortunate accident, but the grand jury, receiving evidence that Jones had thrown the spirits willfully, indicted him, Remington, and Tackerbury for murder. Andrew Bradford used the opportunity to attack the Masons: on August 4 the *American Weekly Mercury* printed an unfriendly article from a London journal.

At the trial in January 1738 Franklin appeared as a witness for the prosecution. Jones and Remington were found guilty of manslaughter; the first was burned in the hand and released; the latter was granted a limited pardon;[1] while Tackerbury was acquitted. In a report of the attorney general's pleading, a writer in the *Pennsylvania Gazette*, February 7, declared that the act that killed Rees was murder and should have been punished as such. To these strictures "C.D." replied in the *Mercury*, February 14, reviewing the testimony at the trial and particularly calling attention to Franklin's conduct. Franklin, he said, had read the blasphemous oath several days before the fatal June 13 and "was pleased to express his Approbation thereof by a most hearty Laughter, and in friendship desired to have the further perusal of it; which in several Companies he diverted himself with the Reading of, and being informed how D.R. had been initiated in the Garden, he candidly saluted him by the name of *Brother*, and to encourage him in it gave him a Sign, as they term it, and congratulated him on being admitted into the *Brotherhood*, and desired to have Notice to be present at the Diversion of Snap-Dragon." To these charges Franklin replied in his own defense in the *Gazette*, February 15.[2]

Some very false and scandalous Aspersions being thrown on me in the *Mercury* of Yesterday, with regard to Dr. Jones's Affair, I find my self obliged to set that Matter in a true Light.

Sometime in June last, Mr. Danby, Mr. Alrihs, and my self were appointed by the Court of Common-Pleas, as Auditors to settle an Affair, between Dr. Jones and Armstrong Smith, then depending in said Court. We met accordingly at a Tavern in Market-Street on the Saturday Morning before the Tragedy was acted

1. Remington's plea to the Council for pardon, with the terms of the Council's action, is in *Pa. Col. Recs.*, IV, 276–7.

2. The episode is related, with the full text of all the newspaper articles referred to in this headnote, in Julius F. Sachse, *Benjamin Franklin as a Free Mason* (Phila., 1906), pp. 49–71.

in the Doctor's Cellar. Dr. Jones appeared, and R-------n as his Attorney, but Smith could not readily be found. While we waited for Smith, in order to hear both Parties together; the Doctor and R-----n began to entertain us with an Account of some Diversion they had lately had with the Dr's. Apprentice, who being desirous of being made a Free-Mason, they had persuaded him they could make him one, and accordingly had taught him several ridiculous Signs, Words and Ceremonies, of which he was very fond. Tis true I laugh'd (and perhaps heartily, as my Manner is) at the *Beginning* of their Relation, but when they came to those Circumstances of their giving him a violent Purge, leading him to kiss T's Posteriors, and administring to him the diabolical Oath which R------n read to us, I grew indeed serious, as I suppose the most merry Man (not enclin'd to Mischief) would on such an Occasion. Nor did any one of the Company, except the Doctor and R------n themselves, seem in the least pleas'd with the Affair, but the contrary. Mr. Danby in particular said, *That if they had done such Things in England they would be prosecuted.* Mr. Alrichs, *That he did not believe they could stand by it.* And my self, *That when the Young Man came to know how he had been impos'd on, he would never forgive them.* But the Doctor and R-------n went on to tell us, that they design'd to have yet some further Diversion, on pretence of raising him to a higher Degree in Masonry. Re------n said it was intended to introduce him blindfold and stripp'd into a Room where the Company being each provided with a Rod or Switch should chastize him smartly; which the Doctor oppos'd, and said He had a better Invention; they would have a Game at *Snap-Dragon* in a Dark Cellar, where some Figures should be dress'd up, that by the pale Light of Burning Brandy would appear horrible and frighten him d-----bly. Soon after which Discourse the young Man himself coming in to speak with his Master, the Doctor pointed at me, and said to him, *Daniel, that Gentleman is a Free-Mason; make a Sign to him.* Which whether he did or not, I cannot tell; for I was so far from *encouraging him* in the Delusion, or *taking him by the Hand,* or *calling him Brother,* and *welcoming him into the Fraternity,* as is said, that I turned my Head to avoid seeing him make his pretended Sign, and look'd out of the Window into the Garden: And all those Circumstances, with that of my *desiring to have Notice that I might be present at the Snap-Dragon,* are absolutely false and groundless. I was acquainted with, and had a Respect for the young Lad's Father, and thought it a Pity his Son should be so impos'd upon, and therefore follow'd the Lad down Stairs to the Door when he went out, with a Design to call him back and give him a Hint of the Imposition; but he was gone out of sight and I never saw him afterwards; for the Monday Night following, the Affair in the Cellar was transacted which prov'd his Death. As to the Paper or Oath, I did desire R------n when he had read it to let me see it; and finding it a Piece of a very extraordinary Nature, I told him I was desirous to shew it to some of my Acquaintance, and so put it in my Pocket. I communicated it to one, who mention'd it to others, and so many People flock'd to my House for a Sight of it, that it grew troublesome, and therefore when the Mayor sent for it, I was glad of the Opportunity to be discharg'd from it. Nor do I yet conceive that it was my Duty to conceal or destroy it. And being subpena'd on the Tryal as a Witness for the King, I appear'd and gave my Evidence fully, freely and impartially, as I think it becomes an honest Man to do. And I may call every one to whom I read that Paper, to witness, that I always accompanied it with Expressions of Detestation. This being the true State of the Case, I think I may reasonably hope, that I am so well known in this City, where I have liv'd near 14 Years, as that the false and malicious Insinuations contain'd in the *Mercury,* will not do the Injury to my Reputation that seems intended.   B. FRANKLIN

***p.s. I suppose A.B. will answer for himself.

We whose Names are hereunto subscribed, do certify, That we were present at the Time and Place above-mentioned, when Dr. Jones and J---n R------n related their Proceedings with Daniel R--s; and we do very well remember, that they were not countenanc'd or encourag'd by any Person present, but the contrary. And that Benjamin Franklin in particular *did speak against* it, and did neither approve of what had been *already* done (as related by the Doctor and R--------n) nor desire to be present at what was propos'd to be *farther* done with the said Daniel R--s, as is falsly insinuated in Mr. Bradford's last *Mercury.* And this we declare sincerely and freely, without any other Motive than the Desire of doing Justice to the Reputation of the said Benjamin Franklin. Witness our Hands, this 15th Day of February, 1737,8.

JOHN DANBY,
HARMANUS ALRIHS

The above-named John Danby being sworn upon the Holy Evangelists, and Harmanus Alrihs being duly affirmed, on their respective Qualifications did declare, that the Contents of the above Certificate were true.

Sworn and affirm'd Before me, this 15th of February, 1737,8.[3]

WILLIAM ALLEN

To Josiah and Abiah Franklin

Draft: Historical Society of Pennsylvania[4]

Honour'd Father and Mother[5]   April 13. 1738
I have your Favour of the 21st of March[6] in which you both seem concern'd lest I have imbib'd some erroneous Opinions.

3. The unhappy affair did not end here. "C.D." printed a strong rejoinder in the *Mercury*, Feb. 21, repeating his statements about BF's behavior and answering BF's defense. Far from hastening after Rees to warn him, "C.D." continued, BF did not stir from the room for half an hour; he expressed the opinion that BF's reading the blasphemous oath in company, though with expressions of detestation, smacked more of hypocrisy than of sincerity; and he reminded his readers that it would have been a greater kindness to the boy and his father to inform them or the magistrates before the tragedy, than afterward, how young Rees was to be used and abused. BF made no further public defense. Reports of the affair, however, were reprinted in the New York and Boston newspapers, where BF's parents saw them. They expressed deep concern about his conduct, which BF tried to relieve, April 13.

4. William Duane printed this letter in *Memoirs of Benjamin Franklin . . . with a Postliminious Preface* (Phila., 1834), I, 233, as addressed to Josiah Franklin alone and with substantial differences in sentence order and paragraphing from the draft. Subsequent editors have followed Duane's text.

5. BF adopted another tone in what appears to be an earlier version of this draft, also in Hist. Soc. Pa. Addressed to his father only, it reads:
"I have yours of the 21st of March, with another from my Mother, in which you both seem concern'd for my Orthodoxy. God only knows whether all the Doctrines I hold for true, be so or not. For my part, I must confess, I believe they are not, but I am not able to distinguish the good from the bad. And Knowing my self, as I do, to be a weak ignorant Creature, full of natural Im-

Doubtless I have my Share, and when the natural Weakness and Imperfection of Human Understanding is considered, with the unavoidable Influences of Education, Custom, Books and Company, upon our Ways of thinking, I imagine a Man must have a good deal of Vanity who believes, and a good deal of Boldness who affirms, that all the Doctrines he holds, are true; and all he rejects, are false. And perhaps the same may be justly said of every Sect, Church and Society of men when they assume to themselves that Infallibility which they deny to the Popes and Councils. I think Opinions should be judg'd of by their Influences and Effects; and if a Man holds none that tend to make him less Virtuous or more vicious, it may be concluded he holds none that are dangerous; which I hope is the Case with me. I am sorry you should have any Uneasiness on my Account, and if it were a thing possible for one to alter his Opinions in order to please others, I know none whom I ought more willingly to oblige in that respect than your selves: But since it is no more in a Man's Power *to think* than *to look* like another, methinks all that should be expected from me is to keep my Mind open to Conviction, to hear patiently and examine attentively whatever is offered me for that end; and if after all I continue in the same Errors, I believe your usual Charity will induce you rather to pity and excuse than blame me. In the mean time your Care and Concern for me is what I am very thankful for.

---

perfections, subject to be frequently misled by my own Reasonings, or the wrong Arguments of others, to the Influence of Education, of Custom, of Company, and the Books I read, It would be great Vanity in me to imagine that I have been so happy, as out of an infinite Number of Opinions of which a few only can be true, to select those only for my own Use. No, I am doubtless in Error as well as my Neighbours, and methinks a Man can not say, *All the Doctrines that I believe, are true; and all that I reject, are false*, without arrogantly claiming to himself that Infallibility which he denies to the Pope, with the greatest Indignation.

"From such Considerations as these it follows, that I ought never to be angry with any one for differing in Judgment from me. For how know I but the Point in dispute between us, is one of those Errors that I have embrac'd as Truth. If I am in the Wrong, I should not be displeas'd that another is in the right. If I am in the Right, 'tis my Happiness; and I should rather pity than blame him who is unfortunately in the Wrong."

6. Not found.

As to the Freemasons,[7] unless she will believe me when I assure her that they are in general a very harmless sort of People; and have no principles or Practices that are inconsistent with Religion or good Manners, I know no Way of giving my Mother a better Opinion of them than she seems to have at present, (since it is not allow'd that Women should be admitted into that secret Society). She has, I must confess, on that Account, some reason to be displeas'd with it; but for any thing else, I must entreat her to suspend her Judgment till she is better inform'd, and in the mean time exercise her Charity.

My Mother grieves that one of her Sons is an Arian, another an Arminian. What an Arminian or an Arian is, I cannot say that I very well know; the Truth is, I make such Distinctions very little my Study; I think vital Religion has always suffer'd, when Orthodoxy is more regarded than Virtue. And the Scripture assures me, that at the last Day, we shall not be examin'd what we *thought,* but what we *did;* and our Recommendation will not be that we said *Lord, Lord,* but that we did GOOD to our Fellow Creatures. See Matth. 26.[8]

We have had great Rains here lately, which with the Thawing ·of Snow in the Mountains back of our Country has made vast Floods in our Rivers, and by carrying away Bridges, Boats, &c. made travelling almost impracticable for a Week past, so that our Post has entirely mist making one Trip.

I know nothing of Dr. Crook, nor can I learn that any such Person has ever been here.[9]

I hope my Sister Janey's Child is by this time recovered.[1] I am Your dutiful Son   B F

7. Boston papers had reported Rees's death the preceding summer, and in March 1738 both the *Boston Weekly News-Letter* and *Boston Evening-Post* had reprinted the account of Jones's trial. See above, p. 198.

8. The citation should be to Matt. 25.

9. The editors have not identified Dr. Crook either.

1. Jane Mecom had four children at this time.

Agreement of Directors of Library Company

ADS: Massachusetts Historical Society

[May 22, 1738]

We the Subscribers, Directors of the Library Company for the current Year, do agree to attend all our appointed Meetings, at ½ an Hour past Eight in the Evening until the first Meeting in August inclusive, And from that Time 'till November at Eight in the Evening And from that Time 'till May ensuing at Seven in the Evening, And that for every Failure we will each of us pay to the rest One Shilling. Witness our Hands hereto the Twenty second Day of May 1738.[2]

B FRANKLIN	WM. COLEMAN
T. CADWALADER	HUGH ROBERTS
THOS. HOPKINSON 1738	WILL: ALLEN
ALEX: GRAYDON	RICHARD PETERS

May 22nd. Absent PS. WPl.[3]

June 12th. Absent WA. RP. TC.

July 10th. Absent TC. AG. HR. WA. WP.

Augst. 14. Absent WA. RP. HR. and PS.

Septr. 11. Absent WA. RP. HR. AG. WP. WC. and tardy BF.

Octobr. 9. Absent WA. WC. WP. HR.

Novr. 13. Absent WA. HR. RP. AG. PS. and WC. the last being gone for England.

2. This agreement, differing somewhat from the form used earlier (see above, I, 321), had two worthy purposes: to improve attendance and to increase the Library's income. Apparently it was made annually, for another similar MS, dated May 11, 1741, survives (in Haverford Coll. Lib.) but it will not be printed in this work. Another device was adopted later: absentees were required to send a proxy in the shape of "two bottles of good wine." Thereafter, so one historian of the Library Company relates, "the Directors attended in force with great regularity . . . in the hope that the other Directors would be represented by their proxies." Austin K. Gray, *Benjamin Franklin's Library* (N.Y., 1937), pp. 14–15.

3. The initials in this list are those of Philip Syng, William Plumsted, William Allen, Richard Peters, Thomas Cadwalader, Alexander Graydon, Hugh Roberts, William Parsons, William Coleman, BF, and Samuel Rhoads, who was elected a director, Dec. 11, 1738, to replace William Coleman. Lib. Co. Phila., Minutes.

Decr. 11.   Absent WA. and RP.
Janry. 8.   Absent WA. WP. AG. and TH.
Febry. 12. Absent WA. WP. AG. and PS.
March 12. Absent WA. RP. BF. HR, and tardy SR.

1739

April 9.   Absent WA. RP. HR. and AG.
May 7th.   Absent WA. RP.

To Josiah Franklin

Incomplete draft: Historical Society of Pennsylvania

Honoured Father   [May ? 1738]
I received your kind Letter of the 4th of May in answer to mine
of April 13.[4] I wrote that of mine with a Design to remove or
lessen the Uneasiness you and my Mother appear'd to be under on
Account of my Principles; and it gave me great Pleasure when she
declar'd in her next to me that she approv'd of my Letter and was
now satisfy'd with me.

To John Ladd[5]   Transcript: Historical Society of Haddonfield (N.J.)

Sir   June 12, 1738
I send you the Ladies Library and the other two Vols. of Don
Quixote.
The Homers I have are done by Pope. The Iliads are in 6 Vols.
12mo price 45s. The Odysseys 5 Vols. 12mo price 37s. 6d. I will not
part with them till I hear from you.[6] I am Sir Your most humble
Servant   B. FRANKLIN

4. See above, p. 202. No letter has been found from either of BF's parents in
reply to his of April 13.
5. John Ladd (d. 1770), of Gloucester Co., N.J.; surveyor; justice of the
peace, 1739; elected to the Assembly, 1754; appointed to the Governor's Council, 1763. 1 N.J. Arch., IX, 395; X, 224–5; XII, 415; XV, 97; Warren Ladd, The
Ladd Family (New Bedford, Mass., 1890), pp. 311–14.
6. In Pa. Gaz., May 25, 1738, and later issues, BF advertised a list of books
"Just Imported," which included The Ladies' Library, 3 vols. 12mo., and
Pope's Homer, 11 vols. 12mo. Ladd's purchase of The Ladies' Library and Don

Directors of Library Company to John Penn[7]

MS Minute Book: Library Company of Philadelphia

Honourable Sir,   Philadelphia August 8th. 1738.

The Library Company of Philadelphia beg leave to return their most hearty Thanks for your noble Benefaction of an Air Pump with its costly and curious Apparatus.

Useful and necessary as that excellent Invention must be to a Society whose View is the Improvement of Knowledge, we might have been long without this Advantage if your judicious Generosity had not come in to our Assistance.

It gives us great Pleasure that the Proprietary Family so many other Ways endeared to us, are so early and in so iminent a Manner the particular Benefactors of our Society; the honorable your Brother having not long since bestowed on us a valuable and well-situated Lot of Ground for the Conveniency of a Library Room and Garden.

Permit us to accompany our thankful Acknowlegements of these Favours, with our sincere Assurances of doing all that lies in our Power to merit the Continuance of your Regards.

WILLIAM ALLEN,	THOS. HOPKINSON,
ALEXR. GRAYDON,	WM. PLUMSTEAD,
THOS. CADWALADER,	WM. COLEMAN,
B. FRANKLIN,	HUGH ROBERTS,
RICHARD PETERS,	PHILIP SYNG JNR.

Quixote is recorded in BF's Shop Book (see above, p. 127), June 9, 1738, where is also noted, July 19, his acquisition of "a Homer 11 Vol" for £4 2s. 6d. Sales of other books to Ladd are entered in BF's Ledger D, p. 75 (see below, p. 232).

7. Following their announcement, May 1, that Thomas Penn had presented the Library Company "a large and commodious Lot of Ground" for a building, and that John Penn had just sent it "a valuable Present . . . consisting of an Air Pump, and other curious Instruments of great Use in the Study of Natural Knowledge" (*Pa. Gaz.*, May 4, 1738; see below, p. 210), the Directors, May 8, appointed BF, William Coleman, and Richard Peters to draft an address of thanks. This was presented at the meeting, August 14, approved, and ordered spread on the minutes.

The lot, located on the south side of Chestnut street between Eighth and Ninth, was surveyed to William Allen, James Hamilton, William Plumsted, and BF, as trustees for the Library Company, on January 12, 1738; but it was never used for the purpose. Warrants and Surveys of the Province of Pennsyl-

From Joseph Morgan[8]

ALS: The Royal Society

Mr. Franklin   Maidenhead 5. Octr. 1738

If my Manuscripts[9] be not gone before this comes to you; I have one Small Amendment (which happened thro' too much hast). It is not far from the beginning, where I compare the Heat on Jupiter and the Earth. In Stead of Jupiter *near* 100 times as large in its Face to the Sun; it should be *above* 100 times &c. This yet makes my Argument the better. However it matters not very much. But if it be not too much Trouble, you will oblige me (as you have done all along) if you mend it. I hope in time to be able to make you Amends for the Troubles I put you to, for me Your humble Servant

JOSEPH MORGAN

Addressed: To   Mr Benjamin Franklin   Post Master & Printer in Philadelphia   These

From Joseph Morgan

ALS: The Royal Society

Mr. Franklin   Octobr 11. [1738]

Please to fasten this to the Manuscript of Philosophy.[1]

And if it be gone, be so kind as to inclose it to the Royal Society by another Ship. You will oblige Your Friend and Servant

JOSEPH MORGAN

_____

vania, VII, 182, Dept. of Records, Phila. The air pump was brought over by one Samuel Jenkins, who instructed the Directors in its use. Austin K. Gray, *Benjamin Franklin's Library* (N.Y., 1937), p. 17. Among the Franklin Papers in Lib. Cong. are MS "Directions for the Air Pump," which may be Jenkins' instructions for John Penn's gift. The pump does not survive.

8. On Morgan, see above, p. 35 n.

9. A 22-page MS entitled "Some farther Improvement of the Astronomical Philosophy of Sir Isaac Newton, and others. Containing Observations upon their Discoveries; which did not at first Occur to the Discoverers: the things being new found out." This MS is in the Royal Society, to which it was addressed; it was not printed.

1. The additions referred to, written on the back of the letter, were to be attached to the MS mentioned in Morgan's letter to BF, Oct. 5. A note in the margin of the enclosure seems to be addressed to BF: "I Sent yesterday to the Office: but have since tho't further. And this may suffice."

Addressed: Mr Benjamin Franklin   Post Master in   Philadelphia
A Second

To Isaac Corin[2]   ALS: American Philosophical Society

Mr. Corin   Dec. 22. 1738
   Please to let the Bearer Stephen Potts[3] have a pair of Leather
Breeches, and charge them to the Account of your Friend
                                                    B FRANKLIN

Extracts from the Gazette, 1738

Printed in *The Pennsylvania Gazette*, January 3 to December 28, 1738.

[ADVERTISEMENT] *To accommodate the Publick.* There will be a
Stage Waggon set out from Trenton to Brunswick, twice a Week
and back again, during next Summer. It will be fitted up with
Benches and cover'd over so that Passengers may sit easy and dry.
And Care will be taken to deliver Goods and Messages safe.
   Note. The said Waggon will set out for the first time, from Wil-
liam Atlee's and Thomas Hooton's in Trenton, on Monday the
27th of March next, and continue going every Monday and
Thursday from Trenton, and return from Brunswick every
Tuesday and Friday. Every Passenger to pay *Two Shillings*
and *Six Pence.* And Goods and Parcels at the cheapest Rates.
                                                    [February 7]

[ADVERTISEMENT] Lent above a Twelvemonth ago, the second
Vol. of Select Trials, for Murders, Robberies, Rapes, Sodomy,
Coining, Frauds, and other Offences, at the Sessions-House in the
Old-Bailey: Which not being return'd to the Owner, he desires the

---

2. Isaac Corin's account with BF appears in Ledger D (see below, p. 232).
He inserted an advertisement for a runaway servant in *Pa. Gaz.*, Sept. 23, 1731.
   3. Stephen Potts (d. 1758) was a member of the Junto, a bookbinder, bookseller, and in his last years a tavern keeper. BF first knew him as a fellow
employee at Keimer's and described him in his autobiography as a young
countryman "of uncommon natural Parts, and great Wit and Humour, but a
little idle." BF's ledgers show that the two men had extensive business relations
from 1733 to 1757.

Person who has the Book in possession, to send it to the Printer of this Paper.   [March 7]

We hear from Birmingham in Chester County, that some time last Week a young Man was unfortunately kill'd in the following Manner. He was falling a Tree, which lodged against another, when the But End left the Stump with a Spring, and took him in the Body, drove him 8 or 10 Foot, and then mash'd him against the Earth. He had only time to say, *Lord have mercy on my Soul,* and died immediately.   [March 14]

[ADVERTISEMENT] Left upon Samuel Powel's Wharff sometime in December last, a very good Great Coat, the Owner applying to the Printer, describing the Marks and paying the Charges, may have it again.   [March 14]

[ADVERTISEMENT] CHOICE LINSEED OYL, To be Sold by William Parsons, in Second-Street, and by the Printer hereof.
                                                                              [April 13]

Monday last the Library-Company of this City had their Yearly Meeting, for the Choice of their Officers, paying their Annual Subscription, &c. when they were acquainted, That the Hon. Proprietary THOMAS PENN, Esq; had presented the Company with a large and commodious LOT OF GROUND, whereon to build an House for their Library; and also that the last Ship from London had brought them a valuable Present from the Hon. JOHN PENN, Esq; consisting of an AIR PUMP, and other curious Instruments of great Use in the Study of Natural Knowledge. Both which Donations were exceedingly agreeable to the Company, not only with respect to their Value, but as they shew a Disposition in our greatest Men to encourage the Design of Promoting useful Learning in Pennsylvania.[4]   [May 4]

4. For the Library Company's thanks, which BF helped draft, see above, p. 207.

JUST IMPORTED, And to be Sold by B. Franklin, for Ready Money only; the lowest Price being marked in each Book.

Allen's Synopsis of Physick, 2 vols. *8vo.*
Arburthnot on Aliments.
Atalantis. 4 Vols. *12mo.*
Arabian Nights. 6 Vols. *12mo.*
Bacon's Essays.
Beveridge's Thoughts.
Bailey's Dictionary.
Bradley on Gardening.
Bladen's Caesar.
Clark on the Attributes.
——'s Sermons. 10 Vols. *8vo.*
Characteristicks. 3 Vols. *8vo.*
Crusoe's Life. 2 Vols. *12mo.*
Croxal's Esop.
Congreve's Works. 3 Vols. *12mo.*
Collection of Novels. 6 Vols.
Drelincourt on Death.
Dryden's Virgil. 3 Vols. *12mo.*
—— Fables.
Gravesande's Elements. 2 Vols. *8vo.*
Gay's Fables.
Human Prudence.
Hive. 4 Vols. *12mo.*
Hudibras.
Jacobs's Law Dictionary.
Lock of Human Understanding.
Landlord's Law.
Ladies Library. 3 Vols. *12mo.*
Milton's Paradise lost.
Nelson's Justice. 2 Vols. *8vo.*
Ovid's Epistles.
Otway's Plays.
Pitcairn's Works.
Pembroke's Arcadia.
Pope's Homer. 11 Vols. *12mo.*

Pomfret's Poems.
Prior's Poems. 2 Vols. *12mo.*
Rowe's Lucan. 2 Vols. *12mo.*
Stanhope's Epictetus.
Sherlock on Death.
—— on Judgment.
Seneca's Morals.
Spectators. 8 Vols.
Quincy's Sanctorius.
—— Lexicon.
—— Dispensatory.
Selden's Table-talk.
Tale of a Tub.
Wood's Institutes of the Laws of England.
—— Civil Law.
Wingate's Arithmetick.
Family Instructor.
Telemachus. 2 Vols. *12mo.*
Addison's Works.
Clark's Introduction.
—— Corderius.
Watts's Psalms.
—— Lyric Poems.
Bailey's Exercises.
Eutropius.
Ovidii Tristia.
Accidences.
Polite Philosopher.
Columbarium.
Duck's Poems.
Every Man his own Lawyer.
Beiler's German Grammar.
History of England.
Ward's Young Math. Guide.
Kelly's Navigation.
Cole's Latin Dictionary.
Barclay's Apology.
Vademecum.

With many other Sorts too tedious to mention.
Where also may be had,
Bibles, Testaments, Psalters, Old and New-England Primers,
gilt Paper, mourning Paper, Sealing-Wax, Wafers, Dutch Quills,
Ivory-leav'd Memorandum Books, Folding Sticks, Pounce, Letter
Cases, Pocket Books of several Sizes, Ink-Powder, Spectacles of
several Sorts, Blanks of all Sorts; with most Sorts of Stationary
Ware. [May 25]

This Morning arrived in Capt. Arthur from Antigua, The Hon-
ourable Col. GEORGE THOMAS, our Governor, with his Lady and
Family, and was received with the universal Acclamations of the
People accompanied by a general Discharge of Cannon from the
Hill and the Ships in the Harbour.[5] [June 1]

We have from Burlington a most melancholly Account of the
Death of a Boy of 5 Years old, last Week, who hanged himself on
the Stake of a Fence with a Rope he had been playing with in the
Yard. He was first discover'd by means of the Crying of a younger
Child, *Brother won't speak to me.* 'Tis thought that the abundance of
Discourse he had heard of the late Execution of Negroes for Poi-
soning, had fill'd his Mind, and put him on imitating what he had
heard was done, not knowing the Danger. It is said, that he dreamt
much of that Execution the Night before, and telling his Dream in
the Morning, added, *And I shall die to Day;* which was not then
regarded. [June 15]

[ADVERTISEMENT] Alle diejenigen Pfältzer, die mit dem Capi-
tain Thomas Thomson in dem Schiff genandt Townsend, überge-
kommen sind von Amsterdam, und weder ihre Fracht bezahlet
haben, werden hierbey aufgefordert die Bezahlung eiligst zu en-
trichten by Simon Edgell, Kauffmann, in Philadelphia; Oder aber
erwarten dass man sie nach denen Rechten dieser Provintz verfol-
gen muss. Ein jeder hüte sich für schaden. [June 15]

[ADVERTISEMENT] Lost in the Road from Mr. William Allen's
Fishing-Place to Pensbury, or from Pensbury to Philadelphia, a

5. On Thomas, see above, p. 187 n.

Cornelian Seal set in Gold. Whoever brings it to the Printer hereof, shall be handsomely rewarded. [June 29]

Yesterday Morning died here, and was the same Day decently interred, Madam BROWNELL, Wife of Mr. GEORGE BROWNELL, a Gentlewoman well known and much respected in New-England and New-York, as well as this Province, for her excellent and happy Method of educating young Ladies; in which useful Employment she had been engag'd many Years.[6] [July 6]

[ADVERTISEMENT] Philadelphia, the 3d of the 5th Mo. 1738
This Day the MAYOR and COMMONALTY met in Common Council, and taking into Consideration the Licentiousness, and many Disorders committed in and about this City on the First Day of the Week; did amongst other Things come to a Resolution, that all Barbers who shall hereafter open their Shops, or suffer any Persons to resort to or about their Houses, or otherwise exercise their ordinary Calling on the First Day of the Week, shall be Prosecuted as the Law directs; of which all Master-Barbers and Servants are desired to take due Notice and conform themselves accordingly. [July 6]

We hear that Mr. Robert Bolton is expected to return and open a Dancing-School in this City, considerable Encouragement being given him for that Purpose. [July 13]

[ADVERTISEMENT] All Persons indebted to George Brownell, of this City, are desired to make speedy Payment, he intending to

6. George Brownell advertised in *Boston News-Letter*, March 2, 1713, that he taught "Writing, Cyphering, Dancing, Treble Violin, Flute, Spinnet &c. Also English and French Quilting, Imbroidery, Florishing, Plain Work, marking in several sorts of Stiches, and several other works, where Scholars may board." He was admitted a citizen April 28, 1713. *Records of Boston Selectmen, 1701 to 1715* (Boston, 1884), p. 139. BF, who attended his school, probably in 1715, described him as "very successful in his Profession generally, and that by mild encouraging Methods. Under him I acquired fair Writing pretty soon, but I fail'd in the Arithmetic, and made no Progress in it." In Philadelphia Brownell operated a dry goods store and conducted a school in his house in Second Street, teaching "Reading, Writing, Cyphering, Dancing, Plain-work, Marking, with Variety of Needle-work." *Pa. Gaz.*, Jan. 6, 1736. He was one of BF's customers. Presumably he left Philadelphia after his wife's death.

Depart this Province in a short Time; and those who have any Demands on him are desired to bring in their Accounts that they may
be adjusted.

*₊*N.B. To be Sold by the said George Brownell, several sorts of
Houshold Furniture, as Chests of Drawers, Tables, Chairs, Look-
ing-Glasses, &c. [July 13]

We have the Pleasure of acquainting the World, that the famous
Chinese or Tartarian Plant, called *Gin seng,* is now discovered in
this Province, near Sasquehannah: From whence several whole
Plants with a Quantity of the Root, have been lately sent to Town,
and it appears to agree most exactly with the Description given of
it in Chambers's Dictionary, and Pere du Halde's Account of
China. The Virtues ascrib'd to this Plant are wonderful. [July 27]

[ADVERTISEMENT] Mr. Bolton gives Notice, that having met
with considerable Encouragement, he designs to remove his Family hither and open a SCHOOL about the Beginning of September
next, in which will be Taught, all Kinds of Needle-work, Dancing,
&c. Where also Children may board, as usual with Mr. Brownell.
[August 3]

To the Printer of the Gazette.
Esteemed Friend,

I have given thee some Information, a good while since, of that
excellent Discovery, that hath been found out amongst us, for to
cure the Bite of a Rattle-Snake: It hath now been practised by several Persons, and it never hath failed, but performed the Cure to
Admiration. It would be well to publish it for the Good of Mankind.

The Cure is thus: Take of common Salt, powder it fine, and rub
it with your Fingers over and into the Wound; if you scarrify the
Skin with the Edge or sharp Point of a Knife or Needle, near the
Wound, 'twould do much good, and bind some Quantity of Salt to
the Sore. It giveth speedy Ease, draweth the poysonous Matter
away in large Quantities, and destroyeth the Nature and Effects of
the Poyson. G. B.
[August 10]

[ADVERTISEMENT] Philad. the 14th of the 6th Mo. 1738
All Bakers of Loaf Bread and Housekeepers in the City of Phila-

delphia are hereby advertised, that the Weight of Bread is appointed as follows, and so to continue till there shall be further Reason to alter the Weight, viz.

The 5penny Loaf White Bread, 38 Ounces and three quarters.

The 5penny Loaf of Wheaten or Midling Bread, 60 Ounces Troy Weight, to which all Bakers are required to conform themselves.

[August 17]

[ADVERTISEMENT] Taken or dropt out of a Chaise (as 'tis suppos'd) on the 4th Inst. in Philadelphia, or in the Road from it to Germantown, a new French Book in 12mo. (or less in Size than the small ordinary Bibles) gilt and titled on the back *Jugemens des Savans. Tom. VII.* It is one of a Set of 17 Volumes, cost at first less than 2s. 6d. sterl. and is of very little Value alone. But as the Loss of it would break the Sett, whoever brings it to Edward Shippen in Philadelphia, or to its Owner J. Logan, shall be paid *Six Shillings* for their Trouble. [October 26]

[ADVERTISEMENT] Forasmuch as Mathematical Learning is (and has been in all Ages) promoted in most Parts of the World especially in all great Towns, and generally pursued by the Gentry and those of the first Rank, as a necessary Qualification; it is to be hoped that this flourishing City will follow the Example and give it such Encouragement as it justly deserves.

In order to which there will be taught this Winter, over against Mr. James Steel's in Second-Street, Philadelphia; Reading, Writing, Vulgar Arithmetick, Decimal Arithmetick, Accompts, Euclid's Elements, Practical Geometry, Mensuration, Gauging, Surveying, Algebra, Trigonometry, Geography, Navigation, Astronomy, Dialing, Projection of the Sphere, the Use of Globes, Maps, Quadrants, Scales, sliding Rules, and all other Instruments for the Mathematical Service, by THEOPHILUS GREW, Mathematician.[7]

Where may be had choice green and blue Mantua, and other Silks, very cheap. [October 26]

[ADVERTISEMENT] Lost some Months since, a Mourning Ring, on which was inscrib'd the late Governor GORDON's Name. Who-

---

7. On Grew, see above, p. 29 n. He had advertised a large quantity of imported dry goods in *Pa. Gaz.*, Aug. 31.

ever brings it to the Printer hereof, shall have *Twenty Shillings* for their Trouble. [November 16]

[ADVERTISEMENT] A small manuscript Treatise, upon the *Dry Gripes*,[8] was lately dropt and lost in one of the Streets of this City. Any Person bringing it to the Printer hereof, will very much oblige the Owner, and shall be handsomely rewarded. [November 24]

This Morning about 2 a Clock, a Fire broke out at Mr. Clark's near Black-Horse-Ally, occasion'd by some Brands carelessly left in the Dancing-School Fire-place; but timely Assistance coming, it was soon extinguished. [November 30]

[ADVERTISEMENT] Lent and Lost, the Earl of Clarendon's History of the Rebellion and Civil Wars, Vol. I. It's an Oxford Edition, printed in 1712, and lettered on the Back. Whoever brings it to the Printer hereof, shall be handsomely rewarded.
[December 6]

JUST PUBLISHED, POOR RICHARD'S ALMANACKS, for the Year 1739.[9] Wherein is contained The Lunations, Eclipses, Judgments of the Weather, Spring Tides, Planets Motions, and mutual Aspects, Sun and Moon's Rising and Setting, Length of Days, Time of High Water, Fairs, Courts and observable Days. Together with many witty Hints, Sayings, Verses and Observations, as usual, viz. The Art of Foretelling the Weather. Why he continues to call himself Poor Richard. Teague's Criticism on the First of Genesis. Giles Jolt's Syllogism. John's Wife. Kings and Bears. Miss Cloe's Case. 'Squire Edward's Kindness. The Knave in Grain. Codrus and Caesar. Bright Florella. The ninth Beatitude. On his late Deafness. An infallible Cure for the Toothach. George's fine Fruitbearing Tree. Lower County Teeth. The Emblem of a Friend. Modern Faith. Pinchall's Temperance. A---'s Wit. Life a Journey. Homer's Fate. Sam's Lawsuit, &c. &c. &c.
To which is added,
A most true and unerring PROGNOSTICATION for the Year 1739,

8. Very likely the composition of Dr. Thomas Cadwalader, which BF published in 1745 as *An Essay on the West-India Dry-Gripes*.
9. The 1739 *Poor Richard* was first advertised November 16, but without listing the contents, as here.

relating to the Condition of these Northern Colonies, The Diseases the People will be subject to, and the Quantity of the Fruits of the Earth.

Sold by B. Franklin, Price 3s. 6d. per Dozen. [December 6]

PHILADELPHIA: Printed by B. FRANKLIN, POST-MASTER, at the New Printing-Office near the Market. *Price* 10s. a Year. Where *Advertisements* are taken in, and *Book-Binding* is done reasonably, in the best Manner.

Poor Richard, 1739

> *Poor Richard, 1739. An Almanack For the Year of Christ 1739, . . .* By Richard Saunders, Philom. Philadelphia: Printed and sold by B. Franklin, at the New Printing-Office near the Market. (Yale University Library)[1]

Kind Reader,

Encouraged by thy former Generosity, I once more present thee with an Almanack, which is the 7th of my Publication. While thou art putting Pence in my Pocket, and furnishing my Cottage with Necessaries, Poor Dick is not unmindful to do something for thy Benefit. The Stars are watch'd as narrowly as old Bess watch'd her Daughter, that thou mayst be acquainted with their Motions, and told a Tale of their Influences and Effects, which may do thee more good than a Dream of last Year's Snow.

Ignorant Men wonder how we Astrologers foretell the Weather so exactly, unless we deal with the old black Devil. Alas! 'tis as easy as pissing abed. For Instance; The Stargazer peeps at the Heavens thro' a long Glass: He sees perhaps TAURUS or the great Bull, in a mighty Chase, stamping on the Floor of his House, swinging his Tail about, stretching out his Neck, and opening wide his Mouth. 'Tis natural from these Appearances to judge that this furious Bull is puffing, blowing, and roaring. Distance being consider'd, and Time allow'd for all this to come down, there you have Wind and Thunder. He spies perhaps VIRGO (or the Virgin); she turns her Head round as it were to see if any body observ'd her; then crouching down gently, with her Hands on her Knees, she

1. Words missing from the Preface because of a torn page in the Yale copy have been supplied from the copy in the American Antiquarian Society.

looks wistfully for a while right forward. He judges rightly what she's about: And having calculated the Distance and allow'd Time for it's Falling, finds that next Spring we shall have a fine April shower. What can be more natural and easy than this? I might instance the like in many other particulars; but this may be sufficient to prevent our being taken for Conjurors. O the wonderful Knowledge to be found in the Stars! Even the smallest Things are written there, if you had but Skill to read. When my Brother J--m-n[2] erected a Scheme to know which was best for his sick Horse, to sup a new-laid Egg, or a little Broth, he found that the Stars plainly gave their verdict for Broth, and the Horse having sup'd his Broth; —Now, what do you think became of that Horse? You shall know in my next.

Besides the usual Things expected in an Almanack, I hope the profess'd Teachers of Mankind will excuse my scattering here and there some instructive Hints in Matters of Morality and Religion. And be not thou disturbed, O grave and sober Reader, if among the many serious Sentences in my Book, thou findest me trifling now and then, and talking idly. In all the Dishes I have hitherto cook'd for thee, there is solid Meat enough for thy Money. There are Scraps from the Table of Wisdom, that will if well digested, yield strong Nourishment to thy Mind. But squeamish Stomachs cannot eat without Pickles; which, 'tis true are good for nothing else, but they provoke an Appetite. The Vain Youth that reads my Almanack for the sake of an idle Joke, will perhaps meet with a serious Reflection, that he may ever after be the better for.

Some People observing the great Yearly Demand for my Almanack, imagine I must by this Time have become rich, and consequently ought to call myself *Poor Dick* no longer. But, the Case is this, When I first begun to publish, the Printer made a fair Agreement with me for my Copies, by Virtue of which he runs away with the greatest Part of the Profit. However, much good may't do him; I do not grudge it him; he is a Man I have a great Regard for, and I wish his Profit ten times greater than it is. For I am, dear Reader, his, as well as thy Affectionate Friend,   R. SAUNDERS

2. John Jerman, whose *American Almanack* for 1739 was printed by Andrew Bradford.

Teague's Criticism on the First of Genesis.[3]

Arra, now, what shignifies the making the two great Lights
The shun to rule the Day, and the Mhoon to rule the Nights?
For the shun in the Day-time there ish no Ochashun;
Because we can she vhery whell all over the Nashun.
But for the Mhoons, they are very good in a dark Night,
Becaush, when we can't shee, they give us a Light.

XI Mon. January hath xxxi days.

Giles Jolt, as sleeping in his Cart he lay,
Some pilfring Villains stole his Team away;
Giles wakes and cries—What's here? a dickins, what?
Why, how now?—Am I Giles? or am I not?
If he, I've lost six Geldings, to my Smart;
If not,—odds buddikens, I've found a Cart.

When Death puts out our Flame, the Snuff will tell,
If we were Wax, or Tallow by the Smell.

At a great Pennyworth, pause a while.

As to his Wife, John minds St. Paul, He's one
That hath a Wife, and is as if he'd none.

Kings and Bears often worry their Keepers.

XII Mon. February hath xxviii days.

Lord, if our Days be *few,* why do we spend,
And lavish them to such an evil End?
Or, why, if they be *evil,* do we wrong
Our selves and thee, in wishing them so long?
Our Days decrease, our evils still renew,
We make them *ill,* thou kindly mak'st them *few.*

3. These lines, in correct English, were printed in *Gent. Mag.,* I (1731),
535.

If thou wouldst live long, live well; for Folly and Wickedness shorten Life.

> Prythee isn't Miss Cloe's a comical Case?
> She lends out her Tail, and she borrows her Face.

Trust thy self, and another shall not betray thee.

I Mon. March hath xxxi days.

> Thus with kind Words, 'squire Edward chear'd his Friend:
> Dear Dick! thou on my Friendship mayst depend;
> I know thy Fortune is but very scant;
> But, be assur'd, I'll ne'er see Dick in Want.
> Dick's soon confin'd—his Friend, no doubt, would free him:
> His Word he kept—in Want he ne'er would see him.

He that pays for Work before it's done, has but a pennyworth for twopence.

Historians relate, not so much what is done, as what they would have believed.

> O Maltster! break that cheating Peck; 'tis plain,
> When e'er you use it, you're a Knave in Grain.

II Mon. April hath xxx days.

> For's Country Codrus suffer'd by the Sword,
> And, by his Death, his Country's Fame restor'd;
> Caesar into his Mother's Bosom bare
> Fire, Sword, and all the Ills of civil War:
> Codrus confirm'd his Country's wholesome Laws;
> Caesar in Blood still justify'd his Cause;
> Yet following Kings ne'er 'dopted Codrus' Name,
> But Caesar, still, and Emperor's the same.

> Doll learning *propria quae maribus* without book,
> Like *Nomen crescentis genitivo* doth look.

Grace then thy House, and let not that grace thee.

Thou canst not joke an Enemy into a Friend; but thou may'st a Friend into an Enemy.

Eyes and Priests
Bear no Jests.

III Mon. May hath xxxi days.

> Think, bright Florella, when you see
>   The constant Changes of the Year,
> That nothing is from Ruin free,
>   And gayest Things must disappear.
> Think of your Beauties in their bloom,
>   The Spring of sprightly Youth improve;
> For cruel Age, alas, will come,
>   And then 'twill be too late to love.

He that falls in love with himself, will have no Rivals.

Let thy Child's first Lesson be Obedience, and the second may be what thou wilt.

Blessed is he that expects nothing, for he shall never be disappointed.

Rather go to bed supperless, than run in debt for a Breakfast.

IV Mon. June hath xxx days.

> On his late Deafness.
> Deaf, giddy, helpless, left alone,
> To all my Friends a Burthen grown,
> No more I hear a great Church Bell,
> Than if it rang out for my Knell:
> At Thunder now no more I start,
> Than at the whisp'ring of a F--t.
> Nay, what's incredible, alack!
> I hardly hear my Bridget's Clack.

Let thy Discontents be Secrets.

An infallible Remedy for the *Tooth-ach*, viz. Wash the Root of an aching Tooth, in *Elder Vinegar*, and let it dry half an hour in the Sun; after which it will never ach more. *Probatum est.*

> A Man of Knowledge like a rich Soil, feeds
> If not a world of Corn, a world of Weeds.

V Mon. July hath xxxi days.

> Says George to William, Neighbour, have a Care,
> Touch not that Tree—'tis sacred to Despair;
> Two Wives I had, but, ah! that Joy is past!
> Who breath'd upon those fatal Boughs their last.
> The best in all the Row, without Dispute,
> Says Will—Wou'd mine but bear such precious Fruit!
> When next you prune your Orchard, save for me,
> (I have a Spouse) one Cyon of that Tree.

A modern Wit is one of David's Fools.

No Resolution of Repenting hereafter, can be sincere.

> Pollio, who values nothing that's within,
> Buys Books as men hunt Beavers,—for their Skin.

Honour thy Father and Mother, i.e. Live so as to be an Honour to them tho' they are dead.

VI Mon. August hath xxxi days.

Ships sailing down Delaware Bay this Month, shall hear at ten Leagues Distance a confus'd rattling Noise, like a Shower of Hail on a Cake of Ice. Don't be frighted, good Passengers! The Sailors can inform you, that it's nothing but Lower County Teeth in the Ague. In a Southerly Wind you may hear it at Philadelphia. Witness G.L.M. *cum multis aliis.*

If thou injurest Conscience, it will have its Revenge on thee.

Hear no ill of a Friend, nor speak any of an Enemy.

Pay what you owe, and you'll know what's your own.

Be not niggardly of what costs thee nothing, as courtesy, counsel, and countenance.

Thirst after Desert, not Reward.

VII Mon. September hath xxx days.

> The Sun now clear, serene the golden Skies,
> Where'er you go, as fast the Shadow flies;
> A Cloud succeeds; the Sunshine now is o'er,
> The fleeting phantom fled, is seen no more;
> With your bright Day, its Progress too does end:
> See here vain Man! the Picture of thy Friend.

Beware of him that is slow to anger: He is angry for something, and will not be pleased for nothing.

No longer virtuous no longer free; is a Maxim as true with regard to a private Person as a Common-wealth.

> When Man and Woman die, as Poets sung,
> His Heart's the last part moves, her last, the tongue.

VIII Mon. October hath xxxi days.

> What Legions of Fables and whimsical Tales
> Pass current for Gospel where Priestcraft prevails!
> Our Ancestors thus were most strangely deceiv'd,
> What Stories and Nonsense for Truth they believ'd!
> But we their wise Sons, who these Fables reject,
> Ev'n Truth now-a-days, are too apt to suspect:
> From believing too much, the right Faith we let fall;
> So now we believe—'troth nothing at all.

Proclaim not all thou knowest, all thou owest, all thou hast, nor all thou canst.

Let our Fathers and Grandfathers be valued for *their* Goodness, ourselves for our own.

Industry need not wish.

Sin is not hurtful because it is forbidden but it is forbidden because it's hurtful.[4]

IX Mon. November hath xxx days.

> Pinchall, possessing Heaps of Wealth,
>   Lives miserably poor;
> He says, 'tis to preserve his Health,
>   But means by it, his Store.
> Let Freeman but the Wretch invite
>   To dine on Good-Cheer *gratis,*
> Then he will gorge, like half-starv'd Wight,
>   And cram his *Nunquam satis.*

Nor is a Duty beneficial because it is commanded, but it is commanded, because it's beneficial.

> A—, they say, has Wit; for what?
> For writing?—No; For writing not.

> George came to the Crown without striking a Blow.
> Ah! quoth the Pretender, would I could do so.

X Mon. December hath xxxi days.

>   In Travel, Pilgrims oft do ask, to know
> What *Miles* they've gone, and what they have to go:
> Their Way is tedious and their Limbs opprest,
> And their Desire is to be at rest.
> In Life's more tedious Journey, Man delays
> T'enquire out the Number of his Days:
> He cares, not he, how slow his Hours spend,
> The Journey's better than the Journey's End.

Love, and be lov'd.

4. For BF's use of this sentiment in his autobiography, see Par. Text edit., pp. 148, 232.

224

O Lazy-Bones! Dost thou think God would have given thee Arms and Legs, if he had not design'd thou should'st use them.

A Cure for Poetry,
Seven wealthy Towns contend for Homer, dead,
Thro' which the living Homer beg'd his Bread.

Great Beauty, great strength, and great Riches, are really and truly of no great Use; a right Heart exceeds all.

On the LAW.

Nigh Neighbour to the Squire, poor Sam complain'd
Of frequent Wrongs, but no Amends he gain'd.
Each Day his Gates thrown down, his Fences broke,
And injur'd still the more, the more he spoke;
At last, resolv'd his potent Foe to awe,
A Suit against him he began in Law;
Nine happy Terms thro' all the Forms he run,
Obtain'd his Cause—had Costs—and was undone.

A True PROGNOSTICATION, for 1739.

Courteous Readers,

Having consider'd the infinite Abuses arising from the false Prognostications published among you, made under the shadow of a Pot of Drink, or so, I have here calculated one of the most sure and unerring that ever was seen in black and white, as hereafter you'll find. For doubtless it is a heinous, foul and crying Sin, to deceive the poor gaping World, greedy of the Knowledge of Futurity, as we Americans all are.

Take Notice by the by, that having been at a great deal of pains in the Calculation, if you don't believe every Syllable, Jot and Tittle of it, you do me a great deal of wrong; for which either here or elsewhere, you may chance to be claw'd off with a Vengeance. A good Cowskin, Crabtree or Bulls pizzle may be plentifully bestow'd on your outward Man. You may snuff up your Noses as much as you please, 'tis all one for that.

Well however, come, snite[5] your Noses my little Children; and

5. Snite: blow or wipe one's nose.

225

you old doating Father Grey-Beards, pull out your best Eyes, on wi' your Barnacles, and carefully observe every Scruple of what I'm going to tell you.

Of the GOLDEN NUMBER.

The Golden Number, *non est inventus*. I cannot find it this Year by any Calculation I have made. I must content myself with a Number of Copper. No matter, go on.

Of the ECLIPSES this Year.

There are so many invisible Eclipses this Year, that I fear, not unjustly, our Pockets will suffer Inanition, be full empty, and our Feeling at a Loss. During the first visible Eclipse Saturn is retrograde: For which Reason the Crabs will go sidelong, and the Rope-makers backward. The Belly will wag before, and the A--- shall sit down first. Mercury will have his share in these Affairs, and so confound the Speech of People, that when a Pensilvanian would say PANTHER, he shall say PAINTER. When a New-Yorker thinks to say (THIS) he shall say (DISS) and the People in New-England and Cape-May will not be able to say (COW) for their lives, but will be forc'd to say (KEOW) by a certain involuntary Twist in the Root of their Tongues. No Connecticut-Man nor Marylander will be able to open his Mouth this Year, but (SIR) shall be the first or last Syllable he pronounces, and sometimes both. Brutes shall speak in many Places, and there will be above seven and twenty irregular Verbs made this Year, if Grammar don't interpose. Who can help these Misfortunes!

Of the DISEASES this Year.

This Year the Stone-blind shall see but very little; the Deaf shall hear but poorly; and the Dumb shan't speak very plain. And it's much, if my Dame Bridget talks at all this Year. Whole Flocks, Herds and Droves of Sheep, Swine and Oxen, Cocks and Hens, Ducks and Drakes, Geese and Ganders shall go to Pot; but the Mortality will not be altogether so great among Cats, Dogs and Horses. As for old Age, 'twill be incurable this Year, because of the Years past. And towards the Fall some People will be seiz'd with an unaccountable Inclination to roast and eat their own Ears: Should this be call'd Madness, Doctors? I think not.—But the worst Disease of all will be a certain most horrid, dreadful, malignant, catching, perverse and odious Malady, almost epidemical, insomuch that many shall run Mad upon it; I quake for very Fear when I think on't; for I assure you very few will escape this Disease; which is called by the learned Albumazar,[6] *Lacko'mony.*

Of the FRUITS of the EARTH.

I find that this will be a plentiful Year of all manner of good Things, to those who have enough; but the Orange Trees in Greenland will go near to fare the worse for the Cold. As for Oats, they'll be a great Help to Horses. I dare say there won't be much more Bacon than Swine. Mercury somewhat threatens our Parsley-beds, yet Parsly will be to be had for Money. Hemp will grow faster than the Children of this Age, and some will find there's but too much on't. As for Corn, Fruit, Cyder and Turnips, there never was such Plenty as will be now; if poor Folks may have their Wish.

Of the CONDITION of some Countries.

I foresee an universal Droughth this Year thro' all the Northern Colonies. Hence there will be *dry* Rice in Carolina, *dry* Tobacco in Virginia and Maryland, *dry* Bread in Pennsylvania and New-York; and, in New-England, *dry* Fish and *dry* Doctrine. *Dry* Throats there will be every-where; but then how pleasant it will be to drink cool Cyder! tho' some will tell you nothing is more contrary to Thirst. I believe it; and indeed, *Contraria contrariis curantur.*

R. SAUNDERS

Subscription to Christ Church

MS not found; reprinted from Benjamin Dorr, *A Historical Account of Christ Church, Philadelphia* (New York and Philadelphia, 1841), pp. 71–2.

Philadelphia, May 7th, 1739

Whereas, the Episcopal church of Philadelphia, having been long built, and much out of repair, as well as too small for the con-

6. Albumazar, ninth-century Arabian astronomer, whose name and work were known in seventeenth- and eighteenth-century England principally through Thomas Tomkis' play *Albumazar*, presented 1614, and reprinted and revived several times in the next century. Tomkis' play, reprinted in Robert

227

venient seating of the congregation, it was therefore resolved, by two several vestries, in the year seventeen hundred twenty-seven, that a sum of money should be raised by subscription, for erecting a new, larger and more commodious building; which good design, with much care and industry hath been carried on, the foundation of a steeple laid, and the body of the new church on the outside almost finished;[7] but the said subscription falling short, and insufficient to complete the same, the inside of the church remains unfinished, and many of the congregation yet unprovided with pews for themselves and families; which makes it necessary that some pews, a gallery, and other conveniences, should yet be added, as well as the whole finished; for which pious and good purpose, we whose names are hereunto subscribed, do promise to pay to the church wardens of the said church, or such others as shall be appointed to receive the same for the use aforesaid, the sums of money by us respectively subscribed. In witness whereof we have hereunto set our names the date above written.[8]

Dodsley's *Select Collection of Old Plays* (London, 1725), VII, was the inspiration and pattern for James Ralph's comedy *The Astrologer*, written in 1734 and produced in 1744. *DNB*.

7. For reference to events in the earlier history of the construction of Christ Church, see Dorr, *Historical Account*, pp. 58–67. A note on the location of BF's pew is in *PMHB*, III (1879), 230.

8. The subscription was signed by over 200 persons, of whom Dorr mentions only Governor George Thomas (£50), the rector Archibald Cummings (£20), William Till, Thomas Bourne, John Kearsley, Thomas Leech, Charles Willing, Peter Evans, Andrew Bradford, Thomas Lawrence, William Hellier, Samuel Hasell, William Bell, Richard Peters, BF, George McCall, Robert Assheton, James Humphreys, Richard Nixon, Joseph Shippen, and Joseph Redman. The amount of BF's subscription is not stated. For the connection of the Franklin family with Christ Church, see above, p. 188 n.

Four years later, so slowly did the subscriptions come in, the vestry ordered, April 16, 1743, "that, for the better accommodating the congregation with seats in the church, the west end gallery be forthwith run out, and built entirely over the west aisle." On August 27, 1744, the wardens reported that the church was "now happily finished" and that materials had been purchased and a contract made to rebuild the pews to provide additional seating. Dorr, *Historical Account*, pp. 83, 86.

From Josiah Franklin

MS not found; reprinted from Duane, *Works*, I, 4–5.

Loving Son.   Boston, May 26, 1739

As to the original of our name there is various opinions; some say that it came from a sort of title of which a book, that you bought when here, gives a lively account. Some think we are of a French extract, which was formerly called Franks; some of a free line; a line free from that vassalage which was common to subjects in days of old: some from a bird of long red legs.[9] Your uncle Benjamin made inquiry of one skilled in heraldry, who told him there is two coats of armour, one belonging to the Franklins of the north, and one to the Franklins of the west.[1]

9. Of the possible sources of the family name BF preferred to believe that it came from "franklin," a class of landowners of free but not noble birth, next below the gentry, and was assumed by his ancestors "for a Surname, when others took Surnames all over the Kingdom." Par. Text edit., p. 6; *OED*. The book that gave such a "lively account" of the Franklins' origin may have been Edward Waterhouse, *Fortescutus Illustratus. or A Commentary On that Nervous Treatise De Laudibus Legum Angliae* (London, 1663), p. 388: "And the old Dames in my memory were wont to call their husbands, *my Good Man:* later times more gentilized, discard that name from all mouthes, but those that are plebeian, and though it be enunciative of *Franklaynes,* that is, free-liers and owners of Land . . . yet it is now not much set by, though from this condition of them, there are many now grown into Families, now called *Franklin.* . . . For of this race of men who were and are but plain Good Man, and John, and Thomas, many in Kent, and Middlesex especially, besides *sparsim* in every severall County have been men of Knights estate, who could dispend many hundreds a year, and yet put up to raise Daughters portions; yea, so ambitious are many of them to be Gentlemen, that they by plentifull living obtaine the courtesie of being called Master, and written Gentlemen; and their posterities by being bred to Learning and Law, either in Universities, or Inns of Chancery and Court, turn perfect sparks, and listed gallants, companions to Knights and Esquires, and often adopted into those orders: And from this source, which is no ignoble one, have risen many of the now flourishing Gentry."

1. There were several armorial families in England with the surname Franklin or one of its variants, unrelated to each other, though some had branches in more than one county. Which of these families the person "skilled in heraldry" referred to cannot now be determined. BF continued to inquire about his family and their arms. In July 1742 he acquired a MS alphabet of arms (now in APS) listing many English families, in which the only Franklin arms

However our circumstances have been such as that it hath hardly been worth while to concern ourselves much about these things, any farther than to tickle the fancy a little.

The first that I can give account of, is my great grand father,[2] as it was a custom in those days among young men too many times to goe to seek their fortune, and in his travels he went upon liking to a taylor; but he kept such a stingy house, that he left him and travelled farther, and came to a smith's house, and coming on a fasting day, being in popish times, he did not like there the first day; the next morning the servant was called up at five in the morning, but after a little time came a good toast and good beer, and he found good housekeeping there; he served and learned the trade of a smith.

In queen Mary's days, either his wife, or my grandmother, by father's side, informed my father that they kept their bible fastened under the top of a joint-stool that they might turn up the book and read in the bible, that when any body came to the dore they turned up the stool for fear of the aparitor, for if it

---

described seem to be those of Franklyn of Moore Park, Hertfordshire. BF adopted arms sometime before 1751, which Anthony R. Wagner, Richmond Herald, in a letter to the editors, Dec. 30, 1958, has tentatively identified as those of the Franklin or Frankelyn family of Skipton-in-Craven, Yorkshire, with branches in Bedfordshire and London. The editors, however, have found no connection between this family and BF's ancestors. Mr. Wagner describes these arms as: "Argent on a Bend between two lions' heads erased Gules langued Azure a Dolphin between two Doves Or collared Azure. . . . The accompanying crest was a lucy's head Or erased Gules between two Olive branches Vert." BF's somewhat less formal description appears in an advertisement in *Pa. Gaz.*, June 20, 1751: "Lost . . . a silver seal, with a Coat of Arms engrav'd, containing two Lions heads, two Doves and a Dolphin." Wax impressions of BF's arms, used in sealing his correspondence or attesting his signature on official documents, survive; some printed forms, such as passports issued during his residence in France, also carry an engraved representation. See illustration on facing page. Other members of his family also used the arms for such purposes as a bookplate and a tombstone (Paul L. Ford, *The Many-Sided Franklin*, N.Y., 1899, p. 2; *Heraldic Jour.*, II, 1866, 97, III, 1867, 67), but when his nephew Peter Mecom proposed to stamp them on crown soap, BF drew the line. BF to Jane Mecom, May 30, 1757.

2. Thomas Francklyne (*fl.* 1563–73; Genealogy: A).

THE FRANKLIN ARMS

Above: From a passport printed by Benjamin Franklin

Below: John Franklin's Bookplate

was discovered, they would be in hazard of their lives.[3] My grandfather was a smith also,[4] and settled at Eton [sic] in Northamptonshire, and he was imprisoned a year and a day on suspicion of his being the author of some poetry that touched the character of some great man. He had only one son and one daughter; my grandfather's name was Henry, my father's name was Thomas,[5] my mother's name was Jane. My father was born at Ecton or Eton, Northamptonshire, on the 18th of October, 1598; married to Miss Jane White, niece to Coll. White, of Banbury, and died in the 84th year of his age. There was nine children of us who were happy in our parents, who took great care by their instructions and pious example to breed us up in a religious way. My eldest brother had but one child,[6] which was married to one Mr. Fisher, at Wallingborough, in Northamptonshire. The town was lately burnt down,[7] and whether she was a sufferer or not I cannot tell, or whether she be living or not. Her father dyed worth fifteen hundred pounds, but what her circumstances are now I know not. She hath no child. If you by the freedom of your office, makes it more likely to convey a letter to her, it would be acceptable to me. There is also children of brother John and sister Morris,[8] but I hear nothing from them, and they write not to me, so that I know not where to find them. I have been again to about seeing . . . .[9] but have mist

3. In the autobiography BF says he had this story from his uncle Benjamin. Par. Text edit., p. 14.

4. Henry Franklyn (1573–1631; A.5).

5. Thomas Franklin (1598–1682; A.5.2).

6. Thomas Franklin (1637–1702; A.5.2.1) and Mary Franklin Fisher (1673–1758; A.5.2.1.1).

7. Wellingborough was almost totally destroyed by fire, 1738. A letter from Benjamin Franklin the Elder, March 17, 1724, referring to an earlier fire that destroyed 44 houses in the town, is printed in facsimile in Ford, *Many-Sided Franklin*, p. 92.

8. John Franklin (1643–1691; A.5.2.3) and Hannah Franklin Morris (1654–1712; A.5.2.8). Josiah Franklin, Jan. 11, 1743/4, wrote to a relative, of whom he had heard through BF, and who he believed was his brother John's grandson Thomas (A.5.2.3.1.1). MS, Boston Pub. Lib. In England years later BF established direct contact with this Thomas Franklin and his daughter Sarah, who resided for some time in BF's London home in the 1760s.

9. So in Duane.

of being informed. We received yours, and are glad to hear poor Jammy[1] is recovered so well. Son John received the letter, but is so busy just now that he cannot write you an answer, but will do the best he can.

Now with hearty love to, and prayer for you all, I rest your affectionate father   JOSIAH FRANKLIN

Ledger D, 1739–47

MS Account Book: American Philosophical Society

Ledger D, like Ledger A & B (see above, I, 172), throws a fitful light on Franklin's income, especially from his printing business, and contains incidental information, usually trivial but sometimes significant, on the purchases of some 900 of his customers. A tall, narrow book of 400 pages, bound in parchment, Ledger D contains accounts of credit sales but relatively few records of payments. The entries were presumably transferred from a shop book or journal by a clerk, although there are some by Franklin and a few by his wife. The earliest are dated July 25, 1739; entries are especially frequent for the next three or four years; and almost cease after 1747; at some time during this period Franklin transferred to this ledger other charges, principally for advertisements, from another book. Before he sailed for England in 1757 he collected many outstanding debts; back in America in 1762 and 1763, he collected others; and in 1786, after his return from France, he reviewed his ledger once more, transferring "Every Accompt whereof settlement is necessary" to a Ledger E, which has not been found.[2] The index pages in the front refer not only to Ledger D, but also to another, later, set of accounts; so that not all the names in the index of Ledger D will be found in the body of the volume. An example is: "Braddock General See his Account posted Oct 1755 in Daybook."

The charges recorded here are for the usual printing office wares— paper, ink, legal forms, sealing wax, pasteboard, quills, lampblack, "fountain pens," and books. Whitefield's Journals and Sermons sold well, especially in 1740 and 1741; and there was a steady market for hymnals, testaments, dictionaries, grammars, spellers, almanacs, and collections of the province laws. "Revd Mullinburg Dutch Parson"

1. James Franklin, Jr., BF's nephew (c. 1730–1762; C.11.4), whom he educated and taught the printer's trade.
2. On Ledger E, see above, p. 179 n.

buys a copy of Watts's Sermons; Dr. John Bard is charged £2 for "10 Pictures"; and the painter Hesselius, a regular customer, buys "A Fire-place," which cost £5. On the morning of February 16, 1741, when Mrs. Franklin was in the shop, the *General Magazine* came from the press, and some twenty citizens, led by the Proprietor and the governor, bought copies. The sale of "A Milk Pott," "Alum, Brimstone & Coperas," "¼ Kentle Fish," and "15 lbs. 14 oz. of Feathers" may represent payments in kind, which Franklin disposed of as quickly as possible, or they may have been articles purchased to accommodate a country customer. There are hundreds of five-shilling charges for *Gazette* advertisements, usually for sales, runaway servants, stray horses, lost or stolen property. The following account is typical:

The Honorable James Logan Eqr.

November 1, 1742	for Homer with Barns note 4° Vols	3	10	0
Jan. 24, 1743/4	Law Book in Sheets	1	10	0
	See Fol. 76: Advertisements Two		10	0
April 18, 1744	For Pantheon		8	0
Dec. 17, 1745	Fr Cordery 5s.		5	0
	From Work Book			
1738 Sept. 21	For Advt. Gazette No. 510 Servt run J. Brewer		5	0
Oct. 26	For Do No. 515 Book lost		5	0
1740. Nov. 27	For Do No. 624 Stray Horse		5	0
1743 Oct. 27	For Do No. 776 Chaise Horse		5	0
	For Do Single 200		6	0

Ledger D illustrates Franklin's dealings with many officers and official bodies—the governments and governors of Pennsylvania, New Jersey, and Delaware, the mayor and Council of Philadelphia, the General Post Office. He did much of the printing for the Association of 1747, adding to his reckoning, "Memo. I charge nothing for the printing I did myself, viz. 2000 Plain Truths, 500 Association Papers, 1000 Lottery Schemes, Tickets, &c. for the first Lottery, with paper &c., amounting in the whole to £52. 5. 0 at the common prices." Of particular interest are Franklin's accounts with a score of fellow printers and bookbinders, including Andrew Bradford of Philadelphia, William Bradford of New York, William Daniell of Jamaica, James Davis of North Carolina, his sister-in-law Ann Franklin of Newport, who was one of his best customers for *Poor Richard's Almanack*, Jonas Green of Annapolis, William Hunter of Williamsburg, Samuel

Kneeland of Boston, James Parker of Woodbridge, N.J., William Parks of Williamsburg, Christopher Saur, the German printer of Germantown, and William Strahan and Thomas Osborne, both of London. "Count Zensendorph" made a large payment in advance "for Paper & Printing several Dutch Pamphlets" in 1742.

A few entries have personal interest. Among the accounts Franklin kept meticulously with his various relatives is one that shows how much he advanced for the nursing and funeral expenses of his brother-in-law John Croker's wife. And when the barber George Cunningham settled his bill, the two men made a practical though unusual contract: "Agreed 11 Sept 1750 to shave B Franklin's Head & Face once a Fortnight, and dress his Wig as often as he wants it, for the Gazette."

Ledger D has been fully described, with quotation of most of the significant accounts, in George Simpson Eddy, *Account Books Kept by Benjamin Franklin. Ledger "D," 1739–1747* (N.Y., 1929).

From Simon Meredith[3]   ALS: American Philosophical Society

Sir   July 29 1739
    Please to let my Son Hugh Meredith have the Sum of Eight pounds and place the Same to the Account of your Real Friend And very Humble Servant   SIMON MEREDITH

To Mr. Benjamin Franklin Postmaster in Philadelphia

[*Receipted:*] Receiv'd the above Eight Pounds per me
July 30. 1739   HUGH MEREDITH

[*Receipted:*] Borrowed and receiv'd also of Benjamin Franklin Six pounds more per me   HUGH MEREDITH
£6. —. —.

---

3. Father of BF's former partner, Hugh Meredith. See above, I, 175 n.

From Alexander Spotswood[4]

MS not found; printed in *The Pennsylvania Gazette*, December 11, 1740.

Sir,[5]   Germanna, Octob. 12. 1739

The Part which your Predecessor, Mr. Andrew Bradford, has acted with respect to the Post-Office Accompts, *is no longer to be born with*. The Deputy Post-Masters in Great-Britain account every two Months with the General Post-Office there; and I am obliged every half Year to have the Accounts of the General Post-Office in America made up: But I have not been able to obtain any Account from Mr. Bradford of the Philadelphia Office, from Mid-summer 1734, notwithstanding all the *pressing Demands* that the Comptroller has been *continually* making upon him for *so many Years past*. Wherefore I now *peremptorily direct*, that, upon receipt hereof, you commence Suit against him, without hearkning any more to his *trifling Excuses* and *fallacious Promises*.[6] If he lays any Stress on the Reputation of a Man of Truth and Sincerity, he must *blush* upon a Trial, before his Towns-Men, to have his Letters produced, continually pleading *Sickness*, for his not sending his Accompts: Whereas, upon Enquiry, I am well assured, that, for these two Years past, he has appeared abroad in as good State of Health, as ever he used to

4. Alexander Spotswood (1676–1740), lieutenant colonel in the War of the Spanish Succession, wounded at Blenheim and captured at Oudenarde; as lieutenant governor of Virginia, 1710–22, he was especially and energetically concerned with Indian policy, defense, and western settlement. Appointed deputy postmaster general for North America and the West Indies, 1730, he extended the regular postal service from the north to Williamsburg and increased its efficiency. Just before his death he was appointed major general and second-in-command of the expedition against Cartagena. *DAB;* Leonidas Dodson, *Alexander Spotswood, Governor of Colonial Virginia, 1710–1722* (Phila., 1932); see below, p. 287.

5. BF made this letter public in the course of a quarrel with Bradford and Webbe over their rival magazines. See below, p. 267. The emphasis of the printed version has been retained, though it was probably supplied by BF and was not in Spotswood's MS.

6. Spotswood had removed Bradford from the postmastership of Philadelphia in 1737 because of neglect. BF employed John Webbe to bring the suit that Spotswood ordered. For the operation of the Philadelphia post office, see above, pp. 178–83. Anna J. DeArmond, *Andrew Bradford, Colonial Printer* (Newark, Del., 1949), pp. 33, 105, 228–32, suggests what is probably all that can be said in Bradford's defense.

be. Such an Imposition I think ought not to be passed over, without some Mark of my Resentment; and *therefore* I now *direct,* that you no longer *suffer to be carried by the Post any of his News-Papers, or Letters directed to him, without his paying** the Postage thereof:* Which you are to observe, until farther Orders in that Behalf, from, Sir, Your most humble Servant,

To Mr. Franklin   A. Spotswood

Extracts from the Gazette, 1739

Printed in *The Pennsylvania Gazette*, January 4 to December 27, 1739.

[ADVERTISEMENT] Benjamin Franklin, Printer, is removed from the House he lately dwelt in, four Doors nearer the River, on the same side of the Street.   [January 11]

We hear from the Head of Timber-Creek in the Jerseys, That a Woman there has lately had Five Children, all born alive, within the space of 11 Months, by two Husbands. [January 25]

[ADVERTISEMENT] THE FRENCH TONGUE Compleatly Taught, in the most easy and expeditious Manner; by a Person who has for many Years past taught the same with great Success both in the West-Indies, and in London. He may be spoke with every Day at the Post-Office; and waits on Gentlemen and Ladies at their respective Houses, at convenient Hours.   [February 15]

[ADVERTISEMENT] Stolen on the 15th Instant, by one William Lloyd, out of the House of Benj. Franklin, an half-worn Sagathee Coat lin'd with Silk, four fine homespun Shirts, a fine Holland Shirt ruffled at the Hands and Bosom, a pair of black broadcloth Breeches new seated and lined with Leather, two pair of good worsted Stockings, one of a dark colour, and the other a lightish blue, a coarse Cambrick Handkerchief, mark'd with an F in red Silk, a new pair of Calf skin Shoes, a Boy's new Castor Hat, and sundry other Things.

*The Privilege of Free-Postage was allow'd Mr. Bradford, *on Condition* of his acquitting himself *fairly* of the Office, and *doing Justice* to the Revenue. [*Franklin's footnote.*]

N.B. The said Lloyd pretends to understand Latin and Greek, and has been a School-Master; He is an Irishman, about 30 Years of Age, tall and slim: Had on a lightish colour'd Great Coat, red Jacket, a pair of black silk Breeches, an old felt Hat too little for him, and sewed on the side of the Crown with white Thread, and an old dark colour'd Wig: but may perhaps wear some of the stolen Cloaths above mentioned.

Whoever secures the said Thief so that he may be brought to Justice, shall have *Thirty Shillings* Reward and reasonable Charges, paid by   B. FRANKLIN
[February 22]

We hear that Tuesday Night last, a young Dutchman was married to an old Dutchwoman, who was known to have Money. They had a Fiddle at the Wedding, and when the Bride was about to Dance, the Bridegroom told her he was oblig'd to go out a little Way and would return in a short Time. She danc'd 'till it was late, and then he not appearing, she went to look for him in the Bed-Chamber; where she found to her great Surprize that he had been and taken away her Money, and he has not since been heard of.   [March 22]

We hear from Pensoken, that on the first Inst. one John Collis, being reproach'd by his Acquaintance for suing a Debtor who was unable to pay him, was so stung with Remorse, that he went voluntarily into the River and drowned himself, in about two or three foot Depth of Water.   [April 12]

[ADVERTISEMENT] Great Variety of MAPS and PRINTS Sold by B. Franklin.   [April 19]

[ADVERTISEMENT] CANARY WINE, sweet Oyl, and Lime-juice by the Gallon or lesser quantity, to be Sold by Hugh Roberts, in Second-Street, Philadelphia. Also fine Salt by wholesale or retail.
[May 10]

Yesterday one James Johnson, met a Man riding into Town, who (in Company with another Man, not yet taken) robb'd him in his Journey from North-Carolina to this Place of upwards of *Three Hundred* Pounds, Carolina Money, and a Note for *Fifty* Pounds Sterling; and laid hold of him: The Highwayman beg'd not to be expos'd, and pretended he had marry'd a rich Widow in Town, and would immediately refund the Money, if the other would go with him to his House; on this Pretence he led him to the outside of the Town, then leap'd on his Horse and made his Escape down to the Lower-Ferry, but finding himself closely pursued, and the Boat not ready to go over, he made into the Neck, where he was taken some Hours after; and after an Examination before a Magistrate, committed to Prison.

[May 31]

We are assur'd that the Man now in Prison in this City for a Robbery committed in Carolina, is the same, who under various Names has been guilty of a great Number of Cheats and Rogueries in this and the neighbouring Provinces for several Years past.

[June 14]

[ADVERTISEMENT] Lost on Monday last, somewhere in this City, the Sheath of an Hanger, with a Silver Tip and Hook, and a Knife and Fork with Buck-Horn Handles, fix'd near the Top of it. Whoever brings it to the Post-Office, shall be handsomely rewarded.

[June 14]

[ADVERTISEMENT] Lately found a Pocket Book, with a Bond and other Papers in it; the Owner applying to the Printer hereof, and paying the Charge of this Advertisement, may hear of it again.

[June 21]

[ADVERTISEMENT] Intending with the Leave of my Master, to collect and print the poetical Writings of my deceas'd Father Aquila Rose, I desire all Persons who are possess'd of any of those Pieces in Manuscript, to bring or send them to me at the New-Printing-Office in Market-Street; and I promise to give, in Return for each Manuscript, one of the Printed Collections, assoon as they shall be finished.[7]

JOSEPH ROSE

[June 28]

7. Aquila Rose, characterized by BF as "an ingenious young Man of excellent Character much respected in the Town, Clerk of the Assembly, and a pretty Poet," was Andrew Bradford's journeyman. He also operated a

On the 30th of May past, the Children, Grand-Children and Great-Grand-Children of Richard Buffington, senior, to the Number of One Hundred and Fifteen, met together at his House in Chester County, as also his Nine Sons- and Daughters-in-law, and Twelve Great-Grand-Children-in-law. The old Man is from Great Marle upon the Thames, in Buckinghamshire in Old-England, aged about 85, and is still hearty, active, and of perfect Memory. His eldest Son, now in the Sixtieth Year of his Age, was the first born of English Descent in this Province.   [July 5]

Mr. Franklin,
    The following is a Paragraph contain'd in a Letter I received lately from my Brother Thomas Bond, in Paris, dated Feb. 20. 1738, 9: As I think it will in no small Measure confirm the Character of the Seneca Snake-Root, set forth by Dr. Tennent,[8] com-

---

ferry over the Schuylkill. Par. Text edit., p. 66; *PMHB*, III (1879), 156. He died June 24, 1723, and Bradford's father, to whom BF applied in New York for a job in September, thinking his son might need a journeyman in place of Rose, sent the runaway apprentice to Philadelphia. The position was already filled, so Andrew Bradford directed BF to Keimer, who at that moment was composing an elegy on Rose (printed in Samuel Hazard, *Register of Pa.*, II, Nov. 8, 1828, pp. 262–3). BF subsequently took Rose's son Joseph as an apprentice; by 1741 young Rose seems to have been foreman of the shop. *PMHB*, III (1879), 114–15. His advertisement did not locate all his father's poems, many of which his mother had carelessly lent to friends; but enough were recovered to make a thin volume, *Poems On several Occasions*. Though dated 1740, it was advertised as "just published" in *Pa. Gaz.*, Aug. 13, 1741.

    8. Seneca rattlesnake root (*Polygala senega*) was strongly advocated by John Tennent (see above, p. 155 n), who claimed, in *An Essay on the Pleurisy* (Williamsburg, Va., 1736), to have used it successfully in treating inflammatory diseases of the chest. So convinced was he of its therapeutic value that he arranged with certain apothecaries to provide it to patients gratis. *Va. Gaz.*, Nov. 5, 1736. Most physicians, however, denounced Tennent's claims as baseless theorizing; the dispute was carried into the columns of the *Virginia Gazette*. Tennent went to England, 1737, where he pressed his arguments for the snakeroot; and he submitted an account of it, with specimens, to the French Academy of Sciences. A committee composed of Lémery and Jussieu (probably Antoine Jussieu, professor of botany in the Jardin du Roi) reported favorably, and the Academy arranged to continue its experiments. *Histoire de l'Académie des Sciences*, 1739, 135–9. In November 1738 the Virginia House of Burgesses rejected Tennent's petition for a reward for having made his discovery public, but on recommendation of the Governor and

mon Justice to that Gentleman obliges me to make it known to the Publick. PHINEAS BOND[9]

"The Seneca Snake-Root, was sent from Virginia to Mr. Jussieu, Physician and Professor of Botany to the King, with a Recommendation and the Method of Use in a Pleurisy, and has been frequently tried by him and many others in that Disorder with surprizing Success, and is in great Esteem: He is a Man of Great Reputation and Learning, and told me this himself." [July 26]

[ADVERTISEMENT] A few Days past was lost, a Magnifying Glass set in a Cup of Wood about the Bigness of a Taylor's Thimble. The Finder shall be well rewarded upon bringing or sending it to the Printer. [August 2]

This Gazette Numb. 564 begins the 11th Year since its first Publication; And whereas some Persons have taken it from the Beginning, and others for 7 or 8 Years, without paying me one Farthing, I do hereby give Notice to all who are upwards of one Year in Arrear, that if they do not make speedy Payment, I shall discontinue the Papers to them, and take some proper Method of Recovering my Money. B. FRANKLIN

N.B. No new Subscriber will be taken in for the future without Payment for the first half Year advanc'd. [October 4]

We hear from Macunja in Bucks County, that last Week two

Council the House reconsidered and grudgingly voted £100 currency. Disgusted with this parsimonious recompense, Tennent addressed a "Memorial and Remonstrance" to the Northern Colonies (printed in *Pa. Gaz.*, July 19, 26, Aug. 2, 1739), and once more quit Virginia for London. BF printed "Dr. Tennent's infallible Cure for the Pleurisy" in *Poor Richard's Almanack* for 1740 (see below, pp. 254–5).

9. Phineas Bond (1717–1773) and his older brother Thomas (1713–1784) were both original members of APS, common councilors, trustees of the College of Philadelphia, and physicians to the Pennsylvania Hospital, of which Thomas was, with BF, the principal founder. Thomas studied medicine in Britain and France in 1738–39. *DAB;* Elizabeth H. Thomson, "Thomas Bond, 1713–84: First Professor of Clinical Medicine in the American Colonies," *Jour. Med. Educ.*, XXXIII (1958), 614–24; Thomas Bond to John Bartram, Feb. 20, 1739, Darlington, *Memorials*, p. 316.

Brothers, the youngest about 10 Years of Age, and the eldest about 18, both of them deaf and dumb, went out into the Woods together, where the eldest cut the Throat of the youngest.
[October 18]

Last Week the Rev. Mr. Whitefield[1] landed from London at Lewes-Town in Sussex County, where he preach'd; and arrived in this City on Friday Night; on Sunday, and every Day since he has preach'd in the Church: And on Monday he designs (God willing) to set out for New-York, and return hither the Week after, and then proceed by Land thro' Maryland, Virginia and Carolina to Georgia.
[November 8]

[ADVERTISEMENT] To Be Sold, At the House of the Rev. Mr. Whitefield, In Second-Street (the same in which Capt. Blair, lately dwelt) the following Goods: Being the Benefactions

1. George Whitefield (1714–1770), evangelist; educated at Oxford, where he met Charles and John Wesley and joined their movement, 1735; ordained Anglican deacon, 1736; priest, 1739. He visited Georgia, 1738, and made a second visit to America, 1739–41, when he established an orphan asylum in Georgia, proposed a school for Negroes in Pennsylvania, and, as in England, had extraordinary success preaching in fields and meeting-houses, Anglican churches being generally closed to him. For an account of his strenuous and effective evangelistic visits to Philadelphia in the fall of 1739, see *A Continuation Of the Reverend Mr. Whitefield's Journal from his Embarking after the Embargo. To His Arrival at Savannah in Georgia* (Phila., 1740), pp. 54–92. Whitefield visited Philadelphia again three times in 1740 (see below, pp. 284, 290), and in that year a hall was erected in the city for his use and that of any other Protestant minister who might wish to use it; it was transferred to the trustees of the Academy and College of Philadelphia in 1750. Of his preaching BF wrote, "It was wonderful to see the Change soon made in the Manners of our Inhabitants; from being thoughtless or indifferent about Religion, it seem'd as if all the World were growing Religious; so that one could not walk thro' the Town in an Evening without Hearing Psalms sung in different Families of every Street." Par. Text edit., p. 266. BF printed Whitefield's journals, sermons, and life (as well as controversial pieces against him), and was a strong supporter of his philanthropies. "He us'd indeed sometimes to pray for my Conversion, but never had the Satisfaction of believing that his Prayers were heard. Ours was a mere civil Friendship, sincere on both Sides, and lasted to his Death." *Ibid.*, p. 270. Whitefield returned to America in 1744–48, 1751–52, 1754–55, 1763–65, 1769–70. *DAB; DNB;* Tyerman, *Whitefield;* Stuart C. Henry, *George Whitefield: Wayfaring Witness* (N.Y., 1957).

241

of Charitable People In England, towards Building an Orphan-House In Georgia:

Brass Candlesticks, Snuffers and snuff-Dishes, four, six, eight, ten and twenty-penny Nails, Pidgeon, Duck and Goose Shot, bar Lead, Pistol Powder in quarter and half Barrels, English Duck *Numb.* 1, 2, 3, and 4, English Cordage, Ratling, Worming, Marline and Spun-yarn, Ruggs and Blankets, Duffills strip'd, Drills for Bed-sacking, seven eighths and three quarter Garlix, white Roles, white Hessins, Russia Hempen Ditto; narrow Lawns, Scotch Cloth, cotton Romalls, Seirsuckers, white Dimities, Carradaries, Cherconees, long Romalls, colour'd Ginghams with Trimings, Gorgoroons black, black Persian Taffities, strip'd Linseys, Swanskin Bays, broad Cloth, Shalloons, long Ells, Buttons, Buckrams, and sewing-Silk.   [November 8]

On Thursday last, the Rev. Mr. Whitefield began to preach from the Court-House-Gallery in this City, about six at Night, to near 6000 People before him in the Street, who stood in an awful Silence to hear him; and this continued every Night, 'till Sunday. On Monday he set out for New-York, and was to preach at Burlington in his Way going, and in Bucks County coming back. Before he returns to England he designs (God willing) to preach the Gospel in every Province in America, belonging to the English. On Monday the 26th he intends to set out for Annapolis.   [November 15]

The Rev. Mr. Whitefield having given me Copies of his Journals and Sermons, with Leave to print the same; I propose to publish them with all Expedition, if I find sufficient Encouragement.[2] The Sermons will make two Volumes in twelves, on the same Character with this Advertisement, and the Journals two

2. Whitefield recorded in his journal, Nov. 28, 1739, that "one of the Printers," i.e., BF, had told him that he had already received 200 subscriptions for the journals and sermons. The bibliographical history of Whitefield's journals for 1737–41 is confused. Several men in England and America, BF among them, printed or reprinted various installments; printings of some sections are known today only by contemporary advertisements; occasionally the imprint date on a title page is demonstrably incorrect; in one or two instances page numbering differs between two copies of what otherwise appears to have been the same printing. The following is a list of

George Whitefield

more, which shall be delivered to Subscribers at 2s. each Volume bound. Those therefore who are enclined to encourage this

---

printings by BF of which surviving copies have been located. They are arranged according to the periods they cover.

1. [Dec. 28, 1737–Feb. 19, 1738] *Journal of a Voyage from London to Gibraltar by Geo. Whitefield, A.B. Of Pembroke-College, Oxford. Containing Many curious Observations, and Edifying Reflections, on the several Occurrences that happen'd in the Voyage. The Sixth Edition.* Philadelphia: . . . 1740. Evans 4630.

2. [Feb. 20–May 7, 1738] *A Journal of a Voyage from Gibraltar to Georgia. By Geo. Whitefield, A.B. Of Pembroke-College, Oxford. Containing Many curious Observations, and Edifying Reflections, on the several Occurrences that happen'd in the Voyage.* Philadelphia, . . . 1739. Evans 4453.

3. [May 7–Dec. 8, 1738] *A Continuation Of the Reverend Mr. Whitefield's Journal from His Arrival at Savannah, to His Return to London.* Philadelphia, . . . 1739. Evans 4453.

4. [Dec. 8, 1738–June 2, 1739] *A Continuation . . . from His Arrival at London, to His Departure from thence, on His Way to Georgia.* Philadelphia, . . . 1739. Evans 4453.

(Nos. 2, 3, and 4 bear the imprint date 1739 but were actually delivered to subscribers May 26, 1740 (see below, p. 286). These three installments were continuously paged and bound together. Separates of each also survive, with pagination unchanged.)

5. [June 4–Aug. 3, 1739] *A Continuation . . . During the Time he was detained in England, by the Embargo. Vol. II.* Philadelphia: . . . 1740. Evans 4633.

6. [Aug. 4, 1739–Jan. 10, 1740] *A Continuation . . . from His Embarking after the Embargo. To His Arrival at Savannah in Georgia.* Philadelphia: . . . 1740. Evans 4633.

(Nos. 5 and 6 were continuously paged and bound together. Publication of the volume was announced for August 18 (see below, p. 289). Separates of no. 6 also survive with the pages renumbered.)

7. [Jan. 11–June 10, 1740] *A Continuation . . . from A few Days after his Arrival at Georgia, to His second Return thither from Pennsylvania.* Philadelphia: . . . 1740. Evans 4636. Advertised in *Pa. Gaz.*, Nov. 27, 1740, as "just published."

8. [June 25–Oct. 29, 1740] *A Continuation . . . from A few Days after his Arrival at Savannah, June the Fourth, to His leaving Stanford, the last Town in New-England, October 29, 1740.* Philadelphia: . . . M,DCC,XLI. Evans 4846. Advertised in *Pa. Gaz.*, March 19, 1741, as "just published."

Some bibliographers have erroneously listed a 1741 printing by BF of Whitefield's journal for Oct. 29, 1740–March 11, 1741. BF advertised this "Continuation" for sale but made no claim to have printed it. *Pa. Gaz.*, Nov. 5, 1741.

Work, are desired speedily to send in their Names to me, that I may take Measures accordingly.   B. FRANKLIN
[November 15]

On Friday last the Rev. Mr. Whitefield, arrived here, with his Friends from New-York, where he preach'd eight Times; and on his Return hither preach'd at Elizabeth-Town, Brunswick, Maidenhead, Trenton, Neshaminy and Abingdon. He has preach'd twice every Day in the Church to great Crowds, except Tuesday, when he preach'd at German-Town, from a Balcony to about 5000 People in the Street: And last Night the Crowd was so great to hear his farewel Sermon, that the Church could not contain one half, whereupon they withdrew to Society-Hill, where he preach'd from a Balcony to a Multitude, computed at not less than 10,000 People. He left this City to day, and is to preach at Chester; to morrow at Willings-Town, Saturday at New-Castle, Sunday at Whiteclay-Creek, and so proceed on his Way to Georgia, thro' Maryland, Virginia and Carolina. [November 29]

On Thursday last the Rev. Mr. Whitefield, left this City, and was accompany'd to Chester by about 150 Horse, and preach'd there to about 7000 People; on Friday he preach'd twice at Willings-Town to about 5000; on Saturday at New-Castle to about 2500, and the same Evening at Christian-Bridge to about 3000; on Sunday at Whiteclay-Creek he preach'd twice, resting about half an Hour between the Sermons, to about 8000, of whom about 3000 'tis computed came on Horse-back. It rain'd most of the Time and yet they stood in the open Air: On Monday he was to preach at North-East, and then proceed directly for Annapolis.   [December 6]

JUST PUBLISH'D, POOR RICHARD'S ALMANACKS, for the Year 1740.[3] Containing besides the usual Matters, many pleasant Verses, merry Jokes and wise Sayings, with a Letter to the Author from Titan Leeds, deceas'd; also Dr. Tennent's infallible Method of Cure in the Pleurisy by the Seneka Rattle-Snake Root.

---

3. The *Gazette*, Nov. 15, had announced that the almanacs would be published "on Saturday next," i.e., Nov. 17. "A Third Edition" was announced as "just published" in *Pa. Gaz.*, Jan. 10, 1740.

Note. As the Plant is very plainly described, and may be found in Pensilvania, the Jerseys, New-York, &c. and as the Method of using it is particularly laid down, it is not doubted but this Almanack may be a Means of saving the Lives of Thousands. Sold by B. Franklin at the New Printing-Office, Market street. Price 3*s.* 6*d.* per Dozen, or 5*d.* Single. [December 6]

Thursday last died, Mrs. Dorcas Bradford, Wife of Mr. Andrew Bradford, Printer; and on Saturday Evening was decently interred. Her Death is much lamented by all that knew her.

[December 27]

PHILADELPHIA: Printed by B. FRANKLIN, Post-Master, at the New Printing-Office near the Market. *Price* 10*s.* a Year. Where *Advertisements* are taken in, and *Book-Binding* is done reasonably, in the best Manner.

Poor Richard, 1740

Poor Richard, 1740. An Almanack For the Year of Christ 1740, . . . By Richard Saunders, Philom. Philadelphia: Printed and sold by B. Franklin, at the New Printing-Office near the Market. (Yale University Library)

Courteous Reader,   October 7. 1739

You may remember that in my first Almanack, published for the Year 1733, I predicted the Death of my dear Friend Titan Leeds, Philomat. to happen that Year on the 17th Day of October, 3 h. 29 m. P.M. The good Man, it seems, died accordingly: But W.B. and A.B.[4] have continued to publish Almanacks in his Name ever since; asserting for some Years that he was still living; At length when the Truth could no longer be conceal'd from the World, they confess his Death in their Almanack for 1739, but pretend that he died not till last Year, and that before his Departure he had furnished them with Calculations for 7 Years to come. Ah, *My Friends,* these are poor Shifts and thin Disguises; of which indeed I should have taken little or no Notice, if you had not at the same time accus'd me as a false Predictor; an Aspersion that the more affects me, as my whole Livelyhood depends on a contrary Character.

4. William and Andrew Bradford.

245

But to put this Matter beyond Dispute, I shall acquaint the World with a Fact, as strange and surprizing as it is true; being as follows, viz.

On the 4th Instant, towards midnight, as I sat in my little Study writing this Preface, I fell fast asleep; and continued in that Condition for some time, without dreaming any thing, to my Knowledge. On awaking, I found lying before me the following Letter, viz.

"Dear Friend Saunders,

"My Respect for you continues even in this separate State, and I am griev'd to see the Aspersions thrown on you by the Malevolence of avaricious Publishers of Almanacks, who envy your Success. They say your Prediction of my Death in 1733 was false, and they pretend that I remained alive many Years after. But I do hereby certify, that I did actually die at that time, precisely at the Hour you mention'd, with a Variation only of 5 min. 53 sec. which must be allow'd to be no great matter in such Cases. And I do farther declare that I furnish'd them with no Calculations of the Planets Motions, &c. seven Years after my Death, as they are pleased to give out: so that the Stuff they publish as an Almanack in my Name is no more mine than 'tis yours.

"You will wonder perhaps, how this Paper comes written on your Table. You must know that no separate Spirits are under any Confinement till after the final Settlement of all Accounts. In the mean time we wander where we please, visit our old Friends, observe their Actions, enter sometimes into their Imaginations, and give them Hints waking or sleeping that may be of Advantage to them. Finding you asleep, I entred your left Nostril, ascended into your Brain, found out where the Ends of those Nerves were fastned that move your right Hand and Fingers, by the Help of which I am now writing unknown to you; but when you open your Eyes, you will see that the Hand written is mine, tho' wrote with yours.

"The People of this Infidel Age, perhaps, will hardly believe this Story. But you may give them these three Signs by which they shall be convinc'd of the Truth of it. About the middle of June next, J. J----n, Philomat, shall be openly reconciled to the Church of Rome, and give all his Goods and Chattles to the Chappel, being perverted by a certain *Country Schoolmaster*.[5] On the 7th of September following my old Friend W.B----t[6] shall be sober 9 Hours, to the Astonishment of all his Neighbours: And about the same time W.B. and A.B. will publish another Almanack in my Name, in spight of Truth and Common-Sense.[7]

"As I can see much clearer into Futurity, since I got free from the dark Prison of Flesh, in which I was continually molested and almost blinded with Fogs arising from Tiff,[8] and the Smoke of burnt Drams; I shall in kindness to you, frequently give you Informations of things to come, for the Improvement of your Almanack: Being Dear Dick, Your affectionate Friend,   T. LEEDS"

For my own part I am convinc'd that the above Letter is genuine. If the Reader doubts of it, let him carefully observe the three Signs; and if they do not actually come to pass, believe as he pleases. I am his humble Friend,   R. SAUNDERS

Of ECLIPSES for 1740.

There will be Six Eclipses this Year, . . . [*Details not here reprinted.*]

Some of these Eclipses foreshow great Grief and many Tears among the soft Sex this Year; whether for the Breaking of their Crockery Ware, the Loss of their Loves, or in Repentance for their Sins, I shall not say; tho' I must own I think there will be a great deal of the latter in the Case. War we shall hear but too much of (for all Christians have not yet learn'd to *love one another*) and, I doubt, of some ineffectual Treaties of Peace. I pray Heav'n defend these Colonies from every Enemy; and give them, Bread enough, Peace enough, Money enough, and plenty of good Cyder.

5. To this prediction John Jerman replied in the preface to his *American Almanack* for 1741, which BF printed: "And as for the false Prophesy concerning me, that Poor Richard put in his Almanack the last Year, I do hereby declare and protest, That it is altogether false and untrue; which is evidently known to all that know me, and plainly shews, that he is one of Baal's false Prophets."

6. Probably William Birkett, compiler of *Poor Will's Almanack*.

7. As, indeed, they did: *The American Almanack for the Year of Christian Account, 1740*. . . . By Titan Leeds, Philomat.

8. Tiff: a draught of liquor; thin or small beer.

XI Mon. January hath xxxi days.

> My sickly Spouse, with many a Sigh
> Once told me,—Dicky I shall die:
> I griev'd, but recollected strait,
> 'Twas bootless to contend with Fate:
> So Resignation to Heav'n's Will
> Prepar'd me for succeeding Ill;
> 'Twas well it did; for, on my Life,
> 'Twas Heav'n's Will to spare my Wife.

To bear other Peoples afflictions, every one has Courage enough, and to spare.

> No wonder Tom grows fat, th' unwieldy Sinner,
> Makes his whole Life but one continual Dinner.

An empty Bag cannot stand upright.

XII Mon. February hath xxviii days.

> While the good Priest with eyes devoutly clos'd
> Left on the book the marriage fee expos'd,
> The new made bridegroom his occasion spies,
> And pleas'd, repockets up the shining prize:
> Yet not so safe, but Mr. Surplice views
> The Frolick, and demands his pilfer'd dues.
> No, quoth the man, good Doctor, I'll nonsuit y',
> A plain default, I found you off your Duty?
> More carefully the holy book survey;
> Your Rule is, you should *watch* as well as *pray*.

Happy that nation, fortunate that age, whose history is not diverting.

> What is a butterfly? At best
> He's but a caterpiller drest.
> The gaudy Fop's his picture just.

None are deceived but they that confide.

I Mon. March hath xxxi days.

When Pharoah's Sins provok'd th' Almighty's hand
To pour his Wrath upon the guilty Land;
A tenfold Plague the great Avenger shed;
The King offended, and the Nation bled.
Had'st thou, unaided, Feria, but been sent,
Vial elect, for Pharoah's Punishment,
Thro' what a various Curse the Wretch had run,
He more than heaven's ten Plagues had felt in one.

An open Foe may prove a curse;
But a pretended friend is worse.

A wolf eats sheep but now and then,
Ten Thousands are devour'd by Men.

Man's tongue is soft, and bone doth lack;
Yet a stroke therewith may break a man's back.

II Mon. April hath xxx days.

Says Roger to his Wife, my dear;
The strangest piece of News I hear!
A Law, 'tis said, will quickly pass,
To purge the matrimonial Class;
Cuckolds, if any such we have here
Must to a Man be thrown i' th' River.
She smiling cry'd, My dear, you seem
Surpriz'd! *Pray han't you learn'd to swim?*

Many a Meal is lost for want of meat.

To all apparent Beauties blind
Each Blemish strikes an envious Mind.

The Poor have little, Beggars none;
The Rich too much, enough not one.

III Mon. May hath xxxi days.

> A Carrier ev'ry Night and Morn,
> Would see his Horses eat their Corn:
> This sunk the Hostler's Vails, 'tis true;
> But then his Horses had their Due.
> Were we so cautious in all Cases,
> Small Gain would rise from greater Places.

There are lazy Minds as well as lazy Bodies.

Tricks and Treachery are the Practice of Fools, that have not Wit enough to be honest.

Who says Jack is not generous? He is always fond of giving, and cares not for receiving.—What? Why; Advice.

IV Mon. June hath xxx days.

> How weak, how vain is human Pride!
> Dares Man upon himself confide?
> The Wretch who glories in his Gain,
> Amasses Heaps on Heaps in vain.
> Can those (when tortur'd by Disease)
> Chear our sick Heart, or purchase Ease?
> Can those prolong one Gasp of Breath,
> Or calm the troubled Hour of Death?
>
> The Man who with undaunted toils,
> Sails unknown seas to unknown soils,
> With various wonders feasts his Sight:
> What stranger wonders does he write?

Fear not Death; for the sooner we die, the longer shall we be immortal.

V Mon. July hath xxxi days.

> The Monarch of long regal Line,
> Was rais'd from Dust as frail as mine:

Can he pour Health into his Veins,
Or cool the Fever's restless Pains?
Can he (worn down in Nature's Course)
New-brace his feeble Nerves with Force?
Can he (how vain is mortal Pow'r!)
Stretch Life beyond the destin'd Hour?

Those who in quarrels interpose,
Must often wipe a bloody nose.

Promises may get thee Friends, but Nonperformance will turn them into Enemies.

In other men we faults can spy,
And blame the mote that dims their eye;
Each little speck and blemish find;
To our own stronger errors blind.

VI Mon. August hath xxxi days.

The Man of pure and simple Heart
Thro' Life disdains a double part;
He never needs the screen of Lies
His inward Bosom to disguise.
In vain malicious Tongues assail,
Let Envy snarl, let Slander rail,
From Virtue's shield (secure from Wound)
Their blunted venom'd shafts rebound.

When you speak to a man, look on his eyes; when he speaks to thee, look on his mouth.

Jane, why those tears? why droops your head?
Is then your other husband dead?
Or doth a worse disgrace betide?
Hath no one since his death apply'd?

Observe all men; thy self most.

251

VII Mon. September hath xxx days.

> We frequently misplace *Esteem*
> By judging Men by what they seem.
> With partial Eyes we're apt to see
> The Man of noble Pedigree.
> To Birth, Wealth, Power we should allow
> Precedence, and our lowest Bow:
> In that is due Distinction shown:
> *Esteem is Virtue's Right alone.*

Thou hadst better eat salt with the Philosophers of Greece, than sugar with the Courtiers of Italy.

> Seek Virtue, and, of that possest,
> To Providence, resign the rest.

Marry above thy match, and thou'lt get a Master.

Fear to do ill, and you need fear nought else.

VIII Mon. October hath xxxi days.

> What's Beauty? Call ye that your own,
> A Flow'r that fades as soon as blown!
> Those Eyes of so divine a Ray,
> What are they? Mould'ring, mortal Clay.
> Those Features cast in heav'nly Mould,
> Shall, like my coarser Earth, grow old;
> Like common Grass, the fairest Flow'r
> Must feel the hoary Season's Pow'r.

He makes a Foe who makes a jest.

> Can grave and formal pass for wise,
> When Men the solemn Owl despise?

Some are justly laught at for keeping their Money foolishly, others for spending it idly: He is the greatest fool that lays it out in a purchase of repentance.

IX Mon. November hath xxx days.

> Old Socrates was obstinately Good,
> *Virtuous* by force, by Inclination lewd.
> When secret Movements drew his Soul aside,
> He quell'd his Lust, and stemm'd the swelling Tide;
> Sustain'd by Reason still, unmov'd he stood,
> And steady bore against th' opposing Flood.
> He durst correct what Nature form'd amiss,
> And forc'd unwilling Virtue to be his.

> Who knows a fool, must know his brother;
> For one will recommend another.

> Avoid dishonest Gain: No price
> Can recompence the Pangs of Vice.

> When befriended, remember it:
> When you befriend, forget it.

> Great souls with gen'rous pity melt;
> Which coward tyrants never felt.

X Mon. December hath xxxi days.

> O blessed Season! lov'd by Saints and Sinners,
> For long Devotions, or for longer Dinners;
> More grateful still to those who deal in Books,
> Now not with Readers, but with Pastry-Cooks:
> Learn'd Works, despis'd by those to Merit blind,
> By these well weigh'd, their certain Value find.
> Bless'd Lot of Paper, falsely called *Waste*,
> To bear those Cates, which Authors seldom taste.

Employ thy time well, if thou meanest to gain leisure.

> A Flatterer never seems absurd:
> The Flatter'd always take his Word.

Lend Money to an Enemy, and thou'lt gain him, to a Friend and thou'lt lose him.

Neither praise nor dispraise, till seven Christmasses be over.

COURTS.

I know you Lawyers can, with Ease,
Twist Words and Meanings as you please;
That Language, by your Skill made pliant,
Will bend to favour ev'ry Client;
That 'tis the Fee directs the Sense
To make out either Side's Pretence:
When you peruse the clearest Case,
You see it with a double Face;
For Scepticism's your Profession;
You hold there's Doubt in all Expression.
    Hence is the Bar with Fees supply'd.
Hence Eloquence takes either Side.
Your Hand would have but paultry gleaning;
Could every Man express his Meaning.
Who dares presume to pen a Deed,
Unless you previously are feed?
'Tis drawn, and, *to augment the Cost,*
In dull Prolixity engrost:
And now we're well secur'd by Law,
'Till the next Brother find a Flaw.

Dr. Tennent's infallible Cure for the Pleurisy.[9]

First when the Patient is taken, let ten Ounces of Blood be drawn from the Arm of the Side opposite to that affected with the Disease, and presently after give 3 Spoonfulls of the Decoction of *Rattlesnake-Root,* which must be repeated every six Hours, till the Symptoms abate in a great Degree. But if they should return notwithstanding, which happens sometimes, Bleeding is to be repeated in the same Quantity as at first, and so in like Manner a third, fourth, or fifth time, or oftener; tho' it seldom

9. These paragraphs are taken from John Tennent's "Memorial and Remonstrance," reprinted in *Pa. Gaz.*, July 26, Aug. 2, 1739. For Tennent and the snakeroot, see above, pp. 156–8, 239 n.

happens that it is wanted above twice; which Method answers for the Cure of a Pleurisy, generally speaking: But in particular Cases, where the Patient has a Purging attending the Disorder, give 20 Grains of the Root every three Hours, with 10 Grains of Cinnamon poudered, and as much prepared Harts Horn, observing also to let Blood as often as the Symptoms recur; by which is meant the Pain, Fever, Cough, and Difficulty in breathing. When the Breast is only affected with the Pain, or both Sides and the Breast affected at once, the same Method is to be followed as when one Side only is affected, the Disease being the same notwithstanding of that Difference in the Symptoms. For ordinary Drink, give Hysop Decoction, or a Tea drawn from Marsh Mallard Roots, sweetned with Honey; but in case of a Purging attending the Case, let the Drink be sweetned with double refined Sugar, and the Cinnamon and Harts Horn before prescribed are to be given with the poudered Rattlesnake Root in a little of it; and it is to be observed, that both the Decoction of the Root and Tea are given warm. If the Patient be troubled with a Vomiting, or Nausea, give one spoonful and half of the Decoction every three Hours, or if that should immediately be thrown up, give half a spoonful of the Decoction every Hour; observing in such a Case to bleed, as before advised. There is a Disease called a Pleurisy, wherein Bleeding is of ill Consequence, which may with great Propriety be called a latent or spurious Peripneumony; yet the above Method with the Decoction of the Root, is a very certain one, giving instead of pectoral Teas, a Tea made of Thyme or Marjoram, or rather Rum-punch. This Disease personates a Pleurisy or Peripneumony, to a superficial Observer, the Symptoms being the same, only with this Difference, That the Pulse is always low, which in an inflamatory Pleurisy or Peripneumony, is so only upon the first Invasion, or when the Disease is upon terminating in Death: But it is to be noted for a Mark of this latent Peripneumony, that on its first Approach the Patient is cold, convulsed, and very much inclined to sleep, and also that it attacks in the Autumn after excessive hot Summers attended with much Rain; and towards February, or sooner if the Winter sets in very cold, translates to an inflamatory Pleurisy or Peripneumony. The Operation of this Root is different according to the Circumstances of the Constitution and Disease; sometimes, it is by Vomit, at other times by Sweat, Urine and Stool, and in some Cases, such as a latent Peripneumony, it has none of these Operations in any Degree; yet the Patient is surprizingly recovered, which shews that it strongly attenuates the Blood. The Success of the aforesaid Method is proved from Experience to be so great, that an intermitting Fever is not carried off with more Certainty with Jesuits Bark, than a Pleurisy or Peripneumony with the Seneka Rattlesnake Root. And the Cure often is effected the third Day if the Method be followed up from the first Attack of the Distemper, and also that the Patient will find great Relief in the space of an Hour after the Decoction; tho' every one may not, yet it has that Effect very often: And he further asserts, That whether the Disease be in the Beginning, Increase, or State, the Medicine has like Effects, and answers to perfection the Design of all the Methods prescribed by Authors of the best note for these different Stages.

The Decoction of Seneka Rattlesnake Root is made by boiling three Ounces of it in a Quart of Water over a slow Fire till near half is evaporated; then strain the Liquor thro' a Cloth. The Root must be reduced to a gross Powder, that the Water may fully draw its Efficacy. The Plant grows plentifully in Virginia, Maryland and Pennsylvania, in the Freshes and hilly Grounds, and affects a light and tolerable good Soil. The Root is of a light yellow Colour, resembling Ipecacuana in its Texture and Shape, but is larger, has a strong Pungency without Heat, but does not communicate that Property upon chewing it immediately. The leaves are something like green Tea, and the Stalk is commonly from six to twelve Inches high, on the Top of which are white Flowers something like the Rattles of a Snake, while in Bud, which appear among the first Flowers in the Woods: And there are no Branches from the Stalks, but several Stalks arise from one Root generally, tho' only one Stalk from a Root may be seen sometimes.

The Indian Traders say, That it grows all the way from Canada to South-Carolina, where in both it is very plenty.

From William Dewees, Jr.[1]   ALS: American Philosophical Society

Sir   Janry. the 26th 1739/40
    I Sent you Last week 7½ Reemes of Large Printing Paper and 8
Reemes of Brown Ditto and Now Send you by the Same Barrer
12 Ditto of Corse printing which I would have you Place to the
Cr. of Yours   WM. DEWEES JNR
To Mr. Benjn Franklin this

Note on Closing the Concert Room

Printed in *The Pennsylvania Gazette* May 8, 1740.

Dancing parties and concerts by a musical club, both taking place in a
room kept by the dancing-master Robert Bolton,[2] gave pleasure to
some of Philadelphia's wealthier citizens. But to George Whitefield
and his enthusiastic followers music and dancing were "devilish diversions" and, as such, should be suppressed. Accordingly his traveling
companion William Seward,[3] with Bolton's assent, locked up the room
and took away the key. The episode made "a great Stir"; the gentlemen who had rented the room for their entertainments broke in the
door, accosted Seward "very roughly," and threatened him with a
caning. "What a Hurry Satan puts his *Servants* into," he wrote, "when
their darling *Idols* are opposed?" On Tuesday, April 22, "the Com-

1. William Dewees, Jr. (*c.* 1712–1777), operated a paper mill in Cresham
township on the Wissahickon near Philadelphia after 1736. BF's accounts
with him are in Ledger D (see above, p. 232). Dewees was a son of William
Dewees (1677–1745), who built a paper mill near Germantown in 1710, the
second in America. Dard Hunter, *Papermaking in Pioneer America* (Phila.,
1952), pp. 41–2; Lyman H. Weeks, *A History of Paper-Manufacturing in the
United States, 1690-1916* (N.Y., 1916), pp. 10–11; Ellwood Roberts, ed.,
The Dewees Family (Norristown, Pa., 1905), pp. 21–35, 86–7.
    2. Bolton opened his dancing classes in 1738. See above, p. 213. The con-
certs were presented by a musical club led by Tench Francis. Carl and Jessica
Bridenbaugh, *Rebels and Gentlemen: Philadelphia in the Age of Franklin*
(N.Y., 1942), p. 155.
    3. William Seward (1702–1740), converted as a young man, did lay re-
ligious work in London after 1728, especially reviving charity schools. He
accompanied Whitefield to America, 1739; returned to England, 1740; died
from blows received while preaching in Wales. He was an uncle of Anna
Seward, "the Swan of Lichfield." Tyerman, *Whitefield* 1, 163–6. Seward's
journal of his American visit was published at London, 1740.

pany met to Dance as they used to do," their spokesman asserted. This was the last such weekly assembly scheduled for the season; there was no dance on April 29.

Seward may or may not have known the reason for this omission, but he took the credit, and rejoiced that the forces of righteousness had "taken Satan's strongest Hold in this City." He sent the following note to the *Pennsylvania Gazette*, which Franklin printed on May 1: "Since Mr. Whitefield's Preaching here, the Dancing School, Assembly and Concert Room have been shut up, as inconsistent with the Doctrine of the Gospel: And though the Gentlemen concern'd caus'd the Door to be broke open again, we are inform'd that no Company came the last Assembly Night."[4]

The "gentlemen" were angered by the note's implication that Bolton's patrons had given up their dancing party because of Whitefield's preaching, since nothing was further from the truth. In a sharply-worded protest and explanation, which they asked Franklin to print, they charged Seward with wilfully misrepresenting the facts "in order to . . . spread his Master's Fame, as tho' he had met with great Success among the better Sort of People in Pennsylvania. . . ." Though this protest seemed to Franklin to contain as much vilification as vindication, he printed it, with a short preface.

In my last, at the Request of Mr. Seward, I inserted an Article of News, relating to the shutting up of the Concert Room, &c. which it seems gives great Offence to the Gentlemen concern'd in the Entertainments usually carry'd on there; for tho' the Article is allow'd to be literally true, yet by the Manner of Expression 'tis thought to insinuate something that is not true, viz. *That the Gentlemen forbore meeting on the Night mentioned, as thinking such Entertainments inconsistent with the Doctrine of the Gospel.* I have often said, that if any Person thinks himself injured in a Publick News-Paper, he has a Right to have his Vindication made as publick as the Aspersion. The Gentlemen above mentioned have brought me the following Letter to be inserted in my Paper, believing the Publication of it will be advantageous to their Reputation: And tho' I think there is a good deal of Difference between a *Vindication* and an *Invective;* and that, whatever Obligations a Printer may be under to publish Things of the former kind, he

4. For Seward's account of these events, see his *Journal of a Voyage from Savannah to Philadelphia, and from Philadelphia to England, M.DCC.XL* (London, 1740), pp. 6–7, 21–2, 61.

can be under none with Regard to the latter: Yet, as the publishing of this, will obviate a groundless Report (injurious to that Gentleman) that Mr. Whitefield had engag'd all the Printers not to print any Thing against him, lest his Doctrine and Practice should be expos'd, and the People undeceiv'd; I shall therefore print it as I received it: And when the Publick has heard what may possibly be said in Reply, they will then judge for themselves.[5]

Statement of Editorial Policy

Printed in *The Pennsylvania Gazette*, July 24, 1740.

George Whitefield's doctrine and eloquence had sensational effects throughout the colonies. One of those who resisted him, strongly disapproving his excessive religious emotionalism, was Ebenezer Kinnersley, a Baptist lay preacher in Philadelphia.[6] In a sermon on July 6, 1740, Kinnersley expressed abhorrence of "Enthusiastick Ravings . . . that . . . proceed not from the Spirit of God; for our God is a God of Order, and not of such Confusion. . . ." These sentiments gave great offense, some of the congregation stormed out of the meeting-house "in a most disorderly and tumultuous Manner," and Kinnersley was denounced as an enemy of the Reformation, a tool of Satan, and an opposer of the doctrine of Christ. He refused to recant and apolo-

5. The controversy did not end here. Obadiah Plainman resented the description of anti-Whitefieldians as "the better Sort"; and during the next three weeks he and Tom Trueman disputed the point in the *Gazette* and *Mercury*, until some third party called on them to end the "thin debate." *Pa. Gaz.*, May 15, 22, 29; *American Weekly Mercury*, May 22, 29, June 5, 1740. These letters are of interest principally for their echoes of the old, deep-seated division in Pennsylvania between the "gentlemen" and the "other sort."

6. Ebenezer Kinnersley (1711–1778), born in Gloucester, England; brought to America, 1714, when his father became assistant minister of Pennypack Baptist church at Lower Dublin, near Philadelphia; educated at home; moved to Philadelphia about 1739. He and his brethren were eventually reconciled after this episode, and he was ordained, 1743. He never had his own congregation but was a constituent member of the Philadelphia Baptist church when it formally separated from the Pennypack church, 1746. His subsequent career as a teacher in the Academy of Philadelphia and associate of BF in electrical experimentation is related below. *DAB;* Montgomery, *Hist. Univ. Pa.*, pp. 172–4; I. Bernard Cohen, *Benjamin Franklin's Experiments* (Cambridge, Mass., 1941), pp. 401–8; William B. Sprague, *Annals of the American Pulpit*, VI (N.Y., 1860), 45–7.

gize, and on July 12 the church forbade him to preach again. On July 15 he wrote a strongly-worded defense and justification that concluded with a savage attack on Jenkin Jones, the regular minister of the Philadelphia Baptists. Franklin printed this defense, entitled "A Letter . . . to a Friend in the Country," as a Postscript to the *Gazette*, July 24, prefacing it with his own justification for doing so.[7]

It is a Principle among Printers, that when Truth has fair Play, it will always prevail over Falshood; therefore, though they have an undoubted Property in their own Press, yet they willingly allow, that any one is entitled to the Use of it, who thinks it necessary to offer his Sentiments on disputable Points to the Publick, and will be at the Expence of it. If what is thus publish'd be good, Mankind has the Benefit of it: If it be bad (I speak now in general without any design'd Application to any particular Piece whatever) the more 'tis made publick, the more its Weakness is expos'd, and the greater Disgrace falls upon the Author, whoever he be; who is at the same Time depriv'd of an Advantage he would otherwise without fail make use of, viz. of Complaining, *that Truth is suppress'd, and that he could say* MIGHTY MATTERS, *had he but the Opportunity of being heard.*

The Printers of this City have been unjustly reflected on, as if they were under some undue Influence, and guilty of great Partiality in favour of the Preaching lately admir'd among us, so as to refuse Printing any Thing in Opposition to it, how just or necessary soever. A Reflection entirely false and groundless, and without the least Colour of Fact to support it; which all will be convinc'd of when they see the following Piece from one Press, and the Rev. Mr. Cummings's Sermons against the Doctrines themselves, from the other.[8]

7. Seven members of Jones's congregation, on behalf of the church, published in the *Gazette*, Aug. 14, a statement officially and formally rejecting Kinnersley's aspersions. Kinnersley replied in *A Second Letter to His Friend in the Country*. The two *Letters* were answered in *A Letter to Mr. Ebenezer Kinnersley, from his Friend in the Country;* and Kinnersley rejoined with *A Letter to the Rev. Jenkin Jones*. The pamphlets were all printed at Philadelphia in 1740.

8. Archibald Cummings' *Faith Absolutely Necessary, but Not Sufficient to Salvation without Good Works* was printed by Bradford, 1740. Later BF printed *Remarks on the Several Passages of Mr. Whitefield's Sermons, Journals*

Englishmen thought it an intolerable Hardship, when (tho' by an Act of their own Parliament) Thoughts, which should be free, were fetter'd and confin'd, and an Officer was erected over the Nation, call'd *a Licenser of the Press,* without whose Consent no Writing could be publish'd. Care might indeed be taken in the Choice of this Officer, that he should be a Man of great Understanding, profound Learning, and extraordinary Piety; yet, as the greatest and best of Men may have *some* Errors, and have been often found averse to *some* Truths, it was justly esteem'd a National Grievance, that the People should have Nothing to read but the Opinions, or what was agreeable to the Opinions of ONE MAN. But should every petty Printer (who, if he can read his Hornbook, may be thought to have Learning enough to qualify him for his own Sphere) presume to erect himself into an Officer of this kind, and arbitrarily decide what ought and what ought not to be published, much more justly might the World complain. 'Tis true, where Invectives are contain'd in any Piece, there is no good-natur'd Printer but had much rather be employ'd in Work of another kind: However, tho' many personal Reflections be interwoven in the following Performance, yet as the Author *(who has subscrib'd his Name)* thought them necessary, to vindicate his own Conduct and Character, it is therefore hoped, on that Consideration, the Reader will excuse the Printer in publishing them.

James Franklin:[9] Indenture of Apprenticeship

Printed form, with MS insertions in blanks: American Philosophical Society

[November 5, 1740]

THIS INDENTURE Witnesseth, That *James Franklin late of Newport in Rhodeisland, but now of Philadelphia in Pennsilvania* Hath put himself, and by these Presents, doth voluntarily, and of his own free Will and Accord, put himself Apprentice to *Benjamin Franklin of the City of Philadelphia, Printer* to learn his

---

and Letters, which seem Unsound and Erroneous and very Liable to Exceptions. See *Pa. Gaz.,* Oct. 16, 1740.

9. James Franklin, Jr. (C.11.4), son of BF's brother James. Anticipating his death, the elder James asked BF to educate his son "and bring him up to

Art, Trade, and Mystery, and after the Manner of an Apprentice to serve *the said Benjamin Franklin* from the Day of the Date hereof, for, and during, and unto the full End and Term of *Seven Years* next ensuing. During all which Term, the said Apprentice his said Master faithfully shall serve, his Secrets keep, his lawful Commands everywhere readily obey. He shall do no Damage to his said Master, nor see it to be done by others without letting or giving Notice thereof to his said Master. He shall not waste his said Master's Goods, nor lend them unlawfully to any. He shall not commit Fornication, nor contract Matrimony within the said Term. At Cards, Dice, or any other unlawful Game, he shall not play, whereby his said Master may have Damage. With his own Goods, nor the Goods of others, without Licence from his said Master, he shall neither buy nor sell. He shall not absent himself Day nor Night from his said Master's Service, without his Leave: Nor haunt Ale-houses, Taverns, or Play-houses; but in all Things behave himself as a faithful Apprentice ought to do, during the said Term. And the said Master shall use the utmost of his Endeavour to teach or cause to be taught or instructed the said Apprentice in the Trade or Mystery of *Printing* and procure and provide for him sufficient Meat, Drink, *Cloaths* Lodging and Washing fitting for an Apprentice, during the said Term of *Seven Years, and at the Expiration thereof shall give him one good new Suit of Cloaths, besides his common Apparel* AND for the true Performance of all and singular the Covenants and Agreements aforesaid, the said Parties bind themselves each unto the other firmly by these Presents. IN WITNESS whereof, the said Parties have interchangeably set their Hands and Seals hereunto. Dated the *Fifth* Day of *November* in the *Fourteenth* Year

---

the Printing Business. This I accordingly perform'd, sending him a few Years to School before I took him into the Office." Par. Text edit., p. 254. While BF's apprentice, James "was always dissatisfied [with the clothes he was allowed] and grumbling." Van Doren, *Franklin-Mecom*, p. 43. A bill for the schooling of James and William Franklin is printed below, p. 388. On completing his apprenticeship, James joined his mother Ann as a printer in Newport, R.I., publishing *Poor Job's Almanack* and establishing the *Newport Mercury*, 1758, which she continued after his death, 1762. Thomas, *Printing*, I, 195–6.

of the Reign of our Sovereign Lord *George the second* King of Great-Britain, &c. Annoque Domini One Thousand Seven Hundred and *Forty.*   JAMES FRANKLIN
    Sealed and delivered in
      the Presence of us
    CHRISTOPHER THOMPSON
    RICHARD VERGUSON [*sic*]

Philadelphia: Printed and Sold by B. Franklin, at the New PRINT-ING-OFFICE, near the Market

Endorsed: Jemmy's Indenture

Advertisement of the General Magazine

Printed in *The Pennsylvania Gazette*, November 13, 1740.

The *American Weekly Mercury*, November 6, 1740, printed a long, ambitious "Plan of an Intended Magazine," to be called *The American Magazine, or A Monthly View of The Political State of The British Colonies.* John Webbe, who was to be the editor, probably composed it, though it was signed by Andrew Bradford. Each issue would contain four sheets, or equivalent, of the size the *Mercury* was printed on; the price was 12*s.* a year Pennsylvania currency; and the first number would appear in March, if enough subscriptions were received. A week later Franklin announced his plan to publish *The General Magazine, and Historical Chronicle, for all the British Plantations in America.*[1] It would be the same size as the *American Magazine,* but cost only 9*d.* a copy; and the first issue would appear in January. There was, however, much more to the rivalry than this indicates, as is shown by Franklin's advertisement and the replies it called forth.[2]

1. For a brief general history of the two magazines, see Frank L. Mott, *A History of American Magazines, 1741–1850* (N.Y., 1930), pp. 71–7. The Facsimile Text Society reprinted all issues of each, the *American Magazine* in 1935, the *General Magazine* in 1938. See also Anna J. DeArmond, *Andrew Bradford, Colonial Journalist* (Newark, Del., 1949), pp. 223–39. BF did not mention this publishing venture in his autobiography. Except for the second sentence in the final paragraph, this advertisement also appeared in *Poor Richard's Almanack* for 1741.

2. See below, pp. 265–9, 270–81.

In January next will be published, (To be continued Monthly) *The General* MAGAZINE, *and Historicle Chronical, For all the British Plantations in America:* Containing,

I. Extracts from the Votes, and Debates of the Parliament of Great Britain.

II. The Proclamations and Speeches of Governors; Addresses, Votes, Resolutions, &c. of Assemblies, in each Colony.

III. Accounts of, and Extracts from, all new Books, Pamphlets, &c. published in the Plantations.

IV. Essays, controversial, humorous, philosophical, religious, moral or political.

V. Select Pieces of Poetry.

VI. A concise CHRONICLE of the most remarkable Transactions, as well in Europe as America.

VII. Births, Marriages, Deaths, and Promotions, of eminent Persons in the several Colonies.

VIII. Course of Exchange between the several Colonies, and London; Prices of Goods, &c.

This MAGAZINE, in Imitation of those in England, was long since projected; a Correspondence is settled with Intelligent Men in most of the Colonies, and small Types are procured, for carrying it on in the best Manner. It would not, indeed, have been published quite so soon, were it not that a Person,[3] to whom the Scheme was communicated *in Confidence,* has thought fit to advertise it in the last *Mercury,* without our Participation; and, probably, with a View, by Starting before us, to discourage us from prosecuting our first Design, and reap the Advantage of it wholly to himself. We shall endeavour, however, by executing our Plan with Care, Diligence and Impartiality, and by Printing the Work neatly and correctly, to deserve a Share of the Publick Favour: But we desire no Subscriptions. We shall publish the Books at our own Expence, and risque the Sale of them; which Method, we suppose, will be most agreeable to our Readers, as they will then be at Liberty to buy only what they like; and we shall be under a constant Necessity of endeavouring to make every particular Pamphlet worth their Money. Each Magazine shall contain four Sheets, of common sized Paper, in a small Character: Price

3. John Webbe.

Six Pence Sterling, or *Nine Pence* Pennsylvania Money; with considerable Allowance to Chapmen who take Quantities. To be printed and Sold by B. FRANKLIN in Philadelphia.

John Webbe:[4] The Detection

Printed in *The American Weekly Mercury*, November 20, 1740.

Franklin's advertisement of the *General Magazine*, November 13, accused John Webbe, to whom as prospective editor he had revealed his scheme in confidence, of carrying the idea to Bradford in order to get ahead of Franklin and reap the advantage personally. Webbe responded immediately with this defense and countercharge. The second part of "The Detection," promised for the *Mercury's* issue of November 27, never appeared, because Webbe substituted a discussion of his own literary competence (see below, p. 270) in answer to charges which must have been circulated by word of mouth, for they do not appear in the *Gazette*. On December 4 Webbe renewed his defense, though not by a continuation of "The Detection," and this time accused Franklin of unfair use of his office as postmaster to deny free circulation to the *Mercury* (see below, p. 273). This charge shifted the grounds of controversy and ended the public discussion of the proposed agreement for the production of Franklin's magazine.

THE DETECTION.

Philadelphia Nov. 17. 1740

Tho' Nothing could be more imprudent in Mr. Franklin than to thrust me into his Advertisement,[5] in any Shape whatsoever; yet he has not only thought fit to introduce me there, but has at the same Time accused me, of such Practices, which if I were guilty of, I should not deserve to breath in any Society.

However highly impertinent it may be deemed in Mr. Franklin, to have troubled the Public with any private Difference between him and my self, yet my appearing at this Time, in my own Vindication, cannot be looked upon in the same Light, for as much as it is an absolute Necessity that constrains me to it.

4. John Webbe (or Webb), presumably of Irish birth; conveyancer and lawyer, employed by BF as an attorney to collect Andrew Bradford's post-office indebtedness; author of essays on government in *Pa. Gaz.*, 1736 (see above, p. 145–6), and *A Discourse concerning Paper Money* (Phila., 1743).
5. See above, p. 264.

As Mr. Franklin has now professedly applied his News Paper to the gratifying his own particular Malice by blackening the Reputation of a private Person; it is reasonable to believe that, without a proper Animadversion on such a Proceedure, he will not stop at this single Instance of spitting his Malignity from his Press, but be incouraged to proceed in making use of it as an Engine to bespatter the Characters of every other Person he may happen to dislike.

My endeavouring, then, to expose the Iniquity of this his first Attempt, by detecting the Falshoods insinuated in his Advertisement, does not only concern me in particular, but is the Cause of every Man in general.

These Falshoods are not directly asserted, and therefore I said they were *insinuated,* which is by far the most mischievous Kind of Lying; for the Strokes being oblique and indirect, a Man cannot so easily defend himself against them, as he might do, if they were straight and peremtory. There is something too more mean and dastardly in the Character of an indirect Lyar than a direct one. *This* has the Audacity of a Highwayman, *That* the Slyness of a Pickpocket. Both indeed rob you of your Purse, and both deserve a Gibbet; but, were I obliged to pardon either, I could sooner forgive the *bold* Wickedness of the one, than the *sneaking* Villainy of the other.

The first Falshood, which I shall take Notice of as insinuated by the Gazetteer, is couched in Expressions that at first sight may seem to admit of several Meanings. He says *I advertised his Scheme, or as he calls it afterwards, his Plan, in the* Mercury, *without his Participation tho' it had been communicated to me in Confidence.* He indeed communicated to me his *Desire* of printing a Magazine or a monthly Pamphlet, if I would undertake to compose one. But surely his making the Proposal neither obliged me to the writing of one for him to print, nor restrained me from the printing of it at any other Press without his Leave or Participation. If that were a Consequence, then Mr. Franklin has only to *offer* himself as a Printer of Books or Pamphlets to every Man that he thinks has a Talent for Writing, and they shall from thenceforth be restrained from publishing any Thing without his Consent. The Consequence would be equally ridiculous, if on the publishing the Plan of a monthly Pamphlet Mr. Franklin should call it his

Scheme, because he happened to mention the Word *Pamphlet* to the Writer: Nor would the Absurdity be at all lessened, if instead of Pamphlet Mr. Franklin had dropped the Word *Magazine*. Again, one applies to a Person, that he believes has some Skill in Architecture, for the Draft of an Edifice. Shall he, because of his Application, be entitled to the Merit of the Draft? Suppose his Request was to build him a House, and the Architect in the first Place draws the Plan of it. Shall the other, because he barely proposed a Building in general, be intitled to call the Plan his, when he never dreamt that it was a previous Requisite to the Building?

Tho' Mr. Franklin mentioned to me the composing a Magazine, yet he never once hinted at any Plan to be wrote on which the Work was to proceed. The Absurdity therefore in claiming it for his, on such Grounds, is too evident to be farther insisted on. He must therefore *insinuate* that it was wholly his Scheme, or at least drawn with his Assistance, and that I afterwards clandestinely published it as mine.

What I have asserted, concerning his Share in it, would have entirely rested on the Credit of my own Testimony, which on Mr. Franklin's Denial would have been left at large for every one to believe as they pleased, had I not *accidentally* preserved my rough Draughts contrary to my usual Custom of destroying them the Moment I make a fair Copy, which Custom Mr. Franklin was well acquainted with. The various Alterations and progressive Improvements made in them will evidently demonstrate I could have no Assistance in drawing the Plan but from my own Judgment. Moreover, by a singular Piece of good Fortune, I found, among my neglected Papers, some Minutes of Proposals made to me by Mr. Franklin in his own Hand-writing, a litteral Copy of which immediately follows, which will show that his long projected Scheme was never intended to be carried on by him in any other Capacity than that of a *meer* Printer.

Magazine to consist of 3 Sheets 1000 *to be printed at first. Price* 15*s. a Year, or* 15*d. a piece single.* 12*s. a Doz. to those that sell again.*[6]

6. Note that BF increased the size and lowered the price of his magazine some time after this discussion with Webbe, presumably to undercut Bradford's competition.

B.F. to be at all Expence of Paper, Printing, Correspondence for procuring Materials &c. vending, keeping Accounts &c.

J.W. to dispose the Materials, make Abstracts, and write what shall be necessary for promoting the Thing &c.

The Money received to be divided thus—B.F. for and towards defraying the Expence above mentioned to take first one half, the Remainder to be equally shared between him and J.W: Bad Debts if any to be divided in the same Manner.

To agree for a Term of 7 Years. The above Agreement to be for all under 2000; all above 2000 sold the Money to be equally divided; B.F. to be at all Expence.

On the Delivery of these Proposals he told me he thought himself intitled to the half of the Profits of the Work, besides his Gain as a Printer, for two Reasons. *First,* for that he had a small Letter that no other Printer in America had besides himself. 2dly the Privilege which he had from his being Post-Master. Either of these advantages being wanting, he affirmed the Work could not possibly go on. Tho' I was then utterly ignorant of the Nature of those several Matters, yet, having an entire Confidence in his Sincerity, I did not at all doubt of the Truth of any Thing he told me, and therefore I frankly agreed to his Proposals. But afterwards finding that every Moment of my Time would be necessarily ingrossed in the Execution of the Undertaking, tho' Mr. Franklin who had it long under his Consideration, had told me, that it would only require about 3 or 4 Days in a month; and having also discovered that his Reasons for claiming half the Profits, over and above the Gain accruing to him as a Printer, were groundless and ridiculous: I thought my self, on these Discoveries, even supposing there were no grosser Frauds yet behind to mention, acquitted from my Engagement, tho' it was ingrossed and ready for Execution. But if I had perfected it, yet being drawn in upon such Circumstances, I should have been relieved from such a Contract, in any Country in the World, by a universal Maxim in Equity.

Tho' what I have alledged is strictly Truth, yet I will acknowledge every Particular to be false, If Mr. Franklin can produce any one Instance of my acting an insincere or dishonest Part in the Course of this Transaction, or on any other Occasion whatsoever, either in Respect to him or any one else, except my not suffering my self to be made his Bubble shall be deemed so.

Of what Composition, then, is the Soul of that Man, who, having contrived to make a Property of his Friend, will afterwards charge him with a Violation of Trust, and *coolly* and *deliberately* endeavour to murder his Reputation *in the most publick Manner,* on which his Livelihood, tho' not in the Capacity of a Magazine-Writer, entirely depends.   JOHN WEBBE

(The Remainder of the *Detection* in the next)

From George Whitefield[7]

MS not found; reprinted from *A Select Collection of Letters of the late George Whitefield, M.A.* . . . (London, 1772), I, 226.

Dear Mr. F[ranklin],   Reedy-Island, Nov. 26, 1740
I thank you for your letter.[8] You may print my life, as you desire.[9] GOD willing, I shall correct my two volumes of sermons, and send them the very first opportunity.[1] Pray write to me by every ship, that goes shortly to Charles-Town.

I shall embark for England, GOD willing, about February. I desire I may hear from you there also, as often as possible. I have prefaced Jenks,[2] and *Presumptuous sinners detected.*[3] Mr.

7. On Whitefield, see above, p. 241 n.
8. Not found.
9. *A Brief and General Account Of the First Part of the Life Of the Reverend Mr. Geo. Whitefield, From his Birth, to his Entering into Holy Orders. Written by Himself.* Philadelphia: Printed and Sold by B. Franklin, in Market-Street. M,DCC,XL.
1. As early as Nov. 15, 1739, BF had announced his intention to print Whitefield's sermons and journals; the first volume of each appeared May 26, 1740, and the second, August 18. See above, p. 242, and below, pp. 286 and 289.
2. Probably Benjamin Jenks (1646–1724), whose *Prayers, and Offices of Devotion,* first published in 1707, went through more than twenty editions in the eighteenth century. BF did not print it, however, and Whitefield's preface has not been found. *DNB.*
3. Gilbert Tennent, *A Solemn Warning to the Secure World . . . or the Presumptuous Sinner Detected* (Phila., 1740), had been published at Boston in 1735.

Bradford has the last, because he said he was to print it. You may have it of him. The *Ornaments of the daughter of Sion*,[4] you may have hereafter. Dear Sir, Adieu. I do not despair of your seeing the reasonableness of christianity. Apply to GOD; be willing to do the divine will, and you shall know it. I have heard from Mr. S-----;[5] all is well. To-day several friends have taken leave of me at this place, waiting for a fair wind in order to embark for Georgia. I think I have been on shore 73 days,[6] and have been enabled to travel upwards of 800 miles, and to preach 170 times, besides very frequent exhortations at private houses. I have collected, in goods and money, upwards of £700 sterling, for the Orphan-house; blessed be GOD! Great and visible are the fruits of my late, as well as former feeble labours, and people in general seem more eager after the word than ever. O the love of GOD to Your unworthy friend,
G. W.

John Webbe: Defense Renewed, I

Printed in *The American Weekly Mercury*, November 27, 1740.

The *principal* End proposed by the Plan of a Magazine, lately published in this Paper, was to lay open the Nature of the Constitutions of the several Colonies, and to give a monthly Account of the Alterations made in each, with the Reasons inducing the Legislature for making such Alterations. The Materials, for executing the first Part, are the Charters and Statute Books; and for the second, the Votes and Proceedings of each Colony.

To perform a Work of that Nature, and even to render it highly useful, demanded no greater Skill than what is requisite in a common Solicitor for the drawing up a Brief. *Perhaps* the Plan was an Evidence that the Writer's Capacity extended at least so far. This Conjecture may be strengthened, when it is considered that Mr.

---

4. Probably Cotton Mather's *Ornaments for the Daughters of Zion*, first published at Boston in 1691; a third edition appeared there in 1741, possibly after BF declined to print it.

5. William Seward, who had returned to England. Whitefield could not have heard of his death on October 22. See above, p. 257 n.

6. Whitefield had landed at Newport, R. I., September 14. He reached Savannah December 13, and sailed for England January 16, 1741.

Franklin, rather than be without the Merit, if any, of the Performance, resolved, at all Events, to outdo Bathyllus. Bathyllus claimed some Lines of Virgil before he owned himself to be the Author. The Gazetteer called the Plan his, even after it had been publickly avowed by the Writer. Whether the Scheme discover'd such Qualifications in the Person that drew it up, as are equal to those of an ordinary Sollicitor I know not? (Tho' I believe Mr. Franklin would think it a great disparagement to his Understanding to have it placed on such a Level:) But if the Affirmative in the Question be admitted, it follows that the Publisher of the Plan undertook Nothing that he was unequal to. Yet, tho' he proposed to furnish the Reader with a Narration of Matters of Fact, he was far from promising to give them, with the Graces of Narration. The Graces here meant, consist in the Brevity, Perspicuity and Purity of Expression, in the Symmetry or just Arrangement of the Sentiments, and in the harmonious Disposition of the larger Branches. Nature, when aided by genteel Conversation, has sometimes, tho' rarely, furnished the first; but the two latter can only be obtained by an accurate Study of polite Authors; agreeable to a common Remark which every School-Boy learning his *Rhetorick* must be acquainted with.

In mentioning the Ornaments of Narration, *Transitions* should not be omitted, which, to render natural and easy, sometimes cost no small Pangs to the Writer in the Production; but if he is happily delivered of them, they add great Beauty to his Discourse, and insensibly lead on the Reader in the Perusal of it. Yet they are not always to be made Use of; for it is often necessary to pass abruptly from one Subject to another, and avoid a Connection of Thought, tho' it should spontaneously offer itself. The Justness of these Observations, as they are only founded on my own Experience and on the Result of such Reflections as suggested themselves on this Occasion, is, therefore, not to be relied on: Nor is it to my present Purpose, to enter into any particular Discussion of the Beauties that constitute good Writing; for all that is necessary for me to say at this Time, in Regard to that Subject, is, that the Publisher of the Plan, was not so vain as to think he could touch any of them. He appealed to the Public for the Decision of that Point, by printing his Scheme, and thereby furnished them with Matter sufficient to ground a Judgment upon.

To place in a clear and advantageous Order many various Matters in one short Piece, to handle *some* Points, not of the least Difficulty and Delicacy, with a Justness of Reasoning, and *all* with a Propriety of Expression, was what he attempted in the Plan. The Plan, then, if well performed, was an Evidence that the Superstructure would be well executed, and *Vice versa.* But as he has met with no Incouragements, but rather Discouragments in his proposed Undertaking, he, *therefore,* concludes that the Judicious have passed Sentence on the *Specimen* of his Qualifications for the Work, as *an ignorant, stupid* Performance.

It is a Misfortune to him not to have thought, like the Gazetteer, of inserting in his intended Magazine, *Proclamations* and *controversial* Essays, i.e. Essays towards or Preludes to Controversies, but not the Controversies themselves. Perhaps he might *then,* have as *reasonably* hoped for a Share in the public Favour, as the Gazetteer: For Pieces of such an *extraordinary* Kind cannot fail of Success, being not only *humorous* and *comical,* but extremely *improving,* and highly *suitable* to the Taste of Petty-Chapmen, to whom, provided they take off *large* Quantities of Paper, the Gazetteer has laid himself under a *constant* Obligation of furnishing them with *large* Quantities of Wit.

In Opposition to so inimitable a Writer, it would be a vain Attempt for the other to persist in his Undertaking. Besides that, he is informed that another Magazine, or rather a monthly News-Paper, like that advertised in the *Gazette,* will be carried on by the Printer of the *Mercury.* Therefore, *That* which was proposed by the Plan, is dropped *for the present;* and the Publisher of it humbly craves Pardon of the Public for troubling them with his Proposals. But he cannot help saying that it is a false Representation, occasioned thro' Want of Candour or Want of Attention, for any one to alledge, that he promised to perform, what was an Excess of Vanity in him to pretend to execute: For it appears from the Case, as it is truly stated above, that he undertook Nothing, but what was within the Compass of a very *mean* Capacity, when it falls in with a laborious Disposition.

Should it be objected, that he published his Plan as a Specimen of his Talents for Writing, imagining himself to be possessed of such as were capable of *embellishing* the Work proposed, and therefore a plain Proof of his being a vain, ignorant Pretender: He has several Things to offer in excuse. First, that the Gazetteer who *was* generally reputed a Man of clear Understanding, and fine Observation, highly approved of the Plan, even before it had received it's last Improvements. That the Writer's Offering it to the Judgement of the Public did, by no Means, imply a vain Confidence in his own abilities. And lastly, his great Resignation and Humility in acknowledging the Just Censure passed on his Essay, joined to his hearty Repentance, as well for that as other Sins of the like Kind he has heretofore been guilty of, together with a sincere Promise of Amendment for the future. These Premises being duly weighed and considered, he throws himself on the Mercy of the Public as a proper Object for their Forgiveness. Yet he wou'd not be understood to cut himself off from a necessary Self-defence when his Character is *unfairly* attacked; nor, therefore, from prosecuting the Dispute that now lies between Mr. Franklin and him, which he did not undertake to vindicate himself from being *a bad Writer* (for to that Accusation he has already pleaded GUILTY) but from the Charge of being a *bad Man*. J.W.

(The Remainder of the *Detection* promised in our last is deferred.)[7]

John Webbe: Defense Renewed, II

Printed in *The American Weekly Mercury*, December 4, 1740.

As it is the *indispensible* Duty of every Man to defend his Reputation from unjust Calumny, I was, *therefore*, obliged to step forth to vindicate mine, from the *injurious Insinuations* in the *Gazette*. But, notwithstanding the *Attempt* to destroy my Character, on which my Livelihood entirely depends, I was extremely *careful*, in my Justification, to avoid running into any Matter, but what the Nature of the Charge (not less than a Violation of Trust) and a Self-Defence* rendered *absolutely necessary*. The Facts urged in my Vindication I endeavoured to set forth with all the Clear-

*Every Man has a *natural* Right to defend himself against such as would deprive him of his Life or of the Means of preserving that Life. My Character in Regard to Integrity which Mr. Franklin every Week

7. See above, p. 269.

ness I was capable of, without Artifice or a *studied* Perplexity; and, therefore, if there had been the *least* Misrepresentation, it could have been *most easily* detected. Facts *so stated,* and NOT DENIED, are, according to a *universal* Rule of judging, CONFESSED; and therefore Mr. Franklin's Silence is the *highest* Justification I can desire. *While* he continues in that Humour I shall suppress the Remainder of the Detection. This is a Kindness he could not reasonably expect at my Hands; Considering that he has since my first Letter, in Quality of Post-Master, taken upon him to deprive the *Mercury* of the Benefit of the Post, and will not permit it to travel with his *Gazette,* that charges me with the most infamous Practices. His Resentment against his Brother Printer is altogether unreasonable; for a Printer should be always acquitted from being a Party to any Writing when he discovers the Author, or when the Author subscribes his Name; except the other knows he publishes a Falsehood at the Time, which cannot be supposed to be the Case in Respect to what Mr. Bradford printed for me.

I take this Occasion to return him my sincere Thanks for the Opportunity he has so *generously,* so *humanely,* tho' it was to his own Prejudice, furnished me with, of vindicating myself from the most scandalous Insinuations. But I presume he will not from thence assume to himself a Right of having me at his Mercy hereafter, and to spare or cut my Throat at his Pleasure. On that Presumption, I subscribe my self, with the greatest *Gratitude* and Respect, his most obliged, humble Servant,   JOHN WEBBE

---

endeavours to take away by representing me on the Face of his *Gazette,* as a perfidious Fellow, is the only Support left me, and on which my whole Reliance is for procuring the *Necessaries* of Life. Cicero, in his diffusive, luxuriant Manner, has left us a just and beautiful Description of the Law of *Self Preservation,* Part of which as it is applicable to the present Case, I shall set down in the Words of that great Orator. *Est enim haec, Judices, non scripta sed nata lex: quam non didicimus, accepimus, legimus; verum ex ipsa natura arripuimus, hausimus, expressimus; ad quam non docti, sed facti; non instituti, sed imbuti sumus.* pro Mil.[8]

8. Cicero, *Pro Milone,* IV, 10.

The Postmaster and the Mercury

Printed in *The Pennsylvania Gazette*, December 11, 1740.

The Publick has been entertain'd for these three Weeks past, with angry Papers, written expressly against me, and publish'd in the *Mercury*. The *two first* I utterly neglected, as believing that both the Facts therein stated, and the extraordinary Reasonings upon them, might be safely enough left to themselves, without any Animadversion; and I have the Satisfaction to find, that the Event has answered my Expectation: But the *last*, my Friends think 'tis necessary I should take some Notice of, as it contains an Accusation that has at least a Shew of Probability, being printed by a Person to whom it particularly relates, who could not but know whether it was true or false; and who, having still some Reputation to guard, it may be presum'd, could by no Means be prevail'd on to publish a Thing as Truth, which was contrary to his own Knowledge.

"Mr. Franklin (says the Writer in the *Mercury*) has, *since* my first Letter, in Quality of Post-Master, *taken upon him* to deprive the *Mercury* of the Benefit of the Post, and will not permit it to travel with his *Gazette* which charges me with the most infamous Practices. His Resentment against his Brother Printer is altogether unreasonable; for a Printer should always be acquitted from being a Party to any Writing, when he discovers the Author, or when the Author subscribes his Name; *except* the other KNOWS *he publishes a Falshood* at the Time; which *cannot be supposed to be the Case* in respect to what Mr. Bradford printed for me."[9]

It unluckily happens, that this not only *may be supposed to be the Case,* but *really is the Case,* in respect to this very Paragraph.

For the Truth is, that 'tis now upwards of a Twelvemonth since I refus'd to forward Mr. Bradford's Papers free by the Post, in Obedience to a positive Order from the Hon. Col. SPOTSWOOD, then Post-Master General.[1]

To prevent any Suspicion of the Reality of such an Order, or that I obtain'd it by some Misrepresentations of Mr. Bradford, or that it was given hastily, thro' Caprice, or without just Reason, I

9. See above, p. 274.
1. Bradford, when postmaster, had forbidden the riders to deliver the *Gazette*, until Spotswood directed otherwise. He contrived, nevertheless, to

am sorry I am oblig'd to mention, That his Detaining the Ballance of his Accounts, and his Neglecting to render any Account for a long time, while he held the Post-Office himself, as they were the Occasion of his Removal, so they drew upon him, after long Patience and Forbearance, the Resentment of the Post-Master General, express'd in the following Letter.

[*Here Franklin incorporated the text of the letter from Alexander Spotswood, October 12, 1739, printed above, pp. 235-6.*]

Upon the Receipt of this Letter it was, that I absolutely refus'd to forward any more of Mr. Bradford's Papers free by Post; and from that time to this, he has never offered me any to forward. *This he cannot but* KNOW *to be true.*

I must however do Mr. Bradford the Justice, to vindicate him from an injurious Suspicion which I apprehend may arise on this Occasion, to wit, That he has impos'd that Story on his unhappy Writer, and misled him by a wrong Account of Facts he might be ignorant of. For this, in my Opinion, cannot possibly be: Inasmuch as that Person is thoroughly acquainted with the Affair, was employ'd as Attorney in the Action against Bradford, and had, at the very Time he was writing the Paragraph in Question, the Original Letter from Col. SPOTSWOOD, in his own Possession.

B. FRANKLIN

---

interfere with its distribution though BF circumvented him by bribing the riders to carry it. When he succeeded Bradford as postmaster in 1737, BF did not bar the former's paper, but allowed it to be carried free, on the understanding that Bradford would settle his account with the deputy postmaster general. Bradford's failure to do so brought Spotswood's order, Oct. 12, 1739, suspending the privilege of free postage for the *Mercury*. Par. Text edit., p. 260; Ruth L. Butler, *Doctor Franklin, Postmaster General* (N.Y., 1928), pp. 32-4. John Webbe charged (see below, p. 278) that BF had continued to carry Bradford's paper, despite Spotswood's order, in order to make Bradford dependent on him. The episode is treated from Bradford's point of view in Anna J. DeArmond, *Andrew Bradford, Colonial Journalist* (Newark, Del., 1949), pp. 223-32.

John Webbe: The Postmaster and the Mercury

Printed in *The American Weekly Mercury*, December 18, 1740.

A Particular must imagine himself to be of mighty Consequence, when he thinks his private Differences deserve to be decided at the public Tribunal. But when he is dragged there against his Inclination, every one must acknowledge that he has a Right to be heard in his Turn. This was my Case in Respect to the Scandalous Accusation, which without the least Provocation on my Part Mr. Franklin brought against me.

"There is something very terrible (to use the words of Sir Richard Steel) in attacking a Man in a Way that may prejudice his Character or Fortune." I thought all in general as much concerned in discouraging, as I in particular was in vindicating my self from the unjust Calumny endeavoured to be propagated in the *Gazette*. I therefore warmly, yet I hope justly, resented the *undeserved* Injury, which every Man, in my humble Apprehension of Things, *would,* nay *should* do, in like Circumstances.

The Advertisement that gave Occasion to those Reflections is lately dropped;[2] and Nothing could compensate the Reader for the Loss of so ingenious a Performance, which the Gazetteer, as a Sample of his Abilities for carrying on a Magazine, favoured us with for four Weeks successively, but the wonderful Letter substituted in the Place of it.

Previous to the Remarks I intend to make on it I would premise, That it is true that after the Orders mentioned by the Gazetteer, Mr. Bradford never sent him any of his Papers to be forwarded in the Mail. But it is as true, that, as they were made up in unsealed Packets, he sent them to the Riders who used to distribute them on their several Routs. This Method, which Mr. Bradford was obliged to have Recourse to a considerable Time past for the Conveyance of his News-Papers, was NO SECRET; and consequently could not be *unknown* to Mr. Franklin; and therefore it must be presumed to have had his Approbation. Moreover, I was *well assured* that He had declared, some Time before he laid

2. BF printed the advertisement in the *Gazette*, November 13, 20, 27, and December 4, but omitted it December 11, the day the defense of his conduct as postmaster appeared. On December 25, however, he again published the advertisement with its offending paragraph.

me under the Necessity of writing against him in my own Defence, that as he favoured Mr. Bradford by permitting the Postman to distribute his Papers, he had him therefore *under his Thumb;*
and was confident, in Regard he could at any Time deprive him
of that Privilege, that he would not, if he understood his own
Interest, be prevaild upon to publish any Thing against him the
Gazetteer.

Of this incontestable Proof can be brought, if it should be
denied; for untill it be, as the Fact lies within his own Knowledge
it would be idle to produce it.

Again, Mr. Bradford, on whom I ought to relie, informed me
before I wrote my last, that the Postman who generally carried
his News-Papers lately mentioned he was apprehensive it wou'd
be displeasing to Mr. Franklin, were he to know he distributed
them. Now such Apprehensions which could only be judged to
arise from some Declaration of Mr. Franklin; (whether directly
or indirectly is left to his Choice to say; for either is equal for our
Purpose) being considered with the Information I had of his
previous Resolution to stop the Passage of the *Mercury,* whenever
he should think himself disobliged by it: I therefore, and *justly*
therefore, inferred, That he had already begun to put his Threats
against the *Mercury* in Execution.

Tho' I think this Inference can be maintained upon the *strictest*
Rules of Reasoning; yet, admitting it to be only a very probable
Conjecture, the Event has shown it was made on the justest
Grounds, if it be true, and Mr. Franklin can best tell whether it
be so or no, that he has as well before as after the Publication
of his Letter affirmed, That, supposing the Postmen had distributed the *Mercury,* since Mr. Spotswood's Orders above mentioned, They did it by Corruption, and without our Post-Master's
Approbation. This surely was a Prohibition to them not to receive
it any more. Now, as it sprung from what I wrote in my own
Defence, it will be incumbent on Mr. Franklin to show, what I
defy him to show, that he had greater Reason to forbid the Passage of the *Mercury* on the Publication of my last Letter than on
that of my first; or he must allow us to date this same *Edict* of his
something higher than 2 Weeks ago, which puts the Point out of
Dispute.

This *Edict* in Regard to the Postman was what I meant by depriving the *Mercury* of the Benefit of the Post. And I expressly charge it on Mr. Franklin that he was sensible I so meant before he wrote his abusive Letter, which I call upon him to deny if he can. If I had thought the general Expression had been less favourable to him than this particular Explanation of it, I should not have left it at large as I did.

He NOTWITHSTANDING, partly with a View, as I am apt to imagine, to convince the World of his great Address in Argument, undertook to prove, and did most *elaborately* and UNDENIABLY prove *(what he was sure no Body would deny)* the Receipt of Mr. Spotswood's Orders: I say he well knew those Orders would not be denied; for it was commonly known he had such; besides the Letter in which they were contained, being in my own Custody, I readily delivered up on his sending for it, without *once* pretending it was mislaid, a few Days before the publishing of it in the *Gazette.*

Such an Absurdity would be pardonable, if it *only* arose from his natural Fondness of being thought a man of Sagacity. But because he could not in *one Respect* be said to deprive the *Mercury* of the Advantage of the Post, in as much as he had Orders so to do, that *Therefore* he did not in any *other Respect;* and from thence in express Terms *peremptorily* to charge me with writing and Mr. Bradford with publishing a *wilful* Falsehood, tho' the Gazetteer was thro'ly Sensible at the Time it was not one, is such *a flagrant* Evidence of his great CANDOUR and SINCERITY, as well as of a violent inclination to *defame,* that I think it may be safely left to it self without any farther Animadversion.

We have already examined into our Gentlemans Pretensions to Candour and Veracity. We would now most humbly crave his gracious Permission to consider him in the Capacity of a Writer. Tho' I had wrote much, too much, in his *Gazette,* yet he never favoured me with a Specimen of his Skill that Way, so as to form any certain Judgment of it, before his late Advertisement. I have already pointed out some of the Nonsense of that laboured Piece, which it seems was the Scheme that, to the great Credit of his Learning, he boasts he had been hatching for several Years. I hope he will not insult the Understanding of the Public so much, as to endeavour to palm it upon them again without Correction. For that Reason I would put him in mind of another egregious Blunder, which I desire he will expunge; I mean that Part where he says, *That my declaring an Intention of beginning a Magazine,* tho' above 4 Months after such Notice, *was probably with a View to get the Start of him.* Now this is highly improbable, except waiting so long behind and Starting before signify one and the same Thing.

The Letter now under Consideration is the second Specimen he ever favoured me with of his Abilities as a Writer. I frankly own that I think it far beneath a Criticism. But as he has introduced it with much Solemnity, telling us he undertook it by the Advice of his Friends, I shall therefore animadvert on *some* Passages in it. It would swell my Paper too much to observe on all the Absurdities contained in that Epistle, for it has not one Line of accurate Sense, except what is comprized in the *late* General's Letter, which, after his Decease, the Gazetteer, contrary to all Rules of Honour, and the Laws of Humanity, has taken the *modest* Freedom to Print.

It will be evident to every Man of Attention, That the true Design of publishing it was to defame Mr. Bradford. But the Gazetteer being obliged to conceal that Design and to devise some plausible Reasons for covering it, therefore says, *To prevent any Suspicion of the Reality of such an order,* [This was needless for he knew no one would call the Reality of such an order in Question][3] *or that I obtained it by some Misrepresentation of Mr. Bradford,* [the Gazetteer has here, instead of laying a Suspicion raised one, by going about to obviate Misrepresentations before he was called upon] *or that it was given hastily, thro' Caprice, or without just Reason,* [if the honourable Person was alive, I believe he would not think himself much obliged to this Advocate, for endeavouring to vindicate him from Hastiness, Caprice, or Unreasonableness; since the very Suspicion, which the Printer undertakes to clear the General from, of any one of those Failings, in so great a Character, must be highly injurious to it] *I am sorry I am obliged to mention,* [Absurd again, to express a Concern for being obliged to mention, what he was not under the least Obligation to mention] *That the detaining the Ballance of his accounts and his neglecting to render any account for a long Time, while he held the Post-Office*

3. The brackets, here and following in this paragraph, are in the original.

himself, as they were the Occasion of his Removal, [The Letter no where says so, and Mr. Bradford says he was removed by the *false* Representations, and *private* Sollicitations of the Gazetteer] *so they drew upon him the Resentment of the Post-Master General expressed in the following Letter,* which afterwards ensues. But the Post-Master General on the contrary, plainly declares, that for as much as on Inquiry he found, That the Sickness pleaded by Mr. Bradford was only pretended, he therefore thought that such an Imposition should not be passed over, without some Mark of his Resentment. If Mr. Bradford can prove, as he says he can, that his Sickness was not imaginary, no Body can be Suspected of giving that false Information of his State of Health to the Post-Master General but his Deputy here. It appears from the Scope of the Letter to which I refer, that the honourable Person who wrote it, designed it should be communicated to Mr. Bradford, which he declares never was done. Perhaps the Reason of concealing it from him, 'till after the Post-Master General's Death, was an Apprehension he might be convinced that the Order in it was obtained upon a Misrepresentation of Mr. Bradford, the Suspicion of which Mr. Franklin, tho' not charged with it, thought himself under a Necessity, even of going out of his Way, to clear himself from. I leave the Paragraph with this farther Observation on it, that I never met with so many Blunders and Inconsistencies crowded together in so small a Compass.

I should not discharge the Part of a just Critic, if, in animadverting on the Faults, I should pass over any Excellency in this inimitable Writer. I cannot therefore but highly applaud the *ingenious and concise* Method he has invented for refuting Facts, i.e. Truths, tho' they manifestly prove him to be false and treacherous, *by only telling you that he utterly neglects them.* But as very few can be supposed [to] have a Taste for relishing a Delicacy in Writing so perfectly *new,* I am therefore of Opinion, that the Expression which imediately follows, to wit, *that the Event has answered his Expectation,* or in other Words, that his Method has been generally admired, ought rather to be taken in a hyperbolical than in a litteral Sense; and that, for the true Construction of it, we ought to have Recourse to a certain Figure in Speech, which the French generally call a *Gasconade.*   J. W.

Extracts from the Gazette, 1740

Printed in *The Pennsylvania Gazette*, January 3 to December 25, 1740.

We hear from Georgia by Way of New-York, that the Reverend Mr. Whitefield arrived there in good Health, about the 20th of January; and that he had immediately set 30 Hands to Work about the Orphan House.[4]   [February 28]

The News of the taking of Porto Bello is confirm'd from all Parts, but the Accounts of the Action are so various, that we chuse not to insert any of them, and wait for one that may be depended on.[5]   [March 20]

**Some unforeseen Accidents have a little retarded the Publication of the Rev. Mr. Whitefield's Sermons and Journals; The

4. This project, suggested by Charles Wesley and approved by the Georgia Trustees, was on Whitefield's mind for more than thirty years, keeping him traveling, preaching, and appealing for funds. On his first visit to Georgia in 1738 he had arranged for the instruction of children in two villages, and opened a school in Savannah. Stuart C. Henry, *George Whitefield: Wayfaring Witness* (N.Y., 1957), pp. 39–40. English philanthropists contributed many kinds of goods, which Whitefield sold in Philadelphia for the benefit of the orphan-house, and he got generous financial contributions in the northern and middle colonies in 1739. Reaching Savannah Jan. 10, 1740, he rented a house, where he took in as many orphans as he could find (including some who were adequately provided for otherwise), and on a 500-acre tract ten miles away began the construction of a twenty-room building, an infirmary, and a workhouse. Whitefield himself laid the first brick March 25, naming the establishment Bethesda "because I hoped it would be a House of Mercy to many Souls." Tyerman, *Whitefield*, I, 347–52, 355.

BF thought sending men and materials to Georgia needlessly expensive— he would have preferred to bring the children to existing accommodations in Philadelphia; but, as he fondly recalled in his memoirs, Whitefield's preaching was so persuasive that he contributed all the same. Par. Text edit., pp. 268–70. To answer charges that Whitefield misappropriated the funds he raised, BF reprinted the former's accounts and financial statements of 1741 and 1746, the former as a pamphlet, the latter in *Pa. Gaz.*, April 16, 1746.

5. Admiral Edward Vernon (1684–1757) took Porto Bello November 21–22. His order, Aug. 4, 1740, to mix water with his sailors' daily ration of rum, soon adopted in other squadrons of the British Navy, effected "perhaps the greatest improvement to discipline and efficiency ever produced by one stroke of the pen." *DNB*. Americans, however, know Vernon because an admiring volunteer at Cartagena gave his admiral's name to his Potomac River plantation.

Work is however in great Forwardness, and Notice will be given in this Paper, when they are finish'd and ready to be deliver'd to Subscribers.   [March 27]

Saturday last about One o'Clock a Fire broke out in Mr. Hamilton's fine new Buildings near the Bridge; and the Wind being high, and the wood Work (which was unfinish'd) exceedingly dry'd by the long dry Weather, the whole was in Flames so suddenly and burnt so fiercely, that it was impossible to save any Part. The Loss is very considerable; and is generally regretted, as those Buildings when finish'd would have been a great Ornament to that Part of the Town.[6]   [April 3]

His Majesty's Ship *Colchester* being arrived in Virginia, with Orders from the Court of Great Britain to the several Governors of the Northern Colonies; an Express came in here on Thursday last with those for this Government, and others, which were immediately forwarded for New-Jersey, New-York, Connecticut, Rhode-Island, Massachusetts Bay, Nova Scotia, and Newfoundland. On Monday His Honour our Governor, attended by near 200 Gentlemen, came to the Court-House, where a vast Concourse of People were assembled, and published the King's Declaration of War against Spain, together with the following Proclamation, viz.
                    [Here it follows.][7]
The People express'd their Joy in loud Huzzas; And the Cannon from the Hill, and the Ships in the Harbour, were discharged, while the following Healths were drank, viz. The KING. The Prince and Royal Family. Success to His Majesty's Arms. My Lord Cathcart. Col. Spotswood. Col. Blakeney. Success to the new Levies, and intended Expedition, &c. Plenty of Liquor was given to the Populace; and in the Evening they had a Bonfire on the Hill.
As a Design against some of the rich Spanish Settlements appears exceedingly agreeable to the People in general, and there

6. One of the buildings is said to have been used as a dancing-room. Watson, *Annals*, I, 340.
7. For the text of the proclamation and a brief account of its publication, see *Pa. Col. Recs.*, IV, 396–8.

is truly a great Prospect of Success, it is not doubted but a considerable Body of Men will be raised on this Occasion, even in Pennsylvania.

In our next we shall, from the Books of Geography, give some Account of those Countries against which it is supposed the present Expedition is intended. [April 17]

The middle of last Month the Rev. Mr. Whitefield was at Charlestown, and preached there five Times, and collected at one Sermon *Seventy Pounds Sterling,* for the Benefit of the Orphan-House in Georgia: And on Sunday last (after Ten Days Passage from Georgia) he landed at New-Castle, where he preached Morning and Evening. On Monday Morning he preach'd to about 3000 at Wilmington, and in the Evening arrived in this City; on Tuesday Evening he preach'd to about 8000 on Society-Hill; and preach'd at the same Place yesterday Morning and Evening. . . . [April 17]

On Sunday last the Reverend Mr. Whitefield preached two Sermons on Society Hill, and collected for the Orphans in Georgia, in the Morning £150 10s. and in the Evening, when it's computed there were 15,000 Auditors, £83, in all £233 10s. Currency, which is about £150 Sterling; besides sundry Benefactions sent in since. On Monday he preached at Greenwich and at Gloucester; on Tuesday twice in this City, when the Congregations were much melted: Yesterday he set out for New York. . . .
[April 24]

Since Mr. Whitefield's Preaching here, the Dancing School, Assembly and Concert Room have been shut up, as inconsistent with the Doctrine of the Gospel: And though the Gentlemen concern'd caus'd the Door to be broke open again, we are inform'd that no Company came the last Assembly Night.[8] [May 1]

Last Night the Rev. Mr. Whitefield arrived here, having preach'd at every Place mentioned in our last, and at New York, where he got upwards of £300 by private Donations and publick Collections, for the Orphan-House in Georgia. He preaches here

8. See above, pp. 257–9.

every Day this Week, and takes his leave on Sunday Evening. On Monday he preaches at Darby and Chester, where a Collection is to be made for the Orphan-House. On Tuesday at Wilmington by Ten a Clock precisely in the Morning; and at Whiteclay Creek at four in the Afternoon, where he intends to collect again. On Wednesday by Noon at Nottingham; and from thence he intends to return with all Speed to New-Castle, and to go on board in order to sail for Georgia. He cannot go so far as Dover and Lewis-Town, as proposed in our last, being obliged to hasten as fast as possible to Georgia, that he may have Time to go to New-England, and come from thence hither at the latter End of the Year.

Those who are disposed to send Provisions or Money for the Orphan House, may send it to the House of Mr. Stephen Benezet Merchant, in Second Street.[9]

In most Places where he has been, the Congregations were as numerous again as when he was here last.   [May 8]

[ADVERTISEMENT] Lent and forgot to whom, a Woman's white broadcloth kirb Bridle, double Rein'd.

Whoever brings it to the Printer hereof shall be thankfully rewarded.   [May 15]

[ADVERTISEMENT] Notice is hereby given to all Persons, that there is come to Town, a very Wonderful and surprizing Creature to all Persons in these Parts of the World; and it is in Scripture the very same Creature, which is there called a *Camel*. It is impossible to describe the Creature, and therefore all Persons of ingenious Curiosity have an Opportunity of Satisfying themselves.

The Creature was brought with great Difficulty from the Desarts of Arabia in that Quarter of the World which is called Asia, to New-England; a Curiosity which never was in this Country, and very likely never will be again.

---

9. John Stephen Benezet (1683–1751), Huguenot refugee to London, where he became a Quaker, came to Philadelphia in 1731. Whitefield often stayed at his house. He was one of the nine "trustees for uses" of the "New Building" erected in 1740 (see below, p. 290 n); becoming a Moravian, he moved to Germantown about 1743. George S. Brooks, *Friend Anthony Benezet* (Phila., 1937), pp. 8–22; Par. Text edit., p. 270.

Constant Attendance will be given to all Persons desirous of seeing said Creature at the House of Owen Owen, Esq. at the Sign of the Indian King in Philadelphia. [May 22]

Monday next will be delivered to the Subscribers, two Volumes of the Rev. Mr. Whitefield's Works; viz. One of Sermons and one of Journals.[1] The other Volumes being near finish'd, will be ready in a short Time.

As many People, during the Printing of the Books, have sent in their Names, or subscribed, without paying the first Subscription Money; and as the whole Number of Names far exceeds the Number of Books printed; those Subscribers who have paid, or who bring the Money in their Hands, will have the Preference.

[May 22]

We hear from French-Creek in Chester County, that on Monday last Mr. Robert Grace, a Gentleman of this City, was married to Mrs. Rebecca Nutt, an agreeable young Lady, with a Fortune of Ten Thousand Pound.[2] [May 29]

[ADVERTISEMENT] The Gentlemen who have subscribed to the *Encouragement* of a *Course* of *Philosophical Lectures* and *Experiments,* to be performed by Mr. Greenwood,[3] are desired to meet in the Chamber adjoining to the Library at the State House, on Tuesday next, about 9 a Clock in the Morning, when it is proposed the *Course* should begin, and be continued afterwards, at such Times as the Gentlemen then present shall see fit to deter-

1. See above, p. 242.
2. By this marriage Grace acquired the Warwick Iron Works, in which Mrs. Nutt's father, grandfather, and stepfather had all been associated. Mrs. Thomas Potts James, *Memorial of Thomas Potts, Junior* (Cambridge, Mass., 1874), pp. 29–30, 50–4, 386; see above, I, 209 n.
3. Isaac Greenwood (1702–1745), first Hollis professor of mathematics in Harvard College, 1727–38; author of an arithmetic text and of several papers in *Phil. Trans.* Dismissed from his post for excessive drinking, he conducted a private school in Boston and lectured in other towns. *Sibley's Harvard Graduates,* VI, 471–82; *DAB.* When Greenwood came to Philadelphia, BF requested and the Library Company directors granted the use of a room adjoining its library (in the State House) for his lectures, as well as the use of the Library's air pump for demonstrations. Lib. Co. Phila., MS Minutes, May 28, 1740.

mine: And such Gentlemen who are willing to attend a *Course* at other Times, in the same Place, are desired to leave their *Names* at the Post Office in Philadelphia, where the *Conditions* thereof may be seen, and *Subscriptions* taken in.   [June 5]

[ADVERTISEMENT] TO BE SOLD, A Dutch Servant Man and his Wife, for Two Years and Eight Months, a genteel riding Chair almost new, a Ten Cord Flat with new Sails and Rigging, a Fishing Boat, and sundry Sorts of Houshold Goods. Enquire of the Printer hereof.   [June 5]

We hear from Annapolis in Maryland, that on Saturday last, about 10 in the Evening, after 7 or 8 Weeks Illness, died there the Honourable Alexander Spotswood, Esq; in an advanc'd Age.[4] He served many Campaigns in the late Wars, under the Duke of Marlborough, as Quarter-Master General of the Queen's Armies. After the Peace he was made Governor of Virginia, and since Postmaster General of all the King's Dominions in America; and by a late Appointment, General and Commander in Chief of the Forces to be raised in the Plantations for the Expedition against the Spanish West-Indies. The Loss of a Gentleman of his distinguish'd Bravery, Skill and Experience in military Affairs, at this critical Juncture, must be regretted by all who have at Heart the Interest and Glory of Great Britain.   [June 12]

During the Session of the Presbyterian Synod, which began on the 28th of the last Month, and continued to the third of this Instant, there were no less than 14 Sermons preached on Society-Hill to large Audiences, by the Rev. Messrs. the Tennents, Mr. Davenport, Mr. Rowland and Mr. Blair, besides what were deliver'd at the Presbyterian and Baptist Meetings, and Expoundings and Exhortations in private Houses. The Alteration in the Face of Religion here is altogether surprizing. Never did the People show so great a Willingness to attend Sermons, nor the Preachers greater Zeal and Diligence in performing the Duties of their Function. Religion is become the Subject of most Conversations. No Books are in Request but those of Piety and De-

4. See above, p. 235 n.

votion; and instead of idle Songs and Ballads, the People are every where entertaining themselves with Psalms, Hymns and Spiritual Songs. All which, under God, is owing to the successful Labours of the Reverend Mr. Whitefield.[5]   [June 12]

His Honour our Governor having, in Pursuance of his Majesty's Instructions, some Time since, issued his Warrants for Raising of *eight* Companies of Men in this Government; the Whole were compleated about a Week ago: Four of these Companies being armed, by the Care and Diligence of the British Lieutenants wherewith they are furnish'd, have made a considerable Progress in the new Exercise; and we hear that the other four, during their Stay on the Continent, will henceforth be diligently attended and instructed by the Adjutant of this Battallion.   [August 7]

On Thursday last died here, aged 63 Years, Anne, the Lady of Sir William Keith, Bart. formerly Governor of this Province, and was decently interr'd the Day following.[6]   [August 7]

Notice is hereby given, To all Masters of Servants in the Counties of Philadelphia, Bucks, Chester and Lancaster, who have in any Manner suffered by the late Enlisting of Servants, that they immediately make known their several Grievances to the Constables of their respective Townships, who have Orders to trans-

5. The revival preaching was an accompaniment of the Synod's meeting, not a part of it. The Tennents—William, William, Jr., Charles, and Gilbert —were members of the Synod, as was Samuel Blair, and all were active leaders in the religious awakening. James Davenport, a Congregational minister from Southold, Long Island, became so fanatical a New Light that the Tennents finally denounced him. The Presbytery of New Brunswick had licensed John Rowland, 1738, though the Synod denied that it had the right to do so. The issue raised by Rowland's case led, in the next year, to the split between Old Side and New Side Presbyterians. Leonard J. Trinterud, *The Forming of an American Tradition* (Lund, Sweden, 1949), pp. 81–4; *DAB*; William B. Sprague, *Annals of the American Pulpit*, III (N.Y., 1859), 58–60.

6. Lady Keith's daughter by her first marriage was Ann Diggs, who married Dr. Thomas Graeme of Philadelphia. Their daughter Elizabeth, jilted by William Franklin, subsequently married Henry Hugh Ferguson. Charles P. Keith, "The Wife and Children of Sir William Keith," *PMHB*, LVI (1932), 1–8.

mit the same to Philadelphia, to the Committee of Grievances appointed by the Assembly.[7]   [August 14]

[ADVERTISEMENT] On Monday next, the two last Volumes of the Reverend Mr. Whitefield's Works will be ready to be deliver'd to the Subscribers.[8]

Note, The last Volume of Journals contains his American Journal.   [August 14]

The seven Companies raised in this Province, are all embark'd; and 'tis said the Transports will fall down in a few Days. The Companies are all full, and the Men chearful and in good Heart. They were review'd by his Honour the Governor before they went on board, and perform'd their Exercise to Admiration.

The Company rais'd in the Lower Counties will embark at New-Castle.   [September 18]

[ADVERTISEMENT] TO BE SOLD, At the Post-Office in Market-Street, Wholesale or Retale by the Importer; fine broad Scarlet Cloth, fine broad black Cloth, fine white Thread Hose, and English Sale Duck.   [October 9]

[ADVERTISEMENT] THOMAS GODFREY Proposes during the Winter Season, to teach Navigation, Astronomy, and other Parts of the Mathematicks, at his House in Second-Street.

[October 30]

7. The enlistment of servants became a matter of sharp controversy between the Assembly and Governor Thomas after July 20, when a petition was received from sundry inhabitants of Philadelphia "setting forth the Hardships they suffer, by the Taking and Detaining their Servants, under Pretence of enlisting them in the King's Service." The Assembly, estimating the number so taken at 300, declined to appropriate money for defense until all were discharged. This the governor refused to do and, as he was supported by the Proprietor, the Assembly appointed a committee to draft a petition and remonstrance to the King "and to take proper Proofs to support the same." *Votes and Proceedings,* III, 395, 409; Charles P. Keith, *Chronicles of Pennsylvania* (Phila., 1917), II, 804–8. This notice was inserted under that authority. Among the Franklin Papers in Lib. Cong. is a copy of a legal opinion on the question prepared by Nicholas Fazakerly, Dec. 24, 1740. *DNB.*

8. See above, pp. 242–3.

On Sunday Evening the Rev. Mr. Whitefield, arrived here from Boston, and has preached twice every Day since in a Building erected for that Purpose, 100 Feet long, and 70 broad; the Roof is ready to be put on; and the Whole, 'tis hoped, will in a short time be finished.[9] He proposes to continue in Town all this Week, and to leave us on Monday next: He designs to preach the same Day at Gloucester in the Morning, and at Greenwich, 12 Miles from thence, in the Afternoon. On Tuesday, at two a Clock in the Afternoon, at Piles-Grove. On Wednesday, at two a Clock in the Afternoon, at Cohansie. On Thursday, at two a Clock, at Salem. On Friday, three a Clock in the Afternoon, at Whiteclay-Creek. Saturday, two a Clock in the Afternoon, at Forks Mannor. And, Sunday Morning and Evening at Nottingham. On Monday Evening he intends to embark at New-Castle for Charles-Town, South-Carolina, in his Way to Georgia. On Sunday next, Morning and Evening, after Sermon, Collections

9. This structure, known as the "New Building," was erected by two groups of Philadelphians. One, aware of the city's needs and motivated by Christian principles and English examples, had in mind an elementary school where poor children might be instructed in "useful Literature and the Knowledge of the Christian Religion." The other wanted a free house of worship for Whitefield, who had been barred from most of the churches in Philadelphia since April 1740. The two groups, wisely pooling their resources, named four trustees, who acquired a lot near Fourth and Arch Streets, began construction of a building, and in turn named nine "trustees for uses" to carry out the terms of the trust. BF was not a member of either group of trustees. Whitefield first preached in the unfinished building November 9, and used it regularly on subsequent visits to Philadelphia; other clergymen preached there; and Gilbert Tennent conducted services in it after 1743. Nothing came of the attempts to set up the charity school until 1750, when the trustees of the newly established Academy of Philadelphia acquired the building.

Though the trustees of the New Building were of different faiths and the foundation was nonsectarian, the deed of trust made it clear that the charity school should offer Christian instruction and that the house of worship should be available only to Protestant ministers who were "sound in their Principles, . . . and acquainted with the Religion of the Heart and experimental piety." Edward P. Cheyney, *History of the University of Pennsylvania* (Phila., 1940), 21–7; Montgomery, *Hist. Univ. Pa.*, pp. 109–11. BF exaggerated when he wrote in his memoirs that the building was designed "expressly for the Use of any Preacher of any religious Persuasion who might desire to say something to the People of Philadelphia, . . . so that even if the Mufti of Constantinople were to send a Missionary to preach Mahometanism to us, he would find a Pulpit at his Service." Par. Text edit., p. 266.

are to be made for the Orphans at Georgia: And, in the mean while, those who will contribute Provisions or other Things, may bring the same to the House of Mr. Stephen Benezet, Merchant, in Front-Street.   [November 13]

On Sunday the 16th Instant, the Rev. Mr. Whitefield preach'd his Farewell-Sermon, and collected about £100 Sterl. for the Orphan-House in Georgia. He had been in Town eight Days, and preach'd 16 times in the New Building, besides private Exhortations, &c. The next Morning he set out in order to preach in several Places on both sides the River, and then embark for Georgia on board the Sloop *Savannah,* which went down the River on Monday last, expecting to meet him at Reedy-Island or Lewes-Town.   [November 27]

The Rev. Mr. Whitefield having taken up 5000 Acres of Land on the Forks of Delaware, in the Province of Pennsylvania, in order to erect a Negroe School there, and to settle a Town thereon with his Friends; all Persons who please to contribute to the said School, may pay their Contributions to Mr. Benezet, Merchant, in Philadelphia, Mr. Noble[1] at New-York, Mr. Gilbert Tennent, in New-Brunswick, New-Jersey, or to the Printer of this Paper.
                                        [November 27]

PHILADELPHIA: Printed by B. FRANKLIN, Post-Master, at the NEW PRINTING-OFFICE, near the Market. Price 10s. a Year.

1. Thomas Noble, New York merchant, was one of the "trustees for uses" of the New Building erected this fall. A friend of Whitefield, he left bequests to Bishop Spangenberg of the Moravian Church and to his brother-in-law Rev. William Tennent, Jr. *PMHB*, XXI (1897), 501; N.-Y. Hist. Soc. *Colls.,* 1895, p. 67. On Stephen Benezet, see above, p. 285 n; on Gilbert Tennent, see below, p. 313 n. The school for Negro children was never established. Tyerman, *Whitefield,* I, 377–9.

Poor Richard, 1741[2]

Poor Richard, 1741. An Almanack For the Year of Christ 1741, . . . By Richard Saunders, Philom. Philadelphia: Printed and sold by B. Franklin, at the New Printing-Office near the Market. (Yale University Library)

Of the ECLIPSES, 1741.

This Year there will be but two Eclipses, and those will be of the Sun, the first will happen June the Second Day: The other, November the 27th: Neither of which will be seen in these Parts of the World: But to the present Inhabitants of Cuba, and other Spanish Settlements in the West-Indies, these are like to appear very great Eclipses.[3]

XI Mon. January hath xxxi days.

> Your homely Face, Flippanta, your disguise,
> With Patches, numerous as Argus' Eyes:
> I own that Patching's requisite for you;
> For more we're pleas'd, if less your Face we view:
> Yet I advise, if my Advice you'd ask,
> Wear but one Patch;—but be that Patch a Mask.

> Enjoy the present hour, be mindful of the past;
> And neither fear nor wish the Approaches of the last.

Learn of the skilful: He that teaches himself, hath a fool for his master.

XII Mon. February hath xxviii days.

> The cringing Train of Pow'r, survey;
> What Creatures are so low as they!
> With what obsequiousness they bend!

2. Instead of the "trifling Preface" with which he usually introduced his almanac, BF offered his readers in 1741 a chronology of important dates since the Revolution of 1688.

3. Probably a reference to the joint military and naval expedition against the Spanish Caribbean possessions impending in the autumn of 1740, for which the British Colonies sent troops, and which met with disaster at Cartagena in the spring of 1741.

To what vile actions condescend!
Their Rise is on their Meanness built,
And Flatt'ry is their smallest Guilt.

Best is the Tongue that feels the rein;
He that talks much, must talk in vain;
We from the wordy Torrent fly:
Who listens to the chattering Pye?

Think Cato sees thee.

No Wood without Bark.

I Mon. March hath xxxi days.

Enrag'd was Buckram, when his Wife he beat,
That she'd so often *lousy Knave,* repeat.
At length he seiz'd and drag'd her to the Well,
I'll cool thy Tongue, or I'll thy Courage quell.
Ducking, thy Case, poor Buckram, little mends;
She had her Lesson at her Fingers Ends.
Sows'd over head, her Arms she raises high;
And *cracking* Nails the Want of *Tongue* supply.

Monkeys warm with envious spite,
Their most obliging FRIENDS will bite;
And, fond to copy human Ways,
Practise new Mischiefs all their days.

Joke went out, and brought home his fellow, and they two began
a quarrel.

II Mon. April hath xxx days.

Rash Mortals, e'er you take a Wife,
Contrive your Pile to last for Life:
On Sense and Worth your Passion found,
By DECENCY cemented round;
Let Prudence with Good-Nature strive
To keep Esteem and Love alive;

293

Then, come old Age when e'er it will,
Your *Friendship* shall continue still.

Let thy discontents be thy Secrets; if the world knows them,
'twill despise *thee* and increase *them*.

E'er you remark another's Sin,
Bid your own Conscience look within.

Anger and Folly walk cheek by jole; Repentance treads on both
their Heels.

III Mon. May hath xxxi days.

Fair Decency, celestial Maid,
Descend from Heav'n to Beauty's Aid:
Tho' Beauty may beget Desire,
'Tis thou must fan the Lover's Fire:
For, Beauty, like supreme Dominion,
Is best supported by Opinion:
If Decency bring no Supplies,
Opinion falls and Beauty dies.

Turn Turk, Tim, and renounce thy Faith in Words as well as
Actions: Is it worse to follow Mahomet than the Devil?

Don't overload Gratitude; if you do, she'll kick.

Be always asham'd to catch thy self idle.

IV Mon. June hath xxx days.

When painful Colin in his Grave was laid,
His mournful Wife this Lamentation made;
I've lost, alas! (poor Wretch, what must I do?)
The best of Friends, and best of Husbands too.
Thus of all Joy and Happiness bereft;
And with the Charge of ten poor Children left;
A greater Grief no Woman sure can know.
Who (with ten Children)—who will have me now?

294

Where yet was ever found the Mother,
Who'd change her booby for another?

At 20 years of age the Will reigns; at 30 the Wit; at 40 the Judgment.

Christianity commands us to pass by Injuries; Policy, to let them pass by us.

V Mon. July hath xxxi days.

Nature expects Mankind should share
The Duties of the publick Care.
Who's born for Sloth? To some we find
The Plough-share's annual Toil assign'd;
Some at the sounding Anvil glow;
Some the swift sliding Shuttle throw;
Some, studious of the Wind and Tide,
From Pole to Pole our Commerce guide.

Lying rides upon Debt's back.

They who have nothing to be troubled at, will be troubled at nothing.

Wife, from thy Spouse each blemish hide
More than from all the World beside:
Let DECENCY be all thy Pride.

VI Mon. August hath xxxi days.

Some (taught by Industry) impart
With Hands and Feet the Works of Art;
While some, of Genius more refin'd,
With Head and Tongue assist Mankind:
Each aiming at one common End
Proves to the whole a needful Friend.
Thus, born each other's useful Aid,
By Turns are Obligations paid.

Nick's Passions grow fat and hearty; his Understanding looks consumptive!

> If evils come not, then our fears are vain:
> And if they do, Fear but augments the pain.

If you would keep your Secret from an enemy, tell it not to a friend.

Rob not for burnt offerings.

VII Mon. September hath xxx days.

> The Monarch, when his Table's spread,
> To th' Farmer is oblig'd for Bread;
> And when in all his Glory drest,
> Owes to the Loom his royal Vest:
> Do not the Mason's Toil and Care
> Protect him from th' inclement Air?
> Does not the Cutler's Art supply
> The Ornament that guards his Thigh?[4]

> Bess brags she 'as *Beauty,* and can prove the same;
> As how? why thus, Sir, 'tis her *puppy's* name.

Up, Sluggard, and waste not life; in the grave will be sleeping enough.

Well done, is twice done.

Clearly spoken, Mr. Fog! You explain English by Greek.

VIII Mon. October hath xxxi days.

> All these, in Duty, to the Throne
> Their common Obligations own.
> 'Tis he (his own and People's Cause)
> Protects their Properties and Laws:
> Thus they their honest Toil employ,
> And with Content the Fruits enjoy
> In every Rank, or great or small,
> 'Tis INDUSTRY supports us all.

4. These verses are continued under October.

Formio bewails his Sins with the same heart,
As Friends do Friends when they're about to part.
Believe it Formio will not entertain,
One chearful Thought till they do meet again.

Honours change Manners.

IX Mon. November hath xxx days.

Syl. dreamt that bury'd in his fellow Clay,
Close by a common Beggar's Side he lay:
And, as so mean a Neighbour shock'd his Pride
Thus, like a Corpse of consequence, he cry'd:
Scoundrel, begone; and henceforth touch me not:
More manners learn; and, at a distance, rot.
How! Scoundrel! in a haughtier Tone cry'd he;
Proud Lump of Dirt, I scorn thy Words and thee;
Here all are equal; now thy Case is mine;
This is my Rotting Place, and that is thine.

Jack eating rotten cheese, did say,
Like Sampson I my thousands slay;
I vow, quoth Roger, so you do,
And with the self-same weapon too.

There are no fools so troublesome as those that have wit.

Quarrels never could last long,
If on one side only lay the wrong.

X Mon. December hath xxxi days.

On a Bee, stifled in Honey.
From Flow'r to Flow'r, with eager Pains,
   See the poor busy Lab'rer fly!
When all that from her Toil she gains
   Is, in the Sweets she hoards, to die.
'Tis thus, would Man the Truth believe,
   With Life's soft Sweets, each fav'rite Joy:
If we taste wisely, they relieve;
   But if we plunge too deep, destroy.

Let no Pleasure tempt thee, no Profit allure thee, no Ambition corrupt thee, no Example sway thee, no Persuasion move thee, to do any thing which thou knowest to be Evil; So shalt thou always live jollily: for a good Conscience is a continual Christmass. Adieu.

COURTS.

He that by Injury is griev'd,
And goes to Law to be reliev'd,
Is sillier than a sottish Chouse,
Who when a Thief has robb'd his House,
Applies himself to cunning Men
To help him to his Goods again:
When, all he can expect to gain,
Is but to squander more in vain.
For Lawyers, lest the Bear Defendant,
And Plaintiff Dog should make an End on't,
Do stave and tail with Writs of Error,
Reverse of Judgment and Demurrer,
To let them breath a while, and then
Cry *Whoop*, and set them on again:
Until, with subtil cobweb Cheats,
They're catch'd in knotted Law, like Nets,
In which, when once they are embrangl'd,
The more they stir the more they're tangl'd:
For while their Purses can dispute,
There's no End of th' immortal Suit.   Hud.[5]

Many Persons being at a Loss to know the Plant which is the true INDIAN PHYSICK, *I thought it not amiss to give the Publick a distinct and plain Account of it.*

The Root hath the Appearance of the true *Ipecacuana*, Branching from the Centre every Way near the Top of the Ground, or about two or three Inches deep, from which riseth one Stalk, finely chaneled with redish Lines; from the Sides of which grow alternately, about the Distance of two Inches, from near the Bottom to the Top, three distinct Leaves, two Inches long, and near an Inch broad, finely toothed round the Edges, and pointed at

5. Samuel Butler, *Hudibras*, III, iii, 529–36; I, ii, 161–6; II, iii, 17–22.

the Ends, but joined near the Stalk; out of the Bosom of which ariseth Branches of every Side the Stalk, which are in large Plants again divided into several Branches, and three Leaves joined together accompany the Beginning of every Branch, both which diminish the nearer they are to the Top; where there is commonly, set upon Foot-Stalks half an Inch long, three white Flowers, consisting of five Leaves to each Flower: The Plant groweth from two Foot to four Foot high, in hilly Ground; in these Northern Provinces the whole Plant is bitter in Taste. This is the true INDIAN PHYSICK mentioned in that valuable little Book entituled, *Every Man his own Doctor*,[6] written by a learned Gentleman in Virginia, whom I had a Letter of Recommendation unto from London: I enquired of him, particularly, concerning the *Ipecacuana* mentioned in his Book, and he shewed me a large Quantity of it, which was gathered for his own Practice: He told me, that less than *Sixty Grains* was not a full Dose for a Man. This I mention because many in Pensilvania and Maryland use a Species of the Spurges, which yieldeth Milk when broken, and is a violent Medicine, instead of this which the Gentleman designed.   JOHN BERTRAM[7]

In January next will be published,
(To be continued Monthly)

The General MAGAZINE, and *Historical Chronicle,* For all the British Plantations in America:[8]

Containing,

I.   Extracts from the Votes, and Debates of the Parliament of Great Britain.
II.   The Proclamations and Speeches of Governors; Addresses, Votes, Resolutions, &c. of Assemblies, in each Colony.
III. Accounts of, and Extracts from, all new Books, Pamphlets, &c. published in the Plantations.
IV.   Essays, controversial, humorous, philosophical, religious, moral or political.
V.   Select Pieces of Poetry.

6. For Tennent's *Every Man his own Doctor*, see above, p. 155.
7. John Bartram (1699–1777); see below, p. 378 n.
8. See above, p. 263.

VI. A concise CHRONICLE of the most remarkable Transactions, as well in Europe as America.

VII. Births, Marriages, Deaths, and Promotions, of eminent Persons in the several Colonies.

VIII. Course of Exchange between the several Colonies, and London; Prices of Goods, &c.

This MAGAZINE, in Imitation of those in England, was long since projected; a Correspondence is settled with intelligent Men in most of the Colonies, and small Types are procured, for carrying it on in the best Manner. We shall endeavour, by executing our Plan with Care, Diligence and Impartiality; and by Printing the Work neatly and correctly, to deserve the Favour of the Publick: But we desire no Subscriptions: We shall publish the Books at our own Expence, and risque the Sale of them; which Method, we suppose, will be most agreeable to our Readers, as they will then be at Liberty to buy only what they like, and we shall be under a constant Necessity of endeavouring to make every particular Pamphlet worth their Money. Each Magazine shall contain four Sheets, of common sized Paper, in a small Character: Price *Six Pence* Sterling, or *Nine Pence* Pennsylvania Money; with considerable Allowance to Chapmen who take Quantities. To be printed and sold by B. Franklin in Philadelphia.[9]

Introduction to The New-Year's Gift

Printed in *The New-Year's Gift; or a Pocket Almanack, For the Year 1741*. Philadelphia Printed and Sold by B. Franklin. (Yale University Library)

Franklin printed three almanacs for 1741 in addition to Poor Richard's and John Jerman's. One was a single sheet, another was *A Pocket Almanack . . . Fitted to the Use of Pennsylvania, and the neighbouring Provinces*,[1] and the third was *The New-Year's Gift*. A miniature about three inches by one and printed, like some of the pocket almanacs, in red and black, *The New-Year's Gift* contained much of the essential data of the larger pocket almanacs, as well as a characteristic introduction by the famous philomath Richard Saunders.

9. This paragraph also appeared in John Jerman's almanac for 1741, which BF printed.

1. See below, p. 400.

Courteous Reader,

Thou hast here an Almanack so small, as that it may be carried conveniently in a Corner of thy Pocket-Book, and yet contains many useful Things, viz. All the Days observ'd by the Church, Lunations, Moon's Place, Sun, Moon and Seven Stars Rising and Setting, Length of Days, Eclipses, Fairs, Courts, Births of the Royal Family, &c. The Days of the Month are set down, but the Week Days I tho't needless; the Weeks being separated by black Lines, and the Days of the Week easily discern'd thereby. It needs little Explanation: ☉ rise 7 16. signifies, *The Sun rises 16 minutes after 7.* the like of the Moon and Seven Stars. Day inc. 20 m. signifies, *the Days are increas'd in length 20 minutes;* Day 9 35, means, *the Days are 9 hours 35 minutes long, &c.* To oblige thee the more, I have omitted all the bad Weather, being Thy Friend R. S.

Advertisement in the General Magazine

Printed in *The General Magazine, and Historical Chronicle, for all the British Plantations in America,* I (January 1741), inside cover. (Yale University Library)

After the first announcements in November, Franklin and Bradford both hurried to get their magazines into print, each promising in his paper of February 5 that his would be published "next Week." As it fell out, Bradford's *American Magazine* won the race, coming off the press on February 13. Franklin's *General Magazine* followed on February 16.[2] It carried an "Advertisement" from the publisher.

[February 16, 1741]
Advertisement.

This *Magazine* will be published Monthly; the Paper and Page will be continued of the same Size, that so the Twelve Months

---

2. *Pa. Gaz.*, Feb. 12, 1741. In BF's Ledger D, p. 176 (see above, p. 232), February 16, Deborah Franklin recorded sales of copies of the "magaseen" to a number of customers, including Israel Pemberton, Governor Thomas, the Proprietor Thomas Penn (six copies), Dr. John Bard, "Willkisen Brush-maker," Thomas Godfrey, John Jerman, "Willcox paper maker," William Dewees, Alexander Annand, and Mrs. Margaret Penn Freame, sister of the Proprietor.

may be bound in one Volume at the Year's End, with a compleat Index or Table, which we shall add to the Month of December.

No Care shall be wanting, or Expence spared, to procure the best Materials for the Work, and make it as entertaining and useful as possible. The Character will generally be small, for the sake of comprising much in little Room, but it shall be good, and fairly printed.

An Account of the Export of Provisions from Philadelphia

Printed in *The General Magazine, and Historical Chronicle, for all the British Plantations in America*, 1 (January 1741), 75. (Yale University Library)

Eighteenth-century periodicals contained almost nothing original, and the *General Magazine* was no exception. The printer extracted news from American and English papers, essays from London journals, and laws, proclamations, treaties, debates, and other documents from the proceedings of Parliament and the colonial assemblies. He included verses and excerpts from new books.[3] These selections were, of course, made with reference to the interests of American readers. Accordingly Franklin printed extensive extracts from Robert Beverley's *History and Present State of Virginia*, an account of the colony of Georgia, the manual of arms and infantry evolutions, and many letters about George Whitefield's doctrine and preaching. There were several pieces on colonial economy, such as the plan of a New England manufactory and an interesting analysis of how a loan office would operate. The first number contained statistics on the provisions exported from Philadelphia in 1740, with a comment which, because of its argument and style, the editors believe to have been written by Franklin. The idea of the colonies' value to the mother country, set forth in the concluding sentences, appears in some of his writings during the controversy with Great Britain.

[February 16, 1741]

An ACCOUNT of the Export of Provisions from the Port of Philadelphia, in Pennsilvania, betwixt the 25th of December 1739, and the 25th of December 1740.

---

3. Despite this variety, however, the *General Magazine* lasted only six issues. The *American Magazine* had died with the March issue, the month Bradford originally set for its first appearance.

Wheat, 314,570 and half, Bushels.

Bread, 49 and half, Tons; 7,980 Tierces, 9,573 Barrels, 885 half Barrels, 881 quarter Barrels, and 9 Cags.

Flour, 100 Tierces, 53,970 Barrels, 147 half Barrels.

Barley, 40 Bushels.

Indian Corn, 418 Tierces, 298 Barrels, 126,418 Bushels.

Rye, 17 Barrels, and 1574 Bushels.

Pork, 7 Tierces, 2978 Barrels, 137 half Barrels, 16 Cags.

Bacon, 10 Hogsheads, 218 Tierces, 258 Barrels, 1 Hamper, 5 Boxes, and 700 lb.

Beef, 313 Barrels, 75 half Barrels, 6 quarter Barrels.

Beer, 497 Barrels, 26 half Barrels, 1 Hogshead.

Butter, 1 Tub, 1 Barrel, 371 Firkins, 207 Cags, 1 Box, 4 Pots, and 400 lb.

Fish, 1 Hogshead, 594 Barrels.

Cyder, 2 Hogsheads, 26 Barrels.

Apples, 1 Hogshead, 17 Barrels, 4 Half-Barrels, 2 Cags.

Dry'd Tongues, 1 Barrel, 2 Boxes, 1 Cag.

Potatoes, 2 Barrels.

Hickery Nutts, 3 Barrels.

Pickled Sturgeon, 15 Cags.

Pease, 27 Barrels.

Beans, 4 Barrels.

Cheese, 1 Tierce, 102 single Cheeses, and 3,300 lb.

Hogs Lard, 28 Barrels, 42 half Barrels, 13 quarter Barrels, 46 Cags.

Sage, 1 Chest.

Oats, 4 Hogsheads, 3 Tierces, 370 Bushels.

Onions, 50 Barrels, 730 Bundles, 221 Strings.[4]

The above Account is a Proof of the Fertility of this Province, and of the great Plenty wherewith GOD has bless'd the Industry of the Inhabitants; who in a few Years have made a Garden of a Wilderness, and, besides living well themselves, have so much Food to spare to other Countries. By means of this and the neighbouring *Provision Colonies,* the British Fleet and Forces in the West-Indies are at this Time supplied with Provisions at a moderate Price, while the Enemy is starving in Want; which shows that

4. Additional data on Philadelphia exports in 1740 were printed in the *General Magazine,* 1 (1741), 146.

these Colonies give Great Britain a considerable Advantage over its Enemies in an American War, and will no doubt be an additional Inducement to our Mother Country to continue us its Protection.

Teague's Advertisement

Printed in *The Pennsylvania Gazette*, February 26, 1741; also draft: American Philosophical Society.

Bradford promised in the *Mercury*, February 19, that each number of his *American Magazine* would "contain something more than four Sheets, or an Equivalent to four of such Paper, as the *American Mercury* is printed on; so that there will be not less than fifty two Sheets published in one Year, which will comprehend double the Quantity of Matter (not reckoning the Advertisements) contained in a common News Paper during a like Course of Time. Price single, one Shilling; to Subscribers twelve Shillings per *ann.* Pennsylvania Currency. It seems unnecessary to add that every Body will be at Liberty as being a Thing of Course, to withdraw his Subscription when he pleases. As the principal Part of this Magazine is not a Transcript from printed Copy, but is a Work that requires a continual Study and Application, it cannot be afforded for less Money than is mentioned. But whether it be therefore worth that Money, the Reader *only* has the Right to judge. The News will be inserted in the next, which was omitted this Time, as not being thought proper to repeat, what had been so often told over in other publick Papers. Care is also promised for the Buyer's Sake, as well as from a Regard to the Reputation of the Country, to avoid reprinting any of the Rubbish or Sweepings of Printing-Houses."

Having failed to deter Bradford by charging him with stealing the idea of a magazine and having lost out in the race to publish first, Franklin now tried ridicule, casting Bradford's address to the public into dialect verse.[5]

To the Printer of the Pennsylvania *Gazette*.

Your Adversary has always been shy of us his Country-Folks, and affected to be thought of some other Nation; but the Constraint with which he appears to write, *in Shoes,* and the great *Brogue* on his Pen at other Times, demonstrates him indisputably

5. The verses are discussed by Alfred Owen Aldridge, "A Humorous Poem by Benjamin Franklin," APS *Proc.,* XCVIII (1954), 397–9.

to be a TEAGUE. I think Nonsense in Prose is not quite so agree-able as in Verse, and therefore, in respect to my Countryman, notwithstanding his want of national Affection, I have turn'd his last Performance† into Metre: The Reader, I hope, will excuse the want of Smoothness in my Verses, the Pegasus I ride being a hobbling Jade and a Trotter. I am your Servant,   SHELAH

TEAGUE'S ADVERTISEMENT.

Arra Joy! My montly *Macasheen* shall contain Sheets four,
Or an Equivalent, which is someting more;
So dat twelve Times four shall make fifty two,
Which is twice as much as fifty two Newsh-Papers do:
Prishe shingle *One Shilling*: But shubscribe for a Year,
You shall have it sheaper,* at de shame Prishe, Honey dear:
And if you will but shubscribe to take it de Year out,
You may leave off when you pleashe, before, no doubt.
'Tis true, my Book is dear; but de Reashon is plain,
The best Parts of it ish de Work of my own Brain:⁶
How can odher Men's Writings be wort so much!
Arra! if you tink so, you're no vhery good Shudge.
De Newsh which I left out, becaush it was old,
And had been in odher Papers so often told,
I shall put into my nexsht (do 'tis shince told onesh more)
Becaush 'twill be newer dan it wash before.
For de dear Buyer's Shake,⁷ and de Land's Reputaish'
No Shweepings, but dose of my own Shcull shall have plaish;
And dose, you must tink,⁸ will be vhery fine:
For do dis Advertisement my Printer does Shign,
To tell you de Trute, de Shense is all mine.
                    Signed   A. BRADFORD⁹

†See the *American Weekly Mercury*, Feb. 19.
*The Word *cheaper*, I own, is not express'd in the Original; but it must have been intended to be understood; otherwise, what Encouragement is there to take by the Year, or where is the Inducement to subscribe?

6. These two lines not in draft.
7. Draft: "For my dear Reader's Shake."
8. Draft: "to be shure."
9. To this ridicule Bradford replied with heavy and humorless dignity. In *American Weekly Mercury*, March 5, he took full responsibility for his ad-

From James Logan   Transcript: Harvard College Library (Sparks)

My Good friend B. Franklin,   Stenton May 6. 1741

I return thee all thy Books with my hearty thanks for thy trouble in favouring me with a sight of them, and am highly pleased there are any in the Province who are so fond of such studies, and at the same time so well furnish'd with Cash as to take them all together in their present Condition at those prices. But as I have some knowledge of the unhappy young man that most (not all) of them belonged to, I am sorry he should strain so far as to say the Homer Cost him 4 Moydores. For one of the same, most exquisitely bound was offer'd to me the same year they were printed (1711) for less than one, and I never heard they were much started.[1] I have one of the same Edition of the Herodotus, perfect with all it's maps of which this has not one that was bought of Chr. Bateman[2] for 14 shillings for Wm. Masters, but this has been bound at least a 2d time and only in sheeps skin

---

vertisement of February 19, expressed resentment at BF's invoking national distinctions and prejudices, by mimicking "the Humour of Teague, and in broken Dutch, too," and continued, "I have . . . ever understood that his Majesty's Subjects, however distinguished by Locality of Birth, are nevertheless all properly ranked under the general Denomination of Englishmen, as they are all equally, without the least Exception, intitled to the benefit of the Laws of England, which is as much the Birthright of a Subject that first breathed Air on the Highlands of Scotland, on the Rocks of Kerry, or in the Desarts of America, as of one that was born in the Metropolis of Great-Britain. . . . Since then neither the King nor the Law distinguishes any of the Subjects on Account of the Place of their Birth; [it] cannot therefore justify my Brother-Printer for making such Distinctions; and I shall ever believe that those, who industriously endeavour to keep them up, have no other end in View in it than to Spirit up one Party to domineer over and oppress another Part of his Majesty's Subjects. . . ."

1. Logan began to buy books after his scholarly interests were fired during a visit to England, 1710–11. The Homer referred to may be the Cambridge edit., with Joshua Barnes's notes, 1711 (Logan bought this or another copy from BF in 1742; see above, p. 233); the Herodotus may have been Thomas Gale's folio edit., London, 1679; the Ovid cannot be positively identified.

2. Christopher Bateman, bookseller in Little Britain, London, of whom Logan purchased books for his library and, 1720, for William Masters of Philadelphia. Frederick B. Tolles, "Quaker Humanist: James Logan as a Classical Scholar," *PMHB*, LXXIX (1955), 420, 422; John Nichols, *Literary Anecdotes of the Eighteenth Century*, I (London, 1812), 424 n.

after it had been grossly abused &c. I therefore advise thee by
all means to accept the offer tho' with some considerable abatement, but I would willingly know who the Possessor is to be
of the Ovid, for I want the use of the 3d vol for about a week
at most. I hope notwithstanding it suits us not to deal at present,
Thou wilt still continue thy resolution to favour us with a visit.
Thy real friend   JAMES LOGAN

Cast: Test: 4s. Bats Gramr 10s. Dionys 8s. Pomey 7s. 6d. Mart.
in U.D. 12s. Ovid 2 (of 3) vol. 30s. Quintil: Lond: 7s. 6d. Barnes
Hom: 6s.[?]. Herod: 30s. Tully 40s. Brown of the Muscles 30s.
Vossii Hist: Lat: and Gr: 15s. Epigr: Delectus 4s. Juvenal in U.D.
8s. Heb. Bible Athiae 1661 25s. Zosimus.[3]

3. This is probably a list of the books Logan examined for BF, with the
prices Logan thought were fair: Sebastian Castalio, *Novum Testamentum
Latinum* (Gotha, 1715); or *Novum Jesu Christi Testamentum* (London, 1735);
[Julius Bate], *The Examiner Examined, &c.; with some Observations upon
the Hebrew Grammar* (London, 1739); Dionysius [Halicarnassus], *De Struc-
tura Orationis* (London, 1702); or Dionysius [Periegetes], *Situs Orbis Descriptio* (Paris, 1577); P. F. Pomey, *Pantheum Mysticum* (Utrecht, 1701);
Martial, *Epigramatum libri* XIV [for the Dauphin's use] (London, 1720);
Ovid, *Opera* (Amsterdam, 1649, 1683, or 1702); Quintilian, *Declamationes*,
1686; *Institutiones*, 1555, 1714; or *Declamationes et Institutiones*, 1641; Joshua
Barnes, *Homeri Ilias et Odyssea* (Cambridge, 1711); Herodotus (Basle, 1541;
or London, 1679); Tully [Cicero], *Opera Omnia* ([Lyons], 1596, 4 vols. in
2; or Paris, 1573, 8 vols.; or London, 1681, 2 vols.); John Brown, *Myographia Nova, sive musculorum omnium (in corpore humano hactenus repertorum)
accuratissima descriptio in sex prolectiones distributa* (London, 1684; Leyden,
1687); or *Myographia Nova, or a Graphical Description of all the Muscles in
Humane Body* (London, 1697, 1698); G. J. Vossius, *De Historicis Graecis,
De Historicis Latinis* (Leyden, 1651); [Pierre Nicole], *Epigrammatum Delectus* (Paris, 1659; or London, 1686, and other edits. to the 11th in 1740);
Juvenal, *Satirae* (Paris, 1684, the first of the "Delphine" editions; or London,
1707, 1715, 1728, 1736); *Biblia Sacra Hebraica*, publ. Joseph Athias (Amsterdam, 1661); Zosimus, *Historiae Novae libri* VI (Basle, [1576?]); or *Historiae
Novae libri sex* (Oxford, 1679).

A Short Account of the Library

Printed in *A Catalogue of Books belonging to the Library Company of Philadelphia*. Philadelphia: Printed by B. Franklin, 1741. (Library Company of Philadelphia)

The Directors of the Library Company in 1741 instructed Franklin to print a catalogue of their collection. On July 13 he read them "a Paper containing a Brief Account of the Library, which he said he wrote to fill up a Blank that happens to be at the End of the Catalogue he is printing; of which he desired the Opinion of the other Directors present, and they approved of his Design." This Franklin composition was first identified by Edwin Wolf, 2nd, in the "Bibliographical Note" to a facsimile edition of the 1741 *Catalogue*, Philadelphia, 1956.

[July 13, 1741]

A short Account of the LIBRARY.

The Library-Company was form'd in 1731, by Constitutions or Articles entred into by 50 Persons, each obliging himself to pay 40s. for purchasing the first Parcel of Books, and 10s. *per annum* to defray Charges and encrease the Library.

Ten Directors or Managers of the Library, and a Treasurer, are chosen yearly by Vote, at a General Meeting of the Company.

The Number of Members are now encreased to upwards of 70. Persons enclining to be admitted, apply to any one of the Directors, who nominates them at the next monthly Meeting of Directors; and being allowed, and paying to the Treasurer the Value of a Share at the Time, and signing the Articles, they become Members.

Any Member may borrow a Book for 2, 3, or 4 Weeks, leaving his Note for double Value, and paying a small Penalty if 'tis not return'd at the Time agreed; which Penalties are applied to defraying Charges, or purchasing more Books.

Every Member has an absolute Property in his Share; may devise it in his Will, or dispose of it when he pleases to any Person the Directors approve. And Shares so sold have always hitherto yielded as much as they had cost. As Shares encrease yearly in Value 10s. so much being yearly added by each Subscriber to the Stock of Books, a Share which at first was worth but 40s. is now valued at £6 10s. But for this small Sum, which, laid out in Books, would go but a little Way, every Member has the Use of a Library now worth upwards of £500, whereby *Knowledge* is in this City render'd more cheap and easy to be come at, to the great Pleasure and Advantage of the studious Part of the Inhabitants.

Those who are not Subscribers may notwithstanding borrow Books, leaving in the Hands of the Librarian, as a Pledge, a Sum of Money proportion'd to the Value of the Book borrow'd, and paying a small Acknowledgment for the Reading, which is ap- ply'd to the Use of the Library.

The Library is open and Attendance given every Saturday Afternoon from 4 a Clock 'til 8.

Besides the Books in this Catalogue given to the Library, the Company have been favour'd with several generous Donations; as, a curious Air-Pump, with its Apparatus, a large double Micro- scope, and other valuable Instruments, from the Hon. JOHN PENN, Esq; A handsome Lot of Ground whereon to build a House for the Library, from the Hon. THOMAS PENN, Esq; Proprietaries of the Province; and the Sum of £34 *Sterl.* (to be laid out in Books) from Dr. Sydserfe,[4] late of Antigua.

At present the Books are deposited in the West Wing of the State-House, by Favour of the General Assembly.

It is now Ten Years since the Company was first established; and we have the Pleasure of observing, That tho' 'tis compos'd of so many Persons of different Sects, Parties and Ways of Thinking, yet no Differences relating to the Affairs of the Li- brary, have arisen among us; but every Thing has been con- ducted with great Harmony, and to general Satisfaction. Which happy Circumstance will, we hope, always continue.

Note, *A Copy of the Articles or Constitutions is left in the Library, for the Perusal of all that desire to be more fully informed.*

4. Walter Sydserfe (1692–1760), Scottish-born physician, planter, and member of the Assembly of Antigua; visited England, 1739–44; settled permanently in London after 1745. Vere L. Oliver, *The History of Antigua* (London, 1894–99), I, ci–cii; III, 128, 135.

From William Coats: Deed

Transcript: Department of Records, Recorder of Deeds, City of Philadelphia

July 31, 1741

ABSTRACT: William Coats (spelled here "Coates") of the Northern Liberties of Philadelphia, brickmaker, grants to Benjamin Franklin an irregularly shaped lot in the Northern Liberties (now in Franklin's possession by virtue of a bargain and sale to him, dated the day before), which lot was formerly in the possession of Thomas Todd. The property is described as follows: beginning at a corner of land lately granted to Valentine Standley, extending by the same north 38 degrees east, 24.6 perches to a post; thence by the same and Coats's meadow north $33\frac{1}{2}$ degrees east, 16 perches to a post; thence by the said meadow south 74 degrees east, 9 perches to a post; thence by land lately granted to William Maugridge south $58\frac{1}{2}$ degrees west, 42 perches to a post; thence by a 40-ft. lane or road intended to be laid out, south 64 degrees west, 13 perches to the place of beginning; containing 2 acres 90 perches. Also granted is free access with horses, carts, wagons, etc. along the lane and all rights and appurtenances belonging to the lot. Franklin is to pay Coats £3 4s. rent on August 2 annually with a right to Coats of entry, distraint, and repossession in case of default. Franklin shall not dig clay for brickmaking nor sink saw pits without the grantor's consent. Coats warrants a clear title. Signed by William Coats; witnessed by Wm. Maugridge, Robert Greenway, the latter of whom appeared, February 15, 1757, before Chas. Brockden, justice of the peace, and swore to having seen Coats seal and deliver the indenture and that his own signature as witness was in his handwriting. Two notes in the margin cite decrees of extinguishment recorded "Nov. 14/07" and "Feb. 25–09" respectively.[5]

5. BF used this land as a pasture. It lies between Ninth and Tenth Streets, on the north side of the present Fairmount Avenue, this section of which was called at different times Hickory Lane and Coats Street. In the distribution of BF's real property among the heirs of his daughter Sarah Bache, Jan. 14, 1812, this piece passed to her son Louis Bache (D.3.5), who became responsible for future payments of the ground rent. Department of Records, Recorder of Deeds, City of Philadelphia, Book I C, 19, pp. 9, 16.

From Christopher and Mary Thompson: Deed

Transcript: Department of Records, Recorder of Deeds, City of
Philadelphia

August 1, 1741

ABSTRACT: Christopher Thompson of Philadelphia, bricklayer, and
Mary his wife grant to Benjamin Franklin a lot in Philadelphia (now in
Franklin's possession by virtue of a bargain and sale, dated the day
before), 22 ft. in breadth east and west and 140 ft. in length north and
south, bounded north by Apple Tree Alley, west by other land of
Thompson at about 62 ft. distance from Fifth Street, south by Mulberry (Arch) Street, and east by other land of Thompson, with all
buildings, improvements, and appurtenances. This lot is part of a piece
of land 149.5 ft. in breadth on Mulberry Street by 306 ft. in length
northward therefrom, which William Penn's commissioners patented
to John Willis, August 14, 1705, with 3s. quitrent. John Willis and
Esther his wife granted the whole to Joan Forrest, widow, in fee on
November 22, 1716, and the latter granted it to Thompson in fee on
July 17, 1720. Franklin is to pay a proportionable share of the proprietary quitrent and is to pay Thompson £3 17s., lawful money of
Pennsylvania, rent on March 21 annually, with a right to Thompson of
entry, distraint, and repossession in case of default. Thompson covenants Franklin's possession if the rents are paid as stipulated.[6] Signed
by Christopher Thompson and (by her mark) Mary Thompson;
witnessed by John Knight and Joseph Breintnall. Acknowledged by
Thompson before Chas. Brockden, justice of the peace, February 14,
1757. Recorded, February 16, 1757.

6. This lot lay between Fourth and Fifth Streets. BF's purpose in acquiring
it is not clear. Receipts for the payment of the specified ground rent are in
his Receipt Book (see below, p. 351). On December 13, 1771, in return for a
cash payment of £64 3s. 4d. Thompson's grandson Samuel Parker discharged
him from all future ground rents. In the distribution of BF's real property
among the heirs of his daughter Sarah Bache, Jan. 14, 1812, this lot and
the buildings then on it passed to her son Richard Bache (D.3.7). Department
of Records, Recorder of Deeds, City of Philadelphia, Book I C, 18, p. 391,
and 19, p. 11.

Directors of Library Company to John Penn[7]

MS Minutes: Library Company of Philadelphia

Sir,   Philada. Aug: 3d. 1741
   Your Present to the Library Company of a curious Microscope
and Camera Obscura is received. This fresh Instance of your
Generosity and Regard gives the Company a sensible Pleasure;
and in their Name and Behalf we return you most hearty Thanks.
We hope those Gentlemen who so generously countenanced our
Undertaking may never have Occasion to think their Benefac-
tions misplaced, but that they may perceive Learning, Virtue and
Politeness advance daily under their Influence; which we are
assured, will be more pleasing to them, than the most studied and
elaborate Compliments.
   We are, Sir, Your most obliged humble Servants &c.

From Thomas Hancock[8]   Draft: Boston Public Library

Mr. Benja. Franklin
Sir   Boston Augt. 10th. 1741
   Inclosed you have Coppys of Seven note of hand from Sundry
Persons who have Since Run away in my Debt, and I am Told
are Gon Towards Philadelphia the Jerseys and Penciliania. I have
therefore Taken the Freedom per this Opportunity to ask the
Favor of you to make Inquiery after the within named Gentry,
and if to be found pray Secure them, or Oblige 'em to pay the
money. In Case you meet with any and find it necessary to have

   7. The Directors on July 13, 1741, appointed William Coleman, BF, and
Thomas Hopkinson to prepare a letter to Penn thanking him for his gifts.
The letter was entered on the minutes August 10. For another instance of
John Penn's generosity to the Library, see above, p. 207.
   8. Thomas Hancock (1703–1764), apprenticed to a bookseller and book-
binder in Boston, 1716, opened his own shop in 1723 or 1724. He soon
branched out into paper manufacturing and the export of provisions to the
Newfoundland fisheries, and by 1741 was on his way to becoming one of
the wealthiest citizens of Boston. A generous benefactor of Harvard College,
he left his fortune to his nephew and partner John Hancock, "the Signer."
William T. Baxter, *The House of Hancock: Business in Boston, 1724–1775*
(Cambridge, Mass., 1945); *DAB*.

the original notes of hand write to me and they Shall be Sent you. As you are in the Post office I Thought you would be the most likely to hear off or meet with Some of them. Intreat you to pursue Such measures as you think may be necessary in finding them, and for your Trouble (if you will be So Kind as to undertake for me) I oblige myself to allow you one Quarter part of whatever Sum you obtain for me of the Inclosed notes. You'l please to write me if any Success, being the needfull Concludes Sir your very humble Servant   T H

[*On reverse:*]
James Question is an old man much pock broken.
Thos. Thompson is a tall young man, about 21 years.
Willm. Houston an old man of the Kingdom of I[relan]d.
Willm. Maxwell is a Lusty man about 30 years of Age.
Valentine Downing a Little man with one hand.
Charles Mackay an old man.

Endorsed: To Benj. Franklin Augst. 10. 1741

From Gilbert Tennent[9]

ALS: American Philosophical Society; also transcript: Harvard College Library (Sparks)

Honoured Sir   N.B. [New Brunswick, N.J.], Sept. 22: 1741
    I thank you kindly for your Love in Sending me Some of the

9. Gilbert Tennent (1703–1764), son of Rev. William Tennent who founded the "Log College"; Presbyterian minister at New Brunswick, N.J., since 1726; an effective evangelist, he prepared the way for George Whitefield, who established a close relationship with him and wrote, "Hypocrites must either soon be converted or enraged at his Preaching. He is a *Son of Thunder,* and I find doth not regard the Face of Man." Tennent made several tours through the colonies, 1739–40, meeting with popular success comparable to Whitefield's. His denunciation of conservatism and formalism and his disregard of church discipline, in which he had supporters, produced a schism in the Presbyterian Church, 1741. He was called to Philadelphia, 1743, as minister of a newly organized Presbyterian congregation, holding services for several years in the building constructed for Whitefield (see above, p. 290). *DAB;* Guy S. Klett, *Presbyterians in Colonial Pennsylvania* (Phila., 1937); Charles H. Maxson, *The Great Awakening in the Middle Colonies* (Chicago, 1920).

remarks and of my Sermons on justification as well as the notice you give me of exceptions made against one passage in it (of which I have wrotte an explication in a letter to Mr. Robert Ishburn).[1] Likewise I thank you kind Sir for your favour in Sending the Querists you lately printed,[2] which I am not att present inclind to write any answer to partly because its Stuffd with Satyr and burlesq and partly because I shall have an opportunity of writing on the principal matters contained in it in the vindication of the remarks.

I am oblidgd to you Sir for the pleasure you take in the recovery of my health. May God enable me to improve it to his glory.

I had the pleasure of discoursing a pritie deal with your Brother in his pass thro our place who was well.

I heartily desire that the blessings of heaven may rest upon you and yours and that you may be kept humble notwithstanding of the gifts of nature and providence with which you are favourd, and maybe enabled to improve your uncommon genius for Gods glory your own and others benefit. I offer affectionate Salutation to your whole Self and remain Sir yours   G TENNENT

Addressed: To   Mr Benjamin   Franklin att   Philadelphia   These

1. Robert Ishburn, or Eastburn, blacksmith, converted from Quakerism during the Great Awakening, was a trustee of the hall erected for Whitefield, 1740, and one of the first members of Tennent's Philadelphia congregation, 1743. William W. Hinshaw, *Encyclopedia of American Quaker Genealogy*, II (Ann Arbor, Mich., 1938), 511; *PMHB*, XIX (1895), 132; Watson, *Annals*, III, 309.

2. The references are to Tennent's *Remarks upon a Protestation presented to the Synod of Philadelphia, June 1, 1741* and *A Sermon upon Justification;* and, probably, *The Querists, Part III. or, An Extract of sundry Passages taken out of Mr. G. Tennent's Sermon*. All were printed by BF, who announced them as "just published" in *Pa. Gaz.*, Aug. 6, July 16, and Sept. 24 respectively. Tennent did reply to *The Querists, Part III*, in his *The Examiner, Examined, or Gilbert Tennent, Harmonious* (Phila., 1743, printed by William Bradford).

Accounts with William Bradford, Jr., 1741–55[3]

MS: American Philosophical Society; MS Account Book: Historical Society of Pennsylvania

Franklin's business relations with other printers are suggested by a bill he submitted to the younger William Bradford and by Bradford's account with him.[4] Franklin's bill covers the period from October 27, 1741, when he lent Bradford £1 10s., to September 22, 1747, when the bill he submitted amounted to £70 17s. 10d. Most of Bradford's purchases were of paper, lampblack, pasteboard, and other printing supplies. Fewer than a dozen other charges are recorded—an occasional spelling book, two dozen *Pocket Almanacks* for 1747, Bradford's advertisement "of his Setting up," July 8, 1742,[5] and "for advertising Colledge in N Jersey," August 13, 1747, a charge of one pound because the advertisement was a long one. On the back of the bill are the words: "This Acct has been delivered in but was never settled. BF. Apr. 2. 1757."

Bradford's account book records his side of this business. From June 12, 1742, when Franklin was charged £2 15s. for "1 peice of Calico," to October 3, 1755, when he bought a copy of Isaac Watts's *Reliquae Juveniles: Miscellaneous Thoughts in Prose and Verse* and a copy of *The Young Lady Conducted through Life*, Franklin's purchases from Bradford came to £74 6s. 9d., plus charges for each year of Bradford's

3. William Bradford (1722–1791), grandson of the printer William Bradford of New York and Philadelphia who sent BF to Keimer; nephew and partner, 1739–40, of Andrew Bradford in Philadelphia. In July 1742, young William opened his own printing office (see below, p. 361), and in December, a few days after his uncle's death, established the *Pennsylvania Journal*. Both men called their shops "At the Sign of the Bible." William published the *American Magazine and Monthly Chronicle*, 1757–58, and the *American Magazine, or General Repository*, 1769; and was appointed King's Printer for New Jersey, 1749. He opened the London Coffee-House in Philadelphia, 1754, and an office for marine insurance, 1762. He was a lieutenant in the volunteer company of Associators, 1748. Strongly opposed to the Stamp Act, he attacked BF for acquiescing in it; as an active participant in the revolutionary movement, Bradford served as colonel of Pennsylvania militia and chairman of the Pennsylvania Navy Board. *DAB;* Thomas, *Printing,* I, 241–4; John W. Wallace, *An Old Philadelphian, Colonel William Bradford* (Phila., 1884).

4. The accounts are printed respectively in George S. Eddy, ed., *Account Books Kept by Benjamin Franklin. Ledger "D," 1739–1747* (N.Y., 1929), pp. 45–7, and Wallace, *An Old Philadelphian,* where the charge for BF's subscription to the *Pennsylvania Journal,* 1742–66, is included.

5. See below, p. 361, for this advertisement.

newspaper. With the exception of the calico, rare purchases of paper, and "2 Mizetinto Pictures," Franklin bought only books—spellers, grammars, Latin classics, and standard devotional literature, and a few dozen of the almanacs Bradford printed: his purchase of 26 dozen of Taylor's almanac and two dozen of Birkett's for 1745 was unusually large. Only a few titles are worth noting: Lord Anson's *Voyage round the World;* Wollaston's *Religion of Nature Delineated, The Grub-Street Journal,* John Freind's *Chymical Lectures,* and *Don Quixote.* Bradford has not indicated when or whether Franklin settled the account.[6]

Extracts from the Gazette, 1741

Printed in *The Pennsylvania Gazette,* January 1 to December 29, 1741.

Our River has been fast some time, And we hear from Lewes, that 'tis all Ice towards the Sea as far as Eye can reach. Tuesday and Wednesday last are thought to have been the coldest Days we have had these many Years. [January 8]

Great Quantities of English Half-pence being Imported here, since the falling of our Exchange, to be pass'd as Pennies, some considerable Dealers were apprehensive we should be overstock'd with them, and began last Week to refuse them otherwise than at the Rate of five for four pence. Their Example being follow'd by many of the Shopkeepers, while others continued to take them for pence apiece, it occasion'd Considerable Confusion in small Dealings. And the Bakers refusing to make any more Bread 'till the Money was settled, the Mob rose on Friday Night and went round the Town breaking the Windows of several Merchants and others, and very much disturbed the City. They began to assemble again the Night following; but by the Vigilance and Resolution of some of the Magistrates, they were timely surpress'd, and the City has since remain'd quiet. [January 8]

[ADVERTISEMENT] Very good Iron STOVES to be sold by the Printer hereof.[7] [February 5]

6. Bradford's account includes a charge of five shillings against William Franklin, July 30, 1755, for "3 Jersey Law Books." Wallace has incorrectly included this in his printing of BF's account.

7. Probably not BF's Pennsylvania fire-places. See below, pp. 331, 419-46.

[ADVERTISEMENT] TO BE SOLD, By Anthony Morris, jun. very good Pitt and Sea Coal, at 18 pence a Bushel; at which Price 'tis allowed to be cheaper Fewel for Hearth Fireing than Wood at the present Rates. [February 5]

Just Published, (To be continued Monthly) The General MAGA-ZINE, and *Historical Chronicle,* For January, 1741.[8] Containing

I. Brief *Historical* and *Chronological* Notes of several Princes, States, Governments, &c.
II. Proceedings in the Parliament of Great-Britain on the Affair of *Paper-Money* in the American Colonies.
III. Instructions thereupon sent to the Governors of the Plantations.
IV. New-England Scheme for emitting private Notes to pass in Lieu of Money.
V. Proclamation issued in New-York, relating to the Coin.
VI. Proceedings in the Assembly of Pennsylvania.
VII. Report of the Lords Commissioners for Trade and Plantations, on the last Six Pennsylvania Laws.
VIII. Report of the King's Attorney and Sollicitor General, on one of the said Laws, viz. That relating to the Manner of Taking an Oath.
IX. Act of Parliament for *Naturalizing Foreigners* in the British Colonies.
X. Proceedings of Assembly in New-England.
XI. Accounts of and Extracts from New Books, Pamphlets, &c. published in the Plantations, viz. Sermon to the military Men in Boston; Querists; Answer to the Querists; Lovetruth's Letters to Mr. Whitefield, &c.
XII. Essays on various Subjects from the American News-Papers, viz. Ovid's Cure. Queries on original Sin and Predestination; Observations on those Queries. Effects of dwelling on the Doctrines of Grace in Preaching, &c.
XIII. POETRY, viz. Address to the Deity. A Riddle. On the War. Admiral Hosier's Ghost. Letter from the Spanish Admiral Don Blas. On Mr. Wesley's Sermon on Free-Grace. To a young new-married Couple in Virginia. To the King, on Governor Gooch. Difference of Preachers. To the Author of the *Poor Planter's Physician.* On Hearing Mr. Whitefield.

8. On the *General Magazine,* see above, p. 263.

XIV. *Historical Chronicle*. Prodigious Booty taken by Kouli Kan. Compendium of the News received this Month from Turky, Russia, France, Germany, Great Britain, Ireland, Jamaica, St. Christophers, South-Carolina, Virginia, Maryland, New-England and New-York. Domestic Occurrences. Number of Troops sent on the Expedition by each Colony.

XV. Exchange between the Colonies and London.

XVI. Price current in Philadelphia.

XVII. Account of the Export of Provisions from Philadelphia, Anno 1740.

Printed and Sold by B. FRANKLIN. Price Nine Pence.

[February 19]

Monday last, some Guns were fired from Carpenter's Wharff, in Honour of St. David; but one of them (being overcharg'd with Powder, and besides imprudently ramm'd with rough Stones, which were to be shot at a Cask on the Ice) burst in Pieces, by which Accident Thomas Scot, Mate of the Ship *Phenix*, of Leverpoole, at 20 Yards distance, had his Scull fractur'd, and died in a few Hours.

[March 5]

Just Published, (To be continued Monthly) The General MAGAZINE, and *Historical Chronicle*, For February, 1741. Containing

I. Proceedings of the Parliament of Great-Britain on the Bill for prohibiting the Exportation of Provisions, &c.

II. Crown of England's Title to America prior to that of Spain; or an Account of the Welch Indians.

III. Of the Constitution of Government in Virginia.

IV. Treaty of Peace concluded by the Governor of New-York, between the Six-Nations, and all the Southern and Western Indians.

V. Order of Council in New-York against Exporting Wheat.

VI. Order of Council in Philadelphia against Exporting Provisions to the Foreign Plantations.

VII. Accounts of and Extracts from New Books, Pamphlets, &c. published in the Plantations.

VIII. Essay on Paper-Currency, proposing a new Method for fixing its Value.

IX. The Wandering Spirit.

THE
GENERAL MAGAZINE,
AND
Historical Chronicle,
For all the *British* Plantations in *America.*
[To be Continued Monthly.]

JANUARY, 1741.

ICH DIEN

VOL. I.

PHILADELPHIA:
Printed and Sold by B. FRANKLIN.

X. Dr. Colman's Character of Archbishop Tillotson.

XI. Letter to Mr. Gilbert Tennent, enquiring into the Motives of his late Conduct.

XII. His Answer.

XIII. Some Account of the Effect of his Preaching.

XIV. The new Manual Exercise for the Foot.

XV. Manner of the Children's Spending their Time at the Orphan-House in Georgia.

XVI. Pieces of Poetry, viz. Orphans Hymns. Answer to Riddle in the last *Magazine*. Elegy on Henry Brooke, Esq; Vernon's Answer to Admiral Hosier's Ghost. Geraldino's Answer to Don Blass. &c.

XVII. *Historical Chronicle.*

XVIII. The Number of his Majesty's Ships, Vessels, and Bomb-Ships, now in Pay.

XIX. Price Current in Philadelphia.

XX. Account of sundry Exports from Philadelphia.

Printed and Sold by B. FRANKLIN. Price Nine Pence.

[March 26]

Tuesday last Mr. William Logan, eldest Son of the Honourable James Logan Esq; was married to Mrs. Hannah Emlen, a young Lady of Beauty, Merit and Fortune.[9]   [March 26]

We hear from Lancaster County, that during the Continuance of the great Snow which in general was more than three Foot deep, great Numbers of the back Inhabitants suffer'd much for want of Bread; that many Families of New-Settlers for some time had little else to subsist them but the Carcases of Deer they found dead or dying in the Swamps or Runns about their Houses; and although they had given all their Grain to their Cattle, many Horses and Cows are dead, and the greatest Part of the Gangs in the Woods are dead; that the Deers which could not struggle through the Snow to the Springs are believed to be all dead, and many of those which did get into the Savannahs are also dead, ten, twelve and fifteen being found in the Compass of a

9. William Logan (1718–1776), merchant and farmer. *PMHB*, xxxvi (1912), 1. His bride was the daughter of George Emlen, Philadelphia brewer. Mrs.: mistress, used as a title of courtesy without reference to marital state.

320

few Acres of Land. The Indians fear the Winter has been so fatal to the Deer, Turkeys, &c. in these Northern Parts, that they will be scarce for many Years. We also hear that a young Woman in Derry Township, attempting to get Home (about a Mile) as soon as she came within sight of her Father's House turned out the Horse which she had borrow'd of her Neighbour, as he directed her; but not being able to make Way through the Snow, she threw off her Cloaths, and attempted to return on the Horses Footing; but after much struggling, as appear'd by her Tracts, she froze to Death.   [April 9]

The Subscribers to the Library in Philadelphia are hereby advertised, that Monday the fourth of May ensuing, at Two in the Afternoon, is the Time appointed for the Company's Choice of Directors and a Treasurer for the succeeding Year, and for making the Ninth Annual Payment, in the Library Room belonging to the State-House.

April 16. 1741.   J. BREINTNALL, Secr.
                                                                [April 16]

On Sunday last died the Reverend Mr. Archibald Cummings, Commissary of the Province of Pensylvania, and the Counties of New-Castle, Kent, and Sussex on Delaware, and Minister of Christ-Church in Philadelphia.[1] He was a zealous Assertor of the Principles of the Christian Religion, a Sincere Professor of the Doctrine of the Church of England, a faithful Pastor in his Congregation, an able and instructive Preacher, and an eminent Example of Piety and Goodness through every Step of his Life and Conversation. In short, He was a Person so Universally esteem'd in this Place for his many good Qualities, but especially for his Charity and Moderation towards all Religious Societies of differing Pursuasions, that his Death is much lamented by all Sorts of People.   [April 23]

[ADVERTISEMENT] Lent or taken by Mistake, about two Weeks ago, a Paduasoy Bonnet lin'd with black Silk. This Bonnet being

1. Archibald Cummings had been rector of Christ Church since 1726. Benjamin Dorr, *An Historical Account of Christ Church, Philadelphia* (N.Y. and Phila., 1841), pp. 58–73.

the Second the Owner has lately lost, she has none now to wear: The Possessor is desired to return it soon to the Printer hereof, and shall be thankfully rewarded. [April 23]

Just Published, (To be continued Monthly) The General MAGAZINE, and *Historical Chronicle,* For March, 1741. Containing

I. Continuation of Mr. Beverley's Present State of Virginia.

II. Remainder of the New Manual Exercise.

III. Evolutions of the Foot by Col. Bland.

IV. Substance of the Bill depending in Parliment, for prohibiting the exportation of Provisions.

V. Considerations on the Bill.

VI. Order of Council in Boston, relating to the Exportation of Provisions.

VII. Governor Belcher's Speech to the Assembly of New-Hampshire.

VIII. Governor Morris's Letters to the Collectors of the Customs in New-Jersey.

IX. Second order of Council in Philadelphia, relating to the Exportation of Provisions.

X. New-England Manufactory- or Land-Bank Scheme.

XI. State of the late Dispute between the Upper and Lower House of Assembly in Maryland.

XII. Letter from D.B. to C.C.

XIII. Letter from Theophilus, Relating to the Divine Prescience.

XIV. Letter from Mr. Hugh Bryan, for Correcting which the Rev. Mr. Whitefield is now under Prosecution in Carolina.

XV. New Method for making excellent Mellasses of Apples.

XVI. *Poetical Essays,* viz. The Gardner's Curse. Divine Psalmody. A Ballad to Admiral Vernon. On taking Porto Bello by Admiral Vernon. To the Rev. Dr. Watts, on his Divine Poems. The Raven's colour chang'd. An irregular Ode. An Epigram. The Comparison, the Choice, and the Enjoyment.

XVII. *Historical Chronicle.*

XVIII. Price of Bills of Exchange.

XIX. Price Currant in Philadelphia.

Printed and Sold by B. FRANKLIN. Price Nine Pence.
[April 30]

[ADVERTISEMENT] BOOKS &c. SOLD by B. Franklin, Bibles, several Sizes; Testaments, Psalters, Dyche, Owen's, and Cocker's, Spelling Books; Young Man's Companion, Grammars, Latin and English Dictionaries, Erasmus and Cordery English and Latin; Ruddiman's Rudiments, London Vocabularies, Cato, &c. Dyche and Bailey's Dictionaries; Chambers's Dictionary, Common Prayer-Books, of several Sizes and Sorts, with Companion to the Altar, Supplement, Cuts, &c. Law's serious Call, and Christian Perfection, Erskine's Sonnets, Whitefield's Works compleat 6 Vol. Every Man his own Lawyer, Every Man his own Doctor, (Note, in a short time will be published, *Every Man his own Priest*) Family Instructor, Cole's Dictionary, Nelson's Justice, German Grammars, Quarles's Emblems, Account Books, Paper, Inkpowder, Ink, Ivory-leav'd Memorandum Books, Quills, &c. &c. &c.

[May 21]

Just Published, (To be continued Monthly) The General MAGAZINE, and *Historical Chronicle,* For April, 1741. Containing

I. Remainder of Mr. Beverly's Present State of Virginia.
II. The Lords *Protests,* 1. Concerning certain Clauses proposed to be Part of the Address on the King's Speech.
    2. Concerning the Resolution upon the Orders given to Admiral Vernon.
    3. On the Instructions given to Admiral Haddock.
    4. On augmenting the Army by raising Regiments, rather than additional Men to Companies.
III. Two Speeches in Parliament by W. P-----y, Esq; and Sir R. W-----e.
IV. Proclamation of the Governor of New-York, enjoining a Fast.
V. Another relating to the Fires in that City.
VI. Speech of the Governor of New-York, to the Assembly of that Province.
VII. Assembly's Answer.
VIII. Speech of the Governor of North-Carolina.
IX. Report from the Board of Trade on the Paper Currency of the Plantations.
X. Remarkable Dedication of the History of Georgia.
XI. Letters to the Rev. Mr. Whitefield from the Rev. Mr. Garden, with one of Mr. Whitefield's in Answer.

323

Printed and Sold by B. FRANKLIN. [May 28]

On the 25th of the last Month, the Presbyterian Synod opened their Session in this City; and after several Days spent in Debates on the Rights of Presbyteries, &c. a Protestation was entred into, on the first Instant, and signed by 12 Ministers and 8 Members then present, by which the Rev. Messrs. the Tennents, and their Adherents, are excluded the Synod, and declared to have forfeited their Right of sitting, and voting as Members thereof: The excluded Brethren immediately withdrew, and met by themselves in another Place. 'Tis said, that the Number of the Excluded was nearly equal to that of the Synod remaining. The Protestation, containing the Reasons of their Conduct, is now published by order of the Synod.[2] [June 11]

2. This was the culmination of differences that had been growing for several years in the Synod of Philadelphia. Orthodox ministers, educated in Scotland or New England, were jealous of their rights and of the Synod's powers, and distrusted revivalism and emotional preaching; these became known as the Old Side. The Tennents, Samuel Blair, Eleazer Wales, and others (see above, p. 288 n) had been educated at, or supported, the Log College, were energetic revivalists who preached where they were led, even within the parishes of settled ministers, and demanded only an essential conformity; these became known as the New Side. The occasion of the schism was the refusal of the Presbytery of New Brunswick to comply with the Synod's requirements on education of ministers. A protest signed by twenty members of the Synod, ministerial and lay, was supported by a majority; and the minority severed relations. The Synod was reunited in 1758. Guy S. Klett, *Presbyterians in Colonial Pennsylvania* (Phila., 1937), pp. 146–59.

324

On Sunday the 31st of last Month, the Rev. Mr. Gilbert Tennent preached five Times, to crowded Audiences: And on the Wednesday following, he baptised, at the New-Building, Eight adult Persons, who had been of the People called Quakers, one, as is said, a Preacher. Mr. Whitefield had baptised three at the same Place, when he was last in this City.   [June 11]

[ADVERTISEMENT] Best Glaz'd Press Papers Sold by the Printer hereof.   [June 11]

The same Day [June 24] at a Grand Lodge of Free and Accepted Masons, held for the Province of Pennsylvania, at the Indian King in this City; Mr. Philip Syng was chosen Grand Master for the Year ensuing; Mr. Thomas Boude was appointed Deputy Grand Master, and Mr. Lambert Emerson and Dr. Thomas Bond Grand Wardens.   [June 25]

Saturday next will be Published, (To be continued Monthly) The General MAGAZINE, and *Historical Chronicle,* For May, 1741. Containing

I. The Lords Protests against Sir R. Walpole.
II. Preface to the History of Georgia.
III. Continuation of Mr. Garden's Letters.
IV. Remainder of the Remarks on Mr. Whitefield's New-England Journal.
V. The Governor of Maryland's Speech to both Houses of Assembly.
VI. The Address of the Upper-House of Assembly to the Governor.
VII. The Governor's Answer.
VIII. The Address of the Lower House of Assembly to the Governor.
IX. The Governor's Answer.
X. Extract of the Votes of Assembly of Maryland.
XI. Proceedings of Assembly in New-England.
XII. Governor of New-England's Brief.
XIII. Proceedings of Assembly in New-York.
XIV. Governor of New-York's Speech to the Assembly.

XV. Martha Harward's Letters, &c.
XVI. A Dialogue against ridiculing Personal Defects.
XVII. Answers to the Mathematical Question, &c.
XVIII. Answer [to] the Letter from Theophilus relating to divine Prescience.
XIX. Copy of Part of Sir John Randolph's Will.
XX. *Poetical Essays,* viz. Translation of Mr. Addison's Latin Poem on the Resurrection. To the Memory of Benjamin Needler, Esq; On the Rev. Mr. Tennent's Departure from Boston.
XXI. *Historical Chronicle.*
XXII. Price of Bills of Exchange.
XXIII. Price Currant in Philadelphia.

Printed and Sold by B. FRANKLIN.   [June 25]

[ADVERTISEMENT] Lost about eight Days since, a red Leather Pocket Case, gilt *Constantinople* on the Back, containing a Note of hand payable to Bradley and Co. for £13 and about £5 in Money. Whoever brings it to the Printer hereof, shall have Forty Shillings Reward.   [July 2]

Just Published, (To be continued Monthly) The General MAGA-ZINE, and *Historical Chronicle,* For June, 1741.[3] Containing,

I. The King's Speech to the Parliament, on the 8th of April, 1741.
II. The House of Lords Address to the King.
III. The House of Commons Address to the King.
IV. Proceedings of Assembly in New-York.
V. Governor of New-York's Proclamation.
VI. Proceedings of Assembly in Pennsylvania.
VII. Abstract of the History of Georgia.
VIII. Continuation of Mr. Garden's Letters.
IX. Answer to Mr. Garden's three first Letters.
X. Answer to some particulars of the Remarks on Mr. Whitefield's New-England Journal.
XI. Reply to the foregoing Answer.
XII. Supplement to the History of the Wandring Spirit.
XIII. Of Slander and Detraction, from the Barbadoes Gazette.

3. This was the last issue of BF's *General Magazine.*

On the 4th Instant, died Andrew Hamilton, Esq; and was the next Day inter'd at Bush-Hill, his Country Seat.[4] His Corps was attended to the Grave by a great Number of his Friends, deeply affected with their own, but more with their Country's Loss. He lived not without Enemies: For, as he was himself open and honest, he took pains to unmask the Hypocrite, and boldly censured the Knave, without regard to Station and Profession. Such, therefore, may exult at his Death. He steadily maintained the Cause of Liberty; and the Laws made, during the time he was Speaker of the Assembly, which was many Years, will be a lasting Monument of his Affection to the People, and of his Concern for the welfare of this Province. He was no Friend to Power, as he had observed an ill use had been frequently made of it in the Colonies; and therefore was seldom upon good Terms with Governors. This Prejudice, however, did not always determine his Conduct towards them; for where he saw they meant well, he was for supporting them honourably, and was indefatigable in endeavouring to remove the Prejudices of others. He was long at the Top of his Profession here, and had he been as griping as he was knowing and active, he might have left a much greater Fortune to his Family than he has done: But he spent more Time in hearing and reconciling Differences in Private, to the Loss of his

4. On Andrew Hamilton, see above, I, 333.

Fees, than he did in pleading Causes at the Bar. He was just, where he sat as a Judge; and tho' he was stern and severe in his Manner, he was compassionate in his Nature, and very slow to punish. He was the Poor Man's Friend, and was never known to with-hold his Purse or Service from the Indigent or Oppressed. He was a tender Husband and a fond Parent: But—these are Virtues which Fools and Knaves have sometimes in common with the Wise and the Honest. His free Manner of treating Religious Subjects, gave Offence to many, who, if a Man may judge by their Actions, were not themselves much in earnest. He feared God, loved Mercy, and did Justice: If he could not subscribe to the Creed of any particular Church, it was not for want of considering them All; for he had read much on Religious Subjects. He went through a tedious Sickness with uncommon Chearfulness, Constancy and Courage. Nothing of affected Bravery or Ostentation appeared; But such a Composure and Tranquility of Mind, as results from the Reflection of a Life spent agreeable to the best of a Man's Judgment. He preserved his Understanding and his Regard for his Friends to the last Moment. What was given as a Rule for a Poet, upon another Occasion, may be justly apply'd to Him upon this,

——*Servetur ad imum*
Qualis ab incepto processerit, et sibi constet.

[August 6]

[ADVERTISEMENT] Taken away from a Back-Room of David Evans, in Market-Street, Philadelphia, on Thursday last, A Case of Drawing Instruments, About four Inches and half long: It is desired the same be return'd out of Hand to David Evans or the Printer hereof. The Owner having greater Occasion for it, than the Person that took it away; otherwise such a speedy return would not have been insisted upon.

July 4. 1741.   [August 6]

[ADVERTISEMENT] Lent about a Month or 6 Weeks ago, two Books call'd Law's Christian Perfection, and his Call to devout and holy Life,[5] the Owner's Name at length on a blank Leaf at

5. William Law's *A Practical Treatise on Christian Perfection*, 1726, and *A Serious Call to a Devout and Holy Life*, 1728.

the beginning. The Borrower is desired to return them, for the Owner has now leisure to read them.   [August 6]

[ADVERTISEMENT] Lent about a Month or 6 Weeks ago, two Books, call'd Law's *Christian Perfection,* and his *Call to a devout and holy Life;* the Owner's Name at Length on a blank Leaf at the Beginning. The Borrower is desired to return them to the Owner, which will be thankfully acknowledged by Your Humble Servant,   DEBORAH FRANKLIN
[August 13]

This Day the Honourable THOMAS PENN, Esq; one of the Proprietors of this Province, attended by a great Number of the principal Inhabitants of this City, set out for New-York, in order to embark on Board his Majesty's Ship *Squirrel,* Capt. Peter Warren Commander, for Great-Britain.   [August 20]

JUST PUBLISHED, THE AMERICAN ALMANACK for the Year 1742. By John Jerman, Ph.lomath. Printed and Sold by B. Franklin.
[September 24]

Tuesday last, Samuel Hasell, Esq; Mayor of this City, made the Customary Feast at the Expiration of the Mayoralty, when the Governor, Council, the Corporation, and a great Number of the Inhabitants were entertain'd at the Court-House in the most handsome Manner.   [October 1]

Last Monday died after a lingring Illness Alexander Henry Keith, Esq;[6] at the Seat of his Father-in-Law Anthony Palmer, Esq; He was for several Years Collector of his Majesty's Customs at New-Castle on Delaware, and Son of Sir William Keith, late Lieutenant Governor of this Province, &c. The Day following he was decently interr'd.   [October 8]

On Tuesday last Clement Plumsted, Esq; was elected Mayor of this City for the ensuing Year: When Robert Strettell, William Parsons, William Rawle, Thomas Hopkinson, Samuel Rhodes, and Andrew Hamilton, Son of Andrew Hamilton Esq; lately

6. Alexander Keith was the eldest surviving son and heir apparent to the baronetcy. *PMHB*, LVI (1932), 5.

deceas'd, were chosen Common-Council-Men. And the following Gentlemen were promoted Aldermen, to wit, William Till, Joseph Turner, James Hamilton, and Benjamin Shoemaker. [October 8]

JUST PUBLISHED, THE NEW JERSEY ALMANACK for the Year 1742. By William Ball, Philomath. Printed and Sold by B. Franklin.
[October 22]

[ADVERTISEMENT] All Persons indebted to Doctor Phineas Bond,[7] are desired to make their Payments to Thomas Bond, who is removed to the Sign of the Golden Mortar in Second-Street, a little below the Quakers Meeting-House. [October 29]

[ADVERTISEMENT] John Dabney, Mathematical Instrument Maker from London, In King-Street, Boston, New-England. Makes and Mends all Sorts of Mathematical Instruments, as Theodolites, Spirit Levels, Semicircles, Circumferenters, and Protractors, Horizontal and Equinoctial Sun-Dials, Azimuth and Amplitude Compasses, Eliptical and Triangular Compasses, and all sorts of common Compasses, drawing Pens and Portagratons, Pencil-Cases and parallel Rulers, Squares and Bevils, Free-Masons Jewels, with sundry other Articles too tedious to mention.

N.B. He sets Load-Stones in Silver or Brass, after the best Manner. [November 19]

NEXT WEEK WILL BE PUBLISHED, POOR RICHARD'S ALMANACK for the Year 1742. Printed and Sold by B. Franklin.
[November 26]

Sunday Night last, Count Zinzendorff[8] arrived here from New-York, attended by some of the Moravian Brethren, who

7. Phineas Bond (see above, p. 240 n) went abroad in the fall of 1741 to study medicine.

8. Count Nicolaus Ludwig Zinzendorf (1700–1760), leader of the Moravian Church in Germany, came to Pennsylvania in 1741. Hoping to unite all the German Protestants there, he held several conferences (the accounts of which BF printed), but the separatism of the German congregations and strong opposition from both German and Presbyterian ministers doomed his efforts to early failure. He made three missionary journeys among the Indians and helped to establish Moravian congregations in several Pennsylvania towns as well as in New York. He sailed for England Jan. 9, 1743. *DAB.*

are, with a considerable Number more expected in the Spring, to be settled at Nazareth on the Forks of Delaware.
[December 3]

[ADVERTISEMENT] TO BE SOLD at the Post-Office Philadelphia, The New Invented Iron Fire-Places;[9] Where any Person may see some of them that are now in Use, and have the Nature and Advantages of them explain'd.   [December 3]

NEXT WEEK WILL BE PUBLISHED, THE POCKET ALMANACK, For the Year 1742. Sold by the Printer hereof; Where may be had, Jerman's, Ball's, Leed's, and Poor Richard's Almanacks.
[December 29]

PHILADELPHIA: Printed by B. FRANKLIN, Post-Master, at the New Printing-Office, near the Market.

Poor Richard, 1742

Poor Richard, 1742. An Almanack For the Year of Christ 1742, . . . By Richard Saunders, Philom. Philadelphia: Printed and sold by B. Franklin, at the New Printing-Office near the Market. (Yale University Library)

Courteous READER,
This is the ninth Year of my Endeavours to serve thee in the Capacity of a Calendar-Writer. The Encouragement I have met with must be ascrib'd, in a great Measure, to your Charity, excited by the open honest Declaration I made of my Poverty at my first Appearance. This my Brother *Philomaths* could, without being Conjurers, discover; and *Poor Richard's* Success, has produced ye a *Poor Will*, and a *Poor Robin;*[1] and no doubt *Poor John,* &c. will follow, and we shall all be *in Name* what some Folks say we are already *in Fact*, A Parcel of *poor Almanack Makers*. During the Course of these nine Years, what Buffetings have I not sustained! The Fraternity have been all in Arms. Honest Titan, de-

9. See below, pp. 419–46.
1. *Poor Will's Almanack* was William Birket's, printed by William Bradford in New York and Andrew Bradford in Philadelphia. No copies of the issues for 1741 and 1742 are known. Evans 4894. *Poor Robin's Almanack* was printed by Andrew Bradford in Philadelphia. Evans 4789.

ceas'd, was rais'd, and made to abuse his old Friend. Both Authors and Printers were angry. Hard Names, and many, were bestow'd on me. They deny'd me to be the Author of my own Works; declar'd there never was any such Person; asserted that I was dead 60 Years ago; prognosticated my Death to happen within a Twelvemonth: with many other malicious Inconsistences, the Effects of blind Passion, Envy at my Success; and a vain Hope of depriving me (dear Reader) of thy wonted Countenance and Favour.—*Who knows him?* they cry: *Where does he live?*—But what is that to them? If I delight in a private Life, have they any Right to drag me out of my Retirement? I have good Reasons for concealing the Place of my Abode. 'Tis time for an old Man, as I am, to think of preparing for his great Remove. The perpetual Teasing of both Neighbours and Strangers, to calculate Nativities, give Judgments on Schemes, erect Figures, discover Thieves, detect Horse-Stealers, describe the Route of Run-aways and stray'd Cattle; The Croud of Visitors with a 1000 trifling Questions; *Will my Ship return safe? Will my Mare win the Race? Will her next Colt be a Pacer? When will my Wife die? Who shall be my Husband, and* HOW LONG *first? When is the best time to cut Hair, trim Cocks, or sow Sallad?* These and the like Impertinences I have now neither Taste nor Leisure for. I have had enough of 'em. All that these angry Folks can say, will never provoke me to tell them where I live. I would eat my Nails first.

My last Adversary is J. J----n,[2] Philomat. who *declares and protests* (in his Preface, 1741) that the *false Prophecy put in my Almanack, concerning him, the Year before, is altogether* false and untrue: *and that I am one of Baal's false Prophets.* This *false, false Prophecy* he speaks of, related to his Reconciliation with the Church of Rome; which, notwithstanding his Declaring and Protesting, is, I fear, too true. Two Things in his elegiac Verses confirm me in this Suspicion. He calls the First of November by the

2. Jerman, whose almanacs for 1741 and 1742 BF printed, replied in his 1743 edition, printed by William Bradford: "The Reader may expect a Reply from me to R---- S---rs alias B---- F---ns facetious Way of proving me *no Protestant*. I do hereby protest, that for *that* and such kind of Usage the *Printer* of that witty Performance shall not have the Benefit of my Almanack for this Year. To avoid further Contention, and judging it unnecessary to offer any Proofs to those of my Acquaintance that I am not a Papist, I shall with these few Lines conclude. . . ."

Name of *All Hallows Day*. Reader; does not this smell of Popery?
Does it in the least savour of the pure Language of Friends?[3]
But the plainest Thing is; his Adoration of Saints, which he con-
fesses to be his Practice, in these Words, page 4.

> When any Trouble did me befal,
> To my dear *Mary* then I would call:

Did he think the whole World were so stupid as not to take Notice of this? So ignorant as not to know, that all Catholicks pay
the highest Regard to the *Virgin-Mary?* Ah! Friend John, We
must allow you to be a Poet, but you are certainly no Protestant.
I could heartily wish your Religion were as good as your Verses.

RICHARD SAUNDERS

XI Mon. January hath xxxi days.

> Foot, Horse and Waggons, now cross Rivers, dry,
> And Ships unmov'd, the boistrous Winds defy,
> In frozen Climes: where all conceal'd from Sight,
> The pleasing Objects that to Verse invite;
> The Hills, the Dales, and the delightful Woods,
> The flowry Plains, and Silver-streaming Floods,
> By Snow disguis'd, in bright Confusion lie,
> And with one dazling Waste fatigue the Eye.

Strange! that a Man who has wit enough to write a Satyr; should
have folly enough to publish it.

He that hath a Trade, hath an Estate.

Have you somewhat to do to-morrow; do it to-day.

XII Mon. February hath xxviii days.

> James ne'er will be prefer'd; he cannot bow
> And cringe beneath a supercilious Brow;
> He cannot fawn, his stubborn Soul recoils
> At Baseness, and his Blood too highly boils.
> A Courtier must be supple, full of Guile,

3. Quaker plainness in speech, especially their use of *thee* and *thy*.

333

Must learn to praise, to flatter, to revile
The Good, the Bad; an Enemy, a Friend;
To give false Hopes, and on false Hopes depend.

No workman without tools,
Nor Lawyer without Fools,
Can live by their Rules.

The painful Preacher, like a candle bright,
Consumes himself in giving others Light.

Speak and speed: the close mouth catches no flies.

I Mon. March hath xxxi days.

As honest Hodge the Farmer, sow'd his Field,
Chear'd with the Hope of future Gain 'twould yield,
Two upstart Jacks in Office, proud and vain,
Come riding by, and thus insult the Swain.
You drudge, and sweat, and labour here, Old Boy,
But we the Fruit of your hard Toil enjoy.
Belike you may, *quoth Hodge,* and but your Due,
For, Gentlemen, 'tis HEMP I'm sowing now.

Visit your Aunt, but not every Day; and call at your Brother's,
but not every night.

Bis dat, qui cito dat.[4]

Money and good Manners make the Gentleman.

Late Children, early Orphans.

II Mon. April hath xxx days.

The Winter spent, Joe feels the Poet's Fire,
The Sun advances, and the Fogs retire:
The genial Spring unbinds the frozen Earth,
Dawns on the Trees, and gives the Prim-rose Birth.
Loos'd from their Friendly Harbours, once again,

4. Who gives promptly gives twice.

Our floating Forts assemble on the Main;
The Voice of War the gallant Soldier wakes;
And weeping Cloe parting Kisses takes.

Ben beats his Pate, and fancys wit will come;
But he may knock, there's no body at home.

The good Spinner hath a large Shift.

Tom, vain's your Pains; They all will fail:
Ne'er was good Arrow made of a Sow's Tail.

III Mon. May hath xxxi days.

What knowing Judgment, or what piercing Eye,
Can MAN's mysterious Maze of Falshood try?
Intriguing MAN, of a suspicious Mind,
MAN only knows the Cunning of his Kind;
With equal Wit can counter-work his Foes,
And Art with Art, and Fraud with Fraud oppose.
Then heed ye FAIR, e'er you their Cunning prove,
And think of Treach'ry, while they talk of Love.

Empty Free-booters, cover'd with Scorn:
They went out for Wealth, and come ragged and torn,
As the Ram went for Wool, and was sent back shorn.

Ill Customs and bad Advice are seldom forgotten.

He that sows thorns, should not go barefoot.

IV Mon. June hath xxx days.

Sometimes a Man speaks Truth without Design,
As late it happen'd with a Friend of mine.
Two reverend Preachers talking, one declar'd,
That to preach twice each Sunday was full hard.
To you, perhaps (says t'other) *for I suppose,
That all Men don't with the same Ease compose:
But I, desiring still my Flock to profit,
Preach twice each Sunday,* and make nothing of it.

335

Reniego de grillos, aunque sean d'oro.[5]

Men meet, mountains never.

When Knaves fall out, honest Men get their goods: When Priests
dispute, we come at the Truth.

V Mon. July hath xxxi days.

> Man only from himself can suffer Wrong;
> His Reason fails as his Desires grow strong:
> Hence, wanting Ballast, and too full of Sail,
> He lies expos'd to every rising Gale.
> From Youth to Age, for *Happiness* he's bound;
> He splits on Rocks, or runs his Bark aground;
> Or, wide of Land a desert Ocean views,
> And, to the last, the flying Port pursues.

> Kate would have Thomas, no one blame her can:
> Tom won't have Kate, and who can blame the Man?

A large train makes a light Purse.

Death takes no bribes.

One good Husband is worth two good Wives; for the scarcer
things are the more they're valued.

VI Mon. August hath xxxi days.

> *The Busy-Man's Picture.*
> BUSINESS, thou Plague and Pleasure of my Life,
> Thou charming Mistress, thou vexatious Wife;
> Thou Enemy, thou Friend, to Joy, to Grief,
> Thou bring'st me all, and bring'st me no Relief,
> Thou bitter, sweet, thou pleasing, teazing Thing,
> Thou Bee, that with thy Honey wears a Sting;
> Some Respite, prithee do, yet do not give,
> I cannot with thee, nor without thee live.

5. Abhor chains though they be of gold.

336

He that riseth late, must trot all day, and shall scarce overtake his business at night.

He that speaks ill of the Mare, will buy her.

You may drive a gift without a gimblet.

Eat few Suppers, and you'll need few Medicines.

VII Mon. September hath xxx days.

The Reverse.
Studious of Ease, and fond of humble Things,
Below the Smiles, below the Frowns of Kings:
Thanks to my Stars, I prize the Sweets of Life,
No sleepless Nights I count, no Days of Strife.
I rest, I wake, I drink, I sometimes love,
I read, I write, I settle, or I rove;
Content to live, content to die unknown,
Lord of myself, accountable to none.

You will be careful, if you are wise;
How you touch Men's Religion, or Credit, or Eyes.

After Fish,
Milk do not wish.

Heb Dduw heb ddim, a Duw a digon.[6]

They who have nothing to trouble them, will be troubled at nothing.

VIII Mon. October hath xxxi days.

On him true HAPPINESS shall wait
Who shunning noisy Pomp and State
Those *little* Blessings of the *Great,*
Consults the Golden Mean.
In prosp'rous Gales with Care he steers,
Nor adverse Winds, dejected, fears,
In ev'ry Turn of Fortune bears
A Face and Mind serene.

6. Without God, without anything; with God, with enough.

337

Against Diseases here, the strongest Fence,
Is the defensive Virtue, Abstinence.

Fient de chien, et marc d'argent,
Seront tout un au jour du jugement.[7]

If thou dost ill, the joy fades, not the pains;
If well, the pain doth fade, the joy remains.

IX Mon. November hath xxx days.

Celia's rich Side-board seldom sees the Light,
Clean is her Kitchen, and her Spits are bright;
Her Knives and Spoons, all rang'd in even Rows,
No Hands molest, nor Fingers discompose:
A curious Jack, hung up to please the Eye,
Forever still, whose Flyers never fly:
Her Plates unsully'd, shining on the Shelf;
For Celia dresses nothing,—*but herself.*

To err is human, to repent divine, to persist devilish.

Money and Man a mutual Friendship show:
Man makes *false* Money, Money makes Man so.

Industry pays Debts, Despair encreases them.

Bright as the day and as the morning fair,
Such Cloe is, and common as the air.

X Mon. December hath xxxi days.

Among the Divines there has been much Debate,
Concerning the World in its ancient Estate;
Some say 'twas once good, but now is grown bad,
Some say 'tis reform'd of the Faults it once had:
I say, 'tis the best World, this that we now live in,
Either to lend, or to spend, or to give in;
But to borrow, to beg, or to get a Man's own,
It is the worst World that ever was known.

7. Dog's dung and silver mark will both be one on Judgment Day.

Here comes Glib-tongue: who can out-flatter a Dedication; and lie, like ten Epitaphs.

Hope and a Red-Rag, are Baits for Men and Mackrel.

With the old Almanack and the old Year,
Leave thy old Vices, tho' ever so dear.

COURTS.

Honest Men often go to Law for their Right; when Wise Men would sit down with the Wrong, supposing the first Loss least. In some Countries the Course of the Courts is so tedious, and the Expence so high, that the Remedy, *Justice,* is worse than, *Injustice,* the Disease. In my Travels I once saw a Sign call'd *The Two Men at Law;* One of them was painted on one Side, in a melancholy Posture, all in Rags, with this Scroll, *I have lost my Cause.* The other was drawn capering for Joy, on the other Side, with these Words, *I have gain'd my Suit;* but he was stark naked.

Rules of Health and long Life, and to preserve from Malignant Fevers, and Sickness in general.

Eat and drink such an exact Quantity as the Constitution of thy Body allows of, in reference to the Services of the Mind.

They that study much, ought not to eat so much as those that work hard, their Digestion being not so good.

The exact Quantity and Quality being found out, is to be kept to constantly.

Excess in all other Things whatever, as well as in Meat and Drink, is also to be avoided.

Youth, Age, and Sick require a different Quantity.

And so do those of contrary Complexions; for that which is too much for a flegmatick Man, is not sufficient for a Cholerick.

The Measure of Food ought to be (as much as possibly may be) exactly proportionable to the Quality and Condition of the Stomach, because the Stomach digests it.

That Quantity that is sufficient, the Stomach can perfectly concoct and digest, and it sufficeth the due Nourishment of the Body.

A greater Quantity of some things may be eaten than of others, some being of lighter Digestion than others.

The Difficulty lies, in finding out an exact Measure; but eat for Necessity, not Pleasure, for Lust knows not where Necessity ends.

339

Wouldst thou enjoy a long Life, a healthy Body, and a vigorous Mind, and be acquainted also with the wonderful works of God? labour in the first place to bring thy Appetite into Subjection to Reason.

Rules to find out a fit Measure of Meat and Drink.

If thou eatest so much as makes thee unfit for Study, or other Business, thou exceedest the due Measure.

If thou art dull and heavy after Meat, it's a sign thou hast exceeded the due Measure; for Meat and Drink ought to refresh the Body, and make it chearful, and not to dull and oppress it.

If thou findest these ill Symptoms, consider whether too much Meat, or too much Drink occasions it, or both, and abate by little and little, till thou findest the Inconveniency removed.

Keep out of the Sight of Feasts and Banquets as much as may be; for 'tis more difficult to refrain good Cheer, when it's present, than from the Desire of it when it is away; the like you may observe in the Objects of all the other Senses.

If a Man casually exceeds, let him fast the next Meal, and all may be well again, provided it be not too often done; as if he exceed at Dinner, let him refrain a Supper, &c.

A temperate Diet frees from Diseases; such are seldom ill, but if they are surprised with Sickness, they bear it better, and recover sooner; for most Distempers have their Original from Repletion.

Use now and then a little Exercise a quarter of an Hour before Meals, as to swing a Weight, or swing your Arms about with a small Weight in each Hand; to leap, or the like, for that stirs the Muscles of the Breast.

A temperate Diet arms the Body against all external Accidents; so that they are not so easily hurt by Heat, Cold or Labour; if they at any time should be prejudiced, they are more easily cured, either of Wounds, Dislocations or Bruises.

But when malignant Fevers are rife in the Country or City where thou dwelst, 'tis adviseable to eat and drink more freely, by Way of Prevention; for those are Diseases that are not caused by Repletion, and seldom attack Full-feeders.

A sober Diet makes a Man die without Pain; it maintains the Senses in Vigour; it mitigates the Violence of Passions and Affections.

It preserves the Memory, it helps the Understanding, it allays the Heat of Lust; it brings a Man to a Consideration of his latter End; it makes the Body a fit Tabernacle for the Lord to dwell in; which makes us happy in this World, and eternally happy in the World to come, through Jesus Christ our Lord and Saviour.

Articles of Agreement with James Parker[8]

ADS: American Philosophical Society

[February 20, 1741/2]

ARTICLES OF AGREEMENT[9] indented made the twentieth Day of February in the year of our Lord, One Thousand seven Hundred and Forty-One, Between Benjamin Franklin, of the City

---

8. James Parker (c.1714–1770), apprenticed as a printer to William Bradford of New York, from whom he ran away, 1733, finding employment with BF. He established the *New-York Weekly Post-Boy*, 1743 (continued after 1747 as *New-York Gazette, or Weekly Post-Boy*) and the *Connecticut Gazette*, 1755; published the *Independent Reflector*, 1752–53, *John Englishman*, 1755, and *New American Magazine*, 1758–60; was public printer to New York and New Jersey and printer to Yale College; and was judged by Victor H. Paltsits (in *DAB*) "a better printer than Bradford or Franklin." One of his apprentices was Benjamin Mecom (C.17.3), BF's nephew, who complained, probably unfairly, of his master's ill-treatment. Van Doren, *Franklin-Mecom*, pp. 39–44. Parker opened a printing office in Woodbridge, N.J., 1751, where he was also captain of a troop of horse and lay reader in Trinity Church. BF appointed him postmaster of New Haven, 1754, and controller and secretary of the Post Office in North America, 1757. He named his son Samuel Franklin Parker. The boy lived for a time with BF, who enrolled him in the Academy of Philadelphia, 1752. The elder Parker's personal, business, and official relations with BF produced a large and, because of illness in later years, sometimes depressing correspondence, much of it printed in 2 Mass. Hist. Soc. *Proc.*, XVI (1902), 186–232. *DAB;* Thomas, *Printing*, I, 188–9, 298–305; William Nelson, "Some New Jersey Printers and Printing in the Eighteenth Century," Am. Antiq. Soc. *Proc.*, n.s., XXI (1911), 17–27; Douglas C. McMurtrie, *A History of Printing in the United States*, II (N.Y., 1936), 227–33. Some of BF's accounts with Parker are printed in George S. Eddy, ed., *Account Books Kept by Benjamin Franklin. Ledger "D," 1739–1747* (N.Y., 1929), pp. 91–7.

9. This agreement is practically identical with that with Louis Timothée, Nov. 26, 1733 (see above, I, 339), except that the latter required annual rather than quarterly settlement of accounts and provided that Peter Timothée might succeed his father in the partnership.

of Philadelphia in the Province of Pennsylvania Printer, of the One Part, and James Parker of the said City, Printer, of the other Part: WHEREAS the said Benjamin Franklin, and James Parker have determined to enter into a Copartnership for the Carrying on the Business of Printing in the City of New-York: IT IS THEREFORE covenanted granted and agreed by and between the said Parties to these Presents; and the said Benjamin Franklin and James Parker do each of them covenant, and mutually agree each with the other of them, and to and with the Heirs, Executors and Administrators of the other of them, in Manner following, That is to say

THAT they, the said Benjamin Franklin and James Parker shall be Partners in carrying on the Trade and Business of Printing in New-York aforesaid, for and during the Term of Six Years from the Day on which the said James Parker shall be in Possession of a Printing-Press, Types and Materials in the City of New-York aforesaid, provided by the said Benjamin Franklin, if they the said Benjamin and James shall so long live. That the said Benjamin Franklin, shall be at the sole Charge of providing a Printing-Press with all its necessary Appurtenances, together with Four Hundred Pounds Weight of Letters (if the said James shall require so great a Quantity) and shall cause the same to be transported at his own Risque and Expence, to the City of New-York aforesaid, and to be there put into the Possession of the said James Parker. That the Business and Working Part of Printing, and of Disposing of the Work printed: shall be under the sole Management and Direction of, and performed by the said James Parker or at his Expence. That all Charges for Paper, Ink, Balls, Tympans, Wool, Oyl, and other Things necessary to Printing, together with the Charge of all common and necessary Repairs of the Press and its Appurtenances, and also the Charge of Rent for a Shop, and for so much Room as is necessary to be used in the Management of the Business of Printing aforesaid, shall be divided into three equal Parts, two of which said Parts shall be defrayed by and paid as due from the said James Parker and the remaining Third Part shall be defrayed and allowed to be paid as due from the said Benjamin Franklin, and deducted out of the Income next herein after mentioned. That as Money received or to be received for Printing, or for any Thing done or to be done relating to the Business of Printing aforesaid, by the said James Parker, either as Gratuity, Premium or Reward or Salary, from the Government, or from others, shall be divided into three equal Parts Two of which said Parts the said James Parker shall have for his Care, Management and Performance aforesaid, and the said Benjamin Franklin shall have the remaining Third Part thereof. That for the regular transacting the Affairs in Copartnership aforesaid the said James Parker shall keep fair and exact Books of Accounts of and concerning all Work done and delivered or sold by him, and of all his Receipts and Disbursements relating to the Business of Printing in Copartnership aforesaid, with the Day, Month and Year of each Entry, and submit the same to the View of the said Benjamin Franklin, his lawful Attorney, Executors or Administrators, as often as thereunto required. And that all the Accounts of the Copartners in Copartnership aforesaid, shall be drawn out plain and communicated to each other, and settled once a Quarter, to wit, at Midsummer, Michaelmas, Christmas, and Lady-Day, during the Copartnership aforesaid, or oftner, if either of them the said Copartners shall require it. And that upon such Settlement, the said James Parker shall remit the Part by this Agreement belonging to the said Benjamin Franklin, in such Wares or Merchandizes, or in Bills of Exchange or in Money, as the said Benjamin Franklin shall direct, by Letter or Order under his Hand, on board such Vessel and to such Port, or by such Person or Conveyance as the said Benjamin shall also require, by Letter or Order as aforesaid, at the proper Risque of the said Benjamin. That the said James Parker shall not work with any other Printing Materials than those belonging to the said Benjamin Franklin, nor follow any other Business but Printing, during the Continuance of the Copartnership aforesaid, occasional Buying and Selling excepted. That the Loss by bad Debts shall be divided and sustained by both Parties, in the same Proportion as the Money ought to have been divided by this Agreement, if it had been received. That neither of the said Parties shall reap any Benefit or Advantage by Survivorship, if the other of them shall depart this Life before the Expiration of the said Term of Six Years; but that if the said James Parker shall depart this Life before the Expiration of the said Term, his Executors or Administrators, shall deliver up the

343

Press, Types, and all other Materials of Printing which have been provided by the said Benjamin Franklin, or at his Charge, to the said Benjamin, his certain Attorney, Executors or Administrators, upon Demand, in good Order and Condition, (allowing for the usual Wear and Decay of such Things) as also the Share of Money, Effects and Debts belonging to the said Benjamin by this Agreement. And if the said Benjamin Franklin shall depart this Life before the Expiration of the Term of Copartnership aforesaid, the said James Parker shall continue the Business nevertheless, paying and remitting the Part, by this Agreement belonging to the said Benjamin Franklin, unto the Executors, Administrators, or Assigns of the said Benjamin, they performing all parts of this Agreement to the said James, which the said Benjamin ought to have done, if he had lived. And [at] the Expiration of the Term of Six Years aforesaid, the said James Parker, shall have the Preference of purchasing the said Printing-Press, Types and Materials, if he shall be so disposed, at their present Value, allowing for the Wear thereof which shall be judged a reasonable Abatement, considering the Time they then have been used: But if the said James shall not be inclined to purchase them he shall transport, or cause to be transported to and delivered at Philadelphia, the said Printing-Press, Types and Materials, at his own proper Risque and Charge, to the said Benjamin Franklin, his Executors, Administrators or Assigns. And if any unusual Damage, by bad Usage or Negligence, shall have happened to them the said James shall make it good: But if the Damage be occasioned by some unavoidable Accident, the Loss shall be divided and sustained by both Parties, in the same Manner as the Loss by bad Debts is by this Agreement to be divided and sustained: Provided nevertheless, that if the said Printing Press, Materials and Types which the said Benjamin provides, shall be lost in the Conveyance to New-York, by any Accident of Water or Fire, Enemy or the like; then the Loss thereby shall be wholly sustained by the said Benjamin Franklin, and the Copartnership hereby made, shall be dissolved and abolished, unless the said Benjamin be willing to continue it, and provide another Press and Types as aforesaid, and send them at his own Risque to New-York aforesaid, there to be delivered to the said James Parker Any Thing herein before contained to the Contrary not withstanding.

IN WITNESS whereof the Parties to these Presents have interchangeably set their Hands and Seals hereunto. Dated the Day
and Year first above-written.

JAMES PARKER [Seal]

Sealed and Delivered   B FRANKLIN   [Seal]
in the Presence of us
    ROBT GRACE
    LEWIS EVANS

Endorsed: Articles of Agreement between B. Franklin and James
    Parker Feby. 20. 1741,2

Library Company: Acceptance of the Charter

DS: Haverford College Library

The increasing property of the Library Company suggested that the
time had come to incorporate it.[1] On June 21, 1739, Rev. Richard
Peters informed the Directors that the Proprietor was willing to grant
a charter, and he proposed to have one drafted for their perusal. "This
Discourse of Mr. Peters's was very pleasing to the Directors present,"
the minutes noted. The matter progressed slowly. The Directors approached Thomas Penn informally; they canvassed the subscribers;
and, meeting with general approval, appointed a committee (its composition is not known) to draft a charter. By July 1741, however, when
they were about to lay it before the Proprietor, they learned that some
subscribers felt strongly that they had exceeded their authority "and
were about to obtrude a disadvantageous Charter upon the Company
without their [the subscribers'] Consent." A few wanted no charter
at all. The Directors called a special meeting for August 3, to explain
their acts and purposes and to ask the subscribers to "determine whether
in their opinion a Charter will be of Service to them, and what Method
of Application shall be made Use of to obtain it." Forty-five members
appeared, several were represented by proxies, and after some debate
they unanimously resolved to apply for a charter. The draft the Directors were considering was read article by article, and two changes
were ordered: the Company should reserve specifically the power of
making laws for its own government, and a quorum for making laws
after notice given should be one fourth of the subscribers, instead of
one fifth as proposed. The charter thus amended was transcribed and

1. This account of the charter is taken from MS Minutes, Lib. Co. Phila.

carried to the Proprietor. He referred it to Governor Thomas, who signed it on August 19, 1741.[2]

When the subscribers were asked to signify their acceptance, two new objections were made: the charter did not specifically apply to the successors of the present members, and (doubtless through the scrivener's error) the subscribers were liable not only for their annual 10s. payments but for greater sums "in lieu thereof."[3] The necessary change and correction were made, to the satisfaction of the dissenters; and on March 15 Samuel Rhoads showed the Directors the charter as "fairly engrossed" by Joseph Breintnall. They presented it to Governor Thomas, and he signed it on March 25, 1742. At their annual meeting on May 3 the subscribers approved it unanimously.[4]

[May 3, 1742]

The third Day of May Anno Domini 1742 We the Subscribers Members of the Library Company of Philadelphia being met in pursuance of Notice for that purpose given do thankfully receive and accept of the Charter granted to the said Company by the honourable the Proprietaries of Pensylvania. Witness our Hands.

JNO LANGDALE	SAML. HALE,
JOHN ROBERTS	by his Proxy WM PARSONS
ISAIAH WARNER	NICHS. SCULL,
PHILIP SYNG	by his Proxy WM PARSONS
GEORGE EMLEN JR.	WILLM. MAUGRIDGE,
JOHN JONES JUN.	by his Proxy WM PARSONS
THOS: HOPKINSON 1742	WM. PARSONS
RICHARD PETERS	JAS: MORRIS
WILLIAM PETERS	JOSEPH STRETCH
by his Proxy	ISAAC WILLIAMS
RICHARD PETERS	by his Proxy HENRY PRATT

2. The charters of 1741 and 1742 are in Lib. Co. Phila. That of 1742 was recorded in Patent Book A 10, p. 538, now in Bureau of Land Records, Dept. of Internal Affairs, Harrisburg, Pa. In both charters BF's name is first in the list of the 75 subscribers named.

3. The 1742 charter obligated every member to pay 10s. "on the first Monday in May in every Year forever, and *those who neglect so to do shall pay* such greater Sum or Sums in Lieu thereof at such Times within Twelve Months then next following as by the Laws of the said Company shall be appointed." The italicized words were omitted from the 1741 charter.

4. See below, p. 358. In 1746 BF printed the texts of the charter and by-laws with a list of "Books Added to the Library Since the Year 1741." Evans 5853.

ALEX: GRAYDON
ANDREW HAMILTON
ROBT GREENWAY
SAML: MORRIS
SAML: COATES
BENJA: SHOEMAKER
HUGH ROBERTS
WM: COLEMAN
JOSEPH BREINTNALL
SAML NORRIS
B FRANKLIN
RICHD STANDLEY
TENCH FRANCIS
JOHN READ
ANTH NICHOLAS

HENRY PRATT
EVAN MORGAN
THOMAS SHAW
    by his Proxy JACOB DUCHÉ
JACOB DUCHÉ
CHARLES MEREDITH
    by his Proxy HENRY PRATT
WM CALLENDER
JOSEPH KING
BENJA: PASCHALL
JOHN PASCHALL
WM PLUMSTED
WILL. ALLEN
FRAS. RICHARDSON
ISR: PEMBERTON JUNR:
JAMES HAMILTON
SAMUEL RHOADS
THOS GODFREY
JAMES BINGHAM
WM CROSTHWAITE
THOMAS BOND ⎱ by their proxy
REECE LLOYD ⎰ HUGH ROBERTS
SAMUEL M'CALL
JOHN SOBER

Directors of Library Company to Proprietors and Reply

ADS (address) and draft (reply): Historical Society of Pennsylvania; also
MS Minute Book (address): Library Company of Pennsylvania.

The charter having been accepted, the Directors of the Library Company on May 10 named Franklin, Thomas Hopkinson, and William Coleman to prepare an address of thanks to the Proprietors. On June 14 a draft was presented, read, and approved; but apparently it was not engrossed and signed until July.

July 1742

To the honourable John Penn Thomas Penn and Richard Penn Esquires, true and absolute Proprietaries of the Province of Pennsylvania &c.

The humble Address of the Directors of the Library Company of Philadelphia, in Behalf of themselves and Others the Members of the said Company

May it please the Proprietaries,

WE the Directors of the Library Company of Philadelphia, by the Appointment and Direction of a general Meeting of the said Company, return your Honours most sincere Thanks for the Charter of Privileges to them granted. It is with the greatest Satisfaction we receive this extraordinary Mark of your Favour and Regard; and what heightens the Obligation is, that it was purely the Effect of your own Goodness and Generosity without being solicited: But we have the pleasure to observe, this is not the first Instance of your kind Concern for the Advancement of the Library, even beyond what the Company could have hoped for; And tho' we may be wanting in Expression and suitable Acknowledgments, yet we assure your Honours we have the most grateful Sense of the Benefits received, and of the favourable Regard of our Proprietaries towards us.

The Powers and Privileges now granted us will, without Doubt, very much conduce to the Increase and Reputation of the Library; and as valuable Books come to be in more general Use and Esteem, we hope they will have very good Effects on the Minds of the People of this Province, and furnish them with the most useful kind of Knowledge, that which renders Men benevolent and helpful to one another. Our unhappy Divisions and Animosities, of late, have too much interrupted that charitable and friendly Intercourse which formerly subsisted among all Societies in this Place;[5] but as all Parties come to understand their true Interest, we hope these Animosities will cease, and that Men of all Denominations will mutually assist in carrying on the publick Affairs in such manner as will most tend to the Peace and Welfare of the Province.

B. FRANKLIN	PHILIP SYNG
HUGH ROBERTS	SAMUEL RHOADS
JOSEPH STRETCH	JOHN JONES JR
THOS. HOPKINSON 1742	EVAN MORGAN
JACOB DUCHÉ	SAML: MORRIS

5. The reference is to the bitter controversy between Governor Thomas and the Assembly, and their respective supporters, over appropriations for the war between Great Britain and Spain that broke out in 1739.

Gentlemen

As wee think it our Duty to improve every oppertunity that offers of advancing the Interest of our Province and the welfare of its Inhabitants wee could not but with great pleasure promote an undertaking calculated to form their Minds and influence them to good and Virtuous Actions. If this should be the happy Consequence of forming your Society wee shal have great reason to be highly satisfied with the Assistance wee have given you, and in order to it wee must recommend to you that ever having that design in view that you lay aside all personal dislikes and with a benevolence of disposition which is the greatest ornament of Human Nature endeavour to impress such Principles on the Minds of those who may want direction as may tend to make them easy [and] happy. Wee are well pleas'd by your Address to find these your Sentiments. While you make this your endeavour you may be assured of our ready and Chearfull Assistance.

Endorsed: Ruff answer to Library Company

From Jacob Spicer[6]   ALS: American Philosophical Society

Mr. Franklin,   Cape May Sepr. 20th. 1742
Sir,

The difficulty I have Labour'd under Some time in the management of my Fathers affairs, for want of giving publick notice, Obliges me to desire you would Insert the advertisement Inclos'd,[7]

6. Jacob Spicer (1716–1765), wealthy merchant of Cape May, N.J.; member of the Assembly, 1744–65; contractor for provisioning troops in the French and Indian War. With Aaron Leaming he compiled and edited *The Grants, Concessions, and Original Constitutions of . . . New Jersey*, 1758. Susan S. Meech and Susan B. Meech, *History of the Descendants of Peter Spicer* (priv. printed, 1911), pp. 15–16; 1 *N.J. Arch.*, XXIV, 625. Spicer's miscellaneous notes of household affairs are in 1 N.J. Hist. Soc. *Proc.*, III (1849), 103–4, 193–8. His remarkable ante-nuptial agreement with his second wife, Mrs. Deborah Leaming, is printed in *PMHB*, XXVI (1902), 404–6.

7. The advertisement summoned those with claims against, or debts to, the estate of Major Jacob Spicer (1668–1741), to present their claims or make payment. *Pa. Gaz.*, Oct. 7, 1742, and following weeks. Major Spicer was a member of the New Jersey Assembly, surrogate, and justice of the peace for Cape May. 1 *N.J. Arch.*, XIX, 393 n; 2 N.J. Hist. Soc. *Proc.*, XIII (1894–95), 50–3; Meech and Meech, *History of the Descendants of Peter Spicer*, pp. 13–15.

and for defraying the Charge thereof, I have also Inclos'd Five Shillings, if I mistake not the usual Sum that is Generally given for Services of that Kind, But if in Case it is not Sufficient then I will pay the whole of your demand; unto you or your Order upon the first Notice.

Mr. Flower[8] Inform'd me he had agreed with you for your Gazette for one year on our Joint account, Whereof I have Received Several, and if the usual advance be behind unpaid, Let me know it and that shall be discharg'd also. I am Your Humble Servant   JACOB SPICER

Addressed: To Mr. Benjn. Franklin Printer In Philadelphia These

Card to the Public

Printed in *The Pennsylvania Gazette*, September 23, 1742.

It being asserted in a printed Paper, directed *to the Freeholders of Pennsylvania,* that the Assembly had concealed the State of the publick Accounts from the People, by artfully deferring the Publication of their Minutes, in order to prevent a Detection of some suppos'd Mismanagement of the publick Money;[9] I think I owe this Justice to that Honourable House, as to declare, that I have had the Minutes in my Hands for Publication ever since the Ad-

8. Possibly Samuel Flower.

9. The charge was made during the election campaign of Sept.–Oct. 1742 in an anti-Quaker handbill *To the Free-Holders Of the Province of Pennsylvania,* deploring the continued disagreement between Governor and Assembly which would result in the expiration of the Loan Office. "Under these Circumstances," it asked, "is it not absolutely necessary that the publick Accounts should be strictly examined into? We have a right to know how the publick Money has been Disposed of, and the late Members of the Assembly cannot but know we have, and yet they have hitherto concealed those Accounts from us, in hopes by this Means to prevent a publick Detection of their Mismanagement, if it may not deserve a worse Name, till it will be too late for us to shew a proper resentment. If all was fair, why were not their Minutes published immediately after their last Adjournment? Why is the Publication artfully deferr'd till they have taken their Measures for getting themselves re-elected?"

journment;[1] that I receiv'd no Directions from the House to delay it, nor the least Intimation from any Member, that such Delay would be agreeable; that no Person has been refus'd a Sight of them, and that the sole Cause of the Delay was my Desire of first finishing the Body of Laws,[2] the Minutes being very little enquired after.   B. FRANKLIN

Receipt Book, 1742–64

MS Record Book: American Philosophical Society

As a man of affairs who frequently made large cash payments, Franklin kept a book for receipts, in which he or the creditor would write out a form of acknowledgment which the creditor would sign on receiving payment. He used this book from 1742 until 1757, when he went abroad; his wife kept it until his return in 1762, when he himself resumed it. There are about 300 receipts; the first is dated December 22, 1742, and the last, October 29, 1764, less than a week before he sailed again to England. The MS has only incidental and limited usefulness to biographers and historians.

Among the persons who signed receipts in this volume are William Coats, Robert and Rebecca Grace, Thomas Smith, Christopher Thompson, Timothy Matlack, and John Wister, from each of whom Franklin held or rented property in Philadelphia; Theophilus Grew, the schoolmaster; David Hall, his journeyman and partner; Mathias Meuris, Anthony Newhouse, J. Conrad Schütz, and Thomas Wilcox, papermakers; William Parks, printer of Williamsburg, Va.; Isaiah Warner, who composed and printed in his own shop jobs for other printers; Adolph Young, bookbinder; and several post riders.[3] A few receipts specify the goods or services for which Franklin paid. On May 1, 1744, for example, he paid his barber George Cuningham £5 for "a light Wig"; and on August 20, 1755, he bought "a Greay wigge" for £3. A carpenter charged him £5 14s. 6d. in 1747 for "Stuff and Work of a Shaise House." When he was building a new house in 1763–64 Franklin paid the architect Robert Smith £96 on April 6, 1763, "towards Pur-

---

1. The Assembly adjourned Aug. 28.

2. *A Collection of all the Laws Of the Province of Pennsylvania: Now in Force*, printed by BF by order of the Assembly, 1742.

3. For BF's charges against some of these persons, see his Ledger D, above, p. 232.

chasing Materials," and on November 26 he paid Smith £80 "on Acct. of Building his House." The plastering cost £25. According to an entry of March 28, 1757, Franklin bought a bill of exchange for £1500 sterling before departing for London as agent of the Pennsylvania Assembly. The following receipt is typical in form:

> July 9, 1745. Receiv'd of Benja. Franklin at sundry Times Cash Forty four Pounds to this Day, which with my Diet, &c. to the 20th of June past Twenty-Six pounds, makes in all, Seventy Pounds, per me   DAVID HALL
> £70. 0. 0

I Sing My Plain Country Joan

MS: American Philosophical Society

There can be little doubt that Franklin composed these verses to his wife. They are assigned to him in two different anecdotes, which, though the incidents described are separated by forty years, are not inconsistent. The first, from the family of Franklin's friend John Bard,[4] relates how, at a meeting of some club, possibly the Junto, someone jokingly took exception to the practice of married men singing songs poets had written in praise of their mistresses. Next morning Dr. Bard, who had been one of the company and may have been the expostulator, received the following song from Franklin, with a request that he be ready to sing it at the next meeting.[5] The second anecdote was conveyed to a London magazine by one John Ellis, Jr., in 1807. Franklin was one of the guests at a dinner in Paris at which each person was to compose verses in praise of a wife. When his turn came Franklin had ready this song. He subsequently gave a copy to a woman friend, and told her the circumstances; and she gave them to Ellis to publish.[6]

Franklin himself provided further evidence of his connection with the song. Writing in playful vein to Catharine Ray, September 11, 1755, he informed her that Deborah Franklin "talks of bequeathing me to you as a Legacy; But I ought to wish you a better, and hope she will live these 100 Years; for we are grown old together, and if she has any faults, I am so us'd to 'em that I don't perceive 'em, as the Song says," and he quoted the stanza here inserted next to the last.

4. John Bard (1716–1799), physician of Philadelphia and New York.
5. John McVickar, *A Domestic Narrative of the Life of Samuel Bard* (N.Y., 1822), pp. 18–19.
6. *Monthly Repository of Theology and General Literature*, III (1808), 214.

Finally, the manuscript from which the song is printed here,[7] though not in Franklin's hand, certainly belonged to him. It is preserved among his papers and Deborah has written on the back of one sheet a note of charges to an unknown customer at the New Printing-Office—8d. for an almanac, for example. Carl Van Doren printed the verses without assigning a date, though he mentions that Bard moved from Philadelphia in 1746.[8] If Franklin's "plain Country Joan" was Deborah, the reference to twelve years of marriage would fix the date of composition at about 1742.

Song   [c. 1742]

Of their Chloes and Phillisses Poets may prate
   I sing my plain Country Joan
Now twelve Years my Wife, still the Joy of my Life
   Blest Day that I made her my own,
                    My dear Friends
   Blest Day that I made her my own.

2

Not a Word of her Face, her Shape, or her Eyes,
   Of Flames or of Darts shall you hear;
Tho' I Beauty admire 'tis Virtue I prize,
   That fades not in seventy Years,
                    My dear Friends

3

In Health a Companion delightfull and dear,
   Still easy, engaging, and Free,
In Sickness no less than the faithfullest Nurse
   As tender as tender can be,   My dear Friends

4

In Peace and good Order, my Houshold she keeps
   Right Careful to save what I gain
Yet chearfully spends, and smiles on the Friends
   I've the Pleasures to entertain
                    My dear Friends

7. Both printed versions differ in minor respects from the MS. In addition, in the Ellis version stanzas five and six are reversed, and seven is omitted. The order of the stanzas in the Bard version is 1, 2, 6, 5, 4, 3, 8, with stanza seven omitted. The stanza inserted between seven and eight is that which BF quoted in his letter to Catharine Ray.

8. Van Doren, *Franklin*, p. 148.

5

She defends my good Name ever where I'm to blame,
　Friend firmer was ne'er to Man giv'n,
Her compassionate Breast, feels for all the Distrest,
　Which draws down the Blessing from Heav'n,
　　　　　　　My dear Friends

6

Am I laden with Care, she takes off a large Share,
　That the Burthen ne'er makes [me]⁹ to reel,
Does good Fortune arrive, the Joy of my Wife,
　Quite doubles the Pleasures I feel,
　　　　　　　My dear Friends

7

In Raptures the giddy Rake talks of his Fair,
　Enjoyment shall make him Despise,
I speak my cool sence, that long Experience,
　And Enjoyment have chang'd in no wise,
　　　　　　　My dear Friends

[Some Faults we have all, and so may my Joan,
　But then they're exceedingly small;
And now I'm us'd to 'em, they're just like my own,
　I scarcely can see 'em at all,
　　　　　　　My dear Friends,
　I scarcely can see them at all.]

8

Were the fairest young Princess, with Million in Purse
　To be had in Exchange for my Joan,
She could not be a better Wife, mought be a Worse,
　So I'd stick to my Joggy¹ alone
　　　　　　　My dear Friends
　I'd cling to my lovely ould Joan.

9. "Me," required by the meter, appears in both printed versions.
1. Jug, Jugg: pet name or familiar substitute for Joan; familiar name for a homely woman, the sweetheart of a peasant. *OED.*

Extracts from the Gazette, 1742

Printed in *The Pennsylvania Gazette*, January 6 to December 30, 1742.

[ADVERTISEMENT] Eben aus der Presse gekommen, Authentische Relation von dem Anlass, Fortgang und Schlusse der am 1sten und 2ten Januarii Anno 1741,2. in Germantown gehaltenen. Versammlung einiger Arbeiter derer meisten Christlichen Religionen und vieler vor sich selbst Gott-dienenden Christen-Menschen in Pennsylvania; Ausgesetzt in Germantown am Abend des 2ten obigen Monats. Gedruckt und zu haben bey B. FRANKLIN, um 6 Pens einzeln, und 4 Schilling 6 Pens beym Dutzent.

[January 13]

[ADVERTISEMENT] Just came down from the Furnace, a fresh Parcel of IRON FIRE PLACES; to be sold at the Post-Office.

[January 20]

[ADVERTISEMENT] Just Imported, And to be Sold by John Breintnal, in Chesnut-street, A Choice Parcel of the best Spectacles, Microscopes, large and small Pocket Compasses with Dials, and several other sorts of Goods.   [February 3]

On Saturday last William Bullock was committed to the Goal of this City, on Suspicion of having been the Occasion of the Death of his Negro Boy, about 8 Years old, by beating and whipping him at sundry Times. The Coroner's Inquest upon view of the Body, were of Opinion the Injuries the said Boy had receiv'd from his Master, were the Cause of his Death.   [February 24]

We hear that a Subscription is on foot for the Encouragement of Mr. John Bertram, Botanist, to travel thro' the Province of New-York, Pensylvania, New-Jersey and Maryland, in Search of curious Vegetables, Fossils, &c. of all kinds; which 'tis hop'd will meet with Success, he being a Person exceedingly well qualified, for such an Employment. A more particular Account of the Design will be given in our next.[2]   [March 10]

2. According to Ernest Earnest (*John and William Bartram*, Phila., 1940, pp. 25–6), BF was a principal figure in raising this subscription for Bartram. Nothing is known of its success, but Bartram did continue his botanizing travels, making a journey to the Catskills that summer. Darlington, *Memorials*, p. 160.

No Letters or News-papers came by last Post from Boston, the Post being robb'd a few Miles on this side Seabrook in Connecticut, of both Horse and Mail; but a great Number of Horsemen being immediately sent in pursuit of the Robber, it was not doubted but he would be soon taken.   [March 10]

On Monday last, at a Court of Oyer and Terminer held here . . . William Bullock was . . . try'd for killing his Negro Boy, and found Guilty.   [March 10]

A COPY of the Subscription Paper, for the Encouragement of Mr. John Bartram, promised in our last.

Botany, or the Science of Herbs and Plants, has always been accounted in every Country, as well by the Illiterate as by the Learned, an useful Study and Labour to Mankind, as it has furnished them with Cures for many Diseases, and their Gardens, Groves and Fields with rare and pleasant Fruits, Flowers, Aromaticks, Shades and Hedges.

And as the Wildernesses, Mountains and Swamps in America, abound with Variety of Simples and Trees, whose Virtues and proper Uses are yet unknown to Physicians and curious Persons both here and in Europe; it should be esteem'd fortunate, and a general Benefit, if a Man could be found sufficiently skilful and hardy, who would undertake, as far as in his Power, a compleat Discovery of such Herbs, Roots, Shrubs and Trees, as are of the Native Growth of America, and not described in Herbals or other Books.

And as John Bartram has had a Propensity to Botanicks from his Infancy, and to the Productions of Nature in general, and is an accurate Observator; well known in Pennsylvania, where he was born and resides, to be a Person fitted for this Employment; acquainted with Vegetables and Fossils, and Books treating of them; of great Industry and Temperance, and of unquestionable Veracity; and has by many Ships sent over to some of the Members of the Royal Society in London, at their Request, Plants, Seeds and Specimens, as were new and unknown to them (and received by them as Curiosities) in order to be farther discovered and made useful by the Learned and Ingenious there, who have yearly return'd him Names for them, and Accounts of some of their Virtues; we the Subscribers, to induce and enable him wholly to

356

spend his Time and exert himself in these Employments, have proposed an annual Contribution for his Encouragement; with which he being made acquainted, and it agreeing with his benevolent Temper, he has promised some of us, that if it appears by what shall be subscribed, that he can maintain himself and Family, and defray the Expences he must sometimes unavoidably be at in long Journies for Guides and Assistance, he will without delay dispose his Affairs at Home, and undertake what is desired of him; and that his Searches after Vegetables and Fossils, shall be throughout the Governments of New-York, the Jerseys, Pennsylvania and Maryland; and that whatsoever he meets with worthy of Notice, in the Places and Things before mentioned, and in the Form, Situation and Produce of Mountains, Lakes, Springs, Grottoes, Rivers, &c. he will describe and yearly communicate to the Subscribers in the best Manner he can.

We the Subscribers, do therefore severally promise, for Us, our Heirs, Executors and Administrators, to pay him yearly the Sums annex'd to our Names for three Years next ensuing, he for so long time industriously employing himself in the Premises.

N.B. *Subscriptions are taken in at the Post-Office in Philadelphia. Near £20 a Year is already subscribed.* [March 17]

On Monday about Noon, being in the Time of the General Meeting of Friends, Benjamin Lay,[3] the Pythagorean-cynical-christian Philosopher, bore a publick Testimony against the Vanity of Tea-drinking, by devoting to Destruction in the Market-place, a large Parcel of valuable China, &c. belonging to his deceased Wife. He mounted a Stall on which he had placed the Box of Ware; and when the People were gather'd round him, began to break it peacemeal with a Hammer; but was interrupted by the Populace, who overthrew him and his Box, to the Ground, and scrambling for the Sacrifice, carry'd off as much of it whole as they could get. Several would have purchas'd the China of him

3. Benjamin Lay (1677–1759), sensation-creating eccentric, both physically and mentally; antislavery, vegetarian, prohibition reformer; Quaker trouble-maker; settled in Pennsylvania, 1731, after a varied and colorful career as sailor, merchant, preacher. *DNB; DAB;* Carl and Jessica Bridenbaugh, *Rebels and Gentlemen* (N.Y., 1942), pp. 254–5. BF printed his *All Slave-Keepers . . . Apostates,* 1737 (Evans 4149).

before he attempted to destroy it, but he refused to take any Price
for it. [March 25]

[ADVERTISEMENT] Whereas Numbers of the Dutch People in
this Province, especially of the New Comers, are thro' mere
Poverty unable to furnish themselves with Bibles in their own
Language, at the advanc'd Price those which are brought from
Germany are usually sold at here: Therefore Christopher Sauer,[4]
of Germantown, proposes to print a High Dutch Bible in large
Quarto, and in a Character that may be easily read even by old
Eyes. And several well-meaning People having promised to contribute something towards the Encouragement of the Work in
general, that the Books may be afforded cheaper to real poor Persons whether Servants or others; Notice is hereby given, that the
said Work (God willing) will be begun, about the End of April
next; and that some Judgment may be made of the Quantity
necessary to be printed, all Persons who are enclined to encourage
the Work, or to have one or more of the said Bibles, may subscribe before that Time with the abovesaid Christopher Sauer,
in Germantown, or with Benjamin Franklin, in Philadelphia. 2s.
and 6d. is to be paid down towards each Bible (for which Receipts
will be given) and the Remainder on Delivery of the Books, which,
'tis expected, will be in about a Twelvemonth. If no Charitable
Contributions towards it are received, the Price of each Bible
will not exceed 14 Shillings, and it shall be as much less as those
Contributions will enable the Printer to afford; of which Contributions a fair Account shall be given the Publick. [March 25]

The Library Company of Philadelphia, are desired to meet on
Monday the third Day of May next, at nine o'Clock in the Morning, at the Library, to receive and accept the Charter granted to
the said Company by the Hon. the Proprietaries.[5] At the same

4. Christopher Saur (1693–1758), came to Pennsylvania, 1724, became successively a tailor, farmer, clockmaker, herbalist, and finally, in 1738, a printer
at Germantown, publishing, in German, a newspaper, an almanac, a Bible,
and great quantities of religious and educational literature. He was one of
those who opposed Zinzendorf's scheme to unite the German Protestants, as in
1754 he opposed Provost William Smith's plan for German charity schools.
DAB. He bought paper of BF. George S. Eddy, ed., *Account Books Kept by
Benjamin Franklin. Ledger "D", 1739–1747* (N.Y., 1929), pp. 113–4.
5. See above, p. 345.

time for the better Regulating the Affairs of the Company, it will be propos'd to them to pass the following Laws, viz.

I. *A Law directing the Manner of Admitting new Members.*

By this Law it is propos'd to be enacted, that no Person shall be admitted a Member, without the Approbation of the Directors, and paying the Value of a Share, of which a Certificate is to be given, and a Record made.

II. *A Law for prescribing a just Equality among the Members, and to prevent the Inconveniences that may arise by any Person's holding more than one Share.*

By this Law it is propos'd to be enacted, that no Member shall buy a Share of, or sell a Share to another Member; and if, as Executor, or Administrator of another, he come to a Plurality of Shares, he shall not thereby be entitled to more than one Vote, or to the borrowing of more Books, &c.

III. *A Law for regulating the Elections of Officers, and appointing their Trust and Duty.*

This Law is extracted from and agreeable to the former Constitutions of the Company.

IV. *A Law for ascertaining the Fines for neglecting the yearly Payments.*

By this Law it is propos'd to lay a Penalty of Five Shillings for every three Months Default of making the annual Payments.

V. *A Law for keeping a Record of the Laws and other Transactions of the Company.*

VI. *A Law for preventing any Advantage by Survivorship among the Members of the Library Company.*

The Company is also desired to take Notice, that the same Day (as by the former Constitutions is appointed) is the Day for the Choice of Directors and Treasurer for the ensuing Year, and for making the Tenth annual Payment.

By Order of the Directors.   J. BREINTNAL, Secry.

[April 8]

On Sunday last died after a short Illness, James Merrewether, a Person somewhat obscure, and of an unpromising Appearance,

359

but esteem'd by those few who enjoy'd an Intimacy with him, to be one of the honestest, best, and wisest Men in Philadelphia.

[April 22]

Several bought Servants belonging to the People of this Province, being enlisted by the recruiting Officers, were put on board the *Minerva* for Jamaica: But the Captain believing himself liable to be sued by their Masters if he carried them off, ordered them ashore again; and they refusing to leave the Vessel, the Sheriff by a Warrant from the Chief Justice went yesterday on board with his Officers, took them all and carried them to Prison.

As the enlisting of Servant 's on all hands allow'd to be a great Hardship to the Province, 'tis a Pleasure to observe, that the Proceedings of the Officers in that Respect are now not countenanc'd by the Government.[6]

[April 22]

On Saturday Evening we had a Shower of Rain, attended with fierce Flashes of Lightning and Thunder: At which Time two labouring Men (standing under a Sawyers-Shead, on Society-Hill, to shelter themselves from the Rain) were struck down by a Flash of Lightning: But one of them recovering, found his Companion, Thomas Smith, dead; his Hat was much torn, and part of one of his Shoes torn off; on his Head, Neck, Breast, and the Inside of one of his Thighs were spots which appear'd as if burnt. The Survivor had most of the upper Leather of one of his Shoes torn away, and was burnt several Parts of his Body. [April 29]

Yesterday William Bullock received Sentence of Death for the Murder of his Negro Boy.

[April 29]

[ADVERTISEMENT] Just imported from London, And to be Sold by B. Franklin, at the Post-Office, near the Market in Philadelphia. All Sorts of fine Paper, Parchment, Ink-powder, Sealing Wax, Wafers, fountain Pens, Pencils, Brass Ink horns, Ink-bottles neatly set in Brass, Ink and sand Glasses with Brass Heads, Pounce and Pounce Boxes, curious large Ivory Books, and common ditto, large and small Slates, Gunter's Scales, Dividers, Protractors, Pocket Compasses both large and small, fine Pewter Stands proper

6. See above, p. 288.

for Offices and Counting-houses, fine Mezzotinto and grav'd Pictures of Mr. Whitefield.

Where may be had great Variety of Bibles, Testaments, Psalters, Spelling Books, Primers,Hornbooks, and other sorts of Stationary Ware. [May 20]

[ADVERTISEMENT] Anvils, Vices [sic], London Bristol and blister'd Steel, Iron Pots, Traces, lately imported from England, to be sold by Hugh Roberts, at the Pipe, in Market-street, Philadelphia. [May 20]

We hear from several Parts of the Country, that infinite Multitudes of black Worms or Caterpillars coming out of the Earth, threaten Destruction to the late promising Crops of Corn and Grass; large Fields being in a Day or two cut down and devoured by them, and the Ground laid bare. Considerable Mischief has likewise been done in the Pastures near this City, and many find themselves obliged to mow sooner than they intended, to save what they can. Indeed it behoves People to watch their Fields narrowly, for where no Worms have been seen on one Day, there have been Millions the next. In the Country some People to secure their Fields, run narrow Trenches round them; others where the Worms are already among the Corn, find an Advantage in running thro' the Fields backwards and forwards with Ropes between two Persons, and bending the Corn, thereby shake them down two or three Times a Day; and hope in a few Days their Time will be over. [May 27]

[ADVERTISEMENT] Stray'd, about two Months ago, from the Northern Liberties of this City, a small bay Mare, branded IW on the near Shoulder and Buttock. She being but little and bare-footed, cannot be supposed to be gone far; therefore if any of the Town-Boys find her and bring her to the Subscriber, they shall, for their Trouble, have the Liberty to ride her when they please, from   WILLIAM FRANKLIN
Philad. June 17. 1742. [June 17]

[ADVERTISEMENT] NOTICE is hereby given, that William Bradford, junr. has set up a New Printing-Office in the House that Mr. Andrew Bradford formerly lived, in Second Street, where Printing is done at the most reasonable Rates;[7] And Persons may be supply'd with Bibles, Testaments, Psalters, Primers, Penn's Works 2 vol. fol. Fox's Doctrinals, Elwood's Sacred History, Josephus, Sufferings of the People called Quakers 3 vol. 8vo. Elwood's Life, Bishop Ken's Retired Christian, Seagrave's Hymns, Chauncey's Doctrine of Godliness, Clark on the Promises, Dutton on the new-Birth, ditto on Justification, ditto on Walking with God, ditto's Letters, Baxter's poor Man's Family Book, Sealing Wax, Wafers, Ink-Powder, Paper, Ink, Ink-Horns, lead Pencils, Pocket-Books, Blank Books, Spectacles, Dividers, Gunter-Scales, Parchment, and a Parcel of neat Metzotinto Pictures in Frames and Glasses, &c.

N.B. The said Bradford designs to Publish a weekly News-Paper, Subscriptions for which are taken in by him at his House in Second street. [July 8]

[ADVERTISEMENT] PRINTING DONE on a NEAT and FAIR CHARACTER, and with Expedition, at reasonable Rates, by Isaiah Warner, at his Printing-Office, almost opposite to Charles Brockden's, in Chesnut-Street, Philadelphia.[8] [August 5]

[ADVERTISEMENT] Any Person that wants to purchase Gold, may hear of some to be disposed of for Paper Money, by Enquiring of the Printer hereof. [September 2]

[ADVERTISEMENT] Aufrichtige Nachricht ans Publicum über eine von dem Hollaendischen Pfarrer Johann Philipp Boehmen edirte Laesher Shrift gegen die sogenannten Herrnhuter, das ist die Evangelischen Brüder aus Boehmen und Maehren u.s.f. [sic] welche jetzt in der Forks von Delaware wohnen, herausgegeben von Georg Neisser aus sehlen in Maehren und Schul-meister in Bethlehem. Es wird verkauft in Philadelphia bey David Süssholz, in Second-Street, bey Johannes Wüster und B. Franklin, in Mar-

7. See above, p. 315.
8. Isaiah Warner, Philadelphia printer, was a partner of Cornelia Bradford, 1743; BF did printing for him. C. William Miller, "Franklin's Type: Its Study Past and Present," APS Proc., XCIX (1955), 425–6; Thomas, Printing, I, 245.

ket-street, im Falckenar Schwamm bey Henrich Antes, in Bethlehem bey Georg Neissern.   [September 9]

[ADVERTISEMENT] An honest and diligent Person, that is capable of building a good Paper-Mill, and another that understands
the Making of Paper, are wanted to undertake and carry on that
Business in a neighbouring Colony. Any such Persons that want
Employment, will meet with a Person who will give good Encouragement, if they apply to the Printer of this Paper on the
25th Instant.[9]   [September 16]

Friday last was the Day of General Election throughout this
Province and Territories, according to the Charter; when the
following Gentlemen were chosen, viz. [Here follows the list.]
    At this Election there was a greater Number of Votes, in all the
Counties of this Province, than have appear'd for several Years
past: And (except in Bucks County) the Majority in favour of the
old Assembly was extraordinary. In Lancaster County the highest
Number for the new Candidates was 362, the old had 1480: In
Chester the highest for the new was 99, the old 961: In Philadelphia County the highest for the new was 336, the old 1790.
    In this City, when the People of City and County were as-
sembled in the Market Place, and had just begun the Choice of
Inspectors, a Body of Sailors, suppos'd to be about 70 or 80, collected from several Ships in the Harbour, appear'd at the Foot
of Market-Street, arm'd with Clubs, and huzzaing march'd up
in a tumultuous Manner towards the People. As they were mostly
Strangers, and had no kind of Right to intermeddle with the
Election, and some ill Consequence was apprehended if they
should be suffer'd to mix, with their Clubs, among the Inhabitants,
some of the Magistrates, and other Persons of Note, met them,
and endeavour'd to prevail with them to return peaceably to their
Ships, but without Effect. For they fell on with their Clubs, and

9. Johann Conrad Schütz, Philadelphia papermaker, answered this advertisement of William Parks, printer at Williamsburg, Va. Parks came to
Philadelphia in late September and arranged for Schütz and a carpenter to go
to Williamsburg and build the paper mill. Eddy, *Account Books*, pp. 30–3,
98–104; Dard Hunter, *Papermaking by Hand in America* (Chillicothe, O.,
1950), pp. 54–6.

knocking down Magistrates, Constables, and all others who oppos'd 'em, fought their Way up to the Court-House, and clear'd
the Place of Election, the People retiring into the Market-House
and Second-Street in a kind of Amaze at such unexpected and
unusual Treatment. After the Sailors had triumph'd awhile before
the Court-house, they march'd off, and the People, without pursuing them, continued and finished their Election of Inspectors;
which was no sooner done but the Sailors returning more numerous and furious than at first, fell upon the People a second time,
and knock'd down all they came a-near, several were carried
off for dead, and the Confusion and Terror was inexpressible. But
the Inhabitants, losing at length all Patience, furnished themselves
with Sticks from the neighbouring Woodpiles, and turn'd upon
the Sailors, who immediately fled to their Ships and hid themselves, from whence they were drag'd out one by one, and before
Night near 50 of them were committed to Prison. A good Watch
was kept that Night to prevent any new Tumult, and the City has
ever since been quiet. [October 7]

[ADVERTISEMENT] On Tuesday will be published, John Jerman's Almanack, for the Year 1743. Printed and Sold by William
Bradford, in Second-street. [October 14]

About two Weeks ago, one John Leek, of Cohansie in West-
New-Jersey, after twelve Months Deliberation, made himself an
Eunuch (as it is said) for the Kingdom of Heaven's Sake, having
made such a Construction upon Mat. xix. 12.[1] He is now under Dr.
Johnson's Hands, and in a fair way of doing well. [October 28]

[ADVERTISEMENT] Now in the Press, THE NEW-JERSEY AL-
MANACK for the Year 1743. By William Ball, Philom. To be Sold
by B. Franklin; By whom also will be speedily published Poor
Richard's and Pocket Almanacks. [November 11]

[ADVERTISEMENT] NEW IRON FIRE-PLACES, large and small,
to be Sold by Robert Grace at the Upper End of Market-street,
and by the Printer hereof. [November 11]

1. "For there be Eunuchs . . . which have made themselves Eunuchs for
the kingdom of heaven's sake." Matt. 19:12.

364

Last Night died, after a lingering Illness, Mr. Andrew Bradford, Printer; one of the Common Council of this City.

[November 25]

JUST PUBLISHED, POOR Richard's ALMANACK, for the Year 1743.

[December 2]

Whereas Mary the Wife of Richard Leadame, hath misused her said Husband, and doth run him in debt unnecessarily; this is to warn all Persons against trusting her on his Account, for he will not pay any Debts she shall contract after the Date hereof. Phila. Dec. 14. 1742.   RICHARD LEADAME

[December 14]

Friend Benjamin Franklin, I desire thee to stop the Advertisement in thy last Week's Paper, concerning my Wife; and Print to the Contrary, that my Friends may give her Credit on my Account as usual. I acknowledge I had no Reason to do what I have done: For what I did was entirely thro' others Perswasions, and my own Passion.[2]   RICHARD LEADAME
Dec. 21. 1742.   [December 21]

PHILADELPHIA: Printed by B. FRANKLIN, Post-Master, at the New Printing-Office, near the Market.

Poor Richard, 1743

Poor Richard, 1743. An Almanack For the Year of Christ 1743, . . . By Richard Saunders, Philom. Philadelphia: Printed and sold by B. Franklin, at the New Printing-Office near the Market. (Yale University Library)

Friendly READER,

Because I would have every Man make Advantage of the Blessings of Providence, and few are acquainted with the Method of making Wine·of the Grapes which grow wild in our Woods, I do here present them with a few easy Directions, drawn from some Years Experience, which, if they will follow, they may furnish themselves with a wholesome sprightly Claret, which will keep for several Years, and is not inferior to that which passeth for French Claret.

2. Richard Leadame's marital saga continues below, p. 390.

Begin to gather Grapes from the 10th of September (the ripest first) to the last of October, and having clear'd them of Spider webs, and dead Leaves, put them into a large Molosses- or Rum-Hogshead; after having washed it well, and knock'd one Head out, fix it upon the other Head, on a Stand, or Blocks in the Cellar, if you have any, if not, in the warmest Part of the House, about 2 Feet from the Ground; as the Grapes sink, put up more, for 3 or 4 Days; after which, get into the Hogshead bare-leg'd, and tread them down until the Juice works up about your Legs, which will be in less than half an Hour; then get out, and turn the Bottom ones up, and tread them again, a Quarter of an Hour; this will be sufficient to get out the good Juice; more pressing wou'd burst the unripe Fruit, and give it an ill Taste: This done, cover the Hogshead close with a thick Blanket, and if you have no Cellar, and the Weather proves Cold, with two.

In this Manner you must let it take its first Ferment, for 4 or 5 Days it will work furiously; when the Ferment abates, which you will know by its making less Noise, make a Spile-hole within six inches of the Bottom, and twice a Day draw some in a Glass. When it looks as clear as Rock-water, draw it off into a clean, rather than new Cask, proportioning it to the Contents of the Hogshead or Wine Vat*; that is, if the Hogshead holds twenty Bushels of Grapes, Stems and all, the Cask must at least, hold 20 Gallons, for they will yield a Gallon per Bushel. Your Juice or Must† thus drawn from the Vat, proceed to the second Ferment.

You must reserve in Jugs or Bottles, 1 Gallon or 5 Quarts of the Must to every 20 Gallons you have to work; which you will use according to the following Directions.

Place your Cask, which must be chock full, with the Bung up, and open twice every Day, Morning and Night; feed your Cask with the reserved Must; two Spoonfuls at a time will suffice, clearing the Bung after you feed it, with your Finger or a Spoon, of the Grape-Stones and other Filth which the Ferment will throw up; you must continue feeding it thus until Christmas,

---

*Vat or *Fatt*, a Name for the Vessel, in which you tread the Grapes, and in which the *Must* takes its first Ferment.

†*Must* is a Name for the Juice of the Vine before it is fermented, afterwards 'tis called Wine.

when you may bung it up, and it will be fit for Use or to be rack'd into clean Casks or Bottles, by February.

N.B. Gather the Grapes after the Dew is off, and in all dry Seasons. Let not the Children come at the Must, it will scour them severely. If you make Wine for Sale, or to go beyond Sea, one quarter Part must be distill'd, and the Brandy put into the three Quarters remaining. One Bushel of Grapes, heap Measure, as you gather them from the Vine, will make at least a Gallon of Wine, if good, five Quarts.

These Directions are not design'd for those who are skill'd in making Wine, but for those who have hitherto had no Acquaintance with that Art.

XI Mon. January hath xxxi days.

On the FLORIDA WAR.[3]

From Georgia t'Augustine the General goes;
From Augustine to Georgia come our Foes;
Hardy from Charlestown to St. Simons hies,
Again from thence to Charlestown back he flies.
Forth from St. Simons then the Spaniards creep;
Say, Children, is not this your Play, *Bo-peep?*

How few there are who have courage enough to own their Faults, or resolution enough to mend them!

3. These derisive lines refer to operations on the Georgia-Florida frontier during the War of Jenkins' Ear. In June and July 1740 General James Oglethorpe led an unsuccessful attack upon the Spanish garrison of St. Augustine. Just two years later the Spaniards retaliated with an expedition against St. Simon's Island and Frederica in Georgia. They captured the island fortifications but were defeated by Oglethorpe near Frederica and forced to withdraw. Captain Charles Hardy arrived with a small naval squadron from Charleston too late to assist in the defense of Georgia and returned to his base without pursuing the retreating Spanish naval force. The *Boston Evening-Post,* Oct. 4, 1742, also satirized these inconclusive operations:

> They both did meet, they both did fight, they both did run away;
> They both did strive to meet again, the quite Contrary Way.

Herbert L. Osgood, *The American Colonies in the Eighteenth Century* (N.Y., 1924), III, 504–10; Amos A. Ettinger, *James Edward Oglethorpe: Imperial Idealist* (Oxford, 1936), pp. 234–44.

Men differ daily, about things which are subject to Sense, is it likely then they should agree about things invisible.

XII Mon. February hath xxviii days.

> Democritus, dear Droll, revisit Earth;
> And with our Follies glut thy heighten'd Mirth:
> Sad Heraclitus, serious Wretch, return;
> In louder Grief, our greater Crimes to mourn.
> Between you both, I unconcern'd stand by:
> Hurt, can I laugh? and honest, need I cry?

> Mark with what insolence and pride,
> Blown Bufo takes his haughty stride;
> As if no toad was toad beside.

Ill Company is like a dog who dirts those most, that he loves best.

I Mon. March hath xxxi days.

> From bad Health, bad Conscience, and Parties dull Strife,
> From an insolent Friend, and a termagant Wife,
> From the Kindred of such (on one Side or t'other)
> Who most wisely delight in plaguing each other;
> From the Wretch who can cant, while he Mischief designs,
> From old rotten Mills, bank'd Meadows and Mines;
> From Curses like these if kind Heav'n defends me,
> I'll never complain of the Fortune it sends me.

> In prosperous fortunes be modest and wise,
> The greatest may fall, and the lowest may rise:
> But insolent People that fall in disgrace,
> Are wretched and no-body pities their Case.

Le sage entend à demi mot.[4]

Sorrow is dry.

4. The wise man knows how to take a hint.

II Mon. April hath xxx days.

> A Parrot is for Prating priz'd,
> But prattling Women are despis'd;
> She who attacks another's Honour
> Draws every living Thing upon her.
> Think, Madam, when you stretch your Lungs,
> That all your Neighbours too have Tongues;
> One Slander fifty will beget;
> The World with Interest pays the Debt.

The World is full of fools and faint hearts; and yet every one has courage enough to bear the misfortunes, and wisdom enough to manage the Affairs of his neighbour.

Beware, beware! he'll cheat 'ithout scruple, who can without fear.

III Mon. May hath xxxi days.

> The Snows are gone, and genial Spring once more
>   New clothes the Meads with Grass, the Trees with Leaves;
> And the proud Rivers that disdain'd a Shore
>   Within their Banks now roll their lessen'd Waves.
> Nature seems all renew'd, youthful and gay,
>   Ev'n Luna doth her monthly Loss supply;
> But Years and Hours that whirl our Time away,
>   Describe our State, and tell us *we must die.*

The D---l wipes his B---ch with poor Folks Pride.

> Content and Riches seldom meet together,
> Riches take thou, contentment I had rather.

> Speak with contempt of none, from slave to king,
> The meanest Bee hath, and will use, a sting.

IV Mon. June hath xxx days.

> *Every Man for himself, &c.*
> A Town fear'd a Siege, and held Consultation,
> What was the best Method of Fortification:

369

A grave skilful Mason declar'd his Opinion,
That nothing but Stone could secure the Dominion.
A Carpenter said, Tho' that was well spoke,
Yet he'd rather advise to defend it with Oak.
A Tanner much wiser than both these together,
Cry'd, *Try what you please, but nothing's like Leather.*

The church, the state, and the poor, are 3 daughters which we should maintain, but not portion off.

A achwyno heb achos; gwneler achos iddo.[5]

A little well-gotten will do us more good,
Than lordships and scepters by Rapine and Blood.

V Mon. July hath xxxi days.

Friend Col and I, both full of Whim,
    To shun each other oft' agree;
For I'm not Beau enough for him;
    And he's too much a Beau for me.
Then let us from each other fly
    And Arm-in-arm no more appear;
That I may ne'er offend your Eye;
    That you may ne'er offend my Ear.

Borgen macht sorgen.[6]

Let all Men know thee, but no man know thee thoroughly: Men freely ford that see the shallows.

'Tis easy to frame a good bold resolution;
But hard is the Task that concerns execution.

Cold and cunning come from the north:
But cunning sans wisdom is nothing worth.

5. Let him who complains without cause, be given cause to complain.
6. He that goes borrowing, goes sorrowing.

VI Mon. August hath xxxi days.

On buying a BIBLE.
'Tis but a Folly to rejoice, or boast,
How small a Price thy well-bought Purchase cost.
Until thy Death, thou shalt not fully know
Whether it was a Pennyworth or no;
And, at that time, believe me, 'twill appear
Extreamly cheap, or else extreamly dear.

'Tis vain to repine,
Tho' a learned Divine
Will die *this day* at nine.

A noddo duw, ry noddir.[7]

Ah simple Man! when a boy two precious jewels were given thee, Time, and good Advice; one thou hast lost, and the other thrown away.

Na funno i hûn.
Na wnaid i ûn.[8]

VII Mon. September hath xxx days.

Good Death, said a Woman, for once be so kind
To take me, and leave my dear Husband behind,
But when Death appear'd with a sour Grimace,
The Woman was dash'd at his thin hatchet Face;
So she made him a Courts'y, and modestly sed,
If you come for my Husband, he lies there in Bed.

Dick told his spouse, he durst be bold to swear,
Whate'er she pray'd for, Heav'n would thwart her pray'r:
Indeed! says Nell, 'tis what I'm pleas'd to hear;
For now I'll pray for your long life, my dear.

The sleeping Fox catches no poultry. Up! up!

7. What will be protected by God will be protected completely.
8. Let no man do to another what he would not wish for himself.

371

VIII Mon. October hath xxxi days.

A Musketo just starv'd, in a sorry Condition,
Pretended to be a most skilful Musician;
He comes to a Bee-hive, and there he would stay,
To teach the Bees Children to sing *Sol la fa.*
The Bees told him plainly the Way of their Nation,
Was breeding up Youth in some honest Vocation;
Lest not bearing Labour, they should not be fed,
And then curse their Parents for being high bred.

If you'd be wealthy, think of saving, more than of getting: The Indies have not made Spain rich, because her Outgoes equal her Incomes.

Tugend bestehet wen alles vergehet.[9]

Came you from Court? for in your Mien,
A self-important air is seen.

IX Mon. November hath xxx days.

A Year of Wonders now behold!
Britons despising Gallic Gold!
A Year that stops the Spanish Plunders!
A Year that they must be Refunders!
A Year that sets our Troops a marching!
A Year secures our Ships from Searching!
A Year that Charity's extended!
A Year that Whig and Tory's blended!
Amazing Year! that we're defended!

Hear what Jack Spaniard says,
Con todo el Mundo Guerra,
Y Paz con Ingalatierra.[1]

If you'd have it done, Go: If not, send.

9. Virtue stays when all else goes.
1. Though all the world's at war, there's peace with England.

Many a long dispute among Divines may be thus abridg'd, It is so: It is not so. It is so; It is not so.

X Mon. December hath xxxi days.

> Inclement Winter rages o'er the Plains,
> Incrusts the Earth and binds the Floods in Chains.
> Is the Globe mov'd? or does our Country roll,
> In nearer Latitude to th'artic Pole?
> The Fate of Lapland and its Cold we bear,
> Yet want the Fur, the Sledge and harness'd Deer:
> To punish Guilt, do angry Stars combine
> Conjunct or Opposite, Quartile or Trine?

Experience keeps a dear school, yet Fools will learn in no other.

Felix quem faciunt aliena pericula cautum.[2]

How many observe Christ's Birth-day! How few, his Precepts!
O! 'tis easier to keep Holidays than Commandments.

> Once on a Time it by Chance came to pass,
> That a Man and his Son were leading an Ass.
> Cries a Passenger, Neighbour, you're shrewdly put to't,
> To lead an Ass empty, and trudge it on foot.
> Nay, quoth the old Fellow, if Folk do so mind us
> I'll e'en climb the Ass, and Boy mount behind us:
> But as they jogg'd on, they were laught at and hiss'd,
> What, two booby Lubbers on one sorry Beast!
> This is such a Figure as never was known;
> 'Tis a sign that the Ass is none of your own.
> Then down gets the Boy, and walks by the Side,
> Till another cries, What, you old Fool must you ride?
> When you see the poor Child that's weakly and young
> Forc'd thro' thick and thin to trudge it along.
> Then down gets the Father, and up gets the Son;
> If this cannot please them we ne'er shall have done.
> They had not gone far, but a Woman cries out,

2. Happy is he whom others' experiences make cautious.

O you young graceless Imp, you'll be hang'd, no doubt!
Must you ride an Ass, and your Father that's grey
E'en foot it, and pick out the best of his Way?
So now to please all they but one Trick lack,
And that was to carry the Ass a pick-pack:
But when that was try'd, it appear'd such a Jest,
It occasion'd more Laughter by half than the rest.
Thus he who'd please all, and their Good-liking gain,
Shows a deal of Good-Nature, but labours in vain.[3]

COURTS.

A Person threatning to go to Law, was dissuaded from it by his Friend, who desired him to *consider,* for the Law was chargeable. I don't care, reply'd the other, I will not consider, I'll go to Law. Right, said his Friend, for if you go to Law I am sure you don't consider.

A Farmer once made a complaint to a Judge,
My Bull, if it please you, Sir, owing a Grudge,
Belike to one of your good Worship's Cattle,
Has slain him out-right in a mortal Battle:
I'm sorry at heart because of the Action,
And want to know how must be made Satisfaction.
Why, you must give me your Bull, that's plain
Says the Judge, or pay me the Price of the Slain.
But I have mistaken the Case, Sir, says John,
The dead Bull I talk of, and please you, 's my own:
And yours is the Beast that the Mischief has done.
The Judge soon replies with a serious Face:
Say you so; then this Accident *alters the Case.*

3. Jonas Green reprinted these verses in *Md. Gaz.*, July 7, 1747. BF had told the same story in prose in Apology for Printers (above, I, 199), where, in the end, the ass was thrown into the river.

Articles of the Union Fire Company

MS Minute Book, Union Fire Company: Library Company of Philadelphia

The Union Fire Company's Articles of Agreement of January 31, 1743, are substantially the same as those of 1736 (see above, pp. 150–3), and will not be printed here in full.[4] There are, however, three noteworthy differences. Article I increased the required equipment for each member from two leather buckets and four linen bags for salvage to six buckets, four bags, and "one convenient Fire hook." Article VII raised the membership from 25 to 30. Article IV prescribed in considerably more detail the procedure to be followed in case of an alarm of fire, and also obligated members to respond to a fire in any part of the city, regardless of whose house was endangered. The text of this article follows:

"IV THAT we will all of us, upon hearing of Fire breaking out, immediately repair to the same with our Buckets, Bags and Fire hooks and there employ our best Endeavours to preserve the Goods and Effects of such of us as shall be in Danger, by packing the same in our Bags; and if more than one of us shall be in Danger at the same Time, we will divide our selves as near as may be to be equally helpful; and such of us as may be spared shall assist others. And to prevent as much as in us lies, suspicious persons from coming into, or carrying any Goods out of such Houses as may be in Danger; Two of our Number shall constantly attend at the Doors, untill all the Goods and Effects that can be saved, are packed up and carried to some safe place to be appointed by the Owner, or such of our Company as shall be present, where one or more of us shall attend them 'till they can be conveniently delivered to or secured for the Owner. And upon our first hearing the Cry of Fire in the Night-time we will immediately cause two or more Lights to be set up in our Windows; and such of our Company whose Houses may be thought in Danger shall likewise place Candles in every Room, to prevent Confusion, and that their Friends may be able to give them the more speedy and effectual Assistance. And, moreover, as this Association is intended for a general Benefit, we do further agree, that when a Fire breaks out in any part of this City, though none of our Houses Goods or Effects may be in any apparent Danger, we will nevertheless repair thither with our Buckets, Bags and Fire Hooks, and give our utmost Assistance to such of our Fellow Citizens as may stand in need of it, in the same Manner as if they belonged to this Company: And if it shall appear at the next meeting of the Company after the breaking out of any Fire in this

4. BF printed these Articles and the List of Members, charging the Company £3 5s. Union Fire Co., Minutes, Oct. 31, 1743, Lib. Co. Phila.

City, that any of our Members neglected to attend, with their Buckets, Bags and Fire hooks, or set up Lights as aforesaid, every such neglecting Member shall forfeit and pay to the use of the Company the sum of Two SHILLINGS; unless they can assign some reasonable Cause to the Satisfaction of the Company."

The following twenty-one signers of the Articles of 1736 also signed the Articles of 1743: Samuel Coates, John Armitt, Benjamin Shoemaker, Hugh Roberts, BF, Philip Syng, William Parsons, Richard Sewell, James Morris, Stephen Armitt, William Plumsted, John Dillwyn, John Cooper, Edward Shippen, Lloyd Zachary, Samuel Powel, Jr., Thomas Lloyd, George Emlen, Thomas Lawrence, William Bell, and Joseph Turner. Others who completed the initial group of thirty signers of 1743 were: Charles Norris, Reese Meredith, Samuel Neave, William Logan, Samuel Morris, John Bard, Charles Jones, Peter Bard, and Luke Morris.[5] As each of the original subscribers died or resigned, his name was struck through and another was elected in his place, he signing the articles as others had done, either below their names or, when that page was filled, on another page of the MS Minute Book.

Distribution of the Mail   Draft: American Philosophical Society

This document obviously belongs to the period of Franklin's Philadelphia postmastership, 1737–53. The date 1743 is tentatively ascribed on the basis of a marginal note that the *John*, Captain Mesnard, for New York arrived at Deal on February 10. Stephen Mesnard was captain of the *Britannia* sailing between New York and England in 1740–41, and of the *Charming Hannah* on the same run in 1742. The *New-York Weekly Journal*, Nov. 8, 1742, reports that the *John*, Captain S. Mesnard, has cleared New York for London; it reports May 2, 1743, that Captain Mesnard has cleared New York in the *Carolina* (the vessel of which he was master for the next eight or ten years). It does not report the return of the *John*, but unless she was lost and her captain res-

5. These new members were: Charles Norris (1712–1766), merchant, trustee of the Loan Office, member of the Board of Managers and treasurer of the Hospital; Reese Meredith (1708–1778), merchant, born in England and educated at Oxford; Samuel Neave (*c.* 1707–1774), merchant; William Logan (1718–1776), son of James, merchant and attorney for the Penns, common councilor, provincial councilor; Samuel Morris (1711–1782), merchant, tanner, lawyer, sheriff, common councilor, trustee of Hospital and College; John Bard (1716–1779), physician; Charles Jones, underwriter, city warden; Peter Bard (1714–1769), merchant, owner of Mt. Holly Iron Works; Luke Morris (1717–1793), owner of ropewalk, director of the Philadelphia Contributionship, warden of port of Philadelphia.

cued, she must have returned in April 1743, which she could have done if she was at Deal waiting to enter the Channel February 10. So while the dating of 1743 for this fragment is plausible and may even be sound, it is not conclusive. Further research on the movements of the *John* may provide evidence which the present editors have sought in vain.

It is only negatively relevant that other *Johns*, smaller than ship-size, are reported entering and clearing New York in the 1740's; that a Captain *William* Mesnard was sailing between New York and the West Indies in the same decade; and that a *John*, which may have been Stephen Mesnard's old command, is noted in the *New-York Gazette*, Nov. 5, 1750, but now under Captain Deane.

To accept the 1743 date suggests, however, that Franklin's proposal for a more orderly distribution of ship's mail was never adopted. At least Peter Kalm reported in 1748 how, as soon as the vessel dropped anchor, "many of the inhabitants came on board to inquire for letters. They took all those which they could carry, either for themselves or for their friends. Those which remained the captain ordered to be carried on shore and to be brought into a coffee-house, where everybody could make inquiry for them, and by this means he was rid of the trouble of delivering them himself." Kalm, *Travels*, I, 16. This passage can, of course, be cited as evidence for dating the document *after* 1748.

Philada. April [1743]

Whereas it has been customary for Numbers of People to croud on board Vessels newly arrived in this Port, and into the Houses of the Captains, or Merchants to whom the same belong or are consigned, in quest of Letters, Packets, &c. and under Pretence of taking care of the Letters of their Acquaintance dividing the whole Bag among themselves in a disorderly Manner, and in such Hurry and Confusion that it cannot afterwards be known by whom any Letter that is missing was taken up, and evil-minded Persons have made use of such Opportunities to pocket and embezle Letters of consequence, and either destroy them or delay the Delivery a long time, to the great Damage and Injury of those to whom they were directed; And whereas there is a regular Post-Office in this Place establish'd by Act of Parliament, which is for the Benefit of Correspondence in General, and ought therefore by no Means to be discouraged;[6] We the Subscribers hereunto taking the Premises into Consideration, and being willing that the Office should be

6. "the Rates of Ship Letters being very low and reasonable" originally added here, but struck out.

encouraged,[7] and that the Captains of Vessels should have the Benefit of the Bounty allowed by Law on delivering the Letters they bring into the Office, do hereby desire all Persons Masters of Vessels and others, to put all Letters they may have for us immediately into the Post Office, or deliver them to such Persons as the Postmaster shall send on board for them; and we declare that we shall not take their so doing in the least amiss, but look on our selves more oblig'd by their taking that Method than by their delivering our Letters in any other Manner whatsoever.

[*In the margin:*] The John, Capt. Mesnard for N. York arrived at Deal the 10th of February.

A Proposal for Promoting Useful Knowledge

Broadside: Yale University Library[8]

A proposal Franklin drafted in 1743 to found an academy in Philadelphia, he wrote in his autobiography, came to nothing and was laid aside. "I succeeded better the next Year, 1744, in proposing and establishing a Philosophical Society."[9] Franklin did take a leading part in founding this Society, but the implications that it was his idea and that the Society flourished are not fully supported by the facts.

The botanist John Bartram seems to have been the first in Philadelphia to propose a learned society.[10] He had been corresponding for a decade with naturalists like Gronovius, Mark Catesby, and Sir Hans Sloane in Europe and Cadwallader Colden, John Clayton, and John Mitchell in America. Of all the Philadelphia philosophers, except James

7. BF originally wrote: "the Crown should have its Due."

8. There are transcripts of this document in APS and Royal Society of Arts, London.

9. Par. Text edit., p. 278.

10. John Bartram (1699–1777), a Quaker farmer and self-taught botanist, began a lifelong correspondence with Peter Collinson, the English Quaker botanist, about 1733. Through Collinson he established contact with leading scientists in England and the Continent and became justly famous among them. His published accounts of extensive field trips throughout the West and South, and the botanical garden he established at Kingsessing, near Philadelphia, where he carried on pioneer experiments in hybridization, helped to earn for him Linnaeus' praise as the greatest contemporary "natural botanist" in the world. George III appointed him Botanist to the King in 1765 with an annual stipend of £50. *DAB;* Darlington, *Memorials;* Francis D. West, "John Bartram and the American Philosophical Society," *Pa. Hist.,* XXIII (1956), 463–6.

Logan, he was probably the best known beyond his own city. Early in 1739 he asked Peter Collinson's advice about the formation of a society or even an academy where "most ingenious and curious men" might communicate knowledge of "natural secrets arts and syances." Collinson realized that there were not yet enough learned men in Philadelphia—Bartram had admitted as much—and pointed out that "to draw learned strangers to you, to teach sciences, requires salaries and good encouragement," which were lacking.[11] Meanwhile, he observed, the Library offered many of the advantages of an academy.[1] Bartram, discouraged, seems to have done no more for several years, but in 1743, with Franklin, whose interest in scientific matters was growing, he took the matter up again. Franklin now wrote a proposal for a learned society which embodied both Bartram's ideas and his own.

The immediate response was encouraging. Colden's warm approval determined Franklin "to proceed in the Affair very soon."[2] The Society was organized, probably early in 1744. By March 27, when Bartram sent Colden "one of our proposals," there had been three meetings.[3] Several persons from neighboring provinces were elected to membership; others expressed interest; and a few, in response to the Proposal's invitation, sent scientific papers. Only James Logan held aloof. "I tould Benjamin that I believed he [Logan] would not incourage it," Bartram explained to Colden; "we should have been pleased with his name at the top of our List, as his person in our meetings. However we resolved that his not favouring the design should not hinder our attempt and if he would not go along with us we would Jog along without him."[4]

Stout words were not enough. The first enthusiasm soon passed off. "The Members of our Society here are very idle Gentlemen," Franklin complained to Colden, August 15, 1745; "they will take no

---

The idea for a learned society may have come to Bartram from his friend Cadwallader Colden of New York, who had proposed a similar "Voluntary Society for the advancing of Knowledge" to Dr. William Douglass of Boston in 1728. *Colden Paps.*, I, 272–3. The history of this society of 1743 is clearly and fully related in Brooke Hindle, *The Pursuit of Science in Revolutionary America, 1735–1789* (Chapel Hill, N.C., 1956), pp. 67–73, and Carl Van Doren, "The Beginnings of the American Philosophical Society," APS *Proc.*, LXXXVII (1944), 277–89.

11. Collinson to Bartram, July 10, 1739, Darlington, *Memorials*, p. 132.

1. This aspect of the Library is developed by Dorothy F. Grimm, "Franklin's Scientific Institution," *Pa. Hist.*, XXIII (1956), 437–62.

2. BF to Colden, Nov. 4, 1743, below, p. 387.

3. Bartram's letter to Colden is written on the back of the folio broadside of the Proposal in Yale Univ. Lib. BF franked the sheet for mailing.

4. Bartram to Colden, April 29, 1744, quoted by West in *Pa. Hist.*, XXIII, 465–6.

Pains." Colden commented later that if some had been lazy, others were "too officious." In October Bartram, Franklin, and Thomas Bond were talking of "carrying it on with more dilligence than ever which we may very easily do if we could but exchange the time that is spent in the Club, Chess and Coffee House for the Curious amusements of natural observations."[5] The Society was already moribund by the time Bartram began receiving inquiries about it from his European friends.

But Franklin did not give up easily. He jumped at Colden's suggestion of publishing an American philosophical miscellany which would include the papers that had been submitted to the Society and others which such a periodical might be expected to attract. These plans, also, came to nothing.[6] Franklin was still clinging to the idea of a learned society in 1751 when he solicited Collinson's influence to get him the office of deputy postmaster general for America: one of the beneficial results of his appointment to that post, he pointed out, was that it "would enable me to execute a Scheme long since form'd, of which I send you enclos'd a Copy, and which I hope would soon produce something agreeable to you and to all Lovers of Useful Knowledge."[7]

A PROPOSAL for Promoting USEFUL KNOWLEDGE among the British Plantations in America.

Philadelphia, May 14, 1743.

The English are possess'd of a long Tract of Continent, from Nova Scotia to Georgia, extending North and South thro' different Climates, having different Soils, producing different Plants, Mines and Minerals, and capable of different Improvements, Manufactures, &c.

The first Drudgery of Settling new Colonies, which confines the Attention of People to mere Necessaries, is now pretty well over; and there are many in every Province in Circumstances that set them at Ease, and afford Leisure to cultivate the finer Arts, and improve the common Stock of Knowledge. To such of these who are Men of Speculation, many Hints must from time to time arise, many Observations occur, which if well-examined, pursued and improved, might produce Discoveries to the Advantage of some or all of the British Plantations, or to the Benefit of Mankind in general.

5. Bartram to Colden, Oct. 4, 1745, *Colden Paps.*, III, 160; Colden to Bartram, Nov. 7, 1745, Darlington, *Memorials*, p. 330.

6. Colden to BF, Dec. 1744, below, p. 446; also BF to Colden, Nov. 28, 1745; and Oct. 16, 1746.

7. BF to Collinson, May 21, 1751.

But as from the Extent of the Country such Persons are widely separated, and seldom can see and converse or be acquainted with each other, so that many useful Particulars remain uncommunicated, die with the Discoverers, and are lost to Mankind; it is, to remedy this Inconvenience for the future, proposed,

That One Society be formed of Virtuosi or ingenious Men residing in the several Colonies, to be called *The American Philosophical Society;* who are to maintain a constant Correspondence.

That Philadelphia being the City nearest the Centre of the Continent-Colonies, communicating with all of them northward and southward by Post, and with all the Islands by Sea, and having the Advantage of a good growing Library, be the Centre of the Society.

That at Philadelphia there be always at least seven Members, viz. a Physician, a Botanist, a Mathematician, a Chemist, a Mechanician, a Geographer, and a general Natural Philosopher, besides a President, Treasurer and Secretary.

That these Members meet once a Month, or oftner, at their own Expence, to communicate to each other their Observations, Experiments, &c. to receive, read and consider such Letters, Communications, or Queries as shall be sent from distant Members; to direct the Dispersing of Copies of such Communications as are valuable, to other distant Members, in order to procure their Sentiments thereupon, &c.

That the Subjects of the Correspondence be, All new-discovered Plants, Herbs, Trees, Roots, &c. their Virtues, Uses, &c. Methods of Propagating them, and making such as are useful, but particular to some Plantations, more general. Improvements of vegetable Juices, as Cyders, Wines, &c. New Methods of Curing or Preventing Diseases. All new-discovered Fossils in different Countries, as Mines, Minerals, Quarries, &c. New and useful Improvements in any Branch of Mathematicks. New Discoveries in Chemistry, such as Improvements in Distillation, Brewing, Assaying of Ores, &c. New Mechanical Inventions for saving Labour; as Mills, Carriages, &c. and for Raising and Conveying of Water, Draining of Meadows, &c. All new Arts, Trades, Manufactures, &c. that may be proposed or thought of. Surveys, Maps and Charts of particular Parts of the Sea-coasts, or Inland Countries; Course and Junction of Rivers and great Roads, Situation of Lakes and Mountains, Nature of the Soil and Productions, &c. New Methods of Improving the Breed of useful Animals, Introducing other Sorts from foreign Countries. New Improvements in Planting, Gardening, Clearing Land, &c. And all philosophical Experiments that let Light into the Nature of Things, tend to increase the Power of Man over Matter, and multiply the Conveniencies or Pleasures of Life.

That a Correspondence already begun by some intended Members, shall be kept up by this Society with the ROYAL SOCIETY of London, and with the DUBLIN SOCIETY.

That every Member shall have Abstracts sent him Quarterly, of every Thing valuable communicated to the Society's Secretary at Philadelphia; free of all Charge except the Yearly Payment hereafter mentioned.

That by Permission of the Postmaster-General, such Communications pass between the Secretary of the Society and the Members, Postage-free.

That for defraying the Expence of such Experiments as the Society shall judge proper to cause to be made, and other contingent Charges for the common Good, every Member send a Piece of Eight *per Annum* to the Treasurer, at Philadelphia, to form a Common Stock, to be disburs'd by Order of the President with the Consent of the Majority of the Members that can conveniently be consulted thereupon, to such Persons and Places where and by whom the Experiments are to be made, and otherwise as there shall be Occasion; of which Disbursements an exact Account shall be kept, and communicated yearly to every Member.

That at the first Meetings of the Members at Philadelphia, such Rules be formed for Regulating their Meetings and Transactions for the General Benefit, as shall be convenient and necessary; to be afterwards changed and improv'd as there shall be Occasion, wherein due Regard is to be had to the Advice of distant Members.

That at the End of every Year, Collections be made and printed, of such Experiments, Discoveries, Improvements, &c. as may be thought of publick Advantage: And that every Member have a Copy sent him.

That the Business and Duty of the Secretary be, To receive all Letters intended for the Society, and lay them before the President and Members at their Meetings; to abstract, correct and methodize such Papers, &c. as require it, and as he shall be directed to do by the President, after they have been considered, debated and digested in the Society; to enter Copies thereof in the Society's Books, and make out Copies for distant Members; to answer their Letters by Direction of the President, and keep Records of all material Transactions of the Society, &c.

Benjamin Franklin, the Writer of this Proposal, offers himself to serve the Society as their Secretary, 'till they shall be provided with one more capable.

[Shavers and Trimmers; and To the Publick]

Printed in *The Pennsylvania Gazette*, June 23 and 30, 1743.

The first of these pieces, to which Smyth gave the title "Shavers and Trimmers" when he reprinted both (*Writings*, II, 232–6), appeared in the *Gazette*, June 23, 1743. It was inspired by a barber's advertising the week before that he intended to give up shaving and trimming to confine himself to wigmaking. The essay is a heavy-handed extension of the idea to politicians, lawyers, churchmen, and young girls. Looking into the church, the author asks, "who has been more notorious for shaving and fleecing, than that Apostle of Apostles, that Preacher of Preachers, the Rev. Mr. G.W.?" and he adds that he forbears to make "farther mention of this spiritual Shaver and Trimmer, lest I should affect the Minds of my Readers as deeply as his Preaching has affected their Pockets." This was the only individual reference in the essay. The piece gave such general offense that the author apologized in the next issue of the *Gazette*. The editors believe that Franklin did not write either the essay or the apology. The style is unlike his, and the sneer at Whitefield is both uncharacteristic and inconsistent with the facts of the two men's friendship.[8]

To William Strahan[9]   ALS: Columbia University Library

Sir   Philada. July 10. 1743

Mr. Read[1] has communicated to me part of a Letter from you, recommending a young Man whom you would be glad to see in

8. The editors were led to a re-examination of Shavers and Trimmers by Alfred Owen Aldridge, who communicated his belief, based on style, that BF was not the author.

9. William Strahan (1715–1785), Scottish-born printer of Wine-Office Court, London; admitted to the Stationers' Company of London, 1738;

better Business than that of a Journeyman Printer.[2] I have already three Printing-Houses in three different Colonies,[3] and purpose to set up a fourth if I can meet with a proper Person to manage it, having all Materials ready for that purpose. If the young Man will venture over hither, that I may see and be acquainted with him, we can treat about the Affair, and I make no doubt but he will think my Proposals reasonable; If we should not agree, I promise him however a Twelvemonths Good Work, and to defray his Passage back if he enclines to return to England. I am Sir, Your humble Servant unknown   B FRANKLIN

Addressed: To   Mr Wm Strahan   London

To Jane Mecom   ALS: American Philosophical Society

Dearest Sister Jenny   Philada. July 28. 1743

I took your Admonition very kindly, and was far from being offended at you for it.[4] If I say any thing about it to you, 'tis only to rectify some wrong Opinions you seem to have entertain'd of me, and that I do only because they give you some Uneasiness, which I am unwilling to be the Occasion of. You express your-

---

publisher, agent, adviser of David Hume, Adam Smith, Samuel Johnson, Edward Gibbon, William Robertson, and William Blackstone; published the *Monthly Review*, 1749, and the *London Chronicle*, 1757. He became King's Printer in 1770 and Master of the Stationers' Company in 1774; and was a member of Parliament, 1774–84. In reminiscent mood BF wrote Strahan, Aug. 19, 1784, that he remembered "your observing once to me, as we sat together in the House of Commons, that no two Journeymen Printers within your Knowledge had met with such Success in the World as our selves." What began as a business correspondence continued more than forty years, deepening in confidence and friendship, hardly interrupted by differences over American affairs. Strahan proposed a marriage between his son William and BF's daughter Sarah. *DNB;* [R. A. Austen-Leigh], *The Story of a Printing House* (2d edit., London, 1912); and "William Strahan and his Ledgers," *The Library*, 4th ser., III (1923), 261–87. These ledgers and other records, papers, and correspondence are in the British Museum.

1. James Read, a relative of Deborah Read Franklin, who had met Strahan in London, 1739-40.

2. The young man was David Hall, who came over to Philadelphia the following year. See below, p. 409.

3. BF's own printing house in Philadelphia, Timothy's in Charleston, and Parker's in New York.

4. The occasion of Jane's admonition is unknown.

self as if you thought I was against Worshipping of God, and believed Good Works would merit Heaven;[5] which are both Fancies of your own, I think, without Foundation. I am so far from thinking that God is not to be worshipped, that I have compos'd and wrote a whole Book of Devotions for my own Use:[6] And I imagine there are few, if any, in the World, so weake as to imagine, that the little Good we can do here, can *merit* so vast a Reward hereafter. There are some Things in your New England Doctrines and Worship, which I do not agree with, but I do not therefore condemn them, or desire to shake your Belief or Practice of them. We may dislike things that are nevertheless right in themselves. I would only have you make me the same Allowances, and have a better Opinion both of Morality and your Brother. Read the Pages of Mr. Edward's late Book entitled SOME THOUGHTS CONCERNING THE PRESENT REVIVAL OF RELIGION IN NE. from 367 to 375;[7] and when you judge of others, if you can perceive the Fruit to be good, don't terrify your self that the Tree may be evil, but be assur'd it is not so; for you know who has said, *Men do not gather Grapes of Thorns or Figs of Thistles.*[8] I have not time to add but that I shall always be Your affectionate Brother   B FRANKLIN

P S. It was not kind in you to imagine when your Sister commended Good Works, she intended is [*sic*] a Reproach to you. 'Twas very far from her Thoughts.

From Cadwallader Colden[9]   Draft: New-York Historical Society

Sir   [October 1743]
    Ever since I had the Pleasure of a Conversation with you tho

5. BF first wrote "Salvation or Eternal Happiness," then substituted "Heaven."
    6. See above, I, 101–9.
    7. Jonathan Edwards, *Some Thoughts Concerning the present Revival of Religion in New-England* (Boston, 1742), pp. 367–75. After having discussed "the external Duties of Devotion, such as Praying, Hearing, Singing and attending religious Meetings," Edwards affirms that the "moral Duties, such as Acts of Righteousness, Truth, Meekness, Forgiveness and Love towards our Neighbours . . . are of much greater Importance in the Sight of God, than all the Externals of his Worship. . . ."
    8. Matt. 7:16.

very short by our accedental Meeting on the Road[1] I have been very desirous to engage you in a Correspondence. You was pleas'd to take some notice of a Method of Printing which I mentioned to you at that time and to think it practicable. I have no further concern for it than as it may be usefull to the publick. My reasons for thinking so you will find in the inclosed Copy

---

9. Cadwallader Colden (1688–1776), a prominent member of BF's scientific circle, was born in Ireland of Scottish parents, graduated from the University of Edinburgh, 1705, studied medicine in London, and migrated to Philadelphia, 1710, where he practiced medicine and engaged in business until he moved to New York in 1718. Appointed surveyor general, 1720, member of the Governor's Council, 1721, and lieutenant governor of the province, 1761, he made and forcefully administered policies respecting lands, Indian affairs, trade laws, and the civil service. He was burned in effigy for his determination to enforce the Stamp Act, 1765. In BF's life he appears as a man of science and philosopher. His correspondence with Peter Collinson, John Bartram, and BF shows him to have been a central figure in the American world of science, putting American correspondents in touch with one another, as well as with European scientists like Linnaeus, Gronovius, and Dillenius. Colden himself was the author of a number of treatises, both published and unpublished, on history, botany, mathematics, and medicine. He was a member of APS, 1744. His letterbooks and papers, published in eleven volumes in the *Collections* of the New-York Historical Society, are a rich source of information not only about him but about his and BF's philosopher-friends. *DAB;* Alice M. Keys, *Cadwallader Colden: A Representative Eighteenth Century Official* (N.Y., 1906), pp. 1–26.

1. This meeting presumably took place in Connecticut during BF's journey to or from Boston, which he visited the previous May and June (see below, p. 450 n). Colden spent most of the summer in Connecticut on public business. *Colden Paps.,* III, 23, 25.

In a letter to William Strahan, Dec. 3, 1743, Colden described the meeting, which was the beginning of a long and fruitful friendship for both men: "I accidentally last summer fell into Company with a Printer (the most ingenious in his way without question of any in America). Upon my mentioning my thoughts which I wrote to Mr. Collinson he told me of the Method which had been used in Holland which you likewise mention but he thought the method by types en creuse to be an improvement of that Method and as he is a man very lucky in improving every hint he has done something on this foundation and which I have seen which has puzled all the printers in this country to conceive by what method it is done. As printing is this mans trade and he makes a Benefite of it I do not think my self at liberty to communicate it without his consent tho' as to my own part I have no interest in keeping the secret. . . ." Strahan guessed at once the identity of Colden's new acquaintance. "From the Character you give of him," he replied, May 9, 1744, "I am sure it must be Mr. Franklin you mean, whose Fame has long ago reached this Part of the World, for a most

of a Paper which I last year sent to Mr. Collinson in London.[2] Perhaps my fondness for my own Conceptions may make me think more of it than it deserves and may make me Jealous that the Common Printers are willing to discourage out of private Interest any Discovery of this sort. But as you have given me reason to think you Zealous in promoting every usefull attempt you will be able absolutely to determine my Opinion of it. I long very much to hear what you have done in your scheme of erecting a society at Philadelphia for promoting of usefull Arts and Sciences in America. If you think any thing in my power whereby I can promote so usefull an undertaking I will with much pleasure receive your Instructions for that end. As my son Cadwallader bears this I thereby think my self secured of the pleasure of a Line from you by him.

To Cadwallader Colden

ALS: New-York Historical Society; also transcript: Library of Congress

Sir   Philada. Nov. 4. 1743

I received the Favour of yours, with the Proposal for a new Method of Printing, which I am much pleased with: and since you express some Confidence in my Opinion, I shall consider it very attentively and particularly, and in a Post or two send you some Observations on every Article.

My long Absence from home in the Summer, put my Business

---

ingenious Man in his Way. I have had the Pleasure of corresponding with him lately, and have Sent him by the Mercurey Captain Hargrave, one of my Journeymen, to whom he intends to give the Management of one of his Printing houses. His Name is David Hall." *Colden Paps.*, III, 38, 59. The first letter has been revised slightly by comparison with the MS, in N.-Y. Hist. Soc.

2. A MS copy of this paper is in the Colden Papers, N.-Y. Hist. Soc. It was printed in *Amer. Medical and Philosophical Register*, I (1810–11), 439–45, and reprinted in Sparks, *Works*, VI, 18–24, as though the essay and this covering letter formed a single whole. Colden's proposed new method of printing was a form of stereotyping. Collinson consulted a London printer, who reported that the scheme had been tried before and found "expencive and inconvenient" even for works in continuing demand, and of no profit to authors. As Colden still insisted his scheme was practicable, Collinson asked the London printer William Strahan (see above, p. 383 n) to comment; Strahan wrote out his objections, which Colden accepted. *Colden Paps.*, III, 11, 37–9, 58–9.

so much behind-hand, that I have been in a continual Hurry ever since my Return, and had no Leisure to forward the Scheme of the Society: But that Hurry being now near over, I purpose to proceed in the Affair very soon, your Approbation being no small Encouragement to me.

I cannot but be fond of engaging in a Correspondence so advantageous to me as yours must be: I shall always r[eceive] your Favours as such, and with great Pleasure.

I wish I could by any Means have made your Son's longer Stay here as agreable to him, as it would have been to those who began to be acquainted with him.

I am, Sir, with much Respect Your most humble Servant

B FRANKLIN

Bill from Alexander Annand[3] AD: American Philosophical Society

Mr Benjamin Franklin to Alexr Annand Dr

	£	s	d
To James and William Franklins Schooling[4] from Decr 12th 1738 [to] Decr 1739	£6	00	0
To Wms Do from Decr 12th 1739 to Decr 1743	12	00	0
To firing £1 2s.	01	02	0
To Ovids Epistles 3s.	00	03	0
To Stirlings Cato 2s.	00	02	0
To Corderius 2s. 6d.	00	02	6
To Stirlings Rhetorick 1s.	00	01	0
To Ovids Metamorph: with Min: Notes	00	03	6
To Clarks Æsops Fables 2s. 6d.[5]	00	02	6
Endorsed: Mr Franklins Acct 1738[?]	£19	16	6

3. Scottish schoolmaster. His purchases of books are recorded in BF's Ledger D (see above, p. 232), and in Ledger A & B (see above, I, 172). In *Pa. Gaz.*, Sept. 25, 1740, he advertised books for sale.

4. James Franklin, Jr. (C.11.4) was BF's nephew, for whose education and training as a printer he assumed responsibility after the death of the boy's father James. See above, p. 261. BF's son William (D.1) and James, Jr., were about the same age.

5. "Ovids Epistles" may be either *Epistolae ex Ponto* or *Epistolae Heroïdum.* The other books listed are probably John Sterling's edition of *Catonis Disticha Moralia* and his *System of Rhetoric*, John Clarke's *Corderii Colloquiorum Centuria Selecta* and *Aesop*, and Ovid's *Metamorphoses* with notes by Johann Minellius.

Extracts from the Gazette, 1743

Printed in *The Pennsylvania Gazette*, January 4 to December 29, 1743.

On Wednesday the 5th Instant, about Two in the Morning, a Fire broke out in Water-Street, at the Blockmaker's Shop, near the Rose and Crown; and the Chief Buildings thereabouts being Wood, it presently got to such a Head, that tho' no Industry was wanting, it could not be mastered till 6 or 7 Dwelling Houses, besides Stores, &c. were reduced to Ashes. William Clymer, Blockmaker, John Ryan, Merchant, Thomas Say, Sadler, Thomas Ingram, Tavernkeeper, Robert Hopkins, Baker, and others, were burnt out, and the Fire was so sudden, that some of them sav'd but very little, and others none of their Goods, (except Mr. Say who sav'd almost every thing by the Diligence of the Fire-Company, of which he was a Member.) The Engines and Leather Buckets were of vast Service; a strong Party Wall, with a Battlement above the Roof, contributed very much to the Saving of Mr. Till's new House, and consequently the rest of the Row towards Market-Street, the Wind, tho' there was not much, being that Way. Collections are making for the Sufferers, which we hear amount already to 7 or 8 hundred Pounds; one Gentleman having given 100 Pistoles, and others very considerable Sums.

We hear there are several new Companies erecting in Town for mutual Assistance in Case of Fires.   [January 13]

[ADVERTISEMENT] Lost at the late Fire in Water-Street, two Leather Buckets, marked B. FRANKLIN & Co. Whoever brings them to the Printer hereof, shall be satisfied for their Trouble.
[January 27]

[ADVERTISEMENT] Stolen out of the Governor's House by a Chimney-Sweeper, as is suppos'd, a large plain silver Stock-Buckle of an uncommon Make, and a silver Tea spoon gilt with the Governor's Crest upon it.

Whoever shall bring the said Buckle and Spoon, or either of them, to the Printer, so that the Thief may be convicted, shall be well rewarded.   [February 10]

[ADVERTISEMENT] To be SOLD, A Negro Man Twenty-two Years of Age, of uncommon Strength and Activity, very fit for a Farmer, or a laborious Trade, he understands the best Methods of managing Horses, and is very faithful in the Employment: Any Person that wants such a one may see him by enquiring of the Printer hereof.   [March 10]

Friend Franklin, I have again Necessity for troubling thy News-Paper, about Mary my Wife: It was Force that made me comply with publishing the last Advertisement in thy Paper. Pray insert in thy Paper now, that she abuses me her Husband so much that I cannot live with her: And I forwarn all Persons from Trusting her on my Account, after the Date hereof.[6]
March 15. 1742,3.   RICHARD LEADAME
                                                   [March 17]

[ADVERTISEMENT] Very good Lampblack made and sold by the Printer hereof.   [March 24]

                              Post-Office, Philadelphia, April 14
***After this Week the Northern Post is to set out for New-York on Thursdays at 3 in the Afternoon, till Christmas next.
The Southern Post sets out next Monday Morning at 8, for Annapolis, and continues going every Fortnight during the Summer Season.   [April 14]

The Library Company of Philadelphia, are hereby desired to meet on Monday the Second of May next, at the Library, by Three o'Clock in the Afternoon, to chuse Directors and a Treasurer, and to make the Eleventh annual Payment.
Phil. April 12th. 1743.   J. BREINTNALL, Secry.
                                                   [April 14]

[ADVERTISEMENT] On the 14th of September past absented himself (but suppos'd was entic'd away) from his Master's Service, an Apprentice Lad, named Macaja Carman, about 19 or 20 Years of Age, tall, pale and slim, and often indisposed from a Bruise on the Head. He has been seen at his Brother's Joseph Carman, near the Head of Sassafras River, in Maryland. Now whoever apprehends him, and brings him to the Subscriber, living in the City

6. For earlier light on Richard Leadame's termagant wife, see above, p. 365.

390

of Philadelphia, shall have Three Pounds Reward, and reasonable Charges: And whoever gives me Intelligence of the Person who carried him off, so that I may obtain Justice, shall have Forty Shillings Reward. And I do hereby forwarn all Persons from harbouring and concealing the said Apprentice, as they will answer the same at their Peril.

Philadelphia, May 24. 1743.   JOHN READ
                                                              [June 9]

We hear from divers Parts of the Country, that the Thunderstorm we had last Friday se'nnight in the Night, spread very wide, and burnt several Barns, beside that near Philadelphia, but no Person hurt. 'Tis computed that the Loss of the Owner of that Barn amounted to near £300. A Collection is now making for his Relief, which is the rather to be encouraged, since the Fire did not happen (as many do,) from Carelessness or Negligence.
                                                              [August 25]

[ADVERTISEMENT] The Body of Laws of the Province of Pennsylvania is now finished, with the Charters and a Compleat Index; &c.[7] Those who bespoke them of the Printer while the Work was in hand, are desired to send for them as soon as conveniently may be, that he may know whether he shall have any left for common Sale.   [August 25]

[ADVERTISEMENT] In June last there were lost two Bundles of Indian Ware and Goods, near Capt. Cressop's[8] on Conegoche (of whom the Indians had receiv'd them) as also a fine Gun. Whoever brings them to Conrad Weiser in Tulpehocken, or the Printer hereof, shall have 30 Shillings Reward, with reasonable Charges, and no Questions ask'd.   [August 25]

7. This was *A Collection of all the Laws Of the Province of Pennsylvania: Now in Force. Published by Order of Assembly.* The title page bears the date 1742.

8. Thomas Cresap (c.1702–c.1790), frontiersman and trader, had a stockaded house and store at Conococheague on Antietam Creek near Hagerstown in western Maryland. He later moved farther west to Shawanese Old Town, near Cumberland; this is the place marked on Lewis Evans' map of 1755. Cresap acted as intermediary for Maryland with the friendly Iroquois to the north and the hostile Cherokees to the south. *DAB.*

NEXT WEEK WILL BE PUBLISHED, The Votes and Proceedings of the House of Representatives of the Province of Pennsylvania, for the Year past. To be sold by B. Franklin.   [September 8]

Sunday last died here Samuel Preston, Esq; aged near Four-score Years. He had been a long Time one of the Governor's Council, and Treasurer of the Province, which Stations he supported with Reputation. His Funeral was respectfully attended by the greatest Number of People of all Persuasions, that has ever been seen here on the like Occasion.   [September 15]

JUST PUBLISHED, Poor Richard's Almanack, for the Year 1744: Printed and Sold by B. Franklin.   [November 10]

We are informed that there is a Free-School opened at the House of Mr. Alison in Chester County,[9] for the Promotion of Learning, where all Persons may be instructed in the Languages and some other Parts of Polite Literature, without any Expences for their Education.

We hear also that a new Map of the Province of Pennsylvania is begun, and great Part thereof finished; wherein will be delineated with the greatest Exactness, the several Counties, Townships, Towns, Rivers, Creeks and High-Ways, &c. with the Situation and Extent of the principal Mountains, as far as the Province is yet surveyed: The River Delaware will be laid down as far as it bounds the Province, and the River Susquehannah with its principal Branches near 200 Miles beyond the Inhabitants.

A Map of each County is also intended, by a greater Scale, in which every Tract of Land will be described, according to the original Surveys; and the Names of the Purchasers inserted; By William Parsons, Surveyor General of the said Province.[1]

[November 24]

---

9. Francis Alison (1705–1779), Presbyterian minister at New London, Chester Co., Pa., opened a grammar school there, 1741; he established an academy, 1743, which was recognized by the Synod of Philadelphia and supported by its congregations. He became principal of the new Academy of Philadelphia, 1752, and was vice-provost of the College from 1755 until his death. *DAB.*

1. Parsons' map was never published.

*_{*}*The Northern Post having began his Fortnight Stage, will set out from hence every other Tuesday during the Winter Season.
[December 6]

JUST PUBLISHED, Pocket Almanacks For the Year 1744: Printed and Sold by B. Franklin. [December 20]

A Blazing Star or Comet was discovered here the Beginning of this Week. It appears in the West, and may be seen from Sunset to near Midnight. [December 29]

PHILADELPHIA: Printed by B. FRANKLIN, Post-Master, at the New-Printing-Office, near the Market.

Poor Richard, 1744

Poor Richard, 1744. An Almanack For the Year of Christ 1744, . . . By Richard Saunders, Philom. Philadelphia: Printed and sold by B. Franklin.[2] (Yale University Library)

Courteous Reader,

This is the Twelfth Year that I have in this Way laboured for the Benefit—of Whom?—of the Publick, if you'll be so good-natured as to believe it; if not, e'en take the naked Truth, 'twas for the Benefit of my own dear self; not forgetting in the mean time, our gracious Consort and Dutchess the peaceful, quiet, silent Lady Bridget. But whether my Labours have been of any Service to the Publick or not, the Publick I must acknowledge has been of Service to me; I have lived Comfortably by its Benevolent Encouragement; and I hope I shall always bear a grateful Sense of its continued Favour.

My Adversary J--n J----n has indeed made an Attempt to *outshine* me, by pretending to penetrate *a Year deeper* into Futurity; and giving his Readers *gratis* in his Almanack for 1743 an Eclipse of the Year 1744, to be beforehand with me: His Words are, "The first Day of April next Year 1744, there will be a GREAT ECLIPSE

---

2. Copies of this almanac in the Huntington Library and the Historical Society of Pennsylvania carry in addition at the end of this imprint: "Sold also by Jonas Green, at Annapolis."

of the Sun; it begins about an Hour before Sunset. It being in the Sign Aries, the House of Mars, and in the 7th, shows Heat, Difference and Animosities between Persons of the highest Rank and Quality," &c. I am very glad, for the Sake of these Persons of Rank and Quality, that there is *no manner of Truth* in this Prediction: They may, if they please, live in Love and Peace. And I caution his Readers (they are but few, indeed, and so the Matter's the less) not to give themselves any Trouble about observing this imaginary Great Eclipse; for they may stare till they're blind without seeing the least Sign of it. I might, on this Occasion, return Mr. J----n the Name of *Baal's false Prophet*[3] he gave me some Years ago in his Wrath, on Account of my Predicting his Reconciliation with the Church of Rome, (tho' he seems now to have given up that Point) but I think such Language between old Men and Scholars unbecoming; and I leave him to settle the Affair with the Buyers of his Almanack as well as he can, who perhaps will not take it very kindly, that he has done what in him lay (by sending them out to gaze at an invisible Eclipse on the first of April) to make *April Fools* of them all. His old thread bare Excuse which he repeats Year after Year about the *Weather,* "That no Man can be infallible therein, by Reason of the many contrary Causes happening at or near the same time, and the Unconstancy of the Summer Showers and Gusts," &c. will hardly serve him in the Affair of *Eclipses;* and I know not where he'll get another.

I have made no Alteration in my usual Method, except adding the Rising and Setting of the Planets, and the Lunar Conjunctions. Those who are so disposed, may thereby very readily learn to know the Planets, and distinguish them from each other. I am, dear Reader, Thy obliged Friend,   R. SAUNDERS

The COUNTRY MAN.

Happy the Man whose Wish and Care
A few paternal Acres bound,
Content to breathe his native Air,
In his own Ground.

---

3. John Jerman applied this epithet to BF in his almanac for 1741. See above, p. 332.

Whose Herds with Milk, whose Fields with Bread,
  Whose Flocks supply him with Attire,
Whose Trees in Summer yield him Shade,
          In Winter Fire.

Blest, who can unconcernedly find
  Hours, Days and Years slide soft away,
In Health of Body, Peace of Mind,
          Quiet by Day,

Sound Sleep by Night; Study and Ease
  Together mixt; sweet Recreation;
And Innocence which most does please
          With Meditation.

Thus let me live, unseen, unknown,
  Thus unlamented let me die,
Steal from the World, and not a Stone
          Tell where I lie.

XI Mon. January hath xxxi days.

Biblis does Solitude admire,
  A wond'rous Lover of the Dark;
Each Night puts out her Chamber Fire,
  And just keeps in a *single Spark;*
'Till four she keeps herself alive,
  Warm'd by her Piety, no doubt;
Then, tir'd with kneeling, just at five,
  She sighs—and lets that Spark *go out*.

He that drinks his Cyder alone, let him catch his Horse alone.

Who is strong? He that can conquer his bad Habits. Who is rich?
  He that rejoices in his Portion.

XII Mon. February hath xxix days.

Our youthful Preacher see, intent on Fame;
Warm to gain Souls?—No, 'tis to gain a Name.
Behold his Hands display'd, his Body rais'd;

395

With what a Zeal he labours—to be prais'd.
Touch'd with each Weakness which he does arraign,
With Vanity he talks against the Vain;
With Ostentation does to Meekness guide;
Proud of his Periods form'd to strike at Pride.

He that has not got a Wife, is not yet a compleat Man.

I Mon. March hath xxxi days.

Without Repentance none to Heav'n can go,
Yet what Repentance is few seem to know:
'Tis not to cry out *Mercy*, or to sit
   And droop, or to confess that thou hast fail'd;
'Tis to bewail the Sins thou didst commit,
   And not commit those Sins thou hast bewail'd.
He that *bewails*, and not *forsakes* them too,
Confesses rather what he *means to do.*

What you would seem to be, be really.

If you'd lose a troublesome Visitor, lend him Money.

Tart Words make no Friends: a spoonful of honey will catch
more flies than Gallon of Vinegar.

II Mon. April hath xxx days.

With what a perfect World-revolving Power
Were first the unweildy Planets launch'd along
Th'illimitable Void! Thus to remain
Amid the Flux of many thousand Years,
That oft has swept the busy Race of Men,
And all their labour'd Monuments away:
Unresting, changeless, matchless, in their Course;
To Night and Day, with the delightful Round
Of Seasons, faithful, not eccentric once:
So pois'd, and perfect is the vast Machine!

Make haste slowly.

Dine with little, sup with less:
Do better still; sleep supperless.

Industry, Perseverance, and Frugality, make Fortune yield.

III Mon. May hath xxxi days.

Irus tho' wanting Gold and Lands,
    Lives chearful, easy, and content;
Corvus, unbless'd, with twenty Hands
    Employ'd to count his yearly Rent.
Sages in Wisdom! tell me which
    Of these you think possesses more!
One with his Poverty is rich,
    And one with all his Wealth is poor.

I'll warrant ye, goes before *Rashness; Who'd-a-tho't-it?* comes
sneaking after.

Prayers and Provender hinder no Journey.

IV Mon. June hath xxx days.

Of all the Causes which conspire to blind
Man's erring Judgment, and misguide the Mind,
What the weak Head with strongest Biass rules,
Is *Pride,* that never-failing Vice of Fools.
Whatever Nature has in Worth deny'd,
She gives in large Recruits of needful Pride;
For as in Bodies, thus in Souls we find
What wants in Blood and Spirits, swell'd with Wind.

Hear *Reason,* or she'll make you feel her.

Give me yesterday's Bread, this Day's Flesh, and last Year's Cyder.

V Mon. July hath xxxi days.

All-conq'ring HEAT, oh intermit thy Wrath!
And on my throbbing Temples potent thus
Beam not so hard! Incessant still you flow,

397

And still another fervent Flood succeeds,
Pour'd on the Head profuse. In vain I sigh,
And restless turn, and look around for Night;
Night is far off; and hotter Hours approach.
Who can endure!—

God heals, and the Doctor takes the Fees.

Sloth (like Rust) consumes faster than Labour wears: the used
Key is always bright.

Light Gains heavy Purses.

VI Mon. August hath xxxi days.

Would Men but follow what the Sex advise,
All things would prosper, all the World grow wise.
'Twas by Rebecca's Aid that Jacob won
His Father's Blessing from an elder Son.
Abusive Nabal ow'd his forfeit Life
To the wise Conduct of a prudent Wife.
At Hester's suit, the persecuting Sword
Was sheath'd, and Israel liv'd to bless the Lord.

Keep thou from the Opportunity, and God will keep thee from the
Sin.

Where there's no Law, there's no Bread.

As Pride increases, Fortune declines.

VII Mon. September hath xxx days.

All other Goods by Fortune's Hand are giv'n,
A WIFE is the peculiar Gift of Heav'n.
Vain Fortune's Favours, never at a Stay,
Like empty Shadows, pass, and glide away;
One solid Comfort, our eternal Wife,
Abundantly supplies us all our Life:
This Blessing lasts (if those that try say true)
As long as Heart can wish—and longer too.

Drive thy Business, or it will drive thee.

A full Belly is the Mother of all Evil.

The same man cannot be both Friend and Flatterer.

He who multiplies Riches multiplies Cares.

An old Man in a House is a good Sign.

VIII Mon. October hath xxxi days.

> Be Niggards of *Advice* on no Pretence;
> For the worst Avarice is that of Sense.
> Yet 'tis not all, your Counsel's free and true:
> Blunt Truths more Mischief than nice Falshoods do.
> Men must be taught as if you taught them not,
> And Things unknown propos'd as Things forgot;
> Without *Good-Breeding* Truth is disapprov'd
> That only makes superior Sense belov'd.

Those who are fear'd, are hated.

The Things which hurt, instruct.

The Eye of a Master, will do more Work than his Hand.

A soft Tongue may strike hard.

IX Mon. November hath xxx days.

> Sylvia while young, with ev'ry Grace adorn'd,
> Each blooming Youth, and fondest Lover scorn'd:
> In Years at length arriv'd at Fifty-nine,
> She feels Love's Passion as her Charms decline:
> —Thus Oaks a hundred Winters old
>   Just as they now expire,
>   Turn Touchwood, doated, grey and old,
>   And at each SPARK take Fire.—

If you'd be belov'd, make yourself amiable.

A true Friend is the best Possession.

Fear God, and your Enemies will fear you.

X Mon. December hath xxxi days.

This World's an Inn, all Travellers are we;
And this World's Goods th' Accommodations be.
Our Life is nothing but a Winter's Day;
Some only break their *Fast,* and so away.
Others stay Dinner, and depart full fed.
The deepest Age but *sups* and goes to bed.
He's most in Debt that lingers out the Day;
Who dies betimes has less and less to pay.

Epitaph on a Scolding Wife by her Husband. Here my poor Bridget's
Corps doth lie, she is at rest,—and so am I.[4]

COURTS.

Two trav'ling Beggars, (I've forgot their Name)
An Oister found to which they both laid Claim.
Warm the Dispute! At length to Law they'd go,
As richer Fools for Trifles often do.
The Cause two Petty-foggers undertake,
Resolving right or wrong some Gain to make.
They jangle till the Court this Judgment gave,
Determining what every one should have.
    Blind Plaintiff, lame Defendant, share
    The friendly Law's impartial Care:
    A Shell for him, a Shell for thee;
    The MIDDLE's *Bench and Lawyer's Fee.*

Verses from A Pocket Almanack

Printed in *A Pocket Almanack For the Year 1744. Fitted to the Use of Pennsylvania, and the neighbouring Provinces. . . .* By R. Saunders, Phil.
Philadelphia: Printed and sold by B. Franklin. (Yale University Library)

The 1741 issue of *A Pocket Almanack*[5] had proved so successful that
Franklin continued for some years to publish it. Only about two inches
by four in size, it sometimes appeared in red and black ink and some
copies had interleaved blank pages, to make them practical memoran-

4. An adaptation of Dryden's suggested epitaph.
5. See above, p. 300.

dum books. These pocket almanacs carried astronomical data, weather forecasts, dates of courts' sitting, fairs, Quaker meetings, and royal birthdays, but no introduction, verses, or aphorisms. An exception was the almanac of 1744, in which there were three stanzas, one or two of which were repeated in several subsequent issues.

> War begets Poverty,
> Poverty Peace;
> Peace makes Riches flow,
> (Fate ne'er doth cease.)
> Riches produce Pride,
> Pride is War's Ground;
> War begets Poverty, &c.
> The World goes round.

> Rules for computing Expence.

Compute the Pence but of One Day's Expence;
So many Pounds, Angels, Groats and Pence,
Are spent in one whole Year's Circumference. *Or,*
One Week's Expence in *Farthings,* makes appear
The *Shill.* & *Pence* expended in a Year.

VIRTUE was reckon'd the chief Thing of Old;
Now lies all Merit in SILVER and GOLD:
VIRTUE has lost its Regard in these Times,
While MONEY, like Charity, covers all Crimes.

From James Logan

Transcript: Harvard College Library (Sparks); another transcript: American Philosophical Society

My friend B. F.   Stenton, Feb. 26. 1744
I have this day read over my version of Cicero's Cato Major in thy Print,[6] with my Notes on it, and cannot but applaud thy care but wish thou hadst not begun in pa: 49 with Greek Letter, since thou hadst not enough of the same character to go on with it, for to this alone I must impute the failure. But without thy particular

6. See below, p. 404.

apology it may be suspected by some at least that I understood not the Language. Therefore pray take care to excuse it in the best manner. But in that very little thou hast given there is a mistake, for the word is αὐτοκρατορ with a rho or r instead of an s at last. So in the bottom of page 60 and in the beginning of pa: 61 the word is Thurium, not Thetrium, and pa: 70 l. 7 in the note it should be Actium, not Antium, instead of "it's palling" it should be "in palling" and pa: 94 in the first line of the notes Idea Mater should be in two words which I had forgot. Intemporate pa: 64 and "impetutous" pa: 100 thou of thyself would correct, and perhaps Grentemesnil for Grantemosnil which with the rest ought to be noted. Add also to these, that I desire the last of the five lines in rhyme pa: 24 may be expunged, yet I am somewhat indifferent in this since I actually put it there, but I am not so in having the reader informed, that on reading it over in Print, I find there are some (but very few) mistakes in the Chronology, owing to the well known disputes about the age of Rome, and the Æra of the Birth of Christ, in both which the greatest authors differ 2 or 3 years, and some more: Yet I have differed I perceive only two years in two or three places, tho' I thought I had reduced the whole to an uniformity, but now I find myself mistaken.[7]

Pray do not forget to mention that it was done ten years since in the 60th year of my Age, nearly the same that Cicero was in when he wrote the original, tho' probably he was a year or two older, that it was wrote only for my own diversion and for the entertainment of a friend less skilled in the Language or the History of Rome, and far from the thought of ever seeing it in print, for I well knew there were other English Versions of it, tho' I had then never seen one of them, having left England before I was five and twenty. But I expect to see thy Preface by the Bearer and therefore might have spared this. I am thy real friend   J. LOGAN

7. BF noted all these errors in a table of Corrigenda on p. vi, adding that there were "Also a few Mistakes in the Dates of Lives, &c. the Author having accidentally used different Chronologies, which vary frequently two Years. These are left to the Correction of the Reader; who is also desired to excuse the *Italic* Types used in some Greek Words."

In the earliest impressions the word "only" in line 5, page 27, was printed "ony." BF corrected this before the edition was completely run off, and the error is of importance only to connoisseurs of bibliographical "points."

M. T. CICERO's

CATO MAJOR,

OR HIS

DISCOURSE

OF

OLD-AGE:

With Explanatory NOTES.

PHILADELPHIA:

Printed and Sold by B. FRANKLIN,

MDCCXLIV.

Preface to Logan's Cato Major

M.T. Cicero's Cato Major, or His Discourse of Old-Age: With Explanatory Notes. Philadelphia: Printed and Sold by B. Franklin, MDCCXLIV. (Yale University Library)

Franklin's edition of James Logan's translation of Cicero's *Cato Major* is one of the best known issues of his press, and many have considered it also the handsomest.[8] "I translated that piece," Logan told a friend, "in the Winter of 1732 for my own diversion for I was exceedingly pleased with it, and added the Notes for the Use of a Friend and Neighbour that was not so well acquainted with the Roman History as I was,[9] without any expectation it would ever be printed."[1] Apparently the translation circulated in manuscript among Logan's friends for several years.[2] After Franklin had read a copy, he "Sent to me for leave to pass it through his Press." Logan gave assent, only making some revisions in the text and notes.

This translation was in fact the sixth or seventh that had been made into English, although Logan had seen none of his predecessors' works until after his own was completed. Because he thought one of these versions "ludicrous" and another deficient for want of notes, Logan was "willing to venture mine abroad, and more especially on account of the Notes that illustrated it, besides that it is neatly printed, and I thought was not inferiour to the best of those that I had Seen."

Franklin printed one thousand copies, advertising the book for sale in Philadelphia at 3*s*. 6*d*. on March 21. He sent 300 copies to Strahan, but the book met competition from other translations and sold slowly.[3] Its worth was recognized, however, and it was reprinted in London in 1750, in Glasgow in 1751 and 1758, in Philadelphia in 1758, and in London again in 1778. Not all of these retained the printer's address to the reader which introduced the first edition.

---

8. Frederick B. Tolles, "Quaker Humanist: James Logan as a Classical Scholar," *PMHB*, LXXIX (1955), 431–8; Paul McPharlin, "Franklin's *Cato Major*, 1744," *Publishers' Weekly*, CXLIV (1943), 2111–18.

9. Believed to be Isaac Norris, the elder, of Fairhill (1671–1735).

1. Logan to John Whiston, March 1, 1750. Logan Letter Book, Hist. Soc. Pa.

2. Logan to Thomas Penn, March 6, 1744. Sparks Transcripts, Harvard Coll. Lib.

3. Logan to Peter Collinson, Feb. 28, 1750. Logan Letter Book, Hist. Soc. Pa. As late as 1782 some of this consignment remained unsold. Robert Strange to BF, Feb. 29 [*sic*], 1782.

The Printer to the Reader

Philadelphia, Febr. 29. 1743, 4

THIS Version of CICERO's Tract *de Senectute,* was made Ten Years since, by the Honourable and Learned Mr. LOGAN, of this City; undertaken partly for his own Amusement, (being then in his 60th Year, which is said to be nearly the Age of the Author when he wrote it) but principally for the Entertainment of a Neighbour then in his grand Climacteric; and the Notes were drawn up solely on that Neighbour's Account, who was not so well acquainted as himself with the Roman History and Language: Some other Friends, however, (among whom I had the Honour to be ranked) obtained Copies of it in M.S. And, as I believed it to be in itself equal at least, if not far preferable to any other Translation of the same Piece extant in our Language, besides the Advantage it has of so many valuable Notes, which at the same time they clear up the Text, are highly instructive and entertaining; I resolved to give it an Impression, being confident that the Publick would not unfavourably receive it.

A certain Freed-man of Cicero's is reported to have said of a medicinal Well, discovered in his Time, wonderful for the Virtue of its Waters in restoring Sight to the Aged, *That it was a Gift of the bountiful Gods to Men, to the end that all might now have the Pleasure of reading his Master's Works.* As that Well, if still in being, is at too great a Distance for our Use, I have, *Gentle Reader,* as thou seest, printed this Piece of Cicero's in a large and fair Character, that those who begin to think on the Subject of OLD-AGE, (which seldom happens till their Sight is somewhat impair'd by its Approaches) may not, in Reading, by the *Pain* small Letters give the Eyes, feel the *Pleasure* of the Mind in the least allayed.

I shall add to these few Lines my hearty Wish, that this first Translation of a *Classic* in this *Western World,* may be followed with many others, performed with equal Judgment and Success; and be a happy Omen, that Philadelphia shall become the Seat of the American Muses.

To Cadwallader Colden

ALS: New-York Historical Society; also transcript: Library of Congress

Sir   New York, April 5. 1744

   Happening to be in this City about some particular Affairs, I have
the Pleasure of receiving yours of the 28th past, here.[4] And can
now acquaint you, that the Society, as far as relates to Philadelphia, is actually formed,[5] and has had several Meetings to mutual
Satisfaction; assoon as I get home, I shall send you a short Account
of what has been done and propos'd at those Meetings. The
Members are[6]

Dr. Thomas Bond, as Physician
Mr. John Bartram as Botanist
Mr. Thomas Godfrey as Mathematician
Mr. Saml. Rhodes[7] as Mechanician
Mr. Wm. Parsons as Geographer
Dr. Phineas Bond as General Nat. Philosopher
Mr. Thos. Hopkinson   President
Mr. Wm. Coleman[8]   Treasurer
BF.   Secretary

4. Not found.

5. See above, pp. 378–83.

6. Biographical notes on Thomas and Phineas Bond, Bartram, Godfrey,
Parsons, and Hopkinson appear elsewhere in this and the preceding volume.
See indexes.

7. Samuel Rhoads (1711–1784), carpenter and builder, president of the
Carpenters' Company, 1780–84, supervised the construction of BF's house
in 1764–65. He was a common councilor, alderman, and mayor of Philadelphia, 1774; member of the Assembly, 1761–63, 1770–74; and a delegate to
the First Continental Congress. He was a director of the Library Company
and an original manager of the Pennsylvania Hospital, 1751–81. Henry D.
Biddle, "Colonial Mayors of Philadelphia. Samuel Rhoads, 1774," *PMHB*,
XIX (1895), 64–71.

8. William Coleman (1704–1769), merchant, an original member of the
Junto, who helped BF set up as a printer, 1728, was later a common councilor, clerk of the city court, justice of the peace, and, in 1758, a justice of the
Supreme Court. He was a trustee of the Academy. Of him BF wrote in his
autobiography that he "had the coolest, clearest head, the best heart, and the
exactest morals of almost any man I ever met with." Montgomery, *Hist.
Univ. Pa.*, pp. 107–8.

To whom the following Members have since been added, viz. Mr. Alexander of New York.[9] Mr. Morris (Ch. Justice of the Jerseys.)[1] Mr. Home Secretary of Ditto.[2] Mr. Jno. Coxe of Trenton[3] and Mr. Martyn of the same Place.[4] Mr. Nickolls[5] tells me of several other Gentlemen of this City that incline to encourage the Thing. And there are a Number of others in Virginia, Maryland, Carolina, and the New England Colonies, who we expect to join us, assoon as they are acquainted that the Society has begun to form itself. I am, Sir, with much Respect Your most humble Servant   B FRANKLIN

Addressed: To   The Honbl. Cadwallader Colden Esqr   at   Coldengham

Endorsed: B. Frankilin

9. James Alexander (1691–1756), lawyer, surveyor general and attorney general of New Jersey, member of the New York Council. *DAB;* see BF to Alexander, Aug. 15, 1745.

1. Robert Hunter Morris (*c.*1700–1764), chief justice of New Jersey, 1738–64; governor of Pennsylvania, 1754–56. *DAB.* His career is treated more fully hereafter.

2. Archibald Home (d. 1744), born in Scotland; came to America before 1733; deputy secretary of New Jersey and secretary of the New Jersey Council, 1738; member of the Council, 1741; a poet of some ability, who translated Ovid, Horace, and French poets, composed elegies, and verses in Scots dialect. 1 *N.J. Arch.,* XII, 154–6.

3. John Coxe (d. 1753), lawyer, member of the New Jersey Council, 1746–50. Governor Belcher suspended him in a dispute over appointments and salaries. 1 *N.J. Arch.,* VII, 6, 546–8.

4. David Martin (d. 1751), first marshall of Trenton under the charter of 1745; sheriff of Hunterdon Co., 1747; first rector of the Academy of Philadelphia, 1750–51. Richard Peters described him as "a perfect good scholar, and a man of good temper." Hubertis Cummings, *Richard Peters* (Phila., 1944), p. 146.

5. Richard Nicholls (d. 1775), lawyer, postmaster of New York. N.-Y. Hist. Soc. *Colls.,* 1899, pp. 295–6. He played a useful part by forwarding correspondence among BF, Colden, Bartram, and others.

Benjamin Franklin and Robert Grace to Elliott Benger: Bond[6]

Copy: Land Office, Department of Internal Affairs, Commonwealth of Pennsylvania

[April 25, 1744]

KNOW ALL MEN by these Presents, That We Benjamin Franklin Deputy-Postmaster of the City of Philada. in the Province of Pennsilvania, and Robert Grace of the same Place Merchant are Held and firmly Bound unto the Honourable Elliott Benger, Esqr; Sole Deputy-Postmaster General of all his Majesty's Dominions in America, in the full Sum of Five Hundred Pounds Sterling Money, to be paid to the said Eliott Benger, his Executors, Administrators or Assigns; To the which Payment well and truly to be made, we do bind our Selves, and each of Us, our and each of our Heirs, Executors and Administrators, joyntly and Severally, firmly by these Presents. Sealed with our Seals, dated this Twenty fifth Day of April in the seventeenth Year of the Reign of our Sovereign Lord George the Second King of Great Britain, &c. and in the Year of our Lord One thousand Seven hundred and forty four.

THE CONDITION of this Obligation is such, That if the above bounden Benjamin Franklin shall and do truly and faithfully execute and perform the Office and Duty of Deputy-Postmaster of Philadelphia, so that no Damage thro' his Neglect, Fraud, Malfeasance or Breach of Duty, do arise to the said Elliott Benger,

---

6. BF had been appointed postmaster of Philadelphia, 1737, by Alexander Spotswood, deputy postmaster general for North America. Spotswood was succeeded by Head Lynch (1700–1743), of whom William Byrd wrote that he had been sent from England to Virginia because his family "coud make nothing of Him there, and ever since he came hither, he has lived in a very low Scene of Life, marrying a Sexton's Daughter, and sotting about with the Dregs of the People." *Va. Mag. Hist. Biog.*, XXXVII (1929), 30–31. One of Lynch's acts as deputy postmaster general was to take bonds for faithful performance by the several postmasters. 3 Mass. Hist. Soc. *Colls.*, VII, 86. He was succeeded, 1743, by Elliott Benger (d. 1751), also of Virginia, who likewise promptly required bonds of the postmasters. BF and William Hunter succeeded Benger as joint deputy postmasters general in 1753. Ruth L. Butler, *Doctor Franklin, Postmaster-General* (Garden City, N.Y., 1928), p. 34; Fairfax Harrison, "The Colonial Post Office in Virginia," 2 *Wm. and Mary Quar.*, IV (1924), 88–91.

then this present Obligation to be Void, otherwise to be and remain in full force and Vertue.　　　　　　　B FRANKLIN [Seal]
Signed Sealed and Delivered in　　　　ROBT. GRACE [Seal]
presence of Us
SAM: HOLLAND
N. HOLLAND

On the fourth Day of June 1744 Benjamin Franklin of the City of Philadelphia and Robert Grace within named both personally appeared before me the Subscriber One of the Justices of the Peace for the County of Philada. and Severally Acknowledged the within written Bond to be their Act and Deed and desired the same might be recorded. In Testimony whereof I have hereunto Set my Hand and Seal, the Day and date aforesaid.　　JONA. ROBESON [Seal]

Docketed: Recorded the 6th Day of June 1744

To William Strahan

ALS: Yale University Library; also duplicate: University of Pennsylvania Library

Sir　　　　　　　　　　　　　　　　　Philada. July 4. 1744

I receiv'd your Favour per Mr. Hall, who arriv'd here about two Weeks since, and from the short Acquaintance I have had with him, I am persuaded he will answer perfectly the Character you had given of him.[7] I make no doubt but his Voyage, tho' it has been expensive, will prove advantageous to him: I have already made

7. David Hall (1714–1772), born in Edinburgh; a journeyman first in Watts's printing office in London, then with Strahan. On the latter's recommendation BF employed him as a journeyman, 1744, intending to set him up in a printing office, presumably in the West Indies. Hall's voyage to Philadelphia was expensive, he came down with jaundice, and he thought BF was reserved about revealing his intentions. Replying to Hall's unhappy complaints, Strahan assured him that BF's terms were "very fair," advised him "to trust to his Generosity . . . and he will deal honourably by you," and predicted that Hall would "have all the Reason in the World" to like BF, "for he seems to me by his Manner of writing to have a very good Heart, as well as to be a Man of Honour and Good Sense." Strahan to Hall, March 9, June 22, 1745, MSS, APS. BF's reserve thawed and he became so pleased with his industrious new journeyman, that instead of setting him up in a distant partnership, like Timothy, he made him his partner in Philadelphia, Jan. 1, 1748. "He took off my Hands all Care of the Printing-Office," BF

him some Proposals, which he has under Consideration, and as we are like to agree on them, we shall not, I believe, differ on the Article of his Passage Money.

I am much oblig'd to you for your Care and Pains in procuring me the Founding-Tools; tho' I think, with you, that the Workmen have not been at all bashful in making their Bills. I shall pay a Proportion of the Insurance, &c. to Mr. Read,[8] and send you a Bill of Exchange by the very next Opportunity.

I thank you for Mr. Dobbs's Piece. I wish that publick-spirited Gentleman may live to enjoy the Satisfaction of hearing that English Ships sail easily thro' his expected Passage. But tho' from the Idea this Piece gives me of Capt. Middleton, I don't much like him, yet I would do him the Justice to read what he has to say for himself, and therefore request you to send me what is publish'd on his Side the Question.[9] I have long wanted a Friend in London whose Judgment I could depend on, to send me from time to time

---

wrote in his autobiography, "paying me punctually my Share of the Profits. This Partnership continued Eighteen Years, successfully for us both." Par. Text edit., p. 300. When the partnership expired in 1766, Hall carried on the business with a new partner. As Hall and Sellers, the firm continued to publish the *Gazette* and *Poor Richard's Almanack*, and to print paper money, the Assembly's *Votes and Proceedings*, and the laws of the province. *DAB*. Many of Strahan's letters to Hall, 1750–73, are printed in *PMHB*, x–xii (1886–88), lx (1936).

8. James Read (1718–1793), a relative of Deborah Read Franklin, who had met Strahan in London, 1739–40.

9. The controversy was between Arthur Dobbs (1689–1765), a wealthy, public-spirited Irish landlord, and Christopher Middleton (d. 1770), F.R.S., a scientific navigator, and captain for the Hudson's Bay Company. Dobbs's reading had convinced him that there was a practicable Northwest Passage; he got the Admiralty to organize an expedition of discovery and persuaded Middleton to command it, 1741. On his return, 1742, Middleton reported no passage west from Hudson's Bay, but only a fresh-water river, Wager Strait (now Bay). An anonymous letter led Dobbs to suspect that Middleton had accepted a bribe from the Hudson's Bay Company not "to look in to those Places where he had Reason to expect a Passage" and to conceal his discoveries by falsifying his records and charts, and he made the charge before the Admiralty. Middleton replied publicly in *A Vindication of the Conduct of Captain Christopher Middleton* (London, 1743). Dobbs answered in *Remarks upon Capt. Middleton's Defence* (London, 1744), which is "Mr. Dobbs's Piece" for which BF thanks Strahan. An acrimonious quarrel ensued: Middleton issued four more pamphlets, and Dobbs two. Middleton's reputation

such new Pamphlets as are worth Reading on any Subject (Religious Controversy excepted) for there is no depending on Titles and Advertisements. This Favour I take the Freedom to beg of you, and shall lodge Money in your Hands for that purpose.

We have seldom any News on our Side the Globe that can be entertaining to you on yours. All our Affairs are *petit*. They have a miniature Resemblance only, of the grand Things of Europe. Our Governments, Parliaments, Wars, Treaties, Expeditions, Factions, &c. tho' Matters of great and Serious Consequence to us, can seem but Trifles to you. Four Days since our Naval Force receiv'd a terrible Blow. Fifty Sail of the Line destroy'd would scarce be a greater Loss to Britain than that to us: And yet 'twas only a new 20 Gun Ship sunk, and about 100 Men drowned, just as she was going out to Sea on a privateering Voyage against the King's Enemies.[1] She was overset by a Flaw of Wind, being built too sharp, and too high masted. A Treaty is now holding at Newtown in Lancaster County, a Place 60 Miles west of this City, between the Governments of Virginia, Maryland, and Pennsylvania, on one Side, and the united Five Nations of Indians on the other. I will send you an Account of it when printed, as the Method of doing Business with those Barbarians may perhaps afford you some Amusement.[2]

---

suffered for a time, especially after Dobbs persuaded the Admiralty to send out a second expedition, 1746. Its findings, however, confirmed Middleton's report. Dobbs was governor of North Carolina from 1754 until his death. *DNB; DAB;* Desmond Clarke, *Arthur Dobbs, Esquire, 1689–1765* (Chapel Hill, N.C., 1957).

1. The episode was reported in full in *Pa. Gaz.*, July 5: "Sunday last [July 1] the Tartar, Capt. Mackey, sail'd down the Bay in order to proceed on his Cruise, but being (as 'tis said) over-masted, and not well ballasted, she was unfortunately overset, by a slight Flaw of Wind, near the Capes, and sunk immediately in about 8 Fathom Water. The Captain with about 60 Officers and Seamen were saved in her Long-boat, and went ashore at the Cape; 14 were taken up by Capt. Plasket in a Pilot Boat; and Capt. Claes, who was coming in from Barbadoes, ran his Vessel near the Ship, and took up 47. The rest perished. 'Tis expected she will soon be weigh'd, and with some Alterations, fitted out again, as she is a most extraordinary Sailor; so that we hope our Enemies will hardly hear of the Misfortune, before they find they have no great Reason to rejoice at it."

2. BF printed the treaty, announcing its publication September 6. It is printed in facsimile in Carl Van Doren, ed., *Indian Treaties Printed by Benjamin Franklin, 1736–1762* (Phila., 1938), pp. 41–79. The meeting took place June 22–July 4 at the Court House in the recently incorporated town of Lancaster.

We have already in our Library Bolton's and Shaw's Abridgements of Boyle's Works. I shall, however, mention to the Directors the Edition of his Works at large; possibly they may think fit to send for it.[3]

Please to remember me affectionately to my old Friend Wigate,[4] to whom I shall write per next Opportunity. I am, Sir, Your most obliged humble Servant   B FRANKLIN

Addressed: To   Mr Wm Strahan   Printer   London

To William Strahan   ALS: University of Pennsylvania Library

Sir   July 31. 1744

The above is a Copy of my last (via Corke).[5] This encloses Bills for Twenty Pounds Thirteen Shillings Sterling, for which when receiv'd please to give my Account Credit, and send me by the first Ship a Fount of about 300 lb. weight of good new English Letter, which I shall want to compleat a little Printing house for our common Friend Mr. Hall. I send you per this Ship a Box containing 300 Copies of a Piece I have lately printed here,[6] and purpose to send you 200 more per next Ship.[7] I desire you to take

3. Peter Shaw's abridgement of Boyle's *Philosophical Works* (2d edit., London, 1738) is listed in the Library Company's catalogue of 1741. Richard Boulton's *Works* of Boyle "Epitomiz'd" (London, 1699), was purchased in 1744. The Library acquired the five-volume edition of Boyle's *Works* (London, 1744), about which Strahan had written, in 1769, when it incorporated the collection of the Union Library Company.

4. John Wigate (or Wygate) was a journeyman in Watts's printing office in London when BF worked there, 1725. Better educated than most printers, he was "a tolerable Latinist, spoke French, and lov'd Reading." BF taught him to swim. The two became warm friends, and Wigate proposed that they travel through Europe together. Par. Text edit., pp. 122–4. He was clerk under Middleton on the search for the Northwest Passage, and gave evidence against his commanding officer in the hearings at the Admiralty.

5. As was customary in time of war, BF sent a duplicate of his July 4 letter. By putting it on the same sheet as this letter he saved paper and postage charges.

6. James Logan's translation of Cicero's *Cato Major*.

7. Probably not 200 more copies of the same work, as BF's phraseology would suggest, but 200 copies of the Indian Treaty of Lancaster, which he was then printing. See below, p. 416.

the properest Measures for getting them sold at such a Price as they will readily fetch, and I will take Books of you in Exchange for them. This kind of Commerce may be advantageous to us both, and to Mr. Hall; since if [we] have a reasonable Sale where we live for such Things as we print, what we do over and above, and can get dispos'd of at a foreign Market, is almost so much clear Gain. I have only time to add, that I am, with sincere Regards Your obliged humble Servant   B FRANKLIN

Addressed: To Mr William Strahan Printer in London   Per Capt. Evans   with a Box W S.

To Josiah and Abiah Franklin

ALS: American Philosophical Society[8]

Philada. Sept. 6. 1744

Honoured Father and Mother,

I apprehend I am too busy in prescribing, and meddling in the Dr's Sphere, when any of you complain of Ails in your Letters: But as I always employ a Physician my self when any Disorder arises in my Family and submit implicitly to his Orders in every Thing, so I hope you consider my Advice, when I give any, only as a Mark of my good Will, and put no more of it in Practice than happens to agree with what your Dr. directs.

Your Notion of the Use of Strong Lee I suppose may have a good deal in it. The Salt of Tartar, or Salt of Wormwood, frequently prescrib'd as for cutting, opening and cleansing is nothing more than the Salt of Lee procur'd by Evaporation. Mrs. Stephens's Medicine for the Stone and Gravel, the Secret of which was lately purchas'd at a great Price by the Parliament,[9] has for its principal Ingredient, Soap, which Boerhave[1] calls the most universal Remedy. The same Salt intimately mix'd

8. The MS is mutilated; missing words have been silently supplied from Duane, *Works*, VI, 6.

9. Parliament in 1739 paid Mrs. Joanna Stephens £5000 for her prescriptions, which were, of course, worthless. They are printed in *Gent. Mag.*, IX (1739), 298–9.

1. Hermann Boerhaave (1668–1738), professor of chemistry at Leyden.

413

with Oil of Turpentine, which you also mention, makes the *Sapa Philosophorum,* wonderfully extoll'd by some Chymists, for like Purposes. 'Tis highly probable (as your Dr. says) that Medicines are much alter'd in passing between the Stomack and Bladder; but such Salts seem well fitted in their Nature to pass with the least Alteration of almost any thing we know. And if they will not dissolve Gravel and Stone, yet I am half persuaded that a moderate Use of them may go a great Way towards preventing those Disorders, as they assist a weak Digestion in the Stomack and powerfully dissolve Crudities there, which I have frequently experienc'd. As to Honey and Mellasses, I did not mention them meerly as Openers and Looseners, but also from a Conjecture that as they are heavier in themselves than our common Drink, they might when dissolved in our Bodies, encrease the specific Gravity of our Fluids, the Urine in particular, and by that means keep separate and suspended therein those Particles which when united form gravel, &c. I will enquire after the Herb you mention: We have a botanist here, an intimate Friend of mine, who knows all the plants in the Country.[2] He would be glad of a Correspondence with some Gentlemen of the same Taste with you; and has twice thro' my Hands sent Specimens of the famous Chinese Ginseng, found here, to Persons who desired it in Boston neither of whom have had the Civility to write him a Word in Answer, even to acknowledge the Receipt of it; of which please to give a Hint to Br. John.[3]

We have had a very healthy Summer, and a fine Harvest: The Country is fill'd with Bread, but as Trade declines since the War began,[4] I know not what our Farmers will do for a Market. I am Your affectionate and Dutiful Son   B FRANKLIN

2. John Bartram, who, like other botanists of the time, was enthusiastic about the properties of ginseng root, which was found growing in America.
3. John Franklin (C.8).
4. England declared war on France, March 21, 1744. Generally known as the War of the Austrian Succession, in America it was called King George's War.

To Cadwallader Colden

ALS: Yale University Library

Sir   Philada. Sept. 13. 1744
    Dr. Mitchel,[5] a Gentleman from Virginia, came to Town this
Morning with Mr. Bertram, and we have been together all Day,[6]
which has hindred my Writing to you as I intended. We are to go
to Mr. Logan's tomorrow, when I shall have an Opportunity
of knowing his Sentiments of your Piece on Fluxions.[7] I am Sir
Your most humble Servant   B FRANKLIN

Addressed: To The Honbl Cadwalr Colden Esqr N York Free BF

5. John Mitchell (d. 1768), physician, naturalist, map maker; studied medicine at Edinburgh and settled in Urbanna, Virginia, in the 1720's, where he
became a justice of the peace of Middlesex County. He traveled much in
North America; on his visit to Philadelphia, 1744, he allowed copies to be
made of his treatises on yellow fever (see below, p. 418) and pines. Mitchell
collected and described American plants, many of which he introduced into
the British Isles; corresponded with European and American naturalists;
and became a member of the APS, 1744. After contributing articles on such
varied topics as the opossum, potash, electricity, and race and color to the
Phil. Trans., he was elected Fellow of the Royal Society, 1748. On a voyage
to England in 1746 he was captured by the French and lost all his papers.
From the records of the Board of Trade he prepared an authoritative *Map
of the British and French Dominions in North America*, 1755, that was frequently reproduced. It was used in the peace negotiations of 1782–83 and in
many controversies regarding boundaries and grants, and was reckoned by
Lawrence Martin to be "without serious doubt . . . the most important map
in American history." BF's last surviving letter (to Thomas Jefferson, April
8, 1790) concerns this map. *DAB; DNB;* Theodore Hornberger, "The Scientific Ideas of John Mitchell," *Huntington Lib. Quar.*, x (1946–47), 277–96;
Raymond P. Stearns, "Colonial Fellows of the Royal Society, 1661–1788,"
3 *Wm. and Mary Quar.*, III (1946), 239–40.
    6. In a letter to Colden, Nov. 2, 1744, Bartram gave a pleasant account
of Mitchell's visit to Philadelphia: "He did me the honour of Calling at my
house and staid all night. And I next morning to demonstrate the kindness
and esteem I had for his Company went with him to town and he being an
intire stranger I introduced him into the company of our friend Benjamin to
whose Care I left him for the present. He staid in town near three weeks so
that I had the favour of his Company many times at my house, in the fields
and in the woods, which I was well pleased with. He is an excelent Phisition
and Botanist and hath dipped in the Mathematicks which inclined A Gentleman in Town well known to us to say to me that our docters was but novices
to him. But another person more volatil and more extravangantly expressed
his value for him tould me thay had not the Milioneth part of his knowledge."
Colden Pap., III, 79.
    7. See below, p. 417.

From Cadwallader Colden

Draft: Yale University Library

Sir   New York 17th of Septr. 1744
I have Yours of the 13th and am glad to find by it that you have
an opportunity of conversing with a Gentleman who I believe
is both willing and Capable of promoting your Philosophical
Design.[8] You'l perceive by what you receive on these Sheets[9]
that I have open'd to my self a large Prospect either into Nature
or into Fairyland and I have in my Imaginations made some
steps into the Country but as the whole of this way of thinking
is entirely new I am desirous to lay it step by step before my
Friends for their remarks that thereby I may be either incouraged
to go on in an amusement of this kind or be prevented in throwing away time uselessly which may be better imploy'd (in my
time of life especially). What I now send is only design'd for
your Perusal and Mr. Logan's. I shall take it as the surest mark
of Friendship if both or either of you will take the trouble to
make your remarks [and] give your opinion on this way of thinking without reserve. I am to return home tomorrow. My humble
Service to Mr. Logan and Mr. Bartram. I am

To Mr Benjn Franklin

To William Strahan

ALS: American Philosophical Society

Sir   [Philada.] Sept. 18. 1744
I wrote to you per Capt. Evans, and enclos'd you Bills for
£20.13.0 Sterlg. of which I now send you the Seconds. I sent
you also a Box containing 300 Books I had printed, and by this
Ship I send you 200 Copies of our late Indian Treaty which I
hope will come to hand and sell with you.[1] I will take Books
of you in Exchange for as much of them as you can [get] sold.

8. Dr. John Mitchell.
9. Probably the MS of his essay on the First Causes of Action in Matter.
Two chapters only of this work were printed at New York, 1746; the entire
work of eight chapters was published in London, 1751, as *The Principles of
Action in Matter, the Gravitation of Bodies, and the Motion of the Planets.*
1. *A Treaty, Held at the Town of Lancaster ... In June, 1744* was printed by
BF and advertised for sale in *Pa. Gaz.*, Sept. 6, at 18d. It is reprinted in fac-

416

I wrote to you also for 300 wt. of New English Letter, which I want to compleat a little Printing House for our common Friend Mr. Hall; I hope you will be able to send it per first Vessel in the Spring; What you send please to insure. I am, Sir, Your obliged humble Servant   B FRANKLIN

Addressed: To Mr Wm Strahan Printer London   Per the Pennsylva Galley Capt. Hougstun

To Cadwallader Colden   ALS: New-York Historical Society

Sir   Philada. Oct. 25. 1744
I communicated your Piece on Fluxions[2] to Mr. Logan, and being at his House a few Days after, he told me, he had read it cursorily, that he thought you had not fully hit the Matter, and *(I think)* that Berkley's Objections were well founded:[3] but said he would read it over more attentively. Since that, he tells me there are several Mistakes in it, two of which he has mark'd in Page 10. He says, $x\dot{x}$ is by no Means$=x+\dot{x}$, nor is the Sq. of $10+1=10:2:01$ but$=100+20+1$ and that the Method of Shewing what Fluxions are, by squaring them, is entirely wrong. I suppose the Mistakes he mention'd, if they are such, may have been Slips of the Pen in transcribing. The other Piece, of the several Species of Matter, he gave me his Opinion of in these Words, "It must necessarily have some further Meaning in it than the Language itself imports, otherwise I can by no means conceive the Service of it."[4] At the same time, he express'd a

---

simile in Carl Van Doren, ed., *Indian Treaties Printed by Benjamin Franklin, 1736–1762* (Phila., 1938), pp. 41–79.

2. The MS of Colden's "Introduction to the Doctrine of Fluxions, or the Arithmetic of Infinites" was printed in his *Principles of Action in Matter* (London, 1751), pp. 191–215.

3. [George Berkeley], *The Analyst; or, a Discourse Addressed to an Infidel Mathematician* (London, 1734). For an introduction to the controversy over fluxions, see Florian Cajori, *A History of the Conceptions of Limits and Fluxions in Great Britain* (Chicago and London, 1919), pp. 57–64.

4. James Parker printed the essay in New York in 1746, though the title page is dated 1745, as *An Explication of the First Causes of Action in Matter, and, of the Cause of Gravitation,* and it was reprinted in London and translated into French and German. Colden's theory, however, was universally

high regard for you, as the ablest Thinker (so he express'd it) in this part of the World. I purpose to write to you from N York next Week, and till then must defer saying any further on the last mention'd Piece. Enclos'd I send you a Piece of Dr. Mitchel's (of Virginia) which I caus'd to be transcrib'd while he was here.[5] He desires your Sentiments of it, and to be favour'd with any other Observations you have made on the same Distemper (the Yellow Fever). When you have perus'd it, please to return it. I am, Sir Your most humble Servant   B FRANKLIN[6]

Endorsed: B Frankilin

To William Strahan

ALS: Chicago Historical Society

Sir   Philada. Nov. 2. 1744

I have wrote to you by several Opportunities to acknowledge the Receipt of yours per Mr. Hall with the Things you sent me. I have also remitted you Bills for £20.13.0. Sterl. of which you have the fourths enclos'd. I desired you to send me a Fount of about 300 wt. English and the best Newspapers and Pamphlets constantly. I hope some of my Letters have come to hand, having no time now to copy. When the English comes I shall have a compleat little Printing House for our Friend Hall who is well, as is Mr. Read, and Your obliged humble Servant   B FRANKLIN

P.S. I sent you a Box of Books per Evans.

Addressed: To Mr Wm Strahan   Printer   London   Per favour of   Mr Shoemaker.

---

rejected by mathematicians. Brooke Hindle, *The Pursuit of Science in Revolutionary America, 1735–1789* (Chapel Hill, N.C., 1956), pp. 44–7; Hindle, "Cadwallader Colden's Extension of the Newtonian Principles," 3 *Wm. ana Mary Quar.*, XIII (1956), 459–75.

5. John Mitchell's essay on yellow fever, which the doctor discussed at some length in letters to BF of March (?) 1745, and Sept. 12, 1745.

6. On the bottom of this letter Colden has made the following notes: "Suppose x = 10 and $\dot{x}$ = .1 one tenth not equal to unite as Mr. Logan has it then $(10+.1)^2 = 100+2+.01$. I do not say any where that $x\dot{x} = x + \dot{x}$ for on the contrary $x\dot{x}$ I say is infinitely less than $x+\dot{x}$ or than x for $x+\dot{x}=x$ the difference being infinitely small."

An Account of the New Invented Pennsylvanian Fire-Places

An Account Of the New Invented Pennsylvanian Fire-Places: . . . Philadelphia: Printed and Sold by B. Franklin. 1744. (Yale University Library)

According to his autobiography, Franklin invented the Pennsylvania fireplace in 1742, but the winter of 1739–40 is a more likely date. Writing of it in the summer or fall of 1744, he says that he and his family and friends have enjoyed its warmth "for these four Winters past."[7] He had the plates for it cast by his friend Robert Grace at Warwick Furnace in Chester County. The new fireplaces were generally approved, orders multiplied, and Grace was soon manufacturing them in quantity. They sold for £5 in Philadelphia. The *Gazette* first advertised them December 3, 1741: "To be sold at the Post Office Philadelphia, the New Invented Fire-Places; Where any Person may see some of them that are now in Use, and have the Nature and Advantages of them explain'd." Six weeks later the paper announced that "a fresh Parcel of Iron Fire-Places" had just been received from Warwick Furnace.[8]

Franklin encouraged their sale with a descriptive account for which Lewis Evans made the illustrative diagrams,[9] and a Boston craftsman, probably James Turner, made the engravings. It was announced as "just published" November 15, 1744, though in fact it came from the press several weeks earlier. Grace paid the costs of what was a very successful promotion brochure.[1] "This Pamphlet had a good Effect," Franklin recalled. "Governor Thomas was so pleas'd with the Construction of this Stove, as describ'd in it that he offer'd to give me a Patent for the sole Vending of them for a Term of Years; but I declin'd it from a Principle which has ever weigh'd with me on such Occasions, viz. *That as we enjoy great Advantages from the Inventions of others, we should be glad of an Opportunity to serve others by any Invention of ours, and this we should do freely and generously.*"[2] Grace's agents for

7. See below, p. 440. Van Doren (*Franklin*, p. 142) first noted this.

8. BF offered "Very good Iron Stoves" for sale in *Pa. Gaz.*, Feb. 12, 1741, but it is not certain these were Pennsylvania fireplaces.

9. Adolph B. Benson, ed., *Peter Kalm's Travels in North America* (N.Y., 1937), II, 652–4.

1. George S. Eddy, ed., *Account Books Kept by Benjamin Franklin. Ledger "D", 1739–1747* (N.Y., 1929), pp. 61–3.

2. Par. Text edit., p. 294, where he also tells of a London ironmonger who made some changes in his specifications, patented the result, and made "a little Fortune by it." This may have been James Sharp, who published in London in 1781 *An Account of the Principle and Effects of American Stoves;* . . .

the fireplaces included John Franklin and Richard Clark in Boston, Peter Franklin in Newport, James Parker and James Burling in New York, Lewis Evans in Philadelphia, and James Mitchell in Yorktown, Virginia.[3] Soon other ironmongers were manufacturing and selling them according to the design Franklin refused to patent.[4]

Franklin sent copies of the pamphlet to his friends. Cadwallader Colden forwarded one to Professor Johann F. Gronovius of Leyden with the pleasantly expressed hope that it would not only keep him warm at his studies but preserve his health at the same time.[5] "That invention hath found a great applause in this part of the world," Gronovius replied, "which is the reason that I could not hinder to let it be translated into Dutch, and no doubt soon into French."[6] In 1757 Franklin had his fireplace made and installed in his lodgings in Craven Street, and soon "many Hundreds" were "set up in Imitation of it," in and about London. He sent one to Sir Alexander Dick, with instructions for installing it in his country house near Edinburgh, and recommended it to Lord Kames for his new house at Blair Drummond.[7] His interest in the efficient heating of houses continued throughout his life. In England in 1771 and later in France he devised heating plants for use with coal as fuel which consumed most of their own smoke. Over many years he corresponded with various friends about problems of combustion and heating, and he wrote treatises on these subjects as late as 1785.

His first device, the Pennsylvania fireplace, was efficient for several reasons: it reduced to a minimum the dissipation of heat up the chimney flue; it transmitted heat by radiation and by direct conduction quite as effectively as a conventional fireplace or metal stove of the same capacity could do at that time; equally or more important, it also employed the principle of convection—the creation of a current of air which was then heated and circulated into the room. This principle was not new; about thirty years earlier a Frenchman Nicolas Gauger had used it, as

---

together with a Description of the late Additions and Improvements made to them.

3. Peter Franklin's account with Grace for fireplaces, 1744–45, is in his Ledger, APS. James Parker advertised that he would give copies of BF's pamphlet gratis with all fireplaces sold. *New-York Weekly Post-Boy*, Sept. 11, 1746.

4. Benson J. Lossing, *The Pictorial Field-Book of the Revolution*, I (N.Y., 1851), 328 n.

5. Colden to Gronovius, [Dec., 1744], *Colden Paps.*, III, 91.

6. Gronovius to Bartram, June 2, 1746, Darlington, *Memorials*, p. 355. Antonio Graziosi printed editions in Venice in 1778, 1788, and 1791.

7. BF to Dick, Jan. 21, 1762; BF to Kames, Feb. 28, 1768.

Franklin points out in his pamphlet, in designing a fireplace with a series of ducts built into the back, sides, and hearth, into which outside air, introduced at the bottom, rose as it was heated and from which it passed out into the room through a vent at the top. Franklin embodied the same idea, much simplified, in the "air-box" which he placed directly behind the fire and over which he caused the hot combustion gases and smoke to pass on their way to the chimney. Outside air was drawn in through a duct at the bottom of the stove, circulated through the air-box around a series of baffles, and passed into the room through openings on both sides of the stove near the top.

Later manufacturers of the so-called "Franklin stove" have usually eliminated this air-box, thereby abandoning a centrally important feature of the original model as the inventor conceived it; most "Franklin stoves" made within the last hundred years or so, however convenient and pleasant they may be, are little more than metal fireplaces. No example of an original Pennsylvania fireplace is known by the editors to survive, although a modern replica is to be seen at the Franklin Institute in Philadelphia.

The Franklin stove was judged by its performance, but the pamphlet describing it was judged by quite another standard than the mere utilitarian purpose of its subject. The New York lawyer James Alexander thought it showed the author "to be a man of Sense and of a good Stile."[8] And Franklin's biographer Sydney George Fisher was "inclined to lay down the principle that the test of literary genius is the ability to be fascinating about stoves."[9]

ADVERTISEMENT.

THESE FIRE-PLACES are made in the best Manner, and sold by R. Grace in Philadelphia. They are sold also by J. Parker in New-York, and by J. Franklin in Boston.

The within-describ'd is of the middle and most common Size: There are others to be had both larger and smaller.[1]

AN ACCOUNT OF THE
NEW-INVENTED FIRE-PLACES.

IN these Northern Colonies the Inhabitants keep FIRES to sit by, generally *Seven Months* in the Year; that is, from the Be-

8. Alexander to Colden, Nov. 12, 1744, *Colden Paps.*, III, 83.

9. *The True Benjamin Franklin* (Phila., 1899), p. 170.

1. This "Advertisement" is followed by a short list of errata; the indicated corrections have been silently made in the present reprinting.

ginning of October to the End of April; and in some Winters near *Eight Months,* by taking in part of September and May.

WOOD, our common Fewel, which within these 100 Years might be had at every Man's Door, must now be fetch'd near 100 Miles to some Towns, and makes a very considerable Article in the Expence of Families.

As therefore so much of the Comfort and Conveniency of our Lives, for so great a Part of the Year, depends on the Article of FIRE; since Fuel is become so expensive, and (as the Country is more clear'd and settled) will of course grow scarcer and dearer; any new Proposal for Saving the Wood, and for lessening the Charge and augmenting the Benefit of FIRE, by some particular Method of Making and Managing it, may at least be thought worth Consideration.

THE NEW FIRE-PLACES are a late Invention to that purpose (experienced now three Winters by a great Number of Families in Pennsylvania) of which this Paper is intended to give a particular Account.

THAT the Reader may the better judge whether this Method of Managing Fire has any Advantage over those heretofore in Use, it may be proper to consider both the old and new Methods separately and particularly, and afterwards make the Comparison.

IN order to this, 'tis necessary to understand well some few of the Properties of AIR and FIRE, viz.

I. AIR is rarified by *Heat,* and condens'd by *Cold;* i.e. the same Quantity of Air takes up more Space when warm than when cold. This may be shown by several very easy Experiments. Take any clear Glass Bottle (a Florence Flask stript of the Straw is best) place it before the Fire, and as the Air within is warm'd and rarified, part of it will be driven out of the Bottle; turn it up, place its Mouth in a Vessel of Water, and remove it from the Fire; then, as the Air within cools and contracts, you will see the Water rise in the Neck of the Bottle, supplying the Place of just so much Air as was driven out. Hold a large hot Coal near the Side of the Bottle, and as the Air within feels the Heat, it will again distend and force out the Water. Or, Fill a Bladder half-full of Air, tie the Neck tight, and lay it before a Fire as near as may be without scorching the Bladder; as the Air within heats, you will perceive it to swell and fill the Bladder, till it becomes tight as if full-blown: Remove it to a cool Place, and you will see it fall gradually, till it become as lank as at first.

2. AIR rarified and distended by Heat, is specifically* lighter than it was before, and will rise in other Air of greater Density. As Wood, Oil, or any other Matter specifically lighter than Water, if plac'd at the Bottom of a Vessel of Water, will rise till it comes to the Top; so rarified Air will rise in common Air, till it either comes to Air of equal Weight, or is by Cold reduc'd to its former Density.

A FIRE then being made in any Chimney, the Air over the Fire is rarified by the Heat, becomes lighter and therefore immediately rises in the Funnel and goes out; the other Air in the Room (flowing towards the Chimney) supplies its Place, is rarified in its turn, and rises likewise; the Place of the Air thus carried out of the Room is supplied by fresh Air coming in thro' Doors and Windows, or, if they be shut, thro' every Crevice with Violence, as may be seen by holding a Candle to a Keyhole: If the Room be so tight as that all the Crevices together will not supply so much Air as is continually carried off, then in a little time the Current up the Funnel must flag, and the Smoke being no longer driven up must come into the Room.

1. FIRE† throws out Light, Heat, and Smoke (or Fume). The two first move in right Lines and with great Swiftness; the latter is but just separated from the Fuel, and then moves only as it is carried by the Stream of rarified Air. And without a continual Accession and Recession of Air to carry off the Smoaky Fumes, they would remain crouded about the Fire, and stifle it.

2. HEAT may be separated from the Smoke as well as from the Light, by means of a Plate of Iron, which will suffer Heat to pass through it without the others.

3. FIRE sends out its Rays of Heat, as well as Rays of Light, equally every way: But the greatest sensible Heat is over the Fire, where there is, besides the Rays of Heat shot upwards, a continual rising Stream of hot Air, heated by the Rays shot round on every Side.

*Body or Matter of any sort is said to be *specifically* heavier or lighter than other Matter, when it has more or less Substance or Weight in the same Dimensions.

†i.e. Common Fire.

THESE Things being understood, we proceed to consider the Fire-places heretofore in Use, viz.

1. The large open Fire-places used in the Days of our Fathers, and still generally in the Country, and in Kitchens.

2. The newer-fashion'd Fire-places, with low Breasts, and narrow Hearths.

3. Fire-places with hollow Backs, Hearths and Jams of Iron, (described by Mons. Gauger*) for warming the Air as it comes into the Room.

4. The Holland Stoves, with Iron Doors opening into the Room.

5. The German Stoves, which have no Opening in the Room where they are us'd, but the Fire is put in from some other Room, or from without.

6. Iron Pots, with open Charcoal Fires, plac'd in the middle of a Room.

1. The first of these Methods has generally the Conveniency of two warm Seats, one in each Corner; but they are sometimes too hot to abide in, and at other times incommoded with the Smoke; there is likewise good Room for the Cook to move, to hang on Pots, &c. Their Inconveniencies are, that they almost always smoke if the Door be not left open; that they require a large Funnel, and a large Funnel carries off a great Quantity of Air, which occasions what is called a strong Draft to the Chimney; without which strong Draft the Smoke would come out of some Part or other of so large an Opening, so that the Door can seldom be shut; and the cold Air so nips the Backs and Heels of those that sit before the Fire, that they have no Comfort, 'till either Screens or Settles are provided (at a considerable Expence) to keep it off, which both cumber the Room and darken the Fire-side. A moderate Quantity of Wood on the Fire in so large a Hearth, seems but little; and, in so strong and cold a Draught, warms but little; so that People are continually laying on more.

*In his Tract entitled, *La Mechanique de Feu.*[2]

2. Nicolas Gauger, *La Méchanique du Feu* (Paris, 1713), translated by J. T. Desaguliers as *Fires Improv'd* (London, 1715). BF mentions this work (below, p. 428) as "published 1709," but no edition earlier than 1713 has been found.

424

In short, 'tis next to impossible to warm a Room with such a Fire-place: And I suppose our Ancestors never thought of warming Rooms to sit in; all they purpos'd was to have a Place to make a Fire in, by which they might warm themselves when acold.

2. MOST of these old-fashion'd Chimneys in Towns and Cities, have been, of late Years, reduc'd to the second Sort mention'd, by building Jambs within them, narrowing the Hearth, and making a low Arch or Breast. 'Tis strange, methinks, that tho' Chimneys have been so long in Use, their Construction should be so little understood till lately, that no Workman pretended to make one which should always carry off all the Smoke, but a Chimney-cloth was look'd upon as essential to a Chimney: This Improvement, however, by small Openings and low Breasts, has been made in our Days; and Success in the first Experiments has brought it into general Use in Cities, so that almost all new Chimneys are now made of that sort, and much fewer Bricks will make a Stack of Chimneys now than formerly. An Improvement so lately made, may give us Room to believe that still farther Improvements may be found, to remedy the Inconveniencies yet remaining. For these new Chimneys, tho' they keep Rooms generally free from Smoke, and, the Opening being contracted, will allow the Door to be shut, yet the Funnel still requiring a considerable Quantity of Air, it rushes in at every Crevice so strongly, as to make a continual Whistling or Howling; and 'tis very uncomfortable as well as dangerous to sit against any such Crevice. Many Colds are caught from this Cause only; it being safer to sit in the open Street; for then the Pores do all close together, and the Air does not strike so sharply against any particular Part. The Spaniards have a Proverbial Saying, *If the Wind blows on you thro' a Hole, Make your Will, and take Care of your Soul.*[3] Women, particularly, from this Cause, (as they sit much in the House) get Colds in the Head, Rheums and Defluctions, which fall into their Jaws and Gums, and have destroy'd early many a fine Set of Teeth in these Northern Colonies. Great and bright Fires do also very much contribute to damage the Eyes, dry and shrivel the Skin, and bring on early the Appearances of Old-Age. In short, many of the Diseases proceeding from Colds, as Fevers, Pleurisies, &c. fatal to very great Numbers of People, may be

3. BF printed this aphorism in *Poor Richard's Almanack* for 1736.

ascrib'd to strong-drawing Chimneys, whereby, in severe Weather, a Man is scorch'd before, while he's froze behind.† In the mean time very little is done by these Chimneys towards warming the Room; for the Air round the Fire-place which is warm'd by the

†As the Writer is neither Physician nor Philosopher, the Reader may expect he should justify these his Opinions by the Authority of some that are so. M. Clare, F.R.S. in his Treatise of *The Motion of Fluids*,[4] says, page 246, &c. "And here it may be remarked, that 'tis more prejudicial to Health, to sit near a Window or Door, in a Room where there are many Candles and a Fire, than in a Room without: For the Consumption of Air thereby occasioned, will always be very considerable, and this must necessarily be replaced by cold Air from without. Down the Chimney can enter none, the Stream of warm Air, always rising therein, absolutely forbids it: The Supply must therefore come in wherever other Openings shall be found. If these happen to be small, *Let those who sit near them beware:* The smaller the Flood-gate, the smarter will be the Stream. Was a Man, even in a Sweat, to leap into a cold Bath, or jump from his warm Bed in the intensest Cold, even in a Frost, provided he do not continue over-long therein, and be in Health when he does this, we see by Experience that he gets no Harm. If he sits a little while against a Window, into which a successive Current of cold Air comes, his Pores are closed, and he gets a Fever. In the first Case, the Shock the Body endures is general, uniform, and therefore less fierce; in the other a single Part, a Neck or Ear perchance, is attacked, and that with the greater Violence probably, as it is done by a successive Stream of cold Air. And the Cannon of a Battery, pointed against a single Part of a Bastion, easier make a Breach, than were they directed to play singly upon the whole Face, and will admit the Enemy much sooner into the Town."

That warm Rooms, and keeping the Body warm in Winter, are Means of preventing such Diseases, take the Opinion of that learned Italian Physician, Antonio Portio, in the Preface to his Tract *de Militis Sanitate tuenda*,[5] where, speaking of a particular wet and cold Winter, remarkable at Venice for its Sickliness, he says, "Popularis autem pleuritis quae Venetiis saeviit mensibus Dec. Jan. Feb. ex coeli, aërisque inclementia facta est, quod non habeant hypocausta [*Stove-Rooms*][6]

4. Martin Clare, *The Motion of Fluids, Natural and Artificial* (London, 1735), pp. 224–6. BF probably saw the second edition, 1737.
5. Luca Antonio Porzio, *De Militis in Castris Sanitate Tuenda* (The Hague, 1739), pp. b–b2.
6. Brackets are BF's.

direct Rays from the Fire, does not continue in the Room, but is continually crouded and gather'd into the Chimney by the Current of cold Air coming behind it, and so is presently carried off.

In both these Sorts of Fire-places, the greatest Part of the Heat from the Fire is lost: For as Fire naturally darts Heat every way, the Back, the two Jambs, and the Hearth, drink up almost all that's given them, very little being reflected from Bodies so dark, porous and unpolish'd; and the upright Heat, which is by far the greatest, flies directly up the Chimney. Thus Five Sixths at least of the Heat (and consequently of the Fewel) is wasted, and contributes nothing towards warming the Room.

---

et quod non soliciti sint Itali omnes de auribus, temporibus, collo, totoque corpore defendendis ab injuriis aëris; et tegmina domorum Veneti disponant parum inclinata, ut nives diutius permaneant super tegmina. E contra, Germani, qui experiuntur coeli inclementiam, perdidicere sese defendere ab aëris injuria. Tecta construunt multum inclinata, ut decidant nives. Germani abundant lignis, domusque *hypocaustis;* foris autem incedunt pannis, pellibus, gossipio, bene mehercule loricati atque muniti. In Bavaria interrogabam (curiositate motus videndi Germaniam) quot nam elapsis mensibus pleuritide vel peripneumonia fuissent absumti; dicebant vix unus aut alter illis temporibus pleuritide fuit correptus."

The great Dr. Boerhaave, whose Authority alone might be sufficient, in his Aphorisms mentions, as one antecedent Cause of Pleurisies, *a cold Air driven violently through some narrow Passage upon the Body overheated by Labour or Fire.*[7]

The Eastern Physicians agree with the Europeans in this Point; witness the Chinese Treatise, entitled *Tchang seng,* i.e. *The Art of procuring Health and long Life,* as translated in Pere Du Halde's Account of China, which has this Passage. "As of all the Passions which ruffle us, Anger does the most Mischief; so of all the malignant Affections of the Air, *a Wind that comes thro' any narrow Passage,* which is cold and piercing, is *most dangerous;* and coming upon us unawares, insinuates itself into the Body, often causing grievous Diseases. It should therefore be avoided, according to the Advice of the ancient Proverb, as carefully as the Point of an Arrow."[8] These Mischiefs are avoided by the Use of the new-invented Fire-places, as will be shewn hereafter.

7. [Hermann Boerhaave], *Boerhaave's Aphorisms: Concerning the Knowledge and Cure of Diseases* (London, 1735), p. 238.

8. J[ean] B[aptiste] DuHalde, *The General History of China* (3d edit., London, 1741), IV, 75.

3. To remedy this, the Sieur Gauger gives us, in his Book entitled *La Mechanique de Feu*, published 1709, seven different Constructions of the third Sort of Chimneys mentioned above, in which there are hollow Cavities made by Iron Plates in the Back, Jambs and Hearth, thro' which Plates the Heat passing, warms the Air in those Cavities, which is continually coming into the Room fresh and warm. The Invention was very ingenious, and had many Conveniencies: The Room was warm'd in all Parts, by the Air flowing into it through the heated Cavities: Cold Air was prevented rushing thro' the Crevices, the Funnel being sufficiently supply'd by those Cavities: Much less Fuel would serve, &c. But the first Expence, which was very great; the Intricacy of the Design, and the Difficulty of the Execution, especially in old Chimneys, discouraged the Propagation of the Invention; so that there are (I suppose) very few such Chimneys now in Use. [The upright Heat, too, was almost all lost in these, as in the common Chimneys.][9]

4. The Holland Iron Stove, which has a Flue proceeding from the Top, and a small Iron Door opening into the Room, comes next to be considered. Its Conveniences are, that it makes a Room all over warm; for the Chimney being wholly closed, except the Flue of the Stove, very little Air is required to supply that, and therefore not much rushes in at Crevices, or at the Door when 'tis opened. Little Fewel serves, the Heat being almost all saved; for it rays out almost equally from the four Sides, the Bottom and the Top, into the Room, and presently warms the Air around it, which being rarified rises to the Cieling, and its Place is supplied by the lower Air of the Room, which flows gradually towards the Stove, and is there warm'd and rises in its Turn, so that there is a continual Circulation till all the Air in the Room is warmed. The Air, too, is gradually changed by the Stove-Door's being in the Room, thro' which, part of it is continually passing, and that makes these Stoves wholesomer, or at least pleasanter, than the German Stoves next to be spoke of. But they have these Inconveniences. There is no Sight of the Fire, which is in itself a pleasant Thing. One cannot conveniently make any other Use of the Fire but that of warning the Room. When the Room is warm, People not seeing the Fire are apt to

9. Brackets in the original.

forget supplying it with Fuel 'til 'tis almost out, then, growing cold, a great deal of Wood is put in, which soon makes it too hot. The Change of Air is not carried on quite quick enough, so that if any Smoke or ill Smell happens in the Room, 'tis a long Time before 'tis discharg'd. For these Reasons the Holland Stove has not obtain'd much among the English (who love the Sight of the Fire) unless in some Workshops, where People are oblig'd to sit near Windows for the Light, and in such Places they have been found of good Use.

5. The German Stove is like a Box, one Side wanting. 'Tis compos'd of Five Iron Plates scru'd together; and fix'd so as that you may put the Fuel into it from another Room, or from the Outside of the House. 'Tis a kind of Oven revers'd, its Mouth being without, and Body within the Room that is to be warm'd by it. This Invention certainly warms a Room very speedily and thoroughly with little Fuel: No Quantity of cold Air comes in at any Crevice, because there is no Discharge of Air which it might Supply, there being no Passage into the Stove from the Room. These are its Conveniencies. Its Inconveniences are, That People have not even so much Sight or Use of the Fire as in the Holland Stoves, and are moreover oblig'd to breathe the same unchang'd Air continually, mix'd with the Breath and Perspiration from one anothers Bodies, which is very disagreeable to those who have not been accustomed to it.

6. Charcoal Fires, in Pots, are us'd chiefly in the Shops of Handicraftsmen. They warm a Room (that is kept close and has no Chimney to carry off the warm'd Air) very speedily and uniformly: But there being no Draught to change the Air, the sulphurous Fumes from the Coals [be they ever so well kindled before they are brought in, there will be some][1] mix with it, render it disagreeable, hurtful to some Constitutions, and sometimes, when the Door is long kept shut, produce fatal Consequences.

To avoid the several Inconveniences, and at the same time retain all the Advantages of other Fire-places, was contrived the PENNSYLVANIA FIRE-PLACE now to be described.

This Machine consists of
A Bottom Plate, (i) [*See the Cut*.] [below, p. 445]

1. Brackets in the original.

A Back Plate, (ii)

Two Side Plates, (iii iii)

Two Middle Plates, (iv iv) which join'd together form a tight
   Box with winding Passages in it for warming the Air.

A Front Plate, (v)

A Top Plate, (vi)

These are all of cast Iron, with Mouldings or Ledges where
the Plates come together, to hold them fast, and retain the Mortar
us'd for Pointing to make tight Joints. When the Plates are all in
their Places, a Pair of slender Rods with Screws, are sufficient to
bind the Whole very firmly together, as it appears in *Fig.* 2.

There are, moreover, two thin Plates of wrought Iron, viz. The
Shutter, (vii) and the Register, (viii); besides the Screw-Rods
O P, all which we shall explain in their Order.

(i) The Bottom Plate, or Hearth-Piece, is round before, with a
rising Moulding that serves as a Fender to keep Coals and Ashes
from coming to the Floor, &c. It has two Ears, *F G,* perforated
to receive the Screw-Rods *O P;* a long Air-hole, *a a,* thro' which
the fresh outward Air passes up into the Air-Box; and three
Smoke-Holes *B C* thro' which the Smoke descends and passes
away; also a square Hole *b* for the Bellows; all represented by
dark Squares. It has also double Ledges to receive between them
the Bottom Edges of the Back-Plate, the two Side Plates, and the
two middle Plates. These Ledges are about an Inch asunder, and
half an Inch high; a Profile of two of them join'd to a Fragment
of Plate appears in *Fig.* 3.

(ii) The Back Plate is without Holes, having only a Pair of
Ledges on each Side, to receive the Back Edges of the two

(iii iii) Side Plates: These have each a Pair of Ledges to receive
the Side-Edges of the Front Plate, and a little Shoulder for it to
rest on; also two Pair of Ledges to receive the Side-Edges of the
two Middle Plates which form the Air-Box; and an oblong Air-
hole near the Top, thro' which is discharg'd into the Room the
Air warm'd in the Air-Box. Each has also a Wing or Bracket,
H and *I,* to keep in falling Brands, Coals, &c. and a small Hole
Q and *R,* for the Axis of the Register to turn in.

(iv iv) The Air-Box is compos'd of the two Middle Plates *D E*
and *F G.* The first has five thin Ledges or Partitions, cast on it,

two Inches deep, the Edges of which are receiv'd in so many Pair of Ledges cast in the other. The Tops of all the Cavities form'd by these thin deep Ledges are also covered by a Ledge of the same Form and Depth, cast with them; so that when the Plates are put together, and the Joints luted, there is no Communication between the Air-Box and the Smoke. In the winding Passages of this Box, fresh Air is warm'd as it passes into the Room.

(v) The Front Plate is arch'd on the under Side, and ornamented with Foliages, &c. It has no Ledges.

(vi) The Top Plate has a Pair of Ears *M N*, answerable to those in the Bottom Plate, and perforated for the same Purpose: It has also a Pair of Ledges running round the under Side, to receive the Top-Edges of the Front, Back and Side Plates. The Air-Box does not reach up to the Top Plate by two Inches and half.

(vii) The Shutter is of thin wrought Iron and light, of such a Length and Breadth as to close well the Opening of the Fire-Place. It is us'd to blow up the Fire, and to shut up and secure it a Nights. It has two brass Knobs for Handles *d d*, and commonly slides up and down in a Groove, left, in putting up the Fire-place, between the foremost Ledge of the Side Plates, and the Face of the Front Plate; but some choose to set it aside when it is not in Use, and apply it on Occasion.

(viii) The Register, is also of thin wrought Iron. It is plac'd between the Back Plate and Air-Box, and can, by Means of the Key *S* be turn'd on its Axis so as to lie in any Position between level and upright.

The Screw-Rods *O P* are of wrought Iron, about a third of an Inch thick, with a Button at Bottom, and a Screw and Nut at Top; and may be ornamented with two small Brasses screw'd on above the Nuts.

To put this Machine to work,

1. A false Back of four Inch- (or, in shallow small Chimneys, two Inch-) Brick-work is to be made in the Chimney, four Inches or more from the true Back: From the Top of this false Back, a Closing is to be made over to the Breast of the Chimney, that no Air may pass into the Chimney, but what goes under the false Back, and up behind it.

2. Some Bricks of the Hearth are to be taken up, to form a

Hollow under the Bottom Plate; across which Hollow runs a thin tight Partition to keep apart the Air entring the Hollow, and the Smoke; and is therefore plac'd between the Air-hole and Smoke-holes.

3. A Passage is made, communicating with the outward Air, to introduce that Air into the forepart of the Hollow under the Bottom Plate, whence it may rise thro' the Air-hole into the Air-box.

4. A Passage is made from the back Part of the Hollow, communicating with the Flue behind the false Back: Through this Passage the Smoke is to pass.

The Fire-place is to be erected upon these Hollows, by putting all the Plates in their Places, and screwing them together.

Its Operation may be conceiv'd by observing the following

PROFILE of the Chimney and FIRE-PLACE.

[*see illustration opposite*]

The Fire being made at *A,* the Flame and Smoke will ascend and strike the Top *T,* which will thereby receive a considerable Heat. The Smoke finding no Passage upwards, turns over the Top of the Air-box, and descends between it and the Back Plate to the Holes at *B* in the Bottom Plate, heating, as it passes, both Plates of the Air-box and the said Back Plate; the Front Plate, Bottom and Side Plates are also all heated at the same Time. The Smoke proceeds in the Passage that leads it under and behind the false Back, and so rises into the Chimney. The Air of the Room, warm'd behind the Back Plate, and by the Sides, Front and Top Plates, becoming specifically lighter than the other Air in the Room, is oblig'd to rise; but the Closure over the Fire-place hindring it from going up the Chimney, it is forc'd out into the Room, rises by the Mantle-piece to the Cieling and spreads all over the Top of the Room, whence being crouded down gradually by the Stream of newly warm'd Air that follows and rises above it, the whole Room becomes in a short time equally warmed.

At the same Time the Air, warmed under the Bottom Plate and in the Air-Box, rises, and comes out of the Holes in the Side-Plates, very swiftly if the Door of the Room be shut, and joins its Current with the Stream before mentioned rising from the Side, Back and Top Plates.

432

PROFILE of the Chimney and FIRE-PLACE.

M The Mantle-piece or Breast of the Chimney.

C The Funnel.

B The false Back & Clofing.

E True Back of the Chimney.

T Top of the Fire-place.

F The Front of it.

A The Place where the Fire is made.

D The Air-Box.

K The Hole in the Side-plate, thro' which the warm'd Air is difcharg'd out of the Air-Box into the Room.

H The Hollow fill'd with frefh Air, entring at the Paffage *I*, and afcending into the Air-Box thro' the Air-hole in the Bottom-plate near

G The Partition in the Hollow to keep the Air and Smoke apart.

P The Paffage under the falfe Back and Part of the Hearth for the Smoke.

⇡ ⇡ ⇡ ⇡ ⇡ The Courfe of the Smoke.

The Air that enters the Room thro' the Air-box is fresh, tho' warm; and computing the Swiftness of its Motion with the Areas of the Holes, 'tis found that near 10 Barrels of fresh Air are hourly introduc'd by the Air-Box; and by this Means the Air in the Room is continually changed, and kept at the same Time sweet and warm.

'Tis to be observed that the entring Air will not be warm at first Lighting the Fire, but heats gradually as the Fire encreases.

A square Opening for a Trap-Door should be left in the Closing of the Chimney, for the Sweeper to go up: The Door may be made of Slate or Tin, and commonly kept close shut, but so plac'd as that turning up against the Back of the Chimney when open, it closes the Vacancy behind the false Back, and shoots the Soot that falls in Sweeping, out upon the Hearth. This Trap-Door is a very convenient Thing.

In Rooms where much Smoking of Tobacco is used, 'tis also convenient to have a small Hole about five or six Inches square, cut near the Cieling through into the Funnel: This Hole must have a Shutter, by which it may be clos'd or open'd at Pleasure. When open, there will be a strong Draught of Air through it into the Chimney, which will presently carry off a Cloud of Smoke, and keep the Room clear: If the Room be too hot likewise, it will carry off as much of the warm Air as you please, and then you may stop it intirely, or in part, as you think fit. By this Means it is that the Tobacco-Smoke does not descend among the Heads of the Company near the Fire, as it must do before it can get into common Chimneys.

The Manner of Using this FIREPLACE.

YOUR Cord-wood must be cut into three Lengths; or else a short Piece, fit for the Fire-place, cut off, and the longer left for the Kitchin or other Fires. Dry Hickery, or Ash, or any Woods that burn with a clear Flame, are rather to be chosen; because such are less apt to foul the Smoke-Passages with Soot; and Flame communicates, with its Light, as well as by Contact, greater Heat to the Plates and Room. But where more ordinary Wood is used, half a dry Faggot of Brush-wood burnt at the first making of Fire in the Morning, is very advantageous; as it immediately by its sudden Blaze heats the Plates and warms the Room (which with bad Wood slowly kindling would not be done so soon) and

433

at the same time, by the Length of its Flame turning in the Passages, consumes and cleanses away the Soot that such bad smoaky Wood had produc'd therein the preceding Day, and so keeps them always free and clean. When you have laid a little Back-log, and plac'd your Billets on small Dogs, as in common Chimneys, and put some Fire to them; then slide down your Shutter as low as the Dogs, and the Opening being by that Means contracted, the Air rushes in briskly and presently blows up the Flames. When the Fire is sufficiently kindled, slide it up again.* In some of these Fire-places there is a little six-inch square Trap-door of thin wrought Iron or Brass, covering a Hole of like Dimensions near the Fore-part of the Bottom-Plate, which being by a Ring lifted up towards the Fire, about an Inch, where it will be retain'd by two springing Sides fix'd to it perpendicularly, [*See the Plate, Fig.* 4][2] the Air rushes in from the Hollow under the Bottom Plate, and blows the Fire. Where this is us'd, the Shutter serves only to close the Fire a Nights. The more forward you can make your Fire on the Hearth-Plate, not to be incommoded by the Smoke, the sooner and more will the Room be warmed. At Night when you go to Bed, cover the Coals or Brands with Ashes as usual; then take away the Dogs and slide down the Shutter close to the Bottom-Plate, sweeping a little Ashes against it that no Air may pass under it; then turn the Register, so as very near to stop the Flue behind. If no Smoke then comes out at Crevices into the Room, 'tis right: If any Smoke is perceiv'd to come out, move the Register so as to give a little Draught, and 'twill go the right way. Thus the Room will be kept warm all Night; for the Chimney being almost entirely stopt, very little, if any, cold Air will enter the Room at any Crevice. When you come to re-kindle the Fire in the Morning, turn open the Register before you

*The Shutter is slid up and down in this Manner, only in those Fire-places which are so made, as that the Distance between the Top of the arch'd Opening and the Bottom-Plate, is the same as the Distance between it and the Top-Plate. Where the Arch is higher, as it is in the Draught annex'd, (which is agreeable to the last Improvements) the Shutter is set by, and apply'd occasionally: because if it were made deep enough to close the whole Opening when slid down, it would hide Part of it when up.

2. Brackets in the original. See below, p. 445.

lift up the Slider, otherwise if there be any Smoke in the Fire-Place, it will come out into the Room. By the same Use of the Shutter and Register, a blazing Fire may be presently stifled, as well as secured, when you have Occasion to leave it for any Time; and at your Return, you will find the Brands warm and ready for a speedy Re-kindling. The Shutter alone will not stifle a Fire; for it cannot well be made to fit so exactly, but that Air will enter, and that in a violent Stream, so as to blow up and keep alive the Flames, and consume the Wood, if the Draught be not check'd by turning the Register to shut the Flue behind. The Register has also two other Uses. If you observe the Draught of Air into your Fire-place, to be stronger than is necessary, (as in extream cold Weather it often is) so that the Wood is consum'd faster than usual; in that Case, a quarter, half, or two thirds Turn of the Register, will check the Violence of the Draught, and let your Fire burn with the Moderation you desire: And at the same Time both the Fire-Place and the Room will be the warmer, because less cold Air will enter and pass through them. And if the Chimney should happen to take Fire (which indeed there is very little Danger of, if the preceding Direction be observ'd in making Fires, and it be well swept once a Year; for, much less Wood being burnt, less Soot is proportionably made; and the Fuel being soon blown into Flame by the Shutter (or the Trap-door Bellows) there is consequently less Smoke from the Fuel to make Soot; then, tho' the Funnel should be foul, yet the Sparks have such a crooked up and down round-about Way to go, that they are out before they get at it) I say, if it should ever be on fire, a Turn of the Register shuts all close, and prevents any Air going into the Chimney, and so the Fire may be easily stifled and mastered.

The Advantages of this FIRE-PLACE.

ITS Advantages above the common Fire-Places are,

1. That your whole Room is equally warmed; so that People need not croud so close round the Fire, but may sit near the Window and have the Benefit of the Light for Reading, Writing, Needle-work, &c. They may sit with Comfort in any Part of the Room; which is a very considerable Advantage in a large Family, where there must often be two Fires kept, because all cannot conveniently come at One.

2. If you sit near the Fire, you have not that cold Draught of uncomfortable Air nipping your Back and Heels, as when before common Fires, by which many catch Cold, being scorcht before and as it were froze behind.

3. If you sit against a Crevice, there is not that sharp Draught of cold Air playing on you, as in Rooms where there are Fires in the common way; by which many catch Cold, whence proceed Coughs, Catarrhs,* Tooth-Achs, Fevers, Pleurisies and many other Diseases.

4. In Case of Sickness, they make most excellent Nursing-Rooms; as they constantly supply a Sufficiency of fresh Air, so warmed at the same time as to be no way inconvenient or dangerous. A small One does well in a Chamber; and, the Chimneys being fitted for it, it may be remov'd from one Room to another as Occasion requires, and fix'd in half an Hour. The equal Temper, too, and Warmth, of the Air of the Room, is thought to be particularly advantageous in some Distempers: For 'twas observ'd in the Winters of 1730 and 1736, when the Small-Pox spread in Pennsylvania, that very few of the Children of the Germans died of that Distemper, in Proportion to those of the English; which was ascrib'd by some to the Warmth and equal Temper of Air in their Stove-Rooms; which made the Disease as favourable as it commonly is in the West-Indies. But this Conjecture we submit to the Judgment of Physicians.

5. In common Chimneys the strongest Heat from the Fire, which is upwards, goes directly up the Chimney, and is lost; and there is such a strong Draught into the Chimney, that not only the upright Heat, but also the back, sides and downward Heats, are carried up the Chimney by that Draught of Air; and the Warmth given before the Fire by the Rays that strike out towards

*My Lord Molesworth, in his Account of Denmark, says, That "few or none of the People there, are troubled with Coughs, Catarrhs, Consumptions, or such like diseases of the Lungs; so that in the Midst of Winter in the Churches, which are very much frequented, there is no Noise to interrupt the Attention due to the Preacher. I am persuaded (says he) their *warm Stoves* contribute to their Freedom from these kind of Maladies." *Page* 91.[3]

3. Robert Molesworth, *An Account of Denmark, as it was in the Year 1692* (London, 1694), p. 91.

the Room, is continually driven back, crouded into the Chimney, and carried up, by the same Draught of Air. But here the upright Heat, strikes and heats the Top Plate, which warms the Air above it, and that comes into the Room. The Heat likewise which the Fire communicates to the Sides, Back, Bottom and Air-Box, is all brought into the Room; for you will find a constant Current of warm Air coming out of the Chimney-Corner into the Room. Hold a Candle just under the Mantle-Piece or Breast of your Chimney, and you will see the Flame bent outwards: By laying a Piece of smoaking Paper on the Hearth, on either Side, you may see how the Current of Air moves, and where it tends, for it will turn and carry the Smoke with it.

6. Thus as very little of the Heat is lost, when this Fire-Place is us'd, *much less Wood** will serve you, which is a considerable Advantage where Wood is dear.

7. When you burn Candles near this Fire-Place, you will find that the Flame burns quite upright, and does not blare and run the Tallow down, by drawing towards the Chimney, as against common Fires.

8. This Fire-place cures most smoaky Chimneys, and thereby preserves both the Eyes and Furniture.

9. It prevents the Fouling of Chimneys; much of the Lint and Dust that contributes to foul a Chimney, being by the low Arch oblig'd to pass thro' the Flame, where 'tis consum'd. Then, less Wood being burnt, there is less Smoke made. Again, the Shutter, or Trap-Bellows, soon blowing the Wood into a Flame, the same Wood does not yield so much Smoke as if burnt in a common

*People who have us'd these Fire-places, differ much in their Accounts of the Wood saved by them. Some say five sixths, others three fourths, and others much less. This is owing to the great Difference there was in their former Fires; some (according to the different Circumstances of their Rooms and Chimneys) having been us'd to make very large, others middling, and others, of a more sparing Temper, very small Ones: While in these Fire-Places, (their Size and Draught being nearly the same) the Consumption is more equal. I suppose, taking a Number of Families together, that two thirds, or half the Wood at least, is saved. My common Room, I know, is made twice as warm as it used to be, with a quarter of the Wood I formerly consum'd there.

437

Chimney: For as soon as Flame begins, Smoke, in proportion, ceases.

10. And if a Chimney should be foul, 'tis much less likely to take Fire. If it should take Fire, 'tis easily stifled and extinguished.

11. A Fire may be very speedily made in this Fire-Place, by the Help of the Shutter, or Trap-Bellows, as aforesaid.

12. A Fire may be soon extinguished, by closing it with the Shutter before, and turning the Register behind, which will stifle it, and the Brands will remain ready to rekindle.

13. The Room being once warm, the Warmth may be retain'd in it all Night.

14. And lastly, the Fire is so secur'd at Night, that not one Spark can fly out into the Room to do Damage.

With all these Conveniencies, you do not lose the pleasant Sight nor Use of the Fire, as in the Dutch Stoves, but may boil the Tea-Kettle, warm the Flat-Irons, heat Heaters, keep warm a Dish of Victuals by setting it on the Top, &c. &c. &c.

Objections answered.

THERE are some Objections commonly made by People that are unacquainted with these Fire-Places, which it may not be amiss to endeavour to remove, as they arise from Prejudices which might otherwise obstruct in some Degree the general Use of this beneficial Machine. We frequently hear it said, *They are of the Nature of the Dutch Stoves; Stoves have an unpleasant Smell; Stoves are unwholesome;* and, *Warm Rooms make People tender ana apt to catch Cold.* As to the first, that they are of the Nature of Dutch Stoves, the Description of those Stoves in the Beginning of this Paper, compar'd with that of these Machines, shows that there is a most material Difference, and that these have vastly the Advantage, if it were only in the single Article of the Admission and Circulation of fresh Air. But it must be allowed there has been some Cause to complain of the offensive Smell of Iron Stoves. This Smell, however, never proceeded from the Iron itself, which in its Nature, whether hot or cold, is one of the sweetest of Metals, but from the general uncleanly Manner of using those Stoves. If they are kept clean, they are as sweet as an Ironing-Box, which, tho' ever so hot, never offends the Smell of the nicest Lady: But it is common, to let them be greased by setting Candlesticks on them, or otherwise; to rub greasy Hands on them, and, above all, to spit upon them to try how hot they are, which is an inconsiderate, filthy unmannerly Custom; for the slimy Matter of Spittle drying on, burns and fumes when the Stove is hot, as well as the Grease, and smells most nauseously; which makes such close Stove-Rooms, where there is no Draught to carry off those filthy Vapours, almost intolerable to those that are not from their Infancy accustomed to them. At the same time, nothing is more easy than to keep them clean; for when by any Accident they happen to be fouled, a Lee made of Ashes and Water, with a Brush, will scour them perfectly; as will also a little strong Soft-Soap and Water.

That hot Iron of itself gives no offensive Smell, those know very well, who have (as the Writer of this has) been present at a Furnace, when the Workmen were pouring out the flowing Metal to cast large Plates, and not the least Smell of it to be perceived. That hot Iron does not, like Lead, Brass, and some other Metals, give out unwholesome Vapours, is plain from the general Health and Strength of those who constantly work in Iron, as Furnace-men, Forge-Men, and Smiths; That it is in its Nature a Metal perfectly wholesome to the Body of Man, is known from the beneficial Use of Chalybeat or Iron-Mine Waters; from the Good done by taking Steel Filings in several Disorders; and that even the Smithy Water in which hot Irons are quench'd, is found advantageous to the human Constitution. The ingenious and learned Dr. Desaguliers,[4] to whose instructive Writings the Contriver of this Machine acknowledges himself much indebted, relates an Experiment he made, to try whether heated Iron would yield unwholesome Vapours; He took a Cube of Iron, and having given it a very great Heat, he fix'd it so to a Receiver, exhausted by the Air Pump, that all the Air rushing in to fill the Receiver, should first pass thro' a Hole in the hot Iron. He then put a small Bird into the Receiver, who breath'd that Air without any Inconvenience or suffering the least Disorder. But the same Experiment being made with a Cube of hot Brass, a Bird put into that Air dy'd in a few Minutes. Brass indeed stinks even when cold, and much more when hot; Lead too, when hot, yields a very un-

4. J. T. Desaguliers, *A Course of Experimental Philosophy* (London, 1734–44), II, 557–8.

wholesome Steam; but IRON is always sweet, and every way taken is wholesome and friendly to the human Body——except in Weapons.

That warm Rooms make People tender and apt to catch Cold, is a Mistake as great as it is (among the English) general. We have seen in the preceding Pages how the common Rooms are apt to give Colds; but the Writer of this Paper may affirm, from his own Experience, and that of his Family and Friends who have used warm Rooms for these four Winters past, that by the Use of such Rooms, People are rendered *less liable* to take Cold, and indeed *actually hardened.* If sitting warm in a Room made One subject to take Cold on going out, lying warm in Bed should, by a Parity of Reason, produce the same Effect when we rise; Yet we find we can leap out of the warmest Bed naked in the coldest Morning, without any such Danger; and in the same Manner out of warm Clothes into a cold Bed. The Reason is, that in these Cases the Pores all close at once, the Cold is shut out, and the Heat within augmented, as we soon after feel by the glowing of the Flesh and Skin. Thus no one was ever known to catch Cold by the Use of the Cold Bath: And are not cold Baths allowed to harden the Bodies of those that use them? Are they not therefore frequently prescrib'd to the tenderest Constitutions? Now every Time you go out of a warm Room into the cold freezing Air, you do as it were plunge into a Cold Bath, and the Effect is in proportion the same; for (tho' perhaps you may feel somewhat chilly at first) you find in a little Time your Bodies hardened and strengthened, your Blood is driven round with a brisker Circulation, and a comfortable steady uniform inward Warmth succeeds that equal outward Warmth you first received in the Room. Farther to confirm this Assertion, we instance the Swedes, the Danes, the Russians: These Nations are said to live in Rooms, compar'd to ours, as hot as Ovens;* yet where are the hardy

*Mr. Boyle, in his Experiments and Observations upon Cold, *Page* 684 of Shaw's *Abridgment,* says, " 'Tis remarkable, that while the Cold has strange and tragical Effects at Moscow, and elsewhere, the Russians and Livonians should be exempt from them, who accustom themselves to pass immediately from a great Degree of Heat, to as great an one of Cold, without receiving any visible Prejudice thereby. I remember, being told by a Person of unquestionable Credit, that it was a common

Soldiers, tho' bred in their boasted cool Houses, that can, like these People, bear the Fatigues of a Winter Campaign in so severe a Climate, march whole Days to the Neck in Snow, and at Night entrench in Ice, as they do?

The Mentioning of those Northern Nations puts me in Mind of a considerable *Publick Advantage* that may arise from the general Use of these Fire-places. It is observable, that tho' those Countries have been well inhabited for many Ages, Wood is still their Fuel, and yet at no very great Price; which could not have been if they had not universally used Stoves, but consum'd it as we do, in great Quantities by open Fires. By the Help of this saving Invention, our Wood may grow as fast as we consume it, and our Posterity may warm themselves at a moderate Rate, without being oblig'd to fetch their Fuel over the Atlantick; as, if Pit-Coal should not be here discovered (which is an Uncertainty) they must necessarily do.

WE leave it to the *Political Arithmetician* to compute, how much Money will be sav'd to a Country, by its spending two thirds less of Fuel; how much Labour sav'd in Cutting and Carriage of it; how much more Land may be clear'd for Cultivation; how great the Profit by the additional Quantity of Work done, in those Trades particularly that do not exercise the Body so much, but that the Workfolks are oblig'd to run frequently to the Fire to warm themselves: And to Physicians to say, how much healthier thick-built Towns and Cities will be, now half suffocated with sulphury Smoke, when so much less of that Smoke shall be made, and the Air breath'd by the Inhabitants be consequently so much purer. These Things it will suffice just to have mentioned; let us

---

Practice among them, to go from a hot Stove into cold Water; the same was, also, affirmed to me, by another who resided at Moscow: This Tradition is likewise abundantly confirmed by Olearius. ' 'Tis a surprizing thing,' says he, 'to see how far the Russians can endure Heat; and how, when it makes them ready to faint, they can go out of their Stoves, stark naked, both Men and Women, and throw themselves into cold Water; and even in Winter wallow in the Snow.' "[5]

5. Robert Boyle, *Philosophical Works*, Peter Shaw, ed. (London, 1725), I, 684. Olearius' description appears in slightly different words in his *The Voyages and Travells of the Ambassadors . . . to . . . Muscovy, and . . . Persia* (2d edit., London, 1669), p. 67.

proceed to give some necessary Directions to the Workman who is to fix or set up these Fire-Places.

Directions to the Bricklayer.

THE Chimney being first well swept and cleans'd from Soot, &c. lay the Bottom Plate down on the Hearth in the Place where the Fire-Place is to stand, which may be as forward as the Hearth will allow. Chalk a Line from one of its back Corners round the Plate to the other Corner, that you may afterwards know its Place when you come to fix it; and from those Corners two parallel Lines to the Back of the Chimney: Make Marks also on each Side, that you may know where the Partition is to stand, which is to prevent any Communication between the Air and Smoke. Then removing the Plate, make a Hollow under it and beyond it, by taking up as many of the Bricks or Tiles as you can within your chalk'd Lines, quite to the Chimney-Back. Dig out six or eight Inches deep of the Earth or Rubbish all the Breadth and Length of your Hollow; then make a Passage of four Inches square, (if the Place will allow so much) leading from the Hollow to some Place communicating with the outer Air; by *outer Air* we mean Air without the Room you intend to warm. This Passage may be made to enter your Hollow on either Side, or in the Fore-part, just as you find most convenient, the Circumstances of your Chimney considered. If the Fire-Place is to be put up in a Chamber, you may have this Communication of outer Air from the Staircase; or sometimes more easily from between the Chamber Floor and the Cieling of the lower Room, making only a small Hole in the Wall of the House entring the Space betwixt those two Joists with which your Air-Passage in the Hearth communicates. If this Air-Passage be so situated, as that Mice may enter it and nestle in the Hollow, a little Grate of Wire will keep them out. This Passage being made, and, if it runs under any Part of the Hearth, til'd over securely; you may proceed to raise your false Back. This may be of four Inches or two Inches Thickness, as you have Room, but let it stand at least four Inches from the true Chimney-Back. In narrow Chimnies this false Back runs from Jamb to Jamb, but in large old-fashion'd Chimnies you need not make it wider than the Back of the Fire-place. To begin it, you may form an Arch nearly flat of three Bricks End

442

to End, over the Hollow, to leave a Passage the Breadth of the Iron Fire-Place, and five or six Inches deep, rounding at Bottom, for the Smoke to turn and pass under the false Back, and so behind it up the Chimney. The false Back is to rise till it is as high as the Breast of the Chimney, and then to close over to the Breast;* always observing, if there is a wooden Mantle-Tree, to close above it. If there is no Wood in the Breast, you may arch over and close even with the lower Part of the Breast. By this Closing the Chimney is made tight, that no Air or Smoke can pass up it, without going under the false Back. Then from Side to Side of your Hollow, against the Marks you made with Chalk, raise a tight Partition, Brick-on-Edge, to separate the Air from the Smoke, bevelling away to half an Inch the Brick that comes just under the Air-Hole, that the Air may have a free Passage up into the Air-Box: Lastly, close the Hearth over that Part of the Hollow that is between the false Back and the Place of the Bottom Plate, coming about half an Inch under the Plate, which Piece of hollow Hearth may be supported by a Bit or two of old Iron Hoop; then is your Chimney fitted to receive the Fire-Place.

To set it, Lay first a little Bed of Mortar all round the Edges of the Hollow and over the Top of the Partition: Then lay down your Bottom Plate in its Place (with the Rods in it) and tread it till it lies firm. Then put a little fine Mortar (made of Loam and Lime with a little Hair) into its Joints, and set in your back Plate, leaning it for the present against the false Back; Then set in your Air-Box, with a little Mortar in its Joints; Then put in the two Sides, closing them up against the Air-Box with Mortar in their Grooves, and fixing at the same time your Register; Then bring up your Back to its Place, with Mortar in its Grooves, and that will bind the Sides together. Then put in your Front-Plate, placing it as far back in the Groove as you can, to leave Room for the sliding Plate; Then lay on your Top-Plate, with Mortar in its Grooves also, screwing the whole firmly together by means of the Rods. The Capital Letters *A B D E*, &c. in the annex'd Cut, show the corresponding Parts of the several Plates. Lastly the Joints being pointed all round on the Out-side, the Fire-Place is fit for Use.

*See *page* 19 [433], where the Trap-door is describ'd, that ought to be in this Closing.

When you make your first Fire in it, perhaps, if the Chimney be thoroughly cold, it may not draw, the Work too being all cold and damp. In such Case put first a few Shovels of hot Coals in the Fire-Place, then lift up the Chimney-sweeper's Trap-Door, and putting in a Sheet or two of flaming Paper, shut it again, which will set the Chimney a Drawing immediately, and when once 'tis fill'd with a Column of warm Air, it will draw strongly and continually.

The Drying of the Mortar and Work by the first Fire, may smell unpleasantly; but that will soon be over.

In some shallow Chimneys, to make more Room for the false Back and its Flue, four Inches or more of the Chimney-Back may be pick'd away.

Let the Room be made as tight as conveniently it may be, so will the outer Air that must come in to supply the Room and Draught of the Fire, be all obliged to enter thro' the Passage under the Bottom-Plate, and up thro' the Air-Box; by which Means it will not come cold to your Backs, but be warmed as it comes in, and mixed with the warm Air round the Fire-Place before it spreads in the Room.

But as a great Quantity of cold Air, in extream cold Weather especially, will presently enter a Room if the Door be carelessly left open, 'tis good to have some Contrivance to shut it, either by Means of Screw Hinges, a Spring, or a Pulley.

When the Pointing in the Joints is all dry and hard, get some Powder of Black-Lead, (broken Bits of Black-Lead Crucibles from the Silver-smith's, pounded fine, will do) and mixing it with a little Rum and Water, lay it on, when the Plates are warm, with a hard Brush, over the Top and Front-Plates, part of the Side and Bottom Plates, and over all the Pointing; and as it dries rub it to a Gloss with the same Brush, so the Joints will not be discern'd, but it will look all of a Piece, and shine like new Iron. And the false Back being plaister'd and whitewash'd, and the Hearth redden'd, the whole will make a pretty Appearance. Before the Black Lead is laid on, it would not be amiss to wash the Plates with strong Lee and a Brush, or Soap and Water, to cleanse them from any Spots of Grease or Filth that may be on them. If any Grease should afterwards come on them, a little wet Ashes will get it out.

444

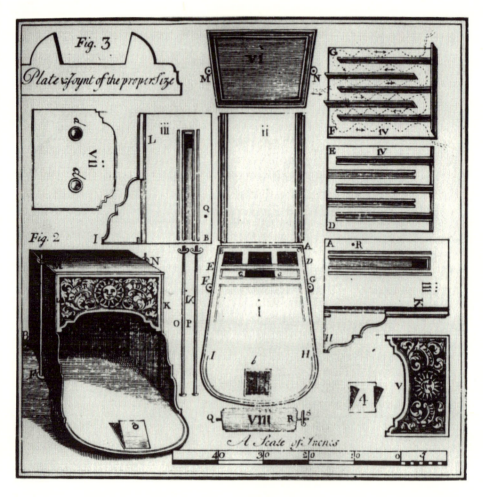

Plate of the Pennsylvania Fireplace

If it be well set up, and in a tolerable good Chimney, Smoke will draw in from as far as the Fore-Part of the Bottom Plate, as you may try by a Bit of burning Paper.

People are at first apt to make their Rooms too warm, not imagining how little a Fire will be sufficient. When the Plates are no hotter than that one may just bear the Hand on them, the Room will generally be as warm as you desire it.

THE END

EXPLANATION of the PLATE,

Referring to the Pages where the several Parts
are describ'd, or their Uses shewn.

		Page
i The Bottom Plate		14 [430]
ii The Back Plate		14 [430]
iii iii The two Side Plates		14 [430]
iv iv The two Plates that make up the Air-box		15 [430]
v The Front Plate		15 [431]
vi The Top Plate		15 [431]
vii The Shutter or Slider	15, 20, 21, 22	[431, 434, 435]
viii The Register	16, 21, 22	[431, 434, 435]
Fig. 2. The Fire-Place put together	16, 35	[431, 443]
3. The Section of a Fragment of a Plate, shewing the quarter-round Regulets that make the Joints		14 [430]
4. The Blower, (Bottom upwards)		21 [434]
OP The two Screw Rods		14 [431]

ƒƒ With the prick'd Lines, shew the Course of the
Air thro' the Windings of the Air-Box.

The Capital Letters show the corresponding Parts of the several Plates.

On the DEVICE of the NEW FIRE-PLACE,
A SUN; *with this Motto,* ALTER IDEM.

i.e. *A second Self;* or, *Another, the same.*

By a Friend.

ANOTHER Sun!—'tis true;—but not THE SAME.
Alike, I own, in Warmth and genial Flame:

But, more obliging than his elder Brother,
This will not scorch in Summer, like *the other;*
Nor, when sharp Boreas chills our shiv'ring Limbs,
Will *this Sun* leave us for more Southern Climes;
Or, in long Winter Nights, forsake us here,
To chear new Friends in t'other Hemisphere:
But, faithful still to us, this *new Sun*'s Fire,
Warms when we please, and just as we desire.[6]

From Cadwallader Colden   Draft: New-York Historical Society

To Mr. Franklin   Decr. 1744

The season of the year advancing in which our Correspondence
from this place with New York becomes more uncertain and my
eldest son going now to New York where he proposes to stay 8 or
10 days I hope you'l excuse my interrupting you in your Business
which I know allows you little time for trifles or amusements. In
your last you gave me hopes that you would soon be able to inform
me of what sentiment Mr. Logan intertains of the Introduction to
Fluxions which was submitted to his perusal. By my last I transmitted to you some thoughts of the Different Species of Matter.
As these thoughts are entirely new and out of the common road of
thinking I have reason not only to be apprehensive that others may
not easily receive the Conceptions but that I may have imposed
on my self and it is for this reason that I have submitted them to
Mr. Logan and your Examination. I have allready shown it to Mr.
Alexander[7] and some steps I have made in applying these thoughts
to the explanation of some phoenomina in which Philosophers
have hitherto not been able to give Satisfaction. He has taken much
more pains in the Examination than could have been expected in
one so deeply engaged in Business and however pleasing his
Sentiments may be to me I have reason to suspect that he may be
biassed by favour to a very long and intimate acquaintance. You
may assure your self that I think and I hope Mr. Logan will believe me in good earnest when I say that there cannot be a stronger

6. These verses were reprinted in *Amer. Mag. and Hist. Chron.* (Boston,
1744), p. 701.
7. James Alexander. See above, p. 407 n.

and surer mark of Friendship than showing to me the mistakes I may have fallen into as it may prevent my exposing my weakness and Ignerance to others. Men often impose sophisms upon themselves which they can not detect without the assistance of others. If the general reasonings be found right I flatter my self you will take more pleasure in examining the application of them to particular phoenomina. As the Winter is the only time that I have leizure to apply my self to speculations I should be glad to know your Sentiments and Mr. Logans assoon as may be either to prevent my throwing away time uselessly or to encourage me to go on in the pursuit of a study which requires much time and leizure more than I can hope for in my life. I know none besides Mr. Logan, Mr. Alexander and your self in this part of the world to whos judgement I can refer any thing of this kind.

I long likewise to know what progress you make in forming your Society. If it meet with obstruction from the want of proper incouragement or otherwise I would have you attempt some other Method of proceeding in your Design for I shall be very sorry to have it entirely dropt. May you not as Printer propose to Print at certain times a Collection of such pieces on the subject of your former proposals which any shall think proper to send you and by way of Speciemen to print such papers as your friends may have communicated to you on your former proposal? For this purpose you may desire a Subscription by all persons indifferently for your Incouragement. I do not propose that every thing be printed that shall be sent. You may communcate them to the best judges with you of the several subjects on which these papers shall happen to be wrote where you are not willing entirely to trust to your own Judgement and if they be found not fit for the press you may return them with remarks or make some excuse for not publishing them. This I expect will in time produce a Society as proposed by giving men of Learning or Genius some knowledge of one another and will avoid some difficulties that allwise attend the forming of Societies in their Beginning. Three hundred Copies may be sufficient at first till it be discover'd what incouragement the undertaking meets with and such a number I cannot doubt will sell.[8] I

---

8. BF was interested in this suggestion, as subsequent correspondence between the two men shows, but he never established such a philosophical periodical.

shall only add that as men naturally have as great a fondness for the Productions of their Mind as for those of their bodies however ill favour'd they be and bear with as much uneasiness to be deprived of the honour of such Productions as to have another assume to be the father of their Children, you must be carefull to acknowlege the receipt of every paper so as that the author may think himself secure from pyratical attempts of others.

To Edward and Jane Mecom

MS not found; reprinted from Jared Sparks, ed., *A Collection of the Familiar Letters and Miscellaneous Papers of Benjamin Franklin* (Boston, 1833), p. 10.

Dear Brother and Sister, Philadelphia, [1744-1745][9]
If you still continue your inclination to send Benny, you may do it by the first vessel to New York. Write a line by him, directed to Mr. James Parker, Printer, on Hunter's Key, New York. I am confident he will be kindly used there, and I shall hear from him every week. You will advise him to be very cheerful, and ready to do every thing he is bid, and endeavour to oblige every body, for that is the true way to get friends.[1]
Dear Sister, I love you tenderly for your care of our father in his sickness.
I am, in great haste, your loving brother, B. FRANKLIN

Extracts from the Gazette, 1744

Printed in *The Pennsylvania Gazette*, January 3 to December 25, 1744.

Wednesday last a Fire broke out in the Roof of a House in Second Street near the Church, but there being sufficient Help at

9. Instead of following Sparks, who dates this letter 1743 (*Works*, x, 471), Van Doren (*Franklin-Mecom*, p. 39) assigns it to 1744-45 for two reasons: The Mecoms' son Benjamin (C.17.3) was 12 at the end of 1744, a usual age for beginning an apprenticeship, even away from home; and Josiah Franklin, whose illness is referred to, was not known ever to have been ill except of the sickness of which he died, Jan. 16, 1745. Par. Text edit., p. 24.
1. That Benny Mecom did not follow his uncle's advice to keep a cheerful temper is shown in a letter from BF to Jane Mecom of 1748.

hand, it was presently extinguished. Axes were observ'd to be of great Use; for when Holes were made in the Shingling, the Water from Engines and Buckets readily enter'd, and did ten times the Service it could otherwise have done.   [January 11]

[ADVERTISEMENT] Proposed by a Society, If due Encouragement be given by Subscriptions, To publish THE IMPARTIAL REFORMER, Containing, Essays serious and entertaining, on Religious and Moral subjects, as well as the common Occurrences of Life, and the various Dispositions, Humours, and Manners of Mankind in these Times. Those who think proper to Encourage the same, are desired to send in their Names to the Printer hereof; and as soon as there is a sufficient Number of Subscribers to defray the Expence of Printing, one Sheet shall be immediately published, and continued once a Fortnight, of which Notice shall be given in the Publick News. Price to each Subscriber Six Shillings per Annum.[2]   [February 2]

[ADVERTISEMENT] Shakespear's Plays in 8 Vol. neatly bound. Sold by the Printer hereof.   [February 16]

May the fst 1744
Than thar is to be a Ras in Taryfar Nak at mr John amerner between His Negor Sharp and a landtarpen townty yards backwards and fordes to Rune the three hetes forty pounds one half wat and half drie bet Carnel John harmar and mastor sone William funeDik Hie Sharaof Nu Cas Conty Ase wch. Thomos Allfree, Jack See and Thomos bufit and prssiler Harod.[3]   [February 22]

LATELY PUBLISHED in Boston, And to be Sold by B. Franklin in Philadelphia, Price, 1s. each. THE *American* MAGAZINE, For the Months of November and December 1743.   [March 1]

JUST PUBLISHED, M. T. Cicero's Cato Major; Or his Discourse

2. The proposed journal was never published.
3. "Taryfar Nak" may be Thoroughfare Neck, near Smyrna, Del.; but the persons named in this example of dialect humor have not been identified. The sheriff of New Castle, 1739–44, was John Gooding; he was succeeded by Gideon Griffith. Henry C. Conrad, *History of the State of Delaware* (Wilmington, Del., 1908), I, 293.

of Old Age. Translated from the Latin; with explanatory Notes, by the Hon. James Logan, Esqr.[4]

Printed and sold by B. Franklin, Price stitch'd in Marble Covers, 3*s.6d.*   [March 21]

[ADVERTISEMENT] A Collection of choice and valuable Books, consisting of near 600 Volumes in most Faculties and Sciences, viz. Divinity, History, Law, Mathematicks, Philosophy, Physick, Poetry, &c. Will begin to be Sold by Benjamin Franklin, for ready Money only, on Wednesday the 11th of April 1744 at Nine o Clock in the Morning, at the Post-Office in Philadelphia; the lowest Price being for Dispatch marked in each Book: Catalogues may be had *gratis,* at the Place of Sale.[5]

Note. *The said Franklin, gives ready Money for any Library or Parcel of Books.*   [March 29]

A Greater Number of Gentlemen having subscribed to Dr. Spencer's first Course of Experimental Philosophy, than can be conveniently accommodated at a Time: He begins his first Lecture of the second Course, on Thursday, the tenth Day of May, at five o'Clock: Subscriptions are taken in at the Post-Office, where a Catalogue of the Experiments may be had gratis.[6]   [April 26]

4. See above, p. 404.

5. The books were listed in *A Catalogue of Choice and Valuable Books, consisting of Near 600 Volumes, in most Faculties and Sciences,* . . . (Phila., 1744, and reprinted in facsimile with a note by Carl Van Doren, 1948).

6. Adam Spencer is one of the least known but possibly most influential men in BF's life. A physician and male midwife, educated at Edinburgh, he came to America with recommendations from Dr. Richard Mead and other London doctors. In Boston he advertised a "Course of Experimental Philosophy" in June 1743, and showed BF, who was visiting there, "some electric Experiments," which, though imperfectly done, "equally surpriz'd and pleas'd me." During the fall and winter of 1743–44 Spencer excited interest in electrical experiments in Newport and New York, where he met Cadwallader Colden; and he delivered at least two courses of lectures in Philadelphia in 1744. It was expected that these would be printed, but they were not. BF and Spencer renewed their acquaintance in Philadelphia, and the lecturer also met Dr. John Mitchell, who was visiting there, and Dr. Thomas Cadwalader, whose *Essay on the West-India Dry-Gripes* (Phila., 1745), he helped revise. Spencer seems to have remained in Philadelphia at least until the spring of 1745. In Parks's *Va. Gaz.,* Jan. 9, 1746, he advertised that he

[ADVERTISEMENT] BOOKS Sold by B. Franklin. Bibles of all sizes, Testaments, &c. young mans companion, horace in usum delphini, creech's ditto, dyche's and bailey's dictionaries, greek and latin testaments, sterling's ovid and rhetorick, buchanan's psalms, clark's erasmus and cordery, lilly's grammar, hoole's parsing ditto, spelling books of all sorts, ward's young mathematician's guide, pardie's Geometry, builders pocket companion, mariner's calendars and compass rectified, quarter waggoners, scales and compasses, love's surveying, protractors, gordon's geographical grammars; gazeteers, boerhave's institutions of physick, shaw's practice of ditto, quincey's dispensatory, edinburgh ditto, cheyne of health, ditto's english malady, becket's surgery, sharp's ditto, cramer of metals, telemachus, stanhope's epictetus, lilly's conveyancer, school of arts, brightland's english grammars, pen's no cross no crown, cruden's concordance, quarles's emblems, pomfret's poems, watt's lyrick poems, seneca's morals, pilgrim's progress in three parts, ditto large edition, bunyan's works two Vols. fol. With great variety of other books. Also slates, inkpowder, paper of all sorts, wax, account books, and all other sorts of stationary ware.

[May 31]

We hear from Dover in Kent County, that Samuel Chew, Esq; Chief Justice of the Government of the Lower Counties, died there

---

would begin a course of experimental philosophy at Williamsburg January 15, and added, "N.B. Catalogues of the Experiments may be had *gratis*, at his House in Williamsburg, where the course is to be performed." At some time, perhaps on Spencer's return from Virginia, BF bought his apparatus and was thereafter able to proceed in electrical experiments "with great Alacrity." In his autobiography, writing in 1788, BF says that he first met "a Dr. Spence" at Boston in 1746; but the man was Spencer and the date was 1743. The facts are fully presented and argued by I. Bernard Cohen, "Benjamin Franklin and the Mysterious 'Dr. Spence,' " *Jour. Franklin Inst.*, CCXXXV (1943), 1–25. See also Par. Text edit., pp. 300–2, 380, 420; Carl and Jessica Bridenbaugh, *Rebels and Gentlemen* (N.Y., 1942), pp. 267–70, 323–4; Cadwalader, *Dry-Gripes*, pp. v, 29. Niels H. deV. Heathcote, "Franklin's Introduction to Electricity," *Isis*, XLVI (1955), 29–35, argues that Spencer's Boston experiments in 1743 interested BF but meant little to him; not until 1746, he believes, when Peter Collinson had sent the Library Company an electric tube, did BF seriously pursue electrical studies and realize the significance of what Spencer had shown him.

last Week; much regretted by all that had the Pleasure of his Acquaintance.[7]   [June 21]

We have the Pleasure to inform our Readers that the News brought hither by two (seeming) Gentlemen from Virginia, of Georgia's being taken (as mention'd in our last) proves not true; a Vessel being arriv'd at New-York in 11 Days from thence, and left all well there. 'Tis pity that any Persons who make the Appearance of Men of Credit, should, as they travel, think it a proper Diversion in such Times as these, to amuse their Countrymen with false Reports, which may prove in many Cases of very pernicious Consequence.   [July 5]

[ADVERTISEMENT] Just arrived from London, And now shown for the Entertainment of the Curious, to six or more Persons, in a large commodious Room, at Mr. Vidal's in Second-street, Philadelphia, The Solar, or Camera Obscura MICROSCOPE, which magnifies Objects to a surprising Degree, and has given universal Satisfaction. Price 18*d.* each Person. Also, the Unparallelled Musical CLOCK, Most beautiful in its Structure, and delightfully playing the choicest Airs, &c. Price 18*d.* each Person.
Bills describing the Particulars, are given gratis *at the Place aforesaid.*   [July 12]

[ADVERTISEMENT] A Course of Experimental Philosophy, begins at the Library-Room, next Monday at five o'Clock in the Afternoon, which will be the last to be performed in this City by Dr. Spencer.
N.B. Any of the Gentlemen who subscribed to the former Courses, may go through this, at half Price, and have as an Addition some *Lectures* on the *Globes.*   [July 26]

7. Samuel Chew (1693–1744), Quaker physician and judge; born in Maryland, moved to Philadelphia, 1732, and to Dover about 1739; appointed chief justice of the Lower Counties (Delaware), 1741. Two addresses to the grand jury on the lawfulness of self-defense against an armed enemy, which BF printed, led to his expulsion from the Society of Friends. Burton A. Konkle, *Benjamin Chew, 1722–1810* (Phila., 1932), pp. 5–48; Evans 4708, 4930.

'Tis computed that there are and will be before Winter 113 Sail of Privateers at Sea, from the British American Colonies; most of them stout Vessels and abundantly well mann'd. A Naval Force, equal (some say) to that of the Crown of Great-Britain in the Time of Queen Elizabeth.   [August 30]

ON MONDAY NEXT WILL BE PUBLISHED, and to be Sold by B. Franklin. The Votes, and Proceedings, of the General Assembly of this Province. Continued by Adjournments, from the seventh Day of May, to the eleventh Day of August, 1744.
                                        [September 20]

[ADVERTISEMENT] Notice is hereby given, That during this Winter Season, between the Hours of Six and Nine, at Night, *Gentlemen* may be Instructed in Euclid's Elements, Algebra, Navigation, Astronomy, Surveying, Gauging, and all other Parts of the Mathematicks. Also in the Day time, Youth are Taught, Reading, Writing, Arithmetick, and Accounts, by Theophilus Grew, at his School in Norris's Alley.   [September 20]

[ADVERTISEMENT] Lost on the Road, betwixt here and Germantown, a light coloured broad cloth short Cloak. Whoever leaves it at the Printer's hereof, shall be handsomely Rewarded.
                                            [October 4]

[ADVERTISEMENT] Lost between the Drawbridge and the Vineyard, a white Stone Seal, set in Gold. Whoever brings it to the Printer hereof, shall receive *Twenty Shillings* Reward.
                                            [October 11]

Last Week a Dutch Waggoner who had wilfully driven over a Chair, in which were two young Women, and a Boy that was unwell, whereby the Child's Scull was fractured, so that his Life is despaired of, was apprehended and committed to the Goal of this City.   [October 18]

[ADVERTISEMENT] To be seen, at the Indian King, in Market Street, Price 1*s.* for Men and Women, and 6*d.* for Children.
A Beautiful Creature, but surprizingly fierce, called a LEOPARD;

453

his Extraction half a Lion and half a Pardeal;[8] his native Place of Abode is in Africa, and Arabia. As he will not stay long in this Place, those who have a Mind to see him are desired to be speedy.

[October 25]

The same Day [Monday last], Michael Milchdeberger, the Dutch Waggoner, who drove his Wagon over a Chair, by which a Boy was wounded so that he died, was burnt in the Hand, the Jury having brought in their Verdict *Manslaughter.*

[November 8]

A Caution to the PUBLICK.

Last Saturday several counterfeit *One Shilling Bills* of New-Jersey were uttered here. The Paper is pretty stiff and good, and some of the Bills have an Impression of a *Sage Leaf,* ill done, upon their Backs. If these Bills are compared with the *True Ones,* both being fair, many Variations may be observed both in the *Signing* and the *Printing,* as the Counterfeits are a very bad Imitation of the *True.* Those who have not both Sorts to look at together, may take notice, that the Figures that make the Ornament or Border at the Bottom of the *False Bills,* which have a Resemblance of a *Flower de Luce* at Top, and something more under, stand apart, which in the *True Bills* stand close; and that in the *False Bills* the first I in the Word *Shilling,* that ends the Bill, is shorter than the last I in that Word; that the second L in the same Word is shorter than the first, and that the G is longer than the other Capitals, and made very open. [November 15]

JUST PUBLISHED, and to be sold by the Printer hereof, the following Books, viz.

I. The Fourth Edition, of *A Preservative from the Sins and Follies of Childhood and Youth,* written by way of Question and Answer. To which are added, some Religious and Moral Instructions, in Verse. By I. Watts, D.D. Price 8*d.*

II. *An Account of the New-Invented Pennsylvanian Fire-Places:* Wherein their Construction and Manner of Operation is particularly explained; their Advantages above every other Method of warming Rooms demonstrated; and all Objections that have

8. Pardeal: probably from the old French "pardil," panther. Frédéric Godefroy, *Dictionnaire de l'ancienne langue française,* v.

454

been raised against the Use of them answered and obviated. With Directions for putting them up, and for using them to the best Advantage. And a Copper-Plate, in which the several Parts of the Machine are exactly laid down, from a Scale of equal Parts. Price 1*s*.

III. *Poor Richard's Almanack,* for the Year 1745.

Of whom also may be had, to compleat Gentlemen's Setts, the American Magazine for April, 1744.   [November 15]

[ADVERTISEMENT] Just Imported, And to be sold by Lewis Evans in Strawberry Alley. Price 1*s*. a Cake.

FINE CROWN SOAP, For the Washing of fine Linen, Muslins, Laces, Silks, Chinces, Calicoes, and for the Use of Barbers.

It cleanses fine Linnen, Muslins, Laces, Chinces, &c. with Ease and Expedition, which often suffers more from the long and hard rubbing of the Washer through the ill Qualities of the Soap they use, than the Wearing. It is excellent for the Washing of Scarlets, or any other bright and curious Colours, that are apt to Change by the Use of common Soap. The Sweetness of the Flavour renders it pleasant for the Use of Barbers.   [November 15]

[ADVERTISEMENT] Saturday next will be published and sold by B. Franklin, The Pocket Almanack, for the Year 1745.

[December 6]

WHEREAS the Nossels of most of the Pumps in Market Street, and several other Streets of this City, were taken out and carried away, on Saturday-night the 24th of this Instant, and at several Times before, by some evil-minded, dissolute Persons; which might have been of most pernicious Consequence, if Fire had happened to break out before they could have been renewed. The Union Fire-Company of Philadelphia, do hereby offer a Reward of FIVE POUNDS to him or her who shall discover (so that they may be convicted at the Mayor's Court) any of the Persons concern'd in removing the said Nossels, or doing any other Damage to the Pumps in the Streets, whereby they may be render'd incapable of discharging Water.

By Order of the Company,   REES MEREDITH, Clerk

[December 14]

455

Last Saturday Night died here Mr. John Acworth, formerly an eminent Wine Merchant in the City of London. [December 18]

We hear that the old Dutch Woman, that prosecuted the young Fellow for a Rape, some time since, is lately married. [December 18]

PHILADELPHIA: Printed by B. FRANKLIN, Post-Master, at the New-Printing-Office, near the Market.

FRANKLIN'S PHILADELPHIA 1723-1776

Property owned by Benjamin Franklin shown in solid black

1. Pennsylvania Hospital, opened 1756

2. Loganian Library, opened 1754-55

3. State House (Independence Hall), occupied 1735

4. Pennsylvania Hospital, 1752-56

5. Graves of Francis Folger Franklin, 1736, and Deborah Franklin, 1774, in Christ Church Burying Ground

6. "New Building," erected 1740; acquired for Academy and College 1750

7. Carpenters' Hall, erected 1770

8. Andrew Hamilton's residence, 1718–c.1727; Israel Pemberton's residence, 1745-54

9. Indian Queen Tavern

10. Franklin's residence, 326 Market St., 1761-65

11. Franklin's house, completed 1765

12. John Read's residence; Samuel Keimer's printing office was next door, 1723-26

13. Prison, erected 1723

14. Franklin's residence, 325 Market St., 1751-61; Post Office(?), 1752-53

15. Masonic Lodge, erected 1755

16. City Tavern, erected 1773

17. James Logan's residence, c.1720–c.1730

18. Indian King Tavern, a meeting place for Junto and Masonic lodge

19. First Presbyterian Church, erected 1704; enlarged 1752

20. Probable site of Samuel Keimer's printing office, 1726-30

21. Andrew Bradford's printing office, 1724-38; William Bradford's printing office, 1742-43

22. Andrew Bradford's printing office, c.1717-24

23. Friends' Meeting Houses: Great Meeting House, 1696-1755; Greater Meeting House, 1755-1804

24. Court House, erected c.1709

25. William Franklin's Post Office, 1753-57

26. Union Fire Company engine probably kept here, 1743

27. Christ Church, erected 1695; enlarged 1727-44

28. Franklin's residence, 1748-50

29. Budd's Buildings

30. William Bradford's printing office, 1743-54

31. Andrew Bradford's printing office, 1738-42

32. London Coffee House, opened 1754

33. William Bradford's printing office, 1754-77

34. Franklin's residence, 141 Market St., 1750-51

35. Franklin's residence, 139 Market St., 1728-39

36. Franklin's residence, 131 Market St., 1739-48; printing office, 1739-65; Post Office, 1739-52

37. Site of early meetings of Library Company

38. Thomas Denham's shop, where Franklin was clerk, 1726-27

39. Crooked Billet Tavern, where Franklin spent his first night, 1723

40. Association Battery (Atwood's Wharf), 1747

41. Tun Tavern, a Masonic meeting place

42. Market Street wharf, where Franklin landed, 1723

43. William Allen's residence

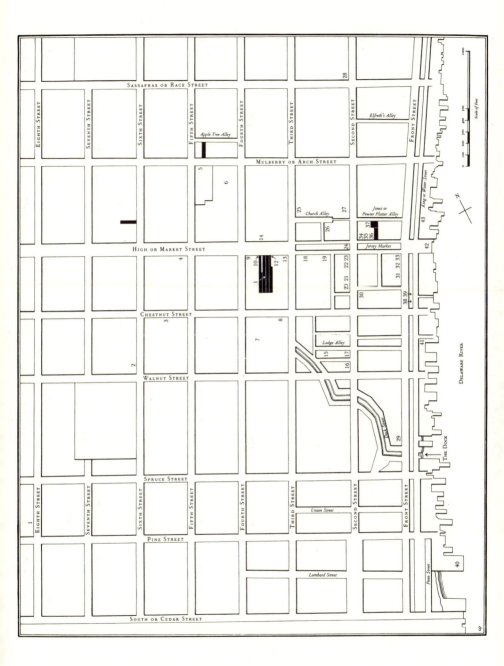

Index

Compiled by David Horne

Edwards, Jonathan, *Some Thoughts Concerning the present Revival of Religion in New-England*, recommended by BF, 385
Ellis, John, reports anecdote on BF's verses, 352
Emerson, Lambert, Grand Warden of Masons, 325
Emlen, George: identified, 154 n.; 320 n.; member of Fire Co., 153; signs acceptance of Lib. Co. charter, 346; signs Fire Co. articles, 376
Emlen, Hannah, marries, 320
"Enigmatical Prophecies": propounded, 144–5; explained, 172
Evans, David: sermon of, 126; instruments stolen from, 328
Evans, Lewis: postal clerk under BF, 180; witnesses Parker partnership agreement, 345; draws diagrams for fireplace pamphlet, 419; sells Pa. fireplaces, 420; advertises Crown soap, 455
Evans, Peter, subscribes to Christ Church, 228 n.
Every Man his own Doctor. See Tennent, John
Extract of the Minutes of the Commission of the Synod, Relating to ... Samuel Hemphil, 37 n.

Faith: basis of Christian communion, 69–71; discussed, 59–60, 107, 111–12, 121–2
Farra, Capt., shipwrecked, 187
Fazakerly, Nicholas, prepared legal opinion on issue of enlistment of servants, 289 n.
Ferguson, Henry Hugh, husband of Elizabeth Graeme, 288 n.
Fire Co. *See* Union Fire Company
Fireplaces, types of, 424–8. *See also* Heating; Pennsylvania fireplace
Fires, news reports of, 132, 158, 189, 216, 283, 389, 448–9. *See also* "Protection of Towns from Fire"; Union Fire Company
Fisher, Mary Franklin, mentioned, 231
Fisher, Sydney George, praises fireplace pamphlet, 421
Fleet, Thomas, orders *Almanacks*, 127
"Florida War," lines on, 367
Flower, Henry: mentioned in *Pa. Gaz.*, 133; notice of death, 158
Flower, Samuel(?), mentioned, 350
Forrest, Joan, mentioned in deed, 311
Foster, James, cited by BF, 120
France, in Polish war, 144 n.
Francis, Tench: leader of Phila. musical club, 257 n.; signs acceptance of Lib. Co. charter, 347

Francklyne, Thomas (fl. 1563–73), mentioned, 230
Franklin: name of, 229; coat of arms, 229–30 n.; family of, 230–2
Franklin, Abiah Folger: letter from, mentioned, 202; letters to, 202–4, 413–14
Franklin, Ann Smith (d. 1763): buys *Almanacks*, 127; BF's accounts with, 233; printer in Newport, 262 n.
Franklin, Benjamin, the Elder (1650–1727), mentioned, 231 n.
Franklin, Benjamin: chronology of life (1735–44), xxv–xxvi; dislikes Andrews' sermons but admires Hemphill's, 27; writes in support of Hemphill against Presbyterian Synod, 28–33, 37–126; quits congregation, 91; sends son William to Grew's school, 29 n.; solicits favor of John Penn for Lib. Co., 33–5; signs as one of original members of Fire Co., 153; death of son, 154; publishes Tennent's *Every Man his own Doctor*, 155, 188; prints 1736 treaty with Six Nations, 160–1, 188, 411, 412 n., 416; commissioned postmaster of Phila., 178; commissioned joint deputy postmaster general, 178; post office records, 178–83; bequeaths outstanding debts to Pa. Hospital, 179 n.; pewholder of Christ Church, 188 n.; role in Daniel Rees affair, 199–202; opinion of Masons, 204; signs Lib. Co. agreement, 205; tardy at Lib. Co. meeting, 205 n.; signs Lib. Co. letter to John Penn, 207; subscribes to Christ Church, 228 n.; inquires into origins of family name, 229 n.; prints Whitefield's journals and sermons, 232, 242–3, 269 n., 282–3, 286, 289; moves residence and printing office, 236; sent to Andrew Bradford by Bradford's father, 239; admires Whitefield, 241 n.; involved in quarrel over Whitefield, 257–61, 270–4; nephew James apprenticed to, 261–3; starts *General Magazine*, 263; prints biography of Whitefield, 269 n.; defends conduct as postmaster, 275–6; prints catalogue and account of Lib. Co., 308–9; buys land in Phila., 310, 311; helps draft address to John Penn, 312 n.; accounts with William Bradford, Jr., 315–16; forms partnership with James Parker, 341–5; name first in subscriber lists of Lib. Co. charters, 346 n.; prints texts of charter and by-laws of Lib. Co., 346 n.; signs acceptance of charter, 347; assists in preparing thanks for Lib. Co. charter, 347; signs address to Penns, 348; denies intent to delay publication of

Sewell, Richard: identified, 153 n.; member of Fire Co., 153; signs Fire Co. articles, 376

Sharp, James, makes fireplaces, 419 n.

"Shavers and Trimmers," erroneously attributed to BF, 383

Shaw, Thomas, signs (by proxy) acceptance of Lib. Co. charter, 347

Shippen, Edward: identified, 153 n.; member of Fire Co., 152 n., 153; signs Fire Co. articles, 376; mentioned, 215

Shippen, Joseph, subscribes to Christ Church, 228 n.

Shoemaker, Benjamin: identified, 153 n.; member of Fire Co., 153; elected alderman, 330; signs acceptance of Lib. Co. charter, 347; signs Fire Co. articles, 376

Shop Book, described, 127–8

Sidi (Shedid Allhazar), Sheik, of Beirut: visits Pa., 188, 188–9 n.; leaves for Barbados, 190

Six Nations, BF prints treaty with, 160–1, 188, 411, 412 n., 416

Sloane, Sir Hans, Bartram corresponds with, 378

Smith, Adam, Strahan publisher of, 384 n.

Smith, Armstrong, BF auditor in court case of, 199

Smith, Robert, signs receipt for BF, 351

Smith, Thomas (d. 1742), killed by lightning, 360

Smith, Thomas (fl. 1746–64), signs receipt for BF, 351

Smith, William, plan for German charity schools, 358 n.

Snakebite, cure for, 156, 164, 214

Snakeroot, as cure for snakebite, 164

Snow, losses caused by heavy fall, 320–1

Soap, an ingredient of medicine for stone, 413

Sober, John, signs acceptance of Lib. Co. charter, 347

Society for Promoting Useful Knowledge. See American Philosophical Society

Socratic dialogue on vicious man. See "Man of Sense"

Solar microscope, exhibited in Phila., 452

Spain, war declared against, 283

Spencer, Adam: biographical note, 450–1 n.; notice of lectures, 450, 452

Spicer, Deborah Leaming, wife of Jacob, 349 n.

Spicer, Jacob (1668–1741), estate of, 349 n.

Spicer, Jacob (1716–65): biographical note, 349 n.; letter from, 349–50

Spotswood, Alexander: biographical note, 235 n.; commissions BF postmaster of Phila., 178, 408 n.; orders post-riders

to carry the *Pa. Gaz.*, 131; forbids post-riders to carry *Mercury*, 275, 276, 278, 279; death, 287; letter from, 235–6

Stage, between Trenton and New Brunswick established, 209

Stamp Act, BF acquiesces to, 315 n.

Standley, Richard, signs acceptance of Lib. Co. charter, 347

Standley, Valentine, mentioned in deed, 310

Steel, James, mentioned, 215

Steele, Sir Richard, mentioned, 146

Stephens, Joanna, medicine for the stone, 413

Stone, medicinal treatment of, 413–14

Story, Thomas, letters to, mentioned, 184 n.

Stoves: BF advertises for sale, 316; types of, 424–8. See also German stove; Holland stove; Pennsylvania fireplace

Strahan, William: biographical note, 383–4 n.; BF's accounts with, 234; corresponds with Colden concerning BF, 386 n.; sells *Cato Major*, 404; reassures Hall of BF's good intentions, 409 n.; BF sends books to, 412, 416; letters to, 383–4, 409–13, 416–17, 418

Strahan, William, Jr., proposal of marriage of BF's daughter to, 384 n.

Stretch, Joseph: signs acceptance of Lib. Co. charter, 346; signs address of thanks to Penns, 348

Strettell, Robert, elected councilman, 329

Sullivan, ———, participant in burlesque masonic ceremony, 198

Sydserfe, Walter: identified, 309 n.; contributes to Lib. Co., 309

Syng, Philip, Jr.: member of Fire Co., 153; absent from Lib. Co. meeting, 205, 206; signs Lib. Co. letter to John Penn, 207; Grand Master of Masons, 325; signs acceptance of Lib. Co. charter, 346; signs address of thanks to Penns, 348; signs Fire Co. articles, 376

Synod of Philadelphia. See Philadelphia Synod

Tackerbury, John, composed burlesque masonic ceremony, 198, 199

Tartar (ship), sunk, 411

Tartar, salt of, medicinal use, 413

Taylor, Jacob, almanacs of, 127, 135

"Teague's Advertisement," verses in brogue, printed in *Pa. Gaz.*, 304–5

Tennent, Charles, leader of religious awakening, 287, 288 n.